A Nation Without Borders

Steven Hahn

A Nation Without Borders

The United States and Its World in an Age of Civil Wars, 1830–1910

The Penguin History of the United States
Eric Foner, Series Editor

VIKING

VIKING
An imprint of Penguin Random House LLC
375 Hudson Street
New York, New York 10014
penguin.com

Illustration credits:

Page 11: Smithsonian American Art Museum, Washington, DC / Art Resource, NY
Pages 32–33, 78, 114, 118–19, 153, 158–59, 192, 260–61, 270, 317, 330–31, 380–81, 401, 448, 501: Library of Congress
Pages 158–59, 233, 362: New York Public Library

ISBN: 9780670024681 (hardcover)
ISBN: 9780735221208 (ebook)

Printed in the United States of America
1   3   5   7   9   10   8   6   4   2

Set in Photina MT Pro
Designed by Francesca Belanger

FOR MY STUDENTS:
Who Teach Me, Inspire Me, and Make Me Proud

Contents

Introduction

In the past two generations, the study of American history has been transformed. Increased attention to the experience of previously-neglected groups, such as women, African Americans, and Latinos, new subfields, including the history of the family and of American capitalism, and new perspectives, notably a "global" approach to U.S. history, have produced an expansion of the cast of characters who populate works of history and striking new insights into the historical narrative. At the same time, the greatly enriched understanding of the American past has inspired laments about a fragmentation of historical understanding, the loss of a sense of the American experience as a coherent whole.

The Penguin History of the United States aims to present, in five volumes, an account of the main themes of American development that reflect this recent revolution in historical scholarship. The authors are historians at the forefront of their respective fields who have demonstrated an ability to present the fruits of their research in a manner accessible to a broad reading public. These works incorporate the experience of diverse groups of Americans while at the same time integrating recent concerns with "older" approaches such as political and intellectual history. They strive to place American history in an international context without losing sight of the distinctive qualities of the American experience. Each volume offers a personal interpretation, and no attempt has been made to impose an artificial uniformity. But taken together the books present an up-to-date narrative of the main themes of American development.

The opening volume, Alan Taylor's *American Colonies*, admirably fulfills the purposes of the series. Ranging across the entire colonial era and devoting attention to all the places that would eventually become part of the United States (including Hawaii and Alaska, not usually included in accounts of these years), Taylor presents a remarkably original historical narrative. His account focuses on the intersections of diverse groups of Native Americans with Spanish, French, Dutch, and English empires and colonists, insisting that all were active agents in shaping the culture, economy, natural environment, and politics of colonial North America. Rather than a simple story of conquest and settlement, Taylor's account shows how power was frequently contested and indeterminate, and how boundaries shifted over time. He makes clear that the history of colonial America was not simply a prelude to national independence, but an era of significance in its own right. No one who reads Taylor's remarkable volume will think the same way about this formative period of our history.

The fifth volume in the series, Joshua Freeman's *American Empire*, also integrates the history of the United States into global processes, while attending to the profound social, economic, and political changes the country experienced in the half century after World War II. He traces both the evolution of Cold War foreign policy, with its successes and failures, and the remarkable economic growth that produced a mass consumer society and, until the 1970s, an expanding standard of living for ordinary Americans. His account attends to the regional variations within the United States and also the homogenization of culture promoted by the advent of television and other forms of mass entertainment. Central to the story is the civil rights revolution, which redrew the boundaries of citizenship and launched a series of movements—second-wave feminism, Latino activism, etc.—that enabled millions to enjoy the promise of American life more fully. But he also details the economic crisis that emerged in the 1970s and the ways it affected Americans' expectations and political outlooks, fueling the rise of Reaganism and the decline of postwar liberalism.

Steven Hahn's book, volume three in the Penguin series, takes its place as a distinguished and original contribution to our understanding of the American past.

Eric Foner, Series Editor

A Nation Without Borders

Prologue

THIS BOOK TELLS a familiar story in an unfamiliar way and, in so doing, challenges our understanding of the past and the future to which it gave rise. *A Nation Without Borders* is a history of the United States and the world with which it was increasingly connected during the near century between 1830 and 1910. These decades witnessed massive transformations in how people lived, worked, thought about themselves, and struggled for sustenance and power. And they witnessed the birth of economic and political institutions that continue to shape the world in which we live.

A listing of some of these changes will remind readers of why this period was so crucial to the making of the United States: The population grew more than tenfold. The geographical boundàries of the country expanded from the Mississippi River west to the Pacific coast and then out into the Pacific itself. Civil warfare erupted. African American slavery, nearly three centuries old, was abolished. Native peoples, who had dominated much of the North American continent, were suppressed and remanded to reservations. The economy and society experienced full-scale industrialization. Massive waves of immigrants from Europe and Asia arrived on the country's shores. Popular movements against the new economic and political order were organized. Wars of conquest were waged against Mexicans, Cubans, and Filipinos. And national power and influence were extended across much of the Western Hemisphere and the Pacific. Beginning as an overwhelmingly agricultural society with a relatively weak central government and relatively independent states and "peripheries," the United States would, during the course of these decades, become an urban and industrial society in which state and federal governments assumed greater and greater roles in the framing of social and economic life. By 1910, as the "long" nineteenth century came to a close, the United States stood as one of the most formidable nations on the globe.

But how was it that these great transformations occurred, and how are we to interpret their significance? The historical literature that seeks to answer these questions is very large and impressive; the volumes on the Civil War alone could fill a good-sized library. And, as one might imagine, there is substantial controversy and disagreement over almost every issue of importance. What was the character of American governance? On what axes did American politics turn? How far did slavery's reach extend, and what was its relation to American economic and political growth? How did the intensifying conflict over slavery turn into civil warfare, and in what ways did civil warfare transform the country? How integral was political violence and conquest to American development? How were relations of class, race, and gender constructed, and what did they contribute to the dynamics of change? When did American industrialization commence, and how rapidly did it unfold? How should we view popular radicalism of the late nineteenth century and its relationship to Progressivism? At what point could the United States be regarded as an empire, and how was empire constituted?

A Nation Without Borders takes up these issues and ties them to a distinctive narrative and analytical arc. It does so by interrogating many of the assumptions that have framed historical treatments of this lengthy period and by shifting the vantage points from which the story may be viewed. To be sure, many of the signal events and actors appear in these pages with the recognition and notoriety due them. But they are joined by others, some scarcely known, who play roles of unexpected consequence. Equally important, rather than looking out from the Northeast, either east across the Atlantic or west across the North American continent—as is ordinarily the case—the book also looks east from the Pacific and trans-Mississippi regions, north from Mexico and the Caribbean basin, and, on occasion, south from Canada. The result, I believe, is a very different sense of the geographies of power, the social and cultural encounters, and the vectors of politics.

It may be helpful here to suggest some of the ways—interpretively—that A Nation Without Borders departs from many historical accounts of this period. The centerpiece of the book is the changing relation between nation and empire in the history of the United States. In this regard, most historians understand a certain sequence: the United States commenced its life as a nation, and over the course of the late nineteenth and early twentieth centuries emerged as an empire too, as it became involved in overseas conquests and markets. A Nation Without Borders suggests something rather different. It argues that the model of governance inherited from the British was empire; that from the birth of the Republic the United States was a union with significant imperial ambitions on the continent and in the hemisphere, many pushed by slaveholders and their allies; that the United States only became a nation, a nation-state—as many others did—in the midst of a massive political and military struggle in the 1860s; and that the new American nation reconfigured the character of its empire, first in the South and the trans-Mississippi West before reaching overseas.

A related set of arguments has to do with the nature of social and political conflict during the first half of the nineteenth century. Almost all previous accounts mark the main divide between areas where slavery was lawful and areas where it was not, between "North" and "South," and identify "sectionalism" as the main axis of politics. Although *A Nation Without Borders* clearly recognizes that distinctive types of slave societies emerged in the Deep South and, to a lesser extent, in the upper South, it also insists that slavery was national, not sectional, during the first six decades of the nineteenth century, that Jim Crow racism initially emerged in the states of the Northeast and the Midwest where slavery was in the process of being formally abolished, that "sectionalism" was less a "fact" of politics than an important political "construct" in the battle over slavery's future, and that the principal struggle of the period was not between the North and the South but rather between the Northeast and the Mississippi Valley for control of the continent and, perhaps, the hemisphere. That struggle joined slaveholding and non-slaveholding expansionists, chiefly in the Democratic Party, and it was the rupture of their alliance that set the stage for secession and war.

The significance of the Mississippi Valley as an alternative developmental zone during the first half of the nineteenth century brings us to yet another interpretive perspective that *A Nation Without Borders* seeks to advance. Until the past several decades, most American historical writing was heavily "exceptionalist": not only in the way it regarded the political standing of the United States in the world, but also in its refusal to look much beyond the nation's boundaries in casting its many stories. More recently, early Americanists, among others (especially slavery scholars), have challenged this analytical isolationism by adopting what they call an "Atlantic" framework. There is very good reason for this move. There can be little doubt that the societies of the North American continent took shape in a context very much owing to the influences of Europe, western and west-central Africa, and the remainder of the Western Hemisphere, all of which touched the Atlantic and increasingly created a complex world of interaction. By now, this framework has not only become well established for the early American field—as Alan Taylor's *American Colonies* shows—but has also had an effect across the nineteenth-century field, especially in relation to the Caribbean basin. *A Nation Without Borders* does not contest this orientation—and the book certainly shows the marks of it in many ways—but it does argue that the Atlantic framework greatly underestimates the importance of the Pacific as an increasingly powerful field of force. Ever since the late eighteenth century, when merchants began to tap into the lucrative trade of the Pacific and Indian oceans, policy makers—across the political spectrum—viewed the Pacific coast of North America as vital to the country's interests and as the gateway to future prosperity and greatness. Indeed, it is impossible to grasp the significance of many of the important events of the nineteenth century—from Texas annexation to the U.S.-Mexican War, to the Civil War, to the developmental projects in the trans-Mississippi West—without recognizing the Pacific as an American destiny, real and imagined.

The issues of empire, slavery, the Pacific, and the struggle for continental and hemispheric dominance between the Northeast and the Mississippi Valley place what we generally call the Civil War and Reconstruction in a rather new and arresting light. *A Nation Without Borders* examines a variety of challenges to the power and authority of the central government of the United States during the years between 1830 and 1861 and how they reshaped the sovereign claims of the government itself. Easily the most important of these challenges came from slaveholders in the Deep and upper South who both wished to protect the world that slavery had made for them and envisioned the possibility of a slaveholding empire spreading across much of the hemisphere. So determined were they to prevail that they first competed for national power and then, when they lost out, launched a rebellion whose suppression would cost more than 700,000 lives and leave long-lasting scars. I term this bloody episode, as many supporters of the Union did at the time, the "War of the Rebellion" (not the "Civil War") and treat the "Confederacy" as a rogue rather than a legitimate state, in good part because no other state power in the world ever recognized it (the terms "Confederate" and "Confederacy" are used sparingly; more frequently, I refer to the "rebellious states").

But the War of the Rebellion was only the largest of many rebellions that either called into question the sovereign authority of the federal government or insisted upon their own claims to sovereignty. These included the resistance of Native Americans to settler colonialism and dispossession, especially in the Second Seminole War of the 1830s and 1840s (the longest American war until Vietnam); the embrace of nullification by reactionary slaveholders in South Carolina in the early 1830s; the efforts of Mormons to limit federal power in the Utah Territory and organize their own State of Deseret in the 1850s; privately financed and directed filibustering operations against Cuba, Mexico, and Central America in the 1840s and 1850s in clear violation of U.S. neutrality law; and the percolation of secessionist sentiment in California, the Midwest, and the City of New York as the Lincoln administration moved to deal with the Confederate rebellion in the winter and spring of 1861. These would be followed during the War of the Rebellion itself by Native American uprisings in the upper plains, copperheadism (white disloyalty to the Lincoln government), violent opposition to the draft and the recruitment of African Americans to fight in the Union army, and resistance to the expansion of federal power more generally. We may, indeed, think of "wars of the rebellions" during the first seven decades of the nineteenth century.

The idea of "wars of the rebellions" raises further questions about what we have come to call Reconstruction. The literature on this complex period—mostly dated from 1863 or 1865 to 1877—has shown enormous sophistication and depth. And it focuses chiefly on the southern states that left the Union and the problems attending political reunification and the transition from slavery to freedom. This surely makes sense. The rebellion was concentrated there, and the institution of slavery was abolished without compensation to slave owners. Pressing issues of land, labor, and belonging had to be solved. But the federal government was also extending its arms across the trans-Mississippi West, and in both the West and the South federal officials—mostly aligned with the Republican Party—prescribed an assortment of conditions concerning labor, faith, family life, discipline, sexuality, property rights, and land use before these regions and their populations would be fully integrated into the new American nation-state. If the conditions were not accepted, various types of punishment were meted out, ranging from repression and confinement (especially involving Native peoples) to disfranchisement and exclusion. It was a massive project of state building that had strong imperial impulses.

It was also a project of capitalist development. There seems to be a good deal of agreement among historians these days that the expansion of capitalism was a central force in the European settlement of the North American continent, especially in a broad crescent stretching from the Chesapeake through the lower Mississippi Valley. There, slave plantations produced staple crops for an international market and, by the nineteenth century, fueled the growth of the entire country. Without question, an Atlantic world of commerce and coercive labor exploitation had come into being at least by the early eighteenth century and deepened its hold by the early nineteenth. Yet *A Nation Without Borders* portrays a much more extended process by which capitalism as a "system" of social relations took hold in the United States.

On the one hand, the book suggests that capitalism encountered major social, political, and cultural obstacles during the first half of the nineteenth century. These included household economies oriented to self-subsistence and local trade, slave labor that defied capitalist forms of production and limited the market for goods and services, and popular hostility to paper money and banks. The period, I argue, witnessed market "intensifications" rather than transformations in the prevailing forms of production, exchange, and social organization. While state and municipal governments played important roles in facilitating commercial expansion—chartering transportation companies and banks, for example—capitalist labor and property relations were only gaining footholds incrementally, in part because the federal government was itself a contested ground of policy making in these regards.

On the other hand, most of the North American continent was populated by Native societies—some economically dynamic and politically aggressive—with divisions of labor, gender relations, social hierarchies, and forms of property and use rights, not to mention ideas about time, space, and spirituality, that bore no resemblance to capitalism. That "middle grounds" of trade could be established between Native Americans and Europeans testified to the flexibility of the Native economic modes but not to the ease with which they could make their peace with capitalist production and exchange. The bitter conflicts erupting almost continuously across the American interior during the nineteenth century were effectively over which form of social organization would prevail. It was only during the War of the Rebellion, when a new type of central state took hold, that the balance decisively tipped.

Indeed, the War of the Rebellion not only allowed for the consolidation of a nation-state but also advanced the interests of new classes of financiers and industrialists who, with the help of their allies in the Republican Party, gave capitalism real traction in the political economy. They especially looked to the trans-Mississippi West as a developmental area. Aided by the army, the courts, Congress, and often local governments, they built a massive network of railroads, took aim at Native societies that stood in their way, organized an array of extractive industries, and tried to keep a growing labor force under their thumbs. Their sights quickly reached into Mexico, Central America, and the Caribbean basin, setting the stage for subsequent ventures in the Pacific. In many ways, the postbellum West and South became, for a time, "colonies" of the Northeast, and they served as proving grounds for a reconfigured imperialism: in their economic and political subordination, in their ruthless exploitation, and in the encounters they offered with various peoples of color, whether Native American, Hispanic, or African American.

But if capitalism gained significant traction, it was also deeply contested for the remainder of the century. And some of the most determined and enduring oppositional movements had strong bases in the South and the West. From the Knights of Labor to the Populists, from the disciples of Henry George and Edward Bellamy to the social democrats and the socialists, these "peripheries" vibrated intensely with popular unrest and political experimentation. Organized principally around "antimonopoly" sensibilities but also heavily infused by the republicanism, socialism, and Marxism that refugees from European revolutions brought with them in the 1870s and 1880s, these movements vied for power at the workplace and in the halls of government. They fashioned searing critiques of capitalist relations and values—and of the political corruption that appeared to sustain them—and hoped to use the levers of the state, locally and nationally, to readjust the balances to favor "producers" over the "moneyed" interests. In some places, they devised remarkable alternatives to the ways of constructing civil and political society. Together, as with the expansion of capitalism, they linked the United States to the worlds of the Atlantic and the Pacific.

These social and political struggles took place at a time when the international economy was cascading through a prolonged depression (from the mid-1870s to the mid-1890s) and were closely related to it. So intense could these conflicts become—the United States had the most violent labor history of any society in the industrializing world at this time—that they commonly involved the deployment of official military and paramilitary forces and contributed to a sense of crisis that was wide and deep. Images of the Paris Commune of 1871— when workers took control of the French capital, sought to enact their own vision of social justice, and then were violently crushed by state authorities—were invoked all around as symbolic of what might be possible and what should be feared. The result was a period, from the 1890s through the first two decades of the twentieth century, of what I call "reconstructions" (customarily known as the Progressive Era): efforts by social, labor, political, and corporate reformers to reconfigure the authority of the state, the property relations of industrial ownership and investment, the organization of work, the universe of political participation, the nature of social responsibility, and the reach of the nation's imperial arms. Following on the defeat of the oppositional movements, the reconstructions also showed the marks of those same movements' influence and social democratic impulses.

By its very title, *A Nation Without Borders* seeks to embody the large global context in which the United States was transformed between 1830 and 1910, one that encompassed the Atlantic, the Caribbean basin, much of Central and South America, and growing parts of the Pacific. The borders of influence, power, and meaning were constantly being traversed. It is impossible to think of anything that went on in the United States during these years (or, for that matter, any other years) in isolation or to think of an international arena that did not increasingly feel the effects of what was happening in the United States.

But *A Nation Without Borders* is also meant to capture the tensions and contradictions between nation and empire. A nation is understood to have clearly defined borders, which delineate sovereignty and belonging. Empires, though they may expand and contract, lack real borders; they are more about vectors, claims, and alliances. *A Nation Without Borders* therefore begins in the 1830s in the contested borderlands of northern Mexico, at the time of what is known as the Texas Revolution, when the United States was not yet a nation but had visions of imperial power. The book ends in the second decade of the twentieth century, again across the lands of northern and central Mexico, as one of the great revolutions of the twentieth century simultaneously defined limits to the imperial reach of the American nation-state and anticipated new challenges the United States would face in the century to come.

Part One

Empire and Union

CHAPTER ONE

Borderlands

Comanche "Horse-backs Camp" (Ta-her-ye-qua-hip).
Photograph by W. S. Soule.

Centers and Peripheries

As he rode northward out of San Luis Potosí at the head of an army of six thousand in early 1836, General Antonio López de Santa Anna intended to crush a rebellion in the state of Coahuila y Tejas and reassert the hold of Mexico's center over the vast stretches of its peripheries, north, east, and south. Born in Veracruz in 1794 to a prosperous creole family, Santa Anna had joined what was then the Spanish army at the age of sixteen and was thereafter embroiled in the convulsive military and political struggles that ushered in Mexican independence and charted the course of a fledgling country.

Santa Anna was haughty, temperamental, and guided chiefly by personal ambitions for power and adulation—he bragged in 1836 that if he found the hand of the U.S. government in the northern unrest, "he could continue the march of his army to Washington and place upon its Capitol the Mexican flag"—and his allegiances swung with the predictability of a weather vane. First a royalist officer battling against the Hidalgo rebellion and its peasant and republican successors, he eventually followed many of his fellow creoles in embracing independence and the constitutional monarchy of Agustín de Iturbide. In a veritable flash, he sided with liberals and federalists in ousting Iturbide, establishing a republic, and fending off a conservative revolt. In 1829, when Spain attempted a reconquest, Santa Anna led Mexican forces in successfully turning the Spanish back, paving the way for his overwhelming election as the country's president in 1833, still aligned, it seemed, with the liberals. He then quickly, and surprisingly, stepped down, leaving the presidency to his liberal vice president, who pursued a reformist agenda designed to trim the sails of the army and the Catholic Church. This time, Santa Anna heeded the appeals of angry conservatives. He helped them topple the regime he had once headed, repealed the liberal reforms, and tried to set the country on a centralist course. In 1836, he commanded not only the Mexican army but also what there was of the Mexican state.

The challenges newly independent Mexico faced from its borderlands were hardly unique. Forged in the cauldron of imperial crises and revolutionary movements that rocked the Atlantic world from the last third of the eighteenth century, Mexico, like other countries that had just emerged in the hemisphere, had to establish its legitimacy and authority over the diverse populations and territory it claimed to control. Although sparked in 1810 by what became a massive and bloody peasant insurrection (the "Hidalgo revolt"), independence, when ultimately achieved in 1821, saw the peasants largely subdued and, as elsewhere in Latin America, a creole elite of landowners, mine owners, merchants, and army officers steering the transition to nationhood. Stretching from the Yucatán,

Tabasco, and Chiapas in the far southeast to Alta California in the far northwest, Mexico had more than twice the landmass of the early United States. And the immense northern regions—perhaps half the size of the entire country—were thinly populated by Spaniards, creoles, and mestizos and defended by a very loose chain of military outposts (presidios) and Catholic missions. There, from the Pacific coast, east across the Great Basin and the Rocky Mountains, and into the southern plains, Native peoples reigned supreme.

From the beginning, Mexican elites, much like their counterparts in the United States, were divided between those who wanted power concentrated in a central state (they were known as centralists in Mexico and federalists in the United States) and those who sought a weaker central state and more regional autonomy (they were known as federalists in Mexico and republicans or anti-federalists in the United States). But unlike the United States, Mexico initially gave rise to a centralist tendency with bases in the army and the Catholic Church, as embodied in the imperious figure of Agustín de Iturbide, who unveiled a Mexican "empire" with himself as emperor. Within months, Iturbide managed to alienate allies and skeptics alike and was quickly routed by federalists. A republican constitution was then crafted in 1824. Modeled to some extent on the Constitution of the United States—there were three branches of government, including a bicameral legislature and a president selected by state legislatures for a four-year term—it went much further in addressing the civil standing of the country's denizens, proclaiming the equality of all Mexicans regardless of race, ethnicity, or social status (though remaining mute about the enslaved of African descent, who could be found working in mining areas and on coastal sugar plantations).

Of perhaps greatest consequence, the constitution divided the country into nineteen states with their own elected governments and four territories (three in the north, including Alta California and Nuevo México), which came under the jurisdiction of the national legislature. Although the Catholic Church retained its monopoly on Mexico's spiritual life and the country's president could claim extraordinary powers in times of emergency, the forces of centralism in Mexico City were clearly weakened and the impulses toward federalism and local autonomy in the states and territories strengthened. In the Yucatán, Sonora y Sinaloa, and especially silver-mining Zacatecas—not to mention very distant Alta California—the federalist disposition thrived, at times manifest in tax resistance and the creation of civilian militias. And, in an effort to secure the northeastern borderlands, the Mexican government offered a variety of incentives to colonists from the United States, who began settling in Coahuila y Tejas during the early 1820s and whose loyalty to the Mexican state was soon suspect.

The task of establishing stable regimes presented enormous challenges for all the new republics of the Western Hemisphere. Haiti, the second to break colonial ties, was rent by deep conflicts between former slaves and former free people of color. They had cooperated long enough to defeat the French, the Spanish, and the British militarily and to end slavery but almost immediately sank into a political maelstrom of assassinations, coups d'état, rival governments, and domestic rebellions—all exacerbated by the diplomatic isolation that had been imposed by the United States and the European powers. Peru, Bolivia, and Chile, emerging independent from anticolonial struggles with Spain, would nonetheless battle each other for years, sometimes by force of arms, over territorial disputes that often unhinged each of their governments. Venezuela's diverse terrain made national integration difficult and turned the office of the presidency into something of a revolving door.

Long boastful of its comparative stability, the United States also suffered more than its share of political turmoil. For the first half decade of independence, the Articles of Confederation provided a shaky foundation of governance (as Shays's Rebellion in western Massachusetts brought home), and even after the Constitution was ratified, questions of federal authority, territorial integrity, and public policy proved bitterly divisive. The British sought their own reconquest, the French and the Spanish schemed with separatists in the Mississippi Valley borderlands, secessionist movements erupted in several areas including New England, Native Americans organized to resist the encroachments of white settlers, and the election of 1800, pitting Thomas Jefferson's Republicans against John Adams's Federalists, threatened to break the Republic apart—though hardly for the last time.

By the late 1820s, Mexican centralists, especially those in the army, had grown increasingly concerned about the centrifugal forces spinning peripheral regions (particularly in the north) out of the orbit of Mexico City. Small revolts against government officials had already erupted in Alta California and Coahuila y Tejas—one, joining Anglos and Cherokees in the ill-fated Republic of Fredonia near Nacodoches in 1826–27, was crushed. Patterns of trade that had long moved from north to south, to markets in Chihuahua, Durango, and Mexico City, were now turning west to east, as merchants in Louisiana and Missouri began to tap the commerce of Tejas and Nuevo México. Traveling across Tejas in 1829, General Manuel de Mier y Terán, commander of the military jurisdiction of northeastern Mexico, thus worried about the dispositions of the American colonists there as well as about the designs of the U.S. government—"The North Americans have conquered whatever territory adjoins them," he observed—and urged concerted state action. Warning that "either the government occupies Tejas now, or it is lost forever," he recommended fortifying the military presence in the north, expanding the coastal trade between Tejas and the rest of Mexico, and attracting Mexican and European settlers to offset the American influence. Partly to stem the flow of American immigration, the Mexican president, Vicente Guerrero, abolished slavery in 1829, and the next year the Congress banned American immigration to the border areas entirely. Although slaveholders in Tejas won exemption from the emancipation decree and the Congress subsequently lifted the immigration ban, Mexico City seemed intent on bringing the northern regions to heel.

But it was not until Santa Anna returned to the presidency in 1834 at the behest of the centralists that a new framework of governance was imposed. Inspired by the conservative "Plan de Cuernavaca" which demanded the repeal of recent liberal reforms and the punishment of those who had enacted them, Santa Anna, together with a newly elected Congress, began to dismantle the federalist constitution of 1824 and undermine the power of the states. It would not be easy to carry through. Predictably, federalist strongholds in Zacatecas and Coahuila resisted tenaciously and forced Santa Anna to intervene militarily. Yet by 1835 the most serious challenge issued from Tejas, where rebellion had long been brewing and where an ascendant rebel faction had embraced the goal of independence. There Santa Anna headed with his army of six thousand in early 1836, far outnumbering the rebel forces and intending to make easy work of it.

Los Indios Bárbaros

When General Santa Anna gazed toward the northern borderlands, he thought about more than the rebellious Texians (Americans in Tejas) and Tejanos (Mexicans in Tejas). He thought, too, about "the savage tribes" (*los indios bárbaros*) who had been waging war in the "frontier departments" and making a mockery of the presumed authority of the Mexican state. The Hidalgo revolt and the decade of brutal conflict into which it plunged Mexico seemed to invite Indian raiding in areas shorn of troops and militias. And although newly independent Mexico looked to make peace, the state's depleted treasury made it very difficult to maintain the gifting rituals that underwrote alliances from the 1780s. Indeed, the effort to limit Indian attacks and advances in the north encouraged the Mexican government to attract the very American colonists who were now causing it so much trouble.

What appeared to Santa Anna and other Mexicans as "savage tribes" were, in fact, constellations of Native bands and confederations that raided, traded, exchanged captives, and fashioned alliances all across the Great Plains and the arid Mexican northwest. Farthest east were relatively sedentary horticultural peoples such as the Wichita, Osage, Pawnee, and Omaha; farthest west were

Navajos, Pueblos, and Utes who formed part of a sprawling Nuevo Méxican trade network built around horses, slaves, woven goods, maize, metals, and guns. But across the southern plains were to be found the hunting and pastoral Kiowas, Lipan Apaches, and, fiercest and most formidable of all, Comanches.

Nomadic, Uto-Aztecan speaking, and originally Shoshone, those who would emerge as Comanches (they called themselves Numunuu, or "the people") began moving out of the northern reaches of the Great Basin in the sixteenth century toward the central plains. By the early eighteenth century, a faction had broken off, headed farther south, and formed a military and political alliance with the Utes that spread havoc among Navajos and Apaches along the northern perimeter of Nuevo México. Most important, they had taken advantage of the horses that became available from the Spanish sometime in the seventeenth century (aided perhaps by the great Pueblo Revolt of 1680) and transformed themselves into extraordinarily able equestrians. With their mounts, their radius for trading and hunting expanded enormously, and the bison now became central to their way of life. What came to be called La Comanchería stretched from southeastern Nuevo México and northeastern Chihuahua across Tejas to the Arkansas River valley. It was a territory larger than western Europe.

At the heart of La Comanchería and of the Great Plains more generally was a distinctive political economy built around bison hunting. Across the many centuries of its unfolding, this political economy saw ever-shifting participants and showed the marks of encounters not only with many different Native peoples but also with European imperial powers. By the early nineteenth century, it included a variety of trading centers, a vast raiding zone chiefly to the south, growing economic contacts with American merchants to the east, and a complex of alliances. The bison served as the main source of food, clothing, and shelter and as an increasingly important article of trade. The raiding zones enabled the accumulation of horses and human captives, both of which were necessary to the hunting of bison, exchanges with trading partners, and the achievement of social status. The alliances helped organize hunting and trade, recognized territorial claims, and directed raiding with greater force and efficiency; they also consecrated relations of power and dependency.

For all of its geographical reach, La Comanchería was very much a decentered society. Its basic unit, the *ranchería*, included up to 250 people, mostly tied by kinship (or fictive kin) relations, and it encompassed the most important activities and hierarchies of the Comanche people as a whole. As in most other Native societies of the plains, gender and age served as the markers for the organization of social, economic, and political life. Adult men had the responsibility for hunting and raiding. Teenage boys took on the laborious tasks of herding and breaking the horses. Women—older and younger—raised the children, processed the bison meat, and cooked the food, but as the hunting economy grew, they became more involved with the horse herds and the bison hides. Indeed, the widening scale of economic activity intensified the demand for labor and thereby made polygyny and enslavement (mainly of captive women and children) increasingly important in Comanche communities. Which is to say that the burdens of a vibrant economy fell heavily on the shoulders of women—captive or not—and accordingly led to a deterioration in their circumstances.

The enslavement of captives—like polygyny—had long been practiced by Comanches and other Native peoples of the plains and Great Basin regions. It was the product of raiding and warfare, and although some adult men were taken into captivity, most of the captives were women and children (Mexican and Indian); the men were regarded as unsuitable to enslavement and instead were killed. Many of the captives were then brought to slave markets and traded, but at least among the Comanche most were kept to work with the horse and mule herds, gather food and wood, cook, and carry out the arduous labor of preparing bison meat and hides: all the more so as the bison economy boomed and the labor available on *rancherías* proved insufficient. Like enslaved captives the world over, these were immediately stripped of their familial and tribal associations and given new names—a ritual of social death and rebirth— though they were regarded as occupying a status distinct from those "born of Comanche." Even so, and unlike enslaved African captives in the Americas (though more like captives and slaves within western Africa itself), they could be assimilated into Comanche families, becoming wives (sometimes in polygynous arrangements), sons and daughters, and eventually spouses, and could play key roles as cultural intermediaries in economic and diplomatic spheres. Some of the males also became mounted warriors and raiders.

The dynamic of the Comanche political economy of the nineteenth century— and of the Native Great Plains more generally—grew out of the demands of equestrian-based bison hunting, ideas about land and wealth, and the pursuit of social prestige and manhood by members of kinship groups and *rancherías*. Comanches sought territorial expansion not to define clear borders or land titles, not to assert cultural superiority, but rather to gain access to the land's resources and to sources of wealth in the form of horses, captives, and trade. Horses were necessary for hunting, and they required extensive pasture lands for nourishment, but horses were also, together with captives, a recognized form of private property (individual property in land had no basis in Comanche society) and personal wealth. Raiding was an important means of acquiring new horses and captives, but it was also the chief avenue for males to achieve social acceptance

and enhance their social standing. *Rancherías* were often on the move owing to
the depletion of pasture, and trading networks enabled Comanches to exchange
surplus livestock and the booty from raids for food supplies, craft goods, and
weapons (including guns and powder). These exchanges and networks linked
Comanches, directly and indirectly, with Native peoples far to the north, west,
and east and opened them to economic relations with Europeans and their
descendants either settled in places like Santa Fe or pressing in from the north
and the east.

Raiding and trading allowed for the accumulation of personal wealth among
Comanches and therefore the development of social distinctions. Building a herd
was a lengthy process, perhaps years in the making, and all of the young men,
irrespective of their families' wealth, were expected to participate in what proved
to be intense competition on battlefields and in collecting the spoils of success.
But by the early nineteenth century, something of an elite had emerged, set
apart by their age and gender, their massive herds, their relative leisure, and the
networks of dependents they could support. Neither rigid nor heritable, social
and economic status nonetheless conferred political power and authority, especially if generosity in the distribution of personal wealth was embraced; among
the Comanche, wealth acquired social meaning chiefly when it was given away.
Through such methods, elite men became leaders of individual *rancherías* (the
leaders were known as *paraibos*) and helped determine when members would
move camp or engage in small-scale raiding.

Although *rancherías* served as the basic units of Comanche society and had a
great deal of independence in decision making, they were part of a larger confederation. Each *ranchería* was aligned with one of four Comanche divisions—Hois,
Tenewa, Kotsoteka, and Yamparika—which together shared language as well
as ideals and sensibilities as to spirituality, personal and communal responsibilities, proper conduct, and the acceptable forms of retribution. They gathered at
certain times of the year to reinforce the bonds between them and engage in
communal hunts, assembling in the largest numbers—often in winter camps in
the thousands—along wooded river valleys. There they staged ceremonies of
cultural cohesion, and their political councils met to settle conflicts and set goals
as to warfare and diplomacy. At this point, decentered Comanche bands composed a powerful army capable of inflicting massive damage on those regarded
as enemies.

By the last quarter of the eighteenth century, the Comanche had emerged as
the dominant power on the southern plains. Their numbers reached, and might
have exceeded, forty thousand, more than the Spanish and mestizo populations
of Tejas and Nuevo México combined. They had pushed Apaches south far
beyond the Canadian River, opened trading relations with Pawnees, Kiowas,

and Cheyennes to the north, turned Native bands to the east into tributary clients, and transformed the northern borderlands of what was then New Spain into raiding domains. Looking southward, the Comanche did not recognize official borders or realms of imperial sovereignty; they rather saw scattered outposts, haciendas, and ranches populated by horses, mules, and potential captives. Theft and trade were not alternative or contradictory activities but rather two sides of the coin of Comanche hegemony.

When the Comanche entered into what would prove to be a long-lasting peace with the Spanish in 1786 (which included a military alliance against the Apache), the very large area of Tejas, Nuevo México, and La Comanchería seemed less a territory divided into discrete political entities than an increasingly integrated economic zone. Navajos and Utes joined the peace as well, making for an extended period of stability and allowing the unhindered movement of goods and people over a great many miles. The alliances were cemented by face-to-face contacts and the exchange of gifts that could be redistributed within each of the Native groups, thereby securing the popular followings of the Native leaders. Although the Spanish imagined that they could gain the upper hand and reduce the Comanche to a position of dependence, it was the Comanche who got the better of the Spanish and defined the boundaries of the relationship. The Comanche advantage became especially apparent in the early years of the nineteenth century as their trading interests partly turned eastward in the direction of American merchants operating through Missouri, Mississippi, and Louisiana and the Mexican independence struggles of the second decade of the nineteenth century made the depleted northern borderlands easy targets for raiding. While Agustín de Iturbide invited a Comanche delegation led by Chief Guonique to attend his coronation in Mexico City and sought to appease the Comanche with a variety of incentives, Mexican governments could not sustain gifting diplomacy at the level Comanches had come to expect. The alliance of more than four decades quickly unraveled, and the Comanche unleashed raids for horses and captives ever deeper into what Mexico considered its terrain: through Coahuila y Tejas, into Chihuahua and Nuevo León, and as far south and east as Durango, Zacatecas, San Luis Potosí, and Tamaulipas.

A Slaveholders' Frontier

Well before Mexican independence, Spanish colonizers had encouraged settlement in Tejas to repel the designs of the Indians, the British, the French, and the Americans. By the early nineteenth century, Tejano enclaves could be found in the northeast around Nacogdoches, along the San Antonio River in the Béxar-Goliad region, and between the Nueces and the Rio Grande rivers, mostly north

and west of Matamoros. But while the Spanish and then the Mexicans imagined an international border created by the Red and Sabine rivers, eastern Tejas
(Texas to the English speakers and writers) remained very much a borderland
marked by murky and competing territorial claims. Known for its rich soils and
access to the Gulf of Mexico, the area caught the attention of the sorts of people
already creating a "cotton kingdom" in what was then the American Southwest of Alabama, Mississippi, Louisiana, and the territories of Arkansas and
Missouri: slaveholders, land speculators, and commercial interests operating in
St. Louis and Independence, Missouri, Natchitoches, Louisiana, and especially
New Orleans.

The cultural and geopolitical liminality of eastern Texas—like that of other
North American borderlands—seemed well embodied in the figure of Moses
Austin, who looked to establish colonies there. Born in Connecticut in 1761,
Austin initially became involved in the dry goods business and moved to Philadelphia to join hands with his brother. Once there, he married into a family with
mining interests and before long was operating a lead mine in western Virginia.
Although he established the village of Austinville, replete with a furnace and
blacksmith shop, he went bust. Undeterred, Austin gazed west: not to territory
claimed by the United States, but rather to what was then upper Spanish Louisiana. By swearing allegiance to the Spanish crown, he managed to get a grant of
one league of land (nearly forty-five hundred acres) and continued his lead-
mining pursuits, branching out into shipping, banking, and merchandising.
A man of aristocratic tastes, Austin had slaves working for him and built a
plantation-style mansion called Durham Hall. But, as in western Virginia, he
also ran up debts that threw his mining operations into jeopardy. Trading on his
adopted Spanish colonial identity even after upper Louisiana became part of the
United States, he then hatched a plan to settle Anglo-Americans in east-central
Tejas and hoped to persuade Spanish officials in San Antonio de Béxar to make
the land available.

Despite the political turbulence created by the Mexican independence struggles, Moses Austin succeeded in being designated an empresario (land contrac-
tor) and was granted a huge tract in the Brazos River valley in 1821, but he
contracted pneumonia and died very soon thereafter. The project then fell to his
son Stephen F. Austin, who managed to negotiate the swirling political currents in Tejas and Mexico City and confirm his title to the land. Looking to
recruit colonists, Austin headed to Louisiana and, owing to the stipulations of
the land grant, could advertise very generous terms: 640 acres for each family
head, an additional 320 acres for the wife and 100 acres for each of the children, together with a square league for the purposes of grazing. Colonists were
given six years to improve the land without being assessed for taxes, and while

they were expected to become Catholics, little effort was made to enforce conversion. Significantly, although antislavery sentiment brewed in Mexico City and legislators both outlawed slave trading and prescribed the emancipation of slave children at age fourteen, Austin was able to offer colonists an extra 80 acres for every slave they brought in.

That Austin moved to evade the direction of change on the slavery question in Mexico suggested that from the first—the hopes of Mexican officials notwithstanding—the axis of Texas colonization turned west to east, rather than north to south. Neither Austin nor other empresarios attracted many settlers from other parts of Mexico; almost all came from the United States, and almost all of them came to Texas from a state where slavery served as the foundation of social, economic, and political life. Some arrived from Kentucky, Tennessee, and Missouri; many more came from the rapidly developing plantation states of Alabama, Mississippi, and Louisiana. They either brought their slaves along or intended to acquire them after they settled, and they were drawn by the lure of land that was cheap and highly suitable for raising cotton. Although the Mexican government wished that they would gradually move into the interior of Tejas and, together with Tejanos, form a line of defense against Comanche raids, the Anglo-Texans clustered chiefly along the Gulf Coast, where the best cotton lands were to be had and relative safety could be assured. They purchased supplies from New Orleans or from merchants in the old Spanish/French trading town of Natchitoches, in north-central Louisiana—not from market centers in Mexico—and sent their livestock and cotton back in the same direction. For all intents and purposes, their activities and orientation blurred whatever there was of a border between Tejas and Louisiana.

Anglo settlers and colonists were, of course, ready to make the political concessions necessary to their economic and familial aspirations. Stephen F. Austin had, himself, become a Mexican citizen and was little interested in seeing Texas joined to the United States. For allies within Mexico, he looked to the liberals and federalists and, with their assistance, sought to block government initiatives deemed hostile to the interests of Anglo-Texans—especially because they might undermine the stability of slavery. A small slaveholder, though never a champion of "the principle of slavery," he quickly came to accept the reality of Texas development. "Texas must be a slave country," he wrote. "Circumstances and unavoidable necessity compels it. It is the wish of the people there and it is my duty to do all I can prudently to favor it."

As early as 1825, the Austin colony could boast a population of nearly two thousand, about one-quarter of whom were slaves, and colonists had drawn a slave code. Other settlements had similar social profiles, and although Mexican authorities would officially prohibit the importation of any more slaves, Anglo immigrants arranged long-term indentures for their bondpeople before they crossed into Tejas, effectively passing government scrutiny and receiving welcomes from the empresarios. Further labor demands drew boatloads of African slaves by way of Cuba to the port of Galveston, escaping the American naval patrols attempting to bring slave smugglers to law. By the 1830s, Anglo-Texans far outnumbered Tejanos and were laying the foundations of a slave plantation society. Perhaps as many as one in four of them owned slaves.

But however successful Stephen Austin might have been in protecting Tejas slaveholders from Mexican officials either in Mexico City or in Saltillo (the capital of Coahuila y Tejas) bent on ridding the country of slaves, the slaveholders did not rest comfortably. By the late 1820s and early 1830s, the central government seemed hostile to their long-term interests and ready to weaken their power base. The emancipation decree of 1829 (from which Texans won exemption) and congressional legislation in 1832 that limited the length of labor contracts to ten years (and thus challenged the use of indentures) were problematic enough; perhaps more threatening was the 1830 ban on further American immigration together with the central state's renewed efforts to collect customs duties and garrison more troops there. The resistance was not long in coming. In 1832, at the very time the Nullification Crisis flared in South Carolina, Anglo-Americans briefly occupied a customs house near Galveston Bay, and more of them (with Austin's help) demanded repeal of the immigration ban and the separation of Tejas from Coahuila. Santa Anna yielded on the immigration issue, and the legislature of Coahuila y Tejas, while refusing to grant separation, nonetheless enacted a series of political reforms that gave the Texans more seats in the state legislature and more control over their local affairs. It might not have been enough to deflate the growing discontent. The Anglo colonists, a government official darkly predicted, "seek nothing more than pretexts for a revolution, whose first object will be separation from Coahuila and afterwards from the Republic."

Imperial Eyes

Texas was not only of interest to slaveholders and aspiring cotton growers who had taken their first turns in the emerging plantation belt of the American Deep South. It had long been of interest to American political leaders who imagined a continental empire before the ink on the Declaration of Independence was dry. After all, the model of governance they had inherited and defended to the last— they rebelled against what they saw as Britain's violations rather than its essence—was imperial, with a metropolitan center loosely coordinating the activities of far-flung and, for the most part, self-regulating outposts. When North

America's version of the Seven Years' War (known on the western side of the Atlantic as the French and Indian War) relieved the French of their claims east of the Mississippi River, it demanded a major effort on the part of British imperial authorities to keep colonial settlers east of the Appalachians and out of Indian country to the west. The Proclamation of 1763 thereby provoked some of the most serious discontent with British rule. Indeed, although they have chiefly been regarded as republicans, many of the architects of American independence— from Franklin and Jefferson to Paine and Madison—looked well beyond the Appalachians and the Mississippi and spoke a language of empire.

It of course required immense conceit to speak of empire when the political integrity of the United States had yet to be established, when the country was only a collection of thinly populated and, largely, semi-independent republics that evinced deep suspicions of centralized authority. But empire simultaneously expressed the aggressive aspirations of white settler populations and the Enlightenment-inspired sense, among sections of the elite and the intelligentsia, that a new political order had been born and was destined to spread across the globe. Empire, too, seemed to offer a solution to the problem of the republic as the eighteenth century saw it: that republics could only thrive in small, culturally cohesive territories; otherwise they tended to become tyrannies. James Madison, in *Federalist* 10, most famously challenged this logic, insisting that only in a large territory could a republic thrive because the many interests that necessarily emerged would make it impossible for any one of them to dominate. Although Madison did not invoke the language of empire there, others, including Thomas Jefferson, understood Madison's ideas in imperial terms and touted them in explaining both the success a geographically expansive American republic would have and the continental horizons it would pursue. That Jefferson the slaveholder could imagine an "empire of liberty" suggested the many contradictions that beset the American project from the first.

Those contradictions were nowhere as plainly in evidence as in the process eventuating in the Louisiana Purchase of 1803, arguably the most far-reaching political and diplomatic event in nineteenth-century America. Imperial-minded political officials, together with western commercial interests, had, since the establishment of American independence, looked greedily and warily on the Mississippi Valley and the port city of New Orleans, understanding both as constituting a main artery of economic prosperity. "There is on the globe one single spot," Jefferson observed shortly after assuming the presidency, "the possessor of which is our natural enemy. It is New Orleans." News that Spain had retroceded control over the Louisiana Territory to France thus stirred great consternation—"The day that France takes possession of New Orleans . . . we must marry ourselves to the British fleet and nation," Jefferson warned—and Jefferson instructed his minister to France, Robert R. Livingston, to offer $2 million for the city. Livingston ended up with all of Louisiana for $15 million.

It was no accident. When the French persuaded the Spanish crown to return Louisiana to them in the Treaty of San Ildefonso in the fall of 1800 (France had been forced to cede the territory to Spain after the Seven Years' War), Napoleon Bonaparte, who had come to power in 1799, imagined the creation of a great empire in the Americas. The empire's center would be in the Caribbean, organized around the rich, sugar-producing colonies of Martinique, Guadeloupe, and St. Domingue, but Louisiana would serve as the vital periphery, a sprawling storehouse of foodstuffs and livestock for the Caribbean plantations and an extended barrier against the incursions of the British and the Americans. True, the sugar islands had been convulsed for the previous decade by massive slave rebellions—the largest in St. Domingue—that had ended slavery, destroyed the plantation economies, and defeated the armies of Britain and Spain. But Napoleon, in his audacity, planned to reverse the wheels of history: to send his grand army to quell the rebellions, arrest the leaders, restore slavery, and make it possible to get the sugar mills up and running again.

He nearly succeeded. Ten thousand troops under the command of Napoleon's brother-in-law Charles Victor Emmanuel LeClerc left France for the Caribbean in early 1802, soon after a peace had been concluded with the British. In short order, LeClerc seemed to pacify St. Domingue and took into custody the island's great rebel leader, Toussaint Louverture, who would die a year later in a frigid cell in the French mountains. But when word of the French intention to restore slavery began to circulate, the officers who had served Toussaint—Henri Christophe and Jean Jacques Dessalines chief among them—reignited the popular rebellion and, with the aid of tropical diseases, decimated the French army. LeClerc perished in November, and the mission collapsed in shambles. "Damn sugar, damn coffee, damn colonies," Napoleon soon thundered. Without St. Domingue, the jewel of the French colonial system, the American empire appeared worthless, and to the enormous surprise of Jefferson's negotiators he offered up the whole of Louisiana.

The moment was replete with ironies of the deepest sort. Jefferson, the slaveholder who saw in the slave rebellion in St. Domingue the incarnation of his greatest fears ("I tremble for my country when I reflect that God is just and that his justice cannot sleep forever") and had effectively given Napoleon the green light to intervene, now scored his biggest political and diplomatic coup thanks to the defeat of Napoleon and the victory of the rebellious slaves. "Santo Domingo," as the political discourse had it, would serve as the terrorizing image for slaveholders throughout the hemisphere who faced the prospect of emancipation, but it also enabled the United States to double its size while introducing a host of new issues and challenges that would shape the remainder of the century. Had the rebellion in St. Domingue gone the way of all others before it—with the crushing defeat of the slaves—Atlantic slavery might well have been reinvigorated, and Napoleon would likely have strengthened his hold on Louisiana, forcing Jefferson, who regarded the "possessor" of New Orleans as "our natural enemy," to contemplate his next move.

As it was, the sale of Louisiana came with an assortment of irregularities and uncertainties. It was not at all clear if Napoleon had the authority to sell the territory or Jefferson to buy it; nor was it clear what property was ultimately conveyed. When the Spanish had retroceded Louisiana to the French in 1800, Napoleon and his foreign minister, Charles de Talleyrand, assured the Spanish king that they would never alienate or transfer the territory to a third country; when the Spanish learned of what had transpired between the French and the Americans, they were justly outraged, all the more so because the French had yet to take full possession of the territory from the Spanish. Napoleon, moreover, moved ahead without consulting the Corps Législatif as French law required him to do. "The sale of Louisiana to the United States was trebly invalid," Henry Adams later wrote with a sardonic eye, "if it were French property, Bonaparte could not constitutionally alienate it without the consent of the Chambers; if it were Spanish property, he could not alienate it at all; if Spain had a right of reclamation, his sale was worthless." For his part, Jefferson's constitutional authority to add new territory to the United States was dubious at best, and he was sufficiently concerned to craft an amendment to the Constitution that advisers prevailed on him to leave in the drawer.

Perhaps most problematic for the future, however, were the ambiguities as to the boundaries of the territory itself. There appeared to be consensus about the Mississippi River as the eastern boundary, although no one knew precisely where the river's source lay, and the Spanish insisted on their claim to the strip of gulf coastal land between Pensacola and the river's edge, known as West Florida. Reeling from the course of events and wary of new intruders on the edges of New Spain (Mexico), the Spanish took a very delimited view, arguing that the United States obtained only a narrow corridor out of New Orleans on the Mississippi River's western side. More generally accepted were boundaries that included the watersheds of the Mississippi, Missouri, Platte, Arkansas, Red, and Canadian rivers, together with other rivers flowing into them, thereby spreading northward into British Canada and westward across the Great Plains and cutting into northern Tejas. Indeed, Andrew Jackson would later insist, in eyeing Mexican Tejas (as Jefferson had earlier thought), that the Louisiana Purchase boundary went as far west and south as the Nueces River—this despite the Adams-Onís Treaty of 1819, which marked the boundary of Louisiana and Tejas at the Sabine River, much farther to the north and east.

Small wonder that Jackson, soon after stepping into the presidency in 1829 and well before the Anglo settlers there had raised much of a tumult, sent Anthony Butler (a Texas land speculator) to Mexico City with instructions to purchase Tejas. Butler told Mexican officials, at Jackson's behest, that Indian violence had exposed Mexico's weakness in the north and that the United States might be forced to seize Tejas for purposes of self-defense; at all events, if Mexico refused to sell, Tejas would soon be lost to settler rebellion. The Mexicans would have none of it and sent Butler packing. But it was just the sort of omen of which General Mier y Terán, touring Tejas around the same time, had warned.

It was also the sort of dilemma that imperial eyes invited, though often refused to see. The principal threat to the destiny of the American republic and empire still seemed to come from the European powers that had long been collecting colonies in the hemisphere and, despite losses, likely wished to continue extending their reach. Although the British failure to subdue the United States in the War of 1812 could be regarded as a turning point, the prospect of hostile forces encircling the country remained a very real one. "Russia might take California, Peru, Chili [sic]," John Quincy Adams, secretary of state in President James Monroe's cabinet, fretted in his diary in 1823, "France, Mexico—where we know she has been intriguing to get a monarch under a prince of the House of Bourbon, as at Buenos Ayres. And Great Britain, as her last resort . . . would take at least the island of Cuba for her share of the scramble. Then what would be our situation—England holding Cuba, France Mexico."

With that in view, Monroe soon announced what would later be called his "doctrine," warning Europeans against further political interventions in the hemisphere. It appeared to be a forceful rejection of colonialism and an implicit endorsement of the moves toward independence that had been unfolding from Venezuela and Colombia up through Mexico in what had been Spanish America. Yet in truth, Monroe only rebuffed the colonial ambitions of "European powers," and he concluded his address by insisting that "the expansion of our population and accession of new States to our Union have had the happiest effects on all its highest interests . . . add[ing] to our strength and respectability as a power . . . admitted by all." Mexico's general Mier y Terán was not alone in recognizing the scope of the imperial vision of the United States. In the words of a British newspaper, "The plain Yankee of the matter, is that the United States wish to monopolize to themselves the privilege of colonising . . . every . . . part of the American continent."

Where Is Indian Territory?

Perhaps no figure embodied the activist projects of the American imperial vision better than Andrew Jackson. Orphaned at an early age in the Carolinas, he read law, moved to middle Tennessee, took up planting, and found his way into state politics and then to Congress. But it was the military that seemed the best vehicle for channeling his ambitions and rage. He detested the British and their Indian allies (owing in good measure to his wounds and his brother's death at the hands of the British during the Revolution), and he sympathized with the aspirations and concerns of the slaveholding class, into which he had risen as a very solid member. The War of 1812 offered him a golden opportunity to make his mark, and although he is best remembered for defeating the British at the Battle of New Orleans, more consequential was his murderous thrashing of the Upper Creeks (also known as Red Sticks for their body and weapon paint) in a series of engagements ending with a bloodbath in 1814 at Horseshoe Bend on the Tallapoosa River in the Alabama Territory. In so doing, Jackson helped destroy the southern wing of Tecumseh's Pan-Indian confederation and forced the Creeks to surrender twenty-three million acres (about two-thirds of their land) to the U.S. government.

But Jackson's biggest military gambit was still to come. Ever since the formation of the American republic, slaveholders in South Carolina and Georgia had been pressuring the federal government to acquire, by diplomacy or force of arms, the Spanish colony of Florida. Although some of their interests were strategic and political (there was worry about British designs), they were mostly concerned about the security of their slave plantations. Spanish Florida, that is, was not merely the bailiwick of an imperial rival. It had also become—with the encouragement of the Spanish crown—a beacon for runaway slaves, who began appearing in the vicinity of St. Augustine in the late seventeenth century, built the town of Gracia Real de Santa Teresa de Mosé in the late 1730s, and formed a complex alliance with the Seminoles (a branch of the Upper Creeks) in the late eighteenth century. Word of the Spanish safe haven circulated widely among slaves in Georgia and Carolina, helping to spark the Stono Rebellion of 1739 and then flight from plantations and farms during the Revolutionary War.

Aggrieved planters formed various raiding parties to retrieve the runaways and in 1812 launched an invasion (known as the Patriot War but in truth an example of what would come to be known as filibustering) aimed at defeating the Spanish and annexing the territory to the United States. With the unofficial aid of U.S. Army troops and gunboats, they laid siege to St. Augustine and were joined in other areas of East Florida by militia companies from Georgia and

Tennessee who vowed to "put to death without mercy" any "negro taken in arms." It was not enough. Runaways and their descendants around St. Augustine, together with Seminoles, some of whom were black, saw the writing on the wall and fought back ferociously. In the Alachua region, they attacked American settlements that cooperated with the invasion and, using guerrilla tactics, struck the invaders serious blows. By the time an American offensive could resume, the political winds had shifted in Washington, D.C., and by early 1814 the "Patriots" learned that they would now be regarded as no more than "trespassers" and annexation would be refused by the U.S. government.

But not for long. The defeat of the Red Sticks and the British in the South during the War of 1812 reconfigured the borderlands of West and East Florida and southern Alabama and Georgia, as both Red Sticks and fugitive slaves looked to regroup. They collected, together with Seminoles, around a makeshift British post at the mouth of the Apalachicola River in Florida's northwestern corner. And once the British evacuated, the blacks remained behind in what became known as Negro Fort, drawing more fugitive slaves from near and far who settled along the river's banks, grew crops, raised livestock, turned back the assaults of slave catchers, and occasionally fired on boats moving on the Apalachicola. Slaveholders on both sides of the Florida line complained bitterly, and when the Spanish governor effectively threw up his hands, the U.S. military stepped in.

In charge was General Andrew Jackson, now commander of the regular army's southern division. He was not confused about what needed to be done. Negro Fort had to be destroyed and the surviving runaways returned to their owners. Jackson sent General Edmund P. Gaines (who would later turn up on the Louisiana-Texas border) to southwestern Georgia; Gaines, in turn, dispatched Lieutenant Colonel Duncan Clinch to attack the fort. The runaways residing nearby fled into the woods, and after Clinch surrounded the fort, rounds from supporting gunboats set off a massive explosion inside that killed almost all of the black defenders. But neither side was done. The black survivors retreated toward the Suwannee River, where they reorganized, began to drill, allied with Seminoles led by Chief Bowlegs, and together plotted revenge for the massacre at Negro Fort. Farther to the west, other Seminole bands in Florida and Georgia rose against American troops after a dispute over the harboring of fugitive slaves ended with the soldiers burning one of their villages (Foul Town) and killing some of the villagers. The borderlands were now ablaze.

In early 1818, Jackson received orders to take charge of operations and—with a force of army regulars, Tennessee militiamen, and Lower Creek warriors (bitter enemies of the Upper Creeks and Seminoles) totaling thirty-five hundred—moved "to chastise a savage foe, who, combined with a lawless band of Negro brigands, have . . . been carrying on a cruel and unprovoked war against the citizens of the United States." It was not much of a contest. The Seminoles were already short of arms and ammunition, and the blacks were heavily outnumbered and only had muskets to fight off long rifles; all were soon in retreat across the Suwannee and then to the south. Jackson occupied the Indian towns, and his troops laid waste to what had been a "fertile country." Then, on his own initiative, Jackson looked to the larger prize of Florida. He captured St. Marks and Pensacola in the west, ransacked Seminole and black villages in the east, captured Spanish fortifications, executed two British subjects who stood accused of aiding and abetting the Indians, and ordered Gaines to take St. Augustine, the last stronghold of Spain. "I assure you," he boasted to the secretary of war, his imperial hunger not yet satisfied, "Cuba will be ours in a few days."

The administration of President James Monroe was not quite ready for Jackson's exploits, and some in the cabinet believed Jackson should be called to account. Monroe initially decided to return the captured territory to Spain, but within a year the weakness of the Spanish position and the likelihood of further American pressure on West Florida and Tejas led Spain to cut its losses. With the Adams-Onís Treaty of 1819, Spain ceded the Floridas (East and West) to the United States and secured the Sabine River (not the Rio Grande as some in Congress were threatening) as the boundary between Louisiana and Tejas. It was not good news for what was left of the Seminoles and their black allies.

Although Andrew Jackson's efforts to extend the boundaries of the United States as far as he could push them and to oust those—Native peoples and fugitive slaves—who might bedevil the project had yet to become settled national policy, they seemed harbingers of the future. Federal officials recognized Indian territorial claims and accepted treaties as the mechanisms to adjust them, but since the founding of the Republic there was little agreement as to how the interests of American settlers and Native peoples might mesh. Owing to their communal ideas of landed property, their mix of hunting and horticulture, which required extensive territory, and their gendered division of labor in which women often did much of the agricultural field work, many Indian societies were regarded as backward and barbaric, relics of earlier ages that stood in the way of civilization's advance. Some policy makers, like Henry Knox, who served as secretary of war in George Washington's cabinet, hoped that Indians could be "civilized": encouraged to abandon hunting and warring, take up farming, learn to read and write, live in nuclear families, embrace Christianity, and adopt Euro-American styles of dress. They would then more readily sell off their "surplus" lands and perhaps find a comfortable place in American society. But, especially after the purchase of the Louisiana Territory, some version of "removal"—the exchange of land east of the Mississippi River for something comparable in size to the west—came to be regarded by most American political leaders as the best option. The question was whether removal would be voluntary or coerced.

Even if they had allies in the U.S. government who accorded Indian tribes sovereign rights and hoped for a mutualist and peaceable resolution of the land questions, the pressure on Native peoples who remained east of the Mississippi mounted steadily. As one European power after another abandoned or was itself forced off the North American continent, the political prospects for Indians (who excelled at playing the Europeans against each other) dimmed. After American independence and particularly after the War of 1812, white settlers and land speculators flooded into what had been Indian country—notably in the Deep South, where the densest Native populations were still to be found—and looked to extinguish Indian claims as quickly as possible and by whatever means necessary. They would receive powerful support from state governments, like that of Georgia, which rejected tribal sovereignty and moved to extend their authority over all people within their designated borders.

Although Protestant missionaries and federal government agents formed part of the mix, it seemed to matter little whether Native peoples tried to reach some accommodation with American cultural proclivities. So the Cherokees learned. Longtime occupants of an area in the southern Appalachians more than 100,000 miles square, the Cherokees were increasingly pressed upon by white settlement over the course of the eighteenth century. Although they established complex trading relations (mostly for deerskins) with the French, the Spanish, and especially the British, they began to cede portions of their land as early as 1721. Their alliance with the British served them well during and after the French and Indian War but left them exposed when Britain accepted the independence of its North American colonies. By the 1790s, the Cherokees appeared under siege, and some of them moved west across the Mississippi River to settle in what was then Spanish Louisiana.

But others, led principally by tribal members who had intermarried with Europeans and Americans, looked to transform their ways. They embraced horse-and-plow agriculture, the ownership of African American slaves, the market economy, a patrilineal family structure, and Christianity. They reformed their political organization in a more centralized direction that included a bicameral legislature, a court system, elective representation, and a bureaucracy. They adopted a written language and a written constitution and published a newspaper. They laid out a capital at New Echota in northwestern Georgia. And their ranks were increasingly marked by social differentiation, with a small elite of planters and slave owners at the top end and a much larger peasant and hunter-gatherer class at the bottom.

Which is to say that by the mid-1820s Cherokee society in the Southeast had come—quite consciously—to look very much like the white American society that surrounded it. Although land was still held in common, reform-minded Cherokees with means built brick or frame-and-clapboard houses, planted orchards, and fenced their fields; they drew up a special legal code to regulate black slaves; and they imagined, in the words of one of their leaders, that "the day would arrive when a distinction between their race and the American family would be imperceptible." There was a substantial price to pay for this orientation. Many of the "full-blooded" Cherokees (about three-quarters of all Cherokees) rejected it, some vociferously. They rebuffed efforts to accumulate wealth and chose instead to keep to themselves.

The Cherokees were not alone in seeking ways to sustain their cultural imperatives while adapting to the circumstances and demands of intensifying American pressure. Nor were they alone in battling among themselves as they attempted to fashion a strategy for the future. In the Ohio River valley during the early nineteenth century, the Algonquian-speaking Shawnees, already residing in multiethnic villages, fractured over the choices they faced: some moved beyond the Mississippi River and the immediate reach of white settlers, and some joined the Pan-Indian movement that Tecumseh and his brother Tenskwatawa (also known as the Prophet) organized to resist American advances and revitalize ties among themselves; but others, led by Black Hoof, began to change their economic practices and avail themselves of opportunities afforded by schools and missionaries. So long as they had sympathetic ears in the halls of the U.S. government, and especially the White House—sympathetic, that is, in accepting some measure of their sovereignty and insisting that removal be voluntary—they could hold their enemies at bay and keep the most divisive of their internal conflicts in check.

But in 1828, in an election that empowered white settlers west of the Appalachians and especially in the South, Andrew Jackson won the presidency, and the bell of doom began to toll. Reflecting the views of many white southerners as well as the governments of Georgia and Alabama, Jackson rejected the idea of Indian tribal sovereignty, supported the right of states to extend their authority over Indian lands, and almost immediately put the federal government on the side of a removal policy the Indians would be unable to stop. Despite opposition from political opponents, especially in New England and the Middle Atlantic, Jackson saw a bill through Congress in 1830 that set aside territory west of the Mississippi for tribal settlement while undermining the legal basis of tribal claims to the east. Although the removal process itself was not elaborated, the federal government agreed to pay for the improvements Indians had made to the lands they surrendered, for the costs of relocation, for protection

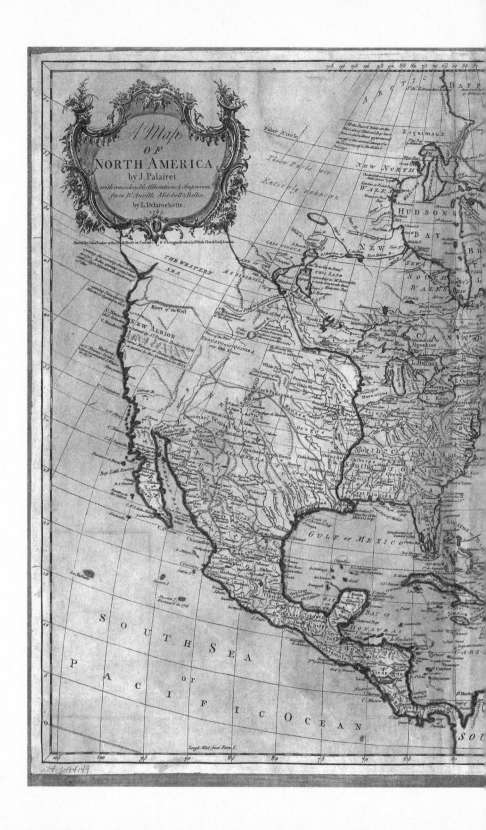

A Map
OF
NORTH AMERICA,
by J. Palairet,
with considerable Alterations & Improvem.ts
from D.r Anville, Mitchell & Bellin,
by L. Delarochette.
1765.

Printed for John Bowles at the Black Horse in Cornhill & S. Carington Bowles in St. Pauls Church Yard, London.

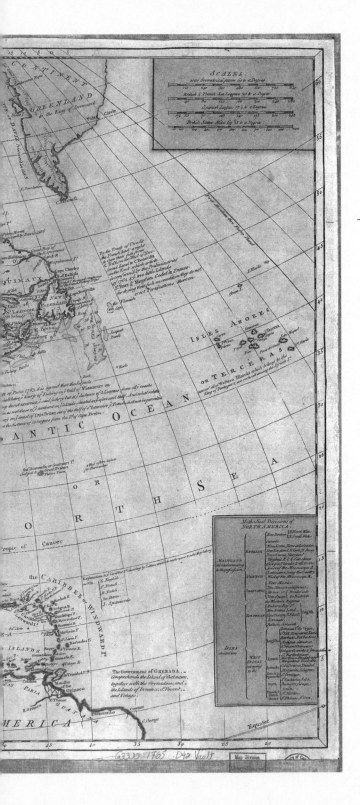

Map of North
America by
J. Palairet.

and care en route, for annuities to tribal leaders and cash for a tribal fund, and for support of various kinds for one year after the tribes arrived in the western districts carved out for them.

Jackson saw removal as the only alternative to the decay and destruction of Native tribes at the hands of whites armed "with their arts of civilization," and thus as a gesture of "humanity and national honor." But he would have battles on his hands, and they would be very costly. In the Great Lakes region, representatives of the Sauk, Fox, and Kickapoo peoples had, between 1800 and 1830, ceded most of their homelands to the U.S. government, much to the consternation of many tribal members. While a moderate faction under the leadership of Keokuk crossed the Mississippi and settled there, in the early 1830s the warrior chief Black Hawk, who had fought with the British during the War of 1812 and whose village was part of the cession, led a band of several hundred back to reclaim land along the Rock River in the northwestern corner of Illinois. Regarding Black Hawk's move as an "invasion," the Illinois governor called out the militia and asked for federal troops, who were then sent from St. Louis under the command of General Edmund P. Gaines, his hands already bloodied in the First Seminole War. The fighting—known as the Black Hawk War—spread across northern Illinois and southern Wisconsin (then part of the Michigan Territory) in the spring and summer of 1832 until the Indians suffered a crushing defeat at the Battle of Bad Axe, ending their resistance. Black Hawk managed to escape and find refuge with the Winnebago before being taken into custody by U.S. authorities and briefly imprisoned in St. Louis; he lived out his few remaining years, very much defeated, on tribal lands west of the Mississippi.

American troops paid a price, though: less in battlefield casualties, which were relatively light, than in the effects of cholera and desertion, which thinned their ranks. Even so, Jackson's removal policy would be far more expensive in Florida. The Seminoles numbered somewhere between five hundred and a thousand in the early 1830s and, unlike other Native peoples east of the Mississippi River, did not stand in the way of white settlement. The First Seminole War had pushed them into south-central Florida, and they did not look to reoccupy land they had been forced to relinquish. They could easily have been left to themselves had it not been for the fugitive slaves and their descendants who lived among them and roiled the slaveholding class of Florida and the Southeast. Slaveholders quite simply wanted the Seminoles sent west and the runaways returned to their owners, and in 1833 a Seminole delegation journeyed to Indian Territory to survey the land they would take up in the larger tract assigned to the Creeks. It appeared that the delegation was satisfied, and the federal government expected the tribe to move there within three years.

But as in other cases of such tribal negotiations, the Seminole negotiators did not have most of the tribe behind them. Many of the Seminoles insisted that the delegates lacked the power to reach a removal agreement and were particularly vexed at the prospect of becoming a minority out in the new Creek country west of the Mississippi. Yet none dug in their heels more fiercely than did the black runaways. Living in their own villages near Seminole encampments, the blacks acknowledged their dependency by paying annual tributes to the Seminole chiefs while also providing valuable services to the Seminoles as interpreters, guides, and fighters. With good reason they looked upon removal with suspicious eyes and feared that rather than trekking west, they would be returned to enslavement. Ordered by the U.S. Army to gather at Tampa Bay in early January 1836, the Seminoles and their black allies chose instead to strike first, attacking sugar plantations along the St. Johns River and annihilating an army command of a hundred men, initiating what has come to be called the Second Seminole War.

The Seminoles were not easy to subdue. More than a year into the fighting, the army had utterly failed to break the Indian-black resistance, because the Seminole leaders Micanopy, Osceola, Wild Cat, Little Alligator, Jumper, and King Philip, together with their black advisers Abraham, John Cavallo, and John Caesar, rallied plantation slaves and put up a formidable defense. One of the American commanders could observe that "this . . . is a negro war, not an Indian war; and if it be not speedily put down, the south will feel the effects of it on their slave population." Before it was all over, the warfare claimed the lives of fifteen hundred American troops and perhaps as much as $40 million (almost three times the price of the Louisiana Territory) in government funds, and the army had to permit many of the black Seminoles to go west rather than be returned to their owners. By 1842, the fighting had ceased (this would be the American state's longest war until Vietnam), and most of the Seminoles had been removed, save for a small group of holdouts who withdrew deep into the recesses of the Everglades.

Cherokee efforts to resist the removal process were less militaristic but no less formidable. Led initially by Chief John Ross, they used their newspaper, the *Cherokee Phoenix*, to keep tribal members informed and to demonstrate their cultural advancement to a wider public; they lobbied in Washington, D.C., by means of petitions and oral arguments; and they brought suit in federal court against the actions of the State of Georgia, insisting on their tribal sovereignty and the political remedies associated with it. The results were not encouraging. The Supreme Court, led by Chief Justice John Marshall, offered mixed rulings in *Cherokee Nation v. Georgia* (1831) and *Worcester v. Georgia* (1832): on the one hand, the Court determined that while the Cherokee did occupy a sovereign status of sorts (they and the other Indian tribes were deemed "domestic, dependent nations"), they had no standing as a foreign state and thus no right to sue Georgia; on the other hand, the Court called "the Cherokee Nation" a "distinct community, occupying its own territory," over which Georgia law had no jurisdiction. A sympathetic chief executive could then have defended Cherokee claims and gone nose to nose with the Georgians. For his part, Jackson regarded the Court's decision as simply one interpretation of the Constitution and refused to enforce it. A possible Native American victory turned into an utter defeat.

Even more troublesome, the removal issue drove a sharp wedge into the Cherokee nation, dividing those who wished to remain in their traditional homelands (Ross was one of them) from those who believed that resistance was pointless and looked to secure the best removal terms possible (they were led by John Ridge and known as the Treaty Party). Ridge managed to gain the upper hand at a crucial moment, and the Treaty of New Echota was signed in very late December 1835, looking toward a removal date in 1838. Although Ross did not give up the fight, the combined pressure of the Jackson administration and the State of Georgia proved impossible to defeat, and what is known as the Trail of Tears eventually brought nearly twelve thousand Cherokees out to Indian Territory (perhaps one-quarter had perished along the way). But the political divisions moved with them, and in a bloody denouement John Ridge and two other Treaty Party leaders (Major Ridge and Elias Boudinot) were brutally murdered by tribal adversaries, who were then pardoned by the larger Ross faction. It was an awful end and an awful beginning.

But where was Indian Territory, and, more precisely, what was it? By the time of the Jackson-era removals, the new states of Arkansas and Missouri—both west of the Mississippi River—had been admitted to the American union, and what was regarded as "Indian" or "Western" territory was an area roughly between the Platte and the Red rivers, to the west of the Arkansas-Missouri state lines. Indian peoples who had found their homelands north of the Ohio River would in turn be located in the northern sections of this territory, while those who had lived below the Ohio, including slaveholding tribes like the Cherokee, Seminole, and Choctaw, would be located to the south (reflecting, in part, the demands of northern congressmen mindful of the line drawn by the Missouri Compromise of 1820—36°30′—which closed the Louisiana Territory north of it to slavery). The United States promised "forever" to "secure and guaranty" the western lands to the resettled Indian tribes and to protect them in their occupancy but did not convey the lands in fee simple. The removal legislation provided instead that if "the Indians become extinct" or abandoned the land, it would revert to the United States.

Yet what would be the political destiny of these newly created territories?

For the previous half century, ever since Congress had enacted the Northwest Ordinance (1787), territories came under the jurisdiction of the federal government while at the same time being viewed as states in the making. They would be administered by congressionally appointed territorial governors and by elected territorial legislatures, and once they achieved the requisite population of sixty thousand, they could write constitutions and apply for statehood. But Indian territories would have no such political arc. They would be supervised by the commissioner of Indian affairs, based in St. Louis, and by the commandants of military bases. Although there had been intermittent talk of a formal Indian state being admitted to the Union, the idea was dropped as soon as the removal policy officially unfolded. For all intents and purposes, Indian Territory was an internal protectorate of the United States marked by impermanent boundaries and obscure lines of governance. It would exist until it was made untenable by the press of white settlement on the outside and the paucity of resources on the inside. Its status was wholly distinct in the United States—set apart and within simultaneously—but an eerie harbinger of America's imperial future.

What Is Texas?

Whatever ambiguities surrounded the status and future of Indian Territory in the United States, Andrew Jackson was quite clearheaded about Texas. He had long believed that Texas formed part of the original Louisiana Purchase and was mistakenly relinquished by John Quincy Adams, secretary of state for James Monroe, in the Adams-Onís Treaty of 1819. Like an assortment of adventurers and political renegades—such as James Wilkinson of Burr conspiracy notoriety—who engaged in filibustering missions there since at least the second decade of the nineteenth century, Jackson eyed Texas with a view to annexation and eventual statehood, and once he assumed the presidency, he wasted little time in pushing forward. Even after his emissary Anthony Butler utterly failed to interest the Mexican government in selling the province, Jackson thought to use the threat of Indian raids into Louisiana and Arkansas as a pretext for invading eastern Texas.

Jackson was not alone. The thriving port city of New Orleans, already the fifth-largest city in the United States and the economic hub of the Caribbean basin, had become a busy crossroads for slave traffickers, financiers, political opportunists, and exiles from failed power struggles looking for new fields of activity. Their horizons stretched from Cuba across to Central America and Mexico, but owing to the Anglo-American colonization of the 1820s Texas seemed especially alluring. New Orleans merchants and factors began to capture the growing Texas cotton trade, as they previously had much of the livestock trade, not to mention the trade in stolen horses and weapons with Indians, Comanches chief among them, in the borderlands of the Red and Sabine rivers. Speculators, some coming in from the Texas town of Nacogdoches, looked to cash in on the sprawling lands made available by the Mexican government. And the New Orleans Association, a business conglomerate, channeled funds in a variety of economic and political directions, including to expeditions hatched by filibusters. Not by accident did Stephen Austin head to New Orleans almost immediately after confirming his empresario grant. From there, from Arkansas, and from other parts of the Deep South, the development and potential acquisition of Texas by the United States seemed increasingly vital both as an outlet for accumulating economic energies and as a zone of protection for the slave system to the east. "A population of fanatical abolitionists in Texas," Austin warned, "would have a very dangerous and pernicious influence on the overgrown slave population of [Louisiana]."

Imperial-minded Americans in New Orleans and the slave South had potential allies among the Anglo-Texans. By the early 1830s, a politically combustible mix was building in the Tejas province, and threats to slavery surely formed part of the explosive package of discontent. Although Texian leaders were divided over whether to seek greater autonomy within the Mexican Republic (they were known as the Peace Party) or to strike for outright independence (they were known as the War Party), all of them feared the rising tide of centralism in Mexico City and the challenges it posed to the social order they had begun to construct. Most were slaveholders, large landholders, land speculators, and cotton growers, and they had watched as the federal and state (Coahuila y Tejas) governments tried to tamper with their labor force, limit the in-migration of Anglo-Americans who shared their aspirations, and recover the customs duties that were not being collected. Through the summer of 1835, they played the principal role in organizing popular unrest and in attempting to create a structure of protest and governance. In November, after military skirmishing had flared between rebellious Texians and Mexican troops, they met in a body—the Consultation—organized an army under the command of Sam Houston (a Jackson ally who arrived in 1832 after stints in Tennessee politics and Cherokee country), and established a provisional government on the basis of the federalist Mexican constitution of 1824. Still, they did not proclaim independence.

But an important shift in the dynamics of the developing rebellion occurred at the same time. As news of the escalating conflict began to circulate in the lower Mississippi Valley and then farther to the east, efforts were made to raise money and troops to support the embattled Texians and advance the prospects of independence from Mexico. Public meetings were held in small towns and large, contributions solicited, paramilitaries mobilized, and visions of an expansive world of plantations and slavery nourished. "The great rage here is the cause of Independence in Texas," a white Mississippian wrote from the village of Louisville. "A great many men are going from this country in expectation of acquiring homes and wealth in the cause [as] the government of Texas offers a large bounty in land for soldiers and their lands I am assured . . . are not surpassed by any in our Southern country for the cultivation of cotton, sugar, etc." Paramilitary units began to arrive from New Orleans and from Georgia, Alabama, and Kentucky. By early 1836 in the vital district stretching from San Patricio to Goliad to San Antonio de Béxar—under the command of James W. Fannin, a wealthy Texas slaveholder—over three-quarters of the soldiers in Texas had arrived only since the previous October. What would come to be known as the Texas Revolution, that is, received decisive aid from a large American filibustering operation.

Andrew Jackson was not long in putting his iron into the Texas fire. Stories have been told for many years that Jackson sent Sam Houston into Texas to promote the cause of annexation. Although no supportive evidence has ever been uncovered—and the stories are probably apocryphal—Jackson did look for an opportunity to enter the fray. The opportunity came in the fall of 1835 when members of the Nacogdoches Committee of Vigilance and Safety appealed to Jackson for protection against Indian attacks, and he sent General Edmund P. Gaines (veteran of the Seminole and Black Hawk wars) and a company of army troops to the Sabine River early the next year. Gaines soon crossed over, occupied Nacogdoches, and remained in place for the next six months.

Whether Gaines would have engaged Mexican troops if they pushed that far into the Tejas northeast or quickly crushed the Texian rebellion is unclear. But when news arrived that General Santa Anna was on his way with a large force, the divisions between War and Peace parties evaporated, and rebellious Texians (Austin among them) embraced independence and the military defense of their territory. Some of them, including hotheads like William Travis and James Bowie, dug in at the Alamo, a large presidio in San Antonio de Béxar (the provincial capital), despite Sam Houston's orders to destroy it and evacuate. Others were with James Fannin around the town of Goliad or with Houston in the vicinity of San Felipe. In the meantime, they prepared for a convention to meet in early March and formally break their ties with Mexico.

Confident as he was that his troops would suppress the rebellion in Tejas, Santa Anna also eyed other vulnerabilities of Texian society. One of them was the looming presence of Indian peoples, especially Cherokee bands and their allies, who had migrated into the Arkansas-Texas borderlands before the coerced removals later in the decade. Mexican officials and Texian leaders alike, including Houston, who had lived for a time among the Cherokee and once had a Cherokee wife, competed for their loyalties with the promise of lands and other accommodations. The Cherokee ultimately split into pro-Mexican and pro-Texian factions. But it was slavery that seemed to represent the soft underbelly of the Texas unrest. "Their intent," one of the Texas rebels said of the Mexican centralists, "is to gain the friendship of different Indian tribes; and if possible to get the slaves to revolt."

The concern was hardly misplaced. In October 1835, as Texians and Mexicans first battled, slaves residing in the Austin settlement along the Brazos River sparked a rebellion that allegedly looked to the redistribution of lands among them. It was brutally repressed by their owners but also served as a reminder of the stakes at play and the dangers involved. More than a few Texians began to warn that Mexican forces intended "to compel you to liberate your slaves," that they would set the "slaves free and loose them upon their families." And, indeed, Mexican officials were not reluctant to suggest, as General Martín Perfecto de Cos did, that the consequences of the Texians' insurrection would "bear heavily upon them and their property." Small wonder that many Texas slaveholders stayed home, keeping close watch over their slaves, rather than join the armed rebels.

Santa Anna recognized the Texians' predicament and pondered how he might best take advantage of it. "There is a considerable number of slaves in Texas also who have been introduced by their masters under cover of certain questionable contracts, but who according to our laws should be free," he observed only days before crossing into the province and meeting the rebels. "Shall we permit those wretches to moan in chains any longer in a country whose kind laws protect the liberty of man without distinction of color?" Imperious in aura and demeanor, Santa Anna might appear among the least likely to launch an assault on slavery and racial exploitation, but the emancipationist sympathies of the Mexican government had clearly circulated among Texas slaves and stoked their anticipation of change in the offing. The "negroes," slaveholders in Brazoria thus noticed, "were on the tip-toe of expectation, and rejoicing that the Mexicans were coming to make them free!" Some of the slaves looked for the first chance to escape from the grips of their owners and head toward Mexican army encampments.

It therefore might have made sense for Santa Anna to steer his forces immediately toward the Texas Gulf Coast, where most of the Texians had settled and the slave population was concentrated. Instead, he and his troops continued northward toward San Antonio de Béxar and the Alamo, where a small band of Anglos and a few of their own slaves were holed up, and laid it siege. Perhaps

Santa Anna wished to begin his operations on terrain that was most familiar (the arid plains rather than the eastern woodlands); perhaps he wanted to make his initial show of strength in what was then the Texas capital. Whatever his logic—and in retrospect the military and strategic value of the Alamo appears minimal—the first results of Santa Anna's invasion seemed auspicious: his troops destroyed the Alamo and killed all of the male defenders (the only two male survivors were slaves), and to the southeast Mexican troops under the command of General José de Urrea overran Texas rebels at San Patricio and then subdued them near Goliad, whereupon all the rebels who surrendered were summarily executed on orders from Santa Anna. Not only was Sam Houston and what remained of the Texas rebel army in hasty retreat, but Anglo-Texians now fearing "extermination" at the hands of the Mexican invaders and a "possible rising of the negroes" fled in a panic that came to be known as the Runaway Scrape.

Yet for all of his ostensible success, Santa Anna paid a heavy price for the track he chose to take. Nearly one-quarter of his troops fell at the Alamo—more than three times the number of Anglo defenders who died inside—and the slaughters he authorized there and at Goliad touched a raw nerve of vengeance among those left to keep the Texas rebellion alive. Believing that he verged on total victory, Santa Anna planned a multipronged attack on Houston and divided his army to carry it out. But the winds of fortune (in this case a captured courier) enabled Houston to learn of Santa Anna's moves, and at Buffalo Bayou on the San Jacinto River, Houston and his nine hundred men struck back. The Mexican army was quickly routed and then subjected to a massacre so fierce that Texas officers could not stop it. Nearly seven hundred Mexican soldiers would die, and several hundred more would be taken prisoner, including General Santa Anna, seized by the rebels while in desperate flight, dressed as a common soldier.

Eager for revenge, many of the rebel troops demanded Santa Anna's execution. Houston had a different idea. In exchange for his life and passage back to Mexico City, Santa Anna would have to agree to Texas independence, order his remaining troops south of the Rio Grande, and seek recognition of Texas by the Mexican Congress. It was a deal he could hardly refuse. Santa Anna signed the Treaty of Velasco ending hostilities and privately promised to press the Mexican government to accept Texas independence. With this, the Republic of Texas—created in convention at Washington-on-the-Brazos in March, by delegates who were younger and had spent less time in Texas than previous leaders, with a constitution resembling the American, though explicitly supporting slavery—had apparently come into being.

But what exactly was the Republic of Texas, and, equally to the point, where was it? Despite Santa Anna's assurances, the Mexican Congress refused to recognize the Texas Republic and regarded itself as still at war with the Texas insurgency. And despite the expectations of the Anglo-Texians that the U.S. government would lend them credibility or move toward annexation, the Jackson administration remained aloof. For all of Jackson's interest in Texas and attempts to find advantage in the unrest there, the outcome of the Texas rebellion posed its own share of challenges. Annexation would be divisive politically and raise the ire of those Americans already building a movement to limit the power of slaveholders and eventually abolish slavery itself. Either annexation or recognition, moreover, would surely court the venom of the Mexican government and threaten warfare that would not unify the United States. Jackson was already counting down the last days of his administration and was reluctant to saddle the new president, and his favored successor, Martin Van Buren, with the burdens that direct involvement with the Texas question would most certainly bring. Although a chargé d'affaires to Texas was appointed moments before Jackson left office, the larger issue of Texas-U.S. relations remained very much unresolved; in Mexican eyes, the Texas Republic simply did not exist.

Then there was the matter of boundaries. The Adams-Onís Treaty had established the Sabine River as the eastern border of the Mexican state of Coahuila y Tejas, and the leaders of the Texas Republic accepted this. But they also defined the southern and southwestern border as the Rio Grande, and a western and northern boundary extending all the way to the 42nd parallel, an immense stretch of territory that no government or confederation save for the Texans—not the United States, not Britain, not France, and certainly not Mexico or the Indian peoples of the southern plains—seemed ready to acknowledge. For the next decade, Texas would be more of an imagined space than a sovereign state, with boundaries that were endlessly porous, ever shifting, and almost impossible to discern. Comanches, Kiowas, Cheyennes, and Arapahos pressed in from the north and the west. Aggressive Texans looked to move against the Indians and even to carry their designs farther into Mexico. And the area between the Nueces and the Rio Grande was neither populated nor politically secured, designated on contemporary maps as the "Mustang or Wild Horse Desert." Texas remained a borderland in the fullest sense, and the struggle over its formal political identity would continue to detonate across the nineteenth century.

CHAPTER TWO

Slavery and Political Culture

Anti-abolitionist mob destroying the printing press of James G. Birney,
Cincinnati, Ohio. *The Anti-Slavery Record*, a monthly published by the
American Anti-Slavery Society, September 1836.

Contesting the Slaveholders' Design

Among the prospective empresarios who sought land grants from Mexican authorities in Tejas during the 1820s and 1830s, Benjamin Lundy was surely the most unusual. Born in New Jersey in 1789 to a family of Quakers, he hoped to establish not a colony of aspiring planters but rather one of freed slaves. Seemingly peripatetic by nature, he had already traveled to Haiti (1825) for the same purpose and then visited the small Wilberforce Colony of fugitive slaves in Ontario, Canada (1831–32), perhaps to take the measure of what such a settlement entailed. Active in the developing antislavery movement since the second decade of the nineteenth century, Lundy moved along a geographical belt encompassing the country's midsection, from Mount Pleasant, Ohio, to St. Louis, Missouri, to Greeneville, Tennessee, and on to Baltimore, Maryland. In the process, he began publishing the *Genius of Universal Emancipation,* one of the earliest and most influential papers devoted to the cause. But Lundy was interested in turning his words into deeds and in demonstrating the superiority of free over slave labor, so he headed to Mexican Tejas on two occasions during the 1830s, imagining that a government with antislavery credentials might be sympathetic to his project. As it happened, he was on the ground as the Anglo-American rebellion came to the boiling point.

Whatever chances Lundy might have had to establish a colony of black freedpeople in Tejas evaporated when rebellious Texans defeated Santa Anna, proclaimed their independence, and wrote a constitution that protected slavery. Indeed, the Texas Republic turned Lundy's emancipationist dream into a potential nightmare, as pro-slavery interests in the United States, with the support of President Andrew Jackson, commenced a vigorous campaign for annexation. Lundy was determined to alert his political allies, as well as the American public more generally, to the perils Texas now posed, and he penned *The War in Texas* (1836) to expose what he regarded as a slaveholders' plot. "It is susceptible to the clearest demonstration," he wrote, "that the immediate cause and leading object of the [Texas revolt] originated in a settled design among the slaveholders of this country to wrest the large and valuable territory of Texas from the Mexican Republic, in order to re-establish the SYSTEM OF SLAVERY; to open a vast and profitable SLAVE-MARKET therein; and, ultimately to annex it to the United States." The ensuing struggle over the future of Texas would lead to war with Mexico and an intensifying crisis over the slavery question.

Benjamin Lundy might have traveled far and wide to find a secure destination for slaves freed from bondage, but his antislavery politics were decidedly gradualist. Although he (like most Quakers) believed that slaveholding was a sin, he thought that any plan of emancipation had to unfold slowly and include the removal of the emancipated black population from the United States. That was why he journeyed to Haiti and Mexican Tejas in search of land and political assistance: unlike many others in the antislavery movement who shared his views, Lundy was planning to enact "colonization" (as it was known) both as a solution to the problem of emancipation and as an encouragement to the advance of emancipation itself. Once freedpeople demonstrated their readiness for freedom and the economic benefits of free labor, slaveholders, he assumed, would be more willing to manumit their slaves.

Lundy's was a version of the program previously unfurled by the American Colonization Society (ACS). Founded in 1816 by elite reformers who worried about the corrosive effects of slavery and wished to envision a distant future when slavery would no longer exist in the United States, the ACS promoted the exile of free people of African descent. To that end, the society established— with financial and political backing from the U.S. government—the colony of Liberia on the west coast of Africa, and by the mid-1820s the first black migrants began to trickle in there and build settlements in uneasy relation to the indigenous populations nearby. ACS organizers included prominent slaveholders like Henry Clay of Kentucky and John Randolph of Virginia, and the membership would boast an array of important political leaders: James Madison, James Monroe, Daniel Webster, John Marshall, Stephen Douglas, and William Seward chief among them; Thomas Jefferson never joined the organization but endorsed its goals. In a significant sense, colonization must be seen in close relation— intellectually and politically, as well as chronologically—to Indian removal, as powerful elements in the developing American imperial project. Both reflected the increasing centrality of racialist thinking and categories together with a growing pessimism as to the prospects for interracial peace. And both reflected a deepening consensus among juridically free Americans that the country— whatever its dimensions—would be ruled in the interests of white people; others would be required to leave or submit.

Benjamin Lundy did not become a member of the ACS, and the *Genius of Universal Emancipation* could be sharply critical of the society's ideas and policies. Yet Lundy's gradualism helped form one of the main currents of emancipationist sensibilities that began to emerge in the last third of the eighteenth century. On the one hand, emancipationiss expressed grave doubts about the ethics and political wisdom of slaveholding; on the other hand, they acknowledged the enormous financial investments and property holdings that slavery involved and, equally consequential, wondered about the slaves' preparedness for freedom. Were slaves ready for a life of freedom, or would they need to be educated into it, socialized in the ways of free society, "civilized"? For a time, emancipationist thought focused on the African slave trade and the repellent images of slave pens, Middle Passages, and slave sales. If the trade were abolished, not only would some of slavery's most ghastly features be eliminated, but slaveholders would be more concerned with the material conditions of their slaves, reliant as they would then be on natural reproduction to replenish their labor force—the first of many steps that might lead to the abolition of slavery itself. Once the trade was indeed officially ended (1808), emancipationists attempted to mobilize sentiment in civil and political society around reforms in slavery's conduct and a gradualist approach—involving implicit or explicit compensation to owners—to slavery's ultimate demise.

What distinguished people like Benjamin Lundy from the more complacent and elitist ACS were not only his humble origins and sympathies for the travail of black slaves but also the urgency he felt the mission demanded. Despite the campaigns against the slave trade and the mounting challenges to slaveholding— bringing with them some notable victories—slavery, like the United States more generally, had shifted into an expansionist phase during the early decades of the nineteenth century. American slave owners and their slaves were moving into the Louisiana Territory, new states (like Missouri) were being admitted to the Union with constitutions that upheld the legality of slave property, and slaveholding Texas loomed on the horizon. Thus, together with seeking land to establish freed black colonies, Lundy headed off on speaking tours of the Middle Atlantic and New England states to rouse public awareness of the threatening circumstances. On one of them, in 1828, he met a young admirer named William Lloyd Garrison.

Garrison came from a modest background in Newburyport, Massachusetts, his father a mariner who fell on hard times and abandoned the family just a few years after Garrison's birth. Raised by a devoted Baptist mother and eventually swept up in the evangelical revivals of the time, he apprenticed as a printer and worked at several newspapers. At the time he met Lundy, Garrison had been drawn to temperance and antislavery, though his emancipationism was of the gradualist sort espoused by the American Colonization Society. Perhaps it was their similar origins (Lundy apprenticed as a saddle maker) and religious zeal; perhaps it was Garrison's skills and experience with the press; at all events, the two seemed to strike up a relationship, and within a month Lundy invited Garrison to Baltimore to help him edit the *Genius of Universal Emancipation*.

Baltimore proved to be an arresting and transforming experience for Garrison. The second-largest city in the United States (next to New York) and a thriving seaport, it was also decidedly in slavery's domain. Although slaveholding in Maryland was concentrated in the countryside south and east of the city, along the eastern and western shores of Chesapeake Bay, roughly one-quarter of Baltimore's population was of African descent, and just under half of it was enslaved.

Here Garrison directly encountered, for the first time, a world organized around slavery: slaveholding, slave hiring, slave punishments, and slave markets. "There is nothing which the curse of slavery has not tainted," he would tell his New England friends of what he saw there. "It rests on every herb and every tree, and every field, and on the people, and on the morals." Yet, even more significantly, Garrison worked and boarded with free people of color in the city who had a far less cautious view of the antislavery project than he had, and he learned that they subscribed in large numbers to the *Genius of Universal Emancipation*, providing a base of support that was essential to the paper's viability. He also read and helped to print in the pages of the newspaper the powerful *Appeal to the Coloured Citizens of the World* written by a free man of color named David Walker. By the time Garrison left Baltimore for Boston in 1830, he had abandoned gradualism and colonization and was ready to take his emancipationist ideas in new, and far more radical, directions.

Garrisonian abolitionism, that is to say, grew out of a soil already nourished by black people, slave and free, and David Walker helps us grasp the complex process and circuits by which this came about. Walker wrote and published his appeal in 1829 in Boston, where he had been since the mid-1820s, active in the interests of antislavery and Boston's black population. He played a role in the organization of the Massachusetts General Colored Association (1828), designed to "unite the colored population" and "meliorate our miserable condition," and he served as a local agent for *Freedom's Journal,* the first newspaper in the United States owned and edited by African Americans, while earning a living by selling used clothing. But Walker was born in the mid- to late 1790s in Wilmington, North Carolina, the son of a free black mother and an enslaved father (and so as a free person), and he spent most of his life moving among dense populations of slaves and free people of color. He appears to have grown to young adulthood in the environs of Wilmington, which reverberated with various forms of slave unrest during the 1790s and early nineteenth century. He then traveled to Charleston, South Carolina, around the time that Denmark Vesey, another free man of color, was talking with slaves and free blacks of political developments relating to slavery at home and abroad, including the Haitian Revolution and the debate over the admission of Missouri to the Union as a slave state, and was charged with plotting a massive slave rebellion. When Walker finally arrived in Boston, some time after Vesey and his alleged conspirators were put to death, he brought with him the fruits of a remarkable education in the black political worlds of slavery and freedom.

Walker's *Appeal* pulsed with anger and erudition, argument and eloquence, threat and forgiveness. It addressed many audiences—white and black, slave and free, American and African diasporic, the living and their ghosts—and constructed a universe of political concern and engagement that was truly internationalist. In prose dotted with classical allusions and historical references and laced with millennial language that reached the pitches of a fevered jeremiad (many of the sentences were punctuated with multiple exclamation points, as if he imagined his readers listening), Walker insisted on the unique barbarity of American slavery, exposed the hypocrisy of slaveholding republicans and Christians, chided slaves for their "wretchedness" and submission, condemned colonization for its moral bankruptcy and self-serving coerciveness, and warned of God's retributive justice. Walker reminded African Americans that their "brethren" were enslaved "the world over" and that their destinies were inextricably tied together. He told them that freedom was their "natural right" and, to claim it, they had to cast off their wretchedness. And, in the *Appeal*'s most audacious move, he took special aim at Thomas Jefferson's ideas of black inferiority and embrace of colonization, predicting that blacks would "contradict or confirm him by your own actions, and not by what our friends have said or done for us."

Yet for all of Walker's outrage and indignation, for all of his adumbrations of turmoil and black triumph—"we must and shall be free, in spite of you . . . God will deliver us from under you. And woe, woe, will be to you if we have to obtain our freedom by fighting"—Walker also offered a vision of redemption and social peace that stood out in an era of racialized removals: "Throw away your fears and prejudices then, and enlighten us and treat us like men, and we will like you more than we do now hate you, and tell us no more about colonization, for America is as much our country, as it is yours.—Treat us like men, and there is no danger but we will all live in peace and happiness together. For we are not like you, hard-hearted, unmerciful, and unforgiving." The *Appeal* revealed a gifted voice and a distinctive political intelligence, but it also distilled passions, languages, and sensibilities that circulated among the people of African descent David Walker encountered in the Carolinas, Massachusetts, and possibly elsewhere in his travels. With riveting perspective, it also showed the marks of struggles against slavery already more than a century old.

Emancipationism in the World of Slaves

David Walker was a publicist and agitator as well as a writer. He intended his *Appeal* to be read not only by the small black population in Boston and New England but also by the very large black, and mostly enslaved, population farther to the south. To that end, he relied chiefly on the networks of communication that people of African descent had long been carving out and secreted copies of the text among black seamen working the coastal trade, at times stitching them in their coats, and had it distributed to a variety of contacts, some known to him personally. Walker was, of course, well aware that few of the slaves were literate, but he also recognized that newspapers, political tracts, or anything of general interest could be read aloud—as was common among all poor and working people—by the few who could claim literacy to the many who could not. Although the evidence is sketchy, the *Appeal* seems to have turned up in port cities from Boston to New Orleans (including Wilmington and Charleston) and excited great alarm among public officials in places where slavery was legal and black people numerous, most notably in Virginia, the Carolinas, Georgia, and Louisiana.

Walker's efforts to circulate the *Appeal* show us what studies of the anti-slavery movement too infrequently acknowledge: that the first and most continuous combatants in the fight against slavery were the slaves themselves. To be sure, none of the slaves had standing in the official arenas of civil and political life. They could not publicly demonstrate their grievances, petition their governments, sue their owners, vote or run for office, publish newspapers and broadsides, or hold political meetings. But there were things they could—and did—do. They could push back against the power and presumed authority of slaveholders. They could build relations and networks across considerable distances. They could flee their plantations and farms and construct settlements they would vigilantly defend (known as maroons). They could make contact and exchange information with slaves and free people of color from other slave societies, often as a result of maritime transport. They could organize small- and large-scale rebellions. And, through their many actions, they could weaken the edifices of enslavement, win the sympathies of people in the ruling populations, attract allies near and far, and eventually create crises for slave regimes. The antislavery movements as we have come to know them were therefore components in a greater battle against slavery, and they might never have arisen had the slaves not prepared the way.

The slaves' movements against slavery, like the more formal movements that would develop in close association with them, were international in their dimensions. They not only encompassed the North and South Atlantic as well as the Caribbean basin but increasingly linked the experiences of slaves and other people of African descent in many different locations and circumstances. After all, the system of slavery moved across, and often defied, national boundaries, and the slaves themselves were among the most frequent transgressors. They were taken across oceans and seas, brought to port cities and remote hinterlands, and traded around the slaveholding colonies owing to the vagaries of markets and the appearance of slave traders. They worked on transoceanic and coasting vessels, accompanied metropolitan armies and colonial militias, labored in seaports—Baltimore, Savannah, New Orleans, Havana, Cap-Français, Kingston, Cartagena, Salvador—that saw heavy international traffic, and served public officials. They also followed owners who migrated to new locales searching for economic opportunities or fleeing political unrest.

Denmark Vesey embodied this transnationalism. Born a slave in the Danish Virgin Islands, he was sold to a ship captain and taken to French St. Domingue for several years before ending up in Charleston, South Carolina, where he won his freedom by means of a lottery. Vesey became multilingual, literate, and very much attuned to the political crosscurrents of the Atlantic. He read to slaves and free blacks from the Bible, the Declaration of Independence, the debates in the U.S. Congress and the South Carolina legislature, and the Charleston papers, and thereby enabled them to view their situations and destinies in relation to thousands of other slaves around the hemisphere. In turn, Vesey's comrades could share these discoveries and insights with others in the workshops and plantations to which they belonged. David Walker might well have been edified in this manner and then carried what he learned far to the north.

Yet owing to their civil and political debilities and the violence required to enforce their submission, the slaves' struggles against slavery more nearly resembled ongoing warfare than recognizable social movements. The warfare could assume the guise of large battles and very public encounters, such as when revolts erupted; most often, it took the form of guerrilla skirmishing as slaves fought with their owners over the rules and governance of their plantations and farms, their ability to develop relations (of kinship, friendship, faith, and strategic alliance) with other slaves, their access to provision grounds and local markets, and the room they could claim to organize communities of different sorts—with wreckage and casualties inflicted on both sides. Over the course of the eighteenth century, as European imperial powers themselves came to blows across the face of the Atlantic world, the warfare grew in scale and ambition. It shifted, generally speaking, from efforts to flee slavery by constructing maroon settlements or finding other safe havens to efforts aimed at defeating slave regimes and at least pushing back the grasp of enslavement.

Indeed, after the Seven Years' War, slaves from the Caribbean basin to northerly New England commenced what would turn into half a century of increasingly interconnected and militant struggle. Beginning with Tacky's Revolt in Jamaica (1760) and slave flight to the British armies during the American Revolution (1770s), this new phase of warfare then exploded in St. Domingue, Guadeloupe, and Martinique in the early 1790s (becoming a successful revolution in St. Domingue by 1804, when the independent Republic of Haiti was proclaimed by victorious slaves and free people of color), further detonated in French Louisiana in 1795, Richmond, Virginia, in 1800 (Gabriel's Rebellion), the plantation parishes of lower Louisiana (this time under U.S. rule) in 1811, Barbados in 1816 (the Easter Rebellion), Florida in 1817–18 (the First Seminole War), Charleston, South Carolina, in 1822 (Vesey's conspiracy), and Demerara in 1823, reaching its climax with Jamaica's massive Baptist War and Nat Turner's far smaller but nonetheless consequential rebellion in Southampton County, Virginia, both in 1831. By the time the smoke cleared, slavery had been abolished in Haiti and Britain's colonial possessions, and an emancipation process had been initiated in the United States, fired as much by aggrieved slaves as by white Americans who could not square the political ideals of their revolution with the continued enslavement of black people.

These blows against slavery did not simply abut chronologically; they fed off each other as information and rumors spread out across the Atlantic and the Caribbean allowing slaves and free blacks to discuss and debate the new political possibilities and decide how they might best advance them. During the American Revolution, free people of color (*gens de couleur libres*) from St. Domingue accompanied French troops and fought with patriot forces in Savannah in 1778, while slaves who had run off to the British ended up in Nova Scotia, England, the British Caribbean, and ultimately Sierra Leone. Rebels in St. Domingue in the 1790s included veterans of the Savannah campaign (Henri Christophe, an eventual leader of the rebellion and then ruler of Haiti, was one of them), and as the rebellion gained ground and slavery collapsed, thousands of refugees—slave owners, slaves, and *gens de couleur libres*—arrived in Havana, Kingston, and Cartagena, but especially in port cities on the North American mainland, stretching from Philadelphia to Baltimore, Charleston, Savannah, Mobile, and New Orleans. Some of the slaves who plotted rebellion in Pointe Coupee Parish, Louisiana, in 1795 and again in 1811 had roots in St. Domingue; the slave blacksmith Gabriel invoked the developing revolution in St. Domingue as he organized a rising in the area of Richmond in 1800; and Denmark Vesey, who had labored briefly in St. Domingue, told slaves and free blacks in his Charleston circle of what had happened there.

Indeed, refugees from St. Domingue arrived in American ports at a very propitious moment. The cotton gin had just been invented, and the beginnings of the short-staple cotton boom led thousands of slaveholders and their slaves into the hinterlands of the Southeast and then into the rapidly developing areas of Alabama, Mississippi, and, with the territorial purchase from France in 1803, Louisiana and the west bank of the Mississippi River. By the second decade of the nineteenth century, an interstate trade was moving thousands of slaves from Virginia, Delaware, and Maryland down to the Gulf Coast; in the end, a million slaves would make this forced migration. Mostly young and male in the early years of the trade—they were needed to do the backbreaking work of clearing fields and building dwellings—these slaves were wrenched out of families and communities that had been constructed over many decades and required to start again in an entirely new environment. But they also brought with them a range of experiences and expectations, and perhaps knowledge of the blows that rebel slaves were meting out to slaveholders. David Walker's *Appeal* showed explicit familiarity with events in "Hayti," and the circulation of the *Appeal* likely extended this familiarity, together with an emerging sense that the institution of slavery was under intensifying attack.

News of the Haitian Revolution was easier to come by for people of African descent in New England and the Middle Atlantic states because there slavery was unraveling and a black civic culture slowly taking shape. But it was a bumpy and contentious process. Slaveholding had a firm legal basis across British North America and was fortified everywhere during the eighteenth century as the Atlantic economy boomed. Although colonies from Pennsylvania on north had relatively few slaves (and small black populations), slave ownership was nonetheless widespread among those most involved in the international market and in public life. Slave trading vessels frequented the port cities, especially Newport, Rhode Island, where a plantation system had developed in nearby Narragansett, and a substantial share of urban households up and down the coast held slaves. The opening came during the American Revolution, in part owing to the ideological and cultural currents of the time and in part owing to slaves who seized the moment: joining patriot military units where it was possible for them to do so and, notably in Massachusetts, petitioning the legislature for freedom in the language of universalism. The Pennsylvania Assembly enacted the first emancipation law in the Americas in 1780, and over the next quarter century Rhode Island, Connecticut, New York, and New Jersey followed suit.

Even so, the hand of hesitation and gradualism made itself felt. Not one of the emancipation statutes freed any slave, providing instead for the liberation of the children of those who were enslaved (known as post-nati emancipation), and only when they reached a certain point in their adulthood: age twenty-one, twenty-five, or twenty-eight depending on the state and their gender. Slave owners thereby received the most productive fruits of slave labor as compensation for the eventual loss of their property, were often relieved of responsibilities for their slaves turned freedpeople, and could coerce their slaves into long-term indentures, which managed to pass emancipationist scrutiny. In Massachusetts and New Hampshire, slavery's end appeared less gradual, though at the same time more confusing, accomplished chiefly through judicial interpretation of state constitutions that in fact made no mention of slavery. The pall of slavery, thickened by the federal Fugitive Slave Law of 1793 (requiring the return of runaways to states where slavery remained legal), consequently continued to hang over all these states, threatening the status of any person of African descent and leaving many hostage to slaveholding authority.

Nevertheless, as the hold of slavery weakened in the New England and Middle Atlantic states, the public and political space available to people of African descent grew. The late eighteenth and early nineteenth centuries saw the establishment of mutual aid societies, Masonic lodges, churches—including the African Methodist Episcopal (AME) Church—and literary clubs. Black writers and publicists began to circulate their personal stories, pen critical essays, reprint the speeches of local leaders, and report on black struggles, such as the rebellion in St. Domingue. Black communities also mobilized to protect newly arrived fugitives, retrieve children illegally retained by former masters, and speed the formal end of enslavement. Their increasing militancy, embrace of direct action, and grassroots appeals contrasted sharply with the elite, tempered, and gradualist demeanor of early—and white—antislavery societies, like the Pennsylvania Abolition Society and the New York Manumission Society, and set the foundation for powerful protests against the program of the American Colonization Society.

The protests erupted quickly, beginning in Philadelphia in 1817, when nearly three thousand blacks packed the AME Bethel Church, and they spread as far south as Baltimore and as far north as Boston, inspiring anger and activism. It was not that African Americans wholly rejected the idea of leaving the United States for more welcoming destinations. They knew firsthand how slavery and an intensifying racism hedged their prospects, and in view of the protracted and often compromised emancipation process that had been unfolding in the Northeast, they could hardly feel optimistic about a future where free labor prevailed. Some had already been attracted to black-led emigration projects (such as that of Paul Cuffe), and in the 1820s several thousand headed off to Haiti. But by the early nineteenth century, most of them had been born in the United States, their labor had enriched the country, and they saw that the American Colonization Society clearly wanted to send them packing, whether or not they wished to depart. At its very best, the ACS envisioned an America without slavery and without blacks, and most white emancipationists greeted the advent of the ACS either with enthusiasm or with silence.

Blacks' critique of colonization and their organized opposition to it pointed the way to new forms of emancipationism. Black leaders regarded colonization as politically objectionable and morally bankrupt, a compromise with both slavery and racism, and recognized that they would have to offer an alternative: that they would have to combat gradualism as to the abolition of slavery as well as the white belief—even among their allies—in black inferiority. During the

1820s, anti-colonization societies sprouted in black enclaves from New England across to the Midwest, and rebuttals to the logic of colonization could be heard in black churches and meetings and read in pamphlets and newspapers like *Freedom's Journal*. David Walker's *Appeal* was therefore the culmination of a challenge more than a decade in the making.

A New Type of Movement

When William Lloyd Garrison began publishing his newspaper, the *Liberator*, in January 1831 and soon thereafter explicitly denounced colonization and helped found the New England Anti-Slavery Society, he joined what had already become a multifaceted antislavery movement that encompassed much of the Atlantic world and, in some cases, had decisively rejected gradualism. The 1780s witnessed the emergence of organized antislavery in both Britain and France (cognizant in each case of what had begun in some parts of the United States), and while initially focused on ending the slave trade, it played an important role in destabilizing their colonial slave systems. Just as slaves shared news and political assessments with one another, white allies constructed a transnational network of communication that broadened the basis of agitation. Indeed, Garrison and others on the American side watched as British efforts to steer a ship of gradualism—ending the slave trade, attempting to enforce the slave trade ban throughout the Atlantic, enacting ameliorative legislation for the colonies—crashed on the shoals of mounting popular protest at home and slave unrest overseas. By the summer of 1833, the British Parliament was ready to stare down the once-formidable West Indian lobby and enact an emancipation bill, though one that called for a six-year transition to freedom and monetary compensation to slave owners.

Garrison's embrace of "immediatism" showed the marks of something more than history's recent lessons, however. Immediatism was less a political program or strategy than a personal commitment: demanding recognition not just of slavery's brutality and inefficiencies but of its sinfulness; insisting upon an acknowledgment not just of the need to mobilize against slavery but of moral responsibility for eradicating it. Immediatism thereby revealed the powerful influence of a major transformation in religious belief, under way for well over a century, and especially the effect of a tide of spiritual enthusiasm that swept across the United States during the early decades of the nineteenth century. Called the Second Great Awakening and advanced by Protestant revivalists like the Reverends Charles Grandison Finney and Lyman Beecher, it built on earlier theological changes that emphasized the work of benevolence and the worth of all human beings regardless of their worldly stations. Yet it also went dramatically further in depicting individuals as moral free agents, capable of corruption or perfectibility, who could establish a personal relationship with God, choose good over evil, achieve salvation, and join the evangelical legions in persuading others to do the same, hastening the day when God's kingdom would come to earth.

To be sure, the evangelical revivals did not "cause" immediate abolitionism; they could just as easily buttress the slaveholding regime. In areas of the United States dominated by slavery and slaveholders, revivalism generally encouraged Christian trusteeship within the context of slave ownership, promoted evangelical missions to the slaves, and nourished a religious and biblical defense of enslavement. But for a generation of young men and women born in New England and the Middle Atlantic—or in places to the west where people from these regions migrated—and who grew up in Presbyterian, Congregational, Quaker, or Unitarian households that valued moral and social responsibility, the revivals offered a vision of human perfectibility and a route of action to help bring it about. Many felt attracted by the idea of social reform, from temperance and education to poverty and prostitution, and some, horrified by the coercive power of slaveholders and the abject dependence forced upon the slaves, came to see slavery as a sin and abolition as a major step toward the coming of God's kingdom. Most of the leading white abolitionists—Garrison, Theodore Dwight Weld, Elijah Lovejoy, Wendell Phillips, Sarah and Angelina Grimké, Elizur Wright, Arthur and Lewis Tappan—either experienced conversion during the revivals or were Quakers. And although districts given over to evangelicalism did not necessarily favor abolitionism, abolitionists could find welcomes only in places that had been evangelized or had Quaker communities.

That Quakerism and evangelical Protestantism helped inspire the turn toward immediatism was of enormous importance to the politics and projects of abolitionism. Garrison and his followers never developed a "plan" for the abolition of slavery, and they never conjured an apocalyptic vision of slavery's end. Most would have had little trouble accepting a version of what New England and the Middle Atlantic had already pursued—emancipation immediately embraced but gradually accomplished—though their orientation was to individuals rather than the state. This is to say that much in the manner of the revivalists themselves the Garrisonians hoped to persuade ("moral suasion" is what they called it) slaveholders and their supporters of the sinfulness of their ways and of the imperative to devote themselves to the task of emancipation. To that end, they chose to mount a campaign, the likes of which had never before been seen in the United States and had only recently been launched in Great Britain: a campaign, constructed from the grass roots, to mobilize public opinion around the righteousness and wisdom of abolitionism.

Organization was crucial. Garrison's New England Anti-Slavery Society represented an important step, but in a sense it resembled previous emancipationist projects. Although the society adopted immediatism, it was based in Boston, brought together journalists, reformers, and genteel professionals who supported the *Liberator*, and followed models of incorporation established by British societies. Two years later, in Philadelphia, sixty-two abolitionists, including Garrison, formed the American Anti-Slavery Society, and while a handful of African American men and Quaker women were in attendance (the women left when the voting commenced and soon convened the Philadelphia Female Anti-Slavery Society), most of the delegates were rising, and urban-based, abolitionist leaders. What made these initiatives historically distinctive was their plan to expand outside major cities, to begin organizing antislavery societies in the hinterlands, and—in Garrison's words—to "scatter tracts like raindrops over the land, filled with startling facts and melting appeals on the subject of Negro oppression." It was a wise and necessary move. After all, the overwhelming majority of the population resided in the countryside, and the cities, even Boston, were especially hostile to abolitionism, dominated as they were by older mercantile elites tied to the international economy and the cotton trade and politically disposed, at best, to colonizationism. "Let the great cities alone," Lewis Tappan advised the abolitionist faithful, "they must be burned down by back fires. The springs to touch in order to move them lie in the country." Young abolitionists as well as formal lecturers soon fanned out to rural towns and villages and to fledgling industrial enclaves, calling anti-colonization meetings, circulating newspapers (like the *Liberator*) and antislavery tracts (like Garrison's stinging *Thoughts on African Colonization*), and encouraging the formation of local antislavery societies. They were remarkably successful. By late 1833, nearly fifty societies had been founded in ten different states, and the pulse of activity was quickening. Within another five years, the number of antislavery societies might have exceeded 1,000 with more than 100,000 members; in Massachusetts alone, there were about 250 societies with roughly 16,000 members.

As Tappan predicted, rural districts proved to be fertile seedbeds of organized abolitionism. But not all of them. Antislavery found its best reception in areas of the New England, Middle Atlantic, and midwestern countryside that had felt the effects of both the rapidly expanding market economy and the evangelical revivals of the Second Great Awakening. These included the farming communities, thriving crossroads villages, and manufacturing towns of the Boston hinterlands and the Connecticut River valley of Massachusetts, Vermont, and New Hampshire; the "burned-over" districts along the Erie Canal and Mohawk River valley in western New York; the Western Reserve of Ohio and the western Pennsylvania border; the Quaker towns surrounding Philadelphia; and eventually the Great Lakes settlements of northern Indiana and eastern Michigan. In 1838, Boston could claim seven antislavery societies, but the rural Massachusetts counties of Essex, Middlesex, and Worcester could claim forty-one, thirty-five, and thirty-two, respectively. The towns of Andover and Abington had as many societies and members (500) each as Boston did, and the factory towns of Lowell and Fall River had several societies and about 450 members each.

The people who stepped forward to embrace abolitionism in these districts did not, for the most part, come from the ranks of the local elites. Rather, they were farmers, skilled tradesmen, factory hands, and shopkeepers, ordinary folk who earned their bread chiefly by the sweat of their brows and who owned relatively little, if any, property. The tradesmen (or mechanics, as they were commonly known) were especially abundant, and their occupations often reflected the economic orientations of their localities: shoemakers in Lynn, Massachusetts, armorers in Springfield, machinists in Worcester, tailors in Utica, New York, and the more skilled of the textile operatives in Fall River and Lowell. Their roads to abolitionism revealed the influence of parents, kin, and clergy and, in all likelihood, the unsettling demands of a growing market economy.

The proliferation of antislavery societies and the circulation of abolitionist newspapers and tracts during the 1830s showed the marks of organizational activity new to the nineteenth century. These were not the voluntary and benevolent associations that communities had long established to care for the poor, the sick, and the deceased among them; nor were they the craft guilds meant, for centuries, to protect the status and livelihoods of artisans—though they provided foundations of familiarity. They were, instead, grassroots institutions looking toward specific social and political ends and employing novel techniques to spread the message and win adherents. They met on a regular basis, raised funds for a variety of projects, sponsored lectures by well-known abolitionists, distributed printed materials supporting the cause, debated divisive issues, boycotted slave-made goods, and had their members try to convert their neighbors. And, like the churches to which many of the activist faithful belonged, the antislavery front included women as well as men. Only the temperance movement of the time bore close resemblance to it.

Nothing seemed more emblematic of grassroots abolitionism in the 1830s than the many petition campaigns that antislavery societies and activists launched. The founding members of the American Anti-Slavery Society had taken the opportunity to petition Congress to abolish slavery in the District of Columbia (where it had jurisdiction) and urge sympathizers to petition state legislatures on the slavery question—a tactic that Benjamin Lundy and some others had already pursued in the 1820s and that tapped into a deep tradition of seeking political redress. All were undoubtedly aware of the enormous effect that antislavery petitioning in Britain had on popular attitudes and public policy there, and they were quick to seize the initiative. Moving door-to-door, whether in small hamlets or larger towns, they began collecting thousands of signatures and soon flooded Congress and statehouses with their calls for abolition, the end to municipal racial discrimination, and the education of black children. By 1838, nearly half a million petitions had been forwarded to Congress alone.

Yet there were equally far-reaching developments within the petition campaign itself. At the outset, the petitioners were overwhelmingly male, a measure of the gendered conventions regarding political citizenship and the male domination of the movement. Women could find no official place in antislavery societies (they were left to form their own) and were rarely afforded the opportunity to speak in public. But by the mid-1830s, more and more women were affixing their names to antislavery petitions, effectively pressing at the boundaries of political practice. Although some had cut their political teeth in the temperance campaign or in the battle against Indian removal (the first mass petition campaign involving women), abolitionist women—even those who organized female antislavery societies—initially turned to more customary projects such as education, fund-raising, religion, and consumer-based actions. Then, with the support of Garrison and some other immediatists, they embraced collective petitioning. Careful as they were to observe certain proprieties—women either submitted their own petitions or signed in columns separate from the men and often adopted a tone of pious deference—they nonetheless stepped out onto new public political terrain and did much of the work that sustained local abolitionism, challenging as that work often proved to be. They also shed special light on what slave women endured, recounting the brutalities, degradations, and "insatiable avarice" they suffered. Many of the abolitionist women were from the families of an emerging middle class of small manufacturers, shopkeepers, clerks, physicians, and ministers who hoped to turn the cultural attributes of domesticity and moral authority to political purpose; some were mill workers and outworkers in search of more personal independence and sensitized to the perils of inordinate power. The repercussions would be enormous both for the advance of women's rights and for the conduct of modern American politics.

Rough Politics

For all of their innovative activities, abolitionists never captured the support of more than a tiny minority of the white American public. Although they helped to demonize slaveholders and what would come to be called the "slave power" in American political life, they also exposed deep unease about emancipationism (and especially immediatism) even in areas of the country where slavery was in retreat. It was not just the abolitionists' moralizing and denunciation of colonization that provoked hostility. Nor was it just their organizational challenges and apparent readiness to defy gender norms. Nor was it just their disregard for the bases of established wealth and economic power. Nor was it just their willingness to imagine a future that included free black people in their midst. It was all of these things. To many white Americans, the abolitionists not only appeared to be demanding the elevation of a degraded subject race but also seemed to be heralding a new—and threatening—social and political order.

Anti-abolitionism took many forms. Abolitionists were denounced in the pages of the press, railed against from the pulpits, and viciously lampooned in broadsides and political cartoons. The case made against them suggested what anti-abolitionists believed was at stake. Abolitionists were deemed "licentious and incendiary," reckless and subversive, revolutionaries who not only invited "all men" to join their crusade but also urged women to "turn their sewing parties into abolition clubs." They had begun, one New Hampshire correspondent fitfully charged, "the agitation of legal, constitutional, or political reform . . . by measures adopted to inflame the passions of the multitude, including the women and children, and boarding school misses and factory girls . . . through organized societies, public meetings, authorized agents, foreign emissaries, regular publications, and the incessant circulation of cheap tracts, pamphlets, handbills, &c." Perhaps most frightening of all, they were "amalgamationists," intent on mixing the races and "mongrelizing" the Anglo-American population with the blood of black inferiors.

Small wonder that the heated language and inflammatory accusations could spark violent attacks. During the mid-1830s, just as abolitionist societies began to multiply across New England, the Middle Atlantic, and the lower Midwest, angry crowds of opponents moved against them. The greatest eruptions came in the larger cities of New York, Philadelphia, Boston, and Cincinnati, but anti-abolitionist violence also spread through smaller urban centers like Utica, New York, Newark, New Jersey, and Concord, New Hampshire, and to country towns like Canterbury, Connecticut, and Berlin, Ohio. Abolitionist conventions were broken up, their property and newspaper presses destroyed, their meeting halls burned to the ground, their bodies tarred and inked, and local blacks (conceived as allies) harassed and beaten. Indeed, any sites of interracialism or any people regarded as "amalgamationists" became vulnerable targets. Although the lethality of these episodes was limited, William Lloyd Garrison was dragged through the streets of Boston, and in the town of Alton, Illinois, the abolitionist editor Elijah Lovejoy was murdered.

Observers and later historians often referred to these explosions of anti-abolitionist violence as "riots" and "mobs," suggesting rage, spontaneity, and disorder. But the social composition and political choreography of anti-abolitionism points instead to more structured political associations and practices. Anti-abolitionist leaders came principally from the ranks of merchants, bankers, lawyers, and public officials whose families were of older stock and more con-servative Protestant religious affiliations (many were Episcopalians) and who were closely identified with a seaboard mercantile economy important to the eighteenth and early nineteenth centuries as well as with the local political establishment. They were regarded as the old elite, the "aristocracy of the North," "prominent and respectable gentlemen," "gentlemen of property and standing." Many were colonizationists. They commonly organized public meet-ings and, through resolutions, handbills, and the press, issued warnings to abo-litionists: that they would not permit their locale to become a "theater" for antislavery "operations"; that abolitionist activities had to be "put down," either by the laws of the state or by the "law of Judge Lynch"; that a gathering of "incendiary individuals" must not be allowed "within corporate bounds"; that the "vital stab" to their prosperity resulting from the "wicked and misguided oper-ations of the abolitionists" had to be "arrested." When, by their lights, the warn-ings were not heeded, the "expostulations and remonstrances" ignored, they proceeded to act in concert.

Directed by the "gentlemen of property and standing," the anti-abolitionist meetings and then "mobs" drew in an array of sympathizers, frequently young and from the lower reaches of the social order, who looked to vent their own hostilities and dissatisfactions—journeymen, laborers, teamsters, and sailors. Together they might choose to disrupt abolitionist assemblies, shouting down speakers and forcing others in attendance to flee. They might set fire to build-ings that housed antislavery newspapers or break in and smash the presses. They might sack the homes and businesses of local antislavery leaders. They might try to run white and black abolitionists out of the city, town, or village, meting out painful and shaming punishments as marks of their resolve. In 1838, they torched Philadelphia's Pennsylvania Hall, newly constructed with the financial support of abolitionists.

Often, the actions of anti-abolitionists were accompanied by a cacophony of shouts, tin horns, clanging pots, and whistles symbolizing the rituals of rough justice that communities had long inflicted upon those accused of transgressing local norms; abolitionists could be pelted with rotten eggs or rocks, further enun-ciating rejection and retribution. On occasion, the anti-abolitionist leadership lost control of events or reorchestrated the choreography, and the violence became especially ugly, more potentially lethal, and almost invariably racialized. Black churches, schools, and settlements could face utter destruction, and black men, women, and children could be subjected to grievous abuse, as the fires of hatred were fanned to a searing heat. The destruction of Pennsylvania Hall, led by a well-dressed crowd, was followed by the demolition of black enclaves in the city. Throughout the early nineteenth century, black people were far more likely than whites to suffer death at the hands of these perpetrators.

Yet anti-abolitionism represented one component in a wider surge of political violence and vigilantism in the 1830s—against Mormons, Catholics, foreigners, slaves, and free people of color—that together suggested how deeply embedded organized violence, coercion, and paramilitarism were in the conduct of American politics more generally. We are, of course, accustomed to focusing on the electoral arena to understand the dynamics of politics and political history, and there can be no doubt that elections and the franchise became more important during the early decades of the nineteenth century. Between the second decade of the nineteenth century and the 1840s, property-owning requirements for voting and office holding were either dropped or modified almost everywhere in the United States, more and more offices became elective rather than appointive at the state and local levels, and mass political parties—developing in close relation to these democratic reforms—emerged for the first time. The participation of eligible voters grew rapidly, and by 1840 it reached a height in national elections (about 80 percent) that would prevail for the remainder of the nineteenth century. Even so, the electoral must be seen as one of several interconnected, and ever shifting, arenas of political activity, and physical intimidation, in various forms, could always be found at the interfaces, if not at the centers.

When, for example, voters made their way to the polls on Election Day, they were ordinarily greeted with a scene that was not for the weak or faint-hearted. Representatives of competing candidates and parties jostled with one another, shouting insults and epithets, lubricated by the alcohol that was always available, as they tried to round up their supporters and strike fear into the opposition. "Each one," an observer of a St. Louis municipal election in 1838 declared, "talking loud and fast . . . bringing forward the voters telling them who to vote for, and challenging the votes of everyone with who they have the faintest shadow of a chance; handing out tickets, crossing out names, with many arguments pro and con, . . . some imitat[ing] the Barking of Dogs and some the Roaring of Bulls, all making as much noise as they could." Scuffling and fighting often broke out, with local toughs in attendance to enforce political discipline, while employers, merchants, and master craftsmen might watch as their employees and clerks deposited their ballots or announced (in viva voce voting) their choices. The weeks preceding an election were usually given over to raucous processions and parades, replete with torches, banners, fifes, and drumbeats, and to militia musters meant to demonstrate the martial basis of political citizenship and the legions of supporters the contestants could command. Not infrequently, the political faithful took the opportunity to inflict physical punishment on their enemies, especially if ethnic or religious antagonisms were added to the mix. Outright "riots" or "mobs," when they occurred—and scores were recorded during this period—seemed far more a matter of electioneering degree than kind.

It was a rough, a rowdy, and very much a male theater of public power, a fierce celebration of the gender exclusions that kept women and other dependents, who did not benefit from political democratization of the time, at the margins or wholly on the outside. It showed that the victors in electoral politics needed the muscle as well as the arguments and organization. And it fed off the rituals of community legitimation and sanction that had governed popular politics long before the franchise assumed importance. For in the face-to-face world of early America—and early modern Europe—power and hierarchy were not just determined by wealth and access, grievances were not merely aired, and justice was not simply enacted. They were performed in ways that had come to be recognizable. The performances could be quiet and didactic, as when members of the local elite entered a church or meeting after everyone else was seated and took their places at the front. But they could also be raucous and harshly edged, as when transients were warned out of a village, informants tarred and feathered, or petty thieves put in the stocks. Plebeians might show their support for a member of the governing class (generally with his encouragement) by taking to the streets in boisterous displays of allegiance or might show their contempt for Catholics by desecrating the symbols of papal authority or destroying a neighborhood convent. By the time of the Revolution, public rituals such as these had become formats of political protest and mobilization and proved ever adaptable to other spheres of conflict. Artisans and journeymen embraced them both in celebrating their trades and in struggling with their employers. Aggrieved leaseholders deployed them against wealthy landlords. Fleeced depositors used them in outbursts against local bankers. And fledgling political parties drew upon them in stoking electoral enthusiasm. After all, how better to distinguish loyalists from enemies?

That electoral politics in the early nineteenth century assumed a martial demeanor—bare-knuckle, coercive, paramilitary—was not only a product of its gendered composition and hypermasculine insistences. The political universe also encompassed arenas of activity that were, in fact, tightly bound up with warlike maneuvers and skirmishing and that gave significant shape to the conduct of elections themselves. Thus, in areas of the United States where substantial populations of slaves were to be found, state and local politics often revolved around efforts to police enslaved laborers and the large stretches of the countryside they might seek to traverse. Here, militia companies and slave patrols were important instruments both for manifesting the power of slaveholders and for herding the energies of white inhabitants (whether or not they owned slaves) who were required to serve. Plantations and farms, where slaves overwhelmingly resided, were important sites of political combat as matters of authority and submission were contested and networks of communication and alliance built. Slaveholders and slaves alike relied on webs of kinship and personal loyalty, extending over property lines and civil divisions, to circulate vital information, establish hierarchies among themselves, and defend their own against attack. Politics thereby meshed electoral practices among the free (and, most prominently, adult male) population with the mechanisms for disciplining the enslaved working class. No wonder that aspiring politicians often sought election or appointment as militia officers and that the smallest units of electoral politics were commonly known as militia districts.

The militia companies and their urban counterparts, like volunteer fire companies, played substantial roles in defining the terrain of local politics and in elaborating the patron-client relations that remained central to political practice and culture even after democratization took hold. If wealth and cultural attainment no longer commanded automatic deference, political ambition nonetheless required an assortment of resources and reciprocities. The abrogation of most property-owning requirements for political participation surely enabled humbler white men to voice their preferences and seek placement, and some positions in counties and municipalities could be economically alluring because of the salaries they paid or the fees they brought. Yet lone voices counted for little, and political office almost always necessitated more powerful sponsors not only because of the demands of electioneering but also because most offices called for the posting of substantial monetary bonds. The county sheriff might have to post a $10,000 bond; the treasurer a bond the size of the county's annual tax revenue. An apparent hedge against corruption and theft, the officer bonds also placed significant hurdles across the path of political preferment. Who but the wealthiest could stand for these sums? Those of more modest means had to rely on better-off sureties; in short, they needed political patrons.

Although patrons expected favors and services from their office-holding clients, they had their own needs as well. Their power and prestige were enhanced by—often required—collections of followers who could offer loyalty, votes, skills, and readiness to intimidate foes, but all of this came at the price of the rewards patrons had to make available: protection, work, credit, loans, assistance in times of trouble. It was a system of vertical allegiances and reciprocal obligations, sometimes mediated by kinship, at once potent and complex, open to differing and conflicting interpretations, not to mention discontent. And rather than disrupting it, the new electoral politics incorporated and effectively institutionalized it. Over the course of the nineteenth century, nothing would so bedevil those social groups and movements that looked for alternatives to the established order as the hardfisted vestiges of patron-client politics, which abolitionists discovered in the face of terrifying crowds called out by "gentlemen of property and standing."

The Slaveholders' Answers

Among America's political patrons of the early nineteenth century, none would have seemed as securely situated as the slaveholding planters who reigned powerfully in a geographical crescent stretching south and west from the Chesapeake to the Mississippi Valley. They owned large tracts of land and at least twenty slaves apiece, and their clients were chiefly small landholders with few or no slaves who were often related to them. They were amply represented in county seats and state legislatures and, owing to the federal ratio that counted slaves as three-fifths of a free person for the purposes of apportionment, had great influence in all the branches of the federal government. People like them—Washington, Jefferson, Madison, Monroe, Jackson—had occupied the presidency almost continuously since the ratification of the Constitution. Some had already moved out to the fertile lands of the Texas Republic; others looked hungrily at Mexico and Cuba.

Yet there was also cause for deep concern. An emancipation process had begun in New England and the Middle Atlantic, and by the 1830s it appeared part of a rising international assault. Slaves had successfully rebelled in St. Domingue and helped establish the second independent—and first black—nation in the Western Hemisphere, and their counterparts in the British Caribbean helped force the metropolitan government in London to accept emancipation there. The specters of "Santo Domingo" and Jamaica (site of the Baptist War) henceforth struck fear into the hearts of slaveholders everywhere, serving as grave reminders of their political vulnerabilities.

In the United States, the Northwest Ordinance had been enacted, the African slave trade had been outlawed, the American Colonization Society, with fantasies of very gradual emancipation, had attracted some prominent slaveholders to its cause, and in Virginia, Maryland, and Tennessee the questions of gradual abolition coupled with colonization now became subjects of public debate, suggesting that emancipationism was spreading ever southward. Since the 1790s, slave unrest had been brewing in Virginia, the Carolinas, and Louisiana and erupted into either large-scale conspiracies or bloody revolts on several occasions. Some members of Congress had begun to oppose the admission of new slave states to the Union and in the Missouri Compromise (1819–21) had managed to close off much of the Louisiana Territory to slaveholding. Most recently, a movement of whites and blacks in the Northeast and the Midwest had come to embrace immediatism, called slavery a sin, and started flooding the mails with their literature and Congress with their petitions.

The response of slaveholders was not uniform, and it depended, in good measure, on the social geography and political culture of their locales. If anything, the challenge of emancipationism revealed both how implicated most of the country was in the system of slave labor and how complex slavery was as a system. As late as the 1830s, slavery and its residues remained alive throughout the United States (due to gradual emancipations and the Fugitive Slave Law) and could be found in a great range of circumstances: in rural and urban settings; in small- and large-scale units; in overwhelmingly white and overwhelmingly black population enclaves; attached to agricultural and industrial activities; involved in different crop cultures; and subject to an array of religious and political influences. In most places outside the southernmost states, slaveholders were still prepared—following Jefferson and the moderate voices of the Virginia dynasty—to regard slavery as an evil and a burden and to speak of a very distant day when it might no longer exist. For while they invariably held the upper hand in their state governments, they had to contend with constituencies of non-slaveholding whites, who resided in districts where slavery did not have much of a foothold (eastern Tennessee and Kentucky, western Virginia and North Carolina, northern Maryland and Delaware) and might have been influenced by small settlements of Quakers and evangelicals. Some of these slaveholders were open to discussing a plan of gradual abolition that would extend over many years and bring compensation to owners of slave property; many more wished to avoid such a discussion entirely and, if they bothered, imagine a protracted process that would move slaves to thriving plantation economies farther to the south and west, thereby "whitening" their counties and states (Jefferson called it "diffusion"); virtually all believed that any acceptable plan would have to be linked with the removal of freed slaves.

In the Southeast and the emerging Southwest—what would come to be called the Deep South—matters had long been different. Slave plantations ruled (or were coming to rule) the social landscape, black majorities (or near black majorities) were the norm, export crops liked cotton, rice, and sugar drove economic growth, and the planter elite was especially powerful. Few slaveholders there had been moved by the Enlightenment currents of the Revolutionary period and, unlike their counterparts in the Chesapeake and farther to the north, rarely manumitted individual slaves. Their representatives at the federal Constitutional Convention insisted that slavery had to be explicitly recognized as well as protected from unwanted government interference. And they remained sensitive about their petty sovereignties and local prerogatives. South Carolina was emblematic in all these regards and took the lead politically and intellectually in challenging federal authority. In 1828, the brilliant and irascible John C. Calhoun, in his "South Carolina Exposition and Protest," argued that the states not simply were sovereign but also had the sovereign right to veto (nullify) federal laws if they determined them to be unconstitutional. Four years later, following Calhoun's lead, South Carolina officials refused to enforce federal tariffs that favored manufacturing at the expense of agricultural interests (and as a consequence threatened to weaken the slave system) and thereby provoked a showdown—known as the Nullification Crisis—with the administration of Andrew Jackson (himself a Tennessee slaveholder).

Although radical slaveholders in South Carolina—at the time called Nullifiers—held sway in their state, they attracted very few supporters elsewhere in the slaveholding United States and were forced, in this instance, to back down. It would be an important lesson for them and for the politics of slavery. What slaveholders almost everywhere in the country during the 1830s could agree upon, however, was that the abolitionist mail and petition campaigns had to be stopped. The future of slavery in the United States, all could see, was becoming a bitterly divisive issue, and when it was raised for public discussion, the divisions seemed to spread and deepen. Abolitionists might have been a despised minority, but their petitions demanded debate in the halls of government, and the literature they sent through the mails could easily get into the hands of non-slaveholders and slaves, encouraging political disaffection on the one hand and, perhaps, "servile insurrection" on the other. By the mid-1830s, with the petition campaign intensifying and a cache of abolitionist material seized by the postmaster in the port of Charleston, the time for a reckoning had been reached.

Despite the broad support that anti-abolitionism attained, these were thorny issues. However objectionable the circulation of abolitionist tracts or petitions might have been, freedom of expression and the right of petition were explicitly protected by the Constitution, and some of the proposals advanced by slaveholding interests and sympathizers seemed heavy-handed violations. The freshman South Carolina representative James Henry Hammond, hoping to put "a decided seal of disapprobation" on the abolitionist petitions, called on his congressional colleagues to outright refuse to receive them. Even President Jackson, who had already had it out with radical South Carolinians, wished to stem the abolitionist tide by prohibiting "under severe penalties, the circulation, in the Southern states, through the mail of incendiary publications." In the end, more temperate voices and less inflammatory solutions prevailed, and a political alliance among slaveholders and anti-abolitionists more generally advanced: Congress, in the so-called gag rule of 1836, agreed to receive abolitionist petitions and then immediately table them so that they would not be considered, and federal authorities (the postmaster general in particular) agreed to tolerate the refusals of local postmasters to deliver abolitionist publications.

Still, for many slaveholders, and especially for those in the Deep South, efforts to hedge in abolitionism did not take the sting out of its moral and political assault. Regarding themselves as modern, cosmopolitan, and devotedly Christian, they reeled at the abolitionists' charges that slavery was a hideous despotism, unfit for a republic, and that they were sadistic tyrants and sinners. To be sure, slavery always had strong and vocal defenders, and slaveholders had long been vigilant not only about protecting their interests and ways of life but also about expanding their power. How else to explain the remarkable success they had in fashioning a constitution that gave slavery a legal basis in every corner of the United States (through the fugitive slave clause), rewarded slaveholders with more political representation than any other group of Americans (through the federal ratio), prohibited the taxation of exports (their greatest source of wealth), empowered the federal government to repress slave rebellions, and refused to halt the African slave trade for two decades. Yet it was only in the 1830s, amid an assortment of disruptions and challenges, that some of them—and their intellectual and clerical allies—began to build an explicit defense of slavery that was simultaneously sacred and secular, tuned to the logic of the Bible and the modern world.

Modern but very much veering toward illiberal. The explicit defense of slavery, what we have come to call the "pro-slavery argument," eagerly embraced the racialist thought that had penetrated more and more of the Atlantic world since the last third of the eighteenth century. In the 1780s, Jefferson, among others, had speculated that black people were innately inferior to white, and during the early nineteenth century, aided by phrenology and other forms of pseudoscience, that speculation took firm hold in academic as well as popular culture. Slavery could thereby be presented as the best means to order a society containing large numbers of people who were destined for little better than a life of menial labor. The "negro," one writer insisted in 1835, "is from his intellectual and moral organization incapable of being civilized or enjoying freedom" and, if freed, would "corrupt the principles of one half of our population and drag them down—down to their own depraved, degraded and disgusting condition." Enslavement, others believed, provided whatever "humanity" slaves might have and enabled them to find their "level." It was a version of racialized arguments that slave and serf owners, from Russia and Prussia to Brazil and Suriname to Cuba and Martinique, deployed in explaining what they regarded as the incapacities of their dependent laborers.

No more, in truth, needed to be said. Certainly not in the early nineteenth-century United States. But much more was said. Drawing upon traditions of an Atlantic conservatism that found outlets in Federalism (associated with the Federalist Party of the early republic) and wider opposition to the radical phases of the French Revolution (anti-Jacobinism), slavery's defenders commenced to reject the egalitarianism that the Declaration of Independence had enshrined. They claimed, as William Harper, reared in Antigua before moving to South Carolina, did, that men were rather born into a state of inequality and "helpless dependence" and that "slavery anticipates the benefits of civilization, and retards the evils of civilization," channeling labor into wealth-producing pursuits. Unlike Jefferson, who worried that slaveholding corrupted both master and slave and ate at the vitals of a republic, they argued that slavery was the necessary basis of a republic, the best means of excluding those not fit to participate, the only way of preventing tyranny. Slavery alone, they suggested, placed a degraded and dependent working class under adequate control and enabled humble white folk to find land and other forms of productive property, thereby escaping exploitation at the hands of white masters and employers. Some would go so far as to call slavery a "positive good" for master and slave alike, an acknowledgment of inherent inferiorities and superiorities, the foundation of economic prosperity, public order, and political progress.

Vital aid came from white ministers, many of whom were from relatively modest backgrounds but nonetheless saw the defense of slavery as integral to the building of Christian community. After all, while they accepted the spiritual equality of all people—and rejected polygenesis, or the separate creation of the races, which won interest in some pro-slavery circles—they understood Christianity in familial terms, with the hierarchy, patriarchal authority, and submission that went along with it. Perhaps their easiest task was demonstrating the compatibility between slavery and the Bible and showing their critics' "palpable ignorance of the divine will," as Virginia's Thornton Stringfellow bellowed. But even more politically effective was the ministers' likening of slavery to other household relations, especially marriage, which both naturalized the subordination that slavery entailed and demonized emancipation as a dire threat to the very foundation of social order. "The true Scriptural idea of slavery," a Mississippi pastor could announce, "is that of patriarchal relations," and masters served as "essentially the head of the household in all relations—the head over the wife—the head over his children—the head over his servants." Therefore, another insisted, the "evils of slavery, like the evils of matrimony, may be traced to the neglect of the duties incumbent upon the individuals sustaining the relation" rather than the relation itself. Abolitionism, like agrarianism, deism, socialism, feminism, and "perhaps other isms," heralded nothing but anarchy.

Ironically, it was Thomas Jefferson, the deist and freethinker, who, in his struggle to come to terms with the problems of slavery and freedom, laid a foundation of later pro-slavery thought. Responding to the appeals of his nephew Edward Coles in the second decade of the nineteenth century, and to others who tried to persuade him to take a public stand against slavery, Jefferson instead lectured them on the realities of the world and the responsibilities of slaveholders in it. The challenge of abolition was too great, at least for his generation, Jefferson concluded, and a solution to it must be left to the future. In the meantime, slaveholders should recognize the duties and obligations that slavery imposed on them and do their best to take care of charges who could not take care of themselves. At once accepting and then rejecting gradualism, Jefferson instead offered Christian trusteeship, which pro-slavery theorists of the 1830s would hold up as the humane alternative to the insecurities and degradations of the free labor market.

Problems of Slavery, Problems of Freedom

White abolitionists had their own version of the effect of slavery on "domestic relations." It corrupted and destroyed them and, for the slave, rendered a family life—a pillar of freedom in the abolitionist view—virtually impossible. A great deal of abolitionist ink was spilled in depicting the many barbarities and brutalities that slaves suffered at the hands of slave owners, and although the lash became a centerpiece of their representations, abolitionists seemed especially focused on the damages done to proper marriage, gender roles, and forms of sexuality. Slave families had no legal basis and could be broken up in an instant; slave men could not be providers and protectors of their wives and children; and slave women were daily exposed to the many sexual predators among their owners. As William Ellery Channing observed in 1835, "Slavery virtually ruptures the domestic relations. It ruptures the most sacred ties on earth. . . . He [the slave man] lives not for his family but for a stranger. He cannot improve their lot. His wife and daughter he cannot shield from insult . . . marriage has not sanctity. It may be dissolved in a moment at another's will."

The result, as many abolitionists saw it, was the slave's descent into a morass of evils. Slavery, according to Lydia Maria Child, seemed to destroy everything it touched, promoting "treachery, fraud, and violence" while "rend[ing] asunder the dearest relations, pollut[ing] the very fountains of justice," and leaving the slave to "his wretched wanderings. . . . They are treated like brutes and all the influences around them conspire to make them brutes." For many abolitionists, "a worse evil to the slave than the cruelty he sometimes endures, is the moral degradation that results from his condition. Falsehood, theft, licentiousness, are the natural consequence of his situation. . . . Cowardice, cruelty, cunning and stupidity, abject submission or deadly vindictiveness" were the bitter "fruits of slavery." Even William Lloyd Garrison, who ordinarily defended blacks against attacks on their character, thought it "absurd . . . to deny that intemperance, indolence, and crime prevail among them to a mournful extent."

It was a biting critique of slaveholding and a devastating portrait of the circumstances in which people of African descent consequently found themselves. Yet at the same time, it raised serious questions about the road to freedom. Were slaves such as these prepared to make the transition? And was the country prepared to accept them? Colonizationists, whose views of black character were strikingly similar, bluntly answered no and called for gradual emancipation and the expulsion of the freedpeople. But what would immediatism have to offer? At no point did abolitionists present a program of emancipation, a way of making immediatism operational. The most radical among them, who rejected formal politics because its arena was contaminated by slavery and slaveholders, hoped to convince individual slaveholders of their sinfulness and Christian obligation to manumit their slaves. Those more open to engagement with the political process might look to mobilize sympathetic voters, force a public reckoning with the slavery question, and compel the federal government to abolish slavery where it had jurisdiction: in the District of Columbia and the federal territories west of the Mississippi River (most agreed that slavery in the states was beyond federal interference). None intended to stir up slave unrest; if anything, they discountenanced slave rebellion and, like Garrison, were "horror struck" by Nat Turner's rising in Southampton County, Virginia.

"Immediatism" did not, therefore, elaborate a clear or rapid route of emancipation, and abolitionists imagined significant cultural work along the way. They spoke of "raising more than two millions of human beings to the enjoyment of human rights, to the blessings of Christian civilization, to the means of infinite self-improvement," of "elevating the slave," of teaching slaves and free blacks "the importance of domestic order and the performance of relative duties in families," of instilling "industry and economy, promptness and fidelity in the fulfillment of contracts or obligations." Some believed that slaves would require guardians, strict controls on their physical mobility, and direct obligations "to labor on the same principles on which the vagrant in other communities is confined and compelled to earn his bread." Many more wondered whether slaves were quite ready "to understand or enjoy" freedom however urgent emancipation was, and they

saw the need for a variety of educational initiatives. Indeed, although abolitionists were virtually alone among free Americans in envisioning a biracial future
and although some of them fought courageously for schooling and civil equality,
few confronted the many challenges of gradual emancipation where it had
occurred or was still occurring. Instead, they often chose pedantry, instructing
blacks to "be industrious, let no hour pass unemployed . . . be virtuous . . . use no
bad language . . . in a word be good Christians and good citizens, that all reproach
may be taken from you." It was a worrisome omen—were abolitionists themselves prepared for emancipation?—and an indication of why many were reluctant to admit black abolitionists to their organizations.

But there were other paths to emancipationism than colonization or immediatism, and they grew out of a wider critique of the American social order that
began to take hold in the 1820s (in the wake of the economic panic of 1819) and
made themselves felt more forcefully in the 1830s. They moved through communitarian experiments, and especially Owenism, that attempted to construct
sets of social relations that would serve as alternatives to the competitiveness,
greed, and exploitation of the market economy. They moved through growing
public hostility to private banks, paper money, and the economic vulnerabilities these new devices introduced. And they moved through a developing opposition, notably among artisans and journeymen in the larger urban centers, to
new concentrations of wealth and power, what might be called "antimonopoly"
sensibilities. While millennial pulses could be felt along some of these paths—
especially the communitarian—evangelical revivalism was by no means a major
influence, and while antislavery would be increasingly important, it began as
one of several issues of concern.

The Scots-born freethinker Frances Wright plotted a number of the intersections. First traveling to the United States in 1818, she greatly admired most
of what she saw but was shocked by her brief encounter with slavery in Washington, D.C.: "The sight of slavery is revolting everywhere, but to inhale the
impure breath of its pestilence in the free winds of America is odious beyond all
that imagination can conceive." Thus, when she returned to the States in 1824
and visited Robert Owen's community, New Harmony, in Indiana as well as
George Rapp's not far away, Wright determined to organize her own social
experiment that would strike a blow at American slavery. Not surprisingly, her
plan showed more of the marks of colonizationism than early immediatism and
indeed was mindful of the need both to compensate slave owners for their losses
and to facilitate the removal of freed slaves. She would purchase a model farm
(she expected to raise money from men of wealth and prominence with the help
of the Marquis de Lafayette, who was in the country at the same time and close
to Wright) and, together with a large group of slaves, have the agricultural work

done in the efficient manner suggested by Rapp's notion of "unified labor," and use the proceeds to emancipate the slaves, pay for their transport to a foreign location, and buy additional slaves to replace them. By her calculations, such an undertaking would "redeem the whole slave population of the United States" in about eighty-five years. To that end, and using her own resources (she failed to attract any investors), she bought 1,240 acres of land near Memphis, Tennessee, but only eight slaves (five men and three women) to labor on them. She called her small colony Nashoba. It was a plan, something in the manner of Benjamin Lundy's, and it failed miserably, due in part to Wright's illness-related absence and the behavior of the managers she left behind. Wright then sold Nashoba to a philanthropic trust and eventually sent the slaves on a chartered ship to Haiti, where they were emancipated (at her expense) and entrusted to the Haitian president, Jean-Pierre Boyer. Yet the experience further radicalized her, not simply on the slavery question, but on the character of the American republic. She spent more time at the community of New Harmony, imbibing the early socialist ideas there, helped to edit Robert Dale Owen's paper, the *New-Harmony Gazette*, and set off on a controversial speaking tour where she heaped scorn on organized religion, the marriage relation, and restrictive divorce laws and advocated for educational reform and an end to capital punishment. In 1829, with Robert Dale Owen and the newspaper in tow, she arrived in New York City.

The moment was propitious. The city was swirling with radical ferment, labor unrest, and an emerging workingmen's movement led by militant journeymen, wage earners, and small master craftsmen that would find its way into electoral politics. The political air had been electrified during the 1820s by the agrarian, antimonopoly, and nascent socialist writings of Thomas Spence, William Thompson, John Gay, Langton Byllesby, and Cornelius Blatchly and by the radical labor theory of value espoused by Philadelphia's William Heighton. It was a lively and welcoming environment for Frances Wright and Robert Dale Owen, who quickly won a following of freethinkers and commenced publishing their paper (renamed the *Free Enquirer*), with the aid of the English-born printer George Henry Evans.

At the intellectual center of the workingmen's movement was Thomas Skidmore, a machinist and inventor originally from the hardscrabble Connecticut countryside who arrived in New York City in 1819 and read deeply in the works of Locke, Rousseau, Jefferson, and Paine, not to mention Gay, Thompson, Blatchly, and Byllesby. Although initially a supporter of John Quincy Adams, Skidmore gravitated to the laboring men and in 1829 (the same year as David Walker's *Appeal to the Coloured Citizens of the World*) published *The Rights of Man to Property!* Best known for its agrarian plan for redistributing landed property and abolishing inheritance, the tract also set its critical sights on the inequities promoted by banking institutions, the public debt, chartered corporations, privately owned and run schools and factories, and an elective franchise that excluded women, blacks, and Indians. It also looked to the prospect of "extinguishing slavery, and its ten thousand attendant evils." Imagining that many slaves were reluctant to "take their freedom if it were given them" because they lacked the property to "support themselves," Skidmore offered a sweeping solution that made a mockery of the colonizationist disposition: include slaves in the "General Distribution," and provide them with "lands and other property."

Skidmore stood out for his agrarian redistributionism, his willingness to maintain private property while equalizing its ownership, but he was not alone in New York radical and labor circles in fashioning an antislavery that owed to political and economic egalitarianism rather than evangelicalism. William Leggett, a native New Yorker who had traveled the West Indies and the Mediterranean in the U.S. Navy and joined William Cullen Bryant at the *New-York Evening Post,* also in 1829, was associated with the "Locofoco"—labor egalitarian—wing of the fledgling Democratic Party and was known to characterize emancipationists as "amalgamators." His main concern was the "money power," the financial predators and their political minions who preyed on farmers, workers, and other producers, and his attacks were withering. But the viciousness of anti-abolitionism jostled his sensibilities, and by the mid-1830s he had come to see "monster slavery" as the most serious aristocratic enemy facing the United States. In moves that shocked most fellow Democrats, Leggett endorsed the American Anti-Slavery Society and called for extending equal rights doctrine (including suffrage) to African Americans. Slavery, Leggett insisted, quite simply ran against the "fundamental article of the creed of democracy, which acknowledges the political equality, and inalienable right of freedom, of all mankind."

Like Leggett, George Henry Evans turned antimonopoly radicalism and support for white labor ("workyism," as it was known in the early 1830s) in the direction of antislavery. English-born and apprenticed as a printer, Evans immigrated to upstate New York and read Tom Paine before coming to New York City and meeting up with Frances Wright and Robert Dale Owen, who, in turn, helped him launch the *Working Man's Advocate.* There he would develop the ideas—less radical than Skidmore's—that would make him perhaps the leading apostle of land reform. But there too he would attack slavery and anti-abolitionists, deride the American Colonization Society ("the most absurd of all absurd projects"), argue for equal treatment of free blacks, and, most remarkable, express sympathy for Nat Turner. "What can be more natural," he wrote, "than human beings destined to perpetual slavery, should commit excesses in attempts to better their condition? And how can the whites be better secured against such excesses than by affording the degraded slaves the prospect of gradual but effectual emancipation, and by capacitating them for the enjoyment of freedom?" In an important sense, Evans's plans to make public lands—homesteads—available to landless settlers fed off the same antimonopoly sentiments that fired his emancipationism. He called his land reform program "Free Soil."

American Maroons

African Americans in the northeastern United States pioneered many of the roads to immediatism. They were the earliest and loudest critics of gradualism and colonization. They built an infrastructure of institutions to coordinate their communities, disseminate important news and ideas, and orchestrate public protest. Black women as well as men became involved in abolitionism, and the fiery Boston activist Maria W. Stewart might have been the first woman to address a "promiscuous assembly"—that is, an audience composed of men and women—when she spoke at the city's African Masonic Hall in February 1833. A small free, economically prosperous, and educated class had emerged among them, especially in Philadelphia, who were concerned both with fighting against slavery and with "uplifting" the poor, uneducated, and dissolute. They became the chief subscribers to abolitionist newspapers and not only helped convince Garrison of the errors of colonizationism but also made their presence felt when he established the New England Anti-Slavery Society and the American Anti-Slavery Society. They also instructed white sympathizers in the international dimensions of abolitionism, annually commemorating the independence of Haiti and the ending of slavery in the British West Indies, as well as the death knells of enslavement in the American states in which they resided.

It appeared, in short, that these African Americans were carving a place for themselves in the developing public political culture and advancing it in a variety of ways. Yet appearances can be deceiving, and in this instance they obscure the very distinctive—and very precarious—political niche in which most of those in the Northeast and the Midwest found themselves. The overwhelming majority of them were at the bottom of the economic ladder, surviving hand to mouth as unskilled laborers and domestics in cities and towns and perhaps as poor tenant farmers and farm laborers in the countryside. They lived in residential clusters usually in the roughest sections of rural and urban areas, if not wholly off to themselves. Many of them had been enslaved or were the children of enslaved parents, and a significant number, especially in Pennsylvania, New York, Ohio, Indiana, and Illinois, were fugitives from states where slavery remained legal; that number would steadily grow. Most important, they were literally besieged by slavery and the many debilities that slavery carried with it. In the United States of the 1830s, any black man, woman, or child anywhere was presumed to be a slave, and owing to gradual emancipations and the federal Fugitive Slave Law the arms of the state were in place to enforce that presumption. Slave catchers, who acted with the sanction or support of white authorities, were regularly on the prowl for runaways, and they often observed no distinction between African Americans who were and were not legally free. As a result, blacks in the Northeast and the Midwest remained in constant fear, and their settlements had to be perpetually alert, perpetually on guard, perpetually self-protective. "After a few years of life in a Free State," William Parker, who fled from Maryland to the rural hinterlands of Pennsylvania, recalled, "I found by bitter experience that to preserve my stolen liberty I must pay, unremittingly, an almost sleepless vigilance."

Fugitive slaves in fact learned quickly that there was no clear dividing line between slavery and freedom in the United States. Lewis Garrard Clarke, a Kentucky slave, successfully fled across the Ohio River and initially "trembled all over" being "on what was called free soil." But when he arrived in nearby Cincinnati and saw "slave dealers . . . who knew me," he concluded that "the spirit of slaveholding was not all south of the Ohio River" and determined, on the advice of an acquaintance, to head to Cleveland and then "cross over to Canada," where he could be sure that "I AM FREE." He was not alone in wondering about the true borders of enslavement. Fleeing into states that had apparently abolished slavery, many runaways discovered that they "were still in an enemy's land," that slaveholders roamed the streets in search of their property, that the "northern people are pledged . . . to keep them in subjection to their masters," and that even "in sight of the Bunker Hill Monument . . . no law" offered them protection. The fugitive Thomas Smallwood spoke bitterly of white abolitionists who "would strenuously persuade" runaways "to settle in the so-called Free States," not recognizing "the influence that slavery had over the entire union." For him and for so many others who attempted escape from captivity, real freedom beckoned only in Canada, Britain, or some other "entirely foreign jurisdiction." "When I arrived in the city of New York," Moses Roper remembered, "I thought I was free; but learned I was not." Roper quickly moved into the surrounding countryside, up the Hudson River valley to Poughkeepsie, on to Vermont, New Hampshire, and Massachusetts. It was all the same, and before long, hearing of a slave catcher on his trail, he "secreted" himself for several weeks until he could get passage on a ship to Liverpool, where he finally felt that he had left "the cruel bondage of slavery."

For African Americans unable or unwilling to leave the United States for a safer destination, organized self-defense became increasingly necessary—all the more so after explosions of anti-abolitionist and racial violence in the early to mid-1830s destroyed some of their communities and frightened off many of their white allies. Very quickly, vigilance committees were established by blacks in the major cities of the northeastern and Middle Atlantic coasts, taking as their responsibility the harboring of fugitive slaves as well as the thwarting of "slave agents and kidnappers." To those ends, they monitored waterfronts for the arrival of runaways or of vessels suspected to be "slavers." They reported on the arrests and abductions of blacks purported to be fugitives and on the whereabouts of slave catchers. And they made efforts to recover fellow blacks who had been carried back into the South.

People like David Ruggles, freeborn in Connecticut in 1810 to a family of artisans and eventually a leader of the New York Vigilance Committee, played key roles both in protecting the many vulnerable African Americans in their midst and in building a grassroots antislavery movement. Availing himself of developing communication networks that linked black settlements over wide areas, Ruggles helped ferry runaways to relatively secure havens—Frederick Douglass was one of them—encouraged subscriptions to abolitionist newspapers, contributed articles and pamphlets in the antislavery cause, and tirelessly pursued kidnappers. In New York and elsewhere, vigilance committees could in fact move toward direct action and armed resistance, mobilizing black members and supporters to rescue fugitives spirited away by bounty hunters and physically drive off those who threatened. In these efforts, the committees, generally headed up by African Americans with skills and means (like Ruggles), were aided by less formal groups of poor, working-class blacks who utilized their own networks based in clustered households and work sites.

Composed heavily of African American men and women who had directly experienced slavery or had escaped from it by flight or manumission of some sort, surrounded by territory in which black enslavement continued to have a significant legal basis, hedged in by civil and political disabilities organized around slavery and race, and subject to regular invasions by armed whites (including constituted police authorities) who tried to kidnap their members, destroy their dwellings and institutions, or utterly drive them out, many black settlements in the Northeast and the Midwest came to resemble what are known as maroons: enclaves of fugitives from slavery. Their public presence might, of course, have been more pronounced, their activities more visible, and their political maneuvering room a bit greater than their counterparts farther to the south in the United States, the Caribbean, and Latin America. But like maroons everywhere, they served as beacons for those attempting to flee their enslavement and as important political meeting grounds for those who found refuge. Here, in an almost unprecedented way, people of African descent who had endured slavery as well as putative freedom, who had lived to the south and to the north, to the east and to the west, in the West Indies and other parts of the Americas, in rural and urban environments, could encounter one another, share perspectives, exchange ideas, and begin to fashion new political languages and political cultures. Together, in the face of precarious circumstances and inveterate public hostility, they waged a militant struggle—of a tenor that few others in the United States were willing or able to embrace—against slavery and the world that slavery had made.

CHAPTER THREE

Markets, Money, and Class

Paper currency issued by Massachusetts state banks.

A Tale of Four Continents

Few cities in the world during the 1830s could rival the economic dynamism of New Orleans. Its population had increased nearly tenfold since the French sold it to the United States in 1803. Its port was jammed with the traffic of hundreds of steamers and flatboats sailing in from the Atlantic and the Caribbean and down the Mississippi River. Its merchant and factorage houses prospered on an import and, especially, export trade that by the mid-1830s well surpassed that of New York City in value, and they drew on the capital of local banks, most of which were newly chartered by the Louisiana state legislature. Boosters like the publisher J. D. B. DeBow exulted in the "rapid and gigantic strides" New Orleans had made, and some predicted that the city was destined to become the economic hub of all the Americas.

The source of the boom that New Orleans rode in the 1830s was not hard to find. Although the sugar plantations that lined the Mississippi to the north and south, and hugged the banks of nearby Bayou Lafourche and Bayou Teche, were the closest, the wharves told the main story, stacked as they were, from late summer to early winter, with bale upon bale of cotton. More than any-thing else, cotton made New Orleans in the first half of the nineteenth century because cotton was remaking large sections of the world. Its cultivation, orga-nized chiefly around large landed estates and slave labor, had spread across the fertile belts of the Deep South and then into the Mississippi Valley in the second and third decades of the nineteenth century and, once harvested, festooned the riverine traffic to the Crescent City before being shipped out to England and France—Liverpool and Le Havre—and secondarily to the American North-east, where it would be turned into yarns, cloth, and other cotton goods for rap-idly growing consumer markets. The profits to be made from cotton culture as the price of the fiber soared in the 1830s fueled human migrations on a large scale (especially from the Chesapeake and the Carolinas, Kentucky and Tennes-see) and land speculation that reached dizzying heights. In 1835–36, the New Orleans cotton market drew in 443,307 bales of cotton from Mississippi and Louisiana alone, almost one-half of all the cotton shipped from the United States.

Then, in what seemed to be an instant, the boom collapsed. Discount rates shot up, and credit, which had been easily available, suddenly tightened. Lenders called in their loans. Debtors ran to convert their paper obligations into specie (gold or silver coin). And banks, which in many cases had overextended them-selves during the boom, were caught short. The price of cotton began to tumble, and the large debts secured by the value of the cotton crop became impossible to collect, driving a stake through the operations of merchants and factors in the cotton trade and eventually through those institutions that propped them up financially. In March 1837, the New Orleans factorage house of Herman, Briggs & Company failed, and soon thereafter the New York lending house of J. L. & S. Joseph & Company, which provided credit to Herman, Briggs, closed its doors. A raft of other firms, especially in the coastal port cities, followed suit. It was a massive financial crisis, now known as the panic of 1837.

Observers at the time and since looked principally to domestic politics to explain what had unfolded, and an easy logic stared them in the face. President Andrew Jackson, a man of considerable means but also deeply suspicious of any authority other than his own, had gone nose to nose with the Philadelphia aristocrat and president of the Second Bank of the United States, Nicholas Biddle, and the fallout appeared to rock the foundations of the expanding American economy. Chartered by the federal government in 1816 for a period of twenty years, the bank, though privately controlled, had become a powerful force under Biddle's stewardship. It served as the depository for Treasury funds and federal tax revenues, circulated notes accepted as legal tender, sold government securities and made loans, established branches in twenty-nine cities, and could keep the growing number of state-chartered banks in check by gathering up their notes and redeeming them for specie. But to Jackson, the bank was a "hydra-headed monster" that corrupted "the morals of our people" and threatened "our liberty," and he determined to slay it. When Congress considered the matter of recharter several years earlier than necessary, he vetoed the bill that Congress passed (but lacked the votes to override) and then proceeded to finish the deed by removing federal deposits from the Bank of the United States and redistributing them to state-chartered banks of his choosing ("pet banks," as they were derisively known).

Jackson's redistribution of federal deposits to state banks appeared—though not by intention—to stoke the fires of inflation and speculation, enabling the banks to print more of their own currency and underwrite the purchase of public lands coming on the market. So too did a burgeoning federal budget surplus, occasioned by a rise in tariff revenues and the boom in land sales, which Jackson thought to spread among the states. When the Jackson administration ultimately moved to rein in the excesses, restricting the circulation of small banknotes and issuing the "Specie Circular," which prohibited the use of paper money for federal land purchases (the government would now only accept gold or silver coin), the bottom, it seemed, quickly and dramatically fell out. It was, according to one critic, like "a tremendous bomb thrown without warning."

Although Jackson's "war" with the Bank of the United States, Specie Circular, and general leadership of hard-money constituencies proved of great importance to the politics and political economy of early nineteenth-century America, they may not explain the panic of 1837 and the severe economic slowdown that carried into the following decade. For that, circuits of investment and exchange encompassing four continents may be better indicators, and at their center was the City of London, the Bank of England, and several large investment houses operating there, Baring Brothers and Brown Brothers chief among them. Despite its late eighteenth-century defeat at the hands of rebellious American settlers, Britain had emerged from the era of the French Revolution and the Napoleonic Wars as the world's premier economic and political power. Its empire remained formidable and vast, stretching across southern Asia, Australia, Canada, and the Caribbean, and London's City—the financial district— became an engine of both domestic and international economic growth. In the second and third decades of the nineteenth century, British investors bought up large blocks of shares in the Second Bank of the United States, ultimately holding about one-quarter of all those in private hands, and they were especially significant in financing many of the costly turnpike, canal, and early railroad projects (perhaps to the amount of $90 million to $100 million) that undergirded the developing infrastructure of the United States. It was an example of the trading relations that continued to bind the British and the Americans together: Britain being the chief market for American goods (especially cotton) and the United States representing a significant market for Britain. In the first half of the 1830s, the volume of Anglo-American trade doubled.

British purchases of American securities promoted the flow of specie, notably gold, from east to west across the Atlantic and, together with other investments, stimulated economic activity in the United States as well as some of the inflationary pressures of the period. But it was the flow of silver from Mexican mines well to the southwest that would be even more consequential. Built on the backs of Afro-Mexicans (many of whom had been enslaved) and indigenous people who labored in the mines of Zacatecas and San Luis Potosí, the silver trade moved through the nearby ports of Tampico and Alvarado (later Veracruz) and out to New Orleans (involved since the Spanish period) and New York. American packet ships brought flour, textiles, carriages, and chairs into Mexico, returning with casks of Mexican coins, silver pesos or "dollars Mex," as some called them. During the 1820s, $3 million to $4 million in silver might be imported annually into the United States from Mexico; during the 1830s, in sharp upticks, the silver imports nearly doubled.

Mexican coins became sufficiently abundant in the United States that Spanish pesos, or dollars, were recognized as a circulating medium and appear to have formed an important part of the country's specie reserves on which banknotes were printed. Mexican silver was also crucial to the developing trade with China. Initiated in the 1780s, the trade brought American ships to the port of Guangzhou (the only one open to foreign merchants), in China's southeast, in search of valuable silks, porcelains, and teas. But because the Chinese had little interest in American goods, they took only silver in payment: all the more so as the trade in opium, which had commenced in the eighteenth century, became extremely brisk in the third and fourth decades of the nineteenth. Linking Bengali poppy producers and Chinese purchasers, and organized by the British East India Company chiefly out of Calcutta, the opium trade could be financed by the silver the Chinese had been accumulating from Americans and various European commercial partners. So large did the opium trafficking become—despite its being officially outlawed in China—that by the 1820s Chinese authorities worried both about the drug's widespread use and about the outflow of silver.

What, in truth, was a massive smuggling operation in southern Asia took a new turn in 1834 when the British government ended the East India Company's mercantile monopoly, effectively opening the India-China trade—in opium (which was legal in Britain) and other goods—to all comers. Among the beneficiaries were American merchants equipped with schooners fast enough to move the opium successfully. Now the debit side of their trading ledgers could be balanced in part with opium rather than silver, which could then be retained in the United States. Together with the increased importation of Mexican silver, this alteration in the specie flow added significantly to American specie reserves in the mid-1830s and to the decade's inflationary spiral.

Before the decade was out, China's Qing emperor determined to crack down on the opium smuggling in Guangzhou and, in the process, provoked an armed conflict—the First Opium War—with the British that would cost the Chinese dearly and extend Britain's empire in the East (to Hong Kong, in this case). But even earlier, in the summer of 1836, British bankers demonstrated that their power moved west as well. Observing a steady decline in its gold reserves (only some of the gold went to the United States), the Bank of England raised its discount rate (interest charged for loans) from 4 percent to 5 percent, forcing merchants and other creditors, including those engaged in the American trade, to contract their business. The international economic dominoes fell first and hardest in New York and New Orleans, where the Anglo-American trade was especially vital, and they generally followed the lines of the Atlantic cotton market, which was heavily dependent on the London-based credit nexus. Although the initial financial rebound was relatively quick, a broad-scale recovery would require more than half a decade.

It is likely that the actions of British bankers and investors reflected not only fears of a deteriorating supply of specie but also diminishing confidence in the American economy and in the apparent economic agenda of Andrew Jackson.

Neither the "bank war" nor the Specie Circular played well in London banking circles, and raised serious questions as to where policy was headed. Indeed, for a time in 1836 British banks refused to receive the paper of any American commercial houses. Yet it was also clear that in the United States trade—particularly foreign trade—was of immense importance, that the cotton economy drove American growth and created intricate webs of finance that covered the Atlantic, and that events in Zacatecas, Guangzhou, Calcutta, and especially London could reverberate powerfully in New York, Boston, Philadelphia, and the rising entrepôt of New Orleans. Less clear was whether the economic panic and the subsequent depression of the late 1830s and early 1840s heralded the end of one economic era and the beginning of another.

Market Intensification

In the 1830s, merchants and large landowners were the dominant actors in American economic life as they had been among people of European descent since their earliest North American settlement. Together, they organized the production and distribution of the goods that circulated in regional and especially international markets and reaped the lion's share of the rewards. In the coastal cities, they controlled the wharves, the shipping, and the warehouses, extended loans and other forms of credit, sold provisions and fineries, employed lawyers, and generally ran the municipal governments. In the countryside, especially where market crops were cultivated in abundance, they owned the most fertile and well-situated lands, exploited the labor of men, women, and children in various states of dependency (slaves, tenants, farm laborers), offered services of several sorts to more humble neighbors, and served as magistrates, militia captains, and political patrons generally. Many of the large landowners found their way into mercantile activities on some scale, while many of the merchants used their earnings to buy land, in either town or country. The opulent town houses in the cities and the great houses in the rural districts symbolized their wealth, power, and presumed authority. Even the early textile mills, in Rhode Island, Massachusetts, and Pennsylvania, depended on the capital that merchants had accumulated in trade.

The dominance of merchants and large landowners spoke of an economic order that had created networks of commerce and colonialism stretching around the globe, provided room for elite-led anticolonial rebellions across the Americas, helped usher in new political unions based on republican principles, and looked to the expansion of market exchange. The dynamism was to be found in the circulation of goods and people, at times over great distances, rather than in major transformations in the ways the goods were produced or the people deployed. Indeed, the very late eighteenth century and the early decades of the nineteenth were marked by the extension and intensification of market economies owing to the growth of population, the elaboration of transportation networks, the advent of new commodities, and the use of state-sponsored and private means of capital formation. Emblematic of the market intensification of the period was the developing cotton economy of the states in the Deep South. The demand for cotton and the potential financial rewards of cotton cultivation drew aspiring growers well into the interior of the Southeast and the Southwest: into upland South Carolina, middle and southwestern Georgia, northern Florida, central Alabama, eastern Mississippi, and the fertile lands of the lower Mississippi Valley. They brought tremendous pressure on the state and federal governments to extirpate Native American land claims, they set off a speculative frenzy in land purchasing, and they provided an enormous market for "surplus" slaves from the general farming areas of Virginia, the Chesapeake, and Kentucky. As was true for other staple crops (tobacco, rice, sugar), cotton was raised chiefly by slave labor and processed for sale on plantations and farms before being sent to cotton factors and merchants in port cities like New Orleans (Charleston, Savannah, and Mobile, too) who organized its shipment to the sites of textile production in Europe and the American Northeast. The availability of easy credit, the printing of paper currency by state banks, and federal policy that (before the Specie Circular) permitted credit purchases together enlarged and intensified market-based involvement and exchanges. But the structures and relations of the market system remained very much what they had been for at least a century.

Much the same could be said for different agricultural regimes around the United States, which were based on the exploitation not of slave but of family and other dependent labor. Closest in character to the slave plantations were the large estates in the Hudson River valley of New York, dating back to the Dutch rule of the seventeenth century, where, by the 1830s, more than a quarter of a million tenant families farmed parcels on long-term leases, producing a mix of market and subsistence crops: wheat (the principal money crop), corn, rye, flax, buckwheat, potatoes, and timber (also marketed). Although wealthy landlords (patroons) like the Livingstons and the Van Rensselaers had cultivated paternalist relations, offering perpetual leases (which could be transmitted generationally) and showing leniency in rent collection in return for political support, by the second and third decades of the nineteenth century the leases had become shorter, the leniency less common, and the tenants more involved in the vagaries of the market to avoid the landlords' squeeze. Before long, more than market participation would be intensified; thousands would rise in a rebellion known as the Anti-Rent movement.

Rebellion did not erupt in the "family farming" areas of the Northeast, Middle Atlantic, Midwest, and backcountry South—Shays's Rebellion (1786) and the Whiskey Rebellion (1791) were the last of these until much later in the nineteenth century—but a similar process of market intensification unfolded nonetheless. Here, free households had long organized economic activity around fee-simple landownership, patriarchal authority, a gender division of labor, and a balance between production for subsistence and—usually local—market exchange. Adult and teenage males cleared land, did most of the heavy field work, tended the hogs, cattle, and draft animals, cut wood, built and repaired fences and structures, hunted and fished; adult and teenage females raised vegetables, egg-laying hens, and small livestock, made cloth, brooms, and hats, churned butter, and prepared food. Planting and harvesting meant long hours of self-exploitation for all family members who raced against the elements to get seeds in or crops out of the ground. Almost invariably, however successful they might be, farm households "swapped work" with neighbors and traded with village merchants and artisans—some of whom were itinerants—for the goods they could not make themselves or wanted from afar. Growing small surpluses enabled them to bring in both cash and store credits. By the latter years of the eighteenth century and surely by the early years of the nineteenth, the pulse of commercial opportunities quickened as the populations of coastal cities increased rapidly, new urban centers rose in the hinterlands of the Middle Atlantic and the Midwest, and mercantile networks extended over greater territory. Agricultural producers in proximity to cities like Boston, New York, Philadelphia, and Baltimore might move to specialize in high-value but perishable goods like dairy products, vegetables, and fruits that could be transported in relatively short order to urban markets. But most who had access to these markets, such as the farming households in the Connecticut River valley of Massachusetts and Connecticut, chose instead to intensify their market involvement. They grew more food crops, such as wheat, for sale, increased their manufacture of homespun and palm-leaf hats, and wove the yarn of local mills into cloth. They did not, by and large, look to expand their operations, hire farm laborers, or take on tenants; only the largest and wealthiest landowners could—and did—do that. Instead, male household heads continued to draw upon the labor of their wives, children, and perhaps an occasional relative or boarder while orienting it further to the production of commodities. Eventually, as farm households came to depend more on store-bought supplies, some of this labor—especially the home manufacturing activities of teenage daughters— became redundant, and the girls might choose to seek work in neighboring households, newly constructed textile mills, or larger urban centers, joining brothers who would not inherit farmland in a swelling rural-to-urban (or, for those bent on the farming life, east-to-west) migration.

The quickening pulse of commerce could be detected far earlier in American cities—particularly those of the Eastern Seaboard and the Gulf Coast—than in much of the countryside (certainly by the last quarter of the eighteenth century), but there, too, market intensification and a ramifying division of labor remained the economic markers well into the 1830s. The artisan shops, which were at the center of urban manufacture, have long been regarded as keystones of this process, and they do provide important indications of what was happening. Thus, as the density and scope of market exchanges increased, master craftsmen, who customarily worked alongside relatively small numbers of journeymen and apprentices (workers who had learned or were learning trade skills), often became more engaged with the purchasing of raw materials and the selling of the finished goods, leaving production in the hands of trusted employees and perhaps a few other journeymen and apprentices at the shop. If demand continued to grow, the shop might be enlarged, more craft workers hired, and outworkers (often women and children laboring in their homes or tenements) brought into the finishing stages by means of runners. New machinery was rarely introduced; handicraft work prevailed, however subdivided it came to be.

To be sure, the course of market intensification varied by trade—printing moved more quickly to mechanization—and in some, such as luxury goods like glass, silver, and fine furniture, the mode of the old artisan shop would endure for a long time to come. But, especially where the mass consumer market was growing rapidly—shoes, the building trades, clothing—the artisan shop was effectively "bastardized" by its expansion (more skilled workers set to different tasks within its walls) and extension (more of the work put out to semiskilled laborers). A pattern of "sweating" became common in larger metropolitan areas as master craftsmen and merchants subcontracted to a range of workers (skilled, semiskilled, male, female, young, old) who would complete their jobs in homes, rooms, or garrets, often being paid by the piece. The needle trades and garment "slop" shops became notorious for sweating, though the system would encompass docks, construction, and other sites of growing economic activity.

The most dramatic signs of early industry, and of the social relations generally associated with industrial capitalism, were to be found not in the urban centers but in the hinterlands where waterpower was abundantly available: the cotton and woolens manufactories or textile mills of the Northeast. By the 1830s, thanks to large investments of merchant capital and technological innovations (some smuggled out of England) that mechanized spinning and weaving, factories that contained within their walls all steps of the production process dotted the fall lines from New Hampshire, Massachusetts, and Rhode Island to Connecticut and Pennsylvania. The laborers came chiefly from the hardscrabble districts of the surrounding countryside, and although they worked for wages under a rhythm set by owners, managers, and especially the unceasing motion of throstles, drawing frames, mules, and looms, there were important ways in which the mills reconfigured—and intensified—long-standing patterns of household manufacture. Most famously, the mills in Lowell, Massachusetts, recruited young, unmarried women, who had customarily done spinning and weaving under the authority of their fathers, to come and live in boardinghouses and turn out yarn and cloth on a scale well beyond anything with which they were familiar.

Elsewhere, the mills relied on whole families who left declining farmsteads or other poor prospects on the land to take up berths in their villages and factories. Even so, the owners mostly looked for operatives among the women and children who had been accustomed to working under patriarchal management and who, they believed, could be paid less and controlled more easily. Mindful of the "dark, satanic mills" of Britain's Manchester and Birmingham, which symbolized the wretched and conflict-ridden road of industrialization, the mill owners hoped to construct something of a pastoral alternative: paternalist in character, rural in setting, tidy in appearance, and relatively peaceful in social relations. Almost commemorating the connection made by cotton, the mill villages seemed most akin to plantations farther to the south, with their residential laborers, their supervisors known as overseers, their machine shops, stores, and churches, and the imposing houses their owners occupied. But the mill owners quickly learned that the workers would push back on the floor or leave at their choosing, and the workers discovered, whether they quickly moved or stayed for a time, that they were now in a new world of wage earning.

Perhaps most indicative of the scope and consequences of market intensification were the swelling pools of casual and manual labor to be found across the American landscape of the early nineteenth century, but especially in cities, in towns, and on multiplying public works projects. Reflecting an Atlantic perimeter of social disruption—encompassing the rural and urban economies of England, Ireland, and northern Europe as well as North America—the pools filled with poor men and women from town and country, enslaved and quasi-free people of African descent, and immigrants from French Canada, Germany, and the British Isles, some of whom still arrived under conditions of indentured servitude. Gender figured quite centrally in the occupational breakdown. The greatest number of women, especially if they were immigrants or African Americans, ended up in domestic service, where they met a burgeoning demand among middling and upper-class families. But the garment trades were becoming close rivals because of a growing market for ready-made clothing and the ability of seamstresses and other female "slop workers" to labor in their households. Still other women operated boardinghouses, worked as street vendors, laundresses, and cooks, and, when necessary, entered the sex trade.

For their part, male laborers found their way to the waterfronts, the construction sites, the transportation networks, the streets, the mines, and the fields, where they lifted, hauled, drove, chopped, carried, hawked, cut, dug, and dredged. Many had the knowledge and skills that came with life on the land, near the sea, or in the towns and cities—they could be regarded as unskilled or semiskilled only in a formal sense—and that they might put to use in a variety of workplace settings. And most faced the problems of seasonality: stretches of un- or underemployment owing to the cycles of weather and trade. Scraping by—for that was what it was—thus required strategies to navigate the slack times by cobbling together a series of work stints and mobilizing the labor of all family members. Poor households that lacked either a male or a female working adult, due to illness, death, or desertion, courted disaster or, at minimum, an extended stay at almshouses that were proliferating in number and size.

But in an important sense, casual labor proved to be the physical engine for the infrastructure that made market intensification possible and wide-ranging in its effect: for the developing transportation networks that extended into the interior, linked rivers and lakes with the coasts, and facilitated the flow of people and goods across distances that had previously been difficult or impossible to traverse. The challenges of transport and communication were widely recognized, including by the federal government, which feared the country's vulnerabilities to foreign invasion. President Thomas Jefferson's visionary Treasury secretary, Albert Gallatin, warning that only "by opening speedy and easy communication through all its parts" could "the inconveniences, complaints, and perhaps dangers" of so "vast [an] extent of territory be radically removed or prevented," thus presented Congress with a remarkable plan in 1808 for building "good roads and canals" into "the most remote quarters of the United States."

Gallatin was well aware of the initiatives that had been undertaken on the local and state levels, most notably the Lancaster Turnpike, completed in 1794, which linked Philadelphia and Lancaster, Pennsylvania, and proved to be a great success. But he was similarly aware of the enormous costs of constructing roads and canals on a large scale and saw federal resources as essential to the task. It was a tough sell. Although the War of 1812 dramatized the need for more and better routes to move troops, if for nothing else, and although some version of Gallatin's plan came before Congress at various times over the following decade, most initiatives were defeated by a combination of regional self-interests and constitutional objections (did the federal government have the authority to carry out such projects?). Only the National Road, connecting Cumberland,

Maryland, and Wheeling, Virginia (and eventually continuing out into Ohio and Indiana), would be built.

The energy and achievements came rather from partnerships of varying types between local (mostly merchant) capital, state and municipal governments, and foreign investors. To advance early road and turnpike development, state legislatures normally chartered private corporations, which in turn financed and organized construction. But when it came to canals, which were far costlier and demanding to build, state and local governments took the lead, raising money by marketing securities in the United States and abroad (especially in Britain). The Erie Canal, an immensely ambitious project that effectively kicked off a three-decade canal boom, won the support of the New York state legislature in 1817. Under the aegis of a state commission, bonds were then sold to cover the multimillion-dollar construction outlays, and subcontractors were hired to carry out the work. By 1825, more than 360 miles had been completed and revenue from canal tolls quickly began to pour into state coffers, enabling the repayment of investors. Other large projects—in New England, Pennsylvania, Maryland, and Ohio—were soon under way, so that by 1840, when railroads increasingly overshadowed them, canals cut through nearly 3,500 miles of the American interior.

Together with proliferating roads and turnpikes, the canals helped to bring the market intensification of the early nineteenth century to its fevered pitch. Tapping deep into the North American hinterlands, these transport networks not only gave farms and mines (especially coal mines) more and easier access to distant markets but also drew metropolitan centers into bitter competition for control of the greatly expanded trade: Boston, Philadelphia, Baltimore, and New York to the east; Rochester, Pittsburgh, Cincinnati, Louisville, St. Louis, and New Orleans to the west and south. All battled for the interior and came to feel the commercial jolts given off by multiplying market exchanges.

The competition for labor to do the building was just as fierce. The transport projects, especially the canals, mobilized workers on a scale unprecedented outside the plantation districts. Builders and contractors seemed ever in search of labor: scouring the countryside, putting advertisements in urban newspapers, offering various inducements. Backbreaking as it was, the work brought decent wages and, above all, steadier employment than was available almost anywhere else for those without trades or special skills. Early on, most of the canal workers were native-born and usually from the surrounding countryside, farm laborers looking for better pay or supplements to what they might make in the fields. But by the 1820s, more and more were recent immigrants from Europe, and particularly from Ireland, who themselves had been pried from the land and cast into a world that new markets were making.

Labor's Coercions

By the mid-1830s, it might have appeared that the political economy of the United States was marked by a fundamental geographical divide. The divide could be traced from the border between Pennsylvania and Maryland (known as the Mason-Dixon Line) in the east, westward along the Ohio River to the Mississippi, then northward to the northern and western borders of Missouri, and then farther westward along the coordinates of 36°30´ to where the Louisiana Territory abutted lands claimed by Mexico and the Texas Republic. South of this line, slavery was supported by the states and secured by the federal government, it organized the production of marketable surpluses for export, and it shaped the social and political power deployed in the free population. North of the line, slavery had been abolished in gradual fashion, and although some African Americans were still officially enslaved, they were rapidly declining in number and, at all events, had never figured very centrally in the production and distribution of either subsistence goods or market commodities. By many measures, "North" and "South" embodied very distinctive labor regimes and therefore seemed to constitute the principal axis of American society and politics.

Yet for those slaves who attempted to escape their captivity by crossing the line between "South" and "North," the reality was far murkier and more unnerving. They discovered in searing ways that the status of slavery attached to their persons wherever they went and that the freedom they sought to grasp could easily slip through their fingers or be violently taken from them. They discovered that they could be pursued, sometimes with great determination, captured or kidnapped, and returned to their owners; that the only safe havens were provided by other fugitives or abolitionist friends, and even these were subject to the invasions of slave catchers and police authorities. They discovered, in short, that slavery remained an American rather than a regional or local institution and that the power of the state—at all levels, almost everywhere—was committed to slavery's preservation.

Slavery's net was cast from the top, and it reinforced or complicated arrangements closer to the ground. The Constitution's fugitive slave clause and, subsequently, the Fugitive Slave Law of 1793, which required that runaways be returned to their rightful owners, put the federal government squarely on the side of sustaining slave ownership and gave slavery a legal basis in all of the American states and territories regardless of what they did about slavery within their particular boundaries. While "northern" states had moved down the path of emancipation, it was not until the 1840s and 1850s that many of them—New Jersey (1846), Pennsylvania (1847), Connecticut (1848), Illinois (1848), and New

Hampshire (1857)—amid judicial confusions and individual exceptions, finally got around to pronouncing slavery dead. Even then, a handful of slaves could be identified in New Jersey as late as 1860. Slaveholders, moreover, expected to take their slaves with them if they needed to travel through states in which slavery had been abolished (say, to New York or Philadelphia to catch a packet ship), and officials in these states generally accommodated their interests—offered "hospitality," in the words of one judge—so long as the slaveholders did not seek to establish residency.

Few succeeded in defying slavery's true geography, though William Parker, who fled enslavement in Maryland, made an impressive and extended effort. He crossed the Pennsylvania line, went into the hinterlands of southeastern Pennsylvania, and settled in Lancaster County, where he headed up a small community of fugitives and other African Americans. Mindful of their vulnerabilities, Parker and his neighbors quickly formed an "organization for mutual protection against slaveholders and kidnappers" and had success in fending off the terrorist raids of local white toughs known as the Gap Gang as well as the incursions of occasional slave catchers. They armed themselves with pistols, rifles, scythes, corn cutters, and other farm tools and learned to summon each other with the sound of a horn. But after one especially fierce fight with a federalized posse looking to take several of them into custody, Parker decided to leave slavery behind in the best way he knew how: he fled to Toronto, Canada.

What made the worlds of slavery and freedom so difficult to distinguish was not only the wide basis that federal authority lent to slavery but also the broad spectrum of coercions that marked labor relations in all corners of the United States. Wherever one looked—at plantations and farms, docks and wharves, shops and garrets, mines and mills, or at farm laborers and tenants, journeymen and apprentices, domestics and outworkers, operatives and common laborers—various forms of legal and customary subordination and dependency prevailed and burdened working people with the direct and coercive power of their employers and with an assortment of vulnerabilities that threw their very survival into question. To be sure, the most burdensome of these relations were to be found in the southern and western parts of the country, and they shaped society and politics there in distinctive ways. But in other regards, the terrain of servitude, compulsion, and dependence was geographically boundless.

Consider how the emancipation process unfolded in the Northeast and the Middle Atlantic. The laws enacted by state legislatures, reflecting fears of instability and threats to property, ignored African Americans who were already enslaved and instead "freed" children born after a certain date and only then when they reached a certain age in adulthood. Masters and slaves could, of course, make their own arrangements for early emancipation, and some of them clearly did. But either way, "freedom" was commonly encumbered with the residues of slavery and servitude. In some cases, emancipated blacks remained within white households as servants; in other cases, they shouldered continuing obligations in return for material or educational support; in still others, they entered indentures, which had passed emancipationist scrutiny owing to the appearance of voluntarism and bound them to labor, sometimes for many years on end. Children, especially poorer ones, were often "bound out" as apprentices or indentured servants, not infrequently for terms extending well into their majority. And in all instances, the indentures were subject to sale. Between 1780, when the Pennsylvania abolition law was passed, and 1820, nearly three thousand people of African descent were indentured in the city of Philadelphia, and in rural Delaware and Chester counties, on the city's outskirts, farm owners widely seized on indentures to increase the supply of cheap and exploitable labor, occasionally purchasing the indentures of slaves emancipated inside or outside the state.

The boundaries between slavery and freedom proved murky and porous in other ways. Rather than revealing a clear line of demarcation, the border areas of the "upper South" and "lower North" were overlaid with ambiguities. Western Pennsylvanians crossed over into neighboring Virginia, purchased slaves at low prices there, brought the slaves back into Pennsylvania, and then emancipated them on condition that they remain in service and, effectively, in conditions scarcely removed from enslavement. There, and elsewhere farther to the west—Ohio, Indiana, Illinois—employers hired slaves from owners in Virginia and Kentucky and worked them for up to a year before sending them back to their masters on the other side of the Ohio River. In Indiana, slaveholders could come with their slaves for up to sixty days and, within the first thirty, arrange for indentures, sometimes lasting for many decades. In the United States of the 1830s, the notion that "free soil" dissolved the chains of slavery—suggested by the famed *Somerset* decision in England in 1772—while making some progress in the lower courts (such as in St. Louis), was generally greeted with skepticism and hostility. It offered little solace or protection to slaves in search of escape.

Gradualism, ambiguity, and halfway houses out of slavery were even more common in states where slave ownership remained very much sanctioned by law. Although the two decades following the American Revolution saw private manumissions on a considerable scale in the states of the Chesapeake, the transition out of slavery there and farther to the south, when it occurred, was much more extended and hedged in by persisting ties and dependencies. In Baltimore, and perhaps in other localities, some slaveholders, hoping to secure labor and discourage flight, postdated deeds of manumission, often years in the future, in return for "faithful" service beforehand. Slaves in perpetuity thereby became "term slaves," such as "a strong healthy mulatto Girl, about sixteen years of age" sold with the proviso that "she has 13 years to serve." Other slaveholders embraced a different but similarly drawn-out strategy: permitting ambitious slaves, willing to follow a long and winding road of self-exploitation and petty accumulations, to purchase themselves (and maybe other family members). Even when slaves were manumitted without explicit encumbrances, they often entered a netherworld of dependency and clientage, looking to their former masters for support and protection in a world in which black people were assumed to be slaves. Those who lacked or rejected such patronage, if they did not leave the state, for all intents and purposes became "slaves of the community" or "slaves without masters."

"Free labor" that would be recognizable to contemporary eyes—and not simply a rhetorical rubric meant to encompass those, like small farmers, who might have worked with their hands and tools but were property owners and employers in their own right—could be found in some significant measure, chiefly in urban areas. It was, above all, a relation characterized by an exchange in which the employee would agree to work for a specified numbers of hours and days in return for a wage, in which the employee could choose to quit without serious penalty, and in which the employer would not deploy physical coercion for purposes of either discipline or labor control. In this sense, free labor was both a political and a social relation, because workers had to be personally unencumbered to enter the exchange of their own volition and employers had to be held accountable for the order they imposed at the workplace.

The relation, therefore, was most likely in evidence among adult males of European descent who could claim ownership of their persons and, perhaps, of some productive property, who had some skills, who had established local residency of some duration, who had achieved civil and political standing, and who, consequently, could appeal to community standards for justice, bring grievances to court, and register their sentiments at the ballot box. Their prospects were most limited in places like Richmond, Charleston, and Savannah, where they competed with slave labor and could be seen as threatening the system of slavery. A strike of puddlers at the Tredegar Iron Works in Richmond over wages and the employment of slaves thus provoked the press to thunder that such demands attacked "the roots of all rights and privileges of the masters and, if acknowledged, or permitted to gain a foothold, will soon wholly destroy the value of slave property." Elsewhere, free laborers were more securely situated, might identify with a transatlantic political culture of working people, and could invoke the language of republicanism ("virtue," "independence," "tyranny," "wage slavery") to express their aspirations and discontents.

Like all categories and ideal types, "free labor" embodied many complexities and contradictions. Its focus on voluntary exchange in the marketplace obscured the historical process that required people to seek work from someone else rather than to work for themselves: a process that might have driven them off the land, reduced their prospects in the shop, rendered their skills less valuable or redundant, limited their inheritances, and in all cases either denied or substantially postponed their access to productive resources that would enable them to labor independently. It also obscured the legal and political advantages that most employers retained and the power they could wield at the workplace once the marketplace exchange was completed. But during the early decades of the nineteenth century, and for a long time thereafter, large numbers of men, women, and children who were putatively "free" were nonetheless also subject to a raft of coercions, to circumstances of servitude, and to the penal reach of the state for contract violations.

At many work sites, apprentices, maritime laborers, sailors, servants, and miners faced physical coercion if they failed to keep up the pace, punishment if they broke equipment, and even imprisonment if they left before the contract expired. Especially in the port cities of Baltimore, Philadelphia, New York, Boston, and Charleston, the jails were loaded with "runaways" of various sorts and ethnicities, none in greater numbers than seamen who would either be forced to complete their terms or remain incarcerated. At other sites, canal diggers, harbor dredgers, workers in the building trades, farm laborers, and domestics could be subject to corporal abuse, coaxed into debt, and fired without pay. Across the country, stints in the workhouse or harsh forms of compulsory labor were regularly meted out to vagrants, paupers, and the unemployed, effectively pressing many working people into the marketplace and anticipating the infamous Black Codes of the post–Civil War era. In some cases, convicts were leased out to transportation projects, undercutting the prospects of those in search of work and strengthening the hands of employers, yet another harbinger of the future.

The vulnerabilities of workers such as these to the compulsions and exploitation that had long been part of the laboring life—and gave the lie to the reach of free labor—reflected their limited civil and political status in the United States of the 1830s. Many were women, children, recent immigrants, and people of African descent who were legally dependent, owned little or no property, had few skills, were subject to the coercive authority of husbands, parents, and masters, were often on the move, had limited access to the courts, and had few, if any, political patrons seeking their support. Their efforts to resist and protect themselves depended on hastily formed alliances and cooperation but more likely on individualized attempts to escape conditions that seemed intolerable and to find better and steadier ones.

Yet during the first half of the nineteenth century—and well beyond it—the entire world of labor was encased by the presumptive power of masters and employers and the presumptive subordination of workers, whether or not they were formally free. Enslavement, which lent masters nearly absolute power, defined the experience of more than three million black workers who grew the crops (tobacco, rice, sugar, and, more than anything else, cotton) that propelled the economic growth of the country. Dependencies owing to gender, which depressed their wages and jeopardized their ability to keep them, left them disfranchised and legally incapacitated, bedeviled many thousands of women (black and white, native-born and immigrant) who tended textile machines, did outwork, sewed ready-made clothing, and served in the households of middle- and upper-class families. Foreign birth or African descent kept a growing proportion of semi- and unskilled workers in liminal civic standing, on the margins of civil and political life, and subject to the whims of employers whose authority dominated the workplace.

But even those whose working lives came closest to the ideal of free labor encountered a structure of power that proved very unfavorable and equally difficult to unsettle. For American labor relations inherited the tradition of the British common law and especially the law of master and servant, which required loyalty and obedience on the part of the worker during the term of a contract and provided for serious legal action in the event of violation. Adjudication of disputes resided wholly with the courts, which, in the early decades of the nineteenth century, were increasingly oriented to commercial growth, influenced by the perspectives of employers, and instrumental in their approach to economic development. When legislatures or municipalities moved in directions more advantageous to workers, and thus showed the political potential of labor, the courts simply chose to ignore them. Equally problematic, the courts embraced the legal doctrine of "entirety," upholding the employer's right to deny any wages if the contract was not entirely fulfilled or if the worker quit early. It made no difference, in the eyes of the court, "whether wages are estimated at a gross sum, or are to be calculated according to a certain rate per week or month, or are payable at stipulated times, provided a servant agree for a definite and whole term."

Still, change was in the air. By the 1820s, some courts were beginning to raise doubts about cases in which workers were effectively compelled to stay on the job in order to retrieve any of the wages due them, and in the process they threw into question the long-standing common-law distinction between voluntary and involuntary servitude—a distinction that had turned voluntary (or contractual) servitude into a species of free labor and only involuntary servitude into a species of slavery. Thereafter, the courts recognized the employer's authority in the workplace so long as it did not involve corporal punishment and so long as employees were allowed to refuse it. The pressure for change had come from workers themselves who brought suit or protested on the job. In so doing, they contributed to a new understanding of the labor relation and eventually to the emergence of new forms of bargaining and adjudication. But that was still a long way off, and despite the rulings as to coercion it would be years before laborers could expect to recover the wages they had earned before they exercised their freedom to quit.

Mediums of Exchange

In December 1790, Alexander Hamilton, secretary of the Treasury in the cabinet of President George Washington, presented a report to Congress that called for the creation of a national bank. Hamilton believed such a bank of "primary importance" to the United States for the administration of finances, the raising of capital, the securing of emergency aid, the support of public credit, and the development of industry. But he was especially interested in the role a national bank could play in establishing the "basis of a paper circulation."

The problem, according to Hamilton, was "that there has been for some time a deficiency of circulating medium," and as a consequence large numbers of producers could do little but engage in barter on the fringes of the market economy. Gold and silver coins (specie) did, of course, change hands, particularly for official purposes. Yet, in Hamilton's view, specie was, in and of itself, "dead stock." Only when deposited in banks could it "acquire an active and productive quality" by enabling investment and the printing of paper money. The "vast tracts of waste land" and the disappointing "state of manufactures" to be seen in various parts of the country seemed to Hamilton evidence of money's limited supply. Expanding mediums of exchange would, that is, advance the march of regional and national markets and draw more and more producers into their wake.

By the 1830s, paper currency was in abundance, though it did not circulate in the manner that Hamilton had envisioned. Rather than being produced and managed by a central, or national, bank, most of the circulating paper was printed and distributed by privately owned banks chartered by individual state legislatures. With differing requirements as to the specie that had to be kept in their vaults and the ratio of specie to the paper issued, the state notes simultaneously permitted an acceleration of market exchanges and created a sea of monetary chaos. Notes printed in one state usually traded at a discount in the others (although the discounts varied from state to state), and their value ultimately depended on the banks' ability to redeem the notes in specie if the note holders presented them. In the early 1830s, well over three hundred state-chartered banks, circulating more than $60 million in notes, operated in the United States, and the federal government provided no oversight of their activities. At best, the Bank of the United States (a partial manifestation of Hamilton's designs) could collect state banks' notes and present them for specie redemption as a way of holding the state banks accountable.

Yet Hamilton's concerns in the 1790s reflected more than limits of supply; they grew out of the circumstances and dynamics of local economies that remained very much in place in the American hinterlands four decades later and suggested that market intensification proceeded fitfully and could meet resistance. Specie and banknotes, together with other paper instruments, were most likely in evidence when trade and other exchange relations transcended localities or occurred in large urban centers. Merchants relied on them in transactions with distant suppliers, master craftsmen and small manufacturers in dealings for raw materials or with distributors of their products, artisans and farmers in selling to strangers. In most cases, some form of credit was involved, and the interest charged would depend on when the notes came due. Without question, these exchanges were becoming more common and encompassed a growing share of the marketplace.

But in smaller towns and villages across the United States, the very types of barter that Hamilton found worrisome—and that he wished to see eliminated—often remained robust. Farmers, craftsmen, shopkeepers, blacksmiths, and tenants, short on cash because there was little of it and they had scant need for it, traded crops for store goods, labor for tools and seed, skilled services for foodstuffs, livestock for shoes, and "swapped work" when the demands of harvesting, building, or fencing were particularly pressing. Although they were increasingly aware of the "prices" being asked and paid for various commodities and frequently kept track of their economic activities in account books (usually with cash equivalents recorded, and sometimes with notes exchanged), they nonetheless were flexible and informal as to the settlement of debts.

Local artisans might accept wheat, fruits, distilled spirits, and raw materials as forms of payment; farmers might take barrels, harvest labor, firewood, and fence rails. In Sugar Creek, Illinois, during the late 1830s, a blacksmith shod horses, sharpened tools, and made nails for a neighboring farmer. In return, he received 15 pounds of veal, 110 pounds of beef, and over 250 pounds of flour. Debts such as these commonly ran for weeks and months—at times for years—on end (nine months in this case), generally with little if any interest charged, occasionally with no expectation that the debts would ever be fully repaid. Store owners, even those engaged with distant wholesalers and creditors, often advertised that they would accept "all kinds of country produce" in exchange for their wares. "When the harvests are in," a Connecticut River valley merchant explained in 1837, "I will accept the tender of grain and goods as may be convenient."

This was plainly not a "subsistence" economy nor one wholly oriented to local communities. Merchandisers brought in supplies from the outside and accumulated debts in the process; tradesmen and farmers looked to send at least some of their products to larger markets and might welcome the arrival of a turnpike or a canal to better facilitate the undertaking. Unpaid debts could cause considerable strain, especially for merchants who, under pressure from their own creditors, were most likely to go to law to recover what was owed them. But it was also a world of face-to-face economic relations in which various producers and shopkeepers met one another in a marketplace governed by shared understandings of how goods were valued and transactions took place. For most of them, "money" was not a specific thing or a universal equivalent or an object of accumulation; it was one of several mediums of exchange and a means of defraying specific obligations (like state taxes), used chiefly to obtain items necessary for production, nourishment, and clothing. Thus, in Ulster County, New York, tradesmen accepted payment in "wheat, rye, Indian corn, as well as cash, or," as they put it, "anything that is good to eat."

Money, as most Americans of the early nineteenth century understood it, came in the form of gold and silver coins. Some of these, since the 1790s, had been imprinted in U.S. mints. Many others were of French, Portuguese, and especially Spanish derivation and still accepted as legal tender (and would be until the late 1850s). By the 1830s, silver and gold were coined or valued at a ratio of roughly sixteen to one and circulated most widely in port cities, where they were utilized in both small- and large-scale transactions. Paper currency was also well known. Since the colonial era, it was circulated, in limited quantities, either by British authorities or by private concerns and, more notoriously, was printed by the Continental Congress and then some of the states to finance the immense costs of the Revolutionary War. But so widespread was their provenance (soldiers were paid with them) and dramatic their depreciation that the "continentals" encouraged disgust with and suspicion of the paper medium more generally. Alexander Hamilton hoped that a national bank would allay those suspicions and lend paper currency a clear basis in specie, though the pushback—which trimmed the plan's sails and then briefly defeated its renewal twenty years later—evinced opposition to the project as well as concerns about its constitutionality.

Whereas specie and "all kinds of country produce" seemed to embody tangible value and conjure a marketplace in which relatively independent producers met to exchange the things they needed for sustenance and comfort, paper currency appeared a creation of dubious value and the medium of a marketplace in which producers were vulnerable and "moneyed men" powerful. For many farmers, craftsmen, laborers, and shopkeepers, paper currency represented—as Hamilton intended—the vortex of a new type of market, one that engulfed territories well outside their own communities and swirled well beyond their control. Although the prospects of gain might be tantalizing—and the overall economic growth of the United States stimulated—the fears of failure and dependence were sobering. As institutions meant to advance this course, banks were thereby eyed, in many quarters, with deep concern, all the more so after a serious financial panic in 1819 was triggered, in part, by the contractionist policies of the Second Bank of the United States. If paper currency were to be regarded as "money," who should be entitled to print it and who to control its value and supply?

These questions and anxieties provided the context for Andrew Jackson's "war" on the Bank of the United States and for the panic of 1837 and its consequences. Jackson's hostility to the bank and its president, Nicholas Biddle, smacked of the personal rivalries and coalition building that routinely energize electoral politics, and its heated rhetoric—"The bank is trying to kill me, but I will kill it!" Jackson told his vice president, Martin Van Buren—could easily be dismissed as masculinist posturing by a wildly masculinist president intent on settling a score. But Jackson's opposition to the bank ran deeper. For a long time, he had looked warily at the operations of private state banks and the influence they could exert over the economy by expanding and contracting the currency, though his greatest animus was directed to the Bank of the United States. Despite the Supreme Court's decision in *McCulloch v. Maryland* (1819), which appeared to uphold its constitutionality, Jackson regarded the bank as an affront to the intentions of the framers and a massive concentration of power "in the hands of a few men . . . a few Monied Capitalists" who could "oppress" the people and "embarrass" the government. And Biddle, with his aristocratic lineage and contempt for public supervision, seemed to embody all that the bank threatened.

Yet Jackson also tapped into wells of popular anti-bank sentiment that had as much to do with social and economic as with political and constitutional issues. In many parts of the United States, paper money and private banking came to symbolize the market intensification that was speeding forward, disrupting customary practices of production and exchange, pressing artisans into circumstances of economic dependence, undercutting the wages of laboring people, and increasing the vulnerabilities of those struggling to maintain the familiar balances between subsistence and the marketplace. Workingmen's associations identified the cause of the banks with the "same men . . . who have always been opposed to our interests," to our "rights of suffrage," and to "almost every other democratic measure that has ever been brought forward in our state or general government," with the "aristocratic and unjust." Yeoman farmers and even slaveholding planters worried about suspensions of specie payments, "the intolerable evils of a fluctuating and depreciated paper currency," and a "system so fraudulent, so anti-Republican," in the sense that banks threatened what they regarded as their independence. Together they began to form a "hard money" tendency in American politics, committed to specie as the basis of exchange and, by extension, to limits on the forces of the market.

As he had previously done in personal duels, Jackson did succeed in "killing" the Second Bank of the United States, not by persuading Congress to reject the bank's recharter but rather by vetoing the bill that provided for it in the summer of 1832. Yet it was in his accompanying veto message that Jackson, assisted by several of his hard-money advisers (including Attorney General Roger B. Taney), articulated the issues that made for such powerful feelings of social unease. He began by identifying the special privileges and "monopolies" that the bank had enjoyed and took care to note the influence that foreigners had obtained through the purchase of bank stock. He went on to raise doubts about the Supreme Court's judgment in *McCulloch v. Maryland* and insisted that "it is as much the duty of the House of Representatives, of the Senate, and of the President to decide upon the constitutionality of any bill or resolution which may be presented to them." But he saved his most stinging and trenchant arguments for last: "It is to be regretted that the rich and powerful too often bend the acts of government to their selfish purposes. Distinctions in society will always exist under every just government. Equality of talents, of education, or of wealth can not be produced by human institutions . . . but when the laws undertake to add to these natural and just advantages artificial distinctions, to grant titles, gratuities, and exclusive privileges, to make the rich richer and the potent more powerful, the humble members of society—the farmers, mechanics, and laborers—who have neither the time nor the means of securing like favors to themselves, have a right to complain of the injustice of their Government."

Jackson's "war" with the Second Bank of the United States, together with his veto of the Maysville Road bill and very tough stance against the nullification campaign in South Carolina, began to shape partisan alignments in the system of formal politics that the democratization of the franchise was producing. Those supportive of Jackson and his policies called themselves Democrats and commenced to organize not only at the upper levels of governance, as was true of the Democratic-Republicans and the Federalists in the early years of the Republic, but also at the grass roots. Those hostile to him and his policies, conjuring the struggle of English parliamentarians of the seventeenth century against their tyrannical king, called themselves Whigs (in battle against "King" Andrew).

But it was less Andrew Jackson than the hardships and discontent caused by the panic of 1837 and its extended aftermath that turned political dispositions based heavily on personal identifications and loyalties into more stable and ideological constituencies. The Whig Party came to appeal to those who were benefiting from the market intensifications of the era; who welcomed the expanded market exchanges and the development of transportation and communication networks even if the government (at all levels) played an important hand in paying for them; who saw banks as promoting capital accumulation and paper money as expanding access to wealth; who looked chiefly to the domestic market as the engine of their advancement and favored protective tariffs to limit foreign competition; and who were drawn to evangelical Christianity and its social reformist impulses. Whigs were to be found in greatest numbers in states that had moved most fully against the institution of slavery, in cities and towns most deeply involved in regional markets, and in rural areas availing themselves of market opportunities as well as swept up in the fires of evangelism. Whig strongholds extended from Massachusetts across the "burned-over" districts of upstate New York, into the Western Reserve of Ohio, and through areas of the upper Midwest where New England migrants settled. They were also in the towns of the interior South and especially in lower Louisiana, where sugar planters sought protection from Caribbean cane growers.

For their part, Democrats appealed to constituencies either harmed or bypassed by market intensifications and left reeling by the effects of the panic. They were dubious about the benefits of expanded market exchanges and suspicious of government involvement in economic infrastructure projects. They regarded banks as privileged institutions that enriched themselves at popular expense and viewed paper money as the means by which banks drew hardworking producers into their grasp. They were oriented either to local or to international markets and opposed protectionism as a threat to their trading relations. And they were generally hostile to the culture of evangelical Protestantism and especially to its reformist initiatives. Democrats were most numerous in the states that supported slavery and/or felt the strong influence of slavery, in port cities that thrived on international trade and had large, multiethnic (and non-Protestant) working populations, and in rural districts either dominated by cotton plantations or on the edges of the market economy and less receptive to evangelical revivalism. Democratic strongholds extended across the countryside of the slave states, into areas of the lower Midwest settled by migrants from the Chesapeake, Virginia, and Kentucky, into the poorer rural sections of New England and the Middle Atlantic, and particularly into the Atlantic cities of New York, Philadelphia, Baltimore, and Charleston.

By the late 1830s and early 1840s, Democrats increasingly fell under the influence of their hard-money (sometimes called Locofoco) wing, setting their sights on the excesses of banking institutions and especially on what they considered the dangers of paper currency. In sections of the country where market economies had long been established (Northeast, Southeast, Middle Atlantic), they pushed to regulate—through the statutory mechanisms of state legislatures—the chartering and operations of banks. But where the boom of the 1830s first drove fledgling economies, only to see them collapse when the boom went bust—much of the cotton Southwest and, most notably, the Mississippi Valley corridor tied to New Orleans—the response was far fiercer and more sweeping: state regulation, the repudiation of debts, and, in some cases, the outright abolition of banks. These were moves that could bring small farmers wary of the marketplace, hard-pressed urban wage laborers, and debt-ridden cotton planters into a political embrace and mark the fissures of American politics along complex economic and cultural lines and the emerging political economy of capitalism.

Making and Remaking Classes

Perhaps the most consequential, though not yet obvious, accompaniment to the market intensification of the early decades of the nineteenth century was the rise and transformation of new social classes. As late as the 1840s, merchants (especially the old, coastal mercantile elite) and large landowners remained the wealthiest Americans and the major economic actors in the Republic, and they had fortified themselves by serving in political offices at all levels of government and constructing a variety of institutions and networks: chambers of commerce, social clubs, schools and colleges, and agricultural societies. But amid the booms and busts of the 1820s and 1830s, their grip loosened, and they began to be challenged from a number of directions. Over the next two decades, those challenges would help to create a massive political crisis.

Some of the challenges emanated from below. In many respects, the organization of labor in the 1830s showed the tenacity of long-established forms and practices. Handicrafts still predominated, machines were not widely in use, and most workplaces were small in scale. But as a measure of the great economic expansions of the period, there were new venues that brought workers together in numbers that had previously been reached only on slave plantations: on canal, turnpike, and railroad projects; in textile mills; at construction sites; on urban labor gangs. The workers did not generally bring special skills to the jobs—

other than brute strength—and overall they were polyglot in social composition. They were white and black, native-born and immigrant, male and female, from town and countryside. Their sense of solidarity was extremely limited; mostly, they lived and worked with those of similar ethnic and religious background and, at times, fought with rival groups of laborers for place, preferment, status, and whatever advantages the jobs might bring.

What they had in common was the experience of working for wages, of transiency and other forms of geographical mobility, of being subject to direct managerial authority (sometimes corporal), and, increasingly, of residing in distinctive settings as to density, gender balance, and cultural sensibility. Indeed, whether in labor camps, mill compounds, or urban enclaves, they seemed, to many observers, to stand apart, to be governed by indiscipline, to follow their own rules as to family responsibility and sexuality, to be alien in character and perhaps threatening in demeanor. A notion of class distinction thereby emerged, less in the self-consciousness of the laborers than in the perception and representations of surrounding communities and denizens. "I never saw anything approaching to the scene before us, in dirtiness and disorder," wrote one offended onlooker of a work encampment along the Illinois and Michigan Canal, "whisky and tobacco seemed the chief delights of the men; and of the women and children, no language could give an adequate idea of their filthy condition, in garments and persons." Herman Melville, too, captured the antinomies—resonant as they were with the images of Britain's "dark, satanic mills"—when writing of a New England paper manufactory: pressed into the "bleak hills . . . against the sullen background of mountain firs," filled with "blank-looking girls . . . blankly folding blank paper" and tending "iron animals . . . mutely and cringingly as the slave serves the Sultan."

Even so, social conflict erupted across these representational oppositions in the 1820s and especially 1830s, triggered by the entrepreneurial competition unleashed by market intensification. Wages—protests against cuts and nonpayment or demands for increases—most often provided the spark, leading to turnouts in textile mills, even among the female operatives in Lowell who would form the Factory Girls' Association, and strikes on canals, docks, railroads, and building sites. But workers also reeled at new circumstances of dependency, unsettling rhythms of labor, wearying hours on the job, and wrenching material vulnerabilities. "We are obliged by our employers to labor at this season of the year, from 5 o'clock in the morning until sunset, being fourteen hours and a half," the operatives in Manayunk, Pennsylvania, complained during the summer of 1833, "at an unhealthy employment where we never feel a refreshing breeze to cool us, overheated and suffocated as we are . . . [by] an atmosphere thick with the dust and particles of cotton. . . . Often we feel ourselves so weak as to be able to scarcely perform our work, on account of the over-strained time we are obliged to labor . . . and the little rest we receive during the night. . . . [I]t requires the wages of all the family who are able to work . . . to furnish absolute wants."

The question of hours, specifically a ten-hour day, stirred labor unrest and more self-conscious forms of class making among workers in the trades, most notably hard-strapped artisans and journeymen, in cities of the coasts and the interior. The organizational impulse was first in evidence in Philadelphia, a birth-place of trade unionism and home to the radical William Heighton, when jour-neymen established the Mechanics' Union of Trade Associations in the fall of 1827. The ripple effects would be powerful and wide-ranging. By the mid-1830s, citywide trade unions and federations had been established in urban centers large and small, east and west—in St. Louis, Cincinnati, Pittsburgh, Louisville, and Cleveland; in Buffalo, Albany, Troy, Newark, and New Brunswick; as well as in New York, Boston, and Baltimore—and union membership spiked to near 300,000, composing somewhere between one-fifth and one-third of all urban journeymen. In the midst of this activity, the National Trades' Union, hoping to advance the prospects of a ten-hour day, was founded.

Equally important, in urban cauldrons of freethinkers, Owenites, and nascent socialists, labor agitation easily crossed into the electoral arenas of poli-tics, and the period saw the proliferation of Workingmen's parties (some spilling into rural towns). Attracting cohorts of master craftsmen, small entrepreneurs, and professionals, though based chiefly on artisans and journeymen, the Work-ingmen fashioned a program that reflected the outlooks and aspirations of petty producers and skilled workers. They called for a variety of reforms: the abolition of imprisonment for debt and of prison labor; the repeal of mechanics' lien laws; and more equitable taxation. They evinced deep hostility to corporate charters for banks and manufacturing companies. They voiced strong support for land reform, principally the availability of cheap homesteads in the West to secure the futures of small producers and relieve the press for employment in the East. Some embraced the more radical agrarianism of Thomas Skidmore (himself a leader of the New York Workingmen). Theirs was an "antimonopoly" political dispensation that both drew upon and fed popular opposition to banks and other concentrations of wealth and power and that imagined more equitable alterna-tives to the developing market society of merchants and speculators.

More equitable, that is, for men of European descent who already had the materials of respectability, especially skills and tools of trade. The Workingmen's movement of the late 1820s and early 1830s had little interest in the men, most of them Irish and African American, who lacked trade skills and spent their energy digging, lifting, and hauling, and it showed relatively little concern for working women in textile mills and urban slop shops. Some in the movement translated their antimonopolism into antislavery, though primarily to safeguard the status and independence of white laboring men. "Wage slavery," not black slavery, was their cause and concern. In turn, they made a fair showing in local elections—gaining the balance of power in some circumstances—before factional disputes, inexperience, and the intervention of political opportunists doomed their efforts. For many labor activists of the time, the experience would sour them on partisan politics and persuade them to steer their trade unions away from the electoral arena; others gravitated to the Locofoco wing of the emerging Democratic Party.

But it would prove a complex fit. Already in the 1830s, the Democratic Party showed the strong, if not dominant, influence of slaveholders, who might have shared the hostility of free laboring folk to banks and corporations, and might have sympathized with their critique of "wage slavery" (this, too, was the slaveholders' view of the social system to their north), yet had a very different vision of the country's future. That vision assumed an increasingly aggressive and expansionist character as the center of gravity of the slaveholding class continued its shift from east to west: from the Tidewater and Low Country of Virginia and Carolina in the early to mid-eighteenth century, into the Piedmont of the Southeast in the late eighteenth and very early nineteenth centuries, and across the states of the Gulf Coast during the second and third decades of the nineteenth century. By the 1830s, the center, intellectually as well as economically, was to be found in the lower Mississippi Valley with the booming city of New Orleans as its crossroads, launching pad, and communications hub.

More than a shifting center of gravity reshaped the slaveholding class. There was an important transformation in social composition as well. To be sure, the slaveholders who directed the building of the Deep South and the Mississippi Valley were not new to the class; their lineages took them back to the Atlantic coast and interior, to the plantation world of the eighteenth century. For the most part, their experience of mastership had been transmitted to them generationally by slave-owning parents and grandparents. They acquired slaves the old-fashioned way: they inherited them or the resources to buy them. The judge and U.S. senator Charles Tait typified this process. Born in Hanover, Virginia, Tait moved with his slaveholding family to Georgia, where he was educated, read law, became active in politics, and presided over a plantation. He eventually sent his son James out to Alabama to purchase land distinguished, he hoped, for its "Fertility, Salubrity, & Navigation," interested as he was in "cotton and slaves." Soon the Tait clan moved to Wilcox County on the banks of the Alabama River. Charles would be appointed a federal judge there; his grandson would continue westward, heading out to Texas in the 1840s. Entry into the slaveholding class, even in the boom times, was not easy for those born outside it. A well-placed marriage was a far better gateway than years of hard work and risk taking.

Still, the slaveholders of the Southwest and the Mississippi Valley infused the class with new and different blood. Most were born after the Revolution and grew to maturity as the battle over slavery began to unfold and as the march of territorial conquest was invigorated. They could thereby look out upon the continent and the hemisphere with a mix of relish and apprehension, cautious to protect their flanks yet eager to pursue a slaveholding empire. They had a roughness that came with getting in on the ground but also a sense of hierarchy and command informed by slaveholding forebears, mixing Faulkner's Thomas Sutpen with South Carolina's Wade Hampton. Theirs was a world constructed chiefly around cotton, rather than rice, tobacco, and sugar, and for all the ebbs and flows of prices they had a confidence derived from their position as the major suppliers on the world market at a time of seemingly endless demand. Few Americans, in fact, were more attentive to the fluctuations of the market, in slaves as well as in cotton. They were on the receiving end of the massive forced march of black men, women, and children—known as the interstate slave trade—and needed to break in thousands of enslaved laborers recently torn from a familiar, if oppressive, environment to the north and the east. In their midst, slavery was at its most grueling and dehumanizing, with back-breaking labor, wildly uneven gender ratios, searing separations, and brutal driving. Perhaps most important, their very ascent owed to policies that annexed lands previously claimed by rival powers and forcibly removed the Native populations who stood in their way. The speculator, labor lord, and conqueror together seemed integral to their makeup.

Indeed, however much they might wish to replicate the lifestyles and cultural attainments of the great planters of the Eastern Seaboard—a Natchez newspaper could complain that the big slaveholders of the district had little interest in the prosperity of the town but rather "sell their cotton in Liverpool; buy their wines in London or Le Havre; their negro clothing in Boston; their plantation implements and fancy clothing in New Orleans"—they would not organize themselves and their yeoman allies around an accommodation with the new realities of an emancipationist tide or around an effort to defend themselves from hostile attack. Rather, they would seek to reset the historical clock, avail themselves of whatever forms of political power might be available, and boldly strike out for control of the continent and the hemisphere.

It might in fact have appeared that the most threatening challenges to the slaveholders' designs had, by the mid-1830s, been defeated or averted. The brutal suppression of Nat Turner's rebellion in Southampton County, Virginia, brought some quiet after several decades of widespread slave unrest, and the abolition process that commenced in the 1780s in New England and the Middle Atlantic hit a wall in the legislatures of Virginia, Maryland, and Tennessee. These appearances would turn out to be deceiving; slave unrest and political mobilization would reassert themselves in new ways and the abolition process would find new avenues of development. But another challenge was already brewing, perhaps less noticeable yet in the end no less formidable: the emergence of a new class of manufacturers, shopkeepers, and commercial farmers with distinctive economic horizons, cultural practices, moral dispositions, and political agendas. They had been rearing their heads in port cities, inland towns, and stretches of the countryside—chiefly in the Northeast and the Midwest—for at least three decades. Now they were beginning to find one another.

Market intensification provided the necessary openings for the formation of this new class, and the ranks of the direct producers offered up the early personnel. In rising urban centers like Lynn, Rochester, Pittsburgh, Cincinnati, Cleveland, St. Louis, and Chicago, as well as in older cities like Boston, New York, Philadelphia, and Baltimore, expanding circuits of trade encouraged well-placed artisans and master craftsmen to move in several new directions. For one thing, they became less involved with the craft work of their shops and more involved in the purchasing of raw materials and in the selling of the finished products, taking on the tasks of suppliers and merchandisers. For another, they began to enlarge and reorganize the operations of their shops, multiplying the division of labor, hiring more journeymen and laborers, and assuming more supervisory responsibilities. Without question, they remained closely associated with their trades, closely connected to the artisans and journeymen in their midst, and closely involved in the productive process. They retained, that is, many of the specific skills, social orientations, and political sensibilities of tradesmen and craftsmen. They regarded themselves as "producers," as people who worked with their hands and their knowledge, who made useful things, who created tangible wealth. But the world of the artisan shop was also unraveling. Although they might still have worked side by side with some of their journeymen, they no longer lived under the same roof. Their residences and neighborhoods were increasingly elsewhere. And they were coming into their own, not as skilled workers, but as employers and manufacturers.

In rural districts along major waterways or newly constructed roads and canals—that is to say, with readier access to supra-local markets—something similar was under way. Many farm owners sought to avail themselves of these opportunities by devoting more of their land to crops they intended to market rather than consume (including newer cash crops like tobacco), by increasing the household manufacture of palm-leaf hats, brooms, or other articles they planned to sell, and, perhaps, by taking in yarns to be woven or shoe leather to be sewn together by female dependents. Other farmers moved along a path of specialization, raising orchard and garden crops, converting improved acreage to pastureland, and focusing on livestock and dairy products. Still others (a very distinct minority), especially those in possession of larger and more fertile tracts, might look to increase their production and improve yields by utilizing better equipment (plows, mowers, seed drills, and reapers) and spreading manures more systematically. The larger landowners also began to hire farm laborers, not so much from the local population and for short stints as from among the landless in nearby market or manufacturing towns or from among tenant households, many of whom were Irish, English, French Canadian, German, or Scandinavian (depending on the location) and contracting for several months, if not an entire year (subject to stiff penalties for leaving before the contract expired).

Shopkeepers and other retailers who traded with these emergent manufacturers and commercial farmers were alike drawn into a new grid of economic activities and relations. Their horizons were regional rather than local, and their connections were with more substantial (and distant) wholesalers and financiers. Their interest in accommodating traditional practices of barter was fast diminishing, and they increasingly preferred (or needed) to operate on more of a strict cash and credit basis. They kept their books, assessed interest, expected to be repaid, and took recalcitrant debtors to court. Together with nascent manufacturers and commercial farmers, they shared a perspective on the American political economy. They welcomed internal improvements to facilitate speedier marketing and communication. They demanded tariff protection against the importation of foreign goods and raw materials that they hoped to supply. They supported public land policies that promoted settlement rather than speculation. And they wanted easier access to capital and other forms of credit. This is to say that they looked inward instead of outward, intent on developing the domestic, rather than the international, market and face of the economy.

Formal politics was therefore an arena in which the members of this new social class met one another and learned of their mutual concerns. Many of them would gravitate to the Whig Party, favorable as it was to an activist state, domestic economic development, tariffs, banks, and transportation projects. These were the elements of the "American System" that the party and its leader, Henry Clay of Kentucky, loudly touted. Yet their arenas of activity and discovery were far more numerous, and none were more important than those tied to evangelical religion. Protestant revivals began to sweep through much of America in the early years of the nineteenth century but reached their greatest pulse during the 1820s and 1830s, especially where the market intensification of the era was being most powerfully felt. Although the reach of revivalism in this overwhelmingly Protestant republic knew no social or racial boundaries, the message of the revivalists seemed to have a special resonance for those women, men, and young people whose fortunes and futures were most clearly linked to the emerging economic order. Preachers such as Lyman Beecher, who moved through Connecticut, Massachusetts, and New York before heading out to Ohio, and Charles Grandison Finney, who set western New York ablaze but also traveled across the Northeast and the Midwest—not to mention across the Atlantic, to England and Wales—no longer spoke in the language of Calvinism, of predestination, of collective sin and helplessness, of the eternal damnation that awaited most human beings whether they chose it or not. They spoke instead in the language of Arminianism, of moral free agency, of rebirth, of personal responsibility for sinfulness, and of the possibility of establishing a direct relationship with God unmediated by ministers or any other members of established hierarchies.

To be sure, the revivalists warned of dangers always lurking, of temptations always presenting themselves, of corruption as the dogged counterpoint of perfection, of the devil as an active force in the world. But they also imagined an immense spiritual transformation that would precede and allow the coming of God's kingdom to earth. For this work, they hoped to recruit a massive army of disciples who would carry the message of Christ's love and convince the doubters that they could choose good over evil and hasten the millennium's arrival. The message, the setting, and the prospects seemed to appeal to a wide swath of American Protestants, especially the young and footloose who searched for new forms of community and those—younger and older—who bore witness to the dynamism and disruption of the market intensification. Yet the evangelical churches began to fill with disproportionate numbers of shopkeepers, small manufacturers, master craftsmen, and artisans, and everywhere they were led to conversion and membership by their wives and daughters. The cultural experience of class in the nineteenth century was, it turns out, deeply gendered.

The central role of women in the making of religious congregations and other venues of spirituality was not distinctive to Protestantism, revivalism, the United States, or the nineteenth century. It was to be found across the centuries, particularly among Judeo-Christian faiths on both sides of the Atlantic, and it reflected both the forms of moral authority that women seized and the means by which they could hold male power in some check. The enormous surge of popular religious enthusiasm in the early decades of the nineteenth century proved no different in these regards. What did prove different was the missionary project with which the faithful were charged and the new openings for public activism that were consequently made available. The associational impulse that the French visitor Alexis de Tocqueville detected in the 1830s was not simply a manifestation of male fraternalism and political bonding; it also had a strong female component, often linked to church and related areas of social reform that brought women (mostly from middling families) by the many thousands into meetings, organizations, and eventually the streets. Some would find their way into abolitionism and ultimately into feminism. Many others would be drawn to missionary societies, Sunday school unions, Bible and tract societies, societies devoted to the fight against prostitution or the use of tobacco, rescue and rehabilitation societies for the poor, the orphaned, and the fallen, and societies aiming at prison and educational reform. But undoubtedly the greatest number rallied to the cause of temperance.

Perhaps more than any other issue of the time, temperance seemed to encapsulate both the threats to the vitals of a rapidly changing society and the character traits increasingly associated with notions of social respectability. Drinking to excess was, in the eyes of many evangelicals, a surrender to the baser passions, a manifestation of lack of self-control, and a cause of poverty, family dissolution, and vice. "What fills the almshouses and jails? What brings you trembling wretch upon the gallows? It is drink." So reflected the former drunkard John B. Gough. At a time when the consumption of alcoholic beverages—both distilled and fermented—reached unprecedented levels, it was regarded in some quarters as the devil incarnate, and critics worried about what they called popular "enslavement" to "demon rum." "Intemperance," the Reverend Lyman Beecher thundered, "is the sin of the land and is coming in upon us like a flood; and if anything shall defeat the hopes of the world it is that river of fire destroying the vital air and extending around an atmosphere of death." Others, deploying the metaphors of disease and contagion, likened it to a cancer "penetrat[ing] the body politic."

The temperance crusade—for a crusade it was and surely the largest social movement of the 1830s—not only promised to turn back the flood and bring peace and prosperity to families and communities or to remove the cancer and restore the health of the social body; it also defined new forms of personal behavior and social comportment organized around the embrace of sobriety: self-discipline, self-restraint, self-control, thrift, and industry—all in contradistinction to the character revealed by submission to alcohol. Some temperance advocates hoped for moderation. More and more pressed for abstinence. They began by reforming their homes and churches, dismissing congregants who drank excessively. They moved on to their places of work, ending traditions of St. Monday, treating at the grog shop, and breaking for a dram. They formed clubs, societies, prayer circles, and maternal associations. And with the help of grassroots politicking, petitioning, and intimidation—carried on by women as well as men—they succeeded in enacting local and state laws prohibiting the manufacture and sale of alcoholic beverages. By the mid-1850s, most of the Northeast and the Midwest were dry.

As the dynamics of the temperance movement suggested, it was in the encounter with the embodiments of social ill that reformers both developed their diagnoses and assessed what set people like themselves apart. Evangelical sensibilities no longer countenanced the notion that social differentiation was the product of either divine providence or ascriptive hierarchy. Rather, in their visits to the almshouses, tenements, brothels, jails, and orphanages, a raft of charitable, philanthropic, and reform societies focused their attention on what they considered individual and group "vices." Not low wages, poor prospects, racial and ethnic discrimination, or underemployment, but idleness, ignorance, drinking, gambling, promiscuous sex, thriftlessness, and family irresponsibility paved the path of criminality, pauperism, and dissipation.

Female reformers were especially concerned for the poor women they saw and met, but even their sympathies reinforced a deepening sense of what separated them. In part, it was their own resistance to the vices they described: their rejection of intemperance, casual sexuality, irreligion, and other profligate ways. Yet it was also their insistence on constructing marriages and family lives that served as counterpoints to the rough, competitive, and destabilizing dynamics of public spaces and marketplaces. It came to be called "domesticity," "separate spheres," and "Victorianism," sets of practices and aspirations that did not so much mark the confinement of women in the early to mid-nineteenth century as announce what distinguished an emerging social group from those below (the laboring classes and the poor) and above them (the upper class of wealthy merchants and estate owners). Thus, in their developing efforts to restrict the size of their families, to educate their children (particularly their sons), and to build social networks among people like themselves, these women simultaneously consecrated a new set of values and character traits and established a basis for the elaboration and reproduction of a new class experience.

New Directions

Their cultural and political associations of the 1830s and early 1840s might have enabled an emerging class of manufacturers, shopkeepers, and commercial farmers to avail themselves of the economic rejuvenation that came soon thereafter. Although there is much debate about when the United States reached its industrial "takeoff" point, there is little doubt that in the wake of the panics and recession of the late 1830s and the first years of the 1840s the economy of the Northeast and the Midwest moved more rapidly in the direction of manufacturing and market agriculture. Between 1844 and 1854, the output of farms, mines, and manufactories grew at a rate that stands out for the entire nineteenth century and both deepened and transformed the linkages that market intensification had been promoting. Indeed, the economic downturn and dislocations might have encouraged a variety of trends—rural to urban migrations, transatlantic immigration, the weakening of fledgling trade unions and artisan producers, the rerouting of capital and credit—that strengthened the position of manufacturers and agriculturalists looking chiefly to the domestic market.

Perhaps the most visible indication of the new directions in which sections of the American economy appeared to be headed was the rapid growth of the railroad. It is true that the first railroads in the United States were built in the 1820s and 1830s, reflecting the efforts of port and interior cities to tap into the trade of their immediate hinterlands. But for the most part, the early roads covered short distances (less than fifty miles), connected existing centers, depended chiefly on locally raised capital, and supplemented existing water transportation. By 1840, about thirty-three hundred miles of track had been laid, almost all of it east of the Appalachians.

The railroad-building boom that commenced in the mid-1840s was of a different character. It established a basic transportation network east of the Mississippi River, increasingly challenging rivers, lakes, and canals as the principal means of transportation, especially in the Northeast and the Midwest. Owing to the immense costs of construction, it also reconfigured an assortment of basic business and financial practices. Capital requirements were generally well beyond the means of individual entrepreneurs, families, or small collections of associates (the bases of most economic enterprises of the time), and so railroad companies developed new and larger organizational structures, began to work with full-time contractors, and needed to seek funding well outside their own regions of operation. Simultaneously, the roads began to recruit a workforce with an enormous range of skills and experiences, and one that grew more than tenfold in the two decades after the panics of 1837 and 1839.

By the 1850s, the new railroad industry played a key role in centralizing the American capital market in New York City, where railroad securities could be bought and sold and a vibrant stock exchange would be established to facilitate the transactions. Ownership and management of the companies would thereby be separated, and forms of accounting and business administration—all of which anticipated the modern corporation—came into use. A variety of technological improvements brought uniformity to the tasks of construction, grading, tunneling, and bridging. Locomotives as well as cars and coaches assumed the designs and functions that would be in place for decades. And although the rails were iron and the track gauges not yet standardized, the railroads turned the dynamics of market intensification into those of industrial transformation.

The new economic features and directions that the railroads encompassed had important resonances in the world of formal politics. Already, the mass political parties that democratization and Jacksonianism helped to construct showed the marks of serious divisions over the future of the American political economy as Whigs and Democrats came to battle about banks, tariffs, governmental activism, and the money supply. But in the aftermath of the panics and recession, more of a coherence in discourse and policy began to emerge. The Whigs, whose strongest bases were to be found in the Northeast, the Midwest, and the urban South, hoped to use the levers of the state and the energies of evangelicalism to advance the march of market relations, intensify the development of the domestic economy, and reconfigure the American character through a mix of moral injunctions, educational initiatives, and political reforms. The Democrats, most formidable in the rural South and the urban North, wished to put the breaks on commercial expansion, limit the powers of the state, curb the cultural projects of evangelicalism, and instead promote the territorial extension of the United States across the continent and, perhaps, throughout the hemisphere. The cultural ambitions of the one and the geographical ambitions of the other would prove to be a very toxic combination.

CHAPTER FOUR

Continentalism

United States Army defeating Mexican forces at the Battle of Monterrey,
September 1846.

Pacific Vistas

Early on the afternoon of October 19, 1842, ships of the U.S. Pacific Squadron sailed into the harbor of Monterey, capital of Mexican California, preparing for conquest. Their chief officer, Commodore Thomas ap Catesby Jones, a Virginian who had been in the naval service since the age of sixteen, fought in the War of 1812, and received command of the squadron a year earlier—a man who, by all accounts, exuded discipline and readiness—was not acting upon orders. Indeed, he appeared to be acting against them. For the two decades since it had been established, the Pacific Squadron looked chiefly to protect American commerce and shipping as far off as the East Indies, and at the time of Jones's assignment the secretary of the navy told him, in no uncertain terms, that "nothing but the necessity of prompt and effective protection to the honor and interests of the United States will justify you in either provoking hostility or committing any act of violence toward a belligerent . . . especially a state with which our country is at peace."

Mexico and the United States were, in fact, at peace in the fall of 1842, but this was not at all clear to Commodore Jones. Political tensions west and south of the Sabine River had reverberated since the early 1830s and especially since the Mexican province of Tejas rebelled against the central government and proclaimed the Texas Republic in 1836. Because most of the Texas rebels were transplanted Americans, the question of "annexation" by the United States immediately surfaced. And although neither the outgoing president, Andrew Jackson, nor his successor, Martin Van Buren, wanted to risk war with Mexico, not to mention domestic political turmoil, by pushing ahead precipitously, the issue hung perilously over the arena of international politics. Not just the United States but Britain and France had designs on Mexican territory, and when the first Whig president, William Henry Harrison of Ohio, died only one month into his term (April 1841), the torch passed to his vice president, John Tyler, a Virginian whose political sensibilities seemed far closer to those of John C. Calhoun and who wished to make the acquisition of Texas central to his legacy and to his bid for formal election in 1844.

Talk of war and interventions of various sorts was therefore rife in the early 1840s, but for Commodore Jones and the Pacific Squadron all eyes were on California rather than Texas. Sparsely populated by Mexicans of European descent (Californios) since the late eighteenth century, the province of California—particularly Alta California—was well beyond the reach of Mexico City, separated by fifteen hundred miles of rugged terrain and formidable bands of Apache, Ute, and Yaqui Indians. The coastline was dotted by a string of declining Franciscan missions and a few lightly defended presidios, and separatist rebellions had already erupted, though without the force or outcome of the one in Tejas. Most important, California boasted a number of fine harbors and took its place on a Pacific coast that had long attracted traders and trappers of Russian, British, and French extraction and increasingly beckoned the political attentions of their governments. California, the Oregon Country, and the southern reaches of Alaska were, after all, both excellent sources of furs and hides and important gateways to Asia. Pacific North America was highly contested territory for the maritime powers of the age.

Jones soon became aware of potentially threatening developments. Sailing into the Peruvian port of Callao in the southern Pacific, he heard of secretive maneuvers by French and British vessels and then received word from the American consul in Mazatlán of pending warfare between the United States and Mexico over the fate of Texas. The alarm bells, in his judgment, had sounded. In early September 1842, with two ships and a third ordered to follow, Jones headed north to California determined to seize every one of California's ports, if war had indeed broken out.

When he sailed into Monterey Bay more than a month later, neither French nor British ships were in evidence. But, his suspicions aroused, Jones decided to demand the surrender of the Mexican garrison and officials there. With a scant twenty-nine soldiers and eleven pieces of cannon to answer Jones's eight hundred men and eighty pieces of cannon, it was no contest, and the Mexicans knew it. Mexican officials capitulated even more quickly than Jones had ordered, and his troops then marched ashore, six abreast, with the naval band playing "Yankee Doodle" and "The Star-Spangled Banner." They settled into the presidio, renamed it in Jones's honor, and raised the American flag.

It seemed to be a glorious and, thankfully, bloodless victory. Yet there was absolutely no evidence that Mexico and the United States were currently at war: nothing in the newspapers that had arrived in Monterey from Mexico City; nothing in the commercial papers of local merchants; nothing in the private correspondence of the inhabitants; not even a wild rumor afloat. Chastened, Jones had little choice but to pack up and restore the status quo ante bellum, which he promptly did. He also wrote apologetically to the new California governor, Manuel Micheltorena, who had already begun to mobilize military commanders in Los Angeles, Santa Barbara, and Sonoma and was himself at the front of six hundred troops heading toward Monterey. The American contingent was instructed by Jones to decamp and reboard their ships, the American flag was lowered and the Mexican raised, and courtesies were exchanged between the two sides. So ended the United States' first invasion of California.

Commodore Jones would eventually be called before his superiors in Washington, D.C., though he would face neither formal charges nor serious reprimands. Instead, the naval brass seemed impressed by his zeal and devotion to duty as he understood it. Small wonder. From the first days of the Republic, power in the Pacific had been central to the continental ambitions of American leaders and policy makers. Well aware of the already thriving trade in eastern and southern Asia—and of the intense jockeying among the British, French, Spanish, and Dutch—they saw the Pacific as a vast source of economic enrichment and the Pacific coast of North America as a gateway to its riches. New England merchants had been active in Asian ports since the 1780s, and they gained an even better footing owing to the European wars of the late eighteenth and early nineteenth centuries. By the late 1830s, whaling ships from New Bedford, Nantucket, and Martha's Vineyard (like the *Pequod* of Melvillean fame) were busy in the northern Pacific, and according to some observers Hawai'i (also known as the Sandwich Islands) was showing the influence of the American Northeast. "Honolulu," the maritime historian Samuel Eliot Morison could write, "with whalemen and merchant sailors rolling through its streets, shops fitted with Lowell shirtings, New England rum and Yankee notions . . . was becoming as Yankee as New Bedford." Thomas Jefferson's eyes were firmly on the Pacific when, in 1803, he instructed Meriwether Lewis that "the object of your mission is to explore the Missouri River, and such principal streams of it, as by its course and communication with the waters of the Pacific Ocean, may offer the most direct and practicable water communication across the continent for the purposes of commerce." Jefferson's views were shared by virtually all of his successors, especially those from John Quincy Adams to James K. Polk. Gaining control of the harbors stretching from San Diego in the south to the Strait of Juan de Fuca to the north represented their major territorial objective.

Nothing appeared more attractive than San Francisco Bay, which came to official American attention before 1820. One American emissary described it as the "most convenient, extensive, and safe harbor in the world" and, not incidentally, "wholly without defense." President Jackson told his Mexican minister, Anthony Butler, in 1835 to negotiate for the "whole bay" in what turned into a failed effort. Although Van Buren made no attempt at acquisition, he did send an expedition to gather information about the Pacific coast and particularly about the harbors there. Tyler's secretary of state, the New Englander Daniel Webster, envisioned San Francisco as extremely consequential for the "numerous Whale Ships and trading vessels . . . which navigate the Pacific." His minister to Mexico, South Carolina's Waddy Thompson, even insisted that Texas was of little value by comparison. "The possession of San Francisco and Monterey," Thompson explained, "would secure the only places of refuge & rest for our numerous fishing vessels, and would no doubt . . . secure the trade of India & the whole Pacific Ocean." Around the time of his inauguration, Polk

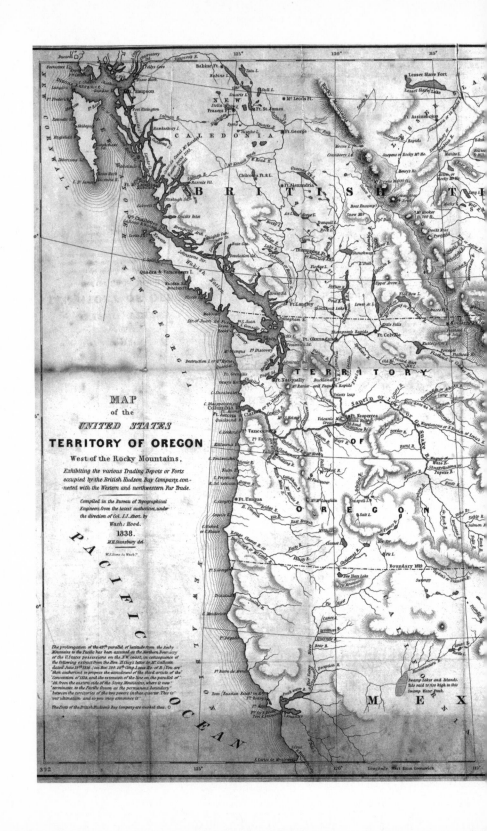

MAP
of the
UNITED STATES
TERRITORY OF OREGON
West of the Rocky Mountains,
Exhibiting the various Trading Depots or Forts occupied by the British Hudson Bay Company, connected with the Western and northwestern Fur Trade.

Compiled in the Bureau of Topographical Engineers, from the latest authorities, under the direction of Col. J.J. Abert, by
Wash: Hood.
1838.
M.H.Stansbury del.

W.J. Stone lo. Wash.ᵗⁿ

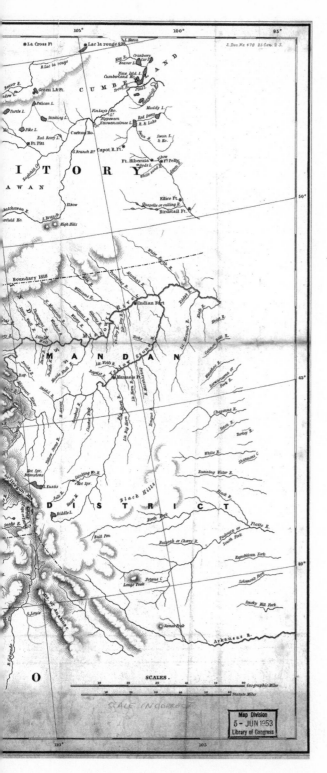

Competing claims of
the United States,
Great Britain, Mexico,
and Native peoples
in the Pacific West,
1838.

thus confided to his naval secretary, George Bancroft, that the acquisition of California sat high on his ambitious list of priorities.

The claims of any of the Europeans, Mexicans, or Americans to the west coast of North America had rather limited foundations, to say the least. Only the Spanish had established settlements, and these—chiefly in response to rumors of British and Russian intentions—were thinly manned. Russian fur traders, having trekked across Siberia in the sixteenth and seventeenth centuries in search of sable, made their way along the Aleutian Islands into the southern Alaskan panhandle in the eighteenth, demanding labor and other forms of tribute from the indigenous peoples; they ultimately established a settlement on Kodiak Island. By 1800, there were all of four hundred Russians living and trading under the auspices of the newly established Russian-American Company, not quite the formidable force the Spanish had feared. For their part, the British touched ground from the west and the east: first, Captain James Cook, sent off by the British Admiralty and the Royal Society, who sailed the coast from Vancouver Island to the Bering Strait in 1778; and subsequently, the fur-trading Hudson Bay Company, moving west from the Great Lakes, across the Canadian prairies, and out to the area between the Columbia River and Vancouver Island (where Cook had spent a month at an inlet he called—mistranslating the name given by the Native people—Nootka). As of 1840, there were fewer than five hundred Hudson Bay Company personnel, more than half of whom were either French, "half-breeds," or Kanakas (from Hawai'i). But even that far surpassed the Americans who had glimpsed the Pacific in 1805 during the Lewis and Clark expedition, had done some trading around John Jacob Astor's post at the mouth of the Columbia River, and numbered fewer than a hundred around 1840, on the eve of overland migrations to the Oregon Country.

If any claims could be well established, they were those of the Native peoples who occupied the area between the Pacific coast and the Rocky Mountains in very substantial numbers. Although only estimates can be ventured, in the latter part of the eighteenth century—at the onset of Euro-American colonizations—more than half a million might have resided in territory that Europeans would name Alta California, the Oregon Country, and Russian Alaska. Showing immense cultural diversity—they spoke well over one hundred languages based in nearly fifteen different language groups—they were mostly to be found in small villages and bands, availing themselves of the environmental abundance. From the north to the south, they called themselves Tlingits, Haidas, Tsimshians, Kwakiutls, Moachats, Salishes, and Tillamooks; Hupas, Yuroks, Shastas, Modocs, Pomos, Esselens, and Salinans; Miwoks, Wintuns, Konkowas, Nisenans, and Yukis; Paiutes, Washoes, Chumashes, Gabrielinos, Tipais, and Serranos; Quechans, Mohaves,

Cahuillas, Luiseños, and Halchidhomas. Depending on the season, they hunted elk, deer, antelope, rabbits, and marine mammals. They gathered nuts, berries, mushrooms, seeds, and acorns. And, especially if they lived north of the 42nd parallel (also marking the accepted border between Alta California and the Oregon Country), they collected enormous quantities of salmon and other fish from the freshwater rivers and streams. Some, like the Nez Perce who were based east of the Cascades and north of the Great Basin along the Snake and Salmon rivers, acquired horses, became outstanding equestrians, and could range as far as the upper plains in search of buffalo. Only in the Colorado River valleys to the southeast were crops like maize, beans, and squash cultivated, showing the influence of horticulturalists in Nuevo México.

Relatively few of the Native Americans of the Pacific West were swept up into the Spanish-Mexican mission complex of Catholic indoctrination and coerced labor (roughly twenty thousand at the time of Mexican independence), and those who were came chiefly from the areas around the missions, along the coast. A good many more became involved, directly or indirectly, in trading networks that linked them with Native bands well into the interior as well as with European and American traders coursing the Atlantic and the Pacific. But most felt the effects of imperial encounter in more lethal ways and often before visible contact: by means of smallpox, malaria, and cholera, which carried away, sometimes with great speed, very large proportions of the Native population. Epidemics might virtually wipe out villages or bands within a few weeks or months, and successive waves of disease wrought long-term havoc. In the fifty years after the arrival of Spanish settlers and Franciscan missionaries, the Indian population of coastal Alta California declined by about 75 percent. Weakened and disoriented, the Native people reorganized, consolidated their villages, and struggled to understand what had happened to them.

The concern of American expansionists, therefore, was not the resistance of the Pacific Indians, who lived in small and decentralized political units and were not known as formidable warriors; it was rather with the plans of the British, who, it was assumed, were in search of more Pacific bases to shore up their developing Asian empire. And, eager as these Americans were to have California, their sights fell too on Oregon, where they had claims to some of the territory recognized by the imperial powers and ambitions to much more of it. A series of international agreements had established the 42nd parallel as the northern boundary of Spanish and Mexican possessions, the 54th parallel as the southern boundary of the Russian, and the 49th parallel as the line separating British and American interests between the Great Lakes and the Continental Divide. West of the divide, south of the 54th parallel, and north of the 42nd was the jointly occupied Oregon Country, with strongest American claims to the area north of the 42nd parallel and south of the Columbia River and strongest British claims north of the 49th parallel and south of the 54th. As American settlers began to move into the Willamette valley in growing numbers during the early 1840s, those claims became stronger still.

In most dispute was the land between the Columbia River and the 49th parallel, which included the valuable Fuca Strait and Puget Sound, one of the great Pacific coast harbors. But with the settler population in Oregon beginning to boom, midwestern Democrats started a new drumbeat, one that rejected any British claims and demanded Oregon for the United States in its entirety. Public meetings assembled from Ohio to Illinois (states that contributed large numbers of Oregon migrants), and a convention in Cincinnati in 1843 declared that Americans had undeniable rights to the territory between California and Alaska. The "whole of Oregon" became an increasingly popular political cry, and Stephen Douglas, a young congressman from Illinois, cried it loudly and belligerently. He wanted to drive "Great Britain and the last vestiges of royal authority from the continent of North America" and create "an ocean-bound republic." So effective did this argument prove to be that its supporters succeeded in including a plank in the 1844 Democratic platform that called for the "reoccupation of Oregon."

Coupled with another plank demanding the "reannexation of Texas," the militant posture on the Oregon question helped the Democrats and their candidate, James K. Polk from Tennessee (a Jackson protégé), eke out a tight election. Polk swept the Deep South, the lower Mississippi Valley (Louisiana, Arkansas, and Missouri), and much of the Midwest, winning Illinois, Indiana, and Michigan, and very nearly winning Ohio. Once in office, Polk appeared to hew to the party line. "Our title to the country of Oregon," he proclaimed at his inauguration, "is 'clear and unquestionable,' and already are our people preparing to perfect that title by occupying it with their wives and children." Yet Polk, unlike hotheaded Douglas, well knew that the "whole of Oregon" bluster risked a war with Britain that would be costly and throw many of his other projects into disarray. He therefore chose to work a compromise by agreeing to extend the 49th parallel boundary west to the Pacific and kept his eyes on the California prize.

Texas and Cotton

British projects loomed even more consequentially when it came to the fate and future of Texas. By the lights of the rebellious Texans, Santa Anna's capitulation after the Battle of San Jacinto secured their independence, and although most seemed intent on joining the United States, their new constitution formed a republic and their new congress established expansive borders, stretching from the Rio Grande in the south to the 42nd parallel in the north. Left unanswered was the question of whether the Texas Republic really existed if no other government recognized it. Whatever Santa Anna's actions (and he would be treated with scorn when he finally returned to Mexico City), the Mexican state, as a Veracruz newspaper put it, "is not aware of the existence of a nation called the republic of Texas but only a horde of adventurers in rebellion against the laws of the government of the republic." The war, in their view, was very much ongoing, and Mexican forces would attempt a reoccupation of their own: in 1838, 1839, and 1842, on the last occasion briefly holding San Antonio and Goliad. The United States seemed no more inclined to offer official recognition—Jackson, in his final message as president, called such a move "impolitic" despite his hope that annexation could be achieved—and neither did Britain, France, or any other European country. Eventually, when Mirabeau B. Lamar, a onetime Georgia nullifier who saw Texas as a "future empire" rather than as one of the United States, succeeded Sam Houston as Texas president, diplomatic arrangements were made with Britain, France, and Holland, as well as the United States. But the geopolitical status of Texas remained in limbo.

The Texas question presented a number of challenges to a union of American states imbued with enormous—and widely shared—territorial ambitions, but at odds as to the sort of union they wished to be. It would have been difficult to find a political leader, of any party or region, who did not envision the United States at least as a continental power, looking out upon both the Atlantic and the Pacific. Indeed, the notion of the country's "manifest destiny to overspread and to possess the whole continent," articulated famously by the Jacksonian journalist John L. O'Sullivan in 1845, was very deeply laid in the political culture and embraced virtually across the political spectrum. The differences had rather more to do with the pace and method of attaining the objective, the political status of newly acquired or conquered territories, the constitutional standing of various subject populations, and the relative power of the country's dominant social classes.

The greatest hesitancy, over the question of Texas and the more general march to the Pacific, was to be found among those associated with the Whig Party in almost any area of the United States. Together, Whigs imagined a gradual process of expansion, after demographic and economic densities had developed in places already settled, achieved through diplomatic means. They also feared the population being spread too thin, drained from the eastern portions of the country to the western, and the new balances of power that might be introduced. Betraying their racialist assumptions, they doubted whether portions of northern Mexico or Cuba could become full-fledged states or whether the Catholic, Indian, and mixed-race denizens of them should be welcomed to the United States—issues for which the Constitution provided few clear directions. Many Whigs in the Northeast and the Midwest were vexed about the addition of new territories and states where slavery would be legal and slave owners would hold sway, shifting the base of political power more decidedly to the lower Mississippi Valley. They saw the slaveholders' hands in the Texas Revolution and the demands for annexation. Whigs in the Southeast worried that slavery in their midst might be undermined and their political influence diminished by the migration of slaveholders and slaves from the Chesapeake, the Carolinas, and Georgia out to Mississippi, Louisiana, Texas, and perhaps other points west and southwest. It was mainly warnings rather than alternatives that Whigs proffered, and their embrace of evangelicalism provided cultural sanction—spreading the personal experience of Christ—for the very projects they wished to oppose.

Some northern Democrats, especially those whose sympathies were moving in the direction of antislavery, shared the Whig misgivings. They were likely associated with the Van Buren—Barnburner, as it was known—wing of the party, or they were East Coast merchants and shippers who looked chiefly to the Atlantic. Yet most Democrats pursued Texas and expansionism with great energy and zeal, fitting well as both did with their political economy and political culture. Enlarging the American landmass and making an "ocean-bound republic" not only promised increased international economic leverage but also could secure the futures of small producers while avoiding the dangers of industrialization and urbanization. To expansionist Democrats, Britain was more than a rival and threatening power; it represented a repugnant path of development, marked by grinding industries, teeming cities, social immiseration, and class conflict. Breathing room in the West thus offered a means of escape to prospective American *voortrekkers*—for *voortrekkers* they were, bound together by race, ethnicity, religion, and a desire for independence like their Afrikaner counterparts, who had migrated into the southern African interior in the nineteenth century on what is known as the Great Trek. It was an opportunity to own land and reassemble their communities, a chance to mix subsistence and commercial agriculture and to flee the grasp of banks and other corporate institutions. They imagined something of an agrarian empire, organized around republican principles, that strengthened rather than undermined the fabric of the American union.

Some Democrats had, as well, a political version of evangelical mission. Believing themselves unique practitioners of democratic values and culture in a world dominated by monarchies and other forms of tyranny, they took it as their responsibility to spread these ideas and institutions across the continent and the hemisphere. In a sense, they combined Jefferson's "empire of liberty" with Madison's *Federalist* 10 and set them to the tasks of the nineteenth century. Their most powerful voices were to be heard in journals like the *Democratic Review* and in organizations like the National Reform Association, which focused on the land question, and they felt a kinship with popular nationalist movements stirring in Ireland, Poland, Italy, Germany, and France. Indeed, as a measure of mutual influence, they would come to call themselves Young America, very much in accord with the many "youth" movements inspired by Italy's Giuseppe Mazzini in the 1830s. "The last order of civilization, which is the democratic, received its first permanent existence in this country," John L. O'Sullivan wrote in the 1840s, "and her example shall smite unto death the tyranny of kings, hierarchies, and oligarchies, and carry the glad tidings of peace and good will where myriads now endure an existence scarcely more enviable than that of beasts of the field." Democracy, he added significantly, "was Christianity in its earthly aspect."

O'Sullivan and Young America provided a language and set of aspirations that could be embraced by expansionists with less lofty ambitions because they generally ignored the "hierarchy" and "tyranny" of slavery and because their understanding of democratic America was so deeply racialized and gendered. The "young American" who would transport "democracy" into new territories was recognizably white, male, probably Protestant, and of martial demeanor— the embodiment of manhood as the nineteenth century prescribed—facing, as he saw it, a world beset by economic backwardness, political lethargy, ignorance, superstition, Catholicism, effeminacy, and racial mixing. Expansionism would defeat the institutions that bred these maladies and offer the benefits of "civilization" for those who wished to seize them. At the very least, it would press those institutions and populations back, weaken them, and allow free and vigorous men (and their families) to find necessary space. How easy it was for the filibusters, adventurers, and speculators, who set their sights on the main chance in an "ocean-bound republic," to wrap themselves in the garbs of democracy and civilizationism.

But for many Democrats, and especially those from the states of the Deep South, the question of Texas had a special urgency. It was not only the lure of more territory, another slave state, and rich cotton land; it was also the threatening alternative to American annexation. With Mexico pressing in from the south, Comanches, Kiowas, Wichitas, and Caddos raiding in the west and the north, and an empty treasury, the future of the fledgling Republic of Texas was in serious doubt. And it appeared as if the British hoped to orchestrate a deal. Indeed, word circulated that in exchange for abolishing slavery and refusing annexation to the United States, Texans could expect British financial and military support as well as the settlement of hostilities with Mexico. After all, the British had already ended slavery in their colonial possessions and hoped to pressure their economic and political competitors to follow them down the path of emancipation. By gaining influence in Texas, they could limit American power in the Gulf of Mexico and, perhaps, in the hemisphere at large. Thus, rather than pushing its boundaries farther to the west and providing for slavery's extension, the United States would have an "abolitionized" troublemaker to its southwest. From his retirement at the Hermitage, Andrew Jackson explained, with his literary finesse, the frightening logic: "Great Britain enters into an alience with Texas—looking forward to war with us, she sends to Texas 20 or 30,000 organising her army near the Sabine . . . marches through Louisiana and Arkansa, makes a lodgment on the mississippi, excite the negroes to insurrection, the lower country falls and with it Neworleans, and a servile war rages all over the southern and western country."

Whatever the truth about British intentions, the new president, John Tyler, was sufficiently concerned to send the editor Duff Green, a close ally of John C. Calhoun's, on a fact-finding mission to London. There, Green claimed to have learned of a vast British design to use Texas to fasten its hold on the world economy and destroy the power of the United States in the process: not so much by abolishing slavery as by challenging American control of the cotton supply. It made a great deal of sense, especially to those who saw a close relation between domestic prosperity and global economic power. "Texas labor, stimulated and fostered by British capital, would soon raise as much cotton as does the United States," the *Daily Madisonian* warned in the spring of 1844, and "would soon either exterminate cotton from our land or limit the market for sale to our own country." Annexation, in turn, would not only offer protection against "servile war" and other hazards of potential British encirclement but also, as Pennsylvania's senator James Buchanan put it, place "within the limits of our broad confederacy all the favored cotton-growing regions of the earth." Texas "will give us the entire control of that great staple, the principal basis of our foreign commerce, and the great conservator of peace of the world," a North Carolina congressman predicted, and so "long as we have control over the cotton trade, we have little to fear from war with European nations."

Sam Houston, leader of the Anglo-Texans favoring annexation, skillfully played the "British card" to press the case. By 1843, Tyler was firmly on board. But the opposition within the United States remained formidable. Neither Whigs nor Barnburner Democrats wished to facilitate British influence in Texas, abandon American imperial ambitions, or jeopardize the cotton economy. If anything, there was a broad consensus across party lines on the centrality of cotton to the country's economic dynamism, and it would define significant limits to social and political change for the duration of the nineteenth century. But they were less convinced by the stories of British intentions and far more worried about both the empowerment of southwestern slaveholders and the very likely prospect of war with Mexico (which still regarded Texas as its territory). They could scarcely have felt comforted when Calhoun, who had become Tyler's secretary of state, linked Texas annexation to the defense and wisdom of black slavery. As a result, a treaty of annexation, which had been negotiated during the spring of 1844, went down to defeat in the U.S. Senate, where it needed a two-thirds vote to secure ratification.

But neither Tyler nor Calhoun was about to give up, even though both had been passed over for the Democratic presidential nomination later that year. Taking heart from the expansionist Polk's victory in November, Tyler decided on a very different tack: to push Texas annexation through in the waning days of his administration as a joint resolution (which demanded only majority support in the House and the Senate) rather than as a treaty. Lame duck that he was, he now had the votes. In late February 1845, days before Polk took his oath, the resolution passed and went back to Texas for its own ratification process. The outcome was hardly in doubt. Voting Texans supported annexation with near unanimity, and in December Texas gained formal admission to the United States.

To be sure, the Texas question exacerbated growing political rifts over the future development of the United States and the place of slavery within it. Abolitionists and other antislavery allies saw the hand of the "slave power" at work and vilified its obvious instrument, the outgoing president, John Tyler, himself a Virginia slaveholder. Several years later, Tyler offered a different assessment. He rejected the charge that in embracing the cause of Texas annexation, he was chiefly interested in advancing the interests of slavery and slaveholders. Texas, he insisted, was "vitally important" to the entire United States because it secured "the virtual monopoly of the cotton plant" (to be grown, as he certainly expected, by slave labor). With that, he proclaimed, the country attained "a greater influence over the affairs of the world than would be found in armies however strong, or navies however numerous."

Political Stage of Warfare

The annexation of Texas by the United States has long been regarded as a precipitant of the war with Mexico that Whigs had warned against. But in truth, warfare against the territory of Mexico had begun at least five years before Texas annexation and six before the United States decided to join in. The decisive event took place near Bent's Fort along the Arkansas River sometime during the first half of 1840, and the parties involved were the entrenched, not the presumptive, powers of the Great Plains, neither the Americans, nor the Texans, nor the Mexicans but the Cheyenne, Comanche, Kiowa, and Arapaho.

They gathered in an effort to settle conflicts that had erupted between them owing to population movements and resulting shifts in the political economy of the plains. The Cheyenne had been heading south from their spiritual center in the Black Hills under pressure from Lakotas invading the area from the east. Along with Arapaho allies, they in turn pushed toward the edges of Comanchería and, traversing the liminal bison hunting grounds between the Platte and the Arkansas river valleys, came into fierce contact with Comanches, Kiowas, and Plains Apaches who had little tolerance for the new intruders. That the Cheyenne and Arapaho could secure guns from two American merchants trading in their midst made the encounters all the more lethal. When, in the late 1830s, a smallpox epidemic added to the tolls that bloodshed was already exacting, it seemed time to reach some sort of accord.

The assembly that subsequently convened involved large numbers of participants and lasted two days. Much of the time was devoted to rounds of gift giving designed to appease those who had lost family and clan members in the fighting and to create a framework of friendship and trust. The Cheyenne and Arapaho brought blankets, guns, ammunition, beads, calico, and brass kettles to exchange; the Comanche and Kiowa brought hundreds of horses and mules. So important and memorable was the gifting that to the present day the Cheyenne refer to the meeting site as Giving Presents to One Another Across the River. But there were significant agreements as well: to joint occupancy of much of the Arkansas River valley, to commercial partnerships that included American traders, and to a political coalition that indirectly involved the Lakota, who had already made an alliance with the Cheyenne. What would be called the Great Peace of 1840 ushered in years of cooperation between these peoples of the plains.

Yet the establishment of a secure peace among Plains Indians also turned warlike eyes, especially those of the Comanche, southward. In the late eighteenth century, the Comanche had made peace with the Spanish and organized trade and diplomacy around San Antonio in the east and Santa Fe in the west. They also formed something of a politico-military alliance against Apaches. Then came the Mexican Revolution and, eventually, Mexican independence, and these relations began to be compromised, in part because of the limited control that the Mexican state held over its peripheries and in part because a depleted Mexican treasury made customary gift-giving diplomacy nearly impossible. The several-decades peace commenced to unravel, and Comanches stepped up raiding in Coahuila y Tejas and other northern Mexican provinces. But continued hostilities with Native bands to the north limited their scope and intensity.

The Texas rebellion and the emergence of the Texas Republic further complicated the political picture. The Comanche engaged in a mix of military and diplomatic encounters, depending on the regime (Houston looked to diplomacy, Lamar to Indian extermination), to defend their hunting grounds, while the Mexicans effectively lost a territorial platform on which they might reconstruct a peace and a buffer against attack. The conclusion of the Great Peace of 1840 thereby freed up the energies of those who had been involved in struggles with the Cheyenne and Arapaho and directed them not to the heavily defended settlements of eastern Texas (which could easily retaliate by driving into Comanchería) but rather to the lightly defended ranches and haciendas below the Rio Grande. Comanche raiding parties began to push deeper and deeper into Mexico—into Chihuahua, Coahuila, Nuevo León, and ultimately as far south as San Luis Potosí—rounding up horses and mules by the thousands and simultaneously laying waste to Mexican settlements in what became bitter fighting. Mounting casualties on both sides only exacerbated the ferocity of the encounters as Comanches made victims of hundreds of herders, field hands, women, and children, of the laborers and their families as well as the proprietors, many of whom were brutalized beyond recognition. Not surprisingly, the surviving inhabitants increasingly fled the pillaged and bloodied countryside for the relative safety of nearby towns. The question of Texas annexation, it appears, only intensified Comanche operations, while farther to the west Apaches, Navajos, and Utes took their own opportunities to strike at the Mexicans.

From the perspective of Mexico City, however, Indian raiding in the north was only one of a number of serious political problems in the early to mid-1840s. Ever since independence, the Mexican state had been rent by turmoil and instability. No social group or political faction appeared able to impose its authority, and both the presidency and the governing framework changed with great frequency by means of coups rather than elections. Although the main political division set federalists (who tended toward liberalism) against centralists (who tended toward conservatism, if not monarchism), the infighting often defied clear dichotomies and was inevitably influenced by two powerful institutions that harked back to the colonial regime: the army and the Catholic Church. At the very moment that the Plains peoples made their Great Peace, Mexico City witnessed the most violent coup attempt in its history, with cannon and rifle fire roaring through the streets for nearly two weeks. The only thing that could be predicted with certainty was the presence, in some political guise, of Antonio López de Santa Anna. Before he was through, he would occupy the office of president on eleven separate occasions.

The instability that racked Mexico City and turned the capital into a battle-ground of political factions had its analogue in social and political unrest that exploded in peripheral areas—Alta California, Sonora, Zacatecas, Yucatán, Puebla, Oaxaca—and worsened the menace of Texas annexation. Some of the unrest, as in Texas, reflected the interest of local elites in greater independence and control over land, labor, and other resources. But equally threatening was growing discontent among the indigenous peasantry. The problems did not revolve principally around exploited and dependent estate laborers, who clearly had grievances of their own. They revolved around peasant villagers who saw their communal holdings come under attack, chiefly from liberally minded elites who wished to turn common into private property that could be bought and sold on the market. This attack was part of a process that had been unfold-ing in Europe and the Americas for two centuries—it was already driving the dispossession of Native Americans in the United States—and while clothed in the language of progress, productivity, civilization, and comparative economic advantage, it promised to destroy the base of customary subsistence and an entire way of life. In the Sierra Gorda, on the Isthmus of Tehuantepec, and, most famously, on the Yucatán Peninsula, the rumblings of what would become explosive insurrections were already being felt.

To be sure, the Mexican state boasted an army formidable by the standards of the Americas. It was considerably larger than the U.S. Army and had been battle-tested on numerous occasions, not only in rebellious Tejas, but also in fending off invasions of Spanish and French troops. Its officer corps showed great élan (not to mention pretentiousness), and the cavalry impressed with its horsemanship and bearing. But in general, the army was poorly equipped and ill-disciplined. Infantry recruits included peasants, vagrants, and prisoners who had been conscripted or coerced into service by other means. They were armed with outmoded weaponry, badly clothed and fed, and, consequently, prone to desertion. The artillery was particularly antiquated and ineffective. Most problematic, the army lacked the numbers and financial resources to meet the challenges that a large, decentralized, insurgent, and territorially threat-ened social order posed. Settlements to the north begged for more protection against Indian raiding, though to little avail; the army remained concentrated in central Mexico. Not surprisingly, provincial governors and bosses looked to establish their own militias and rural police forces.

American policy makers and, through the press, sections of the American public became increasingly aware both of the political dilemmas of the Mexican state and of the punishing raids inflicted by Plains Indians—and with powerful effect. Together, they created a portrait of Mexico and Mexicans etched in weakness, backwardness, cowardice, ignorance, ineptitude, and sloth. Mexicans, in this mind's eye, seemed unable to create free political institutions, protect their territories and families from barbarous attack, build a dynamic economy, dispel superstitions, or educate themselves and their children to the tasks of the new nineteenth-century world. Their lands were arid, sparsely populated, and poorly utilized. Their treasury was depleted by corruption. Their leaders were tyrants who fought among themselves and lorded over submissive followers. The influence of the Catholic Church was blamed, to say nothing of the consequences of race mixing or, as some would have it, "mongrelization." By contrast, "Anglo-Saxons" marched to democracy's beat. They knew how to seize the main chance. They carried the advantages and dispositions of civilization. They could make the deserts bloom. When these very different forces collided, as they did in Texas during the 1830s—a conflict often depicted in racialized terms—who could doubt which side would emerge triumphant?

The American president, James K. Polk, was far less interested in Mexico's near north, where Indians were wreaking havoc, than he was in the far northwest, California primarily, and Nuevo México secondarily. But it is likely that the military successes of the Indians, and the Mexicans' inability to bring them to heel, encouraged him to believe that he could get what he wanted without enormous cost or effort. In the late spring of 1845, he first ordered four thousand American troops under the command of General Zachary Taylor into Texas and down to the Nueces River, with orders to regard any Mexican crossing of the Rio Grande as an act of war. In the fall, he sent the Pacific Squadron to the California coast with instructions to seize San Francisco (Yerba Buena as it was initially known) in the event of armed conflict with Mexico, advising the U.S. consul in Monterey in the meantime to do what he could to encourage disaffected Californians to rebel against Mexican authorities. Finally, he sent an emissary, the Louisiana congressman John Slidell, to Mexico City—which had already severed diplomatic relations with the United States over the annexation of Texas—to explore a negotiated settlement: $20 million for California; $5 million for Nuevo México; and the acceptance of the Rio Grande as the southern and western boundary of Texas in exchange for the assumption of debts owed Americans by the cash-strapped Mexican government.

Polk might have imagined that he was making the Mexicans an offer they could not refuse, but given the tense crosscurrents of Mexican politics it was in fact an offer they could not accept. The sitting president, José Joaquín de Herrera, eager to avoid war, seemed interested in easing the country's financial problems; reports circulated that he might be ready to consider the sale of California and Nuevo México. But even the hint of his willingness to entertain such an option—most conspicuously by allowing Slidell into the country—brought a firestorm of criticism down on him. In short order, he fell victim to a coup orchestrated by one of his generals, the archconservative Mariano Paredes y Arrillaga, who nonetheless had the support of other political factions. The movement of Zachary Taylor's forces across the Nueces to the Rio Grande in early 1846 and a March ultimatum delivered by Slidell closed the last doors to a peaceful settlement. Polk had decided on war, and in the second week of May, after a skirmish on the Rio Grande that resulted in sixteen American casualties, he got it.

The Blood of Continental Destiny

America's war against Mexico, declared by Congress, in the end, with limited opposition in May 1846, has generally been regarded as a relatively minor military affair—more of a showcase for actors who would later play much larger historical roles—that brought major geopolitical rewards. The fighting was over in less than eighteen months, American armed forces occupied Mexico City, and when the smoke cleared, the United States walked away with most of the Mexican northwest, including the prize of California, as well as with a mutually recognized boundary along the Rio Grande in the south of Texas.

But in truth, the U.S.-Mexican War would prove to be one of the costliest, most divisive, and most politically vexing episodes in American history. It involved the full-scale invasion of a foreign country for offensive purposes. It required a major mobilization of military manpower and financial resources. It inflicted depredations and atrocities on the Mexican people, motivated in large measure by bitter racism and anti-Catholicism among American troops. It resulted in an inordinately high rate of American casualties. It raised the prospect of the conquest and acquisition of territory and subject populations that might occupy a distinctive status in relation to the rest of the United States. It reopened increasingly acrimonious questions about the future of slavery and slaveholders in the country. It emboldened some of the most aggressive political and cultural tendencies in American life. And it would leave a legacy of tension, confusion, violence, and militarism around a newly carved U.S.-Mexican "border." It posed, that is, in the most fundamental ways, the problems of continental empire.

President Polk's war message to Congress said nothing about territorial acquisition; it rather made Mexico the provocateur, having "invaded our territory and shed American blood on American soil," and asked Congress "to recognize the existence of war . . . notwithstanding all our efforts to avoid it . . . and to place at the disposition of the Executive the means of prosecuting the war with vigor." But when Secretary of State Buchanan urged Polk to explicitly renounce territorial objectives as a motivation for warfare (chiefly for European consumption), the president found himself "much astonished": "I told him that though we had not gone to war for conquest, yet it was clear that in making peace we would if practicable obtain California and such other portion of the Mexican territory as would be sufficient to indemnify our claimants on Mexico, and to defray the expenses of the war which that power by her long continued wrongs and injuries had forced us to wage."

There was indeed no question that California would be taken at the first opportunity, and the assault would come from several directions. As early as the fall of 1845, Polk and Buchanan warned Consul Thomas Larkin in Monterey (the message arrived the following April) of possible attempts by "foreign governments" to "acquire a control" over California and, aware of American settlers in the Sonoma and Napa valleys—a few hundred merchants, ranchers, trappers, squatters, and distillers—who had grievances against Mexican authorities, urged that he encourage them to follow the example of rebels in Texas. They would, Polk and Buchanan assured him, "be received as brethren." The catalyst, however, appears to have been the arrival—by way of St. Louis, the Arkansas River, and the Great Basin—of the well-connected John C. Frémont (son-in-law of Thomas Hart Benton), who was officially heading a survey expedition of the army engineering corps. It is not entirely clear why Frémont was in California (he had been there on a previous expedition), what his orders were, or what role he played in the subsequent unrest. What is clear is that the rebellious Americans rallied around him and his party and in June 1846 seized the northernmost Mexican outpost in Sonoma. In a separatist action, they proclaimed the Bear Flag Republic. Within days, the rebels looked to Frémont as their leader and prepared to seek annexation by the United States.

Formal annexation would be unnecessary. Almost simultaneously, the Pacific Squadron, this time under the command of the aging commodore John D. Sloat, staged a second American coming at Monterey. Ordered to seize California's ports upon learning of "actual hostilities" between the United States and Mexico, he sailed into Monterey Bay in early July. Like Thomas ap Catesby Jones before him, Sloat and his men marched ashore and raised the American flag without a shot being fired; unlike Jones, he insisted that the flag was there to stay. "Henceforth," Sloat announced without official authorization, "California will be a portion of the United States." Another Pacific Squadron vessel quickly took Yerba Buena and dispatched soldiers to Sonoma, where Sloat's decree was read, the Bear Flag lowered, and the American flag raised. At Sutter's Fort in the Sacramento valley, where he then was, Frémont did the same.

For the next few weeks, it appeared that the Americans would make short and easy work of extending their occupation over the whole of Alta California. In mid-July, Richard Stockton replaced Sloat as squadron commander and, along with Frémont, who incorporated the Bear Flag rebels into the U.S. Army as the California Battalion, quickly headed south. By the middle of August, in the face of minimal resistance, they successfully took San Diego, Santa Barbara, and Los Angeles (which had replaced Monterey as the provincial capital). Most of the Mexican forces retreated into Sonora and Baja California. Both Stockton and Frémont felt confident enough in the outcome of their southern operations to leave a small occupying contingent behind and return to the north.

Additional American military power was on its way from the east. Around the time that the Bear Flaggers rose in Sonoma, the Army of the West, under the command of General Stephen Watts Kearny, left Fort Leavenworth and began an eight-hundred-mile trek toward Santa Fe, intending to bring Nuevo México—Polk's second major territorial objective—under American control. With nearly three thousand troops (most of whom were volunteers) and wagonloads of supplies, Kearny's army made for an imposing sight: so much so that they moved through sections of Comanchería undisturbed and impelled the governor of Nuevo México to disband his militia and flee to Chihuahua without offering a fight. Like Sloat, Kearny raised the flag, proclaimed American occupation, organized a civil government, and declared that Nuevo México would henceforth be known as New Mexico, a territory of the United States. He then set out for California with a force of three hundred, but when he learned that Stockton and Frémont had already occupied the major coastal towns and presidios, he sent more than half of the men back to Santa Fe.

Yet by the time that Kearny and his small battalion arrived in the vicinity of San Diego in early December 1846, after a long and exhausting march, the tables of conquest had been turned, and fighting had commenced anew. Reorganizing on ranchos outside the coastal towns, Californios mobilized popular discontent against the American occupation and the hardfisted policies of local commanders. Within weeks, they retook San Diego, Santa Barbara, Santa Inés, and San Luis Obispo and, in Los Angeles, forced Lieutenant Archibald Gillespie, left in charge there, to sign "articles of capitulation" before sending him packing. When Stockton and Frémont learned of the Californio insurgency and headed south, another insurgency erupted to the north, harassing American troops between Monterey and San Francisco, along the Salinas valley. It would take another several months of concerted efforts—including a costly battle involving Kearny's men at San Pasqual, near San Diego—before the American conquest was secured. The Treaty of Cahuenga, signed in mid-January 1847, resulted in the Californios laying down their arms in return for rights, protection, and freedom of movement. But less than a week later, Pueblo Indians, in alliance with Mexicans, rose in Taos against the American occupation of Nuevo México. They killed and scalped the American-appointed governor and inspired other local conspiracies before Kearny's successor managed to crush them. Sixteen of the rebels who were captured were then tried for murder and treason (despite owing no allegiance to the United States) and hanged.

Popular resentments in Nuevo México appear to have been instigated in good part by the behavior of the volunteers in the American army. It would not be the last time they infuriated civilians. When President Polk sent General Zachary Taylor to the area of the Rio Grande, Taylor's troops were mostly regular enlisted men. Many were recruited on the East Coast, and roughly half were immigrants, chiefly Irish and, to a lesser extent, Germans. They had signed up for five years and, as was true in most military institutions of the time, were subject both to isolation from the mainstream of society and to harsh discipline. Officers could deploy an assortment of corporal and humiliating punishments (flogging was still legal) against those who violated orders, while deserters, if caught, were subject to imprisonment. Under Taylor's command, they pushed General Mariano Arista's Mexican troops back across the Rio Grande and then occupied the town of Matamoros, where volunteers (enlisted for one year), many of whom came from the states of the West and the South with little training, caught up with them. Most arrived by way of New Orleans—perhaps the major staging ground of the war—and often after creating serious commotions there. Over the course of the war, the volunteers would outnumber the regulars by about two to one.

Nonetheless, the regulars did much of the hard fighting, and in the northeast of Mexico they were aided in their objectives by the raiding of Comanches and Apaches. Either potential Mexican manpower had already been eviscerated by the years of Indian attacks, or communities were reluctant to send their men into the Mexican army and leave the home front even more exposed. When, in the fall of 1846, the central government requisitioned the states of Chihuahua, Zacatecas, and Durango for troops to support Santa Anna's forces in San Luis Potosí (expecting to fight Taylor), none were sent. "After we have clamored in vain for many years for help in freeing ourselves from the barbarians who have destroyed the wealth of the state," a Durango newspaper explained, "we have not fielded armies that have been impossible to raise because . . . our brothers have been assassinated by the barbarians, or else fled far away from their fury." At all events, horses and mules that could equip the cavalry and assist the transportation of supplies had been sorely depleted by the raids, and enclaves of Mexican villagers in the northeast had ceased to cooperate with one another.

How much more formidable Mexican military resistance might have been were it not for the Indian warfare is difficult to determine. Without question, Taylor and his men would have met a larger and better supported army and would have had more trouble pacifying the countryside and keeping guerrilla activity in check. As it was, Mexican civilians had reason to look upon the American invaders as possible allies against the Comanche and Apache and might have questioned their own political allegiances were it not for the outrages inflicted by U.S. Army volunteers who were left to garrison the conquered territory. "Our militia & volunteers, if a tenth of what is said be true, have committed atrocities—horrors—in Mexico, sufficient to make Heaven weep, & every American, of Christian morals blush for his country," General Winfield Scott recorded in early 1847. "Murder, robbery, & rape on mothers and daughters, in the presence of the tied up males of the families, have been common all along the Rio Grande." Illdisciplined and facing weak structures of authority (they could elect their own officers), often young and down on their luck, they could run amok with little consequence. One corporal sneeringly described his regiment as "composed of rejected boys, men who were diseased and broken down, some lame and blind in one eye, others were sixty-year old boys" and as "rascally [and] lousy [a] set" as was ever "thrown among decent men." Catholic churches became special targets of their arson and plunder, so much so that the bitter hatreds such desecrations expressed sowed ethnic antagonisms within American ranks and enabled Mexicans to lure several hundred American deserters (most of them Catholic) to their side, composing what became known as the San Patricio Battalion. Believing it "perfectly certain that this war is a divine dispensation intended to purify and punish this misguided nation," one Ohio volunteer only "wish[ed] I had the power to strip their churches . . . and to put the greasy priests, monks, friars and other officials at work on the public highways."

The military occupations of northeastern and northwestern Mexico, together with the political proclamations issued by American occupiers in California and New Mexico, forced the issue of territorial conquest and acquisition that Polk had initially disclaimed and, as Polk might have expected, created a storm of controversy in American politics. The prospect of war with Mexico had stirred dissent from the first, chiefly in the ranks of the Whig Party and among some Barnburner Democrats who bridled at Polk's aggression and feared the political and constitutional challenges a war might bring. Most then held their noses and voted for Polk's war declaration, perhaps imagining that the territorial problem could be averted. The exception was a small group of antislavery Whigs from the Northeast and the Midwest—John Quincy Adams and Ohio's Joshua Giddings prominent among them—who saw the war as a bold move by the slave power and remained steadfast in opposition. But in August 1846, as American troops took charge in California and New Mexico, and as Taylor moved through Reynosa and Camargo on his way to Monterrey, Polk left no doubt about his intentions. He asked Congress for a $2 million appropriation to pay for any "extraordinary" costs incurred in the settlement of the war, which everyone knew to be some sort of territorial adjustment.

That was certainly how David Wilmot understood the appropriation request, and he proved to be an unlikely irritant. A recently elected Pennsylvania congressman from Polk's own party, Wilmot had supported Texas annexation as well as the war with Mexico. But he was also a Van Burenite and offered a rider to the appropriation bill making it "an express and fundamental condition" of any territorial acquisition from "the Republic of Mexico" that "neither slavery nor involuntary servitude shall ever exist in any part of said territory." The language came from the Northwest Ordinance, and Wilmot seemed to have the support of some other anti-slavery Democrats in what came to be called his "proviso." However, Wilmot was no abolitionist. His hope, rather, was to "preserve for free white labor a fair country, a rich inheritance, where the sons of toil, of my own race and own color, can live without the disgrace which association with Negro slavery brings upon free labor." Tellingly, he referred to his rider as the "White Man's Proviso," and it nearly succeeded, winning majority approval in the House of Representatives before dying (without coming to a vote) in the Senate.

Territorial conquest, therefore, was sure to reignite the question of slavery's future in a reconfigured (and greatly enlarged) United States. But there were other serious questions as well, the resolution of which demonstrated how deeply embedded racialist assumptions were—across the political spectrum—in the vision of continentalism and how problematic was the pursuit of empire. After all, what was to become of any of the territory the United States managed to purchase or take from Mexico? Would it assume a territorial status under the jurisdiction of the federal government and, like Louisiana, gradually be divided into states? Would it forever remain a territory or "possession" under direct federal rule? Or would it simply be occupied and unincorporated, run by federally appointed governors and other civil officials, as well as by sections of the military, something in the manner of British India? And what of the people living in the Mexican territories? Would they all have the opportunity to be treated as other Americans were, with the same rights and obligations? Would only certain groups have such an opportunity? Or would none at all, relegated instead to some type of subject status? California appeared to hold out the most appealing prospects for incorporation on the Louisiana model, lightly populated as it was with Mexican citizens, and American military officials seemed to be moving in such a direction from the start of the war. General Kearny had already pronounced New Mexico an American territory. But what of the Mexican northeast or of territories closer to the center? Should the United States seek to take charge of the entire Mexican Republic?

The prospect of massive territorial conquest developed over time. Polk's initial intention, after securing California, New Mexico, and the Rio Grande, was to use the northeastern theater chiefly as a venue to demonstrate American military superiority, demoralize the Mexicans, and force them to accept a peace on American terms. Yet despite suffering a series of defeats, most notably at Monterrey, Chihuahua, and Buena Vista (where Santa Anna had special opportunities to defeat Taylor), the Mexican government refused to negotiate. A new strategy was therefore necessary, one designed to move the military campaign toward Mexico City, far to the south, where a crushing blow would likely put an end to Mexican resistance. For that task—formulated in the fall of 1846—the U.S. Army determined to shift gears and launch an attack by way of the gulf port of Veracruz, effectively reenacting the conquest of the Spaniard Hernán Cortés in the sixteenth century (otherwise the troops would have had to march across hundreds of miles of deserts and mountains in the interior). To lead that campaign, Polk chose General Winfield Scott over Taylor.

Polk would have preferred almost anyone to either Scott or Taylor for the job. Both were Whigs (as was the case for much of the American officer corps) with political aspirations; neither had good working relations with the president. But after consulting with the cabinet and other advisers, who questioned Taylor's suitability, he reluctantly picked Scott. It proved to be a wise choice, at least from a military standpoint. Following a massive amphibious assault just south of Veracruz in early March 1847 (the largest undertaken by Americans before World War II), Scott's troops secured the town after several days of bombardment and then headed west toward Mexico City. The fighting was, at times, fierce, the terrain imposing, and guerrilla harassment—some sanctioned by the Mexican government, some relatively autonomous—effective enough to force Scott to cut loose from his lines of supply and live off the country. Still, despite the challenges, not to mention the departure of many volunteers whose terms of enlistment expired along the way, Scott pushed ahead and in early September entered the Mexican capital. The campaign was, in the judgment of the Duke of Wellington, who followed it closely, "unsurpassed in military annals" and secured Scott's place as one of the greatest of American soldiers.

But Scott's success also invigorated American imperial appetites. The occupation of Mexico City not only put the United States in a very powerful bargaining position; it simultaneously enhanced the opportunity for territorial conquests well beyond anything officially contemplated at the war's outset. Some, in what came to be called the All-Mexico movement, now demanded the entire country as a condition for peace, and a few went so far as to eye all of Central America as well. As might be expected, Democrats—South, West, and East—led the charge, including the editor of the *Brooklyn Eagle*, Walt Whitman, who thought that "fifty thousand fresh troops" would "make our authority respectable." A number of army officers, too, favored an extensive, and permanent, occupation. Yet advocates also came from surprising quarters. The abolitionist Gamaliel Bailey, who had begun to edit the *National Era*, wished to link empire and emancipation much as the British had done. His plan was to offer each of the Mexican states the chance, if it so chose, "to enter into the American Union, upon a footing of equality with the original States." That, he insisted, "would complete our continental boundaries, South, secure a basis of 4,000,000 of square miles for our empire, establish Freedom as the fundamental and unchangeable Law of the North American continent, and give Republicanism the perpetual ascendancy," making the United States "not . . . the robber of a sister Republic, but its greatest benefactor."

Bailey was not alone in imagining annexed Mexican territory as a hedge, "an impassable barrier," in the words of one Bostonian, against "the extension of slavery southward." Mexico, they reminded readers, had already abolished slavery and was not likely to restore it. How better to construct an empire of "free laboring men"? For many slaveholding expansionists, that was the rub. Georgia's *Augusta Chronicle and Sentinel* thought the All-Mexico movement reckless and dangerous, a "death-robed scheme": "Do you wish to be placed at the mercy of ten millions, hostile to you, as enemies and conquerors, in the first place, and as supporters of that institution in the next?" Other voices of the slaveholding interest, especially in the Mississippi Valley and the Southwest generally, often took a more discriminating position, favorably disposed to annexing California and Nuevo México as well as the northeastern tier of Mexican states, where settlement was sparse, but reluctant to push farther south, where the population was denser and the challenges of governance greater. It was not only potential resistance to slavery; it was also the very mix of the inhabitants themselves. South Carolina's John C. Calhoun, who had opposed the war to begin with, warned of the cultural and political mire that awaited annexationists. The United States, Calhoun declared on the floor of the Senate, had never "incorporated any but the Caucasian race. To incorporate Mexico would be the first departure of the kind, for more than half its population are pure Indian and by far the larger portion of the residue mixed blood. Ours is a government of white men."

Calhoun's views, in one form or another, were widely shared. Northern and southern Whigs, whatever their other differences, alike doubted that American institutions could be adapted to what had been Mexican territory or that what they saw as an uneducated, degraded, backward, and superstitious populace could be absorbed by American civil and political society. Worries about annexing a land overrun by Catholics and racial inferiors found expression even among Whigs of an antislavery disposition. But similar reservations on the part of Democrats proved especially telling. The *Democratic Review*, which had chimed the chorus of "manifest destiny," fretted that the "annexation of [Mexico] to the United States would be a calamity" despite the country's "great natural wealth," for it would add five million "ignorant and indolent half-civilized Indians" together with a million and a half "free negroes and mulattoes, the remnants of the British slave trade." "We do not want the people of Mexico, either as citizens or as subjects," Michigan's Lewis Cass told Congress. "All we want is a portion of territory, which they nominally hold, generally uninhabited, or, where inhabited at all, sparsely so, and with a population, which would soon recede, or identify itself with ours."

The All-Mexico movement might have had some supporters inside Mexico itself, among some liberals within the elite who thought that their political aspirations might be better advanced if the country became an American protectorate. It was an example of the bitter factionalism that roiled the Mexican state as American armies pressed in from several directions. Should they fight on and risk both the occupation of the whole country and the destruction of their army? Should they resort to guerrilla warfare and commit to a long process of wearing the Americans down? Should they invite European intervention either to reorganize the state (and perhaps establish a monarchy) or to mediate a settlement? Or should they look to negotiate a peace, recognizing that they would have to rearrange their borders in significant ways?

As the government fled Mexico City in September 1847 to regroup in Querétaro, about one hundred miles to the north, the initiative passed to the *moderado* faction that looked to a peace treaty. In part, it was the surrender of the capital and the resignation of Santa Anna, who had once again come to occupy the presidency, that impelled them in such a direction. But even more consequential were severe rumblings from below. For as the Mexican army turned its attention to the invading Americans, room for popular unrest opened accordingly. The Maya rebellion in the Yucatán had turned into what the governor of the state called a "savage and exterminating war," striking such terror into the local elite—with separatist tendencies of its own—that they asked the United States to intervene (the request was declined). In Puebla, San Luis Potosí, and the Huasteca region of Veracruz, peasant unrest continued to brew, and in Tamaulipas haciendas were burned to the ground and local leaders killed. Whatever else might divide them, liberals and conservatives could unite in their fear of such ongoing social turmoil. By the end of 1847, with a new moderate president selected, they decided to sue for peace.

Military and political options were increasingly narrowing in the United States as well. However enticing further conquests might have been to some of the expansionists, they would require more troops and more money, and although Polk managed to get his appropriation ($3 million in the end) during the summer of 1846, prospects for additional financial support had effectively evaporated by the following summer. The congressional elections of 1846 had seen the Whigs gain narrow control of the House of Representatives and, perhaps more important, registered a shifting public temper on the war. Unease or outright opposition to annexing Mexican territory south of the Rio Grande—expressed in both parties—made more military campaigns pointless. And the occupation itself began to eat at the vitals of the American presence. In his annual message to Congress in December 1847, Polk acknowledged that "the Mexican people generally became hostile to the United States and availed themselves of every opportunity to commit savage excesses on our troops," taking up arms and "engaging in guerilla warfare." Along the corridor between Veracruz and Mexico City, as well as in the north, U.S. commanders had to assign a substantial number of soldiers to fend off guerrillas and other Mexican partisans, and the results were discouraging. More and more of them became concerned about a prolonged occupation and instead turned their hopes to the path of negotiation.

Polk recognized that his maneuvering room was rapidly diminishing. Indeed, the previous spring he dispatched the special envoy Nicholas Trist to join Scott and seek to conclude a treaty of peace. The president insisted upon the cession of Alta California and Nuevo México and the establishment of the Rio Grande as the southwestern Texas border; he also hoped to acquire Baja California and transit rights across the Gulf of Tehuantepec in the south: all for $15 million to $20 million and the assumption of private American claims against Mexico. Trist initially made little progress, and when Mexico City fell, Polk became greedier and more exasperated with Trist, who had developed closer relations with Scott (still a Polk nemesis). But with the *moderados* coming to the fore, Trist saw his opening, ignored a recall order from Washington, and commenced negotiations. In early February 1848, a treaty was signed in the Villa de Guadalupe Hidalgo and then transmitted to Polk, who was furious with Trist but, given the political crosscurrents of the moment, had few cards left to play. He quickly discussed the treaty with his cabinet and sent it to the Senate for ratification.

The Treaty of Guadalupe Hidalgo (as it has come to be known) gave Polk most of what he wanted and all of what he had demanded. The Mexican government ceded Alta California, including the bay of San Diego, Nuevo México (north of the Gila River), and the disputed strip of land between the Nueces and the Rio Grande rivers in Texas to the United States. The American government agreed to pay Mexico $15 million, assume the claims of American citizens, and (in Article XI), as a measure of the damage inflicted on northeastern Mexico by the "savage tribes," accept responsibility for "forcibly restrain[ing]" Indian "incursions" from what was now American territory and for "punish[ing]" what "cannot be prevented." The United States also pledged to outlaw the purchase of Indian captives of Mexican or foreign ancestry by any of its inhabitants and to "rescue" such captives (or any other "stolen property") "within its territory" and "return them to their country, or deliver them to a representative of the Mexican government": ironically, a strike against forms of Indian slavery, and something of the inverse of the Fugitive Slave Law that prevailed in the United States. None of the Native peoples affected were parties to the agreement.

More vexing was the fate of the roughly 100,000 Mexicans (including those Indians regarded by Mexico as "citizens") resident in the newly annexed territories. The treaty allowed them to stay or leave but required them to choose (within a year of its ratification) whether "to retain the title and rights of Mexican citizens, or acquire those of citizens of the United States." At all events, they would be "maintained and protected in the free enjoyment of their liberty and property, and secured in the free exercise of their religion." Still, the question of just when those who disavowed Mexican citizenship would be "admitted . . . to the enjoyment of all the rights of citizens of the United States according to the principles of the Constitution" was left to be determined by Congress in "proper time." Which is to say that, however encouraging the language, Mexicans who remained in what was now the United States necessarily occupied a murky and potentially precarious status as the American government effectively turned its new southwestern borderlands into a zone where many of the occupants could be seen as fugitives, interlopers, and trespassers with unstable political loyalties.

The war, therefore, suggested both the rewards and the costs of America's imperial ambitions. With the ratifications of the Treaty of Guadalupe Hidalgo, the territory of the United States now spanned the North American continent, and the country achieved, as most of its leaders had long sought, a strong and substantial position on the Pacific coast, replete with fine harbors, looking out over the burgeoning trade of eastern and southern Asia. Texas, with its vast prospective cotton fields, was now securely placed within the American union with dimensions that had been demanded. And the lower Mississippi Valley, with New Orleans as its headquarters, was emerging as the epicenter of an expanding empire, eyeing other potential conquests to the south.

Yet the price of empire was also plain for all to reckon. Most Americans could unite over the appeals of an imagined empire, in economic, political, and cultural terms, but the process of empire making proved to be deeply divisive and contradictory. Moving hastily over such enormous space challenged the developmental sensibilities of those who hoped for a more tightly knit political economy. Waging offensive war for territorial ends offended the diplomatic sensibilities of those who thought that the United States represented an alternative to the warmongering that engulfed Europe. Rekindling the issue of slavery's expansion and slaveholders' power outraged the moral and political sensibilities of those who insisted that "empire" be equated with "liberty." And incorporating new populations with complex ancestries confounded the racial and constitutional sensibilities of those devoted to the project of building a "white man's republic." The New England Unitarian and transcendentalist Theodore Parker, who thought the U.S.-Mexican War "mean and wicked," nonetheless believed that the "whole continent" might instead be possessed "fairly": "by the steady advance of a superior race, with superior ideas and a better civilization; by commerce, trade, arts; by being better than Mexico, wiser, humaner, more free and manly." Small comfort indeed for the objects of such beneficence.

But there were human costs, too, that over time have come to be overlooked. American soldiers not only engaged in plunder, depredation, and murder on foreign soil and inflicted very heavy losses on both Mexican soldiers and civilians. They also suffered casualties in unexpectedly high numbers themselves. More than 10 percent of those who served in the U.S. Army—as regulars or volunteers—died (overwhelmingly from disease) in less than two years, and more than 20 percent were either killed, wounded, or otherwise incapacitated. It was, that is—given the short time span of operations—possibly America's deadliest war and a sobering harbinger of what might await later forms of imperial adventurism.

Gold, Globalism, and Ominous Portents

Timing, in affairs small and large, is often everything, and in the American history of California timing could not have been more consequential than it was in the early weeks of 1848. For as Nicholas Trist, in Mexico City, was bringing negotiations that would eventuate in the Treaty of Guadalupe Hidalgo—and California's formal annexation—to a wearying conclusion, an event of immense significance occurred in the foothills of the Sierra Nevada, not too far from the confluence of the American and the Sacramento rivers. There, in late January, an employee of Johann Sutter, a Swiss emigrant turned Mexican citizen who had been granted a very large tract of land in the Sacramento valley and was bent on creating an agro-commercial empire of his own, found, while constructing a sawmill for Sutter, what proved to be gold.

Sutter desperately tried to keep the news from spreading, but to little effect. By March, word of the gold strike reached San Francisco—at first to a skeptical reception—and then, once confirmed, began to move around the vast Pacific basin. Owing to the developing ocean traffic of the day, the news traveled down the west coast of Mexico (though not quite fast enough to disrupt the signing and ratification of the treaty) and South America, reaching as far south as Peru and Chile within a few months, and across to Hawai'i, Australia, and China. For months, in fact, the gold discovery in California remained an effectively Pacific event because, by the customary travel routes (around Cape Horn), the American East Coast was more than twice as far from San Francisco (fifteen to sixteen thousand nautical miles) as Sydney or Canton, nearly three times as far as Valparaiso, four times as far as Callao, and about eight times as far as Acapulco and Honolulu. Before the year 1848 was out, reports of California gold were circulating around the Atlantic, and President Polk, after dismissing them in September, could tell Congress in December that the "accounts of the abundance of gold in that territory are of such an extraordinary character as would scarcely command belief were they not corroborated by the authentic reports of officers in the public service who have visited the mineral area."

News of the gold discovery not only stimulated the imaginations of people across the globe; it also inspired migrations of such range and rapidity as to reduce the term "rush" to something of an understatement. The first to arrive in numbers came, as might be expected, from nearby San Francisco, where, according to observers, nearly the entire male population (and the population was already overwhelmingly male) had packed up and headed east to the foothills by the end of May 1848. They were soon joined by emigrants from Oregon to the north, the Great Basin to the east, and the Mexican state of Sonora to the south. Then came Peruvians and Chileans, Hawai'ians and Tahitians, Australians and Chinese. A bit later came Americans from the Northeast, the Midwest, and the Southwest, English and Irish, Germans and French. Before it subsided, the rush may well have been the most culturally kaleidoscopic event in the history of the United States up to that time, and given the brief duration it might never be surpassed.

Patterns of gold rush migration revealed both the networks of transportation and communication that had been unfolding in the Pacific and Atlantic worlds and the reach of a globalizing economy. Prospective emigrants either had experience with mining (as was true in Sonora, the American Northeast and Midwest, and parts of Europe) or, far more likely, found themselves in a vortex of rapid economic transformations in their home communities that they wished to escape or more fully embrace (central Chile, much of the United States, and the Pearl River delta of southern China). Some signed on or were coerced into working for padrones and entrepreneurs (Chile, Sonora, and Australia); most imagined mining independently, although they often pooled resources or organized companies since the combined costs of transportation and getting started were generally quite high. But whatever their specific origins or social circumstances, the gold rush emigrants swelled the population of non-Native peoples in California, as well as the number of miners, by roughly twenty-fold within five years. In each case, they were almost exclusively males.

Early on, the gold was close to the surface, in deposits called placers, and could be extracted by methods that were labor rather than capital intensive: requiring little more than picks, shovels, buckets, pans, rockers, and sluices—not to mention backbreaking work. Thus, placer mining was conducive to individual and small-group undertakings, often supplemented by the hiring of local Indians (who knew the area well and might have done some mining already). Although slaveholders and labor contractors with larger operations looked for advantages, they could encounter stiff resistance. Especially in the American camps, the miners quickly moved to entrench the position of petty producers and proprietors, establishing districts and attempting to limit both the number and the size of individual claims. In some instances, as on the left bank of the Yuba River, they determined "that no slave or negro should own claims or even work in the mines" and took to enforcing the rules as they saw fit, running out violators and hanging or mutilating those who ignored their warnings. Only when the placer deposits began to be exhausted and the tapping of new veins of gold demanded heavy equipment did the social balances tip away from small mining partnerships and toward industrial forms of organization and finance.

The gold rush did indeed erupt in a liminal political world in which Mexican authority, already very limited, was unraveling and American authority was hardly stronger than a thread. Much of what passed for legal practice was therefore, as with the Yuba miners, created on the ground, and given the stakes involved, the process of establishing, working, and defending claims proved to be an intense scramble, often played out among competing ethnic groups. But the conquest and annexation of California by the United States did leave the American miners—particularly the Anglo-American miners—with the upper hand. They used it both politically and militarily. They engaged in a series of paramilitary contests, known variously as the Chilean War and the French Revolution, to force competitors to abandon their claims and, in the words of one

Englishman who had emigrated from Australia and arrived at the diggings with a Chinese man and a Malaysian, "commenced acts of hostility and aggression on any placer inhabited by coloured people." They regarded the "foreign population" as "trespassers" who "have no right whatever to the soil" and appointed local officials to evict them. Before long, they used government institutions to tax "foreign miners" and control important water rights.

While Anglo-American miners were quick to establish the rudiments of local political authority and resort to the methods of rough justice to enforce their dictates, the complex issues and struggles unleashed by the gold rush in fact propelled California toward more formal organization. Ordinarily, this would have meant a territorial government under federal jurisdiction, but when, in the spring of 1849, the newly appointed military governor called for a convention to write either a territorial or a state constitution—to be determined by the delegates—the momentum had clearly swung in the direction of statehood. After all, the flood of migrants attracted by the gold strikes would leave California with far more than the requisite population to qualify (sixty thousand under the terms of the Northwest Ordinance), and a state government would enable members of the Anglo population, and a variety of Anglo entrepreneurial interests, to craft a framework of political and economic power useful to them. Not surprisingly, the only resistance came from the heavily outnumbered delegates representing southern California (generally Californios) who saw the handwriting on the wall and, in a rearguard effort, unsuccessfully proposed to divide California into a northern state and a southern territory.

Representation at the convention not only favored northern California; it also favored those from the states of the Northeast and the Midwest, who composed the largest bloc of delegates (fully ten of them from New York). There were, accordingly, copies of the state constitutions of New York and Iowa (successfully produced three years earlier) being passed around, from which much of the California document came to be constructed. But with a substantial contingent of delegates who had come from states where slavery remained legal, and who were usually slaveholders themselves, a bitter fight might have appeared imminent. It failed to occur. Reflecting the sensibilities of many of the placer miners, an Irish-born delegate from New York, William Shannon, moved that "neither slavery nor involuntary servitude, unless for the punishment of crimes, shall ever be tolerated in the State." Remarkably, the motion was seconded by William Gwin, a Mississippi slave owner, who nonetheless had great political ambitions (he eyed California's prospective Senate seat) and had taken the temperature of the gold diggings a bit earlier. "In our mines are to be found men of the highest intelligence and respectability performing daily labor," Gwin conceded, "and they do not wish to see slaves of some wealthy planter brought there and put in competition with their labor, side by side." The convention then unanimously approved the Shannon proposal on slavery.

More controversial was an effort, hatched by a delegate from Kentucky, to prohibit "the introduction of free negroes under indentures or otherwise." It was by no means a novel impulse. Most of the states admitted to the Union during the nineteenth century (and some admitted before), whether or not they permitted slavery, enacted a range of "black laws" that either restricted people of African descent from entering the state or demanded large bonds as the price of doing so. The idea was to exclude both members of what was regarded as an inferior race and members of the slaveholding class who could turn their slaves into indentured servants (as had happened in some parts of the East) and soon monopolize the state's resources. Two days of vigorous debate allowed support-ers of a "free negro" ban to warn of the many degradations (including the dump-ing of surplus slaves in California) that awaited white laborers and their communities, though to little avail. The move was defeated, less for high moral purpose than for fear that it might compromise the state's admission. The Cali-fornia Constitution thus proved inhospitable to slaveholders and slaves and was silent on the issue of free people of color (though it restricted the vote to white men, including Californios). Completed by the convention in mid-October 1849 and ratified by voters in mid-November, it went to a deeply divided U.S. Con-gress for the final stage of deliberation.

The issues that stirred Congress over the question of California statehood had reared their heads during the war with Mexico: What would become of the lands ceded to the United States by Mexico? What would become of the people living there? And, most troublesome, would slaveholders be able to migrate to those lands with their slaves? David Wilmot's "proviso" was an opening shot, and although it went down to defeat in 1846, the debate thereby provoked began to lay out the political lines of argument over the future of slavery in the expanding West. In the waning days of his presidency, James K. Polk hoped that territorial governments would be established and the slavery question decided either by the inhabitants of the territories or by the extension of the Missouri Compromise line (36°30′) to the Pacific. Stephen Douglas, a moderate member of Polk's Democratic Party, wanted to move more quickly and dodge the "pro-viso" matter entirely by organizing the entire Mexican cession as one state and admitting it to the Union. But that proposal, which won the support of Polk and some other moderate Democrats, also drew the ire of antislavery Whigs like Joshua Giddings, who insisted upon the "absolute, unconditional, and uncom-promising proviso," and pro-slavery Democrats (Calhounites as well as the aggressive slaveholding interests of the Deep South and the Mississippi Valley), who thought that Douglas's approach had the effect if not the name of the proviso itself. Congress seemed headed for deadlock.

The idea of incorporating most or all of the Mexican cession into one state attracted serious attention among the delegates at California's constitutional convention too. Although the Spanish missions and presidios had hugged the Pacific coast and most of the Californios were to be found there and in the adjacent valleys, Mexican California also included a vast area from the Sierras, across the Great Basin, and into the Rocky Mountains. If an American state of California encompassed most of this territory, some argued, not only would the controversy over the extension of slavery be settled, but the interests of California and the Pacific would be enormously enhanced: especially if, like Texas, California might eventually be subdivided into several states. "So far as I am concerned," William Gwin, one of the proponents of the plan, declared, "I should like to see six states, fronting on the Pacific in California."

It was, for many of the delegates—as it had been for Stephen Douglas—an appealing idea. The stumbling block was a rapidly growing population in the valley of the Great Salt Lake, within the imagined boundaries of a "large" California, who were members of the Church of Jesus Christ of Latter-Day Saints, better known as Mormons after one of their prophets. Mormon migrants began arriving there in the summer of 1847, with their leader, Brigham Young, in search of the security that only extreme social isolation could bring. Founded amid a wave of religious enthusiasm in western New York around 1830 by the Vermont-born Joseph Smith, the Church of Latter-Day Saints preached of the coming millennium and attracted displaced New Englanders from relatively humble backgrounds (they were chiefly small farmers and artisans) who seemed to be seeking both intense spirituality and patriarchal authority. Moving first to Ohio and then on to Missouri and the Illinois bank of the Mississippi River, the Mormons combined religious and communitarian impulses. Adherents of a proselytizing and prophetic faith, they made hundreds of converts; their settlement at what they called Nauvoo, Illinois, numbered more than ten thousand in the early 1840s, roughly the size of nearby St. Louis. But troubles kept following and propelling them on.

On the one hand, Mormons impressed their neighbors with their economic independence and ethic of hard work and thrift. They also gratified local Democrats, with whom they usually voted. Yet their missionary zeal, communal notions, the apparently despotic behavior of Smith, and rumors of sexual irregularities (they had yet to publicly endorse plural marriage but apparently practiced it) alarmed outsiders. In Missouri, when growing harassment led Mormon settlers to establish a paramilitary and fight back, the governor demanded that they be "exterminated or driven from the State." The problems continued in southern Illinois, where, in 1844, Smith and his brother were murdered by an angry mob. Small wonder that when Brigham Young, who succeeded Smith, came out of the Wasatch Mountains with his beleaguered followers and glimpsed the barren-looking and remote Great Salt Lake valley, "unpopulous" and likely to "be coveted by no other people," he decided that "this is the place."

By the spring of 1849, with about five thousand settlers and several colonies under way, the Mormons organized a provisional government called the State of Deseret, with enormous boundaries—stretching to the Pacific coast of southern California to the west, the Rocky Mountains to the east, New Mexico to the south, and Oregon to the north—and applied to Congress for statehood. Although only a few of their members headed to the goldfields, Deseret prospered by provisioning the swelling overland rush that crossed into the Great Basin. A good many of the California miners, and some of their delegates, had therefore made contact with the Mormons and seen "with their own eyes" the formidable and very distinctive communities being built around the Great Salt Lake. How the Mormons of Deseret could be incorporated into a new California state without considerable turmoil was entirely unclear, they surmised, and highly doubtful. As a consequence, the delegates lowered their imperial sights and accepted the Sierra Nevada as California's eastern border. It would not be the last time that the Mormons gave powerful shape to the organization and politics of the trans-Mississippi West.

The idea of admitting California very quickly as a state rather than a territory might have sparked serious conflict in Congress, but it had a surprising supporter in the White House. Zachary Taylor, who led the conquest of northeastern Mexico, though was passed over for the march on Mexico City, managed to parlay (as Polk had feared) his newfound fame into the Whig nomination for the presidency in 1848. He was not a likely Whig candidate. Virginia-born and a relative of James Madison, Taylor had spent his adulthood in the U.S. Army, where he saw action in the War of 1812, the Black Hawk War, and the Second Seminole War before the war against Mexico. He was briefly the father-in-law of Mississippi's Jefferson Davis (his daughter died three months into the marriage) and came to own a large plantation and many slaves in Louisiana. But rather than imagining a slaveholding empire to the west, he doubted that slavery could flourish in the Mexican cession and hoped that by expediting the admission of California (and soon New Mexico) as states, "harmony and tranquility" in the Union might be maintained. Avoiding the issues as much as possible during the presidential campaign enabled him to keep an increasingly unwieldy Whig coalition together and defeat the Democrat Lewis Cass by a million votes in the November election and take office in March (Martin Van Buren, the presidential nominee of the new Free-Soil Party, finished third with about ten percent of the vote). Then Taylor quickly sent a special agent to California to encourage "the formation of any government, republican in its character." By the time the agent arrived, the military governor had already called for a constitutional convention.

In his annual message to Congress that December, Taylor threw his support behind the pending California statehood initiative and convinced some members of the wisdom of his approach. But the pushback was greater still, and amid rancor and threats coming from dissatisfied factions in both parties, the following month saw a flurry of bills that spoke to a number of divisive issues: the Fugitive Slave Law and the rights of fugitive slaves; a boundary dispute between Texas and New Mexico; and the organization of the Mexican cession (including Deseret), especially with respect to slavery. With Taylor holding fast, his Whig rival Henry Clay of Kentucky stepped forward with an alternative package of proposals that eventually became an "omnibus" bill designed "to settle and adjust amicably all existing questions of controversy . . . arising out of the institution of slavery." Clay believed his proposals offered important things to all sides in the slavery dispute. They would admit California on the basis of its recently submitted constitution (which prohibited slavery) while organizing the remainder of the Mexican cession—including Deseret—as federal territories without "any restriction or condition on the subject of slavery," thereby embracing ideas of popular, or "squatter," sovereignty first articulated by Lewis Cass. They would also provide for the abolition of the slave trade (not slavery) in the District of Columbia while protecting the interstate slave trade from congressional oversight and demanding a more draconian fugitive slave law to counteract the "personal liberty laws" passed in some of the states. And they would adjust the southwestern boundary dispute in New Mexico's favor while assuming the outstanding debts of Texas.

Over the next six months of debate on Clay's proposals and then the omnibus bill, Americans not only heard the last orations of Clay, Daniel Webster, and John C. Calhoun; they also saw how the pursuit of continental empire threw the very survival of the United States into jeopardy. Indeed, they saw that continentalism, by demanding a "settlement" of slavery's future, confounded the very appeal of empire's loose embrace. Participants in the debate, however they interpreted the issues, imagined the vitals of proper society at stake. Free-Soilers (Whig and Democrat) warned of the dire consequences of allowing slavery to spread into the new territories, where, they insisted, it would retard "the growth and prosperity of communities," impair "enterprise," promote "aristocratic tendencies," undermine republican government, and degrade labor to the "worthless and miserable" condition evident among non-slaveholders in its midst. "A high state of civilization, slavery, and prosperity," one announced, "are utterly incompatible; they never did, and never will exist together," and the choice, they believed, was "whether this Government shall be administered in the spirit that gave it birth, or whether . . . this Government become an Aristocracy, based on slave property, and slave representation."

For their part, supporters of slavery's right to expand westward identified in it "a question of our very existence" and inverted the claims of their Free-Soil opponents. Should slavery be restricted to its present limits, they charged, "two races" would be thrown "into a fearful conflict—a conflict which admits of no compromise but death"—and "the Government, instead of being that of the whole Union, would have been converted into a mere machine for the advancement" of hostile interests. Rather than degrading white labor, slavery, they asserted, elevated it; rather than discouraging enterprise, slavery embodied it; rather than weakening a republic, slavery enabled it; rather than promoting social conflict, slavery diminished it. "If, by your legislation, you seek to drive us from the territories of California and New Mexico, purchased by the common blood and treasure of the whole people," the Georgia Whig Robert Toombs thundered, "I am for disunion." The invective and threats would have been worrisome enough even if the votes for the omnibus bill were there, as Clay had been betting. Compromise might have emerged again out of the cauldron of dispute. But, ominously, the votes for such a compromise were not there, and all efforts to reach one appeared doomed.

Then, in midsummer 1850, prospects for a resolution brightened. President Taylor, who wanted California and New Mexico admitted to the Union as states and had no interest in Clay's compromise measures (some feared he might veto the bill if it had managed to pass), died suddenly and was replaced by Vice President Millard Fillmore of New York, who was far more favorably disposed to what Clay was trying to do. Equally important, the Illinois Democrat Stephen Douglas took charge of the legislative process and moved it in a different direction. Recognizing that voting majorities for the compromise package could not be found, he nonetheless believed that if the package were broken into its component parts, majorities could be constructed, with shifting blocs, for each of them individually. With a mix of skill and strong-arming, this is what Douglas proceeded to do, and by the middle of September each piece of the package had been passed by the House and the Senate and signed by an eager Fillmore.

Crisis had been averted, and there was some reason to think that those who hailed the legislation as the "final settlement" of the slavery question might be right after all. Although the package of bills that Douglas saw through Congress hardly represented a "compromise" in any meaningful sense, it did provide a framework for managing the possible expansion of slavery in the newly acquired Mexican cession just as the Missouri Compromise (voted on in similar fashion) did for the Louisiana Territory. And no additional territory remained in dispute.

In the meantime, gold continued to flow out of the California mines in staggering quantities and provided enormous energy to the American and international market economies. Although estimates have varied widely, it appears that between 1850 and 1855 the mines yielded, on average, $131 million annually into what had become a specie-poor environment. The repercussions were to be felt from the farmlands of California to those of Chile, from the peasant villages of southern China to the sugar plantations of Hawai'i, and from the Italian countryside to the countinghouses of Britain. Renewed capital flows across the Atlantic reinvigorated railroad construction in the United States, especially in the Northeast and the Midwest, effecting a decisive shift in the dynamic of development from the coast to the interior and from the export to the domestic market: trimming the sails of the old mercantile elites of the seaboard cities and fortifying new rivals in manufactures, transportation, and trade. Most of all, California gold further whet the appetites of well-placed visionaries who had long been seeking to extend the tentacles of a now sprawling continental empire.

CHAPTER FIVE

Border Wars

CAUTION!!

COLORED PEOPLE

OF BOSTON, ONE & ALL,

You are hereby respectfully CAUTIONED and
advised, to avoid conversing with the

Watchmen and Police Officers
of Boston,

For since the recent ORDER OF THE MAYOR &
ALDERMEN, they are empowered to act as

KIDNAPPERS

AND

Slave Catchers,

And they have already been actually employed in
KIDNAPPING, CATCHING, AND KEEPING
SLAVES. Therefore, if you value your LIBERTY,
and the *Welfare of the Fugitives* among you, *Shun*
them in every possible manner, as so many *HOUNDS*
on the track of the most unfortunate of your race.

Keep a Sharp Look Out for
KIDNAPPERS, and have
TOP EYE open.

APRIL 24, 1851.

Broadside warning black Bostonians of danger after the passage
of the 1850 Fugitive Slave Act.

Stephen Douglas and the Imperial Interior

For all of the energy he expended in shepherding what has come to be known as the Compromise of 1850 through the treacherous terrain of Congress, Stephen Douglas also busied himself during those very months on a project that spoke even more directly to his vision of the American future. It was the Illinois Central Railroad, planned to link the Gulf of Mexico to the Great Lakes by way of Chicago. That Douglas had significant real estate investments in Chicago helps explain some of his enthusiasm for building the road, but the Illinois Central represented far more than a means to line his pockets. Douglas saw the railroad as an important piece in a developing landscape of progress and power, organized around the Mississippi Valley and Chicago in particular, that would secure an "ocean-bound republic" and soon spread southward into the Caribbean basin. Much like the compromise measures, the Illinois Central was designed to promote political and economic unity by forming part of a massive transportation network that would extend to the Pacific and perhaps to the Isthmus of Panama. "If gentlemen desired the perpetuation of this Union," the Georgia Democrat Howell Cobb said of Douglas's effort, "in all probability they could do nothing more effective than to tie the Northwest to the extreme South . . . by a railroad connecting several sections of the country." The bills passed one day apart that September.

Douglas was rapidly emerging at the forefront of a new cohort of political leaders who saw empire as the best way to preserve the American union and, to that end, sought to transform the Democratic Party. They were children of the nineteenth century, born and raised in the East, though often having relocated in the West. They shared the zeal of older Democrats for personal independence, local control, state rights, and geographical expansion but took a more ecumenical view of the market's promises and especially of the government's role in developing the economic infrastructure. Unlike many Whigs, they had little interest in manufacturing or industrialization; their main concern was agriculture and commerce, and they viewed cities chiefly as processing and distribution centers. They regarded America's political institutions as examples to the world and, at least for a time, sympathized with Europe's revolutions of 1848. They had their roots in Young America of the 1840s and would call their opponents Old Fogeys. And they imagined that their imperial ambitions could heal the increasingly serious rifts over the question of slavery. Douglas seemed to embody their personal arcs and political dispositions. He spent his youth in Vermont and upstate New York before moving on to Illinois. There he became a circuit judge, a Democratic Party organizer, a congressman, and then a U.S. senator, and he married into a prominent North Carolina family with land and

slaveholdings as far west as Mississippi. By the early 1850s, fresh off his legislative victories, Douglas set his sights on the presidency, and although his overea-
gerness might have cost him the party's nomination in 1852, he had become
the voice, conscience, and strategist of the youthful imperial faction.

Douglas's vision of an expanding agro-commercial empire centered on the
Mississippi Valley stimulated his interest in a railroad to the Pacific and in the
settlement of the trans-Mississippi West. Just as in the case of the Illinois Central, he believed the government had to play a major role both in facilitating
construction (by donating lands to the states) and in offering cheap land to cultivators (he introduced such a bill in 1849). What stood in the way was a large
section of unorganized territory, originally part of the Louisiana Purchase, that
lay immediately west of Missouri, Iowa, and the Minnesota Territory and north
of the Indian reserve. "How are we to develop, cherish, and protect our immense
interests and possessions on the Pacific, with a vast wilderness fifteen hundred
miles in breadth, filled with hostile savages, and cutting off all direct communication?" he asked. "No man can keep up with the spirit of the age who travels on
anything slower than the locomotive, and fails to receive intelligence by lightning. We must therefore have Rail Roads and Telegraphs from the Atlantic to
the Pacific." And as Douglas saw it, "the first steps toward the accomplishment
of each and all of those objects" involved "the extension of the laws of the United
States in the form of Territorial governments."

It was no accident that Douglas chaired the Senate's Committee on Territories. As early as 1844, while still in the House of Representatives, he had introduced a bill for the organization of the Nebraska Territory (adopting an Indian
name predicated on the eradication of Indian claims) and did so again four
years later, this time from the Senate. Others offered up similar bills, only to
follow Douglas down to defeat. By the time that the Iowa senator Augustus C.
Dodge's bill reached the Committee on Territories in December 1853, Douglas
had taken the measure of the problem: the proposed territory lay in that section
of the Louisiana Purchase from which the Missouri Compromise had excluded
slavery, and representatives from the slaveholding states refused to support its
organization. As one Missourian put it, "If we can't all go there on the same
string, with all our property of every kind, I say let the Indians have it forever.
They are better neighbors than the abolitionists, by a damn sight." Hoping to
push ahead as well as curry favor in the slave states, Douglas took the initiative
and reconfigured the Dodge bill by creating two territories (Kansas to the south
and Nebraska to the north) rather than one and explicitly repealing the Missouri Compromise's prohibition. Instead, in the language of the revised bill, "all
questions pertaining to Slavery in the territories and in the new States to be
formed are to be left to the decision of the people residing therein."

"Squatter" or "popular sovereignty," as the policy came to be called, was hardly Douglas's invention. Michigan's Lewis Cass had embraced and developed it during his failed run for the presidency in 1848 (largely in response to the challenges of the Wilmot Proviso and the Free-Soil Party), and the compromise measures of 1850 used it as a principle for organizing the new territories of New Mexico and Utah. Wishful thinking had convinced Douglas that the 1850 compromises had already rendered the Missouri slavery prohibition moot. But Douglas lent popular sovereignty a political significance it had not previously enjoyed and, more to the point, made it central to Democratic Party doctrine of the 1850s. In his view, popular sovereignty accorded with the principles of the Constitution, accommodated the democratic sensibilities of American settlers, and promised to remove the contentious question of slavery from the jurisdiction of the federal government and thus from the reach of federal power.

Douglas did not support the expansion of slavery. He doubted that slavery would flourish west of the Mississippi or that settlers there would choose to welcome it. He strongly objected to the accusation made in some quarters that his bill would "revive and re-establish slavery" where it had been excluded since 1820. But he did believe that the Constitution set down the principle of "nonintervention by Congress with slavery in the States and Territories"—whether in Nebraska or one day in Cuba—and his vision of the American union and empire allowed for (and was fortified by) a "diversity in the local institutions and laws." His concern was for the destiny of white men, and by his lights they were thriving under such a regime. Encompassing both slave and free states, Douglas would later proclaim, the United States grew in population, scale, wealth, and power "beyond any example on earth," becoming "the terror and admiration of the civilized world." The organization of Kansas and Nebraska was yet another step along the march to greatness and popular sovereignty, an example of the political ideals that marked their path.

Militant Arms of Slaveholding Empire

Stephen Douglas was an old pol as well as a political visionary, and he had every reason to be aware of the "democratic" practices that popular sovereignty would unleash, especially when the future of slavery was at stake. Roughhousing and paramilitarism were the norms for campaigns and elections even when the issues were far less contentious; together with ballots printed by the parties, revolvers, knives, bullwhips, cudgels, and alcohol were standard equipment at the polls in many parts of the country. It was an explosive mix under any circumstances.

The principal battleground, everyone knew, would be Kansas. Nebraska was too far to the north and a doubtful host for slavery and the agricultural regime in which it most thrived. Kansas, on the other hand, lay directly to the west of the slaveholding state of Missouri, and its eastern sections appeared promising for staple agriculture. But it would be a scramble of the most intense sort. At the time the Kansas-Nebraska Act was signed into law (May 1854), the new territory of Kansas had a mere eight hundred white settlers, and although it was not entirely clear how popular sovereignty would work—at what point could slavery be either legitimated or excluded—before too long a territorial legislature would have to be elected and a territorial delegate sent to Congress. Populating Kansas as quickly as possible and gaining the upper hand in the territorial electorate thereby became the central project for pro- and antislavery forces alike.

The months following the enabling legislation saw a veritable rush into the territory of Kansas that increased the population tenfold by the beginning of 1855. And pro-slavery sympathizers initially gained the edge. Organizational activity took place as far away as Alabama, and migrants came from there, Georgia, and South Carolina as well as from Kentucky and Tennessee. But easily the largest share crossed over from neighboring Missouri. Overwhelmingly farmers, they came with their families and, perhaps, a slave or two, and if the Salt Creek valley (near Fort Leavenworth) resolutions of the summer of 1854 are any indication, they intended to defend slavery and ward off abolitionists. But in many ways, the most consequential and dangerous contingent was mobilized in Missouri by Self-Defensives, vigilance clubs that aimed to protect slavery in Missouri by extending it westward. They sent migrants into Kansas— generally known as Border Ruffians—who had no intention of settling there; rather, they were male, armed, and planning to remain only long enough to force the territorial elections to the pro-slavery side.

By the time the election for a territorial legislature arrived in March 1855, the Border Ruffians loomed large among prospective voters. Despite a proclamation by the territorial governor, himself a Democrat, which limited the franchise to those who already resided in Kansas (an "actual dwelling") and expected to stay, hundreds of Missourians, often organized into companies, were ferried across the Missouri River in the days before the polling. While a territorial census showed 2,905 eligible voters in Kansas, over 6,000 votes were cast and a pro-slavery legislature selected. Soon after the governor convened the legislators that summer, they enacted a tough slave code for the territory. "It is the duty of the Pro-Slavery Party, the Union-loving men of Kansas territory, to know but one issue, Slavery," they resolved, "and that any party making

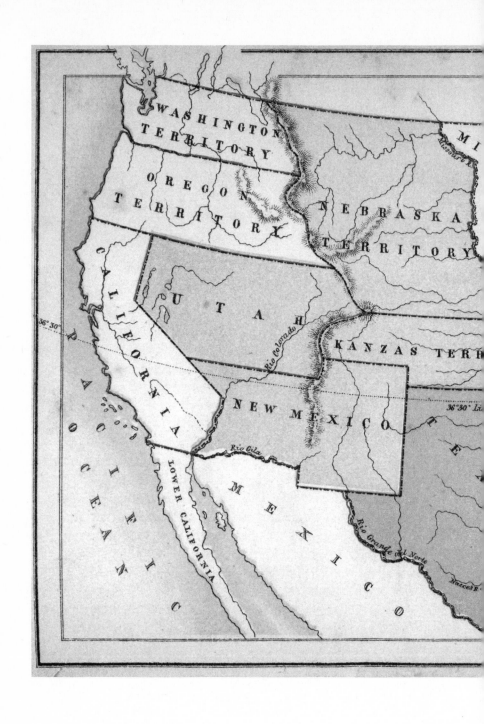

Map of the United States depicting the states where slavery was and was not legal, as well as the territories of the trans-Mississippi West being contested by pro- and anti-slavery forces, 1857.

or attempting to make any other, is, and should be held, as an ally of Abolition-ism and Disunionism."

The paramilitary efforts to claim the Kansas Territory for slavery may be seen as part of a larger project of slaveholding imperialism based chiefly in the lower Mississippi Valley. There the slave regime was most recently established, the master class young and aggressive, and the city of New Orleans long a hub of Caribbean trade, slave marketing, and American filibustering. Much of the support for Texas rebels during the mid-1830s and for U.S. military operations in Mexico during the mid-1840s moved through New Orleans, and although the U.S.-Mexican War ended amid growing public opposition, the 1850s wit-nessed a strong uptick in the beat of slavery expansionism. "I want Cuba, and I know that sooner or later we must have it," the Mississippi senator Albert Gal-latin Brown crowed at the time. "I want Tamaulipas, Potosi, and one or two other Mexican States; and I want them all for the same reason—for the plant-ing or spreading of slavery. And a foothold in Central America will powerfully aid us in acquiring those other States. Yes, I want these countries for the spread of slavery."

Cuba had been of interest to a variety of Americans from early in the nine-teenth century, and by the 1850s economic ties—investments in railroads, banking, and entrepreneurship as well as plantations—were substantial. They involved New England merchants and industrialists together with Deep South slaveholders and made the United States Cuba's most important trading partner next to Spain (and Cuba one of the most important trading partners of the United States). One Connecticut Democrat went so far as to describe Cuba as the "Gibraltar to the American Mediterranean" and predict that the northeastern states could well be the chief beneficiaries of its annexation.

A major boom, it was clear, had been energizing the island. Before the late eighteenth century, Cuba was less of a plantation society and more of a trans-shipment point for Spanish possessions elsewhere in the hemisphere. The majority of the population was free and of European descent, and sugar was raised in relatively limited quantities. Then the British occupation (and eco-nomic liberalization) of Havana during the Seven Years' War got the attention of the Spanish crown. When a slave rebellion turned revolution destroyed the master class in St. Domingue during the 1790s, Cuba began to intensify its plantation complex and import large numbers of African slaves. The island soon emerged as the world's premier sugar producer, with the port of Havana as one of the hemisphere's great trading and urban centers. Annexationists, who included Louisiana sugar planters hoping to absorb Cuban competitors, thus anticipated both a stronger American position in world staple markets and a greatly enhanced American presence in the Caribbean basin, with the dynamic of political economy tipping southward. "Were Cuba annexed," Louisiana's governor imagined during the 1850s, "Havanna [sic] would speedily become the great entrepot of southern commerce, and in a few years would be the rival of New York itself. It would be the nucleus around which would cluster the trade of all the Gulf and many of the South American ports; of all the North and South American Pacific ports, as it passes over the isthmus; and also of the Asiatic and East Indian ports." And Havana, he added, "would be a southern city, a slave-holding city."

Yet fear as well as prospect drove annexationist sentiment. Britain had long been pressuring the Spanish government to suppress the Cuban slave trade (a treaty to that effect was signed in 1817), and American slaveholders worried, just as they had in the case of Texas, that the British would try to effect full-scale emancipation in return for political concessions. The appointment of the abolitionist David Turnbull as British consul in Havana during the early 1840s appeared to be a sign of British intentions and stirred rumors of an emancipationist agreement between Britain and Spain. While the eventual status of an annexed Cuba in the American union was entirely unclear (a state, a territory, something else?), annexation would at least remove Cuba from Britain's orbit of influence and prevent another abolitionized plantation society from taking shape so near to the United States. Small wonder that President James K. Polk, slaveholder and expansionist, authorized his minister to Spain to offer up to $100 million for the island—an offer the Spanish saw no reason to accept.

The acquisition of Cuba remained a goal of Democratic administrations— Franklin Pierce and James Buchanan—throughout the 1850s. "The policy of my administration," New Hampshire's Pierce announced in his inaugural address in 1853, "will not be controlled by timid forebodings of evil from expansion . . . and our attitude as a nation and our position on the globe render the acquisition of certain possessions not within our jurisdiction eminently important for our protection." Pierce filled his cabinet and the diplomatic corps with recognized expansionists from various parts of the country (Jefferson Davis of Mississippi, Caleb Cushing of Massachusetts, James Buchanan of Pennsylvania, Pierre Soulé of Louisiana, and John L. O'Sullivan, August Belmont, and William Marcy of New York). Pierce also requested a $10 million congressional appropriation to pursue the purchase of Cuba from Spain (Congress declined), and then, with his secretary of state, arranged meetings of his European ministers in Ostend, Belgium, and Aix-la-Chapelle, Prussia, to develop a strategy. The result, in the fall of 1854, was the so-called Ostend Manifesto. Invoking the potential dangers of an "Africanized" Cuba and the law of "self-preservation," the manifesto insisted that "Cuba is as necessary to the North American republic as any of its present members" and effectively threatened war if Spain refused to yield the island up. Meant as a confidential dispatch, the manifesto became public and created a firestorm of controversy, undermining Pierce's ambitions. Even so, the annexation of Cuba would remain a centerpiece of Democratic policy, and James Buchanan—a signatory of the manifesto—won election to the presidency in 1856 calling for American "ascendancy in the Gulf."

Most of the activity related to the acquisition of Cuba was in fact generated not by formally elected and appointed officials but by privately operated militaries, known as filibusters (from the French and Spanish terms, *flibustier* and *filibustero*, for freebooter and pirate), who aimed to "liberate" the island by means of armed invasion. Filibustering had a history as long as the American union itself and always in complex relation with official power and territorial ambition. Reflecting both the decentralized nature of federal authority and the relative weakness of the standing army, filibusters had set their sights, variously, on Florida, Louisiana, Canada, Texas, and Mexico as well as Cuba and usually included men of political or military prominence. Some believed they were acting with the blessings of the federal leadership; most hoped to influence American policy by doing what the government was unable or unwilling to do itself. Congress became sufficiently concerned about the international consequences of filibustering that it issued a series of neutrality decrees and then passed the Neutrality Act of 1818. Based on the constitutional authorization to punish "offenses against the Law of Nations" (Article I, Section 8), the law prescribed imprisonment and fines for those within the jurisdiction of the United States who initiated or abetted "any military expedition or enterprise . . . against the territory or dominions of any foreign prince or state, or of any colony, district, or people, with whom the United States are at peace."

Despite the Neutrality Act, the years after the U.S.-Mexican War and the compromise measures of 1850 proved especially fruitful for filibustering expeditions. Interest in Cuba ran high, particularly among slaveholders who bridled at the admission of California to the Union as a non-slave state. Money to finance Cuba operations could be had among wealthy planters in the Deep South and their mercantile allies in New Orleans, while U.S.-Mexican War veterans who had problems returning to civilian life were ready to sign on as the shock troops. No year passed during the decade when an invasion of Cuba, or some other part of the Caribbean basin, was not being planned or carried out. The taking of Cuba was, as a Texan put it, "the paramount enterprise of the age," and John A. Quitman emerged as one of the leading organizers.

Born in New York state in 1798, Quitman ultimately relocated to Natchez, Mississippi, where he practiced law, married into a planting family, and became active in state politics. By the mid-1830s, he owned a large plantation and well over one hundred slaves (he would later have substantial holdings in Louisiana and Texas, too) and served a term as governor. A strong supporter of John C. Calhoun and the nullification movement, Quitman became an early advocate of disunion. But he also saw expansion to the south as an important means for defending slave society and state rights and did not want for militancy or aggressiveness. He participated in the Texas rebellion of the 1830s and later enlisted in the U.S. Army during the war against Mexico, where he commanded brigades under Zachary Taylor and Winfield Scott and served as military governor of occupied Mexico City.

During the late 1840s and very early 1850s, Quitman became involved in Cuban filibustering through the Cuban exile community based in New York City and New Orleans and their leader, the Venezuelan-born Narciso López, who looked to stage an invasion and attract sympathizers on the island. Quitman declined to join the military operation—as did Robert E. Lee and Jefferson Davis when approached—chiefly because he was serving another term as Mississippi's governor, but he did offer financial assistance and strategic advice: so much so that after a force of six hundred filibusters failed in their attack on the Cuban coastal town of Cárdenas, just east of Havana, in 1850 and had to return to the United States, he was indicted along with López by a federal grand jury in New Orleans for violating the Neutrality Act. As was often the case in the trials that followed, the jury refused to convict, and both López and Quitman were free to continue their activities. A year later, López led another expedition, this one of four hundred men, which was supposed to join up with a popular uprising in Puerto Príncipe (now Camagüey) in the east-central region. What they met up with were Spanish government troops who killed or executed many of them, including López.

No longer Mississippi's governor, Quitman now stepped in to fill the leadership vacuum left by López's demise. He attracted impressive levels of support. Together with the remnants of López's followers, Quitman recruited a host of prominent Texans, the governor of Alabama, several Mississippi planters and state legislators, Georgia's Alexander H. Stephens, a raft of Deep South newspapers, and the U.S. senators Judah P. Benjamin of Louisiana and Albert Gallatin Brown of Mississippi. He also worked with John L. O'Sullivan and the labor leader Mike Walsh in New York, both of whom sympathized with the Cuba project. Indeed, administration insiders suggested that Pierce might look the other way despite his public disapproval of filibustering. At all events, Benjamin and Brown in the Senate, along with Louisiana's other senator, John Slidell, sought to suspend the Neutrality Act, effectively giving Quitman the green light.

Although some political voices in the lower Mississippi Valley and the Deep South claimed that Cuba and the Caribbean basin offered far better prospects for the expansion of slavery than did Kansas—the New Orleans *Daily Picayune* observed that popular sovereignty eased the way for Cuba to be "received safely to the Southern States"—the aftermath of the Kansas-Nebraska Act actually unhinged Quitman's Cuba expedition, planned for early 1855. With growing outrage among Whigs and some Democrats in the non-slaveholding states ("I could travel from Boston to Chicago by the light of my own effigy," Stephen Douglas acknowledged of the backlash in the late summer of 1854), Pierce could not allow a filibustering mission to go forward, nor could Quitman's friends in the Senate find the votes to suspend the Neutrality Act. Federal officials began to threaten Quitman and his co-conspirators with legal action, and the president personally discouraged the Mississippian from attempting an invasion while assuring him that the Cuban slave system was well protected internally. With the handwriting obviously on the wall, Quitman shifted his base of political operations to the relative safety of a seat in Congress, though from there he remained a strong proponent of filibustering.

Cuba was not the only target of filibustering and slaveholding imperialism. Partly in response to the flight of their slaves and their failure to secure an extradition agreement with Mexican authorities, Texas slave owners, with the occasional aid of Texas Rangers, launched a series of raids into northern Mexico. "Something must be done for the protection of slave property in this State," the Ranger captain and filibuster John "Rip" Ford demanded, "let the frontier of slavery begin to recede and when or where the wave of recession may be arrested God only knows." At one point, they even backed the Tejano renegade José Carbajal, who wished to establish the separatist Republic of Sierra Madre in Tamaulipas and offered the Americans a free hand in retrieving their slaves. The Knights of the Golden Circle, organized in Kentucky but also based chiefly in Texas, was more ambitious still. It viewed Mexico as an important piece of an expanding slave empire—which would include Cuba, Central America, parts of South America, and much of the remaining West Indies—potentially bringing into the Union twenty-five new slave states. Others, like Duff Green, John Slidell, Pierre Soulé, and Judah Benjamin, conceived of a massive transportation network linking Washington, D.C., with the American Pacific by way of Mexico and could claim a small victory when President Pierce secured nearly fifty thousand square miles south of the Gila River (and a potential railroad route west) in what is known as the Gadsden Purchase of 1853. Mexico, John Quitman proclaimed in the House of Representatives, was but a "waif" awaiting conquest by "some stronger power."

Not all of the filibusters saw themselves as the advance guards of a developing slave empire or as emissaries of slaveholding interests. More than a few sought riches, power, adventure, and the extension of prized institutions in a political culture that presented few constraints and seemed to have cavalier attitudes about territorial borders. Some had gone bust in the California gold-fields, were stumbling around the lower Mississippi Valley, had fled failed revolutions in continental Europe, or were down on their luck (and likely recent immigrants) in cities stretching from the Northeast down through the Gulf Coast. During the 1850s, they were especially active in America's new Southwest, invading Sonora and Baja California (gateways to Mexican silver mines) on several occasions and planning an assortment of related expeditions. Mobile, New Orleans, southern Texas, and San Francisco were their usual staging points, and they could count on favorable receptions—and perhaps fund-raising—almost anywhere in the Deep South. Thus, whether by intention or not, these filibusters were associated with slaveholding concerns, and, when necessary, they made the most of it.

William Walker, who proved the most formidable and successful of them, was a case in point. A Tennessean by birth (1824), Walker studied medicine at the University of Pennsylvania and traveled briefly in Europe before heading off to New Orleans, where he came to practice law and edit a newspaper, the *New Orleans Crescent*. But the death of his wife from cholera and doubtless the discovery of gold led him out to San Francisco in 1849. There he continued with legal and newspaper work and became active in Democratic politics; he also engaged in several duels, which may help explain why, in 1853, he became attracted to filibustering (though his motivations remain a mystery). After the Mexican government denied his request to establish a colony in Sonora, Walker set out with a contingent of about forty-five men to take matters into his own hands. He first moved into La Paz on the southern end of Baja California and declared it an independent republic with himself as president. He then crossed over into Sonora, where the expedition rather ingloriously fell apart and forced his retreat to the United States. When he returned to San Francisco, federal officials put him on trial for violating American neutrality laws, but as was true with John Quitman and many other filibusters, the sympathetic jury refused to convict him. Most important, Walker had achieved an international reputation.

Walker's name certainly came to be known among liberal elites in Nicaragua. Like their counterparts in Mexico, they had been struggling with conservatives since the time of independence from Spain in 1821, and by the 1840s the struggle was joined by peasants, especially in the Pacific zone, who sought to resist the Nicaraguan state's attacks on their subsistence and community rights. Looking to strengthen their hand and imagining that he, as an American, shared their aspirations, the liberals sent representatives to San Francisco to contract for Walker's services. For a time, they were not disappointed. With a filibustering band of nearly sixty men, Walker sailed into the Pacific port of

Realejo in June 1855 and in remarkably short order defeated the conservatives, disbanded the Nicaraguan army, and achieved effective control over the country, though he initially preferred to rule through a puppet regime. Walker won substantial popular support by ending military conscription, and in the rural areas peasants hoped that he would also end the destructive policies of the previous governments. The liberals had offered Walker's followers economic incentives to settle there and thought that they might help put Nicaragua on a path of American-style development. Many of the conservatives also began to see Walker as a man who could keep order and, together with local bosses (caudillos), encouraged him to assume the presidency. Walker himself won the backing of two American entrepreneurs, Charles Morgan and Cornelius Garrison, who were vying with Cornelius Vanderbilt for control of the Nicaraguan transit route from the Caribbean to the Pacific and thus of a vital passageway to California.

Walker's salad days in Nicaragua were not long lived. Through the vehicle of a rigged election in the summer of 1856, Walker ascended to the presidency and moved quickly to destabilize elite opposition and consolidate his power. He commenced to confiscate landed estates and redistribute them to the filibusters, and in September he reinstituted slavery (the only such case in the former Spanish possessions). The purpose, he insisted, was to address a shortage of laborers willing to grow agricultural staples and thereby promote development; the new planter class would be his American followers and future colonists managing a force of African slaves and indentured natives. Although there is little indication that he looked toward annexation or some sort of formal political arrangement with the United States, there is every reason to believe that he wished to win the support of slaveholding elements and their Democratic allies. And, indeed, enthusiasm for Walker steadily mounted in the United States. The Pierce administration briefly agreed to receive Walker's foreign minister, the national convention of the Democratic Party in 1856 endorsed his activities, and American expansionists were raising money for the Walker regime in New Orleans and the Deep South.

Yet in Nicaragua, the foundations of Walker's rule were rapidly disintegrating. Walker's attacks on the Nicaraguan elites united liberals and conservatives as never before and enabled them to form a military pact with Guatemala, Salvador, Costa Rica, and Honduras. Together they launched the "National War" against the Walker regime and began to reclaim the country. Although the Central Americans failed to mobilize the peasantry, Walker's new labor program alienated much of his popular support and left him increasingly isolated. But the deciding blow might have been landed by Cornelius Vanderbilt, who fumed at Walker's alliance with his rivals Morgan and Garrison and started to funnel money and weapons to Walker's enemies. In May 1857, Walker and his men were forced to surrender and then, inexplicably, permitted to leave Nicaragua.

It was a narrow escape, and one misleading in its implications. Walker returned to the United States to great acclaim, especially among Democrats in the slaveholding states, and immediately proceeded to organize a return expedition to Nicaragua. So strong did his support in the Deep South appear—and he cultivated it assiduously—that the *New York Times*, a Republican paper, accused Walker of "laying the basis" for a "Southern Slave Empire." Whatever his ultimate plans, Walker was determined on a restoration to power. After two abortive efforts, he set out for Honduras in the spring of 1860 with the intention of fighting his way into Nicaragua. But this time, he was outnumbered and outmaneuvered. With his back to the wall, he surrendered to an officer of the British navy, hoping that another escape might be possible. No such luck. The British handed him over to the Hondurans, who did not make the same mistake as the Nicaraguans. They acted with summary dispatch: they brought Walker before a firing squad and had him shot dead.

Political Strides of Antislavery

Pro-slavery forces might have gained the early advantage, by means fair and foul, in the settlement and politics of territorial Kansas, but that advantage was almost immediately contested. To be sure, wherever they came from, most of the Kansas migrants had their eyes chiefly on land, farming, and perhaps merchandising or speculative opportunities; aside from Missouri, many had traveled there from Illinois, Indiana, Ohio, Iowa, and Kentucky and regarded economic prospects rather than the fate of slavery as their paramount concern. Even the New England Emigrant Aid Company (NEEAC), organized by Eli Thayer and chartered by the Massachusetts legislature, initially looked to assist prospective settlers in a business venture and provided them with arms largely in association with land disputes that quickly erupted.

But those who feared the further expansion of slavery into the trans-Mississippi West, like their pro-slavery counterparts, recognized the stakes and prepared themselves to keep the Kansas territory out of the grasp of slaveholders. "Come on then, gentlemen of the Slave States," New York's Whig senator William Seward taunted after the passage of the Kansas-Nebraska Act. "Since there is no escaping your challenge I accept it in behalf of the cause of freedom. We will engage in competition for the virgin soil of Kansas, and God give the victory to the side which is stronger in numbers as it is in right." The influx of Missouri Border Ruffians and the corrupt elections that resulted in a pro-slavery territorial legislature made it clear that God would probably give the victory to those stronger in numbers and might, rather than "in right." Together they roused antislavery constituencies across the country and a growing "Free State" faction in Kansas to respond aggressively. In August 1855, free staters gathered in the town of Lawrence—named for the Massachusetts cotton merchant Amos Lawrence, who took charge of the NEEAC from Thayer—and determined to act. They decried the pro-slavery legislature as illegally constituted and decided to hold a constitutional convention in order to establish their own claims and seek admission to the Union as a state.

Within a few months, the free staters had organized the Free State Party, written and ratified a constitution that outlawed slavery but also (in a separate vote) excluded free people of color from the territory, and established a government of their choosing in the western Kansas town of Topeka, several miles up the Kansas River from Lecompton, where the pro-slavery legislature had convened (after short stints at Pawnee and the Shawnee Mission). It was a bold and risky move, all the more so when President Pierce simultaneously termed the Lecompton legislature "legitimate" despite the "irregularities" and the Topeka government "revolutionary" and potentially "treasonable." Indeed, Pierce threatened the Free State movement with the hard fist of military force and requested a congressional appropriation in order to proceed. Only months into 1856, therefore, Kansas had dual governments, each seeking recognition from the federal government and each viewing the other as a set of radical impostors. A disturbing example it was of "squatter sovereignty" in practice.

The developing crisis in Kansas was only the most vivid example of how the battle over slavery's future in the United States was being increasingly joined in political life. During the late 1830s and early 1840s, abolitionists who felt constrained by Garrisonian "moral suasion" and the tactics of legislative petitioning began to look to the formal political arena to advance their cause. They rejected Garrison's view that the Constitution was a compact with slavery and the federal government and electoral process unalterably contaminated by it. Instead, they imagined that federal authority could be deployed not to attack slavery where it existed in individual states (which, they acknowledged, the Constitution protected) but to deprive slavery of support and further sustenance where it had recognized jurisdiction. Congress, they believed, could begin to dislodge slavery in the District of Columbia, in territories such as Florida (before it became a state in 1845), at federal forts, arsenals, and navy yards where slave labor was exploited, and on naval vessels themselves. It could intrude upon the interstate slave trade. It could repeal or otherwise weaken the Fugitive Slave Act. And, of course, it could refuse to admit new slave states as congressmen with antislavery sensibilities had attempted to do ever since the fight over Missouri. In 1840, these political abolitionists organized the Liberty Party and commenced to run candidates for public office including the presidency.

The Liberty Party is generally regarded as little more than a small bridge from the immediatism of the 1830s to the mass antislavery politics of the 1850s. Although well-placed Liberty Party votes shockingly deprived the Whig hero Henry Clay of the presidency in 1844, overall the votes were very few in number, and the party's efforts to educate the electorate on slavery's evils and court political favor fell relatively flat. But, far more important, Liberty Party leaders and intellectuals—Gamaliel Bailey, Thomas Morris, Salmon P. Chase, and Joshua Leavitt among them—began to lay out a political program designed to hem slavery in geographically and eat at its vitals where it continued to exist. They suggested, in contradistinction to Garrison, that the Constitution could be interpreted as an antislavery document, turning freedom into a federal institution and leaving slavery only a local one. Their ideas, anticipated in part by the land reformer George Henry Evans, would find expression in David Wilmot's "proviso" and in the fledgling Free-Soil Party, organized in 1848 by antislavery Democrats and "Conscience" Whigs who lacked the moral fervor of the Libertyites but embraced their strategy of refusing slavery's expansion. Rallying to the cry of "free soil, free speech, free labor, and free men," the Free-Soilers demanded, much as Liberty Party supporters had prescribed, that the federal government "relieve itself of all responsibility for the existence of slavery where the government possesses the constitutional power to legislate" and prohibit "the extension of slavery." Before long, the "nonextension" of slavery, defining a clearer and tighter border around the chattel institution, would emerge as the powerful alternative to popular sovereignty.

Unlike the Liberty Party, the Free-Soilers established a formidable political presence. In 1848, they sent more than fifteen candidates to Congress, including two senators, and their presidential candidate, a reinvented Martin Van Buren, attracted more than a quarter of a million popular votes (but no electoral votes). Although the compromise measures of 1850 sapped some of their momentum, Free-Soil ideas gained traction across New England, the Middle Atlantic, and the Midwest, especially among Whigs who bridled at the enthusiasm their slave state counterparts showed for popular sovereignty and a toughened Fugitive Slave Law. Far more than was true among Democrats at this point, the question of slavery fractured the foundation of Whiggery. When the Kansas-Nebraska Act passed with the votes of Whigs in the slaveholding states, the party collapsed and with it the edifice of electoral politics—known as the Second Party System—that had been erected in the 1820s and 1830s.

Democracy's Gates

Even before the Kansas-Nebraska Act became law, "anti-Nebraska" mobilizations, which brought together disenchanted antislavery Whigs with free state Democrats, began to take shape along a swath stretching from New England to the upper Midwest. In the small town of Ripon, Wisconsin, they went so far as to threaten the organization of a new "Republican" Party to replace the Whigs and supersede the Free-Soilers. Yet as the Whig Party disintegrated and the Second Party System teetered, still another political force seemed far better poised to step into the developing vacuum and refashion opposition to the Democratic Party. It attracted former Whigs who feared slavery's expanding borders, but it derived its energy from growing concerns about border crossings of a different sort. Drawing on very deeply laid traditions of anti-Catholicism, and reflecting doubts about political democracy amid an expanding urban working class, that force was virulently nativist.

Large population migrations moving in westerly and northwesterly directions had been a fact of Atlantic life since the late fifteenth century. In the century and three-quarters before the American Revolution, these routes to North America were taken by roughly 785,000 migrants, perhaps three-quarters of whom arrived in some condition of unfreedom, either African and African-descended slaves or indentured servants from Britain and the European continent (chiefly from parts of Germany).Then, during the first decade of the nineteenth century, the official closing of the African slave trade along with the eruption of the Napoleonic Wars narrowed the currents of migration to a veritable trickle. Only when peace was restored in the middle of the second decade of the nineteenth century did the currents begin to flow again, but this time they also changed in character. Although slavers continued to smuggle small cargoes of slaves into the United States, the migrants were now legally free and, in many cases, had been jettisoned from home communities by overpopulation and the market intensifications of the era. Pushed off the land or reduced to impoverishment by spiraling rents, the subdivision of smallholdings, or some form of enclosure, they joined swelling streams of displaced cultivators from every corner of the world touched by the commercialization of agriculture in seeking new berths. Some, like those from southern and eastern Asia who signed contracts to work sugar plantations in the West Indies, followed the channels of new global empires; others sought to avail themselves of cheap steerage and look for better prospects in Brazil and Argentina to the south or Canada and the United States to the north.

The volume of immigration to the United States grew steadily during the 1820s and 1830s from roughly 10,000 each year to nearly 100,000. A great many of the migrants were Irish, and while early on they tended to be Protestants from the north or Catholics possessing skills and resources, by the mid-1830s most were poor Catholics from the rural south and west best described as unskilled laborers. Whereas German immigrants of the time, who were also substantial in number and increasingly Catholic, often headed to midwestern cities (Cincinnati, Milwaukee, Chicago) and farming areas, the Irish generally enlarged the laboring populations of port cities from Boston, New York, Philadelphia, and Baltimore, to as far south and west as Charleston, Savannah, Mobile, and New Orleans. There they did heavy work on the docks, in the harbors, at construction sites, and on city streets, spilling out into the hinterlands when canals had to be dug, railroad tracks laid, or crops harvested. Already in the 1830s, they might attack free black workers and support the projects of anti-abolitionists; by the early 1840s, nativist organizations (the American Protestant Association and the American Republican Party) began to surface, and vicious nativist riots exploded, especially in Philadelphia's Kensington and Southwark districts.

But the late 1840s and early 1850s saw an influx of immigrants that, to this day, remains unprecedented in scale relative to the size of the American population. Between 1845 and 1854, nearly 3 million Europeans arrived, ranging from 200,000 to 450,000 each year and amounting to about 15 percent of the country's total inhabitants in the mid-1840s. Roughly half came from Ireland owing to a blight that destroyed the potato crop (the staple of the Irish peasant diet) and eventually claimed a million lives. Known as the Great Famine, it might have reduced Ireland's population by more than 20 percent through starvation and emigration and appears to have set in motion a longer-term demographic decline that would not be arrested for well over a century. Not surprisingly, most of those who left were poor rural folk, Catholic in faith, with few goods and no savings. Perhaps as many as a third spoke only Gaelic.

The impact of this dramatically elevated outpouring of people would have been notable under any circumstances, but it flooded into a simmering cauldron of tension, anxiety, and conflict. The ethnic clashes of the early 1840s were still lodged in urban memory, and to these were added new local antagonisms over school funding, Bible reading, Catholic Church property, and temperance, all of which stoked anti-Catholicism. Most troubling to native-born and Protestant observers, however, was the question of politics and political power. With loose requirements for voting—there was no registration, and in many places it was enough simply to declare one's intention to become naturalized—many of the new immigrants, especially the Irish Catholics, quickly aligned with the Democratic Party. It made sense for them to do that. The Democrats were neither evangelicals nor interested in waging cultural warfare over matters of schooling, drinking, workplace demeanor, and forms of entertainment. They were ready to offer patronage in the way of jobs and protection in exchange for votes. And they seemed to sympathize with the struggles of workingmen against both their employers and their black competitors. Small wonder that the Democrats managed to grab the reins of power in many large cities and, for the most part, dominate the executive and legislative branches of the federal government.

Beginning as a secret fraternal organization called the Order of the Star Spangled Banner, the "Know-Nothings" (the derivation of the moniker is not entirely clear) thus looked to combat what they saw as the growing power of Catholic immigrants and their political patrons. Yet for all the ethnic tension in the air, it required the passage of the Kansas-Nebraska Act and the collapse of the Whig Party to catapult the Know-Nothings (officially constituted as the American Party) from relative obscurity into national political prominence. They found their strongest following in the urban Northeast, where Irish immigration had its greatest effect, and they tended to attract the support of an emerging bourgeoisie and petite bourgeoisie that had previously sided with the Whigs: merchandisers and small manufacturers, clerks and skilled workers, who had come of age during the 1840s and early 1850s and had been made uneasy both by the renewed aggressiveness of slaveholders and by what they viewed as the political "corruption" governing urban life.

The Know-Nothings did not press to limit the flow of immigration, but they did seek to limit the political influence that immigrants could wield, proposing to extend naturalization from five to twenty-one years, confine public office holding to the native-born, and set literacy requirements as a condition for exercising the franchise. As early as the fall elections of 1854, the Know-Nothings swept to power across New England and registered impressive gains in Pennsylvania and Indiana; in Massachusetts, they took full control of the government. With such a rapid and remarkable ascent, they seemed ready to replace the Whigs as the main opponents of the Democrats on the country's stage.

That the Know-Nothings offered a political landing pad for Whigs troubled by the Kansas-Nebraska Act and the apparent sympathy of Catholic immigrants for slaveholders clearly limited the party's larger ambitions. Indeed, while the Know-Nothings' identification with antislavery and temperance, as well as with anti-Catholicism, increased their appeal for rural (and especially evangelical) voters in the Northeast and parts of the Midwest, it gained them little help—and considerable hostility—among Whigs in the slaveholding states. But the rise of the Know-Nothings must also alert us to a developing backlash against the democratic impulses of the 1820s and 1830s as the impact of early industrialization was making itself felt and the composition of the urban working class was being reconfigured. The Know-Nothings, that is, exemplified a series of efforts to narrow, strengthen, and more closely patrol the borders of official political life.

In an important sense, the United States began to face, during the 1840s and 1850s, the domestic political challenge that was besetting Britain and much of the European continent: whether to admit putatively free but economically dependent adults into the arenas of formal politics. The comparative ease with which most American states had eliminated property-owning requirements for voting and office holding, creating adult white male suffrage, reflected the wide access to property among small producers, the limited development of a class of wage earners, and the relative ethnic homogeneity of the population in the early Jacksonian era. Not incidentally, the most serious battle over the democratization of the franchise occurred in Rhode Island, the state where industrialization and urbanization had advanced the furthest. But the reckonings would not be long in coming.

Chafing at their exclusion from political society outside northern New England and the indifference of their white antislavery allies, African Americans from the Middle Atlantic across to the Midwest began to press for a civil and political equality that was blatantly denied them. Their vulnerability was well in evidence. Many were fugitives from enslavement or the children of enslaved parents; almost all were to be found at the bottom reaches of the economic order, claiming little property and working as unskilled, casual, or domestic laborers, very much like the Irish. They already suffered discrimination and exclusion in various arenas of public life—especially in schools and on public transportation—and in the newer states of both the lower and the upper Midwest "black laws" officially denied them residency. But in the 1830s and 1840s, some of their leaders met in conventions and less formal assemblies, in cities and towns large and small, to express their grievances and mobilize support. They reminded neighboring whites of their American birth and many contributions to the country's development, and they urged fellow blacks to improve themselves, work diligently, learn to read and write, and look after their families. Most of all, they denounced the projects of colonizationists and called for (in some cases demanded) the extension of the franchise.

Unlike those of white men in humble circumstances earlier in the century, these demands for suffrage fell on deaf or hostile ears. Not only did African Americans utterly fail in their quests for equality and voting rights; they often lost ground. In Pennsylvania, as well as in North Carolina and Tennessee, where free people of color had been able to cast ballots, the expansion of the white male franchise was accompanied by the elimination of the black. Only in Rhode Island were gains made, and even then they were minimal: suffrage came in the 1840s with such heavy property qualifications that all but a handful of black men remained political outcasts. Indeed, together with the new Fugitive Slave Law of 1850 and growing interest in the slave states in further circumscribing the worlds of free people of color there, the defeat of African Americans in their efforts to gain admission to the official arenas of politics reflected their increasingly perilous position and prospects: as members of a despised race and degraded section of the working class. Their alienation from American society and their militancy on the slavery question accordingly deepened.

The largest section of the free adult population of the United States denied participation in formal politics was, next to the slaves, the most legally dependent: females. They lived under the rule of patriarchal fathers as children and of patriarchal husbands as adults (with rare exception). When married, they surrendered claims to property and wages to their husbands, were vulnerable to physical abuse, and had few avenues to seek divorce. And when single or married, growing numbers of them entered the labor force as textile operatives, garment workers, outworkers, and domestics—that is to say, often in the most dynamic sectors of the manufacturing economy. Some organized at their workplaces to resist wage cuts and other forms of exploitation. In Lowell, Massachusetts, female textile operatives struck—"turned out" in the language of the time—on two occasions during the 1830s and heard one of their leaders "make a Mary Woolstonecroft [sic] speech on the rights and the iniquities of the 'monied aristocracy.'" But for the most part, the question of their civil and political standing was raised and pursued by their social betters, who had the time, education, social connections, and developing self-confidence to create a women's rights movement.

The road to women's rights invariably passed through the portals of abolitionism. The mobilizations of the 1830s, especially the petition campaigns, created a cadre of female activists aghast at the consequences of male power and increasingly skilled in the workings of grassroots politics. Many of the leaders were Quakers—Sarah and Angelina Grimké, Lucretia Mott, Elizabeth M'Clintock, and Abby Kelley prominent among them—and Garrisonians, some of whom had been excluded from the World Anti-Slavery Conference in London in 1840 on account of their sex. Even more were from middling farm families and a range of Protestant sects who lived in areas that felt the effects of antislavery agitation, often in the form of the Liberty Party or the Barnburner faction of the Democrats. They might have begun to petition state legislatures for civil and political equality as early as 1844. But it was Elizabeth Cady Stanton, residing in the bustling upstate New York town of Seneca Falls, a veteran of the London debacle, and very much at the intersection of legal reform (her father), political antislavery (her husband), and egalitarian abolitionism (her Quaker allies), who sparked the organization of a women's rights convention in her hometown in the summer of 1848.

Radicalism was very much in the air in 1848. That spring, popular revolutions demanding political liberalization and in some cases social democracy exploded in France and across continental Europe and dealt the final blows to slavery in the French colonies and to serfdom west of Russia. Chartism, calling for the democratization of the franchise in Britain, reached its zenith of working-class support. And the Free-Soil Party was organized in the United States. "Thanks to steam navigation and electric wires . . . a revolution cannot be confined to the place or the people where it may commence but flashes with lightning speed from heart to heart [arousing] the world from its stupor," Frederick Douglass observed.

Three hundred women and men including Douglass, all abolitionists, accordingly made their way—on short notice—to Seneca Falls. One hundred of them would sign the "Declaration of Sentiments" (named after the founding document of the American Anti-Slavery Society). A remarkable text crafted by Stanton and the Quaker Elizabeth M'Clintock, the declaration proclaimed that "all men and women are created equal" and pressed for civil and political rights without regard to sex, including "the sacred right of the elective franchise." "We did assemble," Stanton explained, "to protest against a form of government existing without the consent of the governed, to declare our rights to be free as man is free, to be represented in the government we are taxed to support, to have such disgraceful laws as give to man the right to chastise and imprison his wife, to take wages which she earns, the property which she inherits and in case of separation the children of her love, laws that make her the mere dependent on his bounty."

Yet for all the political energy of the moment, the quest for women's rights (local conventions would gather for the next decade), like the revolutions of 1848 in Europe, suffered rejection and defeat. Although married women's property legislation began to advance, especially because it offered cover for the financial woes of men, woman suffrage was thoroughly repudiated in official circles. Like free African Americans and Catholic immigrants, women's rights activists had attempted to redefine the borders of formal politics, making them more inclusive and more compatible with the high-grounded principles of the Declaration of Independence. But like African Americans and Catholic immigrants, they discovered that the borders instead were contracting and becoming harder to traverse.

Defying Slavery's Borders

The brutal repression that followed Nat Turner's failed rebellion in Southampton County, Virginia, in 1831 appeared to close a lengthy period of slave unrest that had begun during the early days of the American Revolution and continued for another half century. Reflecting a complex web of political interconnections, the unrest had intensified in the 1790s (especially in the Carolinas and lower Louisiana) owing to the impact of the Haitian Revolution; erupted again in the second decade of the nineteenth century amid conflicts involving Britain, Spain, and the Seminoles (including a large slave revolt in St. John the Baptist and St. Charles parishes, Louisiana, in 1811); stirred once more in the early 1820s as Congress debated the admission of Missouri as a slave state (with a possible plot organized by Denmark Vesey and his followers in Charleston, South Carolina); and reverberated in many quarters in the late 1820s and early 1830s as David Walker circulated his *Appeal to the Coloured Citizens of the World*, slaves rose by the thousands in Jamaica, and abolitionism established an institutional base in the Northeast. Thereafter, slave unrest seemed to be pushed underground, into more customary and clandestine channels, as the master class consolidated its power over the newly expanded interior of the Deep South. No serious conspiracy would be unearthed on American soil for at least another quarter century.

But if slaves, reckoning the odds against them, largely ceased to imagine direct rebellions against their owners, they began to test the borders of their enslavement in other consequential ways. On land and sea, mostly as individuals and in small groups, they moved into liminal zones where their status was ambiguous or their allies positioned to expose the ambiguities. Did enslavement simply attach to the body, to be carried wherever the slave traveled? What would such enslavement mean in a state or a foreign country that had declared an end to slavery on its soil? Would fugitives from slavery be entitled to legal recourse or gain substantive protection from free abolitionists? Could slaveholders remain at peace with people and governments, in the United States and abroad, who threatened or were inattentive to their property and prerogatives? By traversing sea-lanes and borderlands, slaves not only marked the limits of their masters' authority but also precipitated an assortment of political confrontations that were international in scope. In the process, they led slaveholders to reassess their place in the American union and helped carve a new landscape of politics in the United States.

Among the vehicles of border transgressions were the ships—most often coasting vessels—meant to transport slaves from one American market to another. During the 1830s, three of them, sailing out of Richmond or Charleston and heading toward New Orleans, were swept up by storms and beached in the Bahamas, where slavery was in the process of being abolished by the British Parliament. How would the slaves be regarded, and what law would apply? Despite American protests, British officials, perhaps upholding the logic of the *Somerset* decision, boldly freed all the slaves on the ships, and their government later offered limited indemnification to avoid a diplomatic crisis. Knowledge of these important developments might then have spread among slaves along the eastern seaboard of the United States, or at least to the arrestingly named Madison Washington. A Virginia slave, Washington had escaped to Canada, only to be captured and sold to slave traders when he returned to liberate his wife. Put aboard the *Creole* in 1841 for a voyage from Richmond to New Orleans, Washington had a clear plan. He and 18 other slaves (there were 135 slaves in all) quickly seized control of the ship and steered it to Nassau, where they eventually gained their freedom. It was one of the largest and certainly the most successful of American slave rebellions up to that time.

But the maritime episode that most riveted the American public and revealed the Atlantic world of slavery in its growing complexities began in the waters off Cuba and ended in the Supreme Court of the United States. In late June 1839, two Spaniards purchased fifty-three slaves in Havana and boarded them on a ship built in Baltimore, *La Amistad*, for a brief trip to the plantation district around Puerto Príncipe. But on the third day out, two of the slaves, Cinqué and Grabeau, led a rebellion that took control of the ship. The captain and the cook were killed, and the Spanish slave traders made prisoners. Cinqué hoped to sail the *Amistad* to Africa but with a limited grasp of navigation was fooled by one of the traders into heading north rather than west. Running short on food and water, the rebels ultimately ran aground on eastern Long Island and were taken into custody by U.S. naval authorities.

It could have been a relatively simple proceeding: Cuban slaves owned by Spanish traders rising in rebellion in Cuban waters had to be returned to the custody of the traders or to Spanish officials. But it turned out that the slave cargo had recently been transported, in violation of an Anglo-Spanish treaty, from the port of Lomboko in Sierra Leone to Cuba, where they were held for two weeks before being brought into the Havana slave market. According to international law, that is, the Africans were legally free, the traders had likely committed a capital offense, and rather than engaging in rebellion, murder, or piracy, Cinqué and his co-conspirators might have been acting in self-defense. The case immediately attracted the interest of American abolitionists in the Northeast, especially the evangelical merchant Lewis Tappan, who began to mount a legal defense as well as a publicity campaign. Still, there was little cause for optimism. The Jacksonian heir Martin Van Buren occupied the White

House and was facing reelection; he wanted nothing more than to dispense with this case, satisfy the Spanish who demanded the black captives return to Cuba, and avoid alienating slaveholding fellow Democrats. Pressure would undoubtedly be brought to bear, and the federal judge who would hear the case—Andrew T. Judson—was a racist Jacksonian Democrat possibly willing to do the president's bidding.

Yet to the surprise and relief of the abolitionists, Judson determined that the captives had been transported illegally, that their rebellion could not be recognized as a crime, and that they were free and should, under Van Buren's auspices, be returned to Africa. Shocked by the ruling—a naval vessel had already been dispatched to ferry the captives to Cuba—the Van Buren administration immediately appealed it to the Supreme Court, where a more favorable outcome could be expected. After all, a majority of the justices hailed from the slaveholding states, and the chief justice, the recently appointed Roger B. Taney, was a Marylander with a slaveholding background. But the defense had enlisted the powerful aid of the former president John Quincy Adams, and what turned into the Court's unanimous opinion was prepared by the associate justice Joseph Story of Massachusetts, who carefully upheld Judson's decision, though at no point challenged the legality of slavery. It would be a defining moment for supporters and opponents of slavery alike, not least Chief Justice Taney.

Less dramatic, though even more consequential, were many small-scale flights of slaves from the grasp of owners in states where slavery remained legal to black settlements in states where slavery had been abolished or was in its very last stages of life. These slaves, like Frederick Douglass, usually fled from "border" areas where slave and non-slave states (or countries) lay in proximity—Maryland, Virginia, Kentucky, Missouri, Louisiana, Texas—and had learned of travel routes, safe havens, collections of allies, forms of demeanor, and sensible destinations that might enable their success. Douglass had "canvassed" with fellow slaves, heard of "Canada, the real Canaan of the American bondmen," and "of Pennsylvania, Delaware, and New Jersey," and discovered that "New York city was our northern limit" and "to go there" risked harassment "with the liability of being hunted down and returned to slavery." Thus, when he finally made his escape in 1838, Douglass stopped only briefly in New York, where he came under the wing of David Ruggles, leader of the New York Committee of Vigilance. Ruggles promptly hid Douglass, helped Douglass reunite with his wife, and, upon learning of Douglass's skills as a caulker, directed him to New Bedford, Massachusetts, where work and a community of African Americans could be found. Often referred to as the Underground Railroad, as something of a transit line between slavery and freedom, such clandestine migrations might better be seen as part of a massive political web, built chiefly by slaves and free people of color, that was energized by networks of communication and directed toward struggles against enslavement and its insidious badges.

Douglass, like many other fugitives from slavery, would align himself with the abolitionist movement and, while admiring Garrison and his loyal followers, take an increasingly militant stance. More than any other people in the United States, fugitives understood the power and violence that undergirded slavery, the temper of slave owners and their white supporters, and the need for vigilance and self-defense wherever they might be. They also understood that so long as the overwhelming majority of African Americans remained in bondage, the prospects for those who had escaped it would be dim. Henry Highland Garnet, who began his life as a Virginia slave before fleeing to Pennsylvania and New York, made that understanding clear in a remarkable address to "the Slaves of the United States" at a black convention in Buffalo, New York, in 1843. Pointing to the many threads of kinship, friendship, and humanity that tied slaves and fugitives together, and celebrating the heroic actions of Denmark Vesey, "the patriotic Nathaniel Turner," the "immortal Joseph Cinque," and "that bright star of freedom Madison Washington," Garnet urged slaves to "arise, arise" and "strike for your lives and liberties."

Garnet's address stirred great controversy at the time it was delivered, but it would not be long before a substantial cut of black abolitionism would come to embrace his perspectives and militancy. An Ohio black convention in 1849 called on "the slave [to] leave the plantation immediately with his hoe on his shoulder" and recommended that David Walker's *Appeal* be combined with Garnet's address in a single volume and circulated widely. Douglass himself conceded at the time that slaves could defensibly murder their owners, and in an 1855 convention in Syracuse that brought radical black and white abolitionists together, he agreed to a demand for the direct "suppression" of slavery. Indeed, after congressional passage of the more repressive Fugitive Slave Law of 1850, African Americans at the grassroots who remained fugitives or had won their freedom revitalized local vigilance committees and in some places formed militia units—known in New York and Cincinnati as the Attucks Guards—to ready themselves for impending battle. Others, including Garnet, who had a change of heart, seemed to give up the fight in the United States and looked instead to emigrate: to West Africa, Haiti, Central and South America, or any location that offered the chance for a better life.

But slave escapes also promoted a new type of militancy in states where slavery had been officially outlawed. Before the 1850s, the work of harboring fugitives and fending off the assaults of slave catchers fell largely to African Americans who, in their settlements and vigilance committees, scouted the docks, patrolled local thoroughfares, tried to rescue blacks being kidnapped, and, if necessary, put up armed resistance. Many of the confrontations were guerrilla skirmishes; some appeared indistinguishable from frontal warfare. Thus, when the Maryland slaveholder Edward Gorsuch, aided by several federal officials, set out with his son and a few neighbors for Lancaster, Pennsylvania, in the late summer of 1851 to recapture four slaves who had run away, they were met by somewhere between 75 and 150 black men and women wielding pistols, rifles, scythes, corn cutters, and other farm tools. In the battle that followed, Gorsuch was killed, his son mortally wounded, and the remaining assailants driven off in what has come to be known as the Christiana Riot.

African Americans would continue to do the heavy lifting of community defense, yet during the 1850s they began to receive concerted support from white antislavery activists. Although most of their neighbors were willing to accept and enforce it, white abolitionists were outraged by the strengthened Fugitive Slave Law, demanding as it did direct federal participation while denying African Americans any means of legal redress. And because the Supreme Court in the *Prigg* case (1842) cast doubt on the constitutionality of personal liberty laws passed by the states, there were few institutional avenues of protest other than noncooperation. Little by little, white abolitionists began to accept the logic of their black counterparts who had long embraced direct action and in numbers of instances joined with them to thwart the reach of slave catchers, disturb the operations of federal commissioners, punish cooperating police officers, and attempt to rescue fugitives who had been remanded to re-enslavement. In Boston and New York, Philadelphia and Syracuse, Cincinnati and Milwaukee, Detroit and Sandusky, Oberlin and Wilkes-Barre, they took to the streets, surrounded jails and federal buildings, hurled taunts and stones, and pressed to take fugitives out of federal hands and ferry them to safety.

Sometimes they succeeded; sometimes they failed. But even when they failed, their efforts could make a searing impression on local observers who had not previously been moved by the moral and political dilemmas of slavery. When, for example, a Virginia fugitive named Anthony Burns was arrested in Boston on a federal warrant in the spring of 1854, black and white abolitionists sprang into action, organizing protest meetings and devising plans of rescue. They also raised money, mobilized legal support, and attempted to purchase Burns's freedom. Nothing worked. Still, with all means of redress exhausted and Burns's supporters defeated, it required "a detachment of the National Lancers, a corps of United States Artillery . . . and [three] of Marines" to clear a path among an estimated fifty thousand angry Bostonians and get Burns on a federal revenue cutter headed south.

The political work of slaves and free people of color in traversing the apparent borders of enslavement captured public attention and sympathy in new and powerful ways—evidenced most famously in Harriet Beecher Stowe's *Uncle Tom's Cabin*—and led many white abolitionists to interrogate their beliefs about the appropriate road to emancipation. As they watched militarized federal posses join hands with slaveholders to recapture runaways—or any person of African descent who appeared to be a runaway—and watched fugitives and their black allies literally battle for their freedom, more and more came to question moral suasion, "nonresistance," and pacifism and to accept violence as a necessary means to abolitionist ends. At the same time, slaveholders saw in the increasing militarism of abolitionism and especially in the efforts to defy the federal law governing fugitive slaves a sign of the Union's dangers and limits. If the laws protecting powerful members of one state would not be observed by the members of another, if legal "comity" would no longer prevail, what good use would the Union any longer serve?

Kansas Ruptured

Nowhere did the question of slavery's future in the United States play out more forebodingly during the 1850s than on the rolling plains of eastern Kansas: not in the streets of Boston or in the newspapers of Charleston or in the port of New Orleans or in the halls of Congress. It was not because fugitive slaves began to flock to Kansas or because big slaveholders and committed abolitionists began to arrive in growing numbers. It was because men of relatively modest means in search of land, prospects, and breathing space chose sides in the belief that their destinies were on the line. Few were morally attached or opposed to slavery; fewer still had any interest in the slaves or African Americans more generally. But many saw either the pro-slavery or the Free State side as the vehicle of their security and the opposition as bent on destroying them. They became, that is, willing shock troops in a struggle for power that linked the trans-Mississippi West with the highest reaches of the American state.

The first really serious warning sign in Kansas was not the incursion of Border Ruffians from Missouri and the fraudulent election of a territorial legislature in March 1855. That was only an exaggerated version of politics as usual in the mid-nineteenth century. Far more ominous was the behavior of the legislature when it then convened. Not only did the pro-slavery majority expel the small contingent of free staters who had won seats, but they quickly passed an "act to punish offences against slave property," which criminalized the expression of antislavery sentiments and prohibited free staters from serving as jurors on any case that might be prosecuted under the law. Having previously urged Missourians to "enter every election district in Kansas . . . and vote at the point of the bowie-knife and revolver," one of their leaders now celebrated laws that "silenced Abolitionists; for in spite of their heretofore boasting, these know they will be enforced to the very letter and with the utmost rigor."

The opposition did not go quietly into the Kansas night. Viewing the territorial legislature as illegitimate, the free staters established newspapers, began to form their own government, and applied for statehood. But because the pro-slavery legislature was accepted by the Pierce administration and theirs deemed revolutionary and treasonous, they understood the precariousness of their position. They could not expect any protection from the "official" authorities and would, instead, have to protect themselves by means of numbers and arms. Any conflict or altercation could easily take on political meaning and escalate rapidly into a full-blown confrontation. Thus, in late 1855 a quarrel over a land claim ended in a murder. The perpetrator, affiliated with pro-slavery elements, avoided arrest while the victim's allies, aligned with the free staters, retaliated by burning the cabins of the accused and his witnesses. Before long, the sheriff, having been thwarted in his efforts to round up the free staters, massed a veritable army of Missourians around the free state town of Lawrence. Only the governor's intervention averted bloodshed (the episode was still called the Wakarusa War), though within weeks the sheriff was back and Lawrence was "sacked": newspaper presses were destroyed, the Free State Hotel (political headquarters for the free staters) was bombarded and torched, and a free state leader's house was burned down.

Among the settlers who responded to the call to defend Lawrence was the peripatetic John Brown. Already an abolitionist zealot who understood the struggle over slavery in biblical terms, Brown had arrived in Kansas from upstate New York several months earlier to join his sons, daughter, and son-in-law at an encampment near the town of Osawatomie (known to locals as Brown's Station). Brown's son John Brown Jr. had written to him of pro-slavery "'Annoyance Associations' whose object is to make Free-State folks all the trouble they can" and who had "armed to the teeth" the "meanest and most desperate men" to "fasten Slavery upon this glorious land, by means no matter how foul." In sum, John Brown Jr. needed more weapons, and Brown agreed to find them and bring them out. But John Brown Jr. was initially in the lead. He could be found at the nexus of the Free State community in the environs of Brown's Station and Osawatomie; he won election as a delegate to the Free State constitutional convention in Topeka and soon thereafter to a seat in the Free State legislature; and he organized local militia units to fight off pro-slavery paramilitarism that continued to claim Free State lives. When the Browns and their allies rode out to defend Lawrence in May 1856, John Brown Jr. was at the head of the company.

Yet from the time of his arrival in Kansas, John Brown Sr. was very much in the fray and increasingly worried about the prospects for the Free Staters. He had long embraced the view to which other abolitionists were now coming: that slavery would only be ended by means of violence. He had formed the League of Gileadites, composed mostly of black fugitives, to resist the Fugitive Slave Law. And he had played a role in the establishment of the Radical Abolition Party. Once in Kansas, he quickly took to the logic of armed self-defense, whether traveling to the polls for an election or joining to protect a town like Lawrence from assault. Brown was, in fact, in Lawrence at the time of the Wakarusa War, and while negotiations to avoid a fight were under way, Free State leaders appointed him a militia captain. But sporadic pro-slavery attacks continued with little response from federal officials, and as he accompanied his sons to Lawrence for the second time, only to learn that they were too late to prevent the sack, he decided to go on the offensive. On the night of May 24, Brown and seven others (including four of his sons—but not John Brown Jr.—and a son-in-law) made their way to a pro-slavery settlement on Pottawatomie Creek and brutally murdered five unarmed men. Their intention, it appears, was to retaliate for what they regarded as a "reign of terror" over the previous months and, in turn, to terrify members of the pro-slavery faction.

Without doubt, the "Pottawatomie massacre," as it was almost immediately termed, showed pro-slavery supporters that the Free Staters, whom they had not considered formidable foes, were armed and dangerous. But they did not come to feel the "restraining fear" as the Browns had hoped. Pottawatomie set off weeks of warfare between militias, posses, and other irregulars who traversed the Kansas countryside harassing their enemies and exacting retribution. John Brown demonstrated no small amount of courage in the fighting, not to mention military skill (he had studied guerrilla warfare), and he did inflict at least one surprising defeat on a band of marauding Missourians. Yet by the time the newly appointed territorial governor John W. Geary (in service in the West during the U.S.-Mexican War) managed to impose a modicum of order that fall, the results had been very costly to Brown and his side. The Brown camp and nearby Osawatomie had been burned, two of Brown's sons who did not participate at Pottawatomie had been roughed up, and Brown's son Frederick had been shot down. A different man might have been chastened, might have retreated or redirected the fight into safer channels. John Brown did neither; transformed by the Kansas crucible into something of a holy warrior, he now looked to continue the struggle with new and more daring plans.

Under indictment for the Pottawatomie murders, Brown soon slipped out of Kansas, but Geary's success in quelling the turbulence in the territory proved short lived. If anything, the effects had already been felt well east of the Mississippi River, shaking the political landscape and, upon reaching Washington, D.C., shattering all sorts of understandings, alliances, and civilities. Perhaps the most shocking episode took place on the floor of the U.S. Senate, just one day after the sack of Lawrence and only hours before Brown swept into Pottawatomie. Massachusetts's Republican senator Charles Sumner had delivered a highly anticipated speech, "The Crime Against Kansas," to packed galleries and crammed doorways over the course of two days. He argued that the Democrats intended to turn Kansas into a slave state at all hazards, that they allowed the territory to be overrun with "assassins" and "thugs," that Douglas's popular sovereignty had ended in "popular slavery," and that Kansas should be admitted to the Union under the Free State constitution drawn up in Topeka. But Sumner also took the opportunity to engage in personal invective, attacking Senators Douglas, James Mason of Virginia, and Andrew P. Butler of South Carolina. Butler, who was not in attendance either day, was called the Don Quixote of slavery, having "chosen [as] a mistress . . . the harlot, Slavery," and derided for his "incoherent phrases," "loose expectoration of speech," and "deviation from truth." Because Butler was unable to defend himself (he was in South Carolina at the time), his cousin and fellow South Carolinian Preston Brooks came over from his seat in the House of Representatives to fill in. Waiting for all the ladies to leave the Senate galleries on the afternoon of May 22, Brooks walked over to Sumner's desk and, in a furious minute, pummeled the senator senseless with his gold-headed cane.

It is not clear if John Brown had learned of the Sumner caning before going off to Pottawatomie, and it was by no means the first or last time that members of Congress would assault one another in their respective chambers. Ironically, Brooks, a man of modest talents, though some humor, had previously proposed that congressmen check their firearms before walking onto the House floor. But in the context of the Kansas bloodshed, the assault on Sumner catalyzed moral and political indignation on both sides of the slavery dispute and seemed to exemplify the extreme peril that suffused the country. Showered with honorary canes, Brooks became a hero to the ardent defenders of slavery and the very embodiment of slavery's villainy to the opponents. "I do not see how a barbarous community and a civilized community can constitute one state," Ralph Waldo Emerson exclaimed. "I think we must get rid of slavery, or we must get rid of freedom."

Yet the damage from Kansas not only deepened the wedge between slavery's supporters and its opponents; it also began to crack the foundations of the Democratic Party, which still encompassed the slaveholding and non-slaveholding states and had appeared to reach some consensus on popular sovereignty as a formula for the territories. No one felt the cracking more ominously than Stephen Douglas. An architect of popular sovereignty and an aspirant for the presidency, Douglas had hoped that the promise of an expanding American empire could redirect the battle over slavery's future. While Kansas might or might not reject slavery (he expected that Kansans would), there was New Mexico and possibly Utah for slaveholders, not to mention lands farther to the south and in the Caribbean, and there was the vast territory of the northern plains (Iowa and Minnesota were already organizing for admission as states) and the Northwest for those who sought free soil. But popular sovereignty, at the very least, had to seem popular, and the pro-slavery forces in Kansas, already outnumbered in the population, were making a mockery of it. Despite the efforts of the territorial governor Geary and then of the Mississippian Robert Walker, who replaced him after the Democrat James Buchanan won the presidency in 1856, to maintain a truce, the "official" pro-slavery legislature in Lecompton called for a constitutional convention (boycotted by the Free State side) in the spring of 1857, wrote a state constitution protecting slavery that fall, and then submitted it to Congress for approval.

Buchanan, who marched to the drumbeats of slaveholders, tendered his support, describing the Free Staters as in "rebellion against the government." Douglas was furious. Decrying the "trickery and juggling" of the Lecompton faction, he warned Buchanan that such a course risked the Democratic Party's survival in the non-slaveholding states and that he would mobilize opposition to the admission of Kansas under the pro-slavery constitution. "I desire you to remember," Buchanan icily responded, "that no Democrat ever yet differed from an administration of his own choice without being crushed." When it came to a vote in Congress, Douglas seemed to prove Buchanan a poor prognosticator. Although the Senate approved the admission of Kansas, the House turned it back by a slim margin, effectively ending the bid for pro-slavery statehood. But in truth, Buchanan saw the weak spot in Douglas's project. Reflecting on a monumental decision of the Supreme Court the previous March, he crowed that "slavery exists in Kansas by virtue of the Constitution of the United States" and that "Kansas is therefore at this moment as much a slave state as Georgia or South Carolina."

Slavery Without Borders?

Buchanan had known of—in fact had interceded in—a pending ruling of the Court in the case of *Scott v. Sandford* even before he was inaugurated president on March 4, 1857. Indeed, Buchanan's inaugural address, delivered after Chief Justice Roger Taney administered the oath of office, both acknowledged "a difference of opinion" over the workings of popular sovereignty and declaimed that the problem was "a judicial question" to "be speedily and finally settled" by the Court. Two days later, as Buchanan expected, the Court declared what the settlement would be. What he did not anticipate was how violently it would shake the foundation of the Union: so violently that the reverberations are still being felt today.

The Supreme Court's momentous decision grew out of a suit brought by the most obscure of men and women. Dred Scott was born a slave in Virginia sometime around the turn of the nineteenth century, though neither his date of birth nor his original name is known. Scott's owner, Peter Blow, operated a farm encompassing over eight hundred acres in Southampton County (later the scene of Nat Turner's slave rebellion) but like many members of the master class searched for new opportunities, especially in the rapidly growing Deep South and Mississippi Valley. Accordingly, in 1818, Blow moved his family and slaves to the Alabama black belt, where they commenced raising cotton for the burgeoning international market. Twelve years later, they moved once again, though this time to a very different type of location and a very different type of undertaking—to a city rather than to the countryside, to St. Louis, Missouri, where Blow opened a boarding-house grandly called the Jefferson Hotel.

Peter Blow was in his early fifties at the time of his move to St. Louis and apparently in poor health. Perhaps this was why he chose to give up planting and take up hotel keeping. At all events, he died in 1832 with five slaves as part of his estate. Although the disposition of the Blow estate remains murky in detail, by late 1833 one of the slaves (who might have been called Sam by the Blows) had been sold to a surgeon in the U.S. Army named John Emerson. That slave has come to be known to history, though for reasons still unclear, as Dred Scott.

Emerson was hardly the typical slaveholder. Born in Pennsylvania at the turn of the nineteenth century (he might have been roughly the same age as Scott), he received medical training at the University of Pennsylvania (like William Walker) and ended up in St. Louis in the early 1830s after having spent some time in other slaveholding states. There Emerson gained appointment as an army surgeon and was soon on his way, with his newly acquired slave, Dred Scott, in tow, to Fort Armstrong on Rock Island in the state of Illinois. That Emerson purchased Scott while already in the U.S. Army and with the full expectation of taking him on assignment suggests not only how commonplace slave ownership could be in many walks of life but also how deeply implicated the federal government was in the support and protection of black enslavement.

After a brief tenure at Fort Armstrong (about two and a half years), during which time he also bought some land in the neighboring Iowa Territory,

Emerson was transferred to Fort Snelling, far up the Mississippi River, in what was then the Wisconsin Territory. Befitting his status, Scott went along, although while at Snelling he met a slave woman named Harriet Robinson, owned by the local Indian agent. Scott and Robinson soon married (in a civil ceremony, highly unusual for slaves), and while Emerson won reassignment to Jefferson Barracks in St. Louis, they remained behind, hired out at the fort. Eventually, the Scotts rejoined Emerson at Fort Jesup, Louisiana, where he had again been transferred and where he met and married Eliza Irene Sanford, also of St. Louis and the daughter of a transplanted Virginian. A return trip to Fort Snelling followed, during which—and north of Missouri—the Scotts' first child, Eliza, was born, then back again to St. Louis, where Emerson left his wife and the Scotts before heading off to Florida, still caught in the grips of the Seminole War. He would be away for two years; Irene Emerson and the Scotts stayed on her father's estate outside St. Louis, although the Scotts might have been hired out once more and Dred might have renewed contact with the Blow family, especially Peter Blow's son Taylor, with whom he had apparently been close.

John Emerson finally returned to St. Louis, and now to civilian life, in late 1842 and, after failing to establish a medical practice there, headed off with his wife, though not with the Scotts—they had been hired out to Irene's brother-in-law at Jefferson Barracks in St. Louis—to Davenport, Iowa, near to where he had previously purchased land, and he started to build a house. The Emersons soon had a daughter, but John had begun to suffer from the complications of what appeared to be late-stage syphilis (contracted many years earlier) and died a short time later. By will, he left his estate, including the slaves Dred and Harriet, to Irene, who, in 1846, retrieved them from her brother-in-law and promptly hired them out in St. Louis to a Samuel Russell. Many slaves had, of course, been forced to move with their migratory owners, whether owing to the orders of the U.S. government or to the cycles of economic and family life. And many, particularly if they resided in cities like St. Louis or in general farming areas of the upper South, had a regular experience of being hired out. Yet the Scotts had, in their coerced travels, crossed a remarkable assortment of borders, not only between states and territories, but also between areas where slaveholding, supposedly, was and was not legal. In April 1846, before a state circuit court sitting in St. Louis, Dred and Harriet Scott determined to test the meaning of those borders and sue for their freedom.

How the Scotts' suit was initiated has never been clear. Was it the idea of friends and sympathizers, like the Blow family, in St. Louis, or was it the idea of Dred and Harriet Scott, who then sought the legal and financial assistance of sympathetic whites? Or was it a collaborative effort from the outset? In all likelihood, we will never know. But some things are clear. Although Missouri was a slaveholding state, it also perched on the border between slave and non-slave states, and St. Louis was one of three cities in the slave states (Baltimore, Maryland, and Wilmington, Delaware, being the others) that could boast public antislavery activity. There were lawyers, politicians, newspaper editors, ministers, and free people of color who spoke out against slaveholding and did some work against it. Even more important, over the previous two decades growing numbers of African American slaves had filed petitions for their freedom in St. Louis courts—more than three hundred by 1860—on the grounds that, like the Scotts, they had been taken by their masters over to bordering Illinois or some other free state zone and resided there before being brought back. Some of the petitions were successful, validated not only by the local circuit courts but by the state supreme court, thereby establishing important legal precedent. Given the time the Scotts spent in areas where slavery was not institutionally accepted and especially their experience being hired out there and in St. Louis, they would surely have learned significant lessons about the geopolitics of slavery and heard about the freedom suits being brought and won.

As a measure of this network of communication and knowledge, the Scotts' suit followed the standards and logic of those coming before: it was not, in fact, a suit by "slaves" for their "freedom" but rather a suit for damages charging "trespass," "assault," and "false imprisonment," based on the notion that the Scotts were already free owing to their residency on free soil and that Irene Emerson illegally held them in slavery and "beat, bruised, and ill-treated" them. But although their prospects were favorable and the attorneys for Irene Emerson worried, the Scotts were in for a long legal haul. At the first circuit court trial, the jury found for Emerson on a technicality, and instead of having to appeal, the Scotts were granted a new circuit court trial. This time the outcome was very different, with the jury finding for Scott and declaring him a free man. Now the ball was in Emerson's court, and she immediately appealed the verdict to the Missouri Supreme Court.

The timing was not good for the Scotts. The temper and personnel of the court had been shifting in a way that was far less receptive to the freedom suits, and when the Scotts' case came up in late 1851, controversy continued to brew over the congressional compromise measures of the previous year. A few months later, by a 2–1 vote, the state supreme court judges ruled against the Scotts, arguing, in effect, that while the soil in Illinois and the Wisconsin Territory might be free, the condition of slavery "reattached" in Missouri. But most unsettling was the rhetoric of the majority opinion. "It is a humiliating spectacle," the lead judge wrote, "to see the courts of this State confiscating the property of her own citizen by the command of *foreign* law [emphasis added]. If Scott is freed, by what means will it be effected, but by the constitution of Illinois, or the territorial laws of the United States." "Times," he then lamented, had come to see "not only individuals but States . . . possessed with a dark and fell spirit with respect to slavery . . . [and] it does not behoove the State of Missouri to show the least countenance to any measure which might gratify this spirit." Confiscation. Foreign law. Dark and fell spirit.

The tenor of the majority opinion in Missouri suggests what might have been coursing through the minds of the U.S. Supreme Court justices—five of whom were from the slave states—when the *Scott* case was argued on appeal (rather belatedly) in February 1856. The appeal, as it turned out, was not from the Missouri Supreme Court decision in *Scott v. Emerson* but from a lower federal court ruling in a separate filing known as *Scott v. Sanford,* John Sanford having become executor of John Emerson's estate (and possibly the owner of the Scotts) when Irene Emerson moved east and remarried around 1850 (Sanford's name was later misspelled in the Supreme Court record). Chief Justice Taney, already witness to the *Amistad* case, was increasingly incensed about "Northern insult and Northern aggression," and although many of the justices seemed reluctant to insert themselves too deeply into the struggle over slavery, the *Scott* case offered them an opportunity to issue a sweeping decision and settle some scores: all the more so as the border war in Kansas crackled and Sanford's lawyers, following Stephen Douglas's tack in the Kansas-Nebraska Act, raised the issue of the constitutionality of the Missouri Compromise line.

On the most important question for Dred and Harriet Scott and their (now two) children, the Supreme Court, by 7–2 in early March 1857, rejected their suit and determined that they were still enslaved. By the majority's lights, the laws of Missouri applied to Dred Scott after his return from Illinois, and because, as a slave, he was a citizen of neither Missouri nor the United States "within the meaning of the Constitution," he had no right to bring suit in either jurisdiction's court. That, of course, could have been the end of it: dismissal on jurisdictional grounds. But Taney and some of the justices chose to go much further, and in other rulings and opinions, none of which managed to garner seven votes, they dramatically advanced the political interests of slaveholders in the American union and relegated all people of African descent born in the United States to subaltern status.

At the time the Constitution was ratified, Taney wrote in a section of the opinion that secured only three votes, black people were regarded as inferior to white and therefore, whether slave or free, had no rights that white Americans "were bound to respect" and could not be citizens of the United States. But far more consequential on the political stage of the time (as it was not yet clear what a citizen of the United States was), Taney went on, with greater support from the justices (six votes), to declare the Missouri Compromise unconstitutional because it denied slaveholders the right to their property without due process of law and thereby violated the Fifth Amendment. "If the Constitution recognises the right of property of the master in a slave and makes no distinction between that description of property and other property owned by a citizen," Taney intoned, "no tribunal, acting under the authority of the United States . . . has a right to draw such a distinction, or deny to it the benefit of the provisions and guarantees which have been provided for the protection of private property against the encroachments of the Government."

Shock and outrage greeted the *Dred Scott* decision in antislavery circles, and that sense has, for the most part, been handed down over the years to students of the case and the period. They regard it as infamous, perhaps the worst decision the Supreme Court ever made, a deeply wrongheaded and illegitimate rendering of the Constitution. On political and social justice grounds, such a judgment can hardly be doubted. Yet Taney's reading did not really fall outside the mainstream of American jurisprudence up to that time, as Garrisonians, insisting that the Constitution was contaminated by slavery, would have been quick to acknowledge. Most judges, whether in the slave or non-slave states, would have shared Taney's views on black civil and racial debilities and it would be hard, if not impossible, to find any court that did not deny African Americans both state and American citizenship. "It is cause of real gratification," Chief Justice John Marshall of Virginia could wax in 1834, "that in the Northern and middle States, the opinion of the intelligent on this delicate subject, on which the Slave-holding States are so sensitive, accords so entirely with that of the South."

The question of federal power in the territories was surely more contested, though Taney's argument that constitutional rights, including those to personal property, were just as vital in the territories as in the states would have commanded broad support across the country. Stephen Douglas would have had no serious dispute with this view, and it could easily have accorded with popular sovereignty. But Taney took the logic one step further, insisting that if the Constitution did not permit Congress to restrict slaveholders from a federal territory, neither did it allow a "Territorial Government" to do the same: "It could confer no power on any local Government, established by its authority, to violate the provisions of the Constitution."

For slaveholders, Taney's doctrine in *Dred Scott* was an enormous boost to their confidence and prospects. It meant that in the vast expanse of federal territory in the trans-Mississippi West no borders to slavery could be erected and that even the borders imposed by some of the states might be of questionable constitutionality. After all, in the legal world of *Dred Scott*, on what basis could a "citizen" of one state be denied rights to his property if he moved across another state or decided on a brief residency there? But for Douglas, Taney's doctrine was a source of immense trouble. It challenged the credibility of the popular sovereignty formula, cast doubt on his entire project of joining union and empire, and jeopardized his standing in the eyes of Democratic slaveholders and non-slaveholders alike. And although it probably never crossed his mind, the deed was done not so much by an irascible chief justice as by determined Missouri slaves and a great many others like them.

CHAPTER SIX

Death of a Union

Depiction of Deep South leadership in the movement for secession, 1861.

The Language of Nation

In 1858, Stephen Douglas was completing his second term in the U.S. Senate and readying himself for a reelection campaign and a possible run at the presidency in 1860. He had been serving in Congress since the early 1840s, and Illinois had been an extremely reliable Democratic state. Whigs never managed to carry the state in a presidential election, and the Democrats had effectively controlled the legislature and the governorship during the 1840s and 1850s. Given his national visibility and efforts to make Illinois a vital hub in an expanding American empire, Douglas might have expected to reclaim his Senate seat fairly easily.

But the winds of political change were blowing in new directions across the Northeast and the upper Midwest, and the gusts were already being felt on the Illinois prairie. Ever since 1854, when Douglas orchestrated the passage of the Kansas-Nebraska Act with the support of most fellow Democrats together with Whigs from the slaveholding states, antislavery Whigs (often known as Conscience Whigs) along with free state Democrats had been searching for a new political home. A good many of the Whigs, especially those in New England and the Middle Atlantic, initially gravitated toward the emergent Know-Nothings, concerned as they were with the power of immigrants and slaveholders and with promoting suitable standards of personal comportment in public and private life. For a time, it appeared that nativism might enable former Whigs from various parts of the country to find an acceptable meeting ground and prepare to renew their battles with the Democrats. Yet as it did almost everywhere else in the 1850s, the slavery question intruded itself into the vitals of Know-Nothingism and quickly doomed the party's prospects for bridging the slaveholding and non-slaveholding states.

For all intents and purposes, Whigs from the slaveholding states were cut adrift in the increasingly turbulent seas of American politics, but their counterparts from the non-slaveholding states found a capacious berth in the fledgling Republican Party. First organized in the upper Midwest as part of the "anti-Nebraska" protests of 1854, the party gradually began to attract support and build a coalition. Like the Whigs, the Republicans looked to domestic economic development and regarded an active federal government as an important component of success. Although many had imperial eyes, they imagined a more slowly unfolding and densely interconnected empire than did their Democratic counterparts. They favored protectionism to bolster American manufactures, the rapid advance of transportation and communication networks, and the promotion of a vibrant commercial banking sector. For the most part, they also sympathized with the reform impulses of the period—whether temperance, education, or asylums—in the hope of encouraging a socially useful American character, and many continued to show the marks of the anti-Catholicism that had left a long and deep imprint in American political culture. Like the free state Democrats who might have been influenced by George Henry Evans, the Republicans favored land policies meant to hasten the settlement of the trans-Mississippi West by family farmers and to that end began to embrace "homestead" legislation.

Yet the most powerful force that drew them together and would continue to define their central project was antislavery. Some had cut their teeth on political abolitionism and the Liberty Party. Others came to the Republicans through the vestibules of the Free-Soil Party or Conscience Whiggery. Many more were concerned by the aggressiveness of what they called the "slave power" and its apparent designs on the American union: the tough new Fugitive Slave Law that slaveholders extracted in 1850; the notorious Kansas-Nebraska Act that repealed the Missouri Compromise; and then the *Dred Scott* decision, which both testified to slavery's hold on the branches of the federal government and threatened to secure much of America's territory for slaveholders. Together, the Republicans met in convention in 1856 and nominated John C. Frémont as their candidate for the presidency.

For a new political party, the Republicans made a very good showing in 1856, winning about one-third of the popular vote and more than a hundred electoral votes (the Know-Nothings also fielded a candidate, the former Whig president Millard Fillmore, who did surprisingly well). Although they failed to carry Illinois, the Democratic margin there was only about nine thousand votes (four percentage points), and, even more impressively, the Republicans succeeded in wresting the state governorship from the Democrats. By 1858, the Republicans would be ready to challenge Stephen Douglas with a candidate who had spent little time in elective office but who, from a base in the state capital of Springfield, had become one of the party notables, in good measure because of his growing attacks on Douglas and popular sovereignty. His name was Abraham Lincoln.

Lincoln did not come to the Republican Party by way of the Liberty or Free-Soil Party. From his political youth, he had been a staunch Whig and eyed organized antislavery with wariness and mistrust. Born in Kentucky before moving with his family across the Ohio River, first to Indiana and then to Illinois, Lincoln admired Henry Clay and was chiefly concerned with the protective tariff. He served briefly in the Illinois state legislature and one term (1847–49) in the U.S. House of Representatives, all the while devoting attention to a law practice given over mainly to civil litigation (debts, railroads, land titles, domestic disputes). Ambitious as he was, Lincoln remained active in Whig politics, but the public notice he would win came as a result of his increasing outspokenness on the issue of slavery.

The origins of Lincoln's discomfort with slavery are not entirely clear—his Baptist parents had an aversion to slavery, though other relatives owned slaves—and he certainly lived most of his life on slavery's border without much trouble. Slave hiring and "servant" trading were hardly unknown in southern Illinois, and racist exclusions were state policy. Lincoln himself was not above indulging in racist language, and he had a hard time imagining a future in which white and black people would live together in peace. But for an effectively self-educated man, Lincoln was remarkably well read in political economy; he appeared to have been influenced by the antislavery Whig Joshua Giddings while serving in Congress; and, when there, he did draft a bill providing for the gradual abolition of slavery in the District of Columbia (it was never introduced). By the early 1850s, Lincoln seemed to share the perspective of moderate free stater, acknowledging that the Constitution protected slavery in the states where it had been deemed legal while objecting to slavery's expansion into the territories of the trans-Mississippi West. Although he had no idea how slavery might be abolished where it existed, he seemed to believe that any plan of abolition would be gradual (as in the northern states), involve compensation of some sort to slave owners, and be followed by the voluntary exile of the freed population, better known to Whigs and then Republicans as colonization.

But it was in the fall of 1854, in response to the Kansas-Nebraska Act, that Lincoln came to be recognized as "a powerful speaker." Looking for the opportunity to take on Douglas, he spent "weeks in the State Library, pumping his brain and his imagination for points and arguments," and then went before large audiences at Bloomington, Springfield, and Peoria (where Douglas spoke, too). Rejecting the idea that black people could be "politically and socially our equals," he nonetheless condemned the constitutional logic of popular sovereignty, told of the founders' moves against slavery, and warned of slavery's likely expansion into Kansas and other territories. Yet Lincoln also shifted to higher ground, pointing to the rise of "liberal part[ies] throughout the world," insisting that "there can be no moral right in connection with one man's making a slave of another," and suggesting the American hypocrisy of "fostering Human slavery and proclaiming ourselves, at the same time, the sole friends of Human Freedom." "Our republican robe is soiled and trailed through the dust," he thundered, and he urged that it be "repurif[ied]" and the Declaration of Independence "re-adopt[ed]."

Before long, Lincoln would be actively involved in building the Illinois Republican Party and making a name for himself in party circles. He joined his colleagues in the state and elsewhere in denouncing the Dred Scott decision and

the Taney Court and in June 1858 was selected by the Republican state convention as the party's candidate for the U.S. Senate seat held by Stephen Douglas. In
accepting the nomination, Lincoln continued to rail against *Dred Scott* and its
implications for "squatter" sovereignty, but he also reflected powerfully about a
"house divided against itself." "The government cannot endure, permanently
half slave and half free," he intoned. "Either the opponents of slavery, will arrest
the further spread of it, and place it . . . in course of ultimate extinction; or its
advocates will push it forward, till it shall become alike lawful in all the States,
old as well as new—North as well as South."

These ideas would frame the seven debates that Lincoln and Douglas had in
the late summer and early fall of 1858. Douglas aggressively attempted to tar
Lincoln with the brush of antislavery radicalism and racial egalitarianism,
arguing that Lincoln favored "the unconditional repeal of the Fugitive Slave
Law," opposed "the admission of any more Slave States," and wished to confer
"upon the negro the rights and privileges of citizenship." For his part, Lincoln
accused Douglas of betraying the intentions of the founders and the spirit of the
Declaration of Independence and pressed him on the implications of *Dred Scott*
for the viability of popular sovereignty (was it now even possible for a territory
to prohibit slavery?).

But running through the speeches and rejoinders, the points and counterpoints, was a thread of argument and contention that the notion of a "house divided" spun out. Indeed, Douglas repeatedly criticized Lincoln's apparent
insistence on "uniformity among the institutions of the different States" and
mocked Lincoln's view that a "house divided against itself cannot stand." The
United States "has stood thus divided into free and slave States from its organization up to this day," Douglas crowed during the third debate at Jonesboro. What
had been the result? "During that period we have increased from 4 millions to
30 millions of people," Douglas reminded the audience, "we have extended our
territory from the Mississippi to the Pacific Ocean; we have acquired the Floridas
and Texas, and other territory sufficient to double our geographical extent . . .
we have arisen from a weak and feeble power to become the terror and admiration of the civilized world; and all this has been done under a Constitution which
Mr. Lincoln thinks . . . cannot stand." "Our Government," Douglas proclaimed,
"was formed on the principle of diversity in local institutions and laws, and not
on that of uniformity."

Lincoln denied that he countenanced "uniformity," but in truth he, along
with growing numbers of Republicans, had begun to speak what may be regarded
as a "language of nation" as opposed to languages of "union" and "empire" that
had largely prevailed since American independence. To be sure, languages of
nation could be heard from very early on, especially in some numbers of *The*

Federalist (most notably the contributions of John Jay) and in corners of Federalism and Whiggery. But the predominant conception of the United States was of a union or confederation of states collectively engaged in the pursuit of an empire whose borders were never clearly set. How much power and authority the states might have and how quickly and continuously the borders of empire might expand were subject to regular dispute, all the more so as the question of slavery came to figure centrally. Yet, whether they were Whigs or Democrats, slaveholders or non-slaveholders, political leaders tended to agree that the principal relationships in constitutional life involved the federal government and the states, on the one hand, and the states and individuals, on the other. Therefore, neither the federal Constitution nor the federal courts could coherently explain what a citizen of the United States was (though the Taney Court found a way to decide what a citizen was not); citizenship together with political rights, most agreed, was a matter for the states.

It was in political antislavery's search for a constitutional argument that the language of nation began to develop in meaningful ways. And it was men like Salmon P. Chase, Thomas Morris, and Gamaliel Bailey—all from west of the Appalachians and initially associated with the Liberty Party—who began to craft the political grammar. Although they conceded that the Constitution offered slavery various protections where it already existed, they insisted that the founders believed that freedom and equality were the natural conditions of humankind and slavery no more than a temporary and discordant institution. They pointed out that the words "slave" or "slavery" never appeared in the Constitution's text and that the various euphemisms deployed—"other persons" or "persons bound to labor and service"—testified to the framers' unease. Equally consequential, they proclaimed that the Constitution and the federal government were made by the "people" and not by the "states" and that it was the people in whom sovereignty inhered. Freedom was "national," they declared, and slavery was only "local." "The Constitution found slavery and left it a State institution—the creature and dependent of State law—wholly local in its existence and character," Chase wrote. "It did not make it a national institution."

The use of the term "nation" was not the essential component of the language of nation; it could be little more than a stand-in for "union" and "confederation," a political synonym of sorts, and usually was. For that matter, Lincoln and other Republicans seemed to use the term "union" far more frequently than "nation." What infused the language of nation was rather a vision or description of the United States: as a territory with recognized borders and sets of principles, laws, and institutional arrangements over which the federal government ruled directly, without the mediations of other sovereign or sovereign-claiming entities. Just as slaveholders rankled some evangelical Christians because they stood between God and the individual slave, thus preventing the slave from choosing the path of salvation and postponing the coming of God's kingdom, so did they rankle antislavery nationalists because they stood between the government (the people) and the slave, and thus between a country corrupted by slavery and one committed to freedom.

In essence, Stephen Douglas and Abraham Lincoln were both right. There was room for slavery and a multiplicity of separate sovereignties—for "diversity"—in an empire or union. But there was no such room in a nation or nation-state. That was the rub.

The Embrace of Secession

By the time Lincoln was articulating a language of nation, very different languages and projects had gained traction in the slaveholding states. Most widely in evidence was a language of region or "section," an idea of a "South" that had a collective identity and set of economic and political interests, not to mention a sense of cultural distinctiveness. The framers, in convention in 1787, could of course speak of a South and of southern concerns as they attempted to construct a constitutional edifice acceptable to representatives from various parts of the Union, and the invocation of regionalism or sectionalism could be heard in numerous political venues during the early republic. But it was only in the 1830s that sectionalism began to become central to the political vocabulary of the United States, and this was because both pro-slavery and antislavery moved into new phases and sought to attract popular support.

Abolitionists and other antislavery partisans played an important role here, especially as they mounted an economic and political critique of slave labor and contrasted the tendencies to be found where slavery did not and did prevail: "freedom" as against "serfdom," "freeholds" as against "tenancies," "democracy" as against "despotism," "education" as against "ignorance," "progress" as against "stagnation." Some would refer to a "North" above the Mason-Dixon Line and the Ohio River where slavery had been eradicated and free labor thrived, and to a "South" below them marked by aristocratic hierarchies, social degradation, and cultural retrogression. Indeed, the political discourse of antislavery effectively erased the long history the Northeast and the Midwest had with slavery and emancipation and instead sought to mark a sharp divide between evolving worlds.

Pro-slavery political leaders and intellectuals, especially from the Southeast and the Gulf Coast, joined the discursive process. It was in part a response to new questions about the wisdom and morality of slaveholding and in part a perception of potentially shifting balances of political and economic power. At the time of the Constitution's ratification, Americans widely believed that the Union's population was moving in a southwesterly direction, strengthening the position of those areas where slavery and the plantation system held sway. The rapid expansion of white settlement and slaveholding across the Deep South and into Texas certainly breathed new vitality into the slave regime. But by the 1830s, it was also clear that the states where slavery had been abolished or was under attack were growing even faster and that in a developing international age of emancipation slavery's long-term prospects might be in serious jeopardy. After all, the revolution in Haiti and then the abolition of slavery in the British West Indies unsettled even the richest and most confident slaveholders and vastly complicated the future of the Caribbean and thus the security of American slavery.

The idea of a "South" was many things—and its characteristics are debated to this day—but from the 1830s on it was in good measure a political argument joined to economic interests and cultural dispositions. It was meant to mediate the tensions between the very local and particularist sovereignties that slavery embodied (the relation of master and slave and the rights of states in which slavery was embedded) and the collective concerns of slaveholders who might have grown different crops and presided over different demographic orders: that is to say, slaveholders in Kentucky as well as Alabama, Maryland as well as South Carolina, Virginia as well as Louisiana. The "South" took shape as a political representation, as a region or "section" where slavery had legal sanction, organized the political economy, and fended off the initial dynamic of emancipationism. It came forth in the increasingly militant defense of slavery and especially in the critique of "free labor society," in the articulation of opposition to protective tariffs and support for free trade, in the insistence on maintaining at least a parity of "slave" and "free" states in the Union and on claiming new territories that would be open to slavery, and in the proliferation of literary and commercial journals devoted to the region. In an important sense, the "South" was a central feature of the emerging consciousness of the slaveholding class, though one as riven with contradictions as the politics of slaveholding itself.

The political idea of the "South" developed alongside theories of empowerment that focused on states and households. South Carolina's John C. Calhoun most famously combined a defense of slavery and local rights in his writings on state sovereignty and nullification, but his was only the most powerful and finely elaborated argument. "State rights" became the political mantra for slaveholders, for their representatives, and for Democrats more generally, though far more than their counterparts in the "North" southern Democrats believed that the states, in their sovereign capacity, had created the Union and retained their sovereign authority. But for slaveholders large and small, state rights had palpable meaning principally in relation to the power they presumed to exercise not only over their slaves but also over other household dependents: their wives, children, and others who might reside under their roofs. Not surprisingly, they associated abolitionism with other challenges to patriarchal household authority, women's rights and temperance chief among them.

For all of his efforts to delimit the powers of the federal government and weaken the ties that bound the states to it, Calhoun remained a unionist. He understood nullification as a constitutional means for preserving the United States and defending "minorities" within it in the face of conflicting property regimes. But South Carolina Nullifiers did threaten secession if President Andrew Jackson tried to wage war against them, and although none of the other slaveholding states were ready to lend their support to such an option, secession was thereafter on the political table. During the remainder of the 1830s and for most of the 1840s, there it sat, quietly, as the slaveholders' representatives battled, among themselves and with those from the non-slaveholding states, about the goals and means of empire, the annexation of Texas and Cuba, the extent of conquest in Mexico, and the best vehicles for stanching abolitionism— especially its British form—in the gulf. These were the years in which cotton became king, princely fortunes were made, and slavery again seemed to be on the march.

Yet as the American war against Mexico drew down and the country had to decide what to do with the territory it had forcibly acquired, slaveholders saw increasingly ominous signs. There was the Pennsylvania Democrat David Wilmot's proviso to exclude slavery from all parts of the Mexican cession. There was the successful attempt of the newly elected Whig president and war hero, Zachary Taylor (ironically, a slaveholder from Louisiana), to have California immediately admitted with a free state constitution. And there was the half loaf of popular sovereignty embedded in the 1850 compromises as formulated by the northern Democrats Stephen Douglas and Lewis Cass.

Militant slaveholders, taking their cue from Calhoun, saw these developments as the handwriting on the wall and looked to organize a united "southern" response in defense of their "rights." Some, increasingly called fire-eaters— Robert Barnwell Rhett and James Henry Hammond of South Carolina; William Lowndes Yancey of Alabama; John A. Quitman of Mississippi; and Edmund Ruffin and Nathaniel Beverley Tucker of Virginia, prominent among them—had already embraced disunion as the only viable means for protecting slavery; others wished to consider the "South's" options, with the goal of unifying the political leadership of the slave states and influencing the debate over the congressional compromises. First gathering in Mississippi, they called for a convention to meet in Nashville, Tennessee, in June 1850.

For the most part, the Nashville Convention was a flop. The organizers intended to attract a strong representation from the slave states and to keep South Carolina in the background, because the Carolinians had a well-earned reputation for unilateral radicalism. They failed on both accounts: most of the delegates came from the Deep South (none from Maryland, Delaware, Kentucky, Missouri, North Carolina, or Louisiana), and as might have been expected, South Carolina sent the largest and best-recognized delegation. To make matters worse for them, the defeat of the Wilmot Proviso and the death of an ailing Calhoun had shifted the tenor of congressional deliberation toward moderation. All that would come out of the Nashville Convention was an assortment of threatening words together with resolutions invoking "southern" rights, supporting the extension of the Missouri Compromise line to the Pacific coast, and vowing to reassemble in the near future.

If slaveholding militancy seemed to have been defeated and South Carolina once again isolated, secessionism, quietly discussed for a number of years, had nonetheless gained new life. Secessionists from the Deep South and Virginia had begun to create something of a political network. "I find the feeling among the Southern members for a dissolution of the Union—if the antislavery [measures] should be pressed to extremity—is becoming much more general than at first," the Georgia congressman Alexander H. Stephens observed in December 1849. "Men are now beginning to talk of it seriously, who, twelve months ago, hardly permitted themselves to think of it." Secessionists had also learned some hard, albeit valuable, lessons. Disunion, which had come to seem so necessary to them, would require a concerted campaign if it were to win significant public support. Secessionists would have to use the hustings, the newspapers, political clubs, and civic associations to disseminate their ideas and explain their logic. As an Alabama secessionist put it, "The great difficulty is to make the Masses see beyond their noses . . . [and] we must have time." They would also have to fill state and local offices with secessionist advocates and sympathizers, who could be in a position to shape opinion and ready constituencies for action. And they would have to recognize that a concerted or unified movement might not at first be possible, that one state might have to provide the spark, after which, in the words of John Quitman, "an active and cordial union of the whole South would be instantly effected, and a complete Southern confederacy organized."

In the months after the Nashville Convention and the passage of the compromise measures, the political prospects for secessionism looked remote, to say the least. Unionism was in the ascendancy across the United States, and many slaveholding politicians spoke of the compromises as the "final settlement" of the slavery question. Whigs and moderate Democrats from the slaveholding states began to form "union" parties and swept all before them in the ensuing state elections. But if the secessionists were humbled by the initial avalanche of ballots, they gained certain advantages from the magnetism of moderation: as unionist Democrats joined hands with Whigs, secessionists were left in charge of the state and local apparatus of the Democratic Party, particularly in the Deep South. They now had a free hand to push forward their candidates for county governing boards, legislatures, and governorships, as well as influence the editorships and editorial policies of Democratic newspapers. Over time during the 1850s, as the political center eroded and the Kansas-Nebraska Act sealed the demise of the Whig Party, the secessionists would be well placed both to convince many southern voters of the legitimacy of disunion and then to help orchestrate the circumstances that would make disunion appear the only sensible alternative. They were building a political movement from the ground up and the top down and by the mid-1850s were in an extremely strong structural position.

Even the ostensible high points of southern unionism and moderation betrayed the ideological inroads of secessionism. Thus, when a convention in Georgia assembled after the compromise measures of 1850 were enacted, the delegates pledged to "abide by [them] as a permanent adjustment of this sectional controversy." Yet the remaining resolutions of their "Georgia Platform" couched the pledge in solemn warnings: "The state of Georgia will and ought to resist even (as a last resort) to the disruption of every tie that binds her to the Union, any action of Congress upon the subject of slavery in the District of Columbia, or in places subject to the jurisdiction of Congress incompatible with the safety and domestic tranquility, the rights and honor of the slave-holding states, or any refusal to admit as a state any territory hereafter applying, because of the existence of slavery therein, or any act, prohibiting the introduction of slaves into the territories of Utah and New Mexico, or any act repealing or materially modifying the laws now in force for the recovery of fugitive slaves." A short leash it was that these "unionists" gave to their counterparts in the non-slaveholding states.

But what lent secessionism its energy and momentum was not only the constitutional argument and sense of impending crisis in the Union; it was also a vision of expansion and modernity that looked to the West, the Caribbean, Mexico, and Central America and took stock of political currents that might have started flowing the slave South's way. Whatever the victories of emancipationism since the late eighteenth century, Deep South slaveholders could reasonably believe that on a world stage antislavery might have run its course. By the mid-1850s, a variety of popular insurgencies in the Atlantic world had been defeated—most notably the revolutions of 1848 in continental Europe and

Chartism in Britain—and the aftermath of slavery in the Caribbean and Latin America seemed so problematic in the social and economic "disorder" it produced that even former champions of abolitionism expressed disenchantment; they made relatively easy peace with the importation of indentured and otherwise bound workers to help re-staff sugar estates from Jamaica to the Peruvian coast. Haiti, perhaps the most disturbing symbol of a world turned upside down, had been cordoned into diplomatic and economic isolation where it stagnated under the burdens of rural impoverishment and political authoritarianism. If anything, political conservatism seemed fortified both by the backlash against popular revolution and by the economic expansion of the period that strengthened the hands and lined the pockets of merchants, bankers, and manufacturers on both sides of the Atlantic. The accelerating Industrial Revolution thereby created a booming world market for cotton in which the American slave states were the major suppliers and the slaveholding planters among the principal beneficiaries.

Although some of the secessionists glanced backward and hoped to recover a rural world lost, the increasingly consequential among them exhibited no such nostalgia. By and large, secessionism—at least outside South Carolina—proved most appealing to young, upwardly mobile slaveholders who imagined a prosperous future for themselves if slave property could be secured and the boundaries of slave territory were capable of being enlarged. Many were already in areas of the Deep South experiencing dynamic growth, and their horizons were to the south and the west. They likely delighted in the forays of filibusters, cast eager eyes on Cuba, and exulted in the cults of militarism and masculinity. They favored developing the South's transportation infrastructure and hoped to see a transcontinental railroad built across a southern route. Some would even support the reopening of the African slave trade so that men like them could expand their labor force and non-slaveholders might have the opportunity to join the slaveholding class. So long as their representatives wielded power in the federal government, they might be able to follow these paths within the Union; if the government passed into hostile hands, new directions would have to be taken.

Not by accident were many of the radical secessionists—the "fire-eaters"—self-made men who began their adult lives as social and political outsiders. And none seemed to be more in tune with the aspirations of rising slaveholders of the Deep South and the Mississippi Valley than J. D. B. DeBow. Born in Charleston, South Carolina, in 1820 to a merchandising family that had emigrated from New York, DeBow worked as a store clerk and schoolteacher before attending the College of Charleston and reading law. But, as one of his contemporaries observed, "he was a born statistician, with a dash of the man of letters," and during a stint with the *Southern Quarterly Review* began to imagine a commercial journal devoted to the interests of the slave states. After floating the idea in Charleston, he decided to move out to New Orleans, where prospects seemed better, and in early 1846 commenced publishing the *Commercial Review of the South and West*, later and better known as *DeBow's Review*.

Although DeBow was not an early champion of secession, he was a great defender of slavery and a strong advocate of slavery's suitability to many walks of economic life. Hardly enamored of the wistful view of a plantation South, DeBow pressed for economic diversification, agricultural reform, and railroad development as the path to modernization and regional strength. He regularly attended commercial conventions in the slave states, opened the pages of his *Review* to extended discussions of improved farming methods and economic experimentation, and favored popular education. Most of all, he beat the drums for geographical expansion and envisioned southern slaveholders moving into Mexico, Central America, and the Caribbean basin. Addressing "the interest in slavery of the southern non-slaveholder," DeBow saw slaveholding empire as a means to enable white men who did not own slaves to join the master class, even suggesting that the slave trade might be reopened to better promote both slavery's march and white social mobility.

Mindful of reaching a large audience, DeBow initially stepped carefully around the issue of disunion, toward which the logic of his projects clearly turned. Still, he supported the Nashville Convention, believed that the compromise measures of 1850 threatened the safety of the slave South, and saw the Republican Party as fixed on excluding slaveholders "from every area of national growth." Fittingly, he came out for secession at the Knoxville Commercial Convention in 1857, where he urged political unity and insisted that the South had the resources "to maintain the rank of a first class power, wherever it should be deemed necessary, to establish a separate confederation." Couched in optimism as well as foreboding, it would prove a powerful argument.

Subterranean Expectations

Among those who took keen note of the intensifying political battle over slavery was a slave named William Webb. Born in Georgia in the mid-1830s, Webb was taken out to Mississippi by his master and then moved several times between Mississippi and Kentucky owing to the changing fortunes of his master's family. Along the way, Webb found God, sought God's graces, and assumed a prophetic stance. But around the time that "Fremont was running for President," he became involved in political debates and discussions in the slave quarters. Posting guards to warn of slave patrols and taking oaths (on pain of death) to maintain secrecy, Webb and his fellow slaves "held great meetings and had speeches among themselves" and "put all their trust in Fremont to deliver them from bondage."

Frémont's defeat proved disheartening—a "great anger arose among the colored people," Webb remembered, while the slaveholders "rejoiced"—though not politically debilitating. The slaves "began to study how they would get free," and they would meet "to try some other way to get free from their cruel bondage." Making "speeches among themselves," they considered "what steps they would take." Some, Webb wrote, "would speak about rebelling and killing, and some would speak and say, 'wait for the next four years,'" imagining the "next President would set the colored people free." Equally important, they looked to create a network of communication so that slaves in the vicinity and across far greater distances could be informed and coordinate their understandings and activities. Webb himself continued organizing when he was sent off to Kentucky, calling together twelve leaders on each plantation and combining folk religion (passing around bags of roots and "marching around the house seven times") with political prognostication. "I told them that Fremont was a small light, and it would keep burning till it was spread over the whole world," he recalled, adding that "slaveholders down in Mississippi are very uneasy, and by what I saw, I think there is a great light coming, and it will be here sooner than we expect." Within a short time, Webb claimed that he had "friends all over the country" and "was receiving news from a great many states."

William Webb's account demonstrated slave knowledge of both the substance and the cycles of American politics. He and the slaves he lived among in Mississippi and Kentucky plainly recognized John C. Frémont as a potential ally in the fight against slavery and knew something of the official political calendar ("wait for the next four years"). But although Webb's is an especially rich representation, it opens our eyes to a world of subterranean politics that enabled slaves to sense the pulse of change, register their expectations, and play a part in the struggle for power in the United States. Especially alert to signs of conflict among whites, they sought to gather intelligence and assess its meanings; with the advent of mass electoral politics together with the explosive growth of print media, their opportunities for political edification accordingly increased.

Slaves gleaned political information in a great many ways: from white politicians they overheard during court days, militia musters, and campaigns; from newspapers and smuggled tracts (such as David Walker's *Appeal to the Coloured Citizens of the World*) that could be read by the handful of them who were literate; from forced migrants like William Webb who arrived from other states and localities; from slaveholders who expressed their fears and concerns within earshot; and from fugitives who returned to ferry more slaves to black settlements to the north. Most often, they learned about politics from other slaves who had mobility, who worked in the plantation house, who were hired out in towns and on docks, who were coachmen, boatmen, and tradesmen, and who then brought news back to the quarters. In the process, slaves in many parts of the southern states constructed political narratives and discourses of expectations—stories about the terrain of politics, about friends and enemies, about their prospects for freedom, and about what freedom would bring them. And while they often imagined an emancipation brought forth by the work of God or one of God's earthly agents, they readied themselves to assist when that day of judgment came.

The political dynamic often joined—in the United States as well as in other slave societies of the hemisphere—news of some consequential event with rumors of impending, or recently proclaimed, emancipation. Thus, black preachers in eastern North Carolina attempted to convince their congregations in the early 1820s (apparently with some success) that "the national government had set them free and that they were being unjustly held in servitude." This was, significantly, the very moment when the debate over Missouri's admission to the Union embroiled the country and rang "a firebell in the night" even louder than Thomas Jefferson might have feared. Could the slaves have believed, given the frets of their owners and reports of the votes in Congress, that opponents of Missouri's admission as a slave state had greater designs and had carried the day, only to see their victory blocked on the ground in the South? Slaves in Charleston, South Carolina, might have reached a similar conclusion in 1822 after hearing that the state legislature had taken up the question, not of emancipation, but of private manumission. Hence the alarm provoked by Denmark Vesey and his political circle of slaves and free people of color.

Hotly contested presidential elections, even with no obvious connection to the slavery issue, could also stir expectations. The bitter contest of 1800 between John Adams and Thomas Jefferson, when many Americans worried that the Union teetered on the brink of dissolution and civil war—together with the more than decade-long revolution in St. Domingue—provided the context for Gabriel's massive conspiracy in the vicinity of Richmond, Virginia. Years later, according to the recollections of a fugitive slave, "there came a report from a neighboring plantation," just before the election of 1836, "that if Van Buren was elected, he was going to give all the slaves their freedom." Indeed, the rumor "spread rapidly among the slaves," prompting great "rejoicing" and identifications with "the children of Israel." In Georgia in 1840, William Henry Harrison's campaign led some slaves to assert boldly that if Harrison "became President of the United States, they should have their freedom."

It is difficult to know whether slaves had some sense of Adams's and Jefferson's different views on the Haitian Revolution (Adams entertained an alliance with Toussaint Louverture; Jefferson looked to destroy Toussaint's regime), or whether they had heard about Van Buren's opposition to Texas annexation, or whether they made something of Harrison's Whig affiliation and Ohio residence. But what they seemed to glimpse was that their owners might have confirmed enemies and they potential allies. This was what the Georgia politician Howell Cobb surmised during the presidential election of 1844, when the Liberty Party fielded a candidate. The "negroes," he recorded, "are already saying to each other that great men are trying to set them free and will succeed." By the fall of 1856, as the Republican Party chose its first contestant for presidential office, rumors that liberation might be at hand flew so vigorously among the slaves—witness William Webb's account—that they, in turn, sent rumors of slave insurrection circulating among whites. Reports of slaves setting fires, secreting arms, and plotting rebellion came from unnerved slaveholders in virtually all of the slave states but especially from Texas and the rest of the Deep South.

Among slavery's enemies who counted on the slaves' political expectations and willingness to act on them was John Brown. After fleeing from Kansas, Brown began to focus on a far more audacious project: striking a massive blow against the slave regime by enabling slaves to flee their captivity and constitute themselves as a hostile state in the heart of slaveholding territory. The project reflected a growing acceptance among abolitionists that slavery was organized violence and warfare, that formal campaigns and political mobilizations were ineffective against it, and that emancipation would likely require force of arms. "There was a time when slavery could have been ended by political action," Gerrit Smith trenchantly declared. "But that time has gone by—and, as I apprehend, forever. There was not enough virtue in the American people to bring slavery to a bloodless termination; and all that remains for them is to bring it to a bloody one."

While in New England in 1857 raising money and arms for the ongoing Kansas struggle, Brown met and won a sympathetic hearing from some of abolitionism's important activists with means—Franklin Sanborn, George L. Stearns, Thomas Wentworth Higginson, Samuel Gridley Howe, Theodore Parker, and, not surprisingly, Gerrit Smith, together eventually known as the Secret Six—who would provide him with financial support. He also attracted the interest of the black abolitionists Frederick Douglass and Martin Delany, whose disenchantment with the course of antislavery and the position of black people in the United States had deepened. Brown was, after all, a proven fighter in the developing war against slavery; he had helped derail the admission of Kansas as a slave state; and unlike other militant abolitionists he appeared to have a plan and was ready to walk the walk.

The plan, such as it was, might best be described as maroon warfare. Brown would amass a large fighting force, arm it, and, from bases in the Appalachian Mountains, raid slaveholding farms and plantations and rally the slaves to join them. As the Appalachian hideouts swelled in size, they would form governing bodies while continuing to disturb the stability of slavery from Virginia to Alabama by means of armed attacks and slave flight. To that end, Brown, while visiting Douglass in Rochester in early 1858, drew up a "Provisional Constitution" that he would present to an upcoming convention of blacks in Chatham, Ontario, in hopes of winning support and recruits. The constitution pledged "protection" to the "proscribed, oppressed, and enslaved citizens, or of the proscribed and oppressed races of the United States," made all property among them equal and communal, required "labor in some way for the general good," and encouraged all members, "whether male or female," to "carry arms openly." Some in fact saw a resemblance to the politically formidable maroons of Jamaica and the Guianas, and Brown was careful to note that the constitution "shall not be construed so as in any way to encourage the overthrow of any State Government of the United States" or the "dissolution of the Union." Rather, Brown was interested in "Amendment and Repeal" and proclaimed that "our flag shall be the same that our Fathers fought under in the Revolution."

Brown did not believe that slaves would spontaneously join his war once they learned of it. He knew it would be necessary to lay the groundwork, which is what drew him to the area of Harpers Ferry, Virginia. Although Harpers Ferry was best known as the site of a federal arsenal—and thus a source of weaponry—it was also a gateway into the Appalachians and very much in the midst of a long-standing route of fugitive slave escapes. The adjacent areas of Virginia, Maryland, and Pennsylvania had scattered populations of slaves as well as growing enclaves of free people of color, some of whom had worked at neighboring iron foundries. And by all accounts, Brown, who rented a farmhouse near Harpers Ferry in the spring of 1859, began to build a network that included local free black leaders—ministers and tradesmen among them—recognizing as he did that the involvement of African Americans was crucial to the undertaking. Well aware of the militancy of many blacks north of the Potomac River and of their paramilitary activities in pursuit of self-defense, Brown seems to have imagined a potential web of alliance extending out from the edge of the Appalachians into the Maryland and Pennsylvania countryside and then east to Baltimore and Philadelphia. At the very least, there is reason to believe that by the summer of 1859 a good many black people, slave and free, in the Harpers Ferry perimeter knew something of John Brown's intentions.

By the early fall of 1859, Brown decided to commence his war with an attack on Harpers Ferry instead of heading there after raids on slave plantations and farms had begun, as he might initially have planned. Perhaps this was because his recruiting efforts had left him with a smaller fighting force than he had anticipated: the Chatham convention brought him only one volunteer, and despite his eloquent pleas Frederick Douglass refused him (though one of Douglass's companions, Shields Green, chose to join up). Nonetheless, with a growing sense of urgency and just over twenty men—most of whom were white and veterans of Brown's Kansas battles, three of whom were his sons, and five of whom were black—Brown set out for Harpers Ferry on the night of October 16, dispatching a small party to round up slaveholders and liberate slaves nearby.

Although the raid went quite smoothly at first, with Brown and his men successfully taking the armory, cutting telegraph lines, and arming the slaves and free blacks—between twenty-five and fifty of them—who had ventured forth, in the early morning hours of the seventeenth an eastbound train was let through and quickly alerted authorities about a "Negro insurrection" in progress. Before long, local militias and angry town residents had the Brown raiders surrounded and under attack, and U.S. troops under the command of Robert E. Lee and J. E. B. Stuart were on their way. On the morning of October 18, Lee demanded Brown's unconditional surrender and, when that was rejected, ordered the soldiers in. When the smoke finally cleared, ten of Brown's men, including two of his sons, and as many as seventeen of the blacks who had taken up arms with them lay dead or mortally wounded. Five of the raiders, including one of Brown's sons, managed to escape. And five (later two more), including Brown himself, who had sustained head and shoulder injuries, were taken into custody. Less than two months later, after brief trials, they were hanged.

Under the best of circumstances, there was only so much that John Brown could have expected from the slaves in the surroundings of Harpers Ferry. The white population outnumbered the black there by about four to one, and the slaves generally lived on farms, rather than plantations, with, at most, a few of their peers. Communications among them would therefore have been difficult, and the task of organizing a militarily formidable number nearly impossible. Although some slaves and free blacks eagerly took up the arms provided them and fought tenaciously, most others either stayed put or quickly fled back to the relative safety of their quarters. Had Brown and his men managed to collect weapons and escape into the mountains, they might have served as a beacon for fugitives and been able to stage attacks on slaveholdings in adjacent valleys. As it was, they chose to hole up in the armory, and the battle ended quickly.

If anything, in the months before Brown's raid, the slaves and free blacks who heard tell of the project likely puzzled over its character and prospects for success. Brown's was not a familiar name among them. He was not the leader of a political party or visible to them in the antislavery cause (though he might have been discussed in connection with Kansas, but not in a way that would have been palpable). Slaveholders and their political representatives probably did not mention him, nor was the fall of 1859 a season of electioneering when tensions over slavery's future would daily be in evidence. Many of the black folk, slave and free, might have found the plan wanting, ill-advised, or destined for disaster. Others might have decided to wait and see how events unfolded before they decided to act. None would have been amused or comforted by either the brutal suppression of the raid, the public executions of the captured participants, or the role of the federal government in defending the interests of slaveholders. Although they recognized that the raid testified to the heightening of antislavery sentiment and sensed the panic among many of their owners in its aftermath, they would require a more politically powerful confluence of events before seizing the time.

Who Will Rule the State?

When John Brown went to the gallows on December 2, 1859, he prophesied that "the crimes of this guilty land: will never be purged away; but with Blood," and it was easy to imagine that his failed raid was the opening salvo of a wider and more deadly conflagration. A Virginia newspaper likened "Brown and his desperadoes" to a "cancerous disease with which a great part of northern society is polluted," while slaveholders began to organize vigilance committees and warn of other abolitionist emissaries ready to make war against them. For their part, many abolitionists mourned Brown as a great martyr to the cause. Ralph Waldo Emerson, whose embrace of antislavery had steadily strengthened, called Brown "the rarest of heroes, a pure idealist," and a "saint" whose execution would "make the gallows glorious like a cross."

Yet the immediate danger to the Union came less from abolitionist-inspired slave insurrection or the general militarization of the slavery question than from a reconfigured struggle at the heart of formal American politics. Into the early 1850s, the political system was dominated by two parties—the Whigs and the Democrats—with very different outlooks and policies but also with constituencies in every part of the country. The Whigs were more favorably disposed to the exercise of federal power, particularly in the pursuit of domestic economic development, though they won support from some planters and commercial interests in the slave states. The Democrats stood for the supremacy of state and local authority, the vitality of cotton and other staple growers, and aggressive geographical expansionism, but they attracted support from farmers and urban workers in the non-slaveholding states. The disproportionate power that slaveholders were able to wield, owing to the federal ratio and their influence in the Democratic Party, enabled them to limit the reach of the federal government and hedge the developmental designs of manufacturers and bankers (such as the protective tariff) who might benefit at their expense. Still, it was the Democrats who mostly controlled the executive, legislative, and judicial branches of the federal government since the advent of mass politics in the 1820s.

By the late 1850s, however, a very different sort of contest was brewing, with potentially momentous consequences for the future of the Union. On the one hand, the collapse of the Whigs and the rapid rise of the Republicans elevated to the political stage a party organized almost entirely in the non-slaveholding states that was intent upon destroying the "slave power" and advancing the interests of those social groups in the American political economy least dependent on the slave plantation system and most concerned with "national" development: small manufacturers, artisans, farmers oriented to the domestic market, bankers not entangled in the export trade, and skilled workers. Recognizing the political costs of their association with nativism, the Republicans established antislavery—and especially the "non-extension" of slavery into the territories of the trans-Mississippi West—as the common denominator of their electoral mobilizations and looked to attract Protestant immigrants from northern and western Europe, especially Germans and refugees from the failed revolutions of 1848.

On the other hand, the Democratic Party, still national in its composition, increasingly unraveled over the implications of popular sovereignty. The Taney Court in the *Dred Scott* case had insisted that the Constitution protected the rights of slaveholders in the federal territories, and when Stephen Douglas suggested, during his debates with Lincoln, that the people in a territory could nonetheless keep slavery out by refusing to enact a slave code (he termed it "unfriendly legislation"), southern Democrats began to contemplate remedies that demanded a firm hold on federal power. Indeed, in early 1859 Mississippi's Jefferson Davis introduced a set of resolutions in the U.S. Senate proclaiming it "the duty of the Federal Government to afford the needful protection" if the territorial governments did not. Davis, that is, called for a federal slave code. Thus, as the election of 1860 approached, the battle for control of the central state reached unprecedented intensity, with enormous repercussions for the winners and the losers alike.

Had James Buchanan chosen to seek a second term as president, southern Democrats might have been able to win the day. In the election of 1856, Buchanan had soundly defeated Republican and American Party rivals by sweeping all the slave states (with the exception of Maryland, won by Fillmore) along with New Jersey, Indiana, Illinois, California, and his home state of Pennsylvania. Although Buchanan hailed from a non-slaveholding state, he had long been sympathetic to slaveholding interests—especially their imperial interests to the west and the south—and in his message to Congress in 1859 proclaimed that the *Dred Scott* decision clearly established the "right" of "every citizen" to take their "slaves into the common territories" and have them "protected under the Federal Constitution." But Buchanan decided not to run (no president since Andrew Jackson had served a second term) and thereby exacerbated the crisis of unity within the Democratic Party while enhancing the prospects of a Republican takeover.

Stephen Douglas had had his eyes on the presidency for at least a decade, and while he had clashed with Buchanan over the admission of Kansas, he was probably as formidable a candidate as the Democratic Party could field in 1860. He had a strong following in the non-slaveholding states, especially in the crucial Middle Atlantic and lower midwestern corridor, and he had spent years cultivating support in the slaveholding states. He not only crafted compromise measures in 1850 that toughened the Fugitive Slave Law and made slave ownership possible in much of the Mexican cession; he sought (albeit reluctantly) the explicit repeal of the hated Missouri Compromise line when he drew up the bill to organize the territories of Kansas and Nebraska. Most of all, he directed his considerable energies toward turning the Mississippi Valley into the main artery of an agro-commercial American empire and looked very favorably upon slaveholding ambitions in the Caribbean. Throughout, he would retain favor among some prominent leaders in the Deep South, notably in Texas, Louisiana, Arkansas, and Georgia.

But the problems facing Douglas and his party were considerable. Douglas had increasingly alienated radical southern Democrats, first by opposing the admission of Kansas on a constitution (drafted in the town of Lecompton) that legalized slavery, and then by offering settlers troubled by the *Dred Scott* decision a strategy for keeping slavery out of the territories of the trans-Mississippi West. And it was precisely these advocates of "southern rights" who had taken charge of the Democratic Party in their states over the course of the 1850s. When the time came in early 1860, they succeeded in instructing their delegations to the presidential nominating convention to either reject Douglas, demand a federal slave code in the party's platform, or both, and to walk out of the convention if they lost. That the convention would assemble in Charleston, South Carolina, and require the votes of two-thirds, rather than a simple majority, of the delegates for a candidate to win the nomination made Douglas's prospects all the more daunting.

The main fight at the Charleston convention, which commenced in late April, was over the platform rather than the nomination. The southern delegates called for a federal slave code, declaring it "the duty of the Federal Government . . . to protect when necessary, the rights of persons and property in the Territories." The Douglas forces, in turn, would leave it to the Supreme Court to decide "the nature and extent of the powers of a territorial legislature." On this question, only a majority of the convention vote was required, and the Douglas Democrats won what turned out to be a pyrrhic victory. Most of the delegates from the Deep South immediately left, at once registering their discontent and depriving Douglas of the vote total he needed to secure the party's nomination. In the end, the rival delegations reassembled separately and tried to match a candidate to a platform: the "northern" Democrats who wished to leave the territorial question to the determination of the Supreme Court selected Douglas; the "southern" Democrats who demanded a federal slave code chose Kentucky's John C. Breckinridge, the sitting vice president. Both sides denounced "the enactments of State Legislatures to defeat the faithful execution of the Fugitive Slave Law" and expressed support for "the acquisition of the Island of Cuba . . . at the earliest practicable moment."

The challenge for the Republicans was finding a presidential candidate who satisfied the temper of the delegates but could also win the election. William Seward of New York and Salmon P. Chase of Ohio were perhaps the leading candidates, poster boys for the party's antislavery politics, though their chances of winning Pennsylvania and the lower Midwest where antislavery was soft and racism hard, not to mention California and Oregon (admitted as a state in 1859), were questionable. Edward Bates of Missouri was far more conservative, and a nativist to boot, who could attract votes where Seward and Chase were weak, though he clearly put off many of the party faithful. The electoral calculus, therefore, bolstered the prospects of a relative unknown who nonetheless became, in the words of one supporter, "the second choice of everybody": Abraham Lincoln of Illinois.

Lincoln came into the national spotlight when he took on Douglas for the Illinois Senate seat in 1858, and especially when their debates gained wide press coverage. Although he lost, Illinois newspapers began to promote him for the presidency, Republicans in other states began to seek his advice, and, his ambitions energized, by the fall of 1859 he seemed ready to enter the race. To that end, Lincoln soon headed east for a speaking tour designed to increase his visibility and burnish his antislavery credentials in the eyes of Republicans who had their suspicions. Before an audience packed with prominent Republican leaders at the Cooper Institute in New York City, Lincoln thus argued that the country's founders had overwhelmingly viewed slavery as an evil to be confined geographically, that in a conflict between the "rights of property" and the "rights of men" the latter must prevail, and that slaveholders planned "to destroy the Government" unless they won "all points in dispute." Powerfully imploring Republicans to stand by their principles even in the face of southern threats, he urged his listeners to "have faith that right makes might."

Lincoln's Cooper Institute speech would be widely circulated in pamphlet form, and he presented versions of it as he moved through New England, stirring interest and excitement along the way. By the time of the 1860 Republican convention, which, as luck would have it, met in Chicago, Lincoln seemed to have identified a package of arguments that could appeal to a large number of northern voters. Playing off his notion of a "house divided" that could not stand, he warned that if not opposed, slavery's expansion westward would turn into its "nationalization." Reflecting on his experiences with Douglas in 1858, he urged Republicans to avoid association with the flammable issue of "negro equality." Indiana's Schuyler Colfax was not alone in recognizing in Lincoln the most promising means for consolidating a "victorious phalanx" in the coming election. When Seward faltered after the first ballot, Lincoln was in a position to win on the third. No one walked out.

Nor was there a bitter fight over the platform despite some important shifts since 1856. As before, slavery and its possible expansion came front and center, with the party celebrating the Declaration of Independence and heaping scorn on the *Dred Scott* decision, the attempt "to force the infamous Lecompton constitution upon the protesting people of Kansas," the efforts to reopen the African slave trade, and the "threats of disunion." "The normal condition of all territory of the United States is that of freedom," the platform prescribed, "and we deny the authority of Congress, or a territorial legislature, or of any individual, to give legal existence to slavery in any territory of the United States." "The new dogma that the Constitution of its own force carries slavery into any or all of the territories of the United States," it warned, "is a dangerous political heresy . . . [and] revolutionary in its tendency and subversive of the peace and harmony of the country."

But there was more that gestured toward a vision of federal power and social development. The party called for a protective tariff to encourage the country's "industrial interests," a "homestead policy" favoring "actual settlers," river and harbor improvements for the "accommodation and security of an existing commerce," and a "railroad to the Pacific" aided "in its construction" by the federal government. The hope was to secure liberal wages to workingmen, higher prices for agriculturalists, adequate rewards for mechanics and manufacturers, and commercial prosperity and independence for the nation. In effect, the platform was more than a rallying point for Republican voters; it was a blueprint for a new political economy.

In the developing battle between radical parties and political tendencies, one denouncing slavery and slaveholders, the other defending them, and both seeking to use the levers of federal power to advance their goals—a battle that was new to American politics on the presidential stage—there were nonetheless those who looked to preserve some semblance of the status quo. Douglas Democrats clearly imagined a divided house standing well into the future, though they put their eggs in the basket of a Supreme Court that had already ruled against them. Even more urgently, former members of the Whig Party who had not veered to the Democrats in the slaveholding states or to the Republicans in the non-slaveholding ones, and especially those who resided in the "border" states between them, hoped to revive the spirit of conservative compromise that had been embodied by Henry Clay. Calling themselves Constitutional Unionists and led by Clay's successor in the Senate, John J. Crittenden, they criticized the Republicans and the Democrats alike for threatening disaster and promised "to recognize no political principle other than the Constitution of the Country, the Union of the States, and the Enforcement of the Laws." Perhaps they could win enough votes to throw the election into the House of Representatives, where some sage phoenix would rise to save the day. But in a world of robust and novel political dispensations, this seemed about as tired, worn, and irrelevant as the political figures who gravitated to it. When they met in the spring of 1860 to nominate a candidate for the presidency, those most talked about in their ranks (Crittenden, Winfield Scott, Sam Houston, and possibly Edward Bates) were all over the age of sixty-five. Crittenden, who could have gotten the nod if he wanted it, was seventy-two. In the end, the best they could do was the Tennessee slaveholder John Bell, a relatively youthful sixty-four.

The election that followed was the most unusual and spectacular the country had ever witnessed. The Republicans had strong organizations in the non-slaveholding states but little more than outposts in the "border" states of Kentucky, Missouri, Maryland, and Delaware. As for bringing the campaign farther to the south, they could do so only at the risk of their lives; in the view of many slaveholders, they were "Black Republicans" intent on violating every form of social order, all the more so after John Brown's raid put them on special edge. The Breckinridge Democrats had some clout in Connecticut and Pennsylvania (owing to his connections to Buchanan), and especially in Oregon and California, where Democrats had customarily held sway, émigrés from the slaveholding states dominated the political scene, and Joseph Lane, selected as their vice presidential candidate, resided (Oregon). Otherwise, they had little support in the non-slaveholding states. Douglas, breaking with tradition, campaigned tirelessly across the country (though not in the Far West), and he gained some traction in the slaveholding states of Kentucky, Missouri, Louisiana, Arkansas,

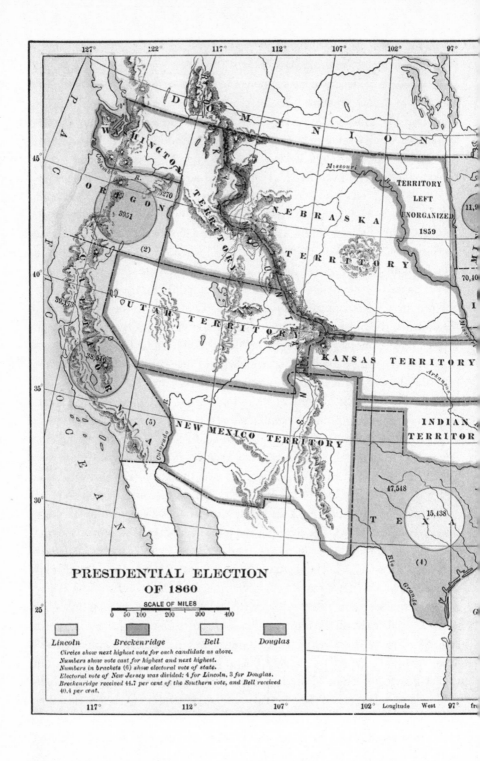

PRESIDENTIAL ELECTION
OF 1860

SCALE OF MILES

0   50 100   200   300   400

Lincoln   Breckenridge   Bell   Douglas

Circles show next highest vote for each candidate as above.
Numbers show vote cast for highest and next highest.
Numbers in brackets (6) show electoral vote of state.
Electoral vote of New Jersey was divided: 4 for Lincoln, 3 for Douglas.
Breckenridge received 44.7 per cent of the Southern vote, and Bell received
40.4 per cent.

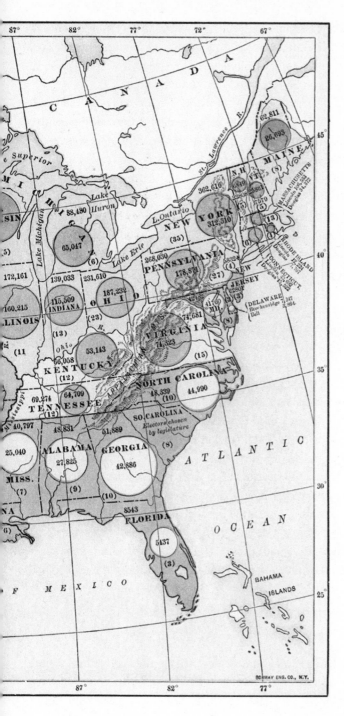

Map of the United States depicting geographical voting strength of presidential candidates in the election of 1860. Dixon Ryan Fox, *Harper's Atlas of American History* (1920).

and Georgia (all, except Georgia, along the Mississippi Valley). But his bases of support were clearly in the non-slaveholding states, particularly outside New England. As for the Constitutional Unionists, their strength was in the slave-holding states and most notably in those of the "border" areas.

Popular interest and participation in the 1860 election had no precedent in the history of the country, nor would it again be reached in the ensuing century and a half and beyond. More than 80 percent of the eligible voters went to the polls, a reflection of the perceived stakes. In some respects, it seemed to be two elections rather than one: Lincoln against Douglas in the non-slaveholding states (where together they won over 90 percent of the votes), and Breckinridge against Bell in the slaveholding states (where together they won well over 80 percent of the votes; Lincoln was not even on the ballot in most of those states). But, in truth, the Republicans and the Breckinridge Democrats best succeeded in mobilizing the electorate around the slavery question and the future of the American political economy; only they managed to win half of the votes in any of the states, and they were the clear front-runners when the electoral votes were tabulated (83 percent of the electoral vote and nearly 60 percent of the popular vote between them).

Had Lincoln faced a united Democratic Party, perhaps a different dynamic would have unfolded. At the very least, he would have lost California and Oregon, where he squeaked out pluralities with about one-third of the vote. Yet he duplicated Frémont's successes of 1856 in New England, New York, and the upper Midwest and, as the party had hoped, managed to peel off enough voters to win small majorities in Indiana and Illinois (51 percent each) and a much larger one in Pennsylvania (56 percent). The American political calculus thus turned in his favor. Despite receiving just under 40 percent of the total popular vote, Lincoln won a decisive majority (59 percent) of the electoral vote and the presidency of the United States. Coupled with sweeps of most legislatures and governorships in the non-slaveholding states and important gains in the House of Representatives, the Republicans were now poised to claim the reins of federal power.

The Slaveholders' Rebellion

Ever since the rise of strong central states, especially in the Euro-Atlantic world of the sixteenth and seventeenth centuries, enclaves of local autonomy and putative sovereignties have pushed back against the new claims of state author-ity. They have resisted demands for burdensome taxes, juridical interference, military conscripts, and other forms of service. Most often, the resistance was based in the countryside—among nobles, landlords, and peasants alike—and it could explode with great ferocity. During the seventeenth century, massive rebellions and civil wars scorched the lands of Britain, Russia, and continental Europe, playing havoc with the designs of absolutism. During the eighteenth and into the early nineteenth century, the arc of resistance shifted chiefly to the Western Hemisphere and the colonial possessions of these states, where slaves warred against the presumed authority of their owners and creoles might come to war against the presumed authority of the European metropolis (although the Vendée in France suggested that the struggle had by no means been played out within the metropolis itself), seeking in both cases to withdraw from what they regarded as an unjust or tyrannical regime.

Not surprisingly, even when New World rebels succeeded—as in the United States, Mexico, much of Spanish Latin America, and Haiti—they either established loosely constructed unions or found it very difficult to impose their authority over various subject populations, let alone over the vast stretches of territory some of them claimed to rule. Almost from the outset, they faced what may be described as "secessionist" movements of small or large scales. Those movements divided Haiti, severed parts of Central America, Texas, and almost the Yucatán from Mexico, and split Gran Colombia into Venezuela, Ecuador, Panama, and Colombia. Those that turned into failed efforts percolated almost continuously across a broad swath of the political geography; some were brutally crushed, while others lived on in other guises.

In the United States, secessionism was in the air from the first—the Revolution itself was a form of secessionism—flaring most prominently in the backcountries of the original states (gaining expression in anti-federalism), in New England during the War of 1812, and in the lower Mississippi Valley of the early republic. Some abolitionists themselves, who viewed the Constitution as a compact with slavery, believed political withdrawal from the Union an appropriate goal, and the conquest of the Mexican cession brought with it a host of challengers ranging from the Mormons in Deseret to Bear Flaggers and Mexican sympathizers in California.

White southerners who embraced secessionism at some point before the election of 1860 thereby took their place alongside what were (and would continue to be) formidable opponents of various central state projects. They were quite cognizant of it, often comparing themselves to the revolutionaries of the American independence movement. They had made concerted efforts to convince other white southerners, especially in the slaveholding leadership, of the dangers that compromise or inaction posed, and they helped orchestrate circumstances that enhanced the prospects of the very political outcome they had been warning against: the Republican assumption of federal power. As the election of 1860 neared, more and more of them publicly asserted that a Lincoln victory would require disunion, and when the day of reckoning arrived, they were well placed to carry out their plans.

All along, the secessionist impulse was most powerful in the states of the Deep South, stretching from South Carolina in the east to Texas in the west. There most slaves lived on plantations, most of the cotton and other staple crops were grown, and most of the country's richest and most influential slaveholders resided. There, too, the dynamic of political and economic life, as well as of the imagined future, turned not toward the states to the north but toward the Caribbean, Mexico, and the new Southwest. With some exceptions, the Deep South boasted the radicals known as fire-eaters and the newspapers and journals that regularly touted secessionism. The movement had a substantial popular base together with the political support to move it ahead. The only question left, once the presidential votes were counted, was how best to proceed.

Secessionists had done so good a job over the previous years that the main issue on the political table of the states in the Deep South was not whether or not to secede but whether to secede as individual states (an expression of their sovereignty) or wait to do so collectively. Supporters of the former were known as immediate secessionists; supporters of the latter as cooperationists. Without doubt, the immediate secessionists were the most dynamic element in the Deep South slaveholding leadership. They recognized that any hesitation might lose them the momentum they had built. They had to move ahead quickly, imagining that popular sentiment was on their side rather than trying to cultivate it. "I do not believe the common people understand it," one secessionist conceded, "but who ever waited for the common people when a great movement was to be made? We must take the move and force them to follow."

As many expected—and as secessionists in other Deep South states hoped— the moment was seized in South Carolina, where a secession convention quickly assembled and even more quickly enacted an ordinance of secession on December 20. By that point, five of the other Deep South states had set the wheels of secessionism in motion, providing for the election of delegates to secession conventions that would gather over the next month and a half, but South Carolina's bold leadership clearly put the winds at the secessionists' backs. They seem to have needed it. Although immediate secessionists appeared focused and poised to move with dispatch and although cooperationists appeared in disarray, the resistance to immediate secessionism was not insignificant. Even in South Carolina, extensive campaigning, together with the organization of active vigilant committees, was necessary to produce a heavy electoral majority. In Mississippi, Florida, and Alabama, cooperationist delegates managed to win somewhere between 35 and 45 percent of the vote (chiefly because of the doubts entertained in non-plantation districts), but in Georgia and Louisiana they won nearly 50 percent (and might have won more than that). In Texas, the sitting governor, Sam Houston, who was not a secessionist, refused to call the state legislature into session, and secessionist leaders had to cobble together a convention (whose legitimacy was in doubt) over the month of January. Not incidentally, where elections for delegates were held, the turnout of eligible voters dropped considerably from its peak in the November presidential election.

Whatever the vote totals (they often proved difficult to tabulate and interpret), immediate secessionists did claim the majority of delegates at the ensuing conventions (in Texas, too), and one by one they embraced disunion with conviction, though, save for South Carolina, not with unanimity. It was a stunning campaign, waged with patience and firmness by radical slaveholders and those who spoke for them. They had organized a rebellion against the authority of the new federal administration and thus against the federal government of the United States more generally, persuading enough of the doubters and enough of the non-slaveholders to accept the outcome without massing against it. Such efforts had failed before, in 1832–33 and in 1850–51, and the prospects for success at any point would have been regarded as dubious. That the secession process could finally move at a dizzying clip given the stakes—far more quickly than American colonists moved against the British government—was truly remarkable. All that was left to the cooperationists, and this after the deeds were done, was an agreement to meet in Montgomery, Alabama, in early February to establish a "union" among themselves.

Given the differences across the Deep South over how to embrace secessionism and especially the strength of immediate state secession, the representatives from all seven of the seceded states moved very expeditiously in Montgomery to establish a "permanent federal government." To be sure, they had a document and structure of governance with which to work—the Constitution of the United States—that their forebears had played a leading role in constructing, and it has been easy to identify similarities between the two, in language and logic. But in truth, the Montgomery convention marked the beginning of a very different project. Although slaveholding delegates at the American Constitutional Convention of 1787 fought mightily to protect slavery and the interests of slave owners, they knew that they were uniting with powerful groups of non-slaveholders and made noteworthy concessions, not least the deployment of euphemisms that kept the language of enslavement out of the document. Not "slaves" but "other persons" or "persons born to labor and service" organized what came to be known as the "federal ratio" and the "fugitive slave clause." While Congress was accorded the power to oversee federal territories and admit (or not admit) new states carved out of them, the U.S. Constitution left open the question of whether slavery could be legal in those new states.

Not so in Montgomery. The Deep South representatives who assembled there invoked some of the flourishing language that had made the Constitution especially memorable—"We the People"—though used it toward very different ends. They regarded themselves as expressing the wills not of the "people" of their now-called Confederate States of America but of the individual states in their "sovereign and independent character." They clearly and boldly inscribed the words "slavery" and "slaves" into the heart of the text, reserved to the new federal government the right to determine the qualifications of eligible voters, and required that any new territory or state wishing to join their Confederacy— and they certainly contemplated an expanding union and empire—make slaveholding legal and allow slaveholders and slaves the right of transit through them. These were powers well in excess of anything the U.S. Constitution granted to its federal government and made it plain whose interests were to be front and center. The representatives in Montgomery, that is, created a government of the slaveholders, by the slaveholders, and for the slaveholders: with no explicit right of secession from it.

Much like the secession conventions meeting first, the Confederate constitutional convention made no provision to submit its work for popular ratification and, given the press of the moment, decided to continue sitting as a "provisional" congress until elections could be held in November. After all, this new Confederacy would need to mobilize politically, economically, and militarily to defend itself against possible, and perhaps imminent, attack. Accordingly, the representatives also chose a president and vice president for their new central state who could then stand for election in the late fall. Mixing the political dispositions of the previous three decades, together with the range of experience they believed necessary, they made two formidable choices. For president, they selected Jefferson Davis of Mississippi, who had been a Democrat (but not a fire-eater), a West Point graduate, a U.S.-Mexican War veteran, a congressman and senator, and a secretary of state. For vice president they selected Alexander Stephens of Georgia, a former Whig and moderate who had served in Congress, came to know Abraham Lincoln, supported Stephan Douglas in 1860, and for a time attempted to put the brakes on secessionism. In many ways, Davis and Stephens were studies in contrasts, and there was little positive chemistry between them. What they shared was an abiding belief that slavery was the "cornerstone" of the supposed Confederate state.

What Is to Be Done?

From the moment that Deep South secessionism moved into high gear, the eyes of the leadership were trained both on the political dynamics of their own states and on the political leanings of the slaveholding states to the north of them. South Carolina's secessionists quickly dispatched emissaries to speak before the Virginia legislature, and networks of communication between all of the slave-holding states buzzed with great intensity. But the enthusiasm for disunion that was plainly in evidence in the Deep South was not to be found outside it. Although all of the slaveholding states boasted advocates for secession, they were a distinct (and in some places overwhelmed) minority in what is generally known as the upper South: the tiers of states that included Delaware, Maryland, Kentucky, Missouri, Arkansas, Tennessee, and North Carolina. It was not because slaveholders had surrendered the leadership of those states or because the attachment to slavery had weakened. In the 1830s, Virginia and Maryland had considered the option of gradual emancipation and soundly rejected it; in 1847, Delaware did the same despite a dwindling population of slaves and a growing population of free people of color. What was different in the upper South were the political economies and political geographies. There slavery was organized on a smaller scale, was less oriented to the production of staple crops, and was more given over to seasonal labor demands and slave hiring. There the black populations were smaller (though in absolute numbers Virginia always had more slaves than any other state) and the non-slaveholding white populations larger. And there, unlike in the Deep South, economic and cultural ties were much stronger to the states of the lower Midwest and the Middle Atlantic. The upper and border South had been the bailiwick of Henry Clay's Whigs, showed only modest interest in imperial adventurism, and was far less enamored of the discourse of "southern rights." In the election of 1860, John Bell and the Constitutional Unionists won most of their votes in these states, and with Lincoln's victory hesitation widely prevailed.

The initial encounter of the slaveholding states of the upper and border South with secessionism could not have pleased the secessionists of the Deep South. In one state after another in the winter and early spring of 1860–61, secession was defeated, by either a refusal to begin the process of formal deliberation (Mary-land, Delaware, Kentucky), the rejection of calls for a convention (Tennessee, North Carolina), or the drubbing of secessionists at conventions that did meet (Virginia, Arkansas). Even the organization of the Confederacy failed to shake the serious doubts and fears—and in some cases the outright unionism—to be found there.

In part, the hesitation in the upper South reflected efforts at compromise and reconciliation that had been hastily advanced in the executive and legisla-tive branches of the federal government. President Buchanan, a longtime favor-ite of slaveholders, used the occasion of his final annual message before Congress in early December to declaim both the legitimacy of secession and his power to do anything about it. "Seldom have we known so strong an argument come to so lame and impotent a conclusion," the *Cincinnati Enquirer* chided. What Buchanan did propose was a constitutional convention to address the issues sundering the Union, and in one form or another the passage of constitutional amendments seemed the vehicle of choice for those seeking to pull back from the precipice of secessionism.

Not surprisingly, Henry Clay's successor in the Senate, Kentucky's John J. Crittenden, stepped forward as a member of the Committee of Thirteen to engineer a solution. He offered a raft of constitutional amendments and resolutions, all designed to defend slave property from hostile attacks or federal emancipationism and to enable its expansion, the centerpiece of which was the extension of the old Missouri Compromise line all the way to the Pacific. Although slavery would be prohibited in states and territories to the north of the line, it would be legal and federally protected to the south, not only in areas "now held," but also in any "hereafter acquired." To make the deal ironclad, the amendments would not be subject to repeal.

There was not much in the "Crittenden Compromise" for those in the antislavery movement who had spent years mobilizing to defeat the "slave power," and Abraham Lincoln, even as president-elect, had no intention of cutting the heart out of Republicanism to appease the slaveholders. Despite his reputation for moderation and his relative inexperience, Lincoln clearly understood that a moment of truth had arrived. Crittenden's proposals, he insisted, "would lose us everything we have gained by the election . . . and put us again on the high-road to slave empire. . . . If we surrender, it will be the end of us. They will repeat the experiment on us ad libitum . . . till we shall have to take Cuba as a condition upon which they will stay in the Union." On the question of slavery's future in the states, Lincoln conceded that it was constitutionally beyond the reach of the federal government. "I have no purpose, directly or indirectly," he said on several occasions, "to interfere with the institution of slavery in the States where it exists. I believe I have no lawful right to do so, and I have no inclination to do so." He was further willing to endorse a constitutional amendment, passed by the House of Representatives and sent out for ratification (the first Thirteenth Amendment) that would have forever prevented the federal government from abolishing slavery there. But "on the territorial question," he was "inflexible." "The tug has to come," Lincoln recognized, "and better now, than any time hereafter."

Lincoln simultaneously rejected the political possibility of secession and feared that what had happened in the Deep South could convulse other parts of the country if federal authority was not asserted. The Union, he believed, was created by the "people" rather than by the states (as the Confederates had inscribed into their constitution) and was therefore "perpetual." "It is safe to assert,"

Lincoln observed in his inaugural address of March 4, "that no government proper, ever had a provision in its organic law for its own termination . . . [and] that no State, upon its mere motion, can lawfully get out of the Union." As a result, self-proclaimed secessionists could not be enacting the sovereign rights of states; they were engaging in rebellion against the United States and had likely dragged much of the white population along with them. The "central idea of secession," Lincoln declared, "is the essence of anarchy" and a mockery of the "majority principle."

In the short run, however, there was good reason for him to act with restraint. More slave states initially rejected secessionism than embraced it (eight to seven), and the fists of federal coercion, if deployed, could well push those eight to reconsider and join the Confederacy. Lincoln somehow imagined that unionist sentiment was not far beneath the surface of public opinion, even in the Deep South, temporarily subdued by secessionist rebels, and, given time and calm, might well resurface and cast secessionism to an ignominious fate. The key was to avoid conflict or related provocations. It was not easy to do, especially as the states of the new Confederacy flexed their sovereign arms by taking control of U.S. property—including arsenals, customhouses, and forts—within their presumed borders. Lincoln had vowed "to hold, occupy, and possess the property and places belonging to the Government" and "to execute in all States . . . the laws of the Union." But for the time being, discretion appeared the better part of valor, and he seemed comfortable with a policy described in the press as "masterly inactivity": refusing either to reclaim property that had been seized by Confederate states or to enforce federal authority in areas of "hostility to the United States."

Fort Sumter proved another matter. Newly constructed and as yet unfinished, Sumter sat in the middle of Charleston Harbor with a small federal force that had abandoned the aging and decrepit Fort Moultrie in December and thus likely avoided the fate of most other U.S. forts located in the new Confederacy. Moultrie was in easy access of the South Carolina mainland and quick Confederate occupation; Sumter would be far more difficult to take and, when completed, could house nearly 150 large guns and almost seven hundred troops. The move was the idea of Major Robert Anderson, a Kentuckian who commanded the fort and, despite southern sympathies, remained loyal to the federal government. It bought him time, though no shortage of trouble, for the very conditions that offered Sumter relative security from occupation left the troops vulnerable when their supplies dwindled. Fort Sumter would have to be provisioned or, as the Confederates demanded, evacuated.

Before he left office, James Buchanan made one effort to reinforce Anderson and his men, sending two hundred troops and supplies aboard an unarmed merchant ship, the *Star of the West*, in early January. They never made it. When the *Star of the West* was sighted coming into Charleston Harbor, Confederate batteries opened fire and drove the ship back out to sea. Anderson did not fire back, so the confrontation did not escalate. But over time, Anderson's position deteriorated, and when Lincoln assumed the presidency, he learned that the time of reckoning had arrived.

Most of the advice Lincoln received from inside his administration counseled retreat. William Seward, the new secretary of state, who already had hopes of upstaging Lincoln, was perhaps the leading advocate for abandoning Fort Sumter, though he initially had plenty of company. Only one member of the cabinet, Montgomery Blair, the postmaster general from Maryland, clearly favored provisioning the fort, and the elderly general in chief of the army, Winfield Scott, thought that holding on to Sumter would require a military expedition of a scale well beyond the country's resources. So confident was Seward in the decision he supported that he leaked word to Confederate emissaries about an impending evacuation.

Outside the administration, however, a different political dynamic quickly unfolded. Word of the possible surrender of Fort Sumter provoked a heated backlash in the states of the Northeast and the Midwest not only among Republicans but among some loyalist Democrats as well. They seemed to recognize that whatever their views on the future of slavery and the specific choreography of the crisis over it, the fate of the Union was now at stake. "If Fort Sumter is evacuated, the new administration is done forever," one correspondent heatedly predicted. "Have We a Government?" more than a few newspaper editors asked, while others more quietly worried about the "gallant band who are defending the country's honor and its flag in the midst of a hostile and traitorous foe." Even the patrician lawyer George Templeton Strong wondered in disgust if "the bird of our country is a debilitated chicken, disguised in eagle feathers." In effect, public opinion was pointedly suggesting that rather than strengthening southern unionists and weakening rebels, abandoning Fort Sumter might well do the opposite. Francis Blair, Montgomery Blair's father, who came to see Lincoln, argued that surrendering the fort would be "virtually a surrender of the Union" and might itself represent a treasonous offense.

Yet there was another looming issue that these demands for the assertion of federal authority could not entirely obscure. The United States, Lincoln appears to have understood, was a sprawling and loosely connected union, with powerful centrifugal forces. The federal government had long been a weak center, and as the country's imperial tentacles spread west and south, the challenges of maintaining a developing empire without a strong metropolis (Jefferson's vision) were increasingly in evidence. An emerging infrastructure of rivers, canals, and especially rails knit some sections of the country more closely together while leaving others either in relative isolation or in potentially different orbits. Keen eyes might have been set on the Pacific coast and new rail lines linking it to the East, but as of 1861 the fastest route out there was by sea around Cape Horn or by sea and land across Central America. Vast territories of the plains, the Southwest, and the Northwest were held chiefly by Native peoples—many of them accomplished warriors and traders—and drew the most immediate attention of white agriculturalists and speculators in the adjacent states of the Midwest and the Far West. Lincoln might have won the electoral votes of all the non-slaveholding states, but his popular vote margins, particularly in the lower Midwest and on the West Coast, were often razor thin and the traditions of localism still well entrenched.

The situation in California encapsulated many of the dilemmas that the Lincoln administration faced. Although very quickly admitted as a "free" state after the Treaty of Guadalupe Hidalgo, California was dominated politically during the 1850s by southern expatriates and sympathizers in the Democratic Party. They controlled the governorship, the legislature, and the congressional delegation and seem to have sailed through the debacle of Kansas-Nebraska much more successfully than Democratic parties in other non-slaveholding states. The local hero John C. Frémont managed to win only 19 percent of the vote on the Republican ticket in the presidential election of 1856, and by 1860 pro-slavery and pro-secessionist sentiment appeared widespread. Milton Latham, the newly elected U.S. senator, took the opportunity of a speech in the spring of 1860 both to defend slavery and to gesture in the direction of disunion: "We in California would have reasons to induce us to become members neither of the southern confederacy nor of the northern confederacy, and would be able to sustain ourselves the relations of a free and independent state." That November, the Breckinridge ticket, which included the pro-slavery Oregonian Joseph Lane, registered large vote margins in southern California, while Lincoln won less than a third of the popular vote statewide. Only the division of the Democrats between Breckinridge and Douglas enabled Lincoln to win the electoral votes of the state. Within weeks, the *San Francisco Herald*, believing the secession of slaveholding states inevitable, imagined California in turn organizing a Pacific or "separate" republic.

California was by no means alone in this regard. State rights sensibilities continued to maintain a strong hold across much of the North, especially the lower North, and important enclaves of pro-slavery and anti-abolition sentiment could be found in the Midwest and the Middle Atlantic. The *Chicago Times* and the *Cleveland Plain Dealer* showed urban support for slavery, while Ohio's *Hamilton Telegraph*, Michigan's *Niles Republican*, Indiana's *New Albany Ledger*, and Peoria, Illinois's *Democratic Union* showed smaller-town and rural support. But the hotbed of southern and slaveholder sympathizing was New York City. Controlled by the Democrats and boasting powerful financial ties to the cotton trade, New York seemed to move into a liminal political status, teetering between the Union and the Confederacy. Antislavery had been gaining ground, but anti-abolitionism had deep and venomous roots, nurtured by an alliance between the old mercantile elite and new Irish Catholic immigrants. Several newspapers, including the highly popular and widely read *New York Herald*, expressed support for slavery as a form of social organization and racial control, and some, like the *New York Journal of Commerce*, thought the acceptance of peaceable secession preferable to armed conflict. Indeed, the Democratic mayor, Fernando Wood, reflecting the liminality, proposed that New York itself secede from the Union and create a free port of entry something in the manner of Bremen or Hamburg in Germany.

As the secession process moved forward in the Deep South during the winter of 1860–61, talk of alternative confederations and separate states or republics spread. Some in the East conceived of a "central confederacy" that would extend from New York to Virginia and harness the economic and political dynamism of the region. In the Midwest, separatism was inspired by fears that the new southern Confederacy would close off the lower Mississippi Valley and leave the states there "slaves and serfs of New England" and the Great Lakes shipping interests. In long-contested Missouri, "leading gentlemen" discussed "the question of the separate independence of that State." The issue, in sum, was not simply whether the United States would split into two different countries if Lincoln failed to enforce the authority of the federal government; the issue was whether the United States might unravel in a variety of ways and leave the North American continent awash in potentially rivalrous states and confederations.

At all events, by the end of March, Lincoln decided to act. The ground was shifting in his cabinet, and although Seward, in a last-ditch effort at delay, urged Lincoln to initiate hostilities with Spain or France, perhaps unifying Americans against a foreign foe, Lincoln instead chose to risk hostilities with the rebellious Confederates and send Major Anderson the supplies he desperately needed. Cleverly choosing to ship only food and clothing, Lincoln ordered an expedition to proceed to Sumter and, on the same day, notified South Carolina's governor, Francis Pickens, of his peaceful intentions. "An attempt will be made to supply Fort-Sumter with provisions only," he informed the governor, "and that, if such attempt be not resisted, no effort to throw in men, arms, or ammunition, will be made, without further notice, [except] in case of an attack on the Fort." Lincoln had no way of knowing how his effort to provide "food for hungry men" would be greeted in the North or the upper South, but by his action he shifted the burden of response to the court of the Confederacy.

Jefferson Davis and his newly assembled cabinet were in much the same position as Lincoln and his. Neither wished to be seen as the provocateur, while both eyed the border states between them with anticipation. Those states were effectively the political battleground, either isolating or strengthening the slaveholders' rebellion. And like Lincoln's, the Davis administration came under growing pressure to take action commensurate with its proclaimed status as an independent confederacy. "The spirit and even the patriotism of the people is oozing out under this do-nothing policy," a newspaper in Mobile warned, and "if something is not done pretty soon . . . the whole country will become so disgusted with the sham of southern independence, that the first chance the people get at a popular election they will turn the whole movement topsy-turvy." Some even insisted that the "shedding of blood" would "change many voters in the hesitating states." As the radical *Charleston Mercury* saw it, "Border southern States will never join us until we have indicated our power to free ourselves."

Davis was ready to agree. Learning from Governor Pickens of Lincoln's move to supply Fort Sumter, he convened his cabinet on April 9 and ordered his commander in Charleston, General P. G. T. Beauregard, to "reduce" the fort before the provisioning expedition arrived. Beauregard then demanded Anderson's surrender and, when this was refused, opened fire in the early morning hours of April 12. Nearly a day and a half later, with the fort ablaze and all his troops exhausted but alive, Anderson gave it up. The last great symbol of U.S. authority in their midst had now fallen to the Confederates.

Lincoln responded without delay. Citing the obstruction of the laws of the United States in South Carolina, Georgia, Alabama, Florida, Mississippi, Louisiana, and Texas "by combinations too powerful to be suppressed by the ordinary course of judicial proceedings, or by the power vested in the Marshals," he called upon "the militia of the several States of the Union" to provide seventy-five thousand men for ninety days service. But it appeared that the militant Confederates were correct about the upper South. Not one of the slaveholding states that remained in the Union agreed to send troops, and most replied with derision and contempt. Kentucky's governor refused to "furnish a single man for the wicked purpose of subduing her sister Southern States," while Missouri's governor termed Lincoln's requisition "illegal, unconstitutional, revolutionary, inhuman." Most seriously, four of the states—beginning with Virginia— quickly revisited the question of secession and chose to embrace it. By early June, North Carolina, Arkansas, and Tennessee, together with Virginia, had severed their connection with the United States and joined the nascent Confederacy. The American union, which had been created seventy years before and spread its empire of slaveholders and non-slaveholders across the continent by military and diplomatic means, had entered its death agony with few prospects of rehabilitation on any familiar basis.

Part Two

Nation and Empire

CHAPTER SEVEN

Birth of a Nation

Execution of thirty-eight Dakota Sioux at Manato, Minnesota, December 26,
1862. They were accused of murdering white settlers during a rebellion earlier
that year. It remains the largest mass execution in American history.
Harper's Weekly, January 17, 1863.

The Westward Reach of the Confederacy

Not long after the ink had dried on the constitution of the Confederate States of America, and weeks before hostilities commenced at Fort Sumter, the eyes of Confederate leaders turned west as well as east and north. The political struggle that eventuated in secession and the formation of the Confederacy had, after all, been over the future of the sprawling trans-Mississippi West, and the Confederate constitution made explicit provision for the incorporation of new territories and states, so long as slavery were legal and the rights of slaveholders respected. Although the territories and states that had been carved out of the Louisiana Purchase, the Mexican cession, and the Oregon boundary settlement still belonged, in theory, to the United States, the Lincoln administration could not assume that they would remain loyal. California and Oregon veered strongly Democratic in politics, boasted substantial numbers of Confederate sympathizers, and already toyed with the idea of organizing a new Pacific coast republic. Mormon Utah had been in a state of rebellion against the federal government in the late 1850s (requiring President Buchanan to send in the army) and now faced a Republican regime that officially regarded polygamy and slavery as the "twin relics of barbarism." The territory of New Mexico, established on a basis of popular sovereignty, for its part had enacted a slave code in 1859 and had southerners placed in the governor's chair and on the territorial supreme court.

Yet Confederate officials, led by the newly designated secretary of state, Robert Toombs, first looked to the Indian Territory that sat adjacent to Texas, Arkansas, and Kansas and particularly to the "Five Civilized Tribes" that had forcibly been exiled there in the 1830s. To be sure, southern white men—slaveholders and non-slaveholders alike—had exerted the military and political pressure that resulted in Indian removal from the Southeast, and the immense costs to the tribes in lives, land, and internal strife could hardly have endeared them to their previous tormentors. But some of the powerful tribal members, especially among the more acculturated, did share an interest in slavery with the Confederacy, were embittered by their experiences with the federal government of the United States, and had reason to hear the entreaties of any emissaries who came calling. It was the renegade Confederacy, not the Union, that quickly decided to pay such calls, and for that assignment they sent Albert Pike.

An Arkansas lawyer and veteran of the U.S.-Mexican War, Pike had come to know his Indian neighbors well. He earlier provided legal assistance for several of the tribes and succeeded in extracting a large monetary settlement for the Creeks. The Davis government authorized him to spend up to $100,000 to secure political and military alliances and was willing to offer far better terms than the tribes enjoyed under the federal government: sovereignty within territorial borders, representation in the Confederate congress, and guarantees of future annuity payments. Although increasingly bitter divisions among the Creeks, the Seminoles, and especially the Cherokees complicated Pike's task, by the end of October 1861 he had reached agreements with at least factions in all the tribes, including for the provision of troops. With lavish gifts and feasting, he then managed to persuade Tonkawas, Caddos, Wacos, Senecas, Osages, Shawnees, and some Comanches farther to the west to put themselves under the protection of the Confederacy. The Comanches even agreed to cease their raiding into Texas. Stand Watie, leader of the Cherokee mixed-blood faction, became a colonel (and later a general) in the Confederate army, and Pike, for his efforts, was rewarded with a brigadier generalship and command of the newly established Department of Indian Territory. While Lincoln initially abandoned the Indian Territory—withdrawing the federal troops who had been stationed there, scoffing at the prospect of enlisting Indian soldiers, and cutting off tribal annuities—the Confederates were reaching west.

And southwest. As Franklin Pierce's secretary of war, Jefferson Davis had been vitally interested in securing a southern route for a transcontinental railroad and, to that end, was instrumental in pressing forward with what became the Gadsden Purchase in 1853: a small but geographically valuable (Davis wanted more) piece of territory in the borderlands of Sonora, Chihuahua, and New Mexico. With secession and the organization of the Confederacy, Davis moved quickly to establish friendly relations with the government of Benito Juárez in Mexico City and to extend Confederate influence into the border regions of northern Mexico, which, he feared, could be subject to Union invasion and further Confederate encirclement. Although Davis's emissary to Mexico City failed miserably, the story in Nuevo León, Coahuila, Tamaulipas, Sonora, and Chihuahua proved more encouraging. Indeed, the governor of Chihuahua suggested privately that he would not permit U.S. troops to march across his state, while the independent-minded governor of Nuevo León and Coahuila raised the prospect of joining the Confederacy outright. The vision of empire continued to exert a powerful hold. "We must have Sonora and Chihuahua," one of Davis's agents in Mexico exulted. "With Sonora and Chihuahua we gain [lower] California, and by railroad to Guaymas render our state of Texas the great highway of nations."

For all the enthusiasm that slaveholding empire had raised in the states—especially the Deep South states—that would form the Confederacy, however, once secession occurred and a Confederate government took shape, a new caution was in evidence. Quickly embattled with the United States and faced with a Union naval blockade along the southern Atlantic and Gulf coasts, Confederate officials desperately needed international recognition and support if they were to survive politically and militarily. Although many were confident that their power in the cotton market dealt them a strong, if not unassailable, diplomatic hand (it became known as King Cotton diplomacy), they knew that aggressive advances in Mexico or the Caribbean would court isolation or hostile intervention from the very countries they needed most: France, Belgium, Russia, Spain, and, most of all, Great Britain. Robert Toombs, along with his successors in the post of secretary of state, took special care to assure the Europeans about Cuba, long in the crosshairs of slaveholding imperialists. "If you should discover that any apprehension exists in the minds of the people of a design on the part of this government to attempt the acquisition of that island in any way," he instructed one of his diplomatic agents, "you will leave no efforts untried to remove such an erroneous belief. It is the policy of the Government of the Confederate States that Cuba will continue to be a colonial possession of Spain."

Both the British and the French governments felt certain that the United States was unraveling and that the Union would be unable to subdue the Confederacy: all the more so after the Union army suffered a shocking early defeat at Bull Run, not far from Washington, D.C., in July 1861. Yet both also knew that any move to offer the Confederacy diplomatic recognition invited retaliation, and likely a declaration of war, from the Lincoln administration. They therefore chose the course of neutrality, aggravating the Union and the Confederacy alike, though the British did lend Confederates the status of "belligerents," enabling international credibility in trading goods and borrowing money. Although Confederates had expected that British and French demand for raw cotton would result in a different political outcome, the bumper cotton harvests of 1858–60 took the immediate pressure off their textile industries and respective governments. The Europeans would wait and see and, increasingly, lean not toward either one of the antagonists but toward negotiations designed to end the fighting and perhaps reassert their influence in North America.

Still, there was the American Southwest and the prospect of extending the Confederacy's reach in that direction. Davis saw New Mexico, with its slave code and Confederate supporters, as a gateway to southern California and the Pacific. He had believed for quite some time that southern Utah would be suitable for growing cotton. And he imagined the mineral wealth of the gold- and silver-mining regions flowing into the Confederate treasury. Indeed, a few years before, as secretary of war, he had arranged to bring seventy-four camels over from North Africa to test their usefulness in the American deserts. But the greatest enthusiasm for the southwestern campaign came from the Confederate Texans who had reluctantly given up claims to sections of New Mexico back in 1850. Led by John R. Baylor, they quickly took charge of federal forts within the boundaries of their state, raising the Confederate flag over Fort Bliss (near El Paso) in July 1861, and then forced the surrender of U.S. troops outside the secessionist New Mexican town of Mesilla. In August, Baylor proclaimed the Confederate territory of Arizona, south of the 34th parallel, that the Confederacy would officially incorporate in early 1862.

An even more ambitious plan was being hatched by Henry Hopkins Sibley, the commander of Texas troops back in San Antonio. A West Point graduate and U.S.-Mexican War veteran who had resigned from the U.S. Army to join the Confederacy, Sibley envisioned an expedition intended not only to seize control of New Mexico and Arizona but also to occupy the gold-mining areas of Colorado and California. With this in mind, he rushed off to Richmond to convince Jefferson Davis of the plan's merits and was so persuasive that he returned to Texas as a brigadier general and "Commander of the Army of New Mexico." "The objective aims and design of the campaign was the conquest of California," one of Sibley's officers later insisted, after which Sibley hoped to set his sights on northwestern Mexico. By the late fall of 1861, Sibley had attracted over three thousand Texas volunteers, marched them toward Fort Bliss, and, in early February 1862, moved into the Rio Grande valley of New Mexico. Within days, he defeated a U.S. force at Valverde, and by mid-March Sibley's troops had taken Albuquerque, hoisted the Confederate flag over Santa Fe, and looked north toward Colorado.

The stakes were high, as U.S. Army officers were themselves quick to concede. Noting that "the real objective" of the New Mexico invasion was "no less than the conquest of California, Sonora, Chihuahua, New Mexico, Arizona, and Utah—and, above all, the possession of all the gold supply on the Pacific coast," Brigadier General Latham Anderson reckoned, "The conquest alone of this vast domain . . . would have insured the recognition of the Confederacy by the European powers." And, Anderson might have added, an independent and increasingly powerful Confederate state.

Remaking the Union

As the election of 1860 approached, secessionists had warned that Abraham Lincoln and the Republican Party intended to create a massive central state that not only would turn its newfound power against slavery and slaveholders but also would intercede in many areas of public and private life. By defying the Constitution and deploying the federal patronage, the "Black Republicans," as many Democrats called them, would turn slave against master, non-slaveholder against slaveholder, wife against husband, and black against white, all in the service of undermining slavery and creating a despotic authority. Secessionists spoke of an "open, unassailable, and powerful influence," of "many thousands of Government officials and employees . . . operat[ing] against the institution of slavery and the interests of slaveholders," of Republicans filling offices "within the Southern States, with their followers and friends," of "the building up in every Southern State of a Black Republican party, the ally and stipendiary of Northern fanaticism, to become in a few very short years the open advocate of abolition." By "the fourth of March next," Robert Toombs intoned at the Georgia secession convention in January 1861, "they will have possession of the Federal executive with its vast power, patronage, prestige of legality, its army, its navy, and its revenue."

In truth, although their party platform conjured an activist state, Republicans and the Lincoln administration had relatively little with which to work. The federal bureaucracy had fewer than thirty-seven thousand employees, most of whom were customs or postal officials and thus worrisome patronage appointments. The U.S. Army had fewer than seventeen thousand men in service, and most were scattered across forts in the trans-Mississippi West. The U.S. Navy had fewer than ten thousand personnel and a rather unimposing fleet of forty-two ships, most of which were patrolling thousands of miles away. To make matters worse, a good many of the trained officers who hailed from Confederate states chose to support the rebellion. There was no central bank and no national currency, aside from gold and silver coins. Most of the money in circulation rather consisted of notes printed by more than fifteen hundred state banks and usually exchanged at a substantial discount. Capital accumulation and investment were carried out by private firms, mercantile houses, and banks marginally (if at all) involved with the federal government and by state and municipal governments that sold bonds; capital flows from European investors remained vital, especially for large infrastructure projects. Federal revenues came principally from tariffs (whose rates had been in decline for nearly thirty years) and public land sales; taxation was minimal at all levels of the government. Democrats across the country were strong supporters of state rights and local control, and Lincoln, insistent as he was on dismissing the constitutional logic of secession and refusing to recognize the Confederacy, was often at pains to concede what was beyond his power as chief of the executive branch: first and foremost to move against the institution of slavery in the states where it remained legal.

Even with the outbreak of hostilities, the horizons of the crisis and the supposed demands on the federal state appeared limited. When Lincoln called for seventy-five thousand troops to subdue the rebellion in the southern states, he asked only for ninety-day volunteers and did so under the auspices of the Militia Act of 1792. He did quickly order a blockade of the southern coastline to cut off

Confederate trading in staple crops and supplies. He did suspend the writ of habeas corpus in the Washington-to-Philadelphia corridor in late April owing to secessionist activity and then imposed martial law in Baltimore after U.S. troops were attacked and the District of Columbia made vulnerable, surrounded as it was on three sides by a slave state—Maryland—teetering on the edge of disunion. And in May, he did call for an additional forty-two thousand volunteers, this time for three years of service, and made provision to increase the size of the regular army and navy by nearly fifty thousand. But with Congress out of session, Lincoln was at once decisive and reserved. He was acting in unprecedented ways and without congressional authority, yet he hardly seemed a tyrant or central state builder in the making.

By early July, when Congress reassembled at his instruction, however, a sobering sense of what lay ahead had set in. Although Lincoln disavowed any intention "to interfere with slavery in the States where it exists," he asked the body to "place at the control of the government . . . at least four hundred thousand men"—they would authorize one million—"and four hundred millions of dollars." Before too long, owing to the requirements of an increasingly destructive and protracted war, the Lincoln administration would take dramatic steps in a variety of areas critical to the political economy of the United States. It would promote the development of a large standing army, a growing manufacturing sector, a new structure of finance and banking, a system of labor in the southern states based on contract rather than enslavement, and an ambitious set of projects in the long-contested trans-Mississippi West. It would also conscript men into the armed forces and challenge the racial exclusions that had been in place since the founding of the Republic. A federal state with an immensely expanded reach and capacity would emerge, connected in significant ways to powerful private interests. What remained to be determined was who would become the real patrons and who the real clients.

Perhaps the most pressing challenge facing the Lincoln administration, aside from mobilizing an army and prosecuting the war against the rebellion, was raising the money to pay for it. Heading that effort was the possibly misassigned secretary of the Treasury, Salmon P. Chase, a former hard-money Democrat who had found his way to Republicanism through the route of antislavery and to the cabinet through Lincoln's determination to keep his friends close but his rivals closer. Rather than attempting to create some version of a central bank, Chase followed a path that the federal government had previously marked out when it needed extra funds: selling securities. And because the European market for those securities had effectively collapsed with the outbreak of fighting, Chase looked to the next best source, the private bankers and investors in Philadelphia, Boston, Providence, and especially New York City.

Both short- and long-term bonds were put on offer, and the initial response encouraged Chase to believe that patriotic motives could fashion the sort of alliance between private creditors and the state that Alexander Hamilton had imagined in the 1790s.

Within months, however, Chase learned that the bankers' patriotism had its limits, and so he devised a plan to sell bonds to a wider public in denominations as low as $50 while seeking help to bring the bigger investors on board. For those tasks, he turned to Jay Cooke. The son of a prominent Ohio family with political connections to Chase, Cooke had recently opened his own banking house in Philadelphia. He had already sold bonds for the State of Pennsylvania and began to exploit his developing financial networks. He convinced many northeastern bankers—first in Philadelphia, soon elsewhere—of the advantages the government bonds could bring (including interest payments in gold and profitable resales within their regions) and then launched popular bond drives replete with patriotic advertising. So successful did Cooke's efforts prove that in the fall of 1862 Chase appointed him general subscription agent for the United States. By war's end, the United States raised about two-thirds of its revenue through the sale of bonds and other securities.

Still, it was not enough to cover the war's spiraling costs. In 1861, Congress enacted a modest tax on incomes over $800 and the next year passed the Legal Tender Act, which authorized the circulation of $150 million (eventually $450 million in total) in noninterest-bearing Treasury notes, known as greenbacks, "receivable for all debts and demands due the United States." Under mounting pressure from western Republicans who cast a critical eye on the Treasury Department's catering to eastern bankers and financiers, Chase also moved toward the construction of a new banking system. Although the banks would remain in private hands (many would be formerly state-chartered banks), they could get national bank charters and print a new national currency if they adhered to a raft of requirements as to specie reserves, loan collateral, and especially the purchase of government securities. In an important sense, the system, legislated by Congress in 1863 and amended in 1864 and 1865, established a stable market for federal bonds and trimmed the sails of state bankers who, like counterfeiters, seemed able to print money at will.

It was not always easy for Secretary Chase and the Republican Congress to keep bankers actively in the game. Indeed, the national banking system provoked enough dissatisfaction among the bankers—especially in New York City—that they succeeded in forcing the government to meet some of their demands. Even so, the financial interests who tied their fates to the federal union, in the bond and gold markets, began to reap windfalls and were poised to find a new and powerful footing if the rebellion were ultimately crushed. Jay

Cooke took only a small commission on the sales he organized, but it would turn into a princely fortune; others, like the young J. Pierpont Morgan, whose family had prospered in the London–New York trading axis and who paid a substitute to serve in the U.S. Army for him, profited handsomely in the secondary securities market, not to mention by investing in arms sales and in gold. A new class of finance capitalists, who were stakeholders in the federal government and oriented to the domestic market, had begun to emerge.

Bankers and private investors were not the only beneficiaries of war-related federal initiatives. Federal contracts brought windfalls to a variety of sectors of the U.S. economy that could supply and transport the troops and that had previously been overshadowed by the wealth and prominence of export merchants and the landed gentry. The 1850s had seen a spike in the building of railroad lines especially in the Middle Atlantic states and the lower Midwest, and these would prove crucial to the conduct of military operations. Although Lincoln could have used his authority as commander in chief to take charge of the roads, he not only chose to leave them in the hands of their managers and shareholders (as a lawyer, he had represented railroad companies) but appointed Thomas A. Scott, vice president of the Pennsylvania Railroad, as an assistant secretary in charge of government transportation. With limited oversight and apparently limitless demand, the railroads had great leeway in making their rate schedules and success in amassing unprecedented profits. And while the Lincoln administration gave the railroad companies wide berth, it also promoted the standardization of track gauges, signals, and freight cars, facilitating later, and better integrated, development. Similar partnerships boosted the fortunes, and encouraged the concentration of ownership, in meatpacking, iron and steel making, ready-made clothing manufacture, coal mining, gun and ordnance production, and blacksmithing in a vital political corridor from southern New England through New York, Pennsylvania, Ohio, and out to Chicago: all the more so as the Republican-controlled Congress, in an effort to raise funds to prosecute the war, turned toward protectionism with the Morrill Tariff of 1861 and continued to raise tariff rates thereafter.

Yet what gave the wartime political economy distinctive traction and provided critical linkages between state and capital formation were policies oriented to the trans-Mississippi West. Ever since the 1840s, congressional leaders across the political spectrum showed growing interest in promoting white settlement in the new western territories and encouraging the construction of railroads to the Pacific. It was the Tennessee Democrat Andrew Johnson who first introduced homestead legislation and the Illinois Democrat Stephen Douglas who pressed to facilitate a transcontinental railroad. Although the question of slavery's expansion doomed these efforts, both Democrats and Republicans included transcontinental railroad planks in their party platforms in 1860, and the departure of most southern Democrats owing to secession left Republicans with the votes to pursue western development as they saw fit. The Homestead Act, passed and signed in 1862, made up to 160 acres of "unappropriated public lands" available to individuals or family heads who would farm them for five years and then pay a small fee; the Pacific Railway Act, enacted the same year, chartered the Union Pacific and Central Pacific Railroad companies and offered enormous incentives in land and financial instruments to build between Omaha, Nebraska, and Sacramento, California.

Touted as a means by which yeoman farmers rather than speculators could populate the rural West and transport agricultural commodities to market, these laws in fact gave the advantage to men of considerable wealth. Much of the public land was to be found in the semiarid plains and the Great Basin where irrigation was a necessity and 160 acres inadequate to the sustenance of farm families. While some imagined that the transcontinental railroad might truly become a publicly held corporation, subject to government oversight and regulation, massive lobbying by railroad promoters put an end to that prospect. Instead, Congress handpicked what would be a privately controlled board of directors and distributed over 100 million acres of land, the use of coal and iron deposits, and millions of dollars in thirty-year bonds to facilitate construction. Many members of Congress in turn received stock and other benefits from the rail companies. It was an unprecedented example of corporate welfare legislation and a harbinger of the priorities Republican officials would continue to support.

A transcontinental railroad made limited economic sense at the time. The "public lands" were populated chiefly by Native Americans who regarded most of the territory as theirs and had little interest in raising crops and livestock for midwestern and eastern markets. Even with the passage of the Homestead Act, there would be relatively little to transport for years. But homestead and railroad legislation were more political than economic in their intent. They were part of a project of bringing the West under control. Well aware of the gold-mining strikes in Colorado in the late 1850s, of gold and silver mines in southern New Mexico and the Sierra Nevada, of California's ports as gateways to the Pacific trade, of secessionist activities all across the trans-Mississippi West, and of Confederate advances into New Mexico, the Lincoln administration took assertive steps to extend its authority. The Republican Congress created the Colorado (1861), Dakota (1861), Nevada (1861), Arizona (1863), Idaho (1863), and Montana (1864) territories and the patronage appointments that went with their governance. It finally admitted Kansas as a free state in 1861 and encouraged Colorado and Nevada to apply for statehood in 1864 (only Nevada gained admission).

It reorganized military districts with a view to raising more volunteers and keeping disloyalty in check. And it ordered the U.S. Army to reclaim Indian Territory, engage in a range of operations meant to subdue Native Americans across the plains, and crush pro-Confederate guerrillas in Missouri.

Lincoln had long been interested in a transcontinental railroad. "There was nothing more important before the nation," he told the engineer Grenville Dodge in 1859, "than the building of a railroad to the Pacific." So concerned was he as president to tie California and the interior West more firmly to the Union that he quickly signed the Pacific Railroad Act, called for even more generous terms to secure private investors, and contemplated the simultaneous construction of three separate lines to the West Coast. It was he who selected Omaha as the road's eastern terminus. The future of the trans-Mississippi West, Lincoln and other Republicans recognized, was the future of a reconfigured union, and both would be determined as the war unfolded, not simply as a result of its outcome.

Rebellion on the Plains

For John Pope, assignment to the Upper Plains was a crushing defeat and a dramatic fall from grace. A West Point graduate, veteran of the U.S.-Mexican War, surveyor and engineer whose father was a federal judge and friend of Lincoln's, Pope had distinguished himself (especially by his own reckoning) in helping to drive Confederate forces out of Missouri in late 1861 and reestablishing U.S. control over the Mississippi River as far south as Memphis in the spring of 1862. Promoted to major general, he had advanced with General Henry W. Halleck to the rail center of Corinth, Mississippi, when Lincoln called him east to command the newly formed Army of Virginia, with fifty thousand men, assembled north of Richmond.

The moment seemed at once desperate and full of promise for the U.S. and Pope. It was now well over a year since the Lincoln administration had called for volunteers to put down the rebellion in the southern states, and as the British and French had predicted, there was perilously little to show for it. Although state governors and their male constituents responded enthusiastically to Lincoln's call, easily filling the quotas, many of the army's commanding officers, especially in the eastern theater, seemed reluctant to lead the soldiers into battle. First Irvin McDowell, who commanded the Army of Northeastern Virginia, and then George B. McClellan, who commanded the reconstituted Army of the Potomac, complained endlessly of their troops' inexperience and their need for more men. When they finally determined to move, the results were disastrous. McDowell, heading out of Washington in hopes of capturing the Confederate capital of Richmond, suffered a devastating defeat at Bull Run (Manassas) in July

1861, which nearly ended with the Confederate capture of Washington. In the spring of 1862, McClellan attempted to take Richmond from the southeast, by way of the Virginia peninsula, and while he outnumbered the Confederates by a considerable margin and came within earshot of Richmond's church bells, he and his army were forced to retreat, in good part because of the clever maneuvering of the Confederate officers on the ground: Robert E. Lee, Thomas "Stonewall" Jackson, and J. E. B. Stuart.

The U.S. Army appeared to be faring better in the western theater, as John Pope's exploits suggested. Control of the Mississippi River was the great prize—as it had been from the time of American independence—and armed forces attacked from the north and the south. They first pushed into Tennessee and Missouri and later sailed up from the Gulf of Mexico and took the crown jewel of New Orleans. The bloody battle at Shiloh, on the Tennessee River, in April 1862, when a surprise Confederate attack nearly overran U.S. troops, managed to maintain the Union momentum, though at very heavy cost. When Pope left Corinth a bit later, the U.S. Army was in a relatively strong position, poised to march toward Vicksburg. In northern Virginia, he joined the troops under his new command and, soon, McClellan's army returning from the peninsula in defeat. Yet another march toward Richmond was contemplated.

Pope behaved as if he were just what the doctor had ordered for the demoralization that beset military, political, and civilian circles. Bragging to his men, "I come to you out of the West, where we have always seen the backs of our enemies," he advised that "success and glory are in the advance, disaster and shame lurk in the rear." No one was impressed, not least George McClellan, who seemed especially irritated by the boastful Pope. After skirmishing for several weeks with portions of Lee's army under the command of Stonewall Jackson, A. P. Hill, and James Longstreet just east of the Blue Ridge Mountains, Pope's army engaged the Confederates in full-scale battle near Manassas Junction, the site of the first, and sobering, Battle of Bull Run, in late August. This time the results were no better: Pope lost sixteen thousand men—dead, wounded, and missing—and, like McDowell before him, was forced to retreat toward Washington, D.C. By all accounts, McClellan hung Pope out to dry, and Lincoln's cabinet called for McClellan's dismissal. Indeed, it appeared that the Confederate rebels were now looking northward to Maryland and possibly Pennsylvania. Lincoln himself regarded McClellan's behavior as "unpardonable" but also recognized that McClellan remained extremely popular with the soldiers and uniquely able "to lick these troops of ours into shape." So, in the end, it was Pope whom Lincoln sent packing, now out to Minnesota, where the Sioux had launched a rebellion of their own.

The rebellion involved the eastern, or Santee, division of the Sioux, roughly sixty-five hundred in all, who were organized into four bands and together called themselves Dakotas. It built upon at least two decades of mounting tensions that turned relatively amicable exchange relations with British, French, and American traders—some of whom had intermarried and been incorporated into Native villages—into hard-bitten political conflicts with various federal officials and white settlers (mostly German, Scandinavian, and Irish immigrants) who hungrily eyed the fertile and game-rich terrain of southern Minnesota. In the process, the Dakotas had ceded millions of acres, which included ancestral grounds, for a strip of reservation land along the Minnesota River, annuity payments, and supplies. Recalcitrance in the American Congress along with corruption among Indian agents and traders then combined to stretch a series of treaties to the breaking point. By the late 1850s, the Dakotas were under great stress and increasingly divided over how best to respond; some of the bands faced starvation.

But the federal government's determination to wage war against the Confederate rebellion caught the attention of many Dakotas and encouraged them to take the measure of the consequences. Although Confederates made no efforts to win them as allies, southern sympathizers in their orbit eagerly told of U.S. defeats, and as federal troops moved in and out of nearby Forts Ridgely, Abercrombie, and Ripley, some Dakota leaders imagined "that the South was getting the best of the fight, and . . . the North would be whipped." When, in August 1862, a U.S. officer came recruiting young men of mixed ancestry ("half-breeds" or "mixed-bloods," as they were called) for military service, one of the chiefs, Big Eagle, concluded that "the whites must be pretty hard up for men to fight the South." "It began to be whispered about," he recalled, "that now would be a good time to go to war with the whites and get the lands back." The sack of a federal warehouse in search of desperately needed food exacerbated tensions. "When men are hungry they help themselves," the influential Dakota leader Little Crow (Taoyateduta) explained. "So far as I am concerned," the Indian agent Andrew Myrick contemptuously shot back, "if they are hungry, let them eat grass."

An unrelated incident that left five white settlers dead and retaliation a certainty finally triggered the decision to rise, and on August 18 Little Crow led a column of warriors toward an agency outpost. There, shouting "kill all the whites!" they overran the place. One of the first of the victims was Myrick, shot as he ran for the woods and offered the retributive justice he had so amply earned: the attacking Dakotas stuffed a tuft of grass in his now-silenced mouth.

Other Sioux war parties spread across the Minnesota countryside enacting lethal vengeance. White settlers were murdered, their farms pillaged and burned, and federal forts threatened. By the end of August, the rebellion had spread west into the Dakota Territory, and alarms were raised farther south into Iowa and Nebraska. Minnesota's governor, Alexander Ramsey, began by mobilizing available troops left in the state and then wired Lincoln and Secretary of War Edwin Stanton for help in the form of men, arms, and horses. "This is not our war," he screeched. "It is a national war." Ramsey was soon joined by his counterparts in Wisconsin, Dakota, Iowa, and Nebraska, who feared that the entire Sioux people, together with the Chippewas and Winnebagos, might soon support the rising. "A few thousand" settlers were "at the mercy of 50,000 Indians should they see proper to fall upon us," the Dakota governor exclaimed, adding his voice to demands that "something must be done at once."

The last thing the Lincoln administration needed in the late summer of 1862 was a western Indian rebellion. U.S. armies had just suffered defeat and grievous casualties at the Second Bull Run; Confederate troops had moved out of Chattanooga and into Kentucky with the hope of establishing a loyal government there; and talk was that the British might be ready to lend the Confederacy diplomatic recognition. Could the soldiers, weapons, and attention possibly be spared? Stanton seemed dubious, especially when Minnesota's governor, Ramsey, requested that state troops be held back from federal service elsewhere, but Lincoln worried that a massive new front in the war might be opening. Rumors of a Confederate conspiracy in the Northwest, a "deep-laid plan" involving "southern emissaries," had been circulating, and some reports had British traders from Canada involved. "Information was received," Lincoln told Congress at one point, "that a simultaneous attack was to be made upon the white settlements by all tribes between the Mississippi river and the Rocky mountains." Thus, Lincoln hastily created the new Department of the Northwest—covering the states of Minnesota, Wisconsin, and Iowa as well as the territories of Nebraska and Dakota—and appointed Major General John Pope as the commander. Shocked and humiliated by what appeared to be his banishment to the West, Pope assumed it was the doing of McClellan. But after complaining to Stanton and Lincoln, he set out for his new headquarters in St. Paul, where he arrived in mid-September.

Pope intended to make quick work of the rebellious Indians. Well aware of the corrupt practices of Indian agents and traders and soured on the treaty process, he determined on a wholly military solution. "It is my purpose," Pope announced, "utterly to exterminate the Sioux if I have the power to do so and even if it requires a campaign lasting the whole of next year. . . . They are to be treated as maniacs or wild beasts, and by no means as people with whom treaties or compromises can be made." Aided by Colonel Henry Hastings Sibley (no relation of the Confederate Sibley) and 270 members of the Third Minnesota Infantry who had surrendered to the Confederates at Murfreesboro, Tennessee, and been paroled, Pope began to have the Sioux rounded up and kept as prisoners of war. Within a month, nearly two thousand Sioux had come under federal control, and both Pope and Sibley determined to exact "a final settlement with all these Indians." Setting up a five-man commission to review evidence on each of the captives and then trying them "for being connected in the late horrible outrages," Sibley soon reported that 303 Indians and half-breeds had been sentenced to hang.

Pope and Sibley seemed satisfied with what they had done and were prepared to carry out a mass execution. But Lincoln and his cabinet had serious misgivings. On the one hand, Minnesota was a strong Republican state, and the settlers there cried for revenge. On the other hand, Lincoln worried about the scale and severity of the punishment and insisted on reviewing the trial transcripts before the executions were carried out. He was shocked by what he found: the rush to judgments, the lack of evidence or eyewitness testimony, and the bitter tempers of the commissioners. Despite political pressures to permit the commission to proceed, Lincoln slowly whittled down the number of Indians condemned to death, in some cases offering pardons or reprieves. He eventually agreed to the execution of thirty-eight men. The hangings took place on December 26; they remain the largest official mass execution in the history of the United States.

Yet in some ways, the federal Congress—with Lincoln's assent—subsequently dealt more devastating blows. In early 1863, it voided all treaties with the Dakota Sioux, effectively stripping them of their reservation along the Minnesota River, abrogating all claims they might have, terminating the payment of annuities, and forcing them out of the state and onto the open plains, along Crow Creek, in southeastern Dakota Territory. There they would be joined by two thousand Winnebagos, suspected of participating in the Sioux rebellion, and, like the Sioux, pushed out of Minnesota by the actions of Congress. As for Pope, he learned some important lessons about the temper of Minnesota settlers and their political leaders. Initially proclaiming that the war was over, Pope was greeted with howls of protest from "angry whites all along the frontier" who demanded "that the war shall now be offensive . . . until the whole accursed are crushed."

If Pope had his way, he would have hastily departed for the East and the thick of the war against the Confederates, a suitable reward, in his mind, for success in completing his assignment. Instead, he was left in the West and so decided to launch a new campaign, beginning in the spring of 1863, against the Sioux in the Dakota Territory. By early July, Little Crow was dead, his scalp brought back for display at the Minnesota Historical Society, and the federal war against the Indians of the trans-Mississippi West, which would last for more than another two decades, had commenced.

The Slaves' Rebellion

At the very moment he decided to send John Pope out west to suppress the Sioux rebellion, President Lincoln was preparing a momentous executive order on the slavery question in the United States. When, precisely, he embraced the idea for such an order we do not know; what we do know is that he presented it to his cabinet in July and waited for a U.S. military victory before moving ahead publicly. The order, issued in his capacity as president of the United States and commander in chief of the army and navy, gave the rebellious states until January 1, 1863, to lay down their arms. Otherwise, all of their slaves would be "thenceforth, and forever, free." Excluded from the order would be the "slave-states . . . not then in . . . rebellion against the United States," where Lincoln offered federal assistance for "the immediate or gradual abolishment of slavery," "voluntarily adopted," "within their respective limits" and for the colonization of "persons of African descent." Announced on September 22, 1862, shortly after the Battle of Antietam (something less than a clear U.S. victory), the order was known as the Preliminary Emancipation Proclamation.

Lincoln did not come to this position easily or without significant struggle. Although he had long been committed to keeping slavery out of the federal territories of the trans-Mississippi West, he was equally committed to keeping federal hands off slavery in the states and, as best he could, slavery out of the War of the Rebellion. Despite the regular entreaties of abolitionists—black and white—to seize this unique and world-historic opportunity; despite the dismal military situation that seemed to require fresh injections of political energy; and despite the efforts of Britain and France to press for an armistice and thus an acceptance of Confederate independence, Lincoln proved reluctant to destroy the Confederacy's very foundation. In part, his hesitation was a reflection of the murkiness of slavery's borders in the United States, with some states and their powerful leaders simultaneously beholden to slavery and to the Union. Lincoln desperately needed to keep states like Kentucky out of the Confederacy, and he knew that a precipitous move against slavery might undermine his strategy. In part, too, his hesitation was a reflection of the racism that abounded across the American continent and could prove as vicious in the "free" as in the "slave" states. Lincoln feared that joining emancipation to the war effort could weaken Union morale and slow enlistment. And in part there was a growing sense internationally, even in onetime antislavery circles, that previous emancipations had been a failure and that the "problem" of substituting free labor for slave remained insoluble.

If anything, Lincoln appeared to bend over backward to court loyal slave-holders, offering them many incentives to support the U.S. or embrace emancipation. Not so for the abolitionists. When abolitionists called for action, he demurred; when they proposed black recruitment for the army, he scoffed; when antislavery officers took the initiative in the field, he reprimanded or dismissed them. Lincoln was especially direct with a black delegation with whom he met in August 1862. "You and we are different races . . . and you are yet far removed from being placed on an equality with the white race," he crassly explained. "But for your race among us there could not be war." Even as he began to contemplate an emancipation process, he imagined it as very gradual (extending over thirty-five years) and involving colonization. Thus, a few weeks before issuing the Preliminary Emancipation Proclamation, he could write in a letter to the Washington *National Intelligencer,* "My paramount object in this struggle is to save the Union, and is not either to save or destroy slavery. If I could save the Union without freeing any slave I would do it, and if I could save it by freeing all the slaves I would do that. What I do about slavery, and the colored race, I do because I believe it helps to save the Union."

As the war unfolded in its increasingly bloody agonies, Lincoln would have anticipated the lobbying of abolitionists, or the petition campaigns of antislavery communities, or the efforts of Radical Republicans in Congress, or the pressure of international politics imploring him to dislodge the cornerstone of the Confederacy. Those were the institutions and vehicles of politics with which he was accustomed and to which he was prepared to respond. What he would not readily have imagined was the source from which the drive for emancipation would most powerfully flow: the slaves themselves.

Lincoln might not have been able to imagine slaves as political actors, but the slaves, as political actors in many parts of the South, had been imagining Lincoln as a political leader for quite some time. Ever since the presidential election campaign of 1860, and especially during the late winter and spring of 1861, reports circulated across the southern states of political attentiveness and restlessness among the slaves. Observers noted the slaves' attraction to "every political speech," their disposition "to linger around" the hustings or courthouse square "and hear what the orators say," and, as if to confirm William Webb's account of his activities in 1856, their interest in collecting information from different sources and deciphering its meaning among themselves. Yet, more significantly still, Lincoln's campaign appeared to promote elevated hopes and expectations among the slaves that he intended "to set them all free."

Information as to the political conflict rupturing the United States was not difficult to come by, especially for those whose ears and eyes had long been attuned to matters affecting their current and future circumstances. There were railroad depots and river docks, courthouse and market days, church services and militia musters, partisan speeches and electoral politicking, where slaves could always be found either with their owners, on hire, or on errand. Most of all, there were the worries of their masters, sometimes expressed with dire predictions of what a Lincoln presidency would bring: abolition, the destruction or confiscation of plantations, racial "amalgamation," a veritable world turned upside down at the hands of "Black Republicans." Lincoln, it seemed, was the mortal enemy of their mortal enemies, and therefore perhaps a friend and political ally.

Indeed, once Lincoln assumed office and determined to crush the slaveholders' rebellion, the slaves' hopes and expectations inspired action. On a plantation near Petersburg, Virginia, a group of slaves celebrated Lincoln's inauguration by proclaiming that they were free and marching off their owner's estate. In northern Alabama, slaves had come to believe that "Lincoln is going to free them all" and had begun "making preparations to aid him when he makes his appearance." A runaway slave in Bossier Parish, Louisiana, told his captors in late May 1861 that "the North was fighting for the Negroes now and that he was as free as his master." "During the campaign when Lincoln was first a candidate for the Presidency," Booker T. Washington, who grew up in western Virginia, later remembered, "the slaves on our far-off plantation . . . knew what the issues involved were," and "when the war was begun . . . every slave on our plantation felt and knew that, though other issues were discussed, the primal one was that of slavery." In the view of a fretful Kentucky slaveholder, the slaves "know too much about [Lincoln], there has been so much talk about the matter all through the State. . . . [They] know as much about it as we do . . . and too much for our own safety and peace of mind."

The Lincoln administration had no interest in encouraging rebellious behavior among slaves in the Confederacy. If anything, the prospect of a war-induced slave rebellion haunted the U.S. side as much as the Confederate, and federal army commanders were directed not only to leave "established institutions" undisturbed as they began to move through the slave states but to "suppress" any slave "insurrections" that might break out. As he marched his Massachusetts troops south into Maryland in April 1861, General Benjamin Butler made the directive explicit, offering to "cooperate" with the governor in checking potential slave unrest there. Slave rebellion would only complicate the main task of subduing slaveholders' rebellion.

But slave rebellion did erupt, though not in the way either the U.S. or the Confederacy had anticipated. It did not erupt (at least at first) with lethal violence against the people and property of the master class; rather, it erupted with small-scale flight (a form of marronage) from the plantations and farms on which they were held captive to the U.S. Army encampments, where they imagined freedom might beckon. These were not the spontaneous actions of individuals; they were the products of collective discussion and organization among the slaves as to the meaning of the war, the intentions of the U.S., the location of the federal army and of Confederate patrols, and the relation between the flight of individuals or small groups and the fate of those left behind. Early on, the slaves were effectively testing their understandings of the war and the Lincoln administration, and runaways depended on both the intelligence and the sustenance that their home communities could provide while intending to lend those communities vital information about what had happened. In an important sense, it was just the sort of thing that John Brown had hoped to see from the slaves in the vicinity of Harpers Ferry, Virginia.

At all events, flight to U.S. lines was a risky undertaking. Slave owners warned their slaves, often with a display of double-barreled shotguns, to stay put. Lincoln planned to enforce the Fugitive Slave Law and initially ordered his military to leave slavery alone. And Union commanders, many of whom were Democrats and hostile to antislavery, had every reason to send runaway slaves back to their masters. Indeed, when slaves rebelled against the demands and authority of their owners and headed to U.S. lines, they presented themselves as allies in what they believed to be a battle against slavery, and like all political emissaries they discovered very quickly that such an alliance was rejected or that the U.S. Army officers did not share their goals. Harry Jarvis, a thirty-year-old slave from Northampton County, Virginia, decided to flee his nasty, gun-toting master in the early spring of 1861 and make his way to the federal outpost at Fortress Monroe, on the Virginia peninsula. It took him more than three weeks, during which time he relied on "friends who kept me informed how things was going on, and brought me food." Finally, after finding a canoe, Jarvis sailed "thirty-five miles across the bay." Arriving at the fort, he took the first opportunity to seek out the commanding general, Benjamin Butler, and "ask him to let me enlist." Butler refused him, saying "it wasn't a black man's war." Rankled, Jarvis shot back that "it would be a black man's war before they got through," though after witnessing a fellow runaway "given up to his master that come for him," he decided to find a safer berth: he hired onto a ship bound for Cuba.

Butler's response to Harry Jarvis might have been anticipated. He was a Democrat who had voted for John Breckinridge in the 1860 election, hardly the man who seemed likely to disrupt the system of slavery or redirect the dynamics of warfare. Yet Butler was also committed to the U.S., to the protection of his troops, and to the task of defeating the slaveholders' rebellion, and when he learned (apparently some time after Jarvis headed off) that the Confederates nearby were exploiting slave labor to build fortifications, he took a different view of "the species of property" seeking refuge within his lines. He declared them to be "contrabands of war" and set the able-bodied among them to work on U.S. fortifications.

By designating runaway slaves as "contrabands," Butler did not challenge the property basis of enslavement. He offered neither freedom nor a blanket policy to cover slaves regardless of their owners' political dispositions. Secretary of War Simon Cameron in fact told Butler later that summer to avoid "interfering . . . with the servants of peaceful citizens" or encouraging "such servants to leave the lawful service of their masters" and thought that the contraband policy would best facilitate "just compensation" to slave owners that "Congress will doubtless provide." But Butler's move did proffer an invitation to slaves who contemplated flight and who might have had their own ideas of what being received into U.S. lines signified. As U.S. armies pushed farther south, first to the coast of South Carolina and then to the lower Mississippi Valley, where densely staffed plantations were to be found, slaves began to appear in the tens and hundreds—sometimes composing entire communities of men, women, and children—increasingly making a mockery of the absolute power their masters claimed to enjoy.

The slaves' rebellious flight forced first federal troops and then the Lincoln administration to deal with a question they preferred to ignore and began to shift the balances of power for the slaves who remained on plantations and farms. The U.S. Congress quickly ratified Butler's contraband policy with the First Confiscation Act in August 1861, and as the war dragged on, Congress and Lincoln took a variety of steps to undermine slavery where they believed they had the authority to proceed: banning slavery in the western territories (upending part of the *Dred Scott* decision); abolishing slavery in the District of Columbia (with monetary compensation to slave owners); prohibiting the use of U.S. soldiers to return runaway slaves to their masters (rejecting the Fugitive Slave Law); and offering federal assistance to any state that would embrace gradual, compensated emancipation. At the same time, slaves who remained in captivity, owing to circumstance or choice, often seized the moment to renegotiate the relations and demands that had governed their lives. With the threat of flight or other disruptions now looming, they pressed for more time in their provision grounds, for more control over the operations of the farm or plantation, and even for small wages or shares of the growing crop. In at least one case, they threatened to hang their owner if he refused to yield.

By the summer of 1862, slavery was in the process of unraveling through official and unofficial means, though mainly as a consequence of the blows that slaves themselves determined to land. But the relation of emancipation—in whatever form—to the war and the future of the United States had still to be decided. Would slavery continue to be destroyed in a piecemeal fashion? Would the power and responsibility for pursuing emancipation continue to be left to the states or to individual slaveholders? What would happen if the War of the Rebellion failed or (as the British and French hoped) an armistice was reached? Not even radical abolitionists, who might have conceded the necessity of violence, had a clear vision of either how slavery should end or who should take the lead in ending it. The only models available were St. Domingue on the one side, where slavery and slave owners perished in the midst of revolution, and various forms of gradualism on the other, which attended to the concerns of slaveholders and generally gave them considerable latitude in supervising the process. Lincoln's desire that the border states take the lead down the road of gradualism, and possibly begin surmounting emancipation's hurdles, was summarily dashed, even by tiny Delaware, which had fewer than eighteen hundred slaves.

Whatever the moment of its germination, Lincoln's new thinking on the slavery question clearly occurred in a context—produced by rebellious slaves and rebellious masters—that demanded a reenvisioning of the war's goals, of the war's methods, and of the country that might emerge from it. Much of the policy initiative came from Radical Republicans in Congress who, in July 1862, succeeded in enacting two transformative pieces of legislation. One, known as the Second Confiscation Act, officially declared the slaveholders' rebellion "treason" and promised severe punishment (including execution) for those who engaged in or assisted it. Named most prominently as culpable parties were the president, vice president, members of the congress, court judges, cabinet officers, and foreign ministers "of the so-called confederate states of America"; rebel army and navy officers; state governors and secession convention members; and anyone who held office under the United States and then subsequently did so under the "so-called" Confederacy.

Equally important, the act made "forever free of their servitude" any slaves owned by rebel masters who came within the "lines of the army" by means of flight, capture, or occupation, and it authorized Lincoln "to employ as many persons of African descent as he may deem necessary . . . for the suppression of the rebellion." The Second Confiscation Act, in sum, was the first law to commit the U.S. government to a policy of general emancipation and to suggest both the use of former slaves to defeat rebel slaveholders and the punishment of participants in the rebellion for treason.

On the same day, Congress also passed the Militia Act of 1862 that made more specific what Lincoln could do to "employ" people of "African descent." It marked an enormous shift in policy. Ever since the founding of the American republic, African Americans (free or slave) had been barred from serving in the federal army and the state militias. Nothing better registered their subaltern status or deprived them of rights claims in a political world in which martial manhood and citizenship went hand in glove. Although blacks had taken part in all of the country's wars—as guides, spies, and translators as well as combatants—their roles were unofficial. When free blacks attempted to enlist in the U.S. Army at the beginning of the Civil War, they were rebuffed by officials at all levels of government, not least the Lincoln administration. "This Department has no intention to call into the service of the Government any colored soldiers," the secretary of war bluntly asserted.

Yet as the war dragged on and contraband camps began to fill with fugitive slaves, initiatives that once seemed fanciful attained unimagined relevance. One was the idea of recruiting slaves and free blacks for military service, which gained traction in official political circles from at least the latter part of 1861 and produced bolder implementations in the field thereafter. During the first months of 1862, Generals David Hunter in South Carolina, John W. Phelps in Louisiana, and James H. Lane in Kansas (where he and Hunter had successfully pressed for recruiting some Native Americans) commenced organizing and drilling black units, much to the annoyance of the Lincoln administration. Yet by midsummer, the wisdom of employing African Americans to the benefit of the Union became irresistible, and, in the Militia Act, Congress authorized Lincoln "to receive into the service of the United States, for the purpose of . . . labor, or any other military . . . service for which they may be found competent, persons of African descent." Initially, the expectation was that black recruits would perform manual labor in the army camps, freeing up white soldiers for combat, and receive pay "according to their respective grades." But the door to arming the slaves had clearly been opened. Before the summer was out, the War Department permitted the New England abolitionist Thomas Wentworth Higginson to organize the First South Carolina Volunteers, a regiment composed entirely of former slaves.

Lincoln's Preliminary Emancipation Proclamation said nothing about arming slaves or any other people of African descent. It opened with a restatement of his intention to prosecute the war until the "constitutional relations" between the United States and the rebellious states were "practically restor[ed]" and immediately went on to offer "pecuniary aid" and the prospect of colonization for those states, no longer in rebellion, that embraced gradual emancipation. Then came the language about making "forever free" all the slaves in the states still in rebellion on January 1, 1863, and the promise, on that date, to designate "the States and parts of states" in that status. For all the power of the moment in which it was issued, the proclamation in many ways summarized what had already been done by Lincoln and Congress—encouraging gradualism in the loyal slave states and extending freedom to the slaves of rebel masters where the army was able to do so—and indeed Lincoln explicitly invoked the Article of

War passed in March 1862 (prohibiting military personnel from returning fugitive slaves) and the Second Confiscation Act to justify his actions. Thus, when January 1, 1863, arrived and the Confederate states, as expected, remained in rebellion, Lincoln could simply have reissued the proclamation with more specific language as to where it did and did not apply. His message to Congress in December, when he continued to emphasize gradual emancipation and colonization, going so far as to advocate constitutional amendments to secure those ends, suggested that he would.

But, remarkably, he did not do so. Even as Lincoln reiterated his interest in gradualism and colonization, his thinking about the Emancipation Proclamation had undergone a dramatic shift. And what he signed on January 1, 1863, was an altogether different document. To be sure, some of the wording of the Preliminary Emancipation Proclamation was included, and Lincoln now exempted the slave states of Delaware, Maryland, Missouri, Kentucky, and the new state of West Virginia—none of which were at war with the Union—the Confederate state of Tennessee (under Union occupation and attempting to form a loyal government), and several counties and parishes in eastern Virginia and lower Louisiana (also under occupation and attempting to form new governments) from its reach. Gone, however, were all references to gradual emancipation or colonization and included, for the first time, was a provision to receive former slaves "of suitable condition . . . into the armed service of the United States." Although the proclamation justified emancipation on the grounds of "military necessity" and said nothing about the position of former slaves in American society, it advanced the radical remedies of abolition without compensation for slave owners and the arming of slaves and free blacks to defeat them in battle.

The repercussions were enormous. Although talk of British mediation did not suddenly cease—in October, the chancellor of the exchequer, William Gladstone, had insisted that the Confederacy "have made a nation"—the Emancipation Proclamation clearly swelled U.S. support in British cities and especially the manufacturing districts, where King Cotton diplomacy had predicted it would crumble amid a cotton famine. Among the strongest supporters were textile workers, some of whom glimpsed a relation between the slaves' political struggles and their own. "We have a general impression amongst us," one of them stated, "that the once despised and enthralled African will not only be set free, but be enfranchised and in spite of his master; and when the slave ceases to be and becomes an enfranchised free man, that then the British workingman's claim may be listened to."

The abolitionist Frederick Douglass had an even broader grasp of what had transpired. Mixing the language of the sacred and the secular, Douglass saw in the Emancipation Proclamation not only providential design but the mark of a new stage in the history of the United States, when a nation seemed to emerge, one in which "the cause of the slave and the cause of the country" had finally been joined. And indeed, since the late eighteenth century, in continental Europe and the Americas, nation-states rose from the ashes of slavery and servility, propelled by their determination to dismantle the petty sovereignties of masters and lords and to claim the military service of freedmen and peasants within their borders. The slaves' rebellion had transformed the objectives of the war and rendered possible a remaking of the United States.

Rebellion in the Rear

From the time of his inauguration, Abraham Lincoln and his administration faced an assortment of rebellions that threatened to take apart the American Union along a number of deeply laid political and social fissures. The slaveholders' rebellion was the most massive and threatening of them, but from the first the United States confronted the prospect of political rebellions in the West, the Midwest, and parts of the urban East that could have fractured the country beyond recognition. Indian rebellion in the upper plains and in Indian Territory looked to take advantage of an apparently weakened federal government to recover ground (and grounds) that had been lost. And slaves who had followed, as best they could, the prolonged battles over the future of slavery in the United States and elsewhere, who had a developing sense of their friends and enemies, and who had recognized that white Americans were hopelessly divided rebelled against their owners' authority once their imagined allies in the federal government struck the initial blow.

But as time wore on, the Lincoln administration had still another rebellion on its hands, this time within the ranks of those who had remained officially loyal to the Union and on whom Lincoln had to rely to fight rebellious slaveholders to a successful end. They were Democrats who in growing numbers mobilized to challenge Republican initiatives on political economy and state building and especially on new war aims organized around the destruction of slavery. To be sure, when hostilities commenced in the spring of 1861, most northern Democrats rallied to the defense of the Union and its government and condemned the militancy and aggressiveness of the Confederates. Among them was Stephen Douglas, who lost no time in denouncing secession, offering his services to Lincoln, and attempting to keep the upper tier of slave states in the Union.

Douglas died suddenly in early June 1861, felled by the exhaustion of the presidential campaign and the crisis of disunion and war, and Douglas's death seemed emblematic of political troubles ahead. The Union's defeat at Bull Run and the massive mobilizations that had begun raised questions both about the war's outcome and about the political consequences of fighting it. Soon joining a small core of Confederate sympathizers who actively spoke out against the war and tried to interfere with its prosecution were a growing number of Democrats who reeled at the dramatic expansion of federal powers, the suspension of the writ of habeas corpus, the enactment of economic legislation that favored banks, manufacturers, and urban interests, and the attacks on Confederate property—especially slave property. They saw a Republican state overreaching its authority and threatening the country with tyranny and racial "amalgamation." They combined a populist opposition to new concentrations of wealth and power with racism and localism. They were to be found in largest numbers in the "butternut" sections of the Midwest (downstate Illinois, Indiana, and Ohio), settled by southern migrants, as well as in ethnically and culturally diverse parts of the Northeast and the Middle Atlantic, especially in New York, Philadelphia, Baltimore, and the coal-mining districts of eastern Pennsylvania. "The Constitution as it is; the Union as it was; the negroes where they are" became their slogan, and they exerted pressure on fellow Democrats who tried to toe a fine line of partisan and patriotic loyalties. Republicans knew them as "copperheads"; Lincoln called their dissidence a "fire in the rear."

Ohio's Clement L. Vallandigham became the poster boy for copperheadism. Born in southern Ohio to a family from Virginia, then marrying into another family from Maryland, Vallandigham was a true denizen of slavery's blurry borders. Like the British and French across the Atlantic, he did not believe that the federal government could subdue the Confederacy and instead called for an armistice, the withdrawal of U.S. troops from the South, and a process of reunification. From the first, he publicly denounced congressional legislation he regarded as unconstitutional and urged opposition to the war. Sensitive to any attacks on civil liberties, Vallandigham nonetheless focused on the fates and futures of white people and was outraged by the Lincoln administration's shift to a "wicked" war of "abolition." In none of this was he unique among the "peace" faction of Democrats. But his verbal skills and self-righteousness set him apart, and in May 1863, after he denounced the war and urged "King Lincoln's" removal from office in a speech at the town of Mount Vernon, Ohio, Vallandigham was arrested by the U.S. Army.

In the view of General Ambrose Burnside (reassigned to the Department of Ohio after disastrous defeats in Virginia a few months earlier), Vallandigham had violated a recent order that promised to treat "as spies or traitors" anyone "within our lines who commits acts for the benefit of enemies of our country." What these acts might be Burnside did not specify, but he insisted that "the habit of declaring sympathy for the enemy," which he regarded as a species of treason, would not be tolerated. Because Lincoln had already suspended the writ of habeas corpus throughout the Union the previous September (the very month he issued the Preliminary Emancipation Proclamation and decided to suppress the Sioux uprising), Vallandigham was tried in a military court and sentenced to prison for the duration of the war. Well aware of the firestorm that Vallandigham's arrest and imprisonment provoked among Ohio Democrats and worried about making him into a martyr, Lincoln quickly commuted the sentence to banishment and had him handed over to Confederates in Tennessee, who rather reluctantly took him in. From there, Vallandigham made his way to Windsor, Ontario, where he received visitors and, seeking vindication, tried to run a campaign for governor of Ohio. The Democrats awarded him the nomination, but the general electorate was in no rush to embrace him. Vallandigham lost in a landslide in the fall of 1863, and the governorship remained in the Republican column.

The Vallandigham case raised a host of thorny questions about the extent of executive war powers, especially well behind the lines of combat, and worries about violations of civil liberties reached into Republican circles. In truth, given the stakes and circumstances, the fist of the Lincoln administration was anything but iron. Arbitrary civilian arrests mostly took place in Confederate territory or in the near border and for the most part involved those suspected of spying, blockade-running, and smuggling. Relatively few Americans on either side of the conflict were jailed for their dissenting beliefs, and Lincoln showed a good deal of restraint when it came to newspapers like the *Chicago Times* and the *New York Atlas*, which regularly howled at his policies and war goals.

Indeed, the catalyst for rebellion in the rear came not from arbitrary detentions or violations of free speech but from the issue of military conscription and its relation to emancipation. When the war began, enlistment—in the U.S. and the Confederacy—was organized at the state and local levels and by officials who had been elected there. Although central governments set quotas, governors were the linchpins in seeing that the quotas were filled, and volunteering drove the process. Men would sign up for a term of service and then, if they survived, would be encouraged to reenlist when their terms ran out. Early on, the combination of patriotic enthusiasm, the defense of family and community, and popular pressure more than sufficed. A large proportion of eligible men stepped forward on both sides, especially in the Confederacy, where invasion from without loomed.

But it was not long before the escalating demands of warfare exposed the limits of such a decentralized system. Within the first year of fighting, most of the sources of volunteering had been tapped, and pressures from the home front in what were still overwhelmingly rural and agricultural societies mounted. Because its population of eligible soldiers (free white men) was roughly one-fifth the size of the Union's and many of its volunteers had enrolled for only twelve months, the Confederacy faced a manpower crisis as early as the winter of 1861–62. The options for finding new ways of stimulating reenlistments were scarce. While the Louisiana Native Guards, a unit of free people of color from New Orleans, had been mustered into service in the spring of 1861 (well before the U.S. made comparable moves), no one initially contemplated using slaves (roughly 40 percent of the Confederate population) for anything other than military or civilian labor. As a consequence, the Confederate congress was forced to enact a draft law in April that required three years of service or extended the terms of the initial volunteers by two years.

Even though it asked the state governors to meet quotas and included numerous exemptions, the Confederate draft provoked controversy and conflict from the start. Many of the governors, especially Joseph Brown in Georgia and Zebulon Vance in North Carolina, found the law an example of the very "despotism" they had embraced secession to avoid and pledged noncooperation. Closer to the ground, soldiers in the ranks often bridled at the Confederacy's intrusion into new domains of coercion and, especially if they were humble non-slaveholders, felt that the burdens of service had been shifted to their shoulders. Legislation, passed several months later, that permitted owners or managers of plantations with twenty or more slaves (the "twenty nigger law," as some called it) to stay out of the military only reinforced that sense. Resistance to the draft began to fester, particularly in districts filled with yeomen and poorer white families, and desertion from the ranks became a gnawing problem.

The prospect of rebellions from within (besides the slave rebellions) thus began to haunt the Confederate leadership. The fear could be detected among self-interested slave owners who refused to allow the government to claim the labor of their slaves or discourage them from growing cotton; among common soldiers who took leave from the front to assist their struggling families at home; among renegades in the hills and hollows who fended off conscription and impressment officers and in some cases joined up with the U.S. Army; and among soldiers' wives who demanded relief and support from the Confederate government and eventually showed their mettle in a wave of food riots. Attempting to build a state—especially a state immediately thrust into war—on the foundation of slaveholding was an enormous gamble even if Confederates had imagined that the winds of history might be blowing in new directions and that slavery and cotton would prove to be sources of strength. By the end of 1863, a few of them began to think the unthinkable and envision a path of emancipation organized around the military enlistment of their slaves.

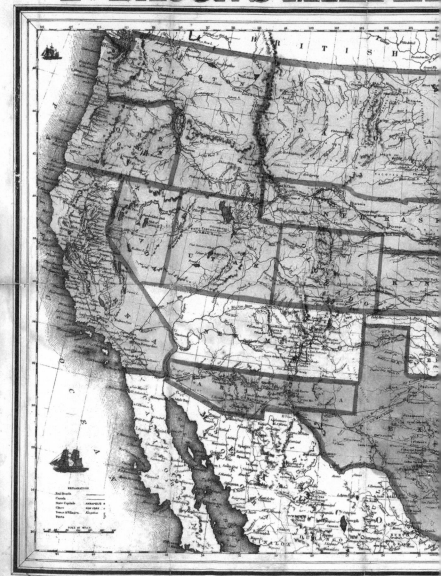

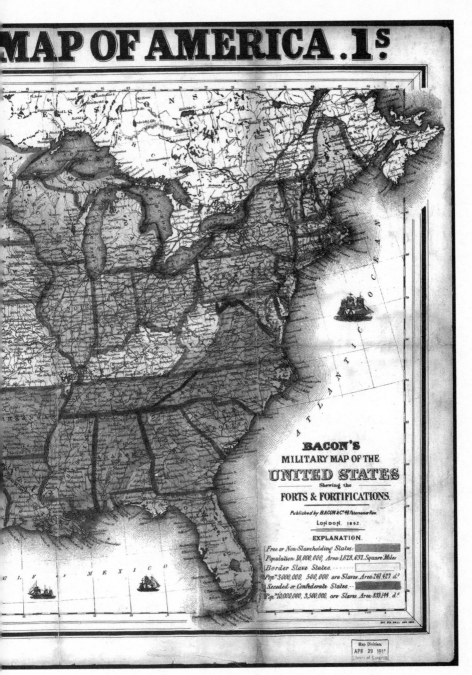

MAP OF AMERICA . 1ˢ

BACON'S
MILITARY MAP OF THE
UNITED STATES
Shewing the
FORTS & FORTIFICATIONS.

Published by BACON & Cᵒ 48 Paternoster Row.

LONDON. 1862.

EXPLANATION.

Free or Non-Slaveholding States:
Population 18,000,000, Area 1,828,637, Square Miles
Border Slave States.
Pop.ⁿ 3,000,000, 500,000 are Slaves Area 261,427 dᵒ
Seceded or Confederate States.
Pop.ⁿ 10,000,000, 3,500,000, are Slaves Area 833,144 dᵒ

The United States during the War of the Rebellion, 1862.

State building had its own logic of peril in the Union, and the resistance to its most direct manifestations was more explosive still. The policies of the Lincoln administration and the Republican Congress not only drew power to the center from the peripheries but also favored certain constituencies at the expense of others. Bond sales enriched a new class of bankers and financiers who then joined forces with railroad developers freshly favored by massive government incentives. Federal contracts provided windfalls for manufacturers in the clothing, food-processing, and armaments sectors. Tariffs and banking legislation favored cities and industry at the expense of the countryside and agriculture. And the inflation that came with printing greenbacks cut into the living standards of skilled—and especially unskilled—workers, many of whom were immigrants from Britain, Germany, and Ireland, traditionally aligned with the Democratic Party.

Social and political tensions were therefore on low simmer in the Union when the Lincoln administration inflamed them by following the example of the Confederates and enacting a military draft that also permitted the hiring of a substitute or the payment of a $300 exemption fee. Implementation came a year later, in the spring of 1863, in good measure because the pool of manpower was larger and the initial terms of service longer. It was greeted with much the same language of opposition—despotism, favoritism, tyranny—that appeared in the south. But the draft also came in the immediate aftermath of the Emancipation Proclamation and the decision to enlist large numbers of African Americans, slave and free, in the U.S. Army, and therefore appeared part of a federal government effort to expand its authority and reorganize the war.

Opposition to the new draft law erupted in Democratic strongholds across the northern states and with special intensity in enclaves of working-class immigrants, especially Irish and Catholic immigrants, who had long been struggling with their employers. Indeed, the draft could become a vehicle of mobilization for workers and employers alike, allowing the former to depict conscription as an example of the tyranny and unfairness of the wartime social order and the latter to call in the troops to break strikes. The anthracite counties of northeastern Pennsylvania, boasting large numbers of Irish-born miners, seethed with conflict over labor and the draft that might have given birth to the feared Molly Maguires.

Yet it was in New York City that the tensions of the moment burst forth in immensely destructive rebellion and savage racial brutality. Beginning on July 13, 1863, what has come to be known as the draft riot in fact moved through several phases over the course of five days. At first, it seemed to be a mass protest aimed at the draft office and was composed chiefly of artisans and skilled workers especially from the building trades. As they streamed along the city's avenues, holding placards demanding an end to the draft, they closed down shops, factories, and other work sites, summoning the laborers there to join in, while some cut down telegraph poles and tore up streetcar tracks. Within a short time, they brought the draft lottery to a halt and cheered the Democratic general and opponent of emancipation George B. McClellan, who resided in the city. But by mid-afternoon on that day, some began to threaten Republican leaders associated in their minds with antislavery, and sections of the demonstrators turned their anger on the police, the offices of the provost marshal, the Republican newspapers, and the houses of wealthy Republicans. Police officers were beaten, property was destroyed, buildings were torched, looting took place, and before the day was out, the Colored Orphanage was burned to the ground and several black men and boys suffered assault.

The vengeance and punishment meted out by some of the protesters on Monday afternoon and evening indicated where things were headed. By Tuesday morning, a good many of the original demonstrators—especially those who had focused on the draft offices and tended to be artisans and journeymen of German and native-born extraction—ceased their activities and, in some cases, joined hands with city officials in attempting to quell the disturbances. From then on, the rebellion was driven principally by Irish-born industrial workers and common laborers, many employed by New York's machine shops, iron foundries, and docks, who vented their rage on those they regarded as villains: abolitionists, social reformers and their institutions, members of the Republican social and political elite, and, increasingly, the population of African descent.

The black population of New York City was neither large, well placed, nor economically secure. In a city of over 800,000 people, they numbered fewer than 13,000 (less than 2 percent). Many were fugitives from enslavement in the South or the offspring of those who had endured enslavement and gradual emancipation in the North. Only a handful had craft skills or property; instead, they worked overwhelmingly as laborers and domestic servants, relegated to the bottom rungs of New York's economic ladder. They lived crowded together in an area encompassing parts of three downtown wards and had been pushed out of the far uptown Seneca Village (where some owned land) to make way for the construction of Central Park. Like most African Americans, they were, during the 1850s, under siege from a variety of directions, and although they had long been active in abolitionist politics, they had few reliable allies outside their own communities.

It did not help that New York City had a history of anti-abolitionist and antiblack violence or that black and Irish workers had already clashed at various work sites, notably at the waterfront, where blacks had recently been employed to break a longshoremen's strike. Nor did it help that New York's Democratic press had been attacking the federal government's "nigger war" or warning that emancipation would flood the city with desperate black competitors for white jobs. Nor did it help that African American men were being enlisted in the army to help carry out what seemed to be the new Republican projects. African Americans, in sum, were exceedingly vulnerable: symbols of the war's most detested policies and of emancipation's most threatening possibilities while left with little protection against their angry enemies.

By the second day, in fact, the rebellion had many of the features of a racial pogrom. Gangs of men and boys, many connected to the families of Irish longshoremen, roved the waterfront rooting out black denizens and murdering black men who came within their grasp in the most grisly fashion: by hanging, stabbing, shooting, stomping, stoning, burning, and mutilating. "Vengeance on every nigger in New York," one vicious mob cried. By the time it was over, eleven black men had been lynched, and hundreds of black men, women, and children were fleeing the city, heading to the relative safety of Brooklyn and New Jersey.

Pitched battles continued in the streets and factories, and the city's police proved unable to gain the upper hand. After all, their ranks had been depleted by the military mobilization, and there were few additional troops available to them. Finally, the War Department stepped in and ordered several regiments of U.S. soldiers from the blood-soaked fields of Gettysburg to occupy New York City in a show of force and determination. It was not easy for them to do. The soldiers had to fight their way in, amid gunfire, flying debris, and ambushes, returning the rioters' fire and in some cases moving tenement to tenement. By Friday, now six thousand strong, they had managed to reestablish control.

Desperate to resume the draft and assert its authority, the Lincoln administration gradually increased the troop strength in the city to twenty thousand. But it did not declare martial law or seek the summary punishment of rioters who clearly engaged in insurrection against the federal government and could be accused of treason. Instead, the administration stood aside when local grand juries refused to indict many of the rioters and allowed the New York City Council to appropriate funds to pay for substitutes or exemptions when drafted men chose not to serve. With leaders of both parties on board and the draft office moved to a strongly Republican ward, conscription started up again on August 19. Quiet prevailed as the names were pulled and more African Americans took flight from the city.

Envisioning a Nation

On November 18, 1863, three months after the draft had resumed in New York City, President Lincoln departed Washington, D.C., for a five-hour train trip, north and west, to Gettysburg, Pennsylvania, from which federal troops had been summoned to quell the insurrection. It was not the sort of thing Lincoln frequently did. Since the time he arrived in Washington for his inauguration in 1861, he rarely left the capital city. But this was a special, if somber, occasion. A cemetery was to be dedicated in Gettysburg, where, the previous July, a massive U.S. Army had turned back an equally massive and ambitious Confederate advance in one of the war's great bloodbaths. Over the course of three days, several thousand U.S. soldiers had been killed and then hastily buried; now they were being reinterred and honored for their heroic deeds. Four train cars carried Lincoln, a few members of his cabinet, and other officials who would be joining governors from several of the loyal states together with local dignitaries and citizens as they assembled the following day to hear the main address by the famed Massachusetts orator and conservative Constitutional Unionist Edward Everett, a former Whig. Lincoln had agreed to make only "a few appropriate remarks."

Although he seemed to be an add-on, Lincoln took his assignment very seriously. For some months, he had been contemplating a speech—and had been urged from several quarters to give one—that would explain the meaning of this long and awful war to a public that had suffered grievous losses and desperately needed perspective on what they had endured and where they were headed. Now he had a special opportunity, and despite later myths about his composing the speech on the train or jotting it last minute on an envelope, he gave it a great deal of thought and saw fit to make several handwritten copies. What he managed to do was offer a deep history of a "nation" that in fact was being born almost as he spoke. And he did it in fewer than three hundred words.

It still required impressive leaps of faith for Lincoln to do this as he stood on the speakers' platform, overlooking the markers of death rather than life and of near calamity for the country he had pledged to protect. The war against the slaveholders' rebellion was more than two and a half years old, and for the most part the story seemed one of unraveling instead of creation: unraveling of the Union, unraveling of political loyalties, unraveling of economic ties, unraveling of slavery, with no clear sense of how the unraveling might be stanched or something new and different constructed. Despite Lincoln's oft-proclaimed goal of "saving the Union," the results on the battlefields offered few signs that this could happen anytime soon, and with an assortment of rebellions on his hands it was increasingly doubtful that there would be much left to save.

Militarily, the best the Lincoln administration could claim for more than two years was stalemate. And the most encouraging results were in the West. The Confederate offensive in the far Southwest, which had proclaimed the new territory of Arizona, had taken Albuquerque and Santa Fe, and had Colorado and possibly California in its sights, eventually stumbled into trouble in late March 1862, though at the hands of an unexpected foe. Initially, the U.S. War Department planned to send a contingent of California volunteers across the southwestern deserts to challenge Henry Hopkins Sibley's rebel soldiers, but the deployment was delayed by problems with secessionists and Confederate sympathizers in southern California itself. By the time the Californians were ready to move, Sibley and his men were already in northern New Mexico. Instead, from Kansas, Major General David Hunter ordered Colorado's territorial governor "to send all available forces that you can," and after a long and dramatic march through high plains and mountains, in snow and freezing weather, the Colorado volunteers surprised the Confederates at Glorieta Pass. Although casualties were relatively light, the damage the Coloradans inflicted was sufficient to send Sibley into retreat, first to the Rio Grande valley of New Mexico and then back to Texas. By the time the California troops were moving east, the job was done, and they were left to occupy Tucson, establish federal authority in Arizona and western New Mexico, and stare down any further Confederate adventures. For the remainder of the war, their main engagements were with bands of Chiricahua Apaches under the powerful chiefs Mangas Coloradas and Cochise.

Union military successes were also achieved in the vital Mississippi Valley. Only days after Glorieta Pass, the federal army and navy reclaimed New Orleans and began fanning out into the surrounding sugar parishes, where unionism had a toehold among Whiggish planters, not to mention among slaves who flocked to their lines and into hastily built contraband camps. To the north, U.S. forces had been pressing in from Tennessee, Missouri, and Arkansas, taking Forts Henry and Donelson, sending the rebels packing at Pea Ridge, surviving another bloodbath at Shiloh, and then taking Memphis. The objective was control of the Mississippi River, but it would not be easy. Vicksburg, strategically overlooking the river, remained a Confederate stronghold, and with the rebels dug in and the rivers and bayous difficult to cross, the varied offensives of Ulysses S. Grant and William T. Sherman were stymied for months on end.

Moving to the east, the military picture became bleaker. The Army of the Cumberland had failed to make much headway in middle Tennessee and in the fall of 1862 had to fend off a bold Confederate invasion of Kentucky that came well within one hundred miles of Cincinnati and almost inaugurated a state government in Frankfort. But the situation in Virginia was nothing short of drastic. Every effort the U.S. Army made to take Richmond—from the north and from the southeast—had been decisively turned back, and after the second defeat at Bull Run in August 1862 rebel troops under Robert E. Lee went on the offensive. Their hope was to move into Union territory, attract some support in the slaveholding state of Maryland, win a military victory, further demoralize the northern public, embolden the peace Democrats, convince Europeans that the Union cause was lost, and perhaps force Lincoln to seek an armistice. It made sense even while entailing serious risk. Northern morale was at a low ebb, state and congressional elections were to take place in November, and McClellan (who, according to Lincoln, had "the slows") was still in charge of U.S. forces.

Lee and his 55,000 men crossed the Potomac River in early September 1862 and marched into Maryland. Their first surprise was the silence that greeted their arrival; sympathetic Marylanders did not come forward. Their second surprise was that owing to sheer luck (the discovery of Lee's plans, carelessly discarded) the U.S. Army was ready for them (though, as usual, McClellan still hesitated). The subsequent battle at Antietam involved over 100,000 men, nearly one-quarter of whom would be killed or wounded, and although there was no clear winner, Lee retreated into Virginia, and Lincoln issued the Preliminary Emancipation Proclamation. But the setback did not cause Lee to reassess the strategy, and in the spring of 1863 he again looked north, this time emboldened by his victory that May at Chancellorsville over U.S. troops who outnumbered him. In the meantime, Alexander Stephens, the Confederacy's vice president, proposed a meeting with Lincoln, under a flag of truce, to discuss prisoner exchanges and a possible peace.

Then, during the first two weeks of July 1863, the dynamics of war and political authority clearly swung toward the Union. In early June, Lee's army began moving north through the Shenandoah Valley and in mid-June again crossed the Potomac River into Maryland, all the while being shadowed by U.S. forces, first under General Joseph Hooker and later under General George Meade, who positioned themselves between the rebels and Washington, D.C. In late June, Lee's troops marched into Pennsylvania and began to feed off the rich fields of southeastern Pennsylvania, taking the opportunity to ransack Thaddeus Stevens's ironworks along the way and eyeing the state capital of Harrisburg. But on July 1, while looking for shoes in the small town of Gettysburg, they encountered U.S. cavalry and commenced what turned into three horrific days of battle. This time, there was no ambiguity about the outcome: on July 3, Lee, having lost one-third of his army, recognized defeat and ordered retreat, not to a safer haven in Pennsylvania or Maryland from which they might strike again on northern soil, but back across the Potomac into Confederate Virginia. Alexander Stephens's mission now seemed pointless; Lincoln, his old friend, refused him safe passage through Union lines.

The next day was July 4, and there was more good and important news. Hundreds of miles to the south and west, another large rebel force, this one under siege for weeks at Vicksburg, finally surrendered to General Grant, giving the U.S. full command of the Mississippi River and effectively severing the Confederacy in two. Lee had hoped that military success in Pennsylvania might relieve the pressure on the rebels in Vicksburg as well as energize copperheads in the Midwest and the Middle Atlantic. The antidraft insurrection in New York City suggested the explosive force that might be bubbling below the surface of the Union had further weakness been exposed. The rebel defeats at Gettysburg and Vicksburg, together with the suppression of the New York insurrection, thus constituted staggering, though not necessarily fatal, blows and encouraged a growing feeling, both in the United States and in Europe, that the Union would likely survive.

But what sort of union might it be? Since the establishment of independence and the founding of the Republic, this was the question with which Americans, at all levels, intensely struggled. Was it a loose confederation of relatively sovereign states? A country in which power was shared between federal and state governments? An empire with many different component parts held together by a weak center and an effervescent idea of destiny? Had the war brought about a major transformation in the very nature—and not simply the composition—of the Union itself? Lincoln and other antislavery Republicans, building upon the political sensibilities of northern Whigs, Liberty Party supporters, and Free-Soilers, had begun to answer this question well before secession and the war by envisioning not just a confederation or a union or an empire but a "nation": a distinctive form of political organization and a distinctive form of state, with specific sorts of territorial reach, political economies, sets of social relations, and cultural projects.

The vision had been conjured, the ideas developed, the arguments made, but when Lincoln began to speak that November afternoon at Gettysburg, he seemed to be announcing a nation's presence. Indeed, he gave the nation a deep historical pedigree (from the time of the Declaration of Independence), lent it a clear political character, and explained the War of the Rebellion not as the moment of the nation's emergence but as the measure of its very survival. "Four score and seven years ago, our fathers brought forth on this continent, a *new nation*, conceived in *liberty*, and dedicated to the proposition that *all men are created equal* [emphasis added].

"Now we are engaged in a great civil war," Lincoln continued, "*testing* whether that *nation*, or any *nation* so conceived and so dedicated, can long *endure*."

He described the cemetery as "a great battle-field of that war" which had become the "final resting place for those who gave their lives that the *nation* might live" and insisted that the "brave men, living and dead, who struggled here, have consecrated it, far above our power to add or detract." Still, it was left to "us the living" to carry on the "unfinished work" that they "so nobly advanced," and the "cause" to which "they gave the last full measure of their devotion" was described by Lincoln with a pithy and riveting eloquence: "that this *nation* shall have a new birth of freedom—and that government of the people, by the people, and for the people, shall not perish from the earth."

At no point in the address did Lincoln speak explicitly of emancipation or political democracy, but in describing the "cause" of the war, he clearly suggested that in his view both would be foundational to the very meaning of the "nation." Yet there were other things left unspoken and unacknowledged that would have a great deal to do with the sort of "nation" this would be. Lincoln said nothing about the Sioux rebellion in the upper plains, its suppression, the execution of alleged participants, the fate of other Indian allies and enemies, or the offensive federal troops were in the midst of carrying out against many of them. Nor did he mention battlefields where newly recruited black troops had fallen in large numbers—especially at Battery Wagner in coastal South Carolina only days after the Battle of Gettysburg—and what place those troops and their communities might have in the "nation" experiencing "a new birth of freedom." Those matters, large, consequential, and contradictory, were still very much left to be decided.

CHAPTER EIGHT

Defining a Nation-State

The 107th United States Colored Infantry Band at Fort Corcoran,
Arlington, Virginia, 1865.

The Fate of the Insurrectionary States

Even before federal armies marched into the rebellious slaveholding states, new Republican policy makers began to contemplate how and in what form the Union might be restored. Insurgents from the states of the Deep South and then the upper South had met in hastily organized conventions, claimed to sever their ties with the United States, formed themselves into what they called the Confederate States of America, and vowed to resist federal coercion in a fight for their independence. But what precisely did this mean in political and constitutional terms, and what powers did the federal government have to act against them? How was the rebellion to be interpreted, and how would this interpretation give shape to a process of reconstruction? And which branches of the government—the executive, the legislative, the judicial—had the proper authority to make the rules?

At the outset, the view of the Lincoln administration, and the dominant view in the Republican Party as a whole, was that secession was constitutionally impossible, that the Union was perpetual, a creation of the people rather than of the states, and that the political crisis of 1860–61 was the work of rebels who had commandeered their respective states and determined to wage war against the federal government in service of their political ends. Imagining that the rebels constituted a powerful minority and that unionism was widespread if temporarily pushed below the surface of public opinion, the administration saw its task as suppressing the rebellion, identifying elements loyal to the United States, and returning control of the affected states to them. The position of the states in the Union would not then have changed, and the laws and institutions of the states and their citizens would remain in place. It was federalism of the type that had prevailed before the rebellion itself, now resurrected in the rebellion's wake.

That is, if the rebellion were defeated quickly and unionism readily in evidence. Early on, this was the expectation. "The States have their status IN the Union," Lincoln told Congress on July 4, 1861, "and they have no other legal status." Yet as it became increasingly clear that the rebellion was militarily formidable and unionists in very short supply—that the war would not be over quickly and Republicans could not count on much of a base of support among white men and their families in rebellious states—such thinking appeared misguided if not politically irrelevant. The dynamics of rebellion, after all, had rendered the seceding states unassimilable to the Union as it had been constituted and certainly to a union governed by the Republican Party. No constitutional fictions could disguise the changes and challenges manifest where the rebels held sway. New thinking proved necessary.

Republicans, chiefly from the Radical camp, thus began to devise a very different argument and perspective. They did not deny that the Union was perpetual or that secession was impossible. What they did deny was that nothing fundamental had happened in the rebellious states. As the Ohio congressman John Bingham put it, the "treasonable civil organization" to be found in those states, "while . . . void against the Federal Government," nonetheless "operates an absolute forfeiture of their powers and rights as States." Senator Charles Sumner of Massachusetts went so far as to claim that by the act of secession the states had effectively "become felo-de-se" (that is, they had committed "suicide") and ceased to exist; many of his colleagues, though less taken with the analogy, came to a similar conclusion: that the rebel states had, in relation to the Union and the central government, been returned to, or "lapsed into the condition of," territories now subject to federal jurisdiction.

"Territorialization," as the argument came to be known, had the advantage of putting the rebellious states into a familiar legal category but did not bring with it any specific plan for reorganizing those states politically. Indeed, numerous ideas and approaches were offered as Congress commenced to debate the question in early 1862, and much of the Union public seemed favorably disposed to some version. Petitions from western New York State demanded that South Carolina, Georgia, and Florida be reduced to territories and reserved for exclusive black settlement (anticipating the Sherman Reserve of 1865). Other northerners, rather less arrestingly, imagined provisional or territorial governments being imposed under congressional auspices. At all events, the "rights" and civil integrity of these states would have been sacrificed and the authority of the federal government consecrated.

Lincoln was not among those Republicans who embraced territorialization. In principle at least, he remained committed to the notion that secession was constitutionally impossible, the states still existed as such, and loyal state governments should be organized as soon as feasible. He was especially interested in reestablishing congressional representation for the rebellious states that had been occupied and could conduct the necessary elections. Yet Lincoln's thinking evolved as well. Now more than a year into the war and with little prospect of an end to the rebellion, he could hardly expect these states to rejoin the Union on their own. Instead, the federal government through its military arm would have to step in and take charge, providing for elections and identifying eligible voters. And as the Lincoln administration and Congress simultaneously committed the war to slave emancipation through legislative and military means, the issue of abolition as a prerequisite for congressional representation now hung over the process. Growing numbers of Republicans, in fact, seemed ready to abandon "territorialization" in exchange for a tougher stand from Lincoln on the slavery question, recognizing that both approaches were predicated on new forms of federal sovereignty.

In this context, Lincoln, shortly after his address at Gettysburg, issued the Proclamation of Amnesty and Reconstruction. More a framework than a clear-cut "plan," and one oriented to ending the war through the stimulation of loyalty and the prospect of self-rule, the proclamation set out guidelines for the establishment of new state governments in the occupied South. Offering pardons to all (with the exception of top Confederate military and political leaders) who would pledge their future allegiance to the United States and support for emancipation, Lincoln provided that when such loyalists composed "not less than one-tenth the number" of those who voted in the presidential election of 1860, they could adopt a new constitution and seek representation in Congress (subject to congressional approval). Given that the proclamation commenced by declaring that "many persons have committed, and are now guilty of treason," Lincoln's terms were remarkably generous and seemed to hark back to his earlier thinking about reconstruction: save, that is, for his instructions as to slavery.

Lincoln's pardon carried the "restoration of all rights of property, except as to slaves," and he expected the new state governments to provide for the "permanent freedom" of the enslaved. Nothing was said about the civil or political status of the former slaves (the voters were those eligible by law in 1860 and thus all white), and Lincoln accepted the likelihood of "temporary arrangement[s] . . . consistent with their present condition as a laboring, landless, and homeless class." As the problem of slavery moved toward resolution, the problem of "freedom" increasingly reared its head. But without invoking his power as commander in chief of the armed forces as he had in issuing the Emancipation Proclamations—alluding instead to his presidential authority "to grant reprieves and pardons for offences against the United States"—Lincoln embarked on a course he had once considered unconstitutional. He asserted the supremacy of the federal government over the states and required them to abolish slavery as a condition for regaining their place in the Union.

Better known as Lincoln's Ten Percent Plan, the proclamation initially enjoyed wide support in Republican circles largely owing to its insistence on emancipation. Yet much of that support quickly dissipated as the policy played out in Louisiana. There, the U.S. Army had gained its second significant foothold in the Deep South (the Sea Islands of South Carolina were the first, captured in November 1861) when New Orleans was taken in April 1862, and by early 1864 loyalist factions were jockeying for advantage. With the help of Lincoln's commanding officer, General Nathaniel Banks, moderates gained the upper hand and wrote a constitution that abolished slavery, concentrated power in New Orleans, and favored white workingmen but did nothing for the civil or political standing of African Americans, free or freed. To the contrary, they asked Congress to provide compensation to loyal slave owners, many of whom were wealthy sugar planters in the surrounding area. The political implications were disconcerting. As the radical reformer Wendell Phillips saw it, Lincoln's policy "leaves the large landed proprietors of the South still to domineer over its politics, and makes the negro's freedom a mere sham." At the very least, it became apparent that claimants under the Proclamation of Amnesty and Reconstruction could be of dubious loyalty and, if quickly readmitted to Congress, threaten Republican power and projects.

Congressional Republicans increasingly embraced two perspectives that brought them into conflict with Lincoln. One was that Lincoln's plan was too hasty and lenient and that, as one Massachusetts congressman insisted, "something more Radical" was needed. Taking a cue from the Pennsylvania Republican Thaddeus Stevens's view that the rebel states constituted a "belligerent power" and an alien enemy that had "abrogated and destroyed all municipal obligations, compacts, constitutions, and laws which were formerly binding," they hoped to slow the readmission process substantially, perhaps indefinitely. The other perspective was constitutional. Pointing to an 1849 Supreme Court decision in *Luther v. Borden* and the constitutional guarantee of a "republican government" in the states (Article IV, Section 4), they claimed it "the exclusive prerogative of Congress—of Congress, and not the President—to determine what is and what is not the established government of the State."

By the early summer of 1864, a bill proposed by Ohio's senator Benjamin Wade and Maryland's congressman Henry Winter Davis became the vehicle for congressional Republicans seeking an alternative to Lincoln's course. Although what was known as the Wade-Davis bill made no move in the direction of black suffrage (still far too controversial in the Union), it did require new state constitutions to "forever prohibit" involuntary servitude, "guarantee . . . the freedom of all persons," disfranchise Confederate officeholders and commissioned military officers, and "extend to all persons" the right to legal justice. But the centerpiece of the bill demanded that a "majority" of "white male citizens" (not one-tenth of 1860 voters) pledge their loyalty to the United States before the wheels of reorganization could go into motion; then only those who never held "civil or military" office under the Confederacy or "voluntarily" took up "arms against the United States" could participate in the elections for state convention delegates or serve as one. Until those conditions were satisfied—and they would not be easy to satisfy—the state would remain under the control of a provisional governor appointed by the president with the consent of the Senate.

With overwhelming Republican support, the Wade-Davis bill passed Congress in early July and was sent to Lincoln's desk for his signature. There it sat. Lincoln did not fundamentally object to the bill's provisions and had no problem if any rebellious state chose to follow them on its own accord. But he feared that if the bill became law, the political process already under way in Louisiana (and perhaps in Arkansas, Tennessee, and Virginia too) could be derailed and the ostensible blows to the rebellion weakened. He refused to sign it before Congress adjourned (an action known as a pocket veto). Unable to contain their fury, Wade and Davis publicly charged him with a "dictatorial usurpation" of congressional authority.

It was the first of many struggles that would play out for another decade between the executive and the legislative branches over basic questions of constitutional power and between warring elements of the Republican Party over the pace and extent of "reconstruction" policy. Yet in all of this, it is easy to lose sight of the momentous shift that was taking place: The U.S. had spent seven decades building an empire with a weak center, constructing a federal union with murky—and multiple—bases of sovereignty, but now the War of the Rebellion was enabling the ruling Republicans to define the boundaries of a nation-state.

The Future of the Freedpeople

How much of an imperial disposition would be maintained or transformed in such a nation-state remained to be seen, though something of its character emerged in relation to the newly freed slaves and the question of their status as free people. None of the emancipatory legislation or decrees—not the Confiscation Acts, not the abolition of slavery in Washington, D.C., or the federal territories of the trans-Mississippi West, not the preliminary or final Emancipation Proclamation—said anything about the civil or political rights of former slaves, who thereby entered a world still reckoning with the *Dred Scott* decision and governed by discriminatory legislation at state and local levels. This was a world of multiple sovereignties in which very few people of African descent had "rights that whites were bound to respect" or could be citizens of the United States. At best, policy makers imagined them, as Lincoln did in his Proclamation of Amnesty and Reconstruction, as laboring people who would now work for "reasonable" wages.

A powerful logic associated freedmen and freedwomen with a life of labor, chiefly on the agricultural lands of the southern states. No one could deny that the cotton plant had fueled the engine of antebellum economic growth, and most policy makers in the Union envisioned a revitalized cotton economy as a central element in the future prosperity of the country. Some saw the opportunity to demonstrate the superior efficiency and productivity of free, as opposed to slave, labor; others were eager to cash in on the high prices that cotton came to fetch. At all events, the availability of black labor was seen to be crucial both to the ending of the war and to the shaping of the peace.

No one established that connection more clearly than the Union general Benjamin Butler. Faced with fugitive slaves heading toward his encampment at Fortress Monroe, Virginia, in the spring of 1861, Butler had declared them to be "contrabands of war" and put them to work building fortifications, a perspective on labor service that would initially be the basis of black military enlistment. A year later, as he confronted the problem of overpopulated contraband camps in lower Louisiana, Butler initiated a "contract labor system," designed, simultaneously, to set former slaves to work and to rehabilitate the plantation sector. Under federal guidelines, contrabands could now be hired out to southern landowners who had taken the loyalty oath or to northerners who had leased or purchased farmland. Receiving small monthly wages and basic subsistence, black laborers would also be subject to close supervision, limited mobility, and penalties for indiscipline: something in the manner of the apprenticeship system that the British had established as a central feature of their emancipation process in the 1830s.

Like the apprenticeship system, contract labor served as one of several testing grounds for the prospects of black freedom. However much they might have denounced slavery as a sin and relic of economic backwardness, even many abolitionists wondered if the slaves were yet "ready" for freedom or if they needed to be "tutored" in its demands and responsibilities. Would the many decades of submission, coercion, exploitation, and brutality that slavery imposed have rendered African Americans too passive and dependent to fend for themselves? Could they be expected to support themselves and respond to economic incentives now that the compulsions and paternalism of enslavement were at an end? Did they understand the nature of private property, of "meum" and "tuum," as one northern observer put it, or would they be prone to thieving? Would they be prepared to organize themselves into family units, embrace the requirements of monogamous marriage, and accept the obligations of parenting after the experience of slavery had officially denied all of this to them? Were they ready to educate themselves and show their faith in a Christian God?

Not surprisingly, the War of the Rebellion energized not only those determined to see American slavery destroyed but also those intent upon transforming the imagined character of slaves into that of free people. The American Missionary Association, deeply involved in the antislavery struggle since its founding in 1846, quickly mobilized missionaries and teachers to head into Union-occupied areas, offer aid of several sorts to the contrabands, and begin acquainting them with the world of freedom: instructing them in literacy, sexual propriety, the values of thrift and industry, the proper roles for men and women, and the vicissitudes of Christian worship. They were joined by an assortment of other reformers, teachers, and missionaries—some associated with other church groups, some with antislavery societies—who braved the dangers and uncertainties of life behind Union lines to commence a "reconstruction" of the slave South as they saw fit.

But the Republican-dominated federal state had related interests of its own. How was the transition from slavery to freedom to be "managed," and how would former slaves be incorporated into a postwar society? What sorts of responsibilities should the state take on, and what should it avoid? How did the travails of slavery shape the dispositions of the emerging freedpeople, and what types of challenges might they pose to social and political order? To address these questions, Secretary of War Edwin Stanton established the American Freedmen's Inquiry Commission in March 1863, soon after the Emancipation Proclamation had been issued. Headed up by Robert Dale Owen, James McKaye, and Samuel Gridley Howe, all with strong reform and antislavery credentials, the commission was to "inquire into the condition of the [emancipated] Colored people . . . and report what means are necessary to give practical effect" to their liberation from bondage and place them "in a condition of self-support and self-defense."

Traveling into the occupied South and Canada, the commissioners interviewed military officials, former slaveholders, and missionaries as well as former slaves and free blacks to take the measure of the task before them. They were relieved to discover that "with rare exceptions" the black "refugees" within federal lines were "loyal men, putting faith in the Government . . . willing to work for moderate wages if promptly paid, docile and easily managed . . . of temperate habits, cheerful and uncomplaining under hard labor whenever they are treated with justice," and "willing to work as long and as hard as white laborers, whether foreign or native born." Acknowledging the "vices" of stealing, lying, and lasciviousness to be found, the commissioners nonetheless blamed them on the circumstances of slavery and expressed confidence that they were "not obstinately rooted" and could be "gradually eradicated by a proper appeal to the self-respect of the newly-made freedman, and by a strict recognition of his rights." Mindful of what were seen as the failures of the British apprenticeship system (which was abandoned after four rather than the prescribed six years), they recommended the establishment of a federal organization, of short-term duration, to supervise the transition out of slavery, provide for "enlightened instruction" and temporary justice courts, assure that "the wages [of freedmen were] promptly and regularly paid," and conduct "a strict and comprehensive system of registration," alerting each freedman "at the time he gives his name, that he must not alter it hereafter, as slaves, when changing owners are in the habit of doing."

The fruit of the commissioners' inquiries appeared in March 1865, when Congress authorized the creation of the Freedmen's Bureau for one year. Charged with supervising the road out of slavery as well as the needs of refugees white and black, the bureau would have agents in each of the rebel states who would help advance the nation's developing principles of freedom. They would see to it that "contract" rather than coercion organized labor relations, that the terms of contracts were fair and mutually understood, that reasonable wages were paid and corporal punishment abandoned, and that laborers and employers carried out their obligations. They would try to settle grievances, establish courts if civil courts were not yet operating, and move to constrain violence and other "outrages" perpetrated against freedpeople. They would also encourage freedmen and freedwomen to register marriages that had existed under slavery and would help establish schools for black children and adults. In an important sense, the bureau was meant to embody the notions that the war was bringing about: that freedom was national, that it would express itself according to certain rules and behaviors, and that it would be cultural as well as legal and political.

Yet there would be far more at play than visions of a road to freedom brought in from the outside and through the auspices of government institutions. The members of the American Freedmen's Inquiry Commission discovered that "the chief object of ambition among the refugees is to own property, especially to possess land, if it only be a few acres," and it proved only one of many things they and other northerners learned that confounded their expectations and complicated their sensibilities. They would come to note that some of the fugitives arrived with goods regarded as their own property, that some seemed to hold fairly complex "notions of liberty," that some espoused "remarkably correct" views "of the leading doctrines of the Bible," that many understood "compensation received for work as a general thing," and that a fair number were "shrewd in their small way" and perhaps "a great deal shrewder and smarter" than poor southern whites. Some former slaves, like Moses Battle of Tennessee, were more direct in contesting northern assessments of their personal qualities. Hearing one philanthropist predict that blacks would not work unless compelled to do so, Battle politely but firmly chided him: "Don't know what for, sir, anybody think that. The colored folks what been keeping up the country. When they had to work all day for their masters, they work all night and Sundays for themselves. Now when its all day to themselves don't know what for they lie down and starve."

Indeed, in a variety of settings across the South, African American men and women emerging from the thralls of slavery demonstrated that they were quite "ready" for freedom and had well-developed ideas as to what their freedom might entail. Along the coast of South Carolina and in southwestern Mississippi—as part of the famous Port Royal and Davis Bend experiments—they continued to cultivate lands they had tended as slaves and established their own forms of self-governance, replete with constitutions, elected officials, and local courts. In the Mississippi Valley, some groups pooled their resources to rent plots of land either from the U.S. government or from northern lessees and impressed observers as "the most successful . . . of all elements." In occupied portions of Virginia and North Carolina, ex-slaves—mostly women, children, and the elderly after the recruitment of black soldiers had begun—gradually turned contraband camps and the immediately surrounding countryside into what one federal official called "African villages of grand proportions," constructing their own shelters, farming land on their own account, building churches and schools, and running stores. In territory still very much in the hands of the rebels, slaves used the many disruptions of wartime, together with the news passing through their communication networks, to renegotiate the rhythms and rules of their captivity, demanding small payments in wages or shares of the crop, more time to cultivate their provision grounds, more control over field work and family affairs. Even on leased plantations, they could battle mightily over the allocation of labor, the crop mix, and the disposition of the harvest, occasionally staging "little rebellion[s]."

Thus, as slaves turned freedpeople struggled to make their aspirations known and to pursue them as best they could, they demonstrated that the transition from slavery to freedom would be deeply contested. They also demonstrated that they could win allies, further fragmenting the ranks of Republican policy makers and their representatives on the ground in the rebellious states. To be sure, most of the teachers, missionaries, and federal officials who encountered freedpeople during the war saw them—and would continue to see them—through the lenses that antislavery literature and racialist images had long provided, and they strove both to elevate freedpeople on the scale of civilization and to prepare them to become reliable workers in a wage-labor economy. But some of the more sensitive and humane among them came to recognize what the images had failed to convey and sympathize politically with what they saw: that, as slaves, African Americans had constructed relationships and expectations as to family, work, and community which resonated more with a world that was eroding than with the political economy the war was creating and which would likely fly in the face of the type of nation building many Republican leaders wished to pursue.

Indian Peoples and the Destiny of the West

The imperial eye of the developing American nation-state gazed west as well as south and on tribal peoples as well as newly emancipated slaves. The threads of policy, contradictory as they were, had, of course, been in place since the founding of the Republic, mixing the carrot of assimilation with the stick of removal and confinement. The reform-minded who regarded Native Americans, as they regarded African Americans, as culturally retrograde, though potentially redeemable, urged that efforts be made at promoting "civilization." They imagined that white teachers could advance literacy, that missionaries could spread Christianity, that Indian men could see the error of their nomadic ways and turn to sedentary agriculture, that communal forms of property could be discarded, and that Indian families could adopt new gender divisions of labor. The result would be some sort of social and cultural absorption.

Yet the projects of the reformers offered little to contest the designs of white settlers and their political allies who hungrily eyed the lands that Indians claimed and had no interest in the goal of absorption or assimilation. If they bothered to articulate their sensibilities, the settlers viewed Indians as hopelessly backward and barbaric, intractable obstacles to "progress," who had to be reduced and pushed out of the way. Even those, like the mixed-blood faction of the Cherokees, who selected the carrot of cultural transformation and came to organize their lives, work, and politics to mimic the whites learned that the stick of retribution was unavoidable. Because the reformers largely accepted the opposition between "progress" and "barbarism" as the settlers defined it, and saw themselves engaged in the struggle to advance the former at the expense of the latter, they could only try to mitigate the worst effects of a process whose ultimate objectives—white territorial expansion, the commodification of land and labor, and the embrace of Christian values—they shared.

The "reservation" thus became the means to resolve the tensions between coercion and civilization. Instead of simply surrendering their land claims or receiving cultural educations where they resided, Indians would agree to cede lands that white settlers desired, move to tracts of land set aside for them by the government, and there, with the help of Indian agents, annuities, and missionaries, embrace the ways of the whites. "Experience . . . has conclusively shown," the Indian commissioner Luke Lea proclaimed in 1859, "that there is but one course of policy by which the great work of regenerating the Indian race might be effected . . . [and it is] that they be placed in positions where they can be controlled," where their "wild energies" and "haughty pride" can be "subdued," where they can "be compelled by stern necessity to resort to agricultural labor" and be "trained in the more ennobling pursuits of civilized life." Beginning with a series of arrangements covering 139 small tribes and bands in California in the early 1850s, such reservations soon became the policy of choice among those in the federal government—on a succession of commissions and in the Interior Department—charged with supervising "Indian affairs."

The centerpiece of this process was, as it had previously been, the "treaty," very much a reflection of the multiple forms of sovereignty that defined the American union and empire. The Supreme Court had, in the 1830s, described Native Americans as members of "domestic dependent nations," something less than full-fledged sovereigns, but effectively distinctive political entities to be neither counted for the purposes of congressional apportionment nor subject to taxation. Although the legal ambiguities hung over every diplomatic engagement and agreement—as one U.S. attorney general put it, "There is nothing in the whole compass of our laws so hard to bring within any precise definition . . . as the relation in which the Indians stand towards this government and those of the States"—the language of the treaties themselves, referring to Indian signatories as "nations" or "tribes" or "confederated tribes," implicitly acknowledged some measure of sovereign authority that Native groupings could exercise over their members and embody in relation to the federal government.

Yet treaty making almost invariably created divisions—sometimes deep ones—among the Indians who entered into it, and the eruption of the War of the Rebellion unhinged the relations and understandings that supported the undertaking. Almost immediately, the Five Civilized Tribes in Indian Territory, many slaveholders among them, made formal alliances with the Confederacy that simultaneously recognized their sovereignty and encouraged their political and military participation. By mid-May 1861, Chickasaws and Choctaws were sending troops, and before long pro-Confederate Cherokees were driving pro-Union Cherokees, Creeks, and Seminoles into neighboring Kansas. By November 1861, the Confederacy defined Indian Territory as one of its military departments, and Cherokees like Stand Watie gained commissions in the Confederate army. That the Lincoln administration quickly stopped annuity payments, refused to recruit Indian soldiers, and withdrew all federal troops from Indian Territory only entrenched the new circumstances of official belligerence. Indeed, in July 1862, Congress permitted Lincoln to terminate treaties with any tribe "in actual hostility to the United States."

Several months earlier, Lincoln thought better of abandoning Indian Territory and determined to reoccupy it. A decisive Union victory at Pea Ridge in northwestern Arkansas in March 1862 against a combined Confederate-Indian force opened the way and, even more significantly, symbolized the militarization of federal Indian policy. The ball was now in the court of U.S. Army commanders who had little patience for the niceties of diplomacy and more interest in bringing about the desired results through the method they knew best: force. In Minnesota, General John Pope had nothing but scorn for treaty making and the entire Indian "system" more generally. He wanted authority over Indian matters shifted from the Interior to the War Department, federal Indian agents marginalized, and sizable military posts established that would help to "concentrate," isolate, and surround tribes once they had been defeated.

Out in the Department of New Mexico, Brigadier General James Carleton, who had marched his troops southeast across the desert from California to intercept Confederate advances, took a similar view after encounters with Navajos and Apaches. Acknowledging the objective of "gathering them little by little on to a reservation, away from the haunts, and hills, and hiding places of their country," and teaching them "literacy," the "arts of peace," and the "truths of Christianity" so that "they will acquire new habits, new ideas, new modes of life," Carleton nonetheless insisted that "the purpose now is never to relax the application of force with people that can no more be trusted than you can trust the wolves that run through their mountains." It was not idle talk. Like Pope, he scoffed at the idea of signing treaties with hostile Native peoples and instead believed that they had to be pursued without mercy until beaten into submission. "There is to be no council held with the Indians nor any talks," Carleton told subordinate officers who were about to engage the Mescalero Apaches. "The men are to be slain whenever or wherever they can be found . . . [and] if they beg for peace, their chiefs and twenty of their principal men must come to Santa Fe [knowing] that you will keep after their people and slay them until you receive orders to desist." Mangas Coloradas, one of the powerful Apache leaders, felt the lethal brunt of this disposition. Lured into a trap by soldiers waving a white flag of truce, Coloradas was brutally tortured and shot to death; then, in a gruesome ritual of imperial science, his body was decapitated and his large head sent east, to the Smithsonian Institution, where it found a place among a growing collection of Indian bones and artifacts: symbols of the knowledge making that brute power and conquest enabled.

The aggressiveness of Carleton and Pope in the apparent service of "civilization" and the Union was indicative of an increasingly ironfisted and violence-ridden politics that spread across the plains commencing in 1862. Carleton not only put several thousand Mescalero Apaches and Navajos (themselves enemies) onto the small reservation of Bosque Redondo in eastern New Mexico but ruled his department in a dictatorial fashion, intimidating territorial officials and eventually earning what the *Weekly New Mexican* described as "the detestation and contempt of almost the entire population of the territory." An equally autocratic regime took shape in the Colorado Territory under the auspices of Governor John Evans, an Illinois transplant who was also a director of the newly established

Union Pacific Railroad. Less concerned about Confederate sympathizers in his midst (vocal but not substantial in number) than about the hunting and raiding of the Cheyenne and Arapaho, Evans believed that the suppression of Indian resistance was key to luring the transcontinental line through Denver. In John Chivington, who commanded a regiment of Colorado volunteers and had successfully led them against Confederate invaders at Glorieta Pass in New Mexico, he found a kindred spirit.

But if Evans and Chivington assumed that brutal attacks could force the Indians into submission, they miscalculated. By the summer of 1864, Cheyennes, Arapahos, Kiowas, Comanches, and Sioux had commenced a general uprising across a broad swath of the plains and interrupted traffic and communication along both the Santa Fe and the Overland trails. "I am now satisfied," Evans feverishly warned the commissioner of Indian affairs in Washington, D.C., "that the tribes of the plains are nearly all combined in this terrible war," and he predicted that "it will be the largest Indian war this country has ever had, extending from Texas to the British lines [Canada]." Frustrated by the inadequate response of federal officials, Evans retracted an earlier promise to protect friendly bands and urged white Coloradans to take matters into their own hands, exterminating hostile Indians "wherever they may be found." Chivington needed no more prompting. In late November, he and a force of seven hundred volunteers marched to Sand Creek, southeast of Denver, fell upon an encampment of Cheyenne and Arapaho who had already submitted to military authorities, and murdered them.

Word of the Sand Creek Massacre spread quickly and only intensified the outrage of the Plains Indians. In early 1865, parties of Cheyenne, Arapaho, and Sioux commenced attacks on major trailheads, ranches, and stage depots. Sometimes moving in bands as large as a thousand, they cut telegraph lines, burned settlements, and attacked supply trains along the northern and southern branches of the Platte River in the Nebraska and Colorado territories, effectively cutting off Denver—not to mention Salt Lake City and San Francisco—from overland communication with the East. "At night the whole valley was lighted up with the flames of burning ranches and stage stations," a survivor of Sand Creek who rode with a Cheyenne raiding band later recalled. So widespread and destructive was the havoc that Ulysses S. Grant, now general in chief of the U.S. Army, reorganized the western military districts and put Pope in command of the new Division of the Missouri (embracing the previous Departments of Missouri, Kansas, and the Northwest). For his part, Pope began to plan a major campaign for 1865 designed to suppress the rebellious Indians and reopen the roads and other thoroughfares that passed through Indian country.

News of the Sand Creek Massacre spread east as well, and although initial reports (especially Chivington's) depicted the episode as a military triumph, competing evidence that, in the words of the chair of the Senate's Indian Affairs Committee, would "make one's blood chill and freeze with horror" established an increasingly persuasive counter-narrative. Quickly succumbing to public pressure, both Congress and the military launched investigations that would depict Sand Creek as "the scene of murder and barbarity . . . of the most revolting character" and John Chivington as having "disgraced the veriest savage." Blows were clearly struck at the militarization of federal Indian policy, serious questions were raised about the army's ability to rein in its own forms of terror, and the ways of the "humanitarian" reformers gained in credibility.

President Lincoln did lend a sympathetic ear to the entreaties of Henry B. Whipple, the Episcopal bishop of Minnesota who was fast becoming the leading advocate for the reform of the Indian system; after hearing Whipple out, Lincoln pledged, "If we get through this war and I live, this Indian system shall be reformed." But Lincoln also wholly embraced the image of Indians as "savages" and found it difficult to imagine them as part of the "people of the United States." In language eerily similar to what he offered black leaders visiting him at the White House—"You and we are different races"—Lincoln told tribal leaders in the spring of 1863 of the "great difference between this pale-faced people and their red brethren both as to numbers and the way in which they lived." "The pale-faced people," he explained, "are numerous and prosperous because they cultivate the earth, produce bread, and depend upon the products of the earth rather than wild game for subsistence." Thus, just as he once concluded that "colonization" was the proper solution to the dilemmas of white and black in the United States, so he regarded "the plan of concentrating Indians and confining them to reservations" as the "fixed policy of the government."

Reinforcing this "fixed policy" was Lincoln's powerful perspective on the relation of the War of the Rebellion to the development of the trans-Mississippi West. In his annual message of December 1864, he noted "the steady expansion of the population, improvement, and government institutions over the new and unoccupied portions of our country . . . scarcely checked . . . by our great civil war," the "great enterprise of connecting the Atlantic with the Pacific States by railways and telegraph lines," and the "numerous discoveries of gold, silver, and cinnabar mines" reaching "one hundred millions in value." He thereby hoped to provide a "proper government of the Indians" to render the West "secure for the advancing settler." With a new and ominous twist on the concept of the "house divided," Lincoln had earlier proclaimed that "a nation may be said to consist of its territory, its people, and its laws" and "that portion of the earth's surface which is owned and inhabited by the people of the United States, is well adapted to be the home of one national family; and it is not well adapted for two, or more. Its vast extent, and its variety of climate and productions, are of advantage, in this age, for one people, whatever they might have been in former ages."

The Jacobin Arm and Peasant Dream

The question of who the "people of the United States" were, of how membership in the "national family" would be determined, was raised not only by Indians reluctant, in the words of the Sioux leader Big Eagle, to "give up their life and live like the white men" but also by people of African descent already in rebellion against their owners as well as against a larger regime of discrimination and oppression that had reached every corner of the country. Ever since the 1820s and 1830s, fugitives from slavery together with their free black allies had been pressing state and national authorities to end their cooperation with slaveholders and reject the markers of subaltern status that African Americans were forced to bear. Meeting in their localities and at larger conventions, they demanded equal standing in civil society, access to education and other institutions in the public sphere, and the right to vote on the same basis as whites. But it was the arming of rebellious slaves to aid in crushing the renegade Confederacy that shifted the tenor of discourse and the horizon of possibility.

The military recruitment of African Americans, slave and free, came in the face of deep traditions of exclusion and then wartime rebuffs from political and military officials despite their need for thousands of volunteers. The entreaties of free black leaders like Frederick Douglass and of abolition-minded officers in the U.S. Army came to little; if anything, they courted a range of disapprobation and discipline from the commander in chief. It was the slaves, therefore, who appeared to accomplish what their allies were failing to do: by fleeing the sites of their captivity in numbers scarcely anticipated by U.S. officials and flooding contraband camps and other military encampments. A chaplain in the Army of the Tennessee could compare the volume of "Negroes" who "abandoned" neighboring "cotton plantations" and headed to "Yankee" lines to "an army in themselves." Contract labor and other leasing arrangements offered one means of alleviating the demographic pressure, but as manpower shortages steadily bedeviled the U.S. project, black recruitment emerged as an option that could no longer be ignored. In July 1862, Congress passed the Militia Act, and shortly thereafter the War Department permitted the establishment of a slave regiment, the First South Carolina Volunteers.

Yet, significantly, full-scale mobilization had to await the Emancipation Proclamation of January 1, 1863. Only then did the Lincoln administration allow northern governors to begin enrolling black men living in their states (a good many of whom were fugitive slaves and their children), and nearly three-quarters of those between the ages of eighteen and forty-five came forward (32,671), a much higher proportion than was the case among eligible northern white men. By far the greatest number of black soldiers, however, came to be recruited in the slave states, and especially in the slave states of the Confederacy. Totaling 140,313, they would compose a growing portion of the U.S. Army: well over 10 percent and in some departments nearly half of it. Thus emancipation not only came as a war measure but was directly tied to the military recruitment of black men who, by their participation, gained freedom for themselves as well as for their mothers, wives, and children (by virtue of a congressional resolution in March 1865), consecrating a gender hierarchy central to the political and cultural vision of the new nation-state.

Initially, federal officials imagined that black troops would serve chiefly behind the lines—"constructing entrenchments or performing camp service or any other labor," in the words of the Militia Act—thereby enabling more of the white troops to do the fighting. But before very long, this distinction evaporated, and African Americans, in substantial numbers, were to be found armed and in the heat of battle. The heat, in fact, came from several directions. Although black recruitment helped destroy many of the petty sovereignties and parochialisms characteristic of slavery and overrode racist exclusions associated with military service in the United States, black soldiers continued to face an assortment of challenges behind their own lines. Their units—combat and otherwise—were segregated from those of white troops. With a few exceptions, they were denied the opportunity to become commissioned officers. They were put to work doing the most degrading tasks in camp and, as a consequence of their presumed status as laborers, paid less than one-half of their white soldiering counterparts. And they were often treated with derision and contempt by white officers and enlistees alike. Remarking on the question of "negroes [doing the] fighting," Governor Samuel J. Kirkwood of Iowa could pointedly assert, "When this war is over & we have summed up the entire loss of life it has imposed on the country I shall not have any regrets if it is found that a part of the dead are niggers and that all are not white men."

Attitudes like Kirkwood's enabled some white commanders to order black troops into militarily hopeless situations, believing that their bodies were more expendable than white ones. But this was only part of the special lethality that encompassed the black experience of armed combat. However much many black men who had been slaves relished the opportunity to help crush the Confederacy and the system of enslavement on which it rested, they were vulnerable to retribution not shared by their white allies. Quite simply, the Confederacy regarded "slaves taken in federal Uniform" as "in flagrant rebellion," not to be "recognized in any way as soldiers subject to the rules of war," and therefore meriting the "condign punishment" for "slaves in armed insurrection." In late November 1862, even before the mass recruitment of black soldiers had begun on the Union side, the Confederate president, Jefferson Davis, ordered his commanders to turn over "all negro slaves captured in arms . . . to the executive authorities of the respective States to which they belong to be dealt with according to the laws of said States": laws that invariably prescribed re-enslavement or execution.

Although exceptions could be made for African American soldiers who had been free when the war started, and although Confederate officials came to discourage public executions by the states, preferring re-enslavement or forced military labor, Confederate officers had a great deal of latitude in the field. This did not bode well for black men in arms. The most notorious episode came in 1864 when General Nathan Bedford Forrest (later one of the organizers of the Ku Klux Klan) had scores of black troops massacred after they surrendered at Fort Pillow in Tennessee. But the murder of captured black soldiers on a smaller scale was widespread. "It was understood among us," one Confederate soldier wrote in 1864 from North Carolina, "that we take no negro prisoners." Small wonder that blacks fought with a special ferocity. "There is," one northern observer reported, "death to the rebel in every black mans eyes."

The ferocity and determination were not without significant effect. Blacks steadily dispelled doubts in Union policy-making circles that slavery had rendered them too cowardly and ill-disciplined to fight. In major engagements at Milliken's Bend and Port Hudson in the lower Mississippi Valley and at Battery Wagner in South Carolina—all during the spring and summer of 1863—they faced down vicious enemy fire and performed valiantly, if not heroically. They would soon appear in most theaters of the war, digging trenches, guarding encampments, skirmishing with Confederate guerrillas, and partaking in full-scale combat, especially in Virginia as the army commanded by General Ulysses S. Grant battled to defeat rebel forces under Robert E. Lee. In that the arming of African American men came at a time of military stalemate and low morale in much of the North, their participation proved to be a tipping point in the war, fortifying the U.S. and weakening the Confederacy. The rapidly circulating reports of black resolve under Confederate fire, of tenacious fighting in the riskiest of circumstances, of remarkable courage in the heat of battle, and of tremendous casualties and savagery inflicted by their former masters simultaneously bolstered the élan of black troops and challenged the racial attitudes of white northerners. "We called upon them in the day of our trial, when volunteering had ceased, when the draft was a partial failure, and the bounty system a senseless extravagance," the army colonel Norwood P. Hallowell later reflected. "They were ineligible for promotion, they were not to be treated as prisoners of war. Nothing was definite except that they could be shot and hanged as soldiers. Fortunately . . . they were equal to the crisis; that the grand historic moment which comes to a race only once in many centuries came to them, and they recognized it."

The political ramifications might have been as great as the military. Contraband camps and then U.S. Army regiments drew African Americans together in numbers that dwarfed the size of their plantations and farms (which rarely had more than fifty slaves and usually fewer than ten) and from a range of settings and conditions far wider than they had ever encountered. The Fifty-seventh U.S. Colored Infantry, raised in Arkansas, included enlistees born in twelve other states, Tennessee chief among them. The Twenty-third, raised in Virginia, boasted men born in nine other southern states, three northern states, the District of Columbia, and the British colony of Jamaica. The famed Fifty-fifth Massachusetts had recruits born in at least sixteen different states and three foreign countries. In these units, that is, they could meet former slaves from the loyal as well as the rebel South, free people of color from the southern and northern states (and even from the West Indies), and white officers who had spent years in the antislavery movement or had fled as political refugees from failed revolutions in Europe. In these units, they could follow the progress of the war, become conversant with the course of federal policy, and discuss their previous experiences and future prospects. In these units, they could discover forms of authority and loyalty other than those prescribed by their masters or by their small communities. And in these units, mixing secular and spiritual concerns, they could obtain the rudiments of literacy. U.S. Army lines thus made for the first large-scale African American political meeting grounds enabled by the war and emancipation. "The general aim and probable consequences of this war," Thomas Wentworth Higginson observed, "are better understood in [my black] regiment than in any white regiment."

But if on one level the military created an increasingly well-disciplined and self-conscious army of liberation and unification, it also revealed tensions between the political goals of black soldiers and the policies of the federal government. The tensions were almost immediately in evidence and soon manifest on a number of fronts: in struggles over combat status, pay, promotion, and other forms of discrimination and exclusion that testified to the subordinate position still envisioned for African Americans in a post-emancipation United States. Best known and organized—and led chiefly by northern black troops and their allies in public life—was the battle against discriminatory pay ($7 per month for black privates as opposed to $16 per month for white ones), itself rooted in the expectation that blacks would serve mainly as military laborers rather than as combat troops. By refusing any pay until wage scales were equitably adjusted (while avoiding, save in one instance, mutiny or resignation), they captured the attention and sympathy of the northern public and, in June 1864, obtained a substantial measure of congressional redress. In the process, black soldiers (slave and free) began to express alternative visions of civil and political society, well in advance of those embraced by most federal officials or Republican leaders, that included new ideas of equality, citizenship, and social justice.

The decisive contribution of an armed black soldiery to the emergence of what can be regarded as a "Jacobin" political orientation may be seen at a series of important political gatherings in 1864 and 1865. In Syracuse, New York, on October 4, 1864, 150 black leaders representing seventeen states and the District of Columbia opened what was termed "the most truly national black convention" that had ever been held. Nine years had passed since the last one, and with it much of the gloom and divisiveness that had then been in evidence. Instead, emigrationists like Henry Highland Garnet and integrationists like John Mercer Langston shared the presiding platform and drew up the "Declaration of Wrongs and Rights." Citing the "unquestioned patriotism and loyalty of colored men" who, "without pay, without bounty, without prospect of promotion, without protection of the government, vindicated their manhood," they demanded the "immediate and unconditional" abolition of slavery, a "fair share" of lands, some made available by the Homestead Act of 1862, and the "full measure of citizenship." Before adjourning, they created the National Equal Rights League to further press their "just claims."

Three months later in Nashville, Tennessee, where a movement for political equality had been growing since the advent of federal occupation, sixty-two "colored citizens" petitioned white unionists then meeting in a state constitutional convention "to abolish the last vestige of slavery by the express words of your organic law" and to extend the franchise. Proclaiming that "freedom is the natural right of all men," they explained that they "knew the burdens of citizenship and are ready to bear them" and that they saw in the sacrifice of "near 200,000 of our brethren . . . in the ranks of the Union army" the basis for action and confidence. "If we are called on to do military duty against the rebel armies in the field," they asked, "why should we be denied the privilege of voting against rebel citizens at the ballot-box?"

At the very moment Nashville blacks formally posed this question, a convention opened in New Orleans, inspired by the prior assembly in Syracuse, that captured the tenor of the political moment with special power. Composed of nearly one hundred delegates, many from the ranks of the city's free people of color (the proceedings were recorded in English and French) but some also from "the country parishes," the convention was presided over by a man who seemed to embody the war's revolutionary dynamics: James H. Ingraham. Born a slave and freed at the age of six, Ingraham was a carpenter by trade who had learned to read and write, a captain in the U.S. Army who had fought bravely at Port Hudson, and a delegate at the earlier Syracuse convention. Insisting that "we must ask our rights as men" and "take a bold and general position," Ingraham reminded the delegates of the "contempt" with which they were treated by the Louisiana state legislature organized under Lincoln's Ten Percent Plan and advised that they send their claims to the U.S. Congress, which "alone has the power" to grant them. After several days of discussion and debate, during which they also protested the practice of segregation on railroad cars in New Orleans, the convention established the structure for the Equal Rights League with chapters in many localities and made the case for civil and political rights based on the notion of a national citizenship. "If we are not citizens why make soldiers of us?"

As the convention came to an end, the *New Orleans Tribune,* designated as the official organ of the Louisiana Equal Rights League and having described Ingraham as "the Mirabeau of the men of color," announced the inauguration of "a new era." "It was the first political move ever made by the colored people of the state acting in a body" and "the first time that delegates of the country parishes . . . came to this city to act upon political matters," the *Tribune* maintained. "There seated side by side the rich and poor, the literate and educated man and the country laborer hardly released from bondage, distinguished only by the natural gifts of mind" and "united in a common thought" of "liberation from social and political bondage." "We must come out of the revolution," the *Tribune* implored, with the French precedent very much in mind, "not only as emancipationists, but as true republicans."

Several hundred miles away, another meeting, this one in Savannah, Georgia, hinted at broader revolutionary impulses and at social dispositions more peasant-like than Jacobinical. The Union general William T. Sherman had arrived there with his troops, following his march from Atlanta, with hundreds of poor black refugees in tow, only to learn that reports had him manifesting "an almost criminal dislike to the negro" very much against "the wishes of the Government." Visiting in January 1865, Secretary of War Stanton confirmed "these thoughts," and Sherman quickly called a meeting of twenty black ministers for the purpose of consultation and action. All of the ministers who attended were "class-leaders, deacons, and divines" in black churches, almost all had been born and raised in Georgia or the Carolinas, three-quarters had been slaves, and more than half had spent at least a portion of their lives in the rural districts. Selecting the sixty-seven-year-old Baptist minister and former slave

Garrison Frazier as their spokesman, they offered a different picture of their aspirations and sense of political belonging. Describing slavery as "receiving by irresistible power the work of another man," and freedom as "placing us where we could reap the fruit of our labor, take care of ourselves, and assist the government in maintaining our freedom," Frazier believed that "the way we can best take care of ourselves is to have land, and turn it by our own labor." And he expressed a clear desire "to live by ourselves . . . rather [than] scattered among the whites . . . for there is a prejudice against us in the South that will take years to get over."

Frazier said nothing about civil or political rights, about citizenship, about thrift, diligence, marriage and family, or fair wages for work. He did not speak in the language of formal politics, of the nation-state, or of the marketplace. He rather imagined a future of agricultural independence, landed proprietorship, and partnership with the "government" and spoke in a language of community, self-reliance, and collective governance. His vision, widely shared among slaves at the moment of emancipation, had far more in common with what has been called a "peasant dream" than with the political economy that Stanton and the Lincoln administration hoped to bring about. Yet, remarkably, four days later and hoping to meet "the pressing necessities of the case," Sherman issued Special Field Orders No. 15, "reserv[ing] and set[ting] apart for the settlement of the negroes . . . the islands from Charleston south, the abandoned ricefields along the rivers for thirty miles back from the sea, and the country bordering the St. John's River, Florida," to be subdivided "so that each family shall have a plot of not more than forty acres of tillable ground." It was 400,000 acres of the richest plantation land in the southern states, effectively destroying the haughty coastal ruling class and possibly laying the foundation of a new social order.

When Was the Slaveholders' Rebellion Defeated?

The arming of African American slaves seemed indicative of the Union's new resolve both to defeat the slaveholders' rebellion and to destroy their social base of slavery. It was indicative, too, of how the resources available to the Lincoln administration slowly made their significance felt: in railroad transportation, iron and coal production, the manufacture of firearms, ammunition, and ordnance, the raising of foodstuffs and livestock, and manpower, occasioned in part by the decades-long flow of European immigrants to the Northeast and the Midwest. The U.S. armed forces were able to mobilize twice as many men as their Confederate counterparts and to feed, clothe, and supply them in ways that the rebels—despite impressive efforts to create a manufacturing sector—simply could not. Eventually, men of foreign birth and African descent would compose more than half of the Union army. Equally important, Lincoln finally found military leaders, Ulysses S. Grant and William Tecumseh Sherman in particular, who shared his vision of how the war needed to be fought and who battled relentlessly to crush the rebel armies.

It was a shift of no small consequence. Before the summer of 1863, the military outcome of the war and the fate of the Union that was the United States seemed in serious doubt. Robert E. Lee and his troops, fresh from stunning victories at Fredericksburg and Chancellorsville in Virginia, readied themselves for another offensive across the Potomac and into Maryland and Pennsylvania. A major military triumph on northern soil might deflate Union morale beyond repair, release pressure on the besieged Confederates at Vicksburg, and leave Lincoln with few options other than to seek a truce and perhaps to abandon the sweeping emancipation his proclamation had anticipated. After all, the English and the French, unwilling to recognize the Confederacy diplomatically, still expected Lincoln to fail in his objectives and stood ready to help negotiate an armistice. Then, in fairly quick succession, Lee suffered a devastating defeat at Gettysburg and took his decimated army back into Virginia; thirty thousand hungry and exhausted Confederates surrendered at Vicksburg; and rebel troops were forced out of Tennessee and into northwestern Georgia. The Mississippi River and both of its banks were now in Union hands, cutting off the Confederate west from the east. The lower North, from the District of Columbia and Pennsylvania out to Illinois, was secured from Confederate attack. And the Confederacy's prospects of achieving political independence had substantially darkened.

Yet it was one thing to turn Confederate aggression back and put the rebellion on the defensive and quite another to fully end the rebellion in ways that were mutually recognized. Lincoln sought an "unconditional surrender," but of whom and to what effect? Clearly, he wanted Confederate troops to lay down their arms and the Confederate government to be disbanded, but because he never acknowledged the Confederacy and insisted that the rebellion was one of individuals in the states, what would be required before the rebellion was regarded as over and the authority of the federal government accepted by rebels and their allies? To be sure, by 1864 the Confederacy was under enormous strain on the home front as well as the battlefront. Desperate for soldiers, supplies to feed them, and workers behind the lines, the Confederate government had enacted a draft, imposed a tax in kind on agricultural produce, regulated the crop mix, and authorized provision officers to impress needed goods and labor, all of which exacerbated social tensions and stirred popular resentments.

Slaveholders, who saw centralized political authority as a potential threat to their petty sovereignties, could prove less than cooperative. They had little patience for government demands that they grow corn instead of cotton and allow their slaves to be requisitioned to support the Confederate military. But it was non-slaveholders and their families who suffered most grievously. With adult men and even teenage boys off in the army, women, children, and the elderly were left to bring in the crops and provide for themselves. Growing numbers experienced privation and, given rampant inflation, were unable to purchase necessities in town or at crossroads stores. Some women struck boldly against merchants and planters who hoarded essential supplies—"bread or blood" could be their cry—but many others wrote to husbands and sons about their plight. Unauthorized leaves or outright desertions might follow, further weakening ranks already thinned by casualties and disease. By early 1864, somewhere between one-third and one-half of the Confederate soldiery might have been absent from their units. Indeed, there were signs of wider political discontent, especially where farms rather than plantations predominated, expressing criticisms of the Davis regime, support for peace and "reconstruction," opposition to the Confederacy, and even loyalty to the Union, whose army would recruit about 100,000 white troops from Confederate states. Western North Carolina and Virginia, eastern Tennessee, and northern Georgia seemed most prone to disaffection, but there were rumblings in the hills of Alabama, Mississippi, Arkansas, and Louisiana as well.

The prospect of defeat could even lead those who remained loyal to the rebel cause in radically dissenting directions. One was Patrick Cleburne. An Irish-born lawyer from Arkansas, Cleburne had strongly supported secession and distinguished himself on the battlefield, earning the sobriquet Stonewall of the West and rising to the rank of major general. But after taking part in the Confederate retreat from Tennessee in late 1863, he thought hard about the challenges the rebellion now faced. Calling his fellow officers together, he offered up a rather remarkable analysis and proposal. The soldiers in the ranks, Cleburne argued, "can see no end to" the war "except in our own exhaustion" and, battling an enemy "with superior numbers," were fast "sinking into fatal apathy." No pools of eligible white men were left to be tapped, and as far as he could see, slavery was "our most vulnerable point, a constant embarrassment," and "an insidious weakness" while being a "source of great strength to the enemy." He therefore suggested that the Confederacy "immediately commence training a large reserve of the most courageous of our slaves" and "guarantee freedom within a reasonable time to every slave in the South who shall remain true to the Confederacy."

Enlist the slaves and abolish slavery to salvage the Confederate rebellion! It was a veritable contradiction in terms and regarded by many of Cleburne's fellow officers as "monstrous," "revolting," "infamous," and "hideous." Davis and his cabinet were not amused either and ordered "all discussion and controversy growing out of the" proposal "suppressed." Over time, the idea of recruiting and arming slave soldiers would gain a small following among Confederates— including Lee and Davis—but not enough of one to initiate a genuine policy or envision a road of emancipation, however long. All the rebels were left to do was assume a defensive posture, drag the war out for as long as possible, inflict heavy casualties on the Union side, and hope that the political winds might shift in a more favorable direction.

There was some cause for optimism in this regard. In the fall of 1864, the U.S. would hold regular elections for the presidency and Congress, and the Lincoln administration was in genuine danger from within and without. Radical members of the Republican Party had become increasingly disgruntled with Lincoln's moderation, first on the slavery issue and then on the questions of "reconstruction" (Lincoln had just pocket vetoed the Wade-Davis bill). Salmon P. Chase, the Treasury secretary and one of their number, had long been contemplating a challenge for the nomination, and a small Radical faction supported the candidacy of the onetime party standard-bearer John C. Frémont. It was not a hollow prospect. Almost a quarter century had passed since the last sitting president was renominated by his own party (Martin Van Buren in 1840), and more than three decades since an incumbent was reelected (Andrew Jackson in 1832). Such was the volatility of American electoral politics that Lincoln himself, master politician that he was, entertained grave doubts about his political future.

Renomination did not prove to be the big problem. Lincoln managed to outmaneuver the Chase and Frémont insurgencies in Republican ranks and move into the campaign on a platform calling for the "complete suppression of the rebellion," the "unconditional surrender" of the rebels, and the passage of a constitutional amendment abolishing slavery (the words "Confederate" and "Confederacy" did not appear). He also took the Tennessee Democrat Andrew Johnson, widely lauded for his powerful stand against secession, as his vice president on what the Republicans now called the Union Party ticket: hoping to find more votes among soldiers in the field and war Democrats at home. But Lincoln faced a formidable opponent pursuing a very different set of political goals. For the Democrats nominated the popular Union general George B. McClellan, whom Lincoln had sent into effective retirement months before, and approved a platform written chiefly by the copperhead renegade Clement Vallandigham (back from his brief exile), which condemned Lincoln's "extraordinary usurpation" of power and called for an immediate armistice. No mention was made of slavery or abolition, only the rights of the states and the resto-ration of the "Federal Union of the States."

So convinced were many Republican leaders that the contest was lost that some wished to send a peace commission to Richmond. For his part, Lincoln secretly pledged to work with McClellan, if elected, to "save the Union between the election and the inauguration" because, in Lincoln's view, McClellan would have won "on such ground that he can not possibly save it afterward." "I am a beaten man," Lincoln said with a sigh in late August, "unless we can have some great victory." Grant's Army of the Potomac was not likely to provide it. Soak-ing the Virginia soil in blood (perhaps 100,000 casualties on both sides) as he pursued Lee and his rebel soldiers for two months in the spring of 1864—in the Wilderness, at Spotsylvania Court House, at Cold Harbor—Grant could do no more than put Petersburg and Richmond to siege with little sign of their surren-der in sight. Having "resist[ed] manfully," Lee and his rebel colleagues believed that if they could hold on until "the Presidential election is over," they would "have a new President to treat with."

Almost miraculously, the "great victory" Lincoln looked for did come and only two days after he had pronounced himself a "beaten man." Down in Geor-gia, General William T. Sherman and his army, after a protracted struggle, marched into the strategic rail center of Atlanta on September 3. The city had been torched by retreating Confederates, but Sherman stood triumphant while the rebels were in disarray. The political effect was nothing short of electric. "I have never seen such a lighting up of the public mind," one northern newspaper editor observed. Although Lincoln remained cautious in his political expecta-tions, Atlanta transformed the electoral landscape and, when November polling arrived, brought him and his party an overwhelming victory. Lincoln won 55 percent of the popular vote and every state in the Union except Kentucky, Dela-ware, and New Jersey for a stunning electoral vote majority of 212–21. Espe-cially gratifying was the soldier vote, which went for Lincoln by nearly four to one despite McClellan's standing with the troops. And especially consequential, the Republicans would control three-quarters of the seats in Congress and all of the governorships and legislatures in the states Lincoln carried.

For the rebels, the effect of Sherman's "great victory" was nothing short of disastrous: all the more so when he and his troops moved out of Atlanta and cut a wide swath of destruction along a three-hundred-mile corridor to Savannah, leaving nothing to fortify Confederate soldiers if they tried to return. One news-paper predicted the "gloom" that would now "diffuse over the South," while for South Carolina's Mary Boykin Chesnut, an ardent rebel from the first, the meaning was grimmer still. "Since Atlanta I have felt as if it were all dead within me," she confided. "We are going to be wiped off the earth." In Virginia, morale among Lee's besieged units began to sink so fast and so low that hundreds of men were deserting each week, and many of those who stayed battled on in a manner that Lee called "feeble," displaying a "want of confidence." By late January 1865, Lee was suggesting to Jefferson Davis that his army could not hold out very much longer.

Davis was determined to fight on, even at the price of arming slaves on the Confederacy's behalf and accepting some plan of gradual emancipation. Perhaps this would bring the English and the French into the war on the Confederate side. At most, short of continued warfare, Davis might enter into negotiations with Lincoln "to secure peace to the two countries": that is, based on an implicit recognition of the integrity and independence of the Confederacy. But for much of the Confederate political leadership, both within Davis's cabinet and among the war governors, the chief interest was less in sustaining the rebellion militarily than in cutting a deal that would allow them to hold on to power in their states and localities, maintain their political rights, protect their property from confiscation, and gain immunity from prosecution for secession- and war-related offenses. After four years and hundreds of thousands of casualties, it was a lot to ask, though rumors did circulate suggesting leniency and generosity on Lincoln's part, including compensation to slave owners for the emancipation of their slaves.

Lincoln did leave a variety of hints along such lines, especially when he met with a small Confederate delegation in Hampton Roads, Virginia, in early February 1865. Yet he remained adamant about the bottom line: the unconditional surrender of rebel armies, the "disbanding of all forces hostile to the [Union] government," the "restoration" of "national authority" in all the states, and the abolition of slavery. As Grant's Army of the Potomac increasingly closed in on Lee's battered and bedraggled troops in Richmond and Petersburg, Lincoln told Grant that he was "to have no conference with General Lee unless it be for the capitulation of Lee's army" and was "not to decide, discuss, or confer upon any political question." Those matters would remain in Lincoln's "own hands" and would not be submitted to any "military conferences or conventions." Soon thereafter, Grant initiated a correspondence with Lee, describing what he saw as the "hopelessness" of Lee's situation, his own desire to avoid "any further effusion of blood," and the necessity for Lee to "surrender."

Lee had seen the handwriting on the wall. Although some of the rebels (Davis among them) hoped that he could find a way through U.S. lines, perhaps with the goal of joining up with Joseph Johnston's troops in North Carolina, or "disperse" his own forces to fight on in guerrilla fashion, Lee decided otherwise. Soldiers such as these would, he argued, become "little better than bands of robbers," and "a state of society would result throughout the South, from which it would require years to recover." "I am too old to go bushwhacking," Lee conceded, "and even if it were right to order the army to disperse, the only course for me to pursue would be to surrender myself to General Grant." To that end, Lee, who said he preferred "to die a thousand deaths," agreed to meet with Grant on April 9, 1865, at Appomattox Court House. He could hardly have hoped for better terms. Rebel officers and their men would be paroled, their "arms, artillery, and public property . . . parked and stacked" and turned over to Grant's appointed men, and they would be permitted to return home with their sidearms and "private horses," not to be "disturbed by United States authority so long as they observe their paroles and the laws in force where they reside." No one was taken into custody, and nothing was said of arrests, charges of treason, or punishments of any sort.

Remarkably, Sherman offered far better, and more wide-reaching, terms to Johnston and his troops near Durham Station, North Carolina, about two weeks later. They were terms sketched out by members of Davis's cabinet, though, in accepting most of them, Sherman insisted that they represented the spirit of Lincoln's instructions. Militarily, the rebels would have to disband rather than formally surrender to the U.S. Army and would be permitted to take their arms home, supposedly to be deposited in the arsenals of their own states and made available for later use "to maintain peace and order." Politically, the existing governments in the rebellious states would be recognized as soon as their elected officials took oaths of loyalty to the United States, and the states' inhabitants would be guaranteed their civil, political, and property rights, not to be disturbed "by reason of the late war so long as they live in peace and quiet, abstain from acts of armed hostility, and obey the laws in existence at the places of their residences." Davis—who had not been consulted by Johnston—quickly, though grudgingly, gave his assent, and just as quickly Grant overrode the agreement on orders of his political superiors. Traveling in person to North Carolina, Grant insisted that Johnston accept the same terms presented to Lee at Appomattox.

Both Lee and Johnston seemed to acknowledge that their surrenders amounted to "the end of the Confederacy." But was this, in fact, the end of the slaveholders' rebellion? Jefferson Davis and his cabinet fled Richmond in early April and headed first toward the southern Virginia tobacco town of Danville, where they intended to reestablish their government. There, on April 4, Davis issued a statement urging his people to keep "their energy and spirits" up, arguing that the abandonment of Richmond would have its benefits, and suggesting that the war, far from being lost, had "entered upon a new phase." Now Confederates, no longer tied to defending cities, could take to the hills and wear the U.S.

Army down with guerrilla-style tactics. "Again and again," Davis asserted, "we will return, until the baffled and exhausted enemy shall abandon, in despair, his endless and impossible task." Even when he learned of Lee's and Johnston's surrenders, Davis believed that Confederate troops could still be rallied, and he looked to the trans-Mississippi West, where he imagined linking up with the forces under Edmund Kirby Smith, who had yet to lay down his arms. There, too, perhaps, he could seek an alliance with the Mexican state, now in the hands of a French-imposed monarch, Maximilian, thereby taking up political objectives unsuccessfully pursued in the wake of secession and trading relations that proved beneficial to the rebels since the outbreak of the war.

In the meantime, the U.S. government sustained a tragic and unprecedented blow at the hands of a Confederate sympathizer and conspirator. On the night of April 14, 1865, four years nearly to the day after federal troops at Fort Sumter had themselves surrendered, President Abraham Lincoln was assassinated by John Wilkes Booth. A Maryland-born actor from a prominent theatrical family, Booth not only embraced the Confederate cause and regarded slavery as "one of the greatest blessings that God ever bestowed upon a favored nation" but detested Lincoln as a tyrant and usurper. As hopes for the Confederacy's success began to dwindle in the fall of 1864, Booth made contact with sections of the Confederate secret service—especially active in the border slave state of Maryland—and initially planned to kidnap Lincoln, take him into Virginia, and hold him hostage in exchange for the release of Confederate war prisoners. It was an idea that had been percolating among other Confederate loyalists and spies for quite some time and hinted at the serious danger Lincoln was in as he won reelection and the war appeared to draw to a close. But when Lee surrendered and Booth heard Lincoln speak favorably, on April 11, of extending the franchise to African Americans who were "very intelligent" and "serve our cause as soldiers" ("That means nigger citizenship," Booth scoffed), he determined that this would be Lincoln's "last speech."

Like Jefferson Davis himself, Booth thought that the fortunes of the Confederacy could be turned around by "something decisive and great." After all, Joseph Johnston's troops had not yet surrendered, and the Davis government was on the move, hoping to reorganize itself and reignite resistance. Collecting a small group of co-conspirators, Booth thus plotted to render the U.S. government leaderless by murdering Vice President Andrew Johnson and Secretary of State William Seward as well as Lincoln. The plot very nearly succeeded. When Booth learned that Lincoln would attend a play at Washington's Ford's Theatre on the evening of April 14, he decided to go ahead. Although Johnson escaped harm, Seward was brutally assaulted and Lincoln was shot in the head, lingering for a few short hours before he died. Never before had a president of the United States fallen victim to an assassin.

And never before or since (at least from the time the presidency was subject to popular election) had a president from one political party served with a vice president from another. The potential dilemmas were, at first, less than apparent. Johnson, who ascended to the presidency on Lincoln's death, was from the slave, and then Confederate, state of Tennessee, though he was anything but a member of the slaveholding elite. From a humble background and a tailor by trade, Johnson was also an experienced politician in the tradition of Jacksonian Democrats who saw themselves representing the interests of small landholders and laboring folk—the "producing classes"—and fighting against those they called the speculators and aristocrats. One of the early congressional advocates of homestead legislation, he had a special animosity for the southern planter class and particularly for those who led and supported secession and the Confederate rebellion. He remained loyal to the Union and served as a tough-minded war governor of Union-occupied Tennessee before being elevated to the vice presidency; eventually, he embraced emancipation. Most consequentially, he had promised to "extend no terms of compromise" to the "leading traitors," to see "treason made odious" and "traitors punished." In failing to kill or debilitate Johnson, the Booth conspiracy seemed to accomplish just the opposite of what it intended.

When Jefferson Davis learned of Lincoln's assassination, he blanched. Knowing of Johnson's political temperament and sensibilities, he thought the repercussions would be "disastrous for our people." That fear was widely shared. Indeed, deep apprehension swept the rebel South in the days and weeks following Johnson's accession. Confederate military and political leaders were well aware that they had been deemed traitors by the federal authorities and that thousands of acres of their land were under federal control. With slavery destroyed and the rebellion on its last military legs, would the U.S. now take the next step of wreaking vengeance on them and fully dismantling their society? Observers on the scene noticed the mood of resignation at the time. "They expected nothing; were prepared for the worst; would have been thankful for anything," one of them recorded, believing that "the National Government could . . . have prescribed no conditions for the return of the Rebel States which they would not have promptly accepted."

Radical Republicans seemed heartened by the turn of events. Whereas Lincoln had spoken a language of generosity and reconciliation, Johnson's was a language of punishment and retribution. The Ohio senator Benjamin Wade, who had his own share of disappointments with the Lincoln administration, thought, after hearing Johnson declare treason to be a crime and "crime must be punished," that "there will be no trouble in running the government now." "I believe that the Almighty continued Mr. Lincoln in office as long as he was useful," another Radical exulted, "and then substituted a better man to finish the work." Although some Confederates were still holding out in the field, Johnson could surely have extended martial law, arrested the rebel leadership (Davis was captured by U.S. soldiers in Georgia in early May), set strict terms for the restoration of civil and political rights to the inhabitants of the rebellious states, allowed the Freedmen's Bureau to carry out its assignment of subdividing abandoned and confiscated land, and asked Congress to grant civil equality to people of African descent and the franchise to at least some African Americans. With that, the Confederate rebellion would have been at an end.

Yet in late May 1865, when Johnson issued proclamations outlining his policy, the tone and requirements were very different. He granted blanket amnesty and pardons to all but an elite cut of the Confederate rebels—the restoration of their property (excluding slaves) and their civil and political rights—once they took an oath of loyalty to the United States. Invoking the constitutional guarantee of a "Republican Form of Government," he appointed provisional governors for each of the rebellious states from the ranks of the population who did not actively support secession, and they, in turn, were to oversee the organization of conventions obliged to rewrite state constitutions that had been the political ballast of slave societies. Only those who had been pardoned could participate in elections for convention delegates or sit as delegates themselves. As for the content of the new constitutions, Johnson asked little other than they recognize the abolition of slavery, renounce secession, and render void state debts contracted in aid of the rebellion; he also hinted that he would look favorably on a limited enfranchisement of black men, though said no more. No one of African descent either voted in the elections or served in the conventions.

Those who did not receive automatic pardons were few in number but significant to waging the rebellion and fortifying the slave society of the Confederacy. They included individuals who served as high-level officers and elected officials of the "pretended Confederate government," who left political and judicial positions in the United States to "aid the rebellion," who received educations at U.S. military academies and entered "the rebel service," and who "voluntarily participated in the rebellion" and claimed taxable property in excess of $20,000. Although Johnson said nothing about possible arrests and prosecutions, the rebels denied blanket pardons and amnesty could, in principle, still be punished as traitors. But Johnson also allowed each of them to "make special application" to him and suggested that on review "clemency" would be "liberally extended."

The very rapid and apparent volte-face on Johnson's part surprised many rebels in the South and has confused scholars since, but it is easy to exaggerate what it represented from Johnson's point of view. On the one hand, as Johnson was quick to acknowledge, the policy resonated with the chords that Lincoln had been striking before his death: establishing the authority of the federal government and the illegitimacy of secession, securing the end of slavery, offering rebels the opportunity to demonstrate their loyalty and responsibility, and enabling an expeditious process of political reincorporation. On the other hand, Johnson singled out the rebel leadership for possible punishment far more extensively than Lincoln ever had, and his refusal to grant blanket amnesty and pardons to the rebellious planter class threatened something of an earthquake in the political landscape of the Confederacy: denied the right to vote or hold office, the planters would be dramatically weakened, and a larger and more humble group of landholders, some of whom had owned slaves and some of whom were inclined to unionism, would be strengthened.

The question, then, was whether Johnson would use his pardoning power to work a political transformation in the rebel South or seek to build a new base of support for his policies and eventual reelection (he was a Democrat presiding over a Republican regime and could not count on Republican support for the nomination in 1868). The prospects for a meaningful transformation appeared sufficiently good to keep most Republicans in Johnson's camp even if they thought the new president more lenient than they would have preferred. And Johnson did appoint men as provisional governors who either hailed from non-plantation districts, campaigned for an early peace, or sat out the war; one—Andrew Jackson Hamilton of Texas—even served in the U.S. Army. But over the course of the summer of 1865, Johnson increasingly demonstrated that his political ambitions won out over his interest in political change. Although the Confederate president, Davis, and vice president, Stephens, had been taken into custody, Johnson failed to bring a legal case for treason against them, and as individual applications for pardons began to swamp his desk—most from wealthy planters—he granted almost all of them. What's more, Johnson became a strong advocate for the restoration of landed property that had been confiscated or abandoned, even if former slaves had already begun cultivating it on their own account. When federal officials and Freedmen's Bureau agents sympathetic to the aspirations of the ex-slaves tried to drag their feet in carrying out Johnson's orders, they came under intense pressure to yield.

Yet the most important result of Johnson's policy announcements was to be seen in the rebellious states. For instead of eliciting gratitude and compliance from rebels who once feared a draconian settlement, the policies stirred a brazenness and defiance. In effect, Johnson had put the ball in the rebels' court. Rather than imposing a set of criteria that the rebels and their states had to meet before rejoining the Union, he laid out a series of steps that they were asked to take. Under the best of circumstances, this approach allowed Confederates to demonstrate that their rebellion was at an end and that they accepted the results of the war as the highest federal authorities defined them. But in truth, few of the rebels were prepared to do this, save at the point of a gun or bayonet. And once they were permitted to choose, they had little incentive to bow down for the sake of congressional representation and a formal place in the national government.

The course and outcome of state constitutional conventions and then legislative and local elections in the summer and fall of 1865 could hardly have satisfied even the most generous of Union victors. While most of the elected convention delegates had opposed secession in 1860–61, they generally did not behave in a spirit of cooperation and, especially in the Deep South, might thumb their noses at the Johnson administration. In Mississippi and Alabama, the conventions would only acknowledge that slavery had been abolished, and in Mississippi as well as in Georgia and Florida delegates decided to repeal rather than nullify or repudiate their secession ordinances. The legislatures then selected under the auspices of the new constitutions included large numbers of active rebels, and they quickly began the work of hedging in the world of freedom for the liberated slaves: enacting vagrancy laws, game and fence laws, occupational licensing laws, and laws restricting the civil standing of freedpeople as well as their ability to rent or purchase land. None permitted any African Americans to vote. In counties and municipalities, particularly where the plantation order prevailed, planter clients resumed their places as sheriffs, treasurers, and magistrates. And although most of the congressional representatives chosen by these states had previously opposed secession, the Georgia legislature sent Alexander Stephens, the vice president of the Confederacy, to take a seat in the U.S. Senate. Even as Congress, returning to session in December 1865, refused to seat the southern claimants, the rebels maintained strong measures of control where it mattered most: on the ground. Members of Congress, looking over the unfolding political events of the previous six months, could reasonably ask whether the rebellion had truly been suppressed or whether it had taken new form.

Freedpeople, Confederates, and the Struggle over Land

The course of what is generally termed Presidential Reconstruction, when Andrew Johnson devised and sought to implement policy before Congress reconvened, was contested from the first, not by Radical Republicans in official station, but by African Americans—freeborn and freed—across the rebellious states. Stepping forth into public light from the moments of wartime occupation and military enlistment, they advanced a very different vision of a postemancipation world than either Lincoln or Johnson could embrace. In meetings and processions, through networks of communication and subterranean discourse, they called, variously, for civil rights, full citizenship, the electoral franchise, land, and community independence. In the process, they brought on intense conflict with their former owners and recently disbanded Confederate soldiers in what would prove to be the final battles of the rebellion—paving the way for a new settlement and a new order.

The earliest mobilizations came in southern cities and adjacent areas where the U.S. Army had arrived before the formal surrender of rebel armies began: in New Orleans, Mobile, Norfolk, Wilmington, Nashville, Memphis, and the coastal districts south of Charleston. Political organizations associated with the Republican Party and wartime black initiatives—Union Leagues and Equal Rights Leagues—found another gear and became vehicles of a new political presence. They organized regular assemblies. They introduced leaders from near and far. They explained the role of black troops in destroying slavery and defeating the slaveholders. They bitterly protested abusive and discriminatory treatment at the hands of federal officials and Confederates alike. They framed aspirations and grievances. They tutored thousands of African Americans in the workings of the government, the likely projects of the national administration, and the character of their allies and enemies. And they pressed for entrance into American civil and political society. That large numbers of newly liberated slaves flooded into cities and towns from the surrounding countryside, seeking economic opportunities as well as safety, made the political impact greater still.

Nothing better exemplified the alternatives to Presidential Reconstruction that African Americans attempted to devise than the freedmen's conventions held in most of the rebellious states during the summer and fall of 1865. Led principally by free people of color from the North and the South (some returning to states they had fled as slaves), though including delegates from rural as well as urban districts, they met in the states' capitals or largest cities and sought "to impress upon the white men," as the Reverend James D. Lynch told the Tennessee freedmen's convention, "that we are part and parcel of the American republic." Meant to anticipate, coincide with, or respond to the whites-only state constitutional conventions held under Johnson's auspices, they cast doubt on the legitimacy of Johnsonian Reconstruction. In the resolutions that virtually all of the conventions passed, they emphasized their desire for education, urged all African Americans to follow the path of thrift and respectability, trumpeted their loyalty to the Union and military courage "in the darkest hour of American history," demanded equal standing before the law, and called for, as the president of North Carolina's convention forcefully declared, "the right to carry [their] ballot to the ballot box." Thus, although their proceedings were moderate and conciliatory in tone, a "Jacobinical" spirit could be detected throughout, invigorating terms of emancipation and national unification well out in front of most of their white Republican allies. As the Virginia freedmen's convention saw it, "Any attempt to reconstruct the states . . . without giving to American citizens of African descent all the rights and immunities accorded to white citizens . . . is an act of gross injustice."

But the nature and pulse of struggle vibrated quite differently in the rural areas where the freedpeople still overwhelmingly resided. For there, what circulated at the very time the freedmen's conventions were demanding "equal rights" were mutually reinforcing rumors of a world turned upside down, of a massive redistribution of land, accomplished either by federal government fiat or by armed black insurrection. A powerful logic was at play, at least for the freedpeople. The idea of land reform reflected both their sense of what a just and meaningful emancipation would entail and their expectations of what the federal government would enable. As agricultural people, they associated land with sustenance, independence, and community stability; they would be able to provide for themselves, avoid depending on their former owners for wage work, and build a hub of security around which relations of kinship and friendship might pivot. As slaves, they were well aware that their unrequited labor and superexploitation had given the lands their value and the master class its prosperity; some even recognized their contributions to the economic growth of the larger country. The redistribution of land thereby offered just compensation for the travails of enslavement and for years of tilling the soil without remuneration. "Our wives, our children, our husbands, has been sold over and over again to purchase the lands we now locates on," one Virginia freedman stated, tellingly explaining the political economy. "Didn't we clear the land and raise de crops. . . . And den didn't dem large cities in de North grow up on the cotton and de sugars and de rice dat we made?" "We have a right to [that] land," he insisted.

Other freedpeople understood the land question in spiritual as well as social and economic terms, sometimes invoking the biblical "jubilee" in Leviticus— they called it the "day of jubilo"—which joined freedom with the restitution of land to its rightful claimants. But in all cases, ideas about a "right" to the land and beliefs that such a "right" would be acknowledged were enormously enhanced by the doings of the federal government. Owing to the Confiscation Acts of 1861 and 1862 and Sherman's Field Orders No. 15, the government controlled more than 900,000 acres of rebel land with authority—included in the legislation creating the Freedmen's Bureau—to divide it into 40-acre tracts for distribution among the freedpeople. Land reform appeared to loom as a genuine possibility; freedpeople could hear fretful planters as well as black soldiers in the army of occupation say as much. Even President Johnson's disappointing Amnesty Proclamation and related efforts to have abandoned and confiscated land quickly restored to white owners failed to stanch their expectations. If anything, Johnson's course and the controversy it immediately stirred might well have elevated them.

Indeed, in the early summer of 1865 talk of a general, government-promoted property division began to circulate along the coast of North and South Carolina and then spread rapidly, especially through those areas where freedpeople were to be found in the largest numbers. By November, the eager anticipations of blacks and related apprehensions of whites had been raised in the plantation districts of Virginia, the Carolinas, Georgia, Alabama, and Texas, and more widely still in the Mississippi Valley states of Louisiana, Mississippi, Arkansas, and Tennessee. One Freedmen's Bureau official familiar with the lower Mississippi Valley reported that "a majority of the colored population . . . positively believe that the government would take the plantations, with their old masters who had been in rebel service, cut them up into forty acre parcels, and give them to the colored people." Although some imagined that the day of reckoning could arrive at any time, more and more came to look to the Christmas season, and particularly to Christmas or New Year's Day: the time of the year when gifts were customarily exchanged and the slave owners' claims to sovereign power ritualistically displayed and contested. Not surprisingly, many of the antebellum slave insurrection panics—and the great Jamaican slave rebellion of 1831 that turned Britain toward emancipation—occurred during the Christmas interlude. It was a time of relaxed surveillance and heightened tension.

Yet just as rumors of land redistribution expressed the freedpeople's deepest desires and their imagined alliance with federal officials, so the very prospect of land reform and the black power it would facilitate catalyzed reorganizations of disbanded rebel troops. Planters and white landowning supporters, recently home from the major battlefields, now told of "extravagant ideas of freedom" that former slaves entertained, of a "prevailing idea among them" that the federal government would distribute land, and, especially, of plans devised by the freedpeople to stage an "insurrection" or "general rising" to take the land by force at Christmastime if the federal government refused to act. There was, the landowners insisted, "great apprehension pervad[ing] the countryside," and they placed much of the blame on the shoulders of African American troops in the army of occupation who, they claimed, "emboldened" the freedpeople politically and "demoralized" them at their work.

Here the fatal weaknesses of Johnson's policies became apparent. The white landowners complained loudly to all who would listen but formally brought their concerns to the attention of provisional governors either appointed or elected under Presidential Reconstruction. However much the governors might have opposed secession and kept a low profile during the War of the Rebellion, as natives of their states and men of means, they usually sympathized with the fears of fellow property owners and responded to the alarms being raised. Receiving letters and petitions that described the tense state of affairs and called for the removal of black troops and the authority to mobilize militia companies (to maintain "order" and "overawe the colored population"), the governors in turn contacted federal military officers, Freedmen's Bureau agents, and, if necessary, President Johnson to obtain the desired results. In this, the governors served less as Johnson's state representatives than as the planters' national brokers, presenting their case as a demonstration of public responsibility.

William Sharkey, the Mississippi governor closely identified with the state's planting interest, was especially vocal and persuasive. "The negroes are bold in their threats" and "about Christmas intend a general rising for the purpose of taking the property," he warned Johnson in August 1865. Thus, "to begin preparation for such an emergency and to suppress crime," Sharkey proposed mobilizing "volunteer companies of militia in each county," obtaining control of the "state arms," "organiz[ing] the whole of the militia," and removing black troops as expeditiously as possible. In Alabama, the provisional governor, Lewis E. Parsons, forwarded a similarly worded resolution from the then-sitting constitutional convention recommending the formation of "one or more companies of militia, in each county . . . to aid in repressing disorder and preserv[ing] the public peace."

On orders of Johnson and the Freedmen's Bureau commissioner, General Oliver Otis Howard, bureau agents traveled into the rural districts to "disabuse" the freedpeople of their "false impression" regarding the division of land and "urge them . . . to make [labor] contracts" for the next year. But federal officials also greeted the planters' alarms with more than a little skepticism. One commander in Louisiana reported that the newly organized militia companies "indulged in the gratification of private vengeance and worked against the policy of the Government," while another saw the influence of the "old secessionists" at play. Carl Schurz, a Republican and U.S. Army veteran who served as Johnson's special emissary, was not alone in pleading with the president to prohibit the organization of militias in the rebellious states. Stunning it was, then, when Johnson welcomed what proved to be the official rearming of disbanded Confederate units and the revitalization of the slave patrols. Johnson might have despised the big slaveholders and landholders, but he had no love for the slaves and freedpeople. He imagined a post-emancipation world run by and for white people with blacks as a subordinate laboring class. He also aimed to restore self-government rapidly in the rebellious states through policies that could stimulate a show of loyalty, moderation, and proper conduct demonstrating that the rebellion was truly at an end. But his willingness to allow "an armed posse comitatus organized under your militia law," like his earlier Amnesty Proclamation, only demonstrated that the spirit of rebellion—in fact the rebellion itself—was very much alive. If anything, Johnson effectively gave the green light to vigilantes of several sorts who traversed the countryside brutalizing the freedpeople. Deploying the threat of "insurrection" as shield and sword, the planters and their allies launched a campaign to disarm, disperse, and intimidate rural blacks, hoping to reassign them to the "tender mercies" of white landowners. Any black assembly, any sign of economic independence, any attempt to ignore or reject the conventions of racial subordination, became invitations to harassment or summary punishment. Away from their posts, even black Union soldiers fell vulnerable to vigilante bands that in most cases were reincarnations of formal Confederate units. As one such "party" of whites in Sumter County, Georgia, proclaimed, "they would make their own laws . . . and if the negroes failed to hire and contract upon their own terms before Christmas . . . they would make the woods stink with their carcasses."

Exaggerated as alarms about an imminent black "insurrection" might have been, they nonetheless spotlighted early political activities of freed communities and the developing contests for power that emancipation unleashed. For just as white landowners turned rumors of land redistribution into harbingers of black violence to reassert their local prerogatives, so the freedpeople used the rumors of land distribution to bolster their own bargaining positions. They seemed to be meeting regularly in their "neighborhoods," in some cases "drilling" for means of protection, and at times wrestling with landowners over the terms of their pay or their claims to the land. "Your hands say they will git one half of your crop let them work or not and you cant drive them off for this land don't Bee long to you," a South Carolina overseer told the planter William Alexander Graham in September 1865. Some freedpeople refused to enter into labor agreements for 1866—despite the prodding of planters and Freedmen's Bureau agents alike—for fear of the compulsions they associated with contracts. Many others saw no reason to accept the small remuneration, open-ended responsibilities, and close supervision customarily offered when the New Year might bring the opportunity to farm on their own account. "The Negroes . . . are not inclined to make any contracts until after Christmas," a Tennessee landowner recorded that October. "They seem to expect something to take place about that time, a division of lands or something of the kind."

When the New Year arrived, these Tennessee "Negroes" and many other freedpeople like them were able to sign contracts for better terms than they had originally been accorded: higher monthly pay or larger shares of the crop, access to provision grounds, lower rents on their housing. But in signing the contracts, they also acknowledged that the "promise" of land distribution would not be fulfilled nor the "threat" of a Christmas "insurrection" carried out. All that the Christmas season brought them were further rounds of harassment, floggings, and late-night searches. For their part, formerly chastened rebels suddenly felt emboldened to reignite their resistance to federal authority and carve out a favorable post-emancipation order. Johnson granted most of them amnesty and the restoration of landed property that had fallen into federal hands, but they nonetheless responded to his few political demands with grudging acceptance and often outright defiance. U.S. Army commanders bowed to planter requests and removed black soldiers from trouble spots in the rural areas. Freedmen's Bureau agents tried to dispel rumors of impending property division and pressure freedpeople into contracting. Southern legislatures commenced restricting black opportunities for either economic independence or civil equality, and in South Carolina and Mississippi (the two states with black population majorities) they enacted draconian "Black Codes" that, along with related laws in Alabama, struck one Freedmen's Bureau assistant commissioner "as the revival of slavery." Locally, planters and other landowners met together and agreed to enforce labor contracts, punish "vagrants," limit competition for laborers among themselves, prohibit the renting or selling of land to freedmen, and provide for regular policing.

Presidential Reconstruction was clearly in disarray, and the support Johnson had once received from a wide swath of Republican officeholders was unraveling. His early policies regarding pardons and the restoration of rebel property caused consternation in the ranks of abolitionists and Radical Republicans, and the disposition of southern constitutional conventions on the matters of slavery, secession, and black rights raised wider doubts about the wisdom of Johnson's course. But nothing troubled or incensed more northerners or pushed more moderate and conservative Republicans toward disenchantment if not outright opposition than the epidemic of violence against blacks and white unionists that exploded amid rumors of federal land reform and Christmas insurrection. Reported extensively in the northern press and on lecture circuits that drew large audiences, the violence and "outrages" of the summer and fall of 1865 seemed to directly threaten what were thought to be the results of the war and rupture the boundaries of northern tolerance. "The most favorable opportunity was afforded to the southern people," the *Cincinnati Daily Gazette* editorialized in early December, "but the spirit in which this was responded to was a rebellious one."

Congress overwhelmingly appeared to agree. When the Thirty-ninth Congress reconvened the first week of December 1865, it refused to admit the claimants sent by the rebellious states, formed the Joint Committee on Reconstruction, and began in earnest to contest Johnson's policies and presumptive executive authority. Recognizing that rebels who had been defeated militarily might claim victory on terrain of their own choosing, the Republican Congress now determined to seize the initiative and bring the rebellion to a different sort of end.

Radical Nationhood

Nearly a year earlier, Congress had taken a dramatic step in asserting its authority and extending the reach of federal power, though much of the impetus came from outside its walls. Pressure had been building among abolitionists and other antislavery activists to secure an emancipation that was universal and unassailable. As early as the spring of 1863, the Women's Loyal National League led by Susan B. Anthony and Elizabeth Cady Stanton launched a massive petition drive that would collect about 400,000 signatures. By the end of that year, congressional Republicans and a small number of their Democratic colleagues were ready to act. Recognizing the limits of the Emancipation Proclamation (it did not abolish slavery in all of the states) while fearing that its legal status as a war measure might render it vulnerable to judicial attack after the war, they resolved to craft an abolition amendment to the Constitution. It was not an easy process. Republicans had initially looked for a statutory means of ending slavery in the United States but struggled over the logic of a move that clearly stretched the Constitution to its limits. Some advanced the argument—as they had over early Reconstruction—that secession had remanded the rebellious states to the status of territories or "conquered provinces"; others embraced the Constitution's guarantee (Article IV, Section 4) of a "Republican Form of Government" to every state.

Eventually, an amendment appeared to be a more effective and formidable instrument, though as the Senate Judiciary Committee began its work in January 1864, conflict arose over what such an amendment should include and how far it should go. Should the amendment's language be confined to the abolition of slavery within the presumed borders of the United States, or should it speak as well to the civil status of those emancipated. No one took a more expansive view than the Massachusetts senator Charles Sumner. Influenced by the Declaration of the Rights of Man and of the Citizen unfurled in revolutionary France and perhaps familiar with the French emancipation decree of 1794, Sumner proposed that the amendment not only abolish slavery without compensation to slaveholders but also stipulate that "all people are equal before the law," a clear gesture in the direction of full citizenship for blacks. Unfortunately, he did not sit on the Judiciary Committee, and its chair, Lyman Trumbull of Illinois, paid him no mind. The result was an amendment that adopted the language of the Northwest Ordinance of 1787 and said nothing about equality or citizenship: "Neither slavery nor involuntary servitude except as a punishment for crime whereof the party shall be duly convicted, shall exist within the United States, or any place subject to their jurisdiction." The amendment did thereby prohibit slavery in any future territory of the United States (quite the opposite of the Confederate constitution) and, in Section 2, granted Congress the "power to enforce" it "by appropriate legislation."

Although the congressional power of enforcement may appear a bureaucratic add-on, it was the source of great consternation among most northern Democrats, not to mention now former slaveholders. For good reason. It lent the federal government sovereign power beyond anything previously enjoyed under the Constitution and threw open the door for any number of initiatives as to the civil and political status of freedpeople that the amendment failed to spell out. If slavery and involuntary labor were prohibited, what type of legislation would be necessary to "enforce" the prohibition? Would the "Black Codes" that the rebellious states were beginning to construct invite federal intervention on this account, and would the Republican majority use the enforcement power to press the matters of citizenship and the franchise? The Mississippi legislature regarded the amendment's enforcement clause as "a dangerous grant of power [which] might admit federal legislation in respect to persons, denizens and inhabitants of the state," and legislators in South Carolina and Alabama feared that the amendment would "confer upon Congress the power to Legislate upon the political status of the Freedmen."

The fears were justified. While President Johnson, Secretary of State William Seward, and war Democrats were quick to argue that the amendment would end rather than initiate conflicts "respecting rights acquired by the negroes," most Republicans—even those who rejected Sumner's approach to the amendment—saw the opportunity to demonstrate that freedom meant more, as the Ohio congressman James A. Garfield put it, than "the bare privilege of not being chained." Citing the amendment's enforcement clause, Republicans moved just as quickly to give freedom substance. In early 1866, they drafted and passed two bills: one extending the life of the Freedmen's Bureau and authorizing its agents to protect freedpeople in the "civil rights belonging to white people"; and one (the Civil Rights Bill of 1866) prescribing that "all persons born in the United States and not subject to any foreign power, excluding Indians not taxed, are hereby declared to be citizens of the United States" and specifying the rights and privileges citizenship entailed. Those included the rights of free labor, property ownership, and equal standing before the law, short of the suffrage. Together these bills seemed to insist that the end of slavery demanded an explicit reconfiguration of subject status, that citizenship would be defined and granted by the federal government, and that *Dred Scott* was no longer the law of the land.

Johnson vetoed both bills as "strides towards centralization," partly in hopes of isolating the Radical Republicans and building support among Democrats and conservative Republicans. But the vetoes boomeranged, unifying Republican ranks around the ends of defending their own power and removing Johnson's meddlesome hand from their policy objectives. As on the issue of slavery, this meant another constitutional amendment. In truth, proposals for constitutional amendments on questions relating to emancipation had been flooding into Congress since the Thirteenth Amendment was ratified. The stakes were high. The Republican Party was barely organized in the former slave states, and the end of slavery appeared to mean that the federal ratio, which counted slaves as three-fifths of a free person for the purposes of congressional apportionment (and, by extension, for the determination of electoral votes), would no longer be operative. Now former slaves would count as five-fifths, like all free people, the states of the South would gain more representation, and if freedmen did not achieve civil and political standing, the former slaveholders and their allies could have much more political power in the country than they had before the rebellion. It was a recipe for Republican defeat and possibly slaveholder revanchism.

African Americans had struggled to put black political rights on the table of discussion for decades and, especially from the time of their enlistment in the U.S. Army, made compelling arguments about the relation of soldiering and political citizenship. A growing number of Republicans, on grounds ranging from principle to opportunism, came to embrace their cause. But how far should such a political revolution go in what was truly a Jacobinical moment? What would the compass of citizenship be in the sort of state that was under construction? Woman suffrage activists, with deep ties to abolitionism, had fought spirited but losing battles for the franchise before the war and then put aside their political aspirations to support the Union and emancipation. Now a springtime of peoples was in the air, a sense that the old boundaries of civil and political life were being pressed and redefined as never before, and a fruitful moment for extending the revolution might well have arrived, a moment, as Elizabeth Cady Stanton put it, to "bury the woman and the negro in the citizen."

As Stanton suggested, woman suffrage advocates hoped to maintain and strengthen, not fracture, their alliance with former slaves. But the very case that African American men made to support their enfranchisement demonstrated the vulnerability of the women's position. By arguing that military service had revealed their courage and manhood, they embraced the gendered political culture of the nineteenth century that masculinized claims for both citizenship and political rights. However much "race" appeared to be the divide and hurdle in the path of universality and equality, it was—as black men seemed to recognize—dependency and femininity that deepened the threshold. Republicans, who mostly imbibed the culture of evangelical Protestantism, regarded male-headed households as the sine qua non of social stability and "separate spheres" as the organizing principle of public and private life. As slavery unraveled during the war, they looked for assurances that former slaves were acquainted with the bourgeois virtues, could respond to market incentives, and would construct their family relations in a morally acceptable hierarchy. Even their radicalism had little in it to make the case for female suffrage. Wendell Phillips, among the most radical in the antislavery camp, could express hope that "in time" he might "be as bold as Stuart Mill and add to that last clause" prohibiting disfranchisement on account of race, color, and previous condition the word "sex." But, he added, "this hour belongs to the negro."

The Fourteenth Amendment that emerged from Congress in June 1866 showed both the reach and the limits of this revolutionary moment. On the one hand, building on the Civil Rights Act of 1866, it established a national citizenry based on birthright and naturalization that offered the same "privileges and immunities" across the many states of the Union as well as the "equal protection of the laws." A more direct and ringing rejection of the world of *Dred Scott* or a more powerful enunciation of Radical Republicanism could hardly be found. The amendment also effectively banned from office anyone who held a political or military position requiring an oath of allegiance to the Constitution and then "engaged in insurrection or rebellion against the same," although Congress could remove the disability by a two-thirds vote.

But the second section of the amendment revealed the boundaries that were still in place. Congress could have taken up the franchise question by establishing a broad principle of political citizenship that the states could not tamper with and that might leave the door open for a more expansive arena of political participation. Instead, Congress took the indirect route on federal authority and the direct route on the matter of gender: it would count the "whole number of persons" in each state for the purposes of apportionment (rejecting the federal ratio) and penalize any state that denied any of its "inhabitants twenty-one years of age and citizens of the United States" the "right to vote" by reducing its congressional representation proportionately. Yet in a move that thrust the dagger into the heart of woman suffrage, the amendment also designated those "inhabitants" as "male," plainly defining the relevant universe of political rights in gender terms and making explicit as never before the exclusion of women from it. So ended an alliance that had helped defeat the rebellion and drive the revolution of emancipation.

Black male suffrage itself remained an unfulfilled Radical goal, and the behavior of southern legislatures elected under Johnson's Reconstruction plan, filled with members who would have been ineligible under the Fourteenth Amendment, suggested that even the threat of lost congressional representation would do little to advance black enfranchisement. After all, the rebellious states had not been readmitted to Congress, and their newly elected leaders were taking care of business—especially as to matters of land and labor—quite nicely nonetheless. All but Tennessee rejected the Fourteenth Amendment (ratification now being the prerequisite for readmission) between the summer and the early winter of 1866–67, citing both the pressure for black suffrage and the exclusion of "the best portion of our citizens." For Radical Republicans like Indiana's congressman George Julian, the lesson was obvious: the rebellious states could not be left to their own devices; they had to be subject to "the strong arm of power, outstretched from the central authority here in Washington."

Julian and the Radicals who shared his political views would benefit from congressional elections in the fall of 1866, which they turned into a referendum on the Fourteenth Amendment, and from Andrew Johnson's political bungling. Setting out on an extended speaking tour that summer—a "swing around the circle," as it came to be known—the president undermined his own standing, not to mention Democratic prospects more generally, by mixing appeals for reconciliation and the rights of the states with bitter harangues against his Republican adversaries. Voters who had never before been treated to presidential campaigning of this sort were shocked and aghast by Johnson's intemperate displays and abandoned him and his party in droves. When the ballots were counted, the Republicans had increased their control of Congress to more than two-thirds of the seats (making it veto-proof), and Andrew Johnson, not the Radicals whom he targeted, appeared isolated.

The Radicalism that emerged from what the *New York Herald* called "the fiery ordeal of a mighty revolution" was now at its pinnacle of influence, and it would meet the last phase of the rebellion on terms far different than either Lincoln, Johnson, or moderate Republicans had contemplated. In the Military Reconstruction Acts, passed overwhelmingly in March 1867, Congress decisively rejected the approach of encouraging rebels to show their loyalty to the Union and permitting them to rebuild their political institutions mostly as they saw fit. Instead, the rebellious states would be divided into five military districts, each under the command of a general in the U.S. Army who would supervise yet another reorganization of state constitutions and governmental structures.

Constitutional conventions would be held, new constitutions would be written, popular ratifications would occur, and elections for local, state, and national offices would be conducted. But this time, black men, most of whom had been slaves only a few years before, would participate as voters and delegates in conventions ordered to enfranchise African Americans on the same basis as whites and ratify the Fourteenth Amendment as conditions of readmission. Congress, that is, demanded the configuration of a radically new body politic in the rebellious states, and one that could secure Republican rule once reunification was completed.

Over the following months, the U.S. Army carried out the first voter registration in American history. It was a daunting and remarkable undertaking, aided by the impressive efforts of federal officers and the enthusiastic response of freed communities. By means of their communication networks, informal organizations, Union Leagues, and Republican emissaries, African Americans mobilized their ranks, streamed to places of registration (often defying the wishes of their employers), helped identify suitable black registrars, challenged the misinformation or indifference of hostile white registrars, and worked to educate and protect those who did not understand the process or feared the consequences of their involvement. "Registration is going on here—negroes all enrolling," grumbled planters from North Carolina to Texas. By the fall of 1867, the rolls of eligible voters had been compiled, and they included an astonishingly high proportion of black adult men: over 90 percent everywhere except Mississippi, where 83 percent registered. Even more consequentially, black voters now composed a substantial portion, if not a majority, of the total electorate in the rebellious states, especially in the counties and parishes where slaveholding planters had long ruled.

The rebellion now appeared to be at an end, and the elements of a new political order in much of the South—and perhaps in the country as a whole—now seemed to be in place (though federal war powers would endure until early 1871). The federal government proclaimed its sovereign authority over the territorial United States. The leading rebels, though escaping arrest and punishment, were politically penalized and marginalized in their home states, and a once-powerful southern bloc in Congress and national political life was left in permanent minority status. A national citizenship had been established and universal manhood suffrage advanced as a principle of political culture. Former slaves and other people of African descent won claims on the reins of power in places where they resided in the largest numbers. And Radical Republicans—America's Jacobins— were in a position to shape the political economy. What had begun as a struggle to subdue an assortment of rebellions, most prominently of slaveholders, turned into a social and political revolution that gave rise to a nation-state.

Still, the full meaning of that revolution and the projects of the nation-state had yet to be determined. Land reform in the rebellious South and woman suffrage in the country at large had tested the limits of change and were repelled. Questions about money, banking, tariffs, and railroads hovered over Congress, asking whose interests the great transformations of war and emancipation would serve. But the harbingers of the future might have been playing out most consequentially in the trans-Mississippi West. With the slaveholders' rebellion defeated, the federal government was more determined than ever to suppress the Indian rebellions that continued to erupt across the plains, the Southwest, and the Northwest. Only a few months after the last of the Confederate armies formally surrendered, the tribes in Indian Territory were made to pay for "making treaties with enemies of the United States" and fighting long and hard alongside them: the Cherokee Stand Watie was the final Confederate general to give up. Addressed by a congressionally appointed commission as "erring children," they learned they would "forfeit all annuities and interests" in their lands and would have to "make new treaties" if they were "willing to be at peace among themselves and with the United States." The treaties required that they set aside lands for the settlement of "friendly tribes in Kansas and elsewhere," form "one consolidated government," grant railroads rights-of-way, and accept not only the "unconditional emancipation of all persons held in bondage" but also "their incorporation into the tribes on an equal footing with original members" (something that had yet to be raised in relation to the emancipation of African American slaves in other parts of the country).

Earlier that summer, the secretary of the interior had spoken more generally about the fate of the Indian peoples of the West and instructed the commissioner of Indian affairs—echoing Lincoln—to "impress upon them in the most forcible terms, that the advancing tide of immigration is rapidly spreading over the country, and that the government has not the power or inclination to check it." "It is in the interests of both races, and chiefly for the welfare of the Indian," the secretary insisted, "that he should abandon his wandering life and settle upon lands reserved to his exclusive use." Nearly three years later, as the first elections under Military Reconstruction were taking place, General William Tecumseh Sherman, who had practiced "total warfare" against the southern rebels and issued Field Orders No. 15 to confiscate and redistribute their lands, traveled out to the Wyoming Territory with the Indian Peace Commission to negotiate an agreement with previously rebellious Sioux and their allies. Known as the Treaty of Fort Laramie and drafted in the spring of 1868, it delineated the boundaries of their reservation, prohibited their occupancy of territory "outside their reservation," and demanded that they "withdraw all opposition to the construction of railroads now being built on the plains."

Not all of the Sioux leaders signed the treaty, and some of the most militant, led by Sitting Bull, continued to raid federal forts along the upper Missouri River that summer and early fall. Elsewhere on the plains, in the Southwest, and in the Northwest, the summer months of 1868 saw Kiowas, Comanches, Cheyennes, Apaches, and Paiutes engage in warfare against what the federal government regarded as "the inevitable law of population and settlement on this continent." Thus, by October, the Indian Peace Commission was ready to take further stock of the situation and urge a dramatic shift in federal policy. "The time has come," the commissioners resolved, "when the Government should cease to recognize the Indian tribes as 'domestic dependent nations' [except owing to existing treaties] . . . and hereafter all Indians should be considered and held to be individually subject to the laws of the United States." Three years later, buried in an Indian appropriations bill, Congress made official what a new nation-state would demand of those who resided within its borders: "Hereafter no Indian nation or tribe within the territory of the United States shall be acknowledged or recognized as an independent nation, tribe, or power with whom the United States may contract by treaty." No competing sovereignty was to exist within the newly consolidated nation. The "reconstruction" of the South and the "reconstruction" of the West thereby formed part of a sweeping national project.

CHAPTER NINE

Capitalism

A formidable armory constructed in New York City for the Seventh
Regiment after the War of the Rebellion, 1868.

Wheels of Capital

Among the economic beneficiaries of the War of the Rebellion, perhaps none stood out more prominently than Jay Cooke. A Philadelphia banker with a modest portfolio in 1861, Cooke used his powerful connections and creative instincts to make a fortune marketing the federal bonds that paid for much of the U.S. war effort. By the late 1860s, with his coffers overflowing, he presided over the formidable Philadelphia banking house of Jay Cooke and Company, with more than three hundred employees, branches in New York and Washington, D.C., and profits exceeding $1 million annually, all the while maintaining close ties to the Republican state.

Indeed, Cooke nearly became Ulysses S. Grant's secretary of the Treasury, a disappointment that stung him. But on September 18, 1873, to the shock of the financial community in the United States, Cooke and Company closed its doors in disgrace, unable to meet its credit obligations, and declared bankruptcy. Almost instantaneously, the New York Stock Exchange was shaken to its core, briefly closing its own doors, and a domino effect of bank failures quickly spread across the country, ushering in a deep and prolonged depression the likes of which had not been seen before.

The immediate source of Cooke's woes was his gamble on investing in the Northern Pacific Railway, meant to link Duluth, Minnesota, and Puget Sound, which Congress had chartered in 1864 as a second transcontinental. Although Cooke initially regarded the investment as "a mere bagatelle," he soon imagined being at the helm of a great northwestern rail corridor, possibly involving the annexation of western Canada, which, to him, "could be done without any violation of treaties" simply by encouraging the "quiet emigration over the border of trustworthy men with families." That the European market for American railroad bonds was drying up did not appear too worrisome to Cooke, for he had shown his genius at marketing bonds to small investors in the United States during the late war.

But in truth, the changing European bond market was a sign of significant troubles in the world of international finance. Capital flows on the Continent had become increasingly interwoven and robust owing to the great economic boom of the 1850s. Germany, the Low Countries, and France saw important industrial gains, while Britain solidified its position not only as the leading industrial power but also as the organizing center of finance capital. Circuits of trade in agricultural commodities—wheat in particular—intensified, especially during and immediately after the American War of the Rebellion, and drew Russia and the Austro-Hungarian Empire into close embrace with neighbors to the west, notably with Paris, which stood second only to London as a source of banking and investment capital. Then, almost at once, cheap American wheat flooded the European grain market, and the settlement of the Franco-Prussian War (a humiliating defeat for France) required large transfers of gold from Paris to Berlin. Grain merchants across northern and central Europe had to hedge their bets and, in some cases, liquidate their assets; newly chartered banks that had depended on French gold suddenly tottered. The Vienna stock market collapsed in May 1873, and the ripple effects were quickly felt in Amsterdam, Berlin, Paris, and London. The Bank of England saw no alternative to raising its discount rate, and over the course of only a few months that rate spiked from 4.5 percent to 9 percent, the highest level in the nineteenth century.

For American financiers like Cooke, this was a rude awakening in what had otherwise been a relatively dreamy ride thanks to help from Congress and the Treasury Department. When major hostilities in the United States ended, the federal government had a raft of important decisions to make about the initiatives it had taken in the midst of war. Would the policies and institutions that had dramatically expanded the reach and authority of the state be maintained, augmented, or scaled back, and whose interests would be privileged in the decision making? Some of the most pressing issues concerned wartime finance, both because a new national banking system had been created and because over $400 million in greenbacks, federally printed, though not redeemable in coin, were now in circulation. Would the banking system be maintained, and would it continue to favor the urban and manufacturing sectors of the economy? Or would the charters be amended to lower capital requirements and permit the extension of loans on the collateral of real estate (giving rural and small-town areas better access)? Would greenbacks remain a circulating medium, the volume increased or decreased as the times demanded, or would they be retired in favor of a specie-based (probably gold) currency? And would the many millions of dollars in government bonds, whose interest was coming due, be payable in greenbacks (favoring debtors) or only in gold (favoring creditors)?

The Republican Party had substantial majorities in Congress and was thus in a position to leave a strong imprint on the nature and course of the postwar political economy. But there were serious divisions in its own ranks over the speed and overall direction of any readjustments, reflecting the complex coalition that the party had constructed. Eastern banking and finance capital, some of which had been sponsored by the Republican government itself, nonetheless hoped to scale back central state authority, free up capital markets, trim the protective tariff, withdraw greenbacks from circulation as quickly as feasible, and have bondholders paid off in gold specie rather than in depreciated greenbacks. Western agricultural producers (farm owners growing chiefly for the domestic market), on the other hand, favored monetary inflation, debt repayment in greenbacks (most of the bondholders were in the East and Europe), protectionism to bolster the national economy, and federal initiatives for infrastructure projects, like railroads, to facilitate the sale and purchase of essential goods. But across the manufacturing belt that stretched from New England through New York and Pennsylvania and out to Illinois, and in the rural and small-town Midwest, there were fractures. The iron producers of western Pennsylvania strongly supported both greenbacks and protectionism, while the textile manufacturers of the Northeast and the Middle Atlantic looked for lower tariff rates and sounder money. In many ways, it was a defining, though usually unrecognized, moment in the unfolding of Reconstruction. Many Radical Republicans who hoped to transform the former slave South while advancing the interests of small producers in the North supported greenbacks and protectionism; more moderate and conservative Republicans, who were closely aligned with industrialists and bankers and eager to resurrect the southern plantation economy, favored moderate tariffs and the return to a specie-based currency. The Radical Charles Sumner of Massachusetts, a onetime free state Democrat, frowned on protectionism and embraced hard money.

For the next three decades, the "money question," which had reared its head in the 1830s, would embroil American politics like no other issue, speaking to the intense battle over the balances of power that would organize the development of the country's economy. But by the late 1860s, harbingers of the outcome—and of the limits of federal Reconstruction—were plainly in evidence. President Andrew Johnson's Treasury secretary, Hugh McCulloch, himself a banker and a sometime advisee of Jay Cooke's, struck the first blow (with considerable Republican support) by pursuing a policy of monetary contraction, retiring greenbacks as they came into the federal Treasury and promoting a mildly deflationary course. Then, in 1869, with the strong backing of eastern Republicans, Congress passed the Public Credit Act, which ensured that the federal government's debt obligations would be paid in specie or specie-backed notes, rather than in greenbacks. These were victories for the larger financial interests and their allies.

Bankers and investors like Jay Cooke could flex their policy muscles so effectively because they were accumulating political loyalists nearly as fast as they were accumulating capital or access to it. To be sure, most Republicans had long favored a developmental vision that involved federal support for infrastructure and manufacturing and that would bring the sprawling territories of the United States under the authority of a new nation-state. For them, the wartime measures providing for a protective tariff, western homesteads, national banks, and transcontinental railroads were less the products of necessity than the consummation of initiatives they had been calling for since the party's founding, now made possible by the departure of so many hostile southern Democrats. But financing railroad projects required more than land grants and guaranteed federal start-up loans. It required almost endless borrowing to keep projects afloat during the extended period of construction. And for this, it was necessary to curry the favor of congressional legislators with handouts such as directorships on railroad boards, selling watered railroad stock, and inventing dummy building corporations. Indeed, the net of corruption and bribery reached out of the legislative and well into the executive branch of the national government.

For Jay Cooke, it came to be a family operation. Long content to reap the rewards of the federal bond market, Cooke began to look elsewhere for investment opportunities as the government commenced retiring its debt and the market with which he was most familiar began to shrink. Like other newly moneyed men of the time, he looked to the railroads, the faltering Northern Pacific in particular. In 1870, Cooke purchased a controlling interest in the road. It came with massive government land grants (fifty million acres), though neither federal cash nor secured bonded debt. He hoped and half expected that the government would come to his financial aid in jump-starting the operation. But revelations of rampant corruption and mismanagement of the transcontinentals were souring the public mood for federal largesse and prompting congressional investigations of some of the more egregious practices, most infamously the Crédit Mobilier (a dummy construction company set up by the Union Pacific Railroad, which offered bribes to members of Congress in return for their funding support). Marketing railroad bonds, at home and abroad, was therefore increasingly difficult even for the likes of Jay Cooke, and when construction on the Northern Pacific consequently slowed, he turned to his brother, Henry. No financial genius, Henry had been running the Washington branch of Cooke and Company, but, more important, in 1867 he also became finance chairman of the Freedman's Savings Bank, chartered by Congress and signed into law by President Lincoln in March 1865.

The Freedman's Bank was not meant to be a commercial investment house. It was part of the federal government's effort to supervise the African American transition out of slavery by encouraging behaviors it associated with responsible free people and wage earners: thrift, hard work, an eye to the future. Not accidentally, the bank was established at the same time as the Freedmen's Bureau. Freedmen and freedwomen would be able to create deposit accounts and build their savings with government guaranteed interest of 6 percent. And although the institution got off to a slow start—freedpeople brought little money out of slavery and had no experience with savings banks—by the late 1860s there were Freedman's Bank branches in several southern cities and a growing number of smaller towns in the rural districts. More impressively still, individual deposits had increased nearly tenfold to well over $1 million, a good bit of it destined for the purchase of land.

When Henry Cooke joined the Freedman's Bank, there were clear restrictions as to how the deposits could be invested. No matter. He quickly went to Congress to have the charter revised and found no shortage of people ready to relax the standards, the Massachusetts senator and Radical Republican Charles Sumner chief among them. Before long, Henry was loaning out the bank's resources left and right and more consequentially sank over $500,000 of its deposits into Jay Cooke and Company for only a 5 percent return. Without knowing it, that is, poor black laborers, tenants, and small landowners had become investors in the house of Cooke and, by extension, in the Northern Pacific Railway. It would not be the last time that the hard-earned dollars of working people sponsored the high-risk adventures of wealthy speculators.

Unfortunately for the freed depositors, Jay Cooke was reluctant to read the handwriting on the wall, in part because of his self-confidence and in part because of his standing with the federal state. Cooke might not have obtained the financial benefits showered on his Union Pacific and Central Pacific counterparts, but he did not lack for important government assistance. Although Northern Pacific track had been inching toward Bismarck in the North Dakota Territory, it was still a long way from Puget Sound, and much of the projected route had not even been surveyed. More problematic, many miles of the route, especially in the Yellowstone River valley of eastern Montana, was home to militant Sioux bands, led by Sitting Bull, who had refused to sign the Treaty of Fort Laramie in 1868 consigning them to reservations and requiring that they allow railroads the right-of-way. Northern Pacific survey parties would clearly need protection from potential attack, and they received it by way of hundreds of U.S. Army infantry and cavalry sent to the area.

This might have been enough to permit the necessary progress, but the renegade Sioux were in no mood to weigh the military balances or bide their time. For them, in the words of Spotted Eagle, another of the Sioux leaders, "it was life or death," and they "would fight it out" regardless of the "consequences." "There will be constant danger West of the [Missouri River]," one of the army officers told the chief railroad surveyor in the spring of 1872, "and it should be impressed on all persons that eternal vigilance is the price for keeping their scalps."

As predicted, the fighting began later that summer shortly after the first troops arrived, and it continued for months, summoning additional soldiers, including the Seventh Cavalry and its flamboyant new commander, George Armstrong Custer, who nearly met his death in an ambush in August 1873. More significantly for Cooke and the Northern Pacific, the military and the survey expeditions acted as magnets for newspaper reporters who followed the action and started to file stories of Indian hostilities against the road and of the road's related financial woes. By late 1872, Cooke and Company was having great difficulty selling bonds to increasingly nervous investors, and the house very nearly failed that December. The news out of the upper plains only worsened thereafter as word of the Northern Pacific's efforts to push "through the country of the warlike Sioux" spread eastward. "Our men and their escort have been resisted and fought by forces of Indians, in such numbers and with such spirit as to stop our work," a Northern Pacific official conceded. "The company's engineers have in effect been driven by Indians out of the Yellowstone Valley." In early September 1873, Custer's close brush with disaster of the previous month became public, and although he managed to escape the ambush in Montana, there would be no such quick recovery for the Northern Pacific. The insurgent Sioux sealed the doom of Jay Cooke, and he took the Freedman's Savings Bank down along with him.

It was a telling historical moment, bringing a period of very dramatic economic change to an abrupt close and setting the foundation for a new system of social and political relations. And the railroad was the embodiment of what had been happening and where things were likely to go. Already in the late 1840s and early 1850s, as the first great railroad boom took off, the outlines were very much in evidence. They showed the emergence of large private companies, supported in various ways by state and municipal governments, which sold bonds and related financial instruments to raise capital, took corporate legal form, created administrative hierarchies, and depended on a sprawling cast of wage workers, from the ethnically diverse construction crews and section hands (most of them recent immigrants) to the semiskilled and skilled workmen who fired the engines, handled the breaks, coupled the cars, drove the locomotives, and staffed the repair shops. It was a model of a developing form of capitalist production and circulation, previously anticipated in other transportation projects, maritime operations, and textiles mills, given new articulations. Whatever the political course of the country, the railroads would have been powerful exemplars of and pacesetters for an American capitalism that was beginning to take hold around mid-century.

But the war and the configuration of a nation-state lent the process new scope, scale, direction, connections, and personnel: in sum, a wholly different character. And at the center was a complex alliance between the financiers and industrialists who had benefited from government business; the legislative and executive arms of the national state; and the higher reaches of the U.S. military. Eventually, the alliance would include the federal and state courts. Finance capital was positioning itself to play an increasingly important role, not only in the construction of the transcontinentals and many other rail lines that would traverse the territory of the United States, but in capitalizing the mines and mills that would help power American industrialization. Financiers looked to accumulate resources, remove obstacles (environmental and human) from their paths, and draw upon the muscle of laborers who had been dislodged from the land and from personal restraints and were now moving around the globe in search of livelihoods. Their eyes were trained especially on the trans-Mississippi West and, with the aid of political allies on both sides of the border, on Mexico and perhaps the rest of the Western Hemisphere. That Promethean project fired the imaginations of ambitious men like the Scots immigrant Andrew Carnegie, who made a fortune in wartime investing (he paid a substitute to avoid military service) through the good offices of the Pennsylvania Railroad's Thomas Scott, but worried about sinking his money directly into railroad stocks. So he did the next best thing. He channeled the fruits of his new fortune into the iron and steel industry, having learned they were the basic materials that made railroad transport possible.

When the speculative bubbles finally burst in 1873 and the railroad boom collapsed, Carnegie fared better than his old boss Tom Scott and certainly better than Jay Cooke or a raft of other financiers who had plunged headfirst into the whirlpool and now could barely come up for air. The consequences were deep, wide ranging, and long lasting. Credit dried up, factories and shops closed or dramatically cut their workforces, wages were slashed, un- and underemployment spiraled, bankruptcies exploded, and household economies unraveled. The cascading crisis ignited more than two decades of political struggle, threatening social upheaval and calling into question many of the basic ways in which the political economy worked. But the alliance that came out of the war would endure, and in many respects become stronger, leaving those who had been enriched and had then run amok to pick up the pieces.

Transformations of the Countryside

Although the development of capitalism is customarily associated with cities and industries, where the production and circulation of commodities and the sources of finance were most clearly concentrated, the transformation of the countryside, in the United States and around the globe, was the necessary foundation for capitalism's rise and sustenance. Until land became an alienable commodity, no longer subject to communal claims and use rights, and until the ties that bound the great mass of humanity to the soil by means of slavery, servility, and community obligation were severed, no mass market in goods or labor could emerge. Several centuries in the making, this transformation escalated very dramatically in the nineteenth, when slaves and peasants were emancipated in Europe and the Western Hemisphere and new markets for land came into being there, in eastern and southern Asia, in sub-Saharan Africa, and around the Mediterranean. Many millions of men, women, and children were thereby turned loose to earn their keep, often moving across expansive territories and oceans, in what became history's largest migrations.

The greatest number, by far, would come to the United States, where they might find work on the docks and construction sites, on the canals and railroads, in the mines, mills, and manufactories, and in the fields of commercial farms. But the American countryside also pulsed with new transformations during and after the War of the Rebellion—deeper and more sweeping than the intensifications of previous decades—which simultaneously evidenced and contributed to the advance of capitalist relations. Nowhere was this more apparent than in the South and the West.

The plantation economies of the former rebellious states were of deep concern to Republican policy makers from the start of the war, and it was there that some of the most convulsive and consequential transformations occurred. The stakes could not have been higher. Cotton and sugar planters were among the wealthiest and most politically powerful of all Americans on the eve of the War of the Rebellion, and the crops that their slave laborers produced proved central to the economic growth of the country as a whole. Merchant and shipping houses from New Orleans to Boston took large earnings from the cotton trade; textile mills from Pennsylvania to Massachusetts depended on the delivery of the cotton fiber to make yarns and cloth. Failure to subdue the rebellion would have had dramatic economic consequences; so would have any set of circumstances that either saw the plantations destroyed or the balance of power shifted from the owners who lorded over them to the workers who made them flourish. Although a handful of Radical Republicans hoped to dismantle the plantation sector (and the planter class with it) through some type of land reform and create a social order in the slave South that more closely mimicked their own, most Republicans believed that a resurrected cotton economy was crucial to the future prosperity of the nation, and they worried that a landed black peasantry would devote their energies to raising food rather than market crops.

The logic of federal policy could be seen, first, with the advent of the contract labor system in 1862, as the U.S. Army simultaneously helped destroy slavery and restore the plantations to production as it took New Orleans and moved up the Mississippi Valley to crush the rebellion there. Abandoned estates were leased or sold either to northerners who were quickly on the scene or to southerners who took an oath of loyalty to the United States. Then able-bodied contrabands were sent to work them for paltry wages or shares of the harvested crop. Some of the northerners had been aligned with the antislavery movement and hoped to demonstrate the superior efficiency of free, over slave, labor; most others looked to cash in on the very high price of cotton (owing to the U.S. naval blockade of the Atlantic and Gulf coasts) and perhaps become absentees in the manner of the West Indian plantocracy. For their part, the southern lessees or loyalists tried to position themselves to ride the transition out of slavery successfully.

Further policy initiatives, from Lincoln's Ten Percent Plan to Johnson's Amnesty Proclamation also aimed to promote the emergence of a loyal class of commercial (white) cotton and sugar growers and imagined former slaves principally as wage laborers on reorganized plantations. Sherman's Field Orders No. 15, which made 400,000 acres of prime rebel land available for black settlement, was soon rolled back, and the Freedmen's Bureau, which did have the official responsibility for redistributing nearly half a million acres of other rebel land held by the federal government, focused chiefly on supervising and enforcing labor contracts. By the fall of 1865, the army of occupation was both disabusing freedpeople of the idea that land would be provided for them before the year was out (around Christmastime, as was widely believed) and attempting to rein in the excesses of white paramilitaries, which intended to repress any black political initiatives toward such an end. The nation-state, under Republican auspices, therefore played a central role in trying to construct the framework for a new labor system in the former slave South, one that would, at least in theory, be based on individual self-ownership, voluntarism, contract rather than compulsion, and the potential rewards of profits and wages.

Yet theory was one thing, practice quite another. Former slaveholders could scarcely believe that the now freedpeople would work without the coercive mechanisms—including the whip—they had long deployed, and many bridled at the prospect of "bargaining" with men and women they had been accustomed to controlling. A South Carolina planter, complaining bitterly about the laziness and "ignorance" of the "negroes" and the sorry state of the crops in the spring of 1865, drew a lesson that many of his counterparts would have ratified: "Labor must be commanded completely or the production of the cotton crop must be abandoned."

Well aware of their owners' views and dispositions, former slaves hoped instead that emancipation would bring the opportunity to work for themselves on lands they could purchase or rent, and they would struggle mightily for the next several decades to realize some semblance of this goal. But in the shorter term, they and their former owners battled day in and day out, and year in and year out, over the new rules of the agricultural system: over the extent of supervision, seasonal obligations, the responsibilities of family members, rent and provisioning, and the form, level, and regularity of pay. Given the deeply conflicting aspirations, the results could be explosive, as the old masters tried to preserve as much of slavery as possible and the newly freed people tried to maintain the gains they had made as slaves while limiting the coercive authority to which they had previously been subjected. The many thousands of grievances lodged at the local offices of the Freedmen's Bureau, by laborers and employers alike, testified to the contested ground of transition.

In the end, the transformation of land and labor relations was multifaceted and uneven, shaped by the crop cultures and organization of production under slavery and by the specific ways in which slavery crumbled during the War of the Rebellion. The most rapid and direct movements toward wage labor came in those areas of the South in which operations were highly capitalized to begin with (the sugar sector of lower Louisiana being the prominent example) or in which labor requirements were highly seasonal, as in areas of the border South increasingly devoted to wheat, livestock, truck, and general farming, especially in the states that were not in rebellion and thus where cash and credit were more readily available. The sugar planters managed to preserve gang labor, pay cash wages, and experiment with Chinese, native white, and Italian workers before strikes and instabilities led them (like their counterparts in Cuba) to build central mills employing black labor. Wealthy rice planters along the southern Atlantic coast, who also had substantial capital investments, did not fare so well. The early occupation of U.S. forces during the war set in motion a train of events—including land redistribution and restoration—that headed toward the irreversible decline of the export sector along with the emergence of one of the largest enclaves of black petty proprietors to be found anywhere in the South. But when the rice industry resurfaced later in the century on the prairies of Louisiana, Texas, and Arkansas, it did so on the basis of outside capital, extensive mechanization, the rental of big parcels of land, and seasonal wage labor.

In the cotton belt, where the rebellion was centered and the cash and credit crunch most pronounced, the hardfisted vestiges of coercion survived most tenaciously. Wage labor had some importance, perhaps more than is generally assumed, especially in northern Florida and the newly developing districts of the Mississippi delta. But in the main, planters and freedpeople fought their way along a path—carved by regular skirmishing, the interventions of state and local governments, the eradication of common use rights, personal violence, and vigilantism—toward sharecropping, in which planters continued to supply the housing, tools, animals, and seed but divided their plantations into a collection of plots to be worked by black households, living scattered about rather than in the old quarters, who would receive a portion of the crop in return for their labor.

However diverse in their forms of organization and settlement—some of which seemed to make a mockery of "free labor"—what all these agricultural economies shared was a new set of social relations that linked farms and plantations across the southern states to proliferating towns and villages nearby and then to centers of finance and political power to the north and the east. Although strong doses of personal domination, extra-economic compulsion, and repression persisted and, in some cases, were fortified over time, they did not formally bind black laborers to the estates or to the direct authority of property holders as had been true under slavery. Instead, they gradually created a class of workers who, while now claiming ownership of their persons, were stripped of means to produce or subsist on their own account and, through the legislative and police powers of the state, were left with few alternatives to laboring in the fields for the landowners. Vagrancy laws required them to have "gainful employment" by a certain date. Anti-enticement laws prohibited employers from luring laborers away with the promise of higher wages and better working conditions. Fence laws extinguished common use rights to unenclosed land for the raising of livestock. Game laws restricted the use of woods and streams for hunting and fishing. Already by the 1870s, southern courts began to confirm the results: sharecroppers, they determined, occupied the legal status of "wage laborers," having no claim to the crop they grew until the landowner settled his other financial obligations.

Yet if planters and other substantial landowners eventually managed to use the levers of the state to secure their property and access to black labor—which made for the bloody ground of local Reconstruction politics—they, too, were part of a new structure of economic and political power. Having rebelled against the authority of the federal government and been defeated, they saw their slaves emancipated without monetary or other types of compensation. Garrisoned by the U.S. Army, they faced martial law and extended military occupation. Perhaps most important, they had forfeited their power at the national level for the foreseeable future. The consequences were enormous. The factorage system that had enabled them to market their cotton and purchase supplies on favorable terms before the war was now in ruins, and they were forced to turn to town and crossroads merchants, themselves dependent on outside sources of capital, for necessary credit and provisions. Owing to the national banking system created during the war and the contraction of greenbacks by the federal Treasury Department, that capital was in short supply in the South, and it could not be loaned on the security of land.

Interest rates were therefore much higher than in other parts of the country, all the more so given the uncertainties of the new labor system. Protective tariffs raised the prices of goods landowners needed to purchase, and they could get little help from the federal government in the face of an increasingly competitive export staple market as landed elites in other post-emancipation societies had succeeded in doing: no resources for attracting immigrant labor, no federally sponsored loans for agricultural modernization or cooperatives to lower the cost of credit, and no price supports for their crops. Now the Republican Party held sway, and it increasingly ruled the nation in the interests of big financiers and big industry in the Northeast and the Midwest. So firmly under the control of national politics and economic power was this triumphalist coalition that few deals had to be cut with the landed classes who would pay the costs of industrialization.

The ways in which the results of the War of the Rebellion transformed the southern countryside and advanced the development of capitalist agriculture could also be seen in areas of the South that had previously been populated by small-scale yeoman farmers, who had chiefly depended on household labor and mixed subsistence with limited market production. Very quickly, new rail lines pushed into these regions—often with the support of Reconstruction governments—linking them with growing urban centers in the South and especially with financial and commercial centers in the Northeast. Towns multiplied along the routes, and merchandisers soon offered venues for selling staple crops and, owing to deepening connections with northern capital markets, credit instruments for encouraging their production. Before long, mortgages or liens on the growing crop and on land and other productive property were executed to secure these debts, drawing yeomen into the international cotton market and giving merchants, some of whom began accumulating land, new power in local and state political life.

Had the cotton economy of the South returned to its antebellum vitality, this process of commercial expansion might well have had wide benefits, at least for white landowners, and slowly augmented the availability of capital and credit. But the wartime blockade of the rebellious states took them out of the international cotton market and provided incentives for cotton production in other parts of the globe where it had formerly been pursued on only a limited scale: in India, Egypt, and Brazil. By war's end, the world cotton supply was

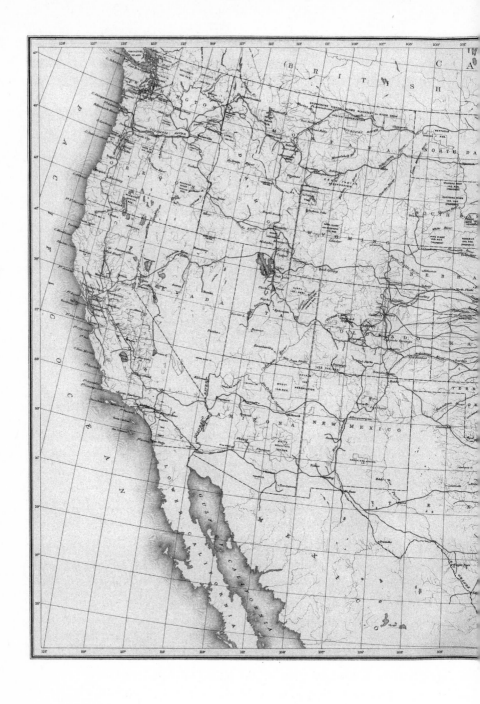

Map of the railroad networks of the United States in 1890.
Henry Gannett, *Statistical Atlas of the United States*, 1898.

growing rapidly, as was true for other important market crops, while demand for the fiber in some of the industrial hubs of Europe and North America was beginning to flatten. By the early 1870s, the international price for cotton, as well as for other agricultural commodities, began to slip. The panic of 1873 and its aftermath only worsened a deflationary spiral that was encompassing more and more producers and proved impossible to escape. Before the century was out, most of the South's cotton was raised by white labor, tenancy and share-cropping became rampant, and growing numbers of white agriculturalists were looking to textile factories and other sorts of regular and seasonal employment to subsist. Although it was difficult to see at the time, the cotton economy of the South was slowly beginning to unravel, and the white and black hands who grew the crop would soon be making greater migrations of their own.

Witnesses to the dramatic transformations of the southern countryside began to reckon that the staple-producing South, once a driving force of American growth, had become something of a colony of the Northeast. Its economy was principally organized around agriculture and the extraction of other raw materials (coal, lumber, phosphates), the products of which would be shipped north for processing and manufacture. The prices fetched for its exports were declining, while the interest charges paid for necessary credit were increasing. And the region now occupied a subordinate position in the structure of national politics, especially in the executive and judicial branches of government. At the very least, the idea of a colonial South, which would also gain important resonance in cultural representations, spoke to the new balances of power in the American political economy that the results of the War of the Rebellion brought into being.

But it was in the trans-Mississippi West that the developmental patterns and transformations most closely approximated a colonial relationship and ultimately served as a foundation for later colonial encounters elsewhere in the hemisphere and the Pacific. This was to be seen in the pivotal role played by the federal government both in promoting the market exploitation of the land and its resources and in exercising direct political authority over the many territories that had been created there (far more formidably and for much longer than was true in the Reconstruction South), and it was to be seen in the new relations of economic power that were swiftly installed. The question of the West's future in the American political economy—whether it would be open to the use of slave labor—had been bitterly contested from the time of the Northwest Ordinance (1787) and, more than any other issue, led to the War of the Rebellion. Now that the rebellion was defeated and the victors in a position to press ahead, the scramble was on.

The driving forces of western development were the railroads, not simply the transcontinentals, which did multiply in number, but also a great many lines that pushed across the vast interior, especially into the mineral-rich districts of Idaho, Montana, Minnesota, and the Dakotas to the north and Colorado, New Mexico, and Arizona to the south. They were energized by the marriage of the government (at federal, state, and local levels) and finance capital, and they drove the expansion of mining and lumbering, not least because they became prodigious consumers of wood (for tracks, rolling stock, and fuel) and then coal (replacing wood to fire the engines). They would be of immense benefit to the emerging iron and steel industries as well. William Jackson Palmer exemplified the connections and process. A native of Delaware who was trained as an engineer, Palmer became convinced of the importance of coal to the country's future and, with the support of the Pennsylvania Railroad's president, J. Edgar Thomson, helped convert the company's locomotives from wood to coal. His relationship with Thomson, and then with Thomas Scott and the young Andrew Carnegie, both also of the Pennsylvania, got Palmer his railroad bearings and access to capital, especially from investors in Philadelphia.

Soon after the war ended, Palmer went out to Colorado with a nose for minerals and a clear vision of what he intended to do. He began buying up coal-rich lands south of Denver (itself a railroad hub) and was soon pointing his own railway, the Denver and Rio Grande, toward the coalfields there. In 1880, he formed the Colorado Coal and Iron Company and shortly thereafter built an integrated iron and steel manufacturing complex in Pueblo. By the end of the century, the company—reorganized as Colorado Fuel and Iron—owned thousands of acres of land, had operations in Wyoming and New Mexico as well as Colorado, employed fifteen thousand workers, and produced three-quarters of Colorado's coal. Sprawling and powerful, Colorado Fuel and Iron was itself bought up in 1902 by one John D. Rockefeller, who already had interests in copper mining along with the newly discovered fossil fuel, petroleum.

The emergence of Colorado Fuel and Iron was symptomatic of the mineral boom that spread across the western interior during the last four decades of the nineteenth century. Gold and silver "rushes" shifted ground from Comstock, Nevada, and Pikes Peak, Colorado, to Idaho, Montana, and White Pine, Nevada, during the 1860s; to the Black Hills of South Dakota, Tombstone, Arizona, and Leadville, Colorado, in the 1870s; to Coeur d'Alene, Idaho, in the 1880s; to Cripple Creek, Colorado, in the 1890s; and then on to northwestern Canada and Alaska. To these may be added important copper strikes in the southwestern borderlands and in Montana during the 1880s and the exploitation of the great ranges of iron ore in Minnesota, Wisconsin, and Michigan in the 1880s and 1890s. What all of these sites had in common—as prefigured by the anthracite districts of northeastern Pennsylvania—were the railroads as sources of both transportation and investment capital, the rise of small urban centers with overwhelmingly male populations and industrial processing tied to the mines, the appearance of multicultural and multiethnic wage-labor forces, and the rapid move toward corporate organization.

The "miners" who initially staked individual or group claims were, for the most part, petty producers, aided perhaps by hired helpers, and they worked close to the surface panning or sluicing for minerals. But when the surface or placer deposits became exhausted, deeper—hard-rock—mining required shafts or pits that were far more capital-intensive to construct and complex to operate. The "miners" were steadily pushed out, replaced by "mine workers" with hierarchies of their own based on skill and ethnicity. Experienced colliers, often from England (Cornwall especially) and Ireland, sat atop a labor pyramid that would also include lesser and unskilled workers from central and eastern Europe, the Mediterranean, Scandinavia, the Iberian Peninsula, and Mexico, with a scattering of African Americans and Chinese. Few of the workers, other than the African Americans, were native-born, and ethnic rivalries of several sorts frequently roiled the camps.

As for the sources of investment and dynamics of ownership, although San Francisco merchants and bankers, themselves beneficiaries of the first of the western gold rushes, helped finance some of the undertakings, it was the northeastern financial houses (particularly in New York and Boston), many already involved in western railroading, that provided most of the capital. Sometimes new rail hubs like El Paso, Albuquerque, and Tucson in the 1880s became gateways to mineral exploitation in the arid hinterlands; oftentimes, the new corporate mine owners became lords of all they surveyed, buying up huge tracts of land, establishing company towns, and taking effective control of the local municipal councils, police, and courts. Names like Harriman, Gould, Morgan, Sage, and Guggenheim hovered over the process. Phelps Dodge, generally known as the Company, held sway in Arizona with mines, refineries, land, and railroad lines. Montana, where copper and the Rockefeller-owned Anaconda Company ruled supreme, was quickly known as a company state. Capitalism and colonialism appeared to go hand in glove.

Much the same could be said for the range cattle industry that exploded across the Great Plains and into the Great Basin in the 1870s and 1880s as the army completed its defeat of Native peoples, railroads pushed across the grassy landscape, and the once immense bison populations collapsed. Rooted in the practices of ranchos and haciendas in northern Mexico, cattle raising had been concentrated in Texas and originally looked for market outlets in the hide and tallow manufactories of the Gulf Coast. But the War of the Rebellion simultaneously saw a massive increase in the size of the cattle herds that could not be brought to market (over four million head by 1865) and the establishment, with the support of railroads and federal food contracts, of large stockyards and meatpacking plants in Chicago. The Union Stock Yard and Transit Company, capitalized at nearly $1 million thanks to Chicago's nine largest railroads and the city's Pork Packers' Association, opened in late 1865.

Availing themselves of cheap land, open-range grazing on the public domain, and small cohorts of skilled wage workers (also known as cowboys), the Texas cattlemen—some of them the emerging cattle "kings" of the panhandle—thus commenced the "long drives" that first headed to Abilene and several other Kansas towns including Dodge City in the western part of the state, prodding herds of as many as twenty-five hundred. Between 1865 and 1885, well over five million head of cattle made the trek north out of Texas, destined for the stockyards of Chicago and, to a lesser extent, St. Louis, Omaha, and Kansas City. But as the railheads multiplied and the spatial conflicts intensified between the cattle drovers and the rapidly increasing agricultural settlements, a new economic configuration came into being. Using the recently patented barbed wire (1874) to contain the livestock and drawing upon substantial supplies of investment capital from the Northeast and Great Britain, large ranches spread through the middle and northern plains, virtually to the foothills of the Rocky Mountains, from Kansas and Colorado up to Wyoming and Montana, and across to the Dakotas (the young Theodore Roosevelt bought two of them there). The Swan Land and Cattle Company, which included nearly thirteen thousand square miles of grazing land in southeastern Wyoming, was organized by Scottish investors in 1883 and managed by Alexander Swan, who had been born in Pennsylvania and handled livestock in Ohio and Iowa before landing in Wyoming with his brothers in 1874. Small wonder that the Wyoming Stock Growers' Association, something in the manner of the Anaconda Company in neighboring Montana, became "the unchallenged sovereign of the Territory of Wyoming."

Large-scale capitalist agriculture, which dwarfed the plantations of the older South, was also the product of the postwar western developmental scramble. The most enduring was to be found in California, where sizable Mexican land grants and the costs of irrigation gave way to huge wheat farms, thousands of acres in size. Heavily mechanized from the outset, with combines and steam-powered tractors in the fields, they were operated by a small corps of managers and full-time laborers supplemented by the work of migrant crews—Chinese, Mexican, southern European—during the harvest. By the 1880s, California ranked second only to Minnesota as a wheat producer in the United States, and the vertical organization of the estates there clearly pointed to the agribusinesses that would dominate the state's central valleys in the twentieth century.

More spectacular still were the "bonanza" farms of the Dakotas that rose phoenixlike from the ashes of depression in the 1870s. Indeed, it was the failure of Jay Cooke's Northern Pacific Railway, having just reached Bismarck in 1873, that planted the seeds of these mega-farms, after the company exchanged its depreciated securities for land grants along the fertile Red River valley. By 1880, the Northern Pacific had disposed of almost 3 million acres of land, much of it to investors from the Northeast and Britain, and "farms" of up to 100,000 acres (the average of all was about 7,000 acres) took shape. As in California, they were heavily mechanized, often run by managers or leaseholders, and reliant on gangs of migrant laborers, some of whom worked seasonally in the lumber camps of northern Minnesota and many moving between city and country in search of work, as they followed the wheat harvest north from Kansas toward the Canadian border. When the subsequent depression of the 1890s threw these highly profitable bonanza operations into crisis, most were parceled off and either sold or rented to farm families, who nonetheless maintained, on a smaller scale, the capitalist relations that agriculture on the Great Plains seemed to require: cultivating large tracts of land with the aid of expensive machines and seasonal hired labor.

The great boom in the production of wheat and other grains from the Great Plains to California not only thrust the trans-Mississippi West into the expanding circuits of international commodity markets but also had transformative consequences for growers in other parts of the United States. Especially hard hit were agriculturalists in the Northeast and along the Atlantic Seaboard whose relatively small and soil-exhausted farms could not compete with their sprawling, capital-intensive counterparts to the west. Struggling to make ends meet by exploiting their own labor and looking for outside sources of cash, many began to abandon or sell their properties, sometimes to the urban middle and upper classes who looked for summer homes or rural retreats. Meanwhile, their sons and daughters increasingly left the countryside. But as the urban population of New England and the Middle Atlantic continued to swell with rural in-migration and new transatlantic arrivals, growing numbers turned from grain to dairy and truck farming to supply the burgeoning food markets of Boston, New York, Newark, Philadelphia, Baltimore, and smaller proximate cities with milk, cheese, fruits, and vegetables. And now, in a similar fashion, though on a much smaller scale than was true in the West, they came to rely on intensive cultivation (plowing and weeding machines along with fertilizers) and migrant labor—sometimes recent European immigrants, sometimes African Americans if they were farther to the south—to bring in the delicate harvest.

Bonanza farming notwithstanding, the staple grains of wheat and corn continued to be raised chiefly by family farmers whose search for breathing space moved the center of production westward from the states of Indiana, Illinois, Wisconsin, and Missouri, onto the prairies of Kansas, Nebraska, Minnesota, and the Dakotas. Unlike the big estates, these farmers generally looked to cultivate grains destined for national and international markets along with a range of other crops and livestock that might be sold regionally or consumed by the farm household itself, much as they had done for years across the antebellum American countryside. That they had long depended on face-to-face exchange relations and local sources of credit enabled them, like peasant producers in many parts of the world, to retain flexibility in the face of market uncertainties (though not to avoid conflicts and lawsuits with their neighbors) and to make strategic shifts in their crop mixes for the sake of maintaining economic independence. Practices such as these organized much of rural life as agricultural settlers migrated across western New York and Pennsylvania and into the Midwest. On the eve of the War of the Rebellion they remained dominant even with the market intensifications of the last antebellum decades.

What changed in the postwar era, and especially after the panic of 1873, was not so much the structure and relations of family farming as the world of exchange and credit in which these farmers engaged. To be sure, prairie agriculture brought a host of challenges that farming east of the Mississippi, with its abundant rainfall, ample woodlands, and more fertile soils had not. Smaller homesteads were no longer sufficient to provide a livelihood, even a modest one. And mechanization, itself hastened by the war (though the patents had mostly been taken out beforehand), required further expense. Yet there were now new sets of financial operatives, new lenders, on the scene, residing no longer in the rural and small-town districts but rather in more distant urban centers, who extended mortgages to cover the costs of land and farm equipment and, in turn, bundled the mortgages and sold them to individual and institutional investors mostly in the Northeast. Perhaps the biggest of the investors ran life insurance companies, many founded in the 1840s and 1850s. They had come to see fields of possibility in the agricultural areas, just as savings banks saw potential depositors among urban workers. Interest rates on these mortgages did not reach the exorbitant levels characteristic of liens in the South; eastern and western rates increasingly converged. But the mortgages had to be paid off in a few years (usually five), and they demanded substantial balloon payments at the end. Thus, somewhat in the manner of the yeomanry in the up-country of the southern states, the circuits of finance capital pressed western farmers to devote more and more of their acreage to staple crops, whether wheat, corn, or, in the upper Midwest, dairy products.

It should be no surprise, therefore, that grains and other agricultural commodities began to flood the market. But the glut was a global, not merely a national, phenomenon. Just as the Great Plains were drawn—by new rail lines, new financial instruments, and many new urban mouths to feed—into the vortex of international trade, so too were the Russian and Austro-Hungarian steppes, the Argentine pampas, the Canadian prairies, and the Australian outback. World wheat production more than doubled during the second half of the nineteenth century, and it grew especially fast between 1870 and 1890. And unlike earlier examples of agricultural expansion, this was both far greater in its geographical reach and far more tenacious in its social grip: not just the extension of the international market economy, but the fastening of capitalist relations.

The Peculiarities of Industrialization

However one chooses to date the advent of American industrialization—with the rise of textile mills in the early nineteenth century, the economic boom that followed the panic of 1837, or the government-supported projects of the war and its immediate aftermath—an important shift occurred between 1860 and 1900. On the eve of the War of the Rebellion, the country's leading industries were oriented to what are called consumer goods, to the production of cottons and woolens, ready-made clothing, boots and shoes, hats, lumber, and flour, as had long been the case whenever agricultural and small-town communities prevailed. Where mechanization or the division of labor had become most advanced (as in textiles and the garment trades), the workforce would chiefly comprise women and children; otherwise, male artisans, journeymen, and skilled craftsmen reigned supreme, sometimes tenaciously, sometimes in the face of rapidly eroding conditions.

By the end of the century, however, a very different industrial economy had taken shape. Consumer goods had been equaled if not surpassed in importance by "capital goods" (iron and steel, machine tools, rubber, petroleum, metal refining, and chemicals); the size and scale of manufacturing establishments had increased substantially; the proportion of the labor force involved in industrial production had jumped severalfold; artisan shops had been marginalized and semiskilled operatives had come to do the greatest share of the work; and the country had emerged as the leading industrial powerhouse in the world. The story is of course familiar, told often in texts and survey lectures. Yet the arc of change was neither smooth nor incremental. New factories often absorbed rather than transformed more traditional methods of production even as they became steadily mechanized, and skilled craftsmen struggled to maintain their technical expertise and traditional authority over the manufacturing process even as their workplaces moved from small shops to much larger shop floors. In many cases, "the manager's brain" remained "under the workman's cap." Battles on several fronts would be necessary before a new industrial order could be consolidated. But whatever the form of organization and wherever the "brains" resided, the wage relation had dramatically extended its reach and rested at the heart of the manufacturing enterprise.

Working for wages had once been imagined as a relatively temporary condition, a stepping-stone on the path to economic independence or settled family life. Young and inexperienced males might labor as apprentices, journeymen, tenants, and farm laborers until they had the resources and tools to set up their shops or cultivate their own farms; females might labor as domestic servants, outworkers, or textile hands until they married and took charge of their own households. Yet as early as the 1870s, there could be no mistaking the trend: two-thirds of productively engaged Americans worked for wages, and the road to independence had become increasingly bumpy and challenging to traverse.

In good part, this was the result of the market intensifications that had swept through town and countryside in the Northeast, the Middle Atlantic, and the Midwest during the decades before the War of the Rebellion and brought larger segments of a rapidly growing population into the new cash and credit nexus. Economic and demographic pressures were simultaneously pushing farm households to produce more crops for sale and encouraging sons and daughters to look elsewhere for work—as New England farm girls had been doing since the second decade of the nineteenth century—to support either the family or themselves. Rural to urban migrations, either seasonal or more permanent, flowed first toward smaller towns in the agricultural districts and then to larger cities along the East Coast and at strategic locations in the interior. New York and Philadelphia grew in size, but not as dramatically as Chicago, Pittsburgh, St. Louis, and Buffalo or, especially, as the small commercial and manufacturing cities of Milwaukee, Minneapolis, Grand Rapids, Terre Haute, Toledo, Syracuse, Jersey City, Bridgeport, and Fall River, where populations doubled and tripled. And there, migrants, whether working jobs as clerks, skilled tradesmen, mill hands, domestic servants, seamstresses, in railroad shops, or on construction crews, mostly labored for wages.

Yet the spread of wage labor was also part of an industrial regime marked by great diversity. The largest cities, which were also important transshipment centers, had the most complex economic foundations (New York, Philadelphia, Chicago). The clothing trades and food processing generally assumed major importance given the needs of the cities' inhabitants and were characterized less by mechanization than by more elaborate divisions of labor. Other types of manufacturing ran the gamut, varying by the commodities being produced and the settings of production. For the most part, they were small- to medium-sized shops and factories owned and operated by individuals and partnerships, but they ran alongside sprawling railroad yards and teeming docks with their hierarchies of employers, supervisors, and workers.

One-industry—or one-industry-dominant—towns were nonetheless to be found in the textile and shoe centers of New England (Lowell, Lawrence, Fall River, and Lynn, Massachusetts; Manchester, New Hampshire), the coal-mining districts of northeastern Pennsylvania and the lower Midwest (Scranton and Wilkes-Barre, Pennsylvania; Braidwood, Illinois), the iron- and steel-making hubs of western Pennsylvania (Pittsburgh and surrounding towns), or places (many in the South and the trans-Mississippi West) where lumber was cut and minerals extracted. But into the 1870s, the pace of industrial development seemed most intense and robust in smaller towns that usually combined manufacturing and transportation with links to the surrounding countryside: Wilmington, Delaware, Trenton, New Jersey, Waterbury, Connecticut, and Providence, Rhode Island, up the Atlantic coast; Schenectady, Utica, Buffalo, and Rochester in western New York; Reading, Harrisburg, and Altoona in central Pennsylvania; Akron, Toledo, Zanesville, and Grand Rapids in Ohio and Michigan; Pueblo, Colorado, Butte, Montana, and Virginia City, Nevada, in the mountain West. Here resided a significant portion of the industrial workforce in postwar America.

The dynamism of smaller industrial towns reflected the persisting importance of craft organization, the limited authority of employers in the production process, and the social composition of the labor force. Although textile mills—incorporated, financed by merchant capital, heavily mechanized, and dependent on semiskilled operatives—are icons of the Industrial Revolution, they remained exceptions to the rule until late in the nineteenth century. Most manufacturing establishments of the 1860s and 1870s were small in scale (fewer than ten employees), owned by men who likely emerged out of the ranks of artisans and master craftsmen, and reliant upon the traditional craft techniques of skilled workers who were chiefly native-born (mining was an exception) and drawn from the town or nearby rural areas. The great influx of Irish immigrants in the 1840s and early 1850s had only begun to tip the ethnic balances of industrial workplaces in the largest cities; elsewhere, native-born workers still predominated, supplemented by skill-bearing immigrants from Britain, Germany, and other parts of northern and western Europe.

Even so, the productive process took a bewildering range of forms, depending in good measure on the nature of the industry and the extent of mechanization.

At times, manufactories would be little more than enlarged artisan shops where employees continued to control the pace and organization of work. At times, highly skilled workers at various stages of production would hire and supervise their own helpers (as with iron puddlers and rollers or coal miners) or would effectively serve as subcontractors inside the manufacturing establishments (as in many machine and munitions shops). At times, as the division of labor became more complex, skilled craft workers labored alongside semiskilled operatives and other machine tenders (as in the partially mechanized shoe industry). At times, a small corps of craftsmen put their wares out to nearby shops or dwellings for finishing (as in high-end clothing). And at times, as in the sweated garment and ready-made clothing trades, labor-intensive piecework in tenements might be tethered to forms of outwork. In all this, the industrial landscape of smaller towns and large cities had a great deal in common, even if it was a raft of forms and contexts.

Thus, while the wage relation had become the common denominator, the markets in which labor was contracted formed something of a patchwork. Although the abolition of slavery effectively "nationalized" the "market" as the arbiter of labor relations, employers and prospective employees usually met each other in marketplaces that were highly localized and fragmented owing to the levels of skill required and to the distribution of workers as to gender, race, and place of birth. Regional wage differentials abounded. Craftsmen, especially those still able to protect their trades (sometimes by means of formal organization), could give significant shape to the conditions of their labor, the wages and benefits they received, and the competition to which they would be subjected. Other sections of the workforce faced greater vulnerabilities but also discrete opportunities depending on the local labor supply. Foreign-born males (about one-third of all industrial workers in 1870) were found disproportionately in iron and steel, textiles, and especially mining, though far less so in printing, lumbering, and milling. Females, irrespective of nationality, were overwhelmingly in the garment and shoe trades, and even there mainly in lesser-skilled jobs. Native-born males who lacked skills or worked in seasonal industries were often on the move, mostly in limited perimeters involving town and country but sometimes over considerable distances; their prospects as to wages and conditions would vary depending on their numbers and whether public works projects were under way and able to bid on their services. For their part, African Americans, nine-tenths of whom lived in the southern states, had few employment possibilities outside agriculture there because of state and local legislation that hedged them in, informal understandings among employers that limited alternatives, and racist practices that knew no regional boundaries and prevented their hiring.

The structural complexities of the labor process and the balkanized character of labor markets deepened the economic crisis of the 1870s and pointed the capitalists who weathered the storm in new directions. In important respects, the panic of 1873 and its aftermath marked less the domino effect of an international market collapse than the end of a business cycle—a "long swing"—of about a quarter century in duration. The indicators were abundant. The dramatic economic growth of the 1840s and 1850s, which peaked somewhere between 1847 and 1854, had begun to slacken during the 1860s despite the demands of war. The value added per worker was in sharp decline. The cost of raw materials was increasing faster than the selling price of manufactured goods. Profits, while strong in some sectors, were lagging or falling in others. And much of the problem seemed related to the organization of manufacturing itself: its small scale that fostered intense competition; its craft methods that limited productivity even as industrial output rose; its volatile labor markets that squeezed manufacturers who were already close to the margin; and the cost of necessary credit. Abram Hewitt, the Trenton ironmaster, could fret that fewer than "ten families in the United States" had been "successful" in his business, and he claimed that "employers generally are very uneasy because manufacturing has not been profitable." Little wonder that Republicans who hoped to advance the interests of small manufacturers and other "producers" championed tariff protection and inflation, fighting against the contraction of greenbacks and a return to the gold standard. Their political defeat, evident well before the panic, would strike a telling blow to this constituency and the world it hoped to preserve.

But the direction of change would be charted on the factory floors and in their offices. Although some of the early forays took place during the 1860s, the 1870s and 1880s saw the beginnings of an extended period of exploration and experimentation in search of alternatives to the traditional methods. Often, the impetus came from owners and managers who started careers outside their particular industry or trade but who had acquired a larger view of the economy, an awareness of technological advances and their potential prospects, a sense of the interconnections between production and marketing on a substantial scale, and a familiarity with new bureaucratic forms of administration. Not surprisingly, more than a few had experience working in railroad companies or in merchandising; some had training as engineers or served in the military. They had become acquainted with the challenges posed by a national and international economy, large-scale organizations, and new means of mobilizing investment capital. They complained that customary practices of manufacture were "chaotic" and "wasteful" and that the costs of production were difficult to determine. They thought that factories were in need of better administration and that organization should be prescribed by managers from above rather than skilled workers from below, especially as those factories grew in size. And they increasingly viewed competition as a major source of their woes, cutting into profits and creating instabilities across the economy.

As organizational innovators, they proceeded on several fronts. They sought to mechanize more and more of the labor process both to increase productivity and to undercut the control traditionally exercised by skilled workers and craftsmen. They attempted to add specialized tasks so that semiskilled operatives could replace craft workers. Some even experimented with techniques that anticipated later assembly lines. They looked to shift supervisory authority away from foremen, who invariably came out of the ranks of artisans or highly skilled workers, and put it more firmly in the hands of their own hired staffs. They tried to implement cost accounting and related administrative methods. And they moved to take charge of as much of the market for their products and to integrate as many stages in the course of production and distribution as possible.

The path was not a smooth one. Skilled workers fiercely defended their places and prerogatives, making for an era of unprecedented labor conflict. Smaller manufacturers and shippers pushed back against the massive concentrations of wealth and power that were being created and undermining their ability to compete. Reformers worried deeply about the social and political price of the great transformation under way. For the next two decades, the changes would be haphazard and difficult to measure and the opposition formidable. But by the end of the century, the balances clearly tilted toward the organizational dynamics of the new industrialism. The size of factories and plants, especially those involved with the production of steel, textiles, machinery, electrical goods, chemicals, and glass, had more than doubled. Some now employed over a thousand workers, and the very largest could employ nearly ten thousand. The horsepower per worker had grown by leaps and bounds—by 8 percent in the 1870s, 13 percent in the 1880s, and 36 percent in the 1890s—and craft workers were steadily being replaced by operatives whose tending skills enabled them to handle machines in a variety of industries. Equally important, the struggle to install more "rational" and "efficient" industrial management and to reorganize the marketplace for labor and products was steadily being won by owners and their technological allies, with significant aid from the state and the courts.

The developing steel empire built by Andrew Carnegie in the 1870s, 1880s, and 1890s exemplified (and often pioneered) this trajectory. A Scottish immigrant from humble roots, Carnegie had no firsthand experience making iron or steel. Indeed, he got his start, through local patronage, in the offices of the Pennsylvania Railroad and cleverly used his connections with the road's vice president, Thomas Scott, to learn about the business and about investing. During the War of the Rebellion, Scott and Carnegie both benefited from the sort of state-sponsored largesse that was empowering others in finance, manufacturing, and transportation. Owing to his superintendence of the Pennsylvania, Scott was appointed assistant secretary of war with special responsibility for government railroads, and he took Carnegie with him to Washington. There Carnegie got an expansive view of a large industrial system while busily amassing money through personal investments in companies directly or indirectly related to the railroads. By the time the war ended, Carnegie was rich and had developed interests not in the railroads but in the industry on which the railroads most depended: iron and steel.

Carnegie's initial involvements with an iron mill and bridge construction company enabled him to glimpse both the long-term prospects and, from his viewpoint, the sorry state of the industry. Despite the enormous demand for iron and steel goods, there was little integration in the production process. Coordination between producers and merchants was poor; when it came to measuring costs, there was outright ignorance. Well aware of the latest technologies—like Bessemer converters—that would enable steel to supplant iron, he managed to construct a mill by 1875 (in the midst of the depression) by raising capital through an extended partnership that the Pennsylvania legislature enabled and by selling rails to the Pennsylvania Railroad (he named the mill after a former Pennsylvania Railroad president, Edgar Thomson). But he also insisted on new accounting techniques and a new hierarchy of management run by men of his own choosing who shared his devotion to cutting costs, especially by holding down wages and substituting machines for skilled workers. Over the next decade and a half, Carnegie expanded his facilities, integrated his operations, diversified his product line, and began to take control of the raw materials flow by purchasing iron ore mines and coke smelters. When the reckoning came in the 1890s, with a bitter strike at his huge plant in Homestead, Pennsylvania, he had a strong hand to play.

As the dominant force in steelmaking, Carnegie relished competition. He had the resources, energy, and personnel, and he expected to win. But few of his counterparts in the industrial world of the latter nineteenth century shared his view. They considered competition destructive and inefficient, a threat to their investments and a nasty inconvenience. Thus, just as owners and managers began to experiment with methods to transform the productive process, so they began to explore new avenues of consolidation. One was incorporation, which enabled companies to raise capital through stock subscriptions, protected investors from excessive liability for company debt, allowed their shares to be traded, separated ownership and management, and provided long-term stability. Corporations did, of course, have a history extending back into the eighteenth century, and hundreds of them were established during the first half of the nineteenth. But these corporations were usually in the public interest—banks and means of transportation—and, for the most part, were specially chartered by state legislatures. Although a few states, beginning with New York, enacted general incorporation laws before the War of the Rebellion, it was during and immediately after the war that most of the others followed suit, suggesting new ways in which states might facilitate private development. For a time, significant questions hung over the process—what exactly was a corporation as a social and legal entity? A great many industrial concerns, Carnegie's included until the 1890s, remained owned by individuals, families, and partnerships. But the vector of change was evident.

Competition proved a thornier problem, all the more so after the panic of 1873, and especially for industries with high fixed costs and limited room to maneuver. After all, competition was celebrated in many quarters as the basis of the market economy and a hedge against the danger of monopolies; political discourse and public policy still favored petty producers and frowned on practices that could do them harm. Yet there was no shortage of experimentation. One of the early experimenters was John D. Rockefeller. Having made thousands of dollars marketing agricultural commodities during the War of the Rebellion—the U.S. Army was one of his customers—Rockefeller turned his attention first to railroads and then to the petroleum that was recently discovered in the northwestern Pennsylvania countryside. With some business partners, he constructed an oil refinery in nearby Cleveland that was soon turning out an impressive fifteen hundred barrels a day. But Rockefeller looked beyond technology to gain the upper hand. He began, as Carnegie did in steel, to buy out rival refineries. He then cut secret deals with railroad companies to reduce their shipping rates for his oil and thereby permit him to sell the oil—chiefly kerosene for lighting at this point—more cheaply in eastern markets. Before long, he offered competitors cash or company stock to join a conglomerate under his control to keep costs and prices in line. It was multifaceted and extremely clever, though also unwieldy and of dubious legality. Little by little, however, he took his company, known as Standard Oil, toward a solution that would have traction.

Even more experimentation involved the railroads themselves. Saddled with enormous construction and equipment costs and heavy debt loads, they could easily buckle when faced with ambitious competitors and destructive rate wars.

This was particularly true for lines east of the Mississippi River—already rocked by the effects of the panic—where most of the track and freight business was still concentrated. The resulting uncertainties chilled the hearts of investors, shippers, and managers alike. "There is no steadiness, no system, no fixedness for anything," the Chicago newspaper editor Joseph Medill complained, "and the whole country is kept to a tremor of expectancy as to whether prices are going up or going down from this unregulated cause." Some of the roads looked to control the shipping end either by buying out the shippers (as occurred in the anthracite region of eastern Pennsylvania) or by offering them special "rebates" for their business. Others leagued together to divide up freight traffic and manage freight rates by forming "pools" and rate associations among themselves. Still others, if they had access to the capital, purchased smaller trunk lines and expanded the reach of their rail network. Greed surely spawned some of the creativity, though, in this case, to relatively limited effect. Pools were notoriously difficult to enforce and, together with rebates, rate fixing, and consolidation, courted public hostility. At all events, further experimentation seemed necessary, and as was true among manufacturers and managers, there was a growing recognition by the 1880s that some sort of system building would be required.

What gave industrialists special leverage over time were migrations on a scale the country had never before seen. The migrants came chiefly from rural areas not in the United States but in southern and eastern Europe and southern Asia. They came from Russia and Poland, Hungary and the Balkans, Greece and Italy, the Iberian Peninsula and the Baltic states, and from southeastern China. They were the products—in many cases the refugees—of forces creating new political economies across much of the globe: transoceanic empires; the expanding reach of international trade; the emancipation of peasants, slaves, and religious minorities; the ensuing commodification of land and labor; the industrialization of northwestern Europe; and the construction of nation-states on the European continent. Well over half of the entire population of Europe was on the move over the course of the nineteenth century, searching for secure berths in the rapidly changing countryside or relocating to the cities where commerce and industry offered the prospect of work. But somewhere between forty and fifty million of them left entirely, for Algeria, Tunisia, Egypt, and the Levant, for Argentina, Uruguay, Brazil, and the Caribbean basin, for South Africa, Australia, and New Zealand, and, in the greatest numbers by far, for North America. Roughly two-thirds of them ended up in the United States, either permanently or temporarily—an influx larger than the entire U.S. population in 1860—joining thousands of migrants from other parts of the world, such as the extended hinterlands of Guangdong, China (most of whom traveled to other parts of southern Asia) and the modernizing stretches of northern Mexico.

The most organized of these migrations, managed mainly by a group of San Francisco–based Chinese merchants known as the Six Companies, brought nearly 200,000 workers (overwhelmingly male) from various parts of southeastern China between the late 1840s and the early 1880s. Making labor arrangements through Six Companies agents once they arrived in San Francisco (it was not formally contract labor, though it had many of the features, including debt), they headed principally to the gold-mining districts of the Sierras, where they received a mixed greeting. By the 1860s, when the surface deposits of the mines had been tapped out, many were hired by railroad companies, the Central Pacific especially, to lay track across the difficult terrain of the interior West. But others were to be found in a range of occupations requiring heavy labor and personal service: on farms and ranches, in factories, and as launderers and domestics. By 1870, they might have composed nearly one-tenth of California's total population and as much as one-fifth of all those gainfully employed there.

The immigration of eastern and southern Europeans was many times larger in scale and far more extended in duration than that of the Chinese. Flowing through the portals of New York City, it was also much less tightly orchestrated. Contract labor assumed very limited importance despite enabling legislation enacted by Congress during the War of the Rebellion, and few labor agents worked on the eastern side of the Atlantic. New steamship companies did post advertisements in European ports as to the opportunities that might be found in the United States, but for the most part migrants followed the trails already carved by their families, villages, and ethnic groups—"chains" of kith and kin as they have come to be known. These were supplemented by the involvement of labor agents and padrones who combed the docks on the western side of the Atlantic to recruit workers (and sometimes strikebreakers) for steel and textile mills and especially for mines, lumber camps, agricultural operations, and railroads in the trans-Mississippi West. Together, international channels of migration and communication such as these helped create new national and international labor markets.

Those many millions of migrants who arrived after the early 1870s not only swelled the size of industrializing American cities but made for growing ethnic enclaves within them. Unlike the British and German immigrants of the first half of the nineteenth century—though very much like the Irish immigrants of the 1840s and 1850s—they had few skills associated with manufacturing, and their cultural traditions—language, religion, forms of sociability—stood them apart from the native-born mainstream. Most of them had been peasants or had lived in agricultural communities destabilized by the spread of commerce and market relations; many imagined short stays in the United States before accumulating the resources to return to their countries of origin. What they all possessed, irrespective of their ethnic and cultural roots, was the muscle and wherewithal to labor long hours at tasks that could be quickly learned and to tend machines that were taking the place of skilled workers and craftsmen.

Threads of Discourse

For all of its associations with historical modernity, the United States offered up a complex cultural environment for the development of capitalism. Although the country's colonial settlement came in the midst of a massive expansion of international—and especially Atlantic—trade, there was something of a redeployment of forms of peasant agriculture and coerced labor that continued to mark the economic life of Europe, from the Atlantic to the Urals and from the Baltic to the Mediterranean, even after the crumbling of feudalism and feudaltype relations. The North American continent was already filled with a diverse array of Native peoples who, like their European counterparts, engaged in warfare and dense networks of exchange but who also had distinctive divisions of labor and ownership regimes that widely rejected private (especially landed) property. The plantations of the Chesapeake and the Carolinas might have faced the Atlantic and contributed to transnational accumulations of capital, but they were worked by black slaves who were tied to their masters and unable to enter any markets of their own volition or necessity. The farming communities that spread across New England and the Middle Atlantic and into the backcountry South depended chiefly on family (dependent) labor, recognized both private property and common use rights, and generally combined subsistence agriculture with the marketing of surpluses. They responded to market opportunities, though often with great caution.

The ambiguous place of expanding markets in the lives of North Americans found powerful cultural expression whether in the Native cosmologies that tied material goods principally to the satisfaction of communal and spiritual needs or in the tenets of Puritanism that saw prosperity as a measure of God's blessings but frowned on greed, worldly vanities, and competitive behavior. The First and Second Great Awakenings—themselves born at moments of social strain and market intensifications—might then have challenged established hierarchies and provided new emphases on human agency and personal responsibility and might have reinforced certain character traits more compatible with a market society and bestowed cultural authority on an emerging middle class. Yet well into the nineteenth century, suspicions of the market's reach, its faceless qualities, its deceptions and duplicitous representatives (exemplified in the figure of the "confidence man"), pervaded popular culture and influenced a range of responses, from communitarian experiments and reassertions of patriarchalism to attacks on banks and paper money. Even among the urban middle classes, the ideology of domesticity and separate spheres consecrated the rough-hewn male world of the market while providing what was thought to be a necessary refuge in the female-dominated and sentimentally laden world of the home.

The political culture offered no clear resolution to the ambiguities of the marketplace and, in many respects, raised formidable doubts about it. While republican ideology fortified the colonial critique of British imperial rule and made possible the creation of a union governed by merchants, gentry, and slaveholders, it also failed to provide a secure place for many of the people on whom the market depended: those who owned little in the way of property and had to do the market's work. The Republic, as political theorists argued, relied for its survival on those who were independent and could know the public good, but it was always threatened by the multitudes who were left without means of subsistence and might form a constituency for tyrants. And independence, as the Americans who embraced republicanism understood it, was defined in economic terms and thus demanded ownership of some sort of productive property. Those who, by circumstance or personal failure, lacked the means of economic independence fell into the category of "dependency," worthy of nothing but fear and scorn and certainly not of any official status in the arenas of politics. They were hardly better than slaves.

Liberal sensibilities and discourses that imagined a rather different world of autonomous individuals pursuing their self-interest could surely be identified in elite political circles by the last quarter of the eighteenth century. James Madison, who, in *Federalist* 10, famously challenged the conventional wisdom by arguing that a republic would be best secured in a large territory (such as the United States) with many diverse interests, no one of which could dominate the others, adumbrated some of the important intellectual lineaments. But it was among the abolitionists and their close allies that the liberal alternative to republicanism would achieve especially powerful articulation and traction. The essence of freedom, abolitionists insisted, was not to be found in the economic independence that republicanism prized or in the virtuous quest for the public good that republicans celebrated; it was rather to be found in the personal independence that self-ownership made possible and, of course, that slavery fundamentally denied. With emancipation, the abolitionist William Jay proclaimed, the slave "is free, and his own master, and can ask for no more." For the Quakers and evangelicals among them, self-ownership enabled individuals to establish direct relations with God or to follow the directives of the inner light. In no other way could God's kingdom come to earth. But for all of the abolitionists, as well as for growing numbers of reformers of the 1830s, 1840s, and 1850s, self-ownership permitted people to act in ways that social harmony and progress demanded: to discipline themselves, improve their circumstances, better their character, respond to material incentives, raise their children properly, cultivate the senses, and look meaningfully to the future.

To be sure, neither abolitionists nor like-minded social reformers of the day saw themselves advancing the interests of capitalism; most shared misgivings about the market's effects then abroad in the culture. They worried especially about the dislocations that market economies appeared to provoke. Yet by effectively detaching "freedom" from republican notions of economic independence and embedding it in individual self-ownership, they implicitly called into question many forms of coercive authority while lending moral legitimacy to the sorts of market relations that could otherwise be eyed with fear and suspicion. By the early postwar era, some, in their rhetoric, would thereby naturalize the "market" as a basic arena of human interaction and regard its dynamics as veritable "laws" of human nature.

They did so in the face of serious challenges to the world as they imagined it. Influenced by the classical political economists from Adam Smith and David Ricardo to John Stuart Mill, these liberals assumed that self-ownership and the pursuit of self-interest would set the balances of society on a self-regulating trajectory to the benefit of all. Indeed, once the thrall of slavery and servitude had been removed, self-ownership would facilitate a liberation as complete as individual character and ambition allowed. William Lloyd Garrison was not alone among abolitionists in believing that with the passage of the Thirteenth Amendment their goals had been achieved and freedpeople now had to fend for themselves. But what if those who labored—on the land in the South or in factories in the North—found self-ownership an empty promise amid inequalities of wealth and resources, not to mention a weak shield against the power and exploitation of their employers? What if they sought to reduce the long hours that they worked or improve their prospects for economic independence through land reform and political rights? What if they rejected the idea that self-ownership and self-interest alone would allow them to fulfill their aspirations and instead demanded the intervention of the state?

These challenges began to tear liberals away from their association with Radicalism. Some had long-standing doubts about the economic policies of the Republican Party, especially its embrace of the protective tariff; some had been wedded to the gold standard and were aghast at the monetary excesses of greenbacks, even in the service of military victory. What they had in common was a personal or family history in the antislavery movement and a cultural heritage in Yankee, Protestant New England. Once the campaign against slavery seemed at an end, their other differences with Radical Republicanism appeared more obvious, all the more so as Radicals pressed for civil and political equality for the former slaves and, in some cases, for land reform. Led by Edwin L. Godkin, David Ames Wells, Charles Eliot Norton, Edward Atkinson, Horace White, Henry Adams, and Francis Amasa Walker, liberal intellectuals came to command the pages of the *Nation* (appropriately founded in 1865), *Harper's Weekly*, the *North American Review*, *Scribner's Monthly*, and the *Atlantic Monthly*—the periodicals most widely read by the northern middle and upper classes—and advance their critique of the ill-conceived or "corrupt" practices they saw around them: whether workers' calls for an eight-hour workday or governments established in the former Confederacy by coalitions of "trashy whites" and "ignorant negroes." Radicals like Wendell Phillips, whose sympathies remained with laboring folk and who continued to embrace state activism on their behalf, were increasingly isolated within the Republican Party.

The cultural and political influence of the liberals gained greater ground in the 1870s owing to convulsions on both sides of the Atlantic. The expansion of trade unionism, the organization of the International Workingmen's Association (1864, also known as the First International), the brief rule of the Paris Commune (1871), and then the panic of 1873 together suggested the great dangers that "class" sensibilities and state-sponsored experimentation might bring. Liberal intellectuals like Godkin soured on the prospects of the freedpeople and questioned their readiness for the rights and responsibilities that had been extended to them. He and other liberals bridled at the inflationary schemes that won support from workers and farmers in the throes of the deep depression. They associated urban political corruption with the teeming population of poor European immigrants. And they increasingly questioned whether popular democracy was the best method of governance in a rapidly industrializing society. Whatever sympathies they might have had for producers, workingmen, and former slaves were now realigned in the direction of employers, wherever they were to be found.

Small wonder that the works of the Englishman Herbert Spencer and the American (of English descent) William Graham Sumner won a warm reception in new elite circles. Born in 1820 to a family of relatively humble, religious nonconformists, Spencer was trained as a civil engineer and, after becoming enamored of developing ideas in physics and biology, sought to combine the two in an ethical system. Although he is regarded as a social Darwinist, Spencer's views both preceded and anticipated Darwinism and suggested that *The Origin of Species* (1859) emerged in an environment in which a good deal of the intellectual material had been prepared in the cauldrons of natural science, political economy, and British industrialism. Appearing in 1851, his first book, *Social Statics*, argued that ethical progress was driven by human adaptation to the conditions of existence. Spencer had little but contempt for those reformers—especially the disciples of Jeremy Bentham—who hoped to use legislation for the goal of social improvement, and he staunchly opposed state interference in either the economy or civil society, especially if it looked to benefit the poor. It was he, not Darwin, who wrote of the "survival of the fittest."

With the publication of his multivolume *A System of Synthetic Philosophy*, commencing in 1860, Spencer won a growing audience in the United States, especially among those who were in, or moving into, the liberal mold. "Mr. Herbert Spencer is already a power in the world," the *Atlantic Monthly* observed in 1864, and he "represents the scientific spirit of the age . . . the principles which . . . will become the recognized basis of an improved society." Over the next three decades, Spencer's ideas became intellectual touchstones for Gilded Age liberals as well as for many of the American thinkers—William James, Josiah Royce, John Dewey—who were coming to maturity and would leave their marks on twentieth-century philosophy and social thought. But the scope of his influence was far wider and deeper. The labor economist John R. Commons, who claimed to have been "brought up on Hoosierism, Republicanism, Presbyterianism, and Spencerism," recalled that during his boyhood "everyone" living in the "eastern section of Indiana" was "a follower of Herbert Spencer who was then the shining light of evolution and individualism." By the turn of the twentieth century, nearly 400,000 copies of Spencer's books had been sold in the United States.

Among those most influenced by Spencer was William Graham Sumner. Very much in the manner of his intellectual mentor, Sumner was the son of an English artisan who had fled the effects of the new factory system, settled—ironically—in the industrializing town of Paterson, New Jersey, and instructed the family in the values of hard work and self-reliance, even though he died impoverished. Twenty years Spencer's junior, Sumner would acquaint college students with Spencerian ideas in the sociology course he taught at Yale, a post he took up in the early 1870s after a short run as an Episcopalian minister. His invocation of a social "struggle for existence" and his role in popularizing evolution have often given Sumner, like Spencer, the label of "social Darwinist," but his thought was as much beholden to classical political economy (his chair at Yale) and Protestant values as to Darwinian natural selection (he never mentioned Darwin in his writings).

Sumner's book *What Social Classes Owe to Each Other* (1883) was a critique of the activism of the state, an encomium to the principles of laissez-faire, and a vilification of the "pauper," a central figure in the political economy of the day who, in Sumner's view, drained taxpayers and the rest of society of their resources. His answer to the question posed by the book's title was "nothing." More generally, Sumner spent a good deal of his time in the 1870s and 1880s writing and speaking against protectionism, reformism, socialism, and government assistance to the poor while participating in the movement for free trade. "The State," he argued, owed nothing to "anybody" except "peace, order, and the guarantee of rights." Only in the face of escalating social conflict in the United States would he move toward an academic interest in cultural folkways (*Folkways* was also the title of the work for which he is best known) and a critique of natural rights and laissez-faire in the service of social order.

Neither Sumner nor Spencer regarded himself as an advocate for the new class of large-scale capitalists coming to power or a cheerleader for the corporate capitalism that was taking shape. Sumner was in fact something of a critic, blaming them for the political corruption that seemed to pervade the state at all levels and for the protectionist policies he detested. If anything, he was a bit of a Jeffersonian at heart and celebrated "the Forgotten Man" of the middle class who went about his job, took care of his family, and asked nothing of the state. Yet he, and especially Spencer, were embraced wholeheartedly by capitalism's contemporary revolutionaries who were fashioning new relations in the workplace and the marketplace and were happy to find a language and scientific basis to explain the logic and wisdom of their projects. The railroad magnate James J. Hill and the petroleum tycoon John D. Rockefeller alike exulted that their fortunes and those of other "large businesses" were "determined by the law of the survival of the fittest" and demonstrated their "superior ability, foresight, and adaptability." "The survival of the fittest," in fact, became something of a catchphrase and mantra for those who came to sit atop the unprecedented wealth they accumulated during the Gilded Age. But it was Andrew Carnegie whose worldview might have been most transformed.

Having abandoned Calvinism and the Swedenborgians (who believed that Jesus Christ embodied God's divinity), though still struggling with issues of "theology and the supernatural," Carnegie found first in Darwin and then in Spencer "light[s] that came in as a flood" and showed him "the truth." Here, it seemed to Carnegie, was a perspective that made sense to him, that saw progress as moral as well as material, industrial society as an improvement over what came before, and "no conceivable end" to man's "march to perfection." "All is well since all grows better" became his "motto," his "true source of comfort." Seeking his way in London literary circles in the early 1880s, Carnegie finally met Spencer, whom he began to shower with attention and gifts. The fruits of what was a personal and intellectual infatuation would be in evidence in Carnegie's best-known essay, published in the *North American Review* in 1889, titled "Wealth."

Both Carnegie and William Graham Sumner were in attendance at a grand banquet held at Delmonico's in New York City to honor Herbert Spencer at the end of his seven-week visit to the United States in 1882. It was, meaningfully, an event that showed the cultural links and sociability between the Gilded Age liberals and the titans of the new industrial age. There was Godkin, Charles Dana, Charles Francis Adams, Carl Schurz, Elihu Root, the philosopher John Fiske, and the prominent ministers who embraced Darwinism, Henry Ward Beecher and Lyman Abbott. There was also the telegraph pioneer and financier Cyrus Field, the iron manufacturer Abram Hewitt, and the railroad executive Chauncey Depew. Together they feted Spencer in the most extravagant of terms; Schurz even suggested that the Civil War might have been avoided if southerners had been familiar with Spencer's *Social Statics*. And together they appeared to be satisfied with—and grateful for—the cultural authority that Spencer had offered them: a way of understanding themselves as the products of natural laws of evolutionary change, and a way of believing that the path of social evolution would be paved not by "struggle," as Darwin had posited, but by immutable and relatively harmonious progress.

Visible and Invisible Hands

It is tempting to see the popular embrace of Spencer and Sumner— as noted by John R. Commons in eastern Indiana and demonstrated by book sales across the entire country—as a manifestation of the new cultural prestige of capitalism, the normalization of social relations and dynamics that were foundational to capitalist development, and the emerging hegemony of a class of industrialists and financiers who had come to preside. Yet there is cause for skepticism. Spencerian ideas won audiences at a time of crisis and intensifying social strife in the very broad Atlantic world, and they would be bitterly contested by working people and petty proprietors in urban and rural places alike who sought, with great determination, either to hold the market at bay or to construct alternative sets of relations and values. Their resistance to the advance of capitalism would define national and international politics during the second half of the nineteenth century and well into the twentieth. Indeed, beyond the educated middle and upper classes across the United States who read the liberal-laced periodicals and heard their ministers, friends, families, teachers, fellow club members, and business partners invoke their logic and vocabulary, there is simply no way of knowing how widely or deeply the culture of capitalism became implanted in this period: east, west, north, or south.

Where intellectual sensibilities favorable to the sustenance and growth of capitalism did become embedded to enormously important effect was in the state and federal judiciary. Here both the legal traditions in which they worked and the political and class orientations that they embodied had a powerful impact. At the federal level, judicial appointees were overwhelmingly Republican, with strong ties to the moderate and conservative wings of the party (Salmon P. Chase, of the Radical camp, who became chief justice of the Supreme Court in 1864, was an exception), and overwhelmingly bourgeois in social background. Their perspectives had been shaped by a world of commerce, manufacturing, or finance, and their educations would have acquainted them with Spencerian and Darwinian ideas, the common law, and the economic instrumentalism of antebellum courts. At the state level, the playing field would seem to have been more level; most judges were elected rather than appointed, with Democrats and Republicans filling these positions. But in fact, once we move away from magistrate and other local courts, the social profiles and legal dispensations of state and federal judges were more alike than different. They came from privileged families or were sponsored by them; they were eager to expand their jurisdictional authority; they rallied around contractual freedoms; and they generally held workers accountable for pushing back against their employers' demands.

The actions of the U.S. Supreme Court, now dominated by Republican justices from the Northeast and the Midwest, are perhaps best known, though not fully appreciated in these terms. In a series of landmark decisions—the Slaughterhouse Cases (1873), *United States v. Cruikshank* (1876), the Civil Rights Cases (1883)—the Court narrowed the reach of the Thirteenth and Fourteenth Amendments, limited the extent of federal citizenship rights, and left freedpeople vulnerable to the violence and discrimination of individuals who, by the justices' reckonings, were subject only to the laws of the states in which they resided. In so doing, the Court strengthened the hands of employers (often former slaveholders) in the southern states who depended on black labor, were accustomed to using coercive methods of exploitation, and commonly resorted to paramilitarism in order to defeat strikes and other African American political mobilizations. At the same time, the Court began to sketch out new doctrines of contract and especially substantive due process (offering protections against government interference) that would not only shape American jurisprudence for years to come but also shield corporations from workers, small-business people, and the political institutions that tried to promote their interests.

But in many ways, it was the lower federal and state courts, through their interpretations of precedent and rulings in specific cases, that proved most effective
in naturalizing relations of the marketplace and enhancing the power of
employers. Indeed, there appeared to be two separate bodies of law, each with
its own principles, that came to govern commerce and manufacturing on the
one side and labor on the other. The law of labor as the courts generally saw it
was deeply laid historically, rooted in the common-law tradition, and still defined
by the centuries-old rules of master and servant, the relics of a precapitalist economic regime marked by servitude and other forms of coerced and dependent
labor. This meant that even when workers entered into contracts voluntarily,
the employer retained a property interest in the worker's labor not simply while
the worker remained on the job but over the course of the "entire" contract
should it be terminated early (the worker quitting) without what was regarded
as "legal cause." It also meant that employers had very limited liability for an
injury or death that a worker suffered owing to a workplace accident: only if it
could be shown that the employer was personally at fault and that the fault was
not shared by the employee ("contributory negligence") or caused by another
employee (the "fellow servant rule"). During the postbellum era, when the
United States achieved the dubious distinction of having the highest incidence
of industrial accidents in the world and when workers in some sectors—like
agriculture—entered into annual contracts, these rules gave employers great
leverage and left employees dangerously vulnerable.

Yet when it came to the realm of the marketplace, courts continued their
moves away from strict common-law precedent (in evidence from earlier in the
nineteenth century) and toward a set of doctrines, based fundamentally on
liberal freedom of contract, that was more flexible and pragmatic. Eventually
captured by the "rule of reason" (distinguishing between reasonable and
unreasonable restraints of trade) in antitrust jurisprudence, in the shorter term
it privileged judge-made (equity) law and invested corporations with legal per-
sonhood and thus with claims to substantive due process owing to the Fourteenth Amendment's due process clause. A rule-as-you-go mentality seemed
increasingly pervasive among judges when it came to commercial activities,
while federal courts began to provide business interests—and especially
corporations—with a haven from state- and locally based lawsuits. Whenever
state legislatures, more subject to popular influence, saw fit to intervene in the
contracting process either by limiting the hours of the legal workday or by outlawing payment in scrip rather than cash, the courts were quick to side with
employers. The Pennsylvania Supreme Court thus found a law requiring remuneration in cash "degrading and insulting" to the workers, for it attempted to
"prevent persons who are sui juris from making their own contracts." It was a

disposition that the U.S. Supreme Court would uphold in the landmark *Lochner* case of 1905.

Where the laws of commerce and labor most clearly intersected was in the arena of collective action, notably strikes, picketing, and boycotts, on the part of workers. Beginning in 1877, federal courts first stepped into the midst of large labor disputes, issuing injunctions against workers who were striking railroad lines between Baltimore and St. Louis. Many of these lines had gone bankrupt after the panic of 1873 and fell into federal receivership, and so the judges justified their decision "to extend our administrative capacity" over the roads on their "public authority for the time being." Over the next two decades, railroad strikes would be the main sites of court injunctions, often in connection with public receivership, though they established a practice that would soon be deployed against striking workers on lines that remained under private control as well as in some other large industries, especially when unions were involved. Before long, judges made use of injunctions to combat the growing incidence of citywide boycotts and sympathy strikes, which mobilized non-union and union workers, together with local residents and small businesses. These were found to be "combinations of irresponsible cabals or cliques" who sought to bring "an end to government."

At times, the injunctive process exposed the close relations between members of the judiciary, particularly at the federal level, and railroad officials and their attorneys. Some judges were, or had been, on the payroll. They might have represented railroad companies in court proceedings, served on railroad boards, or invested in the lines. But more generally it showed a meeting of the minds on the social relations of capitalism, on who was "responsible" and who "irresponsible," on private property and freedom of contract as the foundations of the public good. To be sure, more than a few judges worried about the size and power of new corporations and industrial interests, and they were ready to trim the sails of these giants to the benefit of smaller competitors. Yet they also tended to see labor mobilizations, especially those organized by unions, as far more menacing and destructive, as threats to private property and social order, and as possible manifestations of "communistic" influences that were spreading across the Atlantic. Unlike local officials, including sheriffs and town councilmen, who were part of multi-class communities and might be either sympathetic to striking workers or at least reluctant to move against them, judges were no longer socially embedded and were therefore far more likely to uphold legal principles as they saw them. When necessary, they were also happy to see the troops called in.

The railroad strike of 1877 was not only the largest and most destructive labor conflict in the nineteenth century; it also witnessed, for one of the first times, federal troops deployed to support the interests of capital. They were not the initial resort. All along the rail lines, as workers struck, governors called in militia units, only to find that they either were ineffective or openly fraternized with the strikers. This was a dilemma that hung over the landscape of intensifying social conflict. Secretary of War George McCrary, a Republican who served in the cabinet of President Rutherford B. Hayes and believed that the "Army is to the United States what a well-disciplined and trained police force is to a city," thought that the militias were "unreliable" in the face of "uprisings of large masses of people for the redress of grievances" because "such uprisings enlist in greater or lesser degree the sympathies of the communities in which they occur." Only the "coolness, steadiness, and implicit obedience to orders" of army regulars, he insisted, could deal "with an excited and exasperated mob."

Top-level army officers such as Generals William T. Sherman and Philip H. Sheridan—who had served in the War of the Rebellion and then in the South and the West during Reconstruction—thrilled at the prospect that labor unrest could help them bolster the troops and reform the service, to "Prussianize" it, as Sherman suggested. So too did Emory Upton, an army general and military strategist, who had just returned from an extended tour of Europe determined to professionalize the corps of regulars and marginalize the militia. Congress balked. The Democrats who controlled the House of Representatives after the election of 1874, southerners among them, wanted to scale back, not increase, the number of troops and officers, and they were reluctant to see U.S. soldiers on the ground in the midst of labor disputes. "You had better overhaul all the muskets and pistols in the attic," Sherman groused to his brother the Ohio senator John Sherman, "for a time will soon come when every householder must defend with firearms his own castle."

The initiative thereby fell to the state and local governments, and in some places it was already well along. Large cities like New York and Philadelphia had begun to establish uniformed police forces during the 1840s as their populations expanded with Irish Catholic immigrants and neighborhood watches and patrols proved unable to control the drinking, disorder, and violence that seemed to be exploding around them (they were commonly participants themselves). Often recruited among native- or British-born Protestant artisans whose trades seemed to be weathering the storm of market intensification, the new urban police were instructed in the use of coercion rather than persuasion, carrying billy clubs and showing an intimidating bearing. As one police chief instructed his men, "Never arrest a man until you have licked him in a fair fight first." Although more than a few of these uniformed men remained a part of the turmoil they were meant to patrol, the discipline and steadfastness of the New York police during the brutal draft riots in 1863 won notice from leaders in business and politics. Over the next three decades, the number of patrolmen in cities across the United States grew very rapidly, and some took over a number of activities of interest to municipal authorities, including surveillance of working-class meetings and organizations.

Yet perhaps the most important developments occurred among the state militias, so readily dismissed by the regular army brass. The Democrat Abram Hewitt, now of New York, the manufacturer who won a congressional seat in 1874, led the charge against regular army reform and increased appropriations by proclaiming that the states "should maintain order within their own limits" and warning that the threat of upheaval would be more dire if U.S. Army troops assumed the role of a national police force. But he took the threat very seriously and instead proposed a reinvigoration of state militias, even something of a "national militia system": reform, that is, more from the states up than from the nation down.

As it turned out, Hewitt was preaching to a growing choir. In the immediate aftermath of the railroad strike, the National Guard Association was established "to promote military efficiency throughout the active militia of the United States," and over the next decade and a half states, especially in the developing industrial belt stretching from the Northeast well out into the West, revised their military codes to provide for active and organized units, greatly increased their appropriations, and began to hold annual encampments. New armories were soon built in industrial cities across the country—away from the working-class districts there—to house, train, and supply what were now national guardsmen. The Seventh Regiment Armory in Manhattan was especially formidable, and its architecture captured the new sensibilities that inspired the construction boom: it had the appearance of an enormous fort, "pierced with loop-holes for muskets . . . so constructed as to be defensible at all points against mobs." Nationwide, the number of guardsmen/militiamen grew to over 100,000, and everywhere their main purpose was to serve as state police officers in the control and suppression of labor unrest.

Nowhere did capitalists rely more heavily on the use of force than in the West. And this was because federal, state, and territorial officials alike had deep interests—oftentimes financial—in western developmental projects. Federal troops were sent out to defeat the resistance of Native peoples to railroad building and the white settlement that accompanied it and then were left to protect the lines that were in private hands. National guardsmen were often called in by state and territorial governors to suppress labor disputes on the railroads and in the mines of the interior West, in which they might well have been personally invested. And when these military instruments did not prove sufficient or readily available, a variety of large-scale capitalists—cattle ranchers, mine owners, agricultural operators—turned to hired gunmen, vigilantes, and private armies (something in the manner of the Pinkertons) to enforce their rules and punish their adversaries.

This was a formula quite to the liking of onetime slaveholders, who neither wished to see federal troops on the ground nor pay for an expanded state militia. After all, they were used to controlling their laborers through private and quasi-private means (the discipline inflicted by themselves, their overseers, their drivers, and local slave patrols) and had long seen paramilitarism as a vital accompaniment to organized electoral politics. Vigilantes who either served as their families' clients or were directly attached to the Democratic Party played a central role in patrolling "free" labor and defeating hostile Reconstruction regimes on the local and state levels. By the 1880s, when the geographical expansion of the cotton and timber economies brought an upsurge of migrations on the part of young black laborers, lynch parties looked to enforce the submission that slavery and its generational legacies no longer could. In more than a few cases, lynching victims had run afoul of their employers and were accused of murdering them or members of their families. Sheriffs and justices of the peace generally looked the other way, if they were not directly involved themselves, as lynchers thumbed their collective noses at the "rule of law."

The role of the courts and the widespread use of state- or legally sanctioned violence to manage labor conflict seemed emblematic of American capitalism's complex course during the immediate postwar period. On the one hand, the War of the Rebellion served to energize those forces most committed to advancing a capitalist economy and to defeat those who were most opposed. With enormous assistance from the federal state, capital accumulated rapidly in the hands of a new class of manufacturers and financiers who looked to extend the reach of the market to every corner of the United States (and beyond), and the vital plantation economy of the Deep South was salvaged, resuscitated, and reorganized around social relations that approximated wage labor, at least in their property form. New liberal sensibilities that were wedded to the logic of the marketplace gained considerable influence in middle-class and elite circles, delivering blows to the Radical Republicanism that was at one time attached to them. And the federal and state judiciaries were increasingly staffed by judges who held freedom of contract dear and regarded workers as subject to the authority of their employers while on the job and potentially dangerous to social order while off it.

On the other hand, manufacturers faced serious challenges in attempting to enlarge their workplaces and build new factories, because artisans and skilled workers, on whom they depended, were able to use their technical knowledge and experience to control much of the productive process. Mine owners, east and west, were similarly reliant on highly skilled workers who mostly came from abroad and hired their own helpers to dig the shafts and haul the coal and precious metals. Large landowners in the South were short of cash and credit, owing to the financial system that the Republicans had installed, and produced for an international commodities market that was sinking under the weight of an avalanche of grains and fibers being raised in new market economies around the globe. Even the agriculturalists of the Midwest, the Great Plains, and the Far West, having access to more machinery, were feeling the squeeze from mortgages on their land and low prices for their crops. The panic of 1873 and the ensuing depression not only brought an extended period of economic expansion to a close but also unsettled the social worlds of both capital and labor. The political explosions that followed and the directions and projects that were charted would make for a new national and international political economy.

CHAPTER TEN

Imperial Arms

Grassroots organizing among African Americans in the Deep South after
the coming of the franchise. *Harper's Weekly,* July 25, 1868.

The Federal Reach in the Rebellious South

When Congress passed the Reconstruction Acts over the veto of President Andrew Johnson in March 1867, General Philip H. Sheridan was appointed governor of the newly created Fifth Military District, encompassing Louisiana and Texas. He did not have to move. Once the Confederacy had begun to surrender in the spring of 1865, General in Chief of the Army Ulysses S. Grant relieved Sheridan of command over the Middle Military Division, which included the Shenandoah Valley of Virginia—still smoldering from his scorched-earth policy—and sent him west "to restore Texas, and that part of Louisiana held by the enemy, to the Union in the shortest practicable time." But when Sheridan arrived at his headquarters in New Orleans, he learned that rebel troops under Edmund Kirby Smith had officially surrendered, and so he devoted most of his attention to the Texas-Mexico borderlands where some of the rebels were fleeing into Mexico in hopes of gaining the support of the French-installed emperor Maximilian (himself an Austrian archduke).

Sheridan had little patience either for the rebels in flight or for Maximilian's regime, which he saw as an affront to "republicanism." Like Grant, with whom he had a close relationship, Sheridan understood Maximilian's seizure of power as "a part of the rebellion itself because of the encouragement that invasion has received from the Confederacy." It had to be defeated before the War of the Rebellion could truly be over. Ordering four divisions of cavalry and infantry into Texas, Sheridan looked at least to make a show of force, and his bellicose maneuvers, which seemed to anticipate an invasion, did stir deep concern in the emperor's court. Maximilian soon withdrew his troops from much of northern Mexico, and Confederate plans for a colony in Córdoba collapsed. Quickly reined in by Secretary of State William H. Seward, who had his own imperial ambitions but did not want hostilities with Mexico, Sheridan nonetheless helped ship armaments to the forces of the deposed liberal president, Benito Juárez, who would eventually drive the French out and have Maximilian's head.

Sheridan was one of five U.S. Army generals appointed to impose martial law and oversee the reconstruction and restoration of rebellious states under congressional auspices. He was a good choice. Sheridan insisted on establishing the authority of the federal government, had no interest in appeasing rebels and their collaborators, and believed that the freedom of the former slaves had to be placed on a secure basis. He knew what he was up against. Witnessing rampant "lawlessness" in his district, especially in Texas, and finding "more disloyalty here now than in '61," Sheridan removed civil officials who had climbed into the seats of power under President Johnson's policies, including the governors of both states, and conducted a massive registration of newly enfranchised black voters to facilitate the recasting of the state constitutions and the body politic.

Neither Sheridan nor any of the other military governors—none of whom proved as energetic in the task—had great resources at their disposal. The army of occupation had been steadily dwindling in size since the spring of 1865; left to enforce the Reconstruction Acts were roughly twenty thousand soldiers, most of whom were stationed in or near the larger towns and only thinly scattered across the expanses of the countryside. The Freedmen's Bureau, authorized to take charge of abandoned rebel lands and supervise the implementation of a free labor system, was already having its operations scaled back. Despite hopes that supportive elements could be identified in the southern white population—especially among commercially minded landowners and business interests—few such allies were to be found. Indeed, as in Sheridan's Texas, hostility to the freedpeople, to the Republican project of reconstruction, and to black suffrage continued to simmer if not boil over in many parts of the rebellious South, assuming deadly manifestations in paramilitary organizations like the Ku Klux Klan that came to life with the Reconstruction Acts.

While short on resources, military governors like Sheridan had substantial agendas to fulfill as congressional Republicans extended their imperial arms and demanded that a new framework of social and political relations be adopted by the states previously in rebellion. To be sure, those states had already been remanded to quasi-territorial status when Congress, in December 1865, refused to seat their recently elected delegations. They had been required to acknowledge the end of slavery and were expected, with the Freedmen's Bureau as an arbiter, to move along a path toward free, contractual labor. In 1866, they had been instructed to ratify the Fourteenth Amendment for readmission to the Union (only Tennessee did). Yet even without congressional representation, former rebels and former slaveholders continued to wield a good deal of power in their localities, aided by state legislatures composed of many participants in the rebellion and by county and municipal officials who were sympathetic to them if not wholly in their pockets. There were, in short, few incentives to cooperate with Republican objectives and many opportunities to obstruct them until Congress decided to take matters into its own hands.

Congressional Republicans did have an assortment of allies in their effort to turn the rebellious South and its new citizenries into loyal components of the nation-state they were devising. Many were missionaries and social reformers—black and white—often filled with evangelical fervor, who set up schools and churches designed to advance literacy, the embrace of Christianity, the values of thrift, industry, and materialism, and the formation of patriarchal families among the freedpeople. Many others were U.S. Army officers, often serving in the Freedmen's Bureau or locally based detachments, who offered freedpeople an opportunity to have their grievances redressed and their former owners brought to heel, to find measures of justice and protection against the retribution of the defeated rebels. Some were entrepreneurial types from the northern states, still fired by antislavery zeal, who leased or purchased plantations with hopes of tutoring the former slaves in the ways of contracts while demonstrating the economic superiority of free over slave labor. Together they struggled to set new social standards and cultural terms for the political reunification that was pending.

But in many ways, the most consequential allies were party organizers who traveled into the South to give the Republicans their first real footing and the black constituents they organized to turn that footing into power. Their tasks were critical. When the War of the Rebellion erupted, the Republican Party had little presence in the states where slavery remained legal. Beachheads had been established in some of the border areas—Maryland, Delaware, Kentucky, Missouri—but Republican campaigners knew that they risked their lives farther to the south; Lincoln did not even make it onto the ballot there. Although Lincoln's wartime Ten Percent Plan created openings for the party in Virginia, Arkansas, Tennessee, and Louisiana, had the rebellious states been readmitted under President Johnson's proclamation of 1865—before freedmen gained the franchise—the Democrats would have taken full control, and the Republican Party would have had its congressional initiatives (including the Fourteenth Amendment) hamstrung, if it was not driven from national power entirely.

No organizational vehicle proved more important in this regard than the Union League. Created in 1862 and 1863 to rally public support for the Lincoln administration and the war effort, the league early embraced the practices of both popular and patrician politics. Bound by secrecy, requiring oaths and rituals much in the manner of the Masons, and winning a mass base through local councils across the Midwest and the Northeast, the league also took hold among loyalist elites in Philadelphia, New York, and Boston. Before long, it established fledgling councils in areas of the South that came to be occupied by the U.S. Army, and once major hostilities ended, it continued educational and agitational work chiefly among white unionists who resided in the hill and mountain districts of the South. Committed "to protect, strengthen, and defend all loyal men without regard to sect, condition, or race," the league also began to sponsor political events and open a few councils for the still disfranchised African Americans, principally in larger cities like Richmond, Raleigh, Savannah, Tallahassee, and Nashville.

Once the Reconstruction Acts made provision for a black franchise and voter registration, however, league organizers quickly shifted direction and fanned out into smaller towns and the surrounding countryside, particularly into the plantation districts where African Americans resided in greatest and densest numbers. Associated with the national Republican Party, they were nonetheless a diverse lot. Some of the league activists were northern Radical Republicans with experience in the military and the Freedmen's Bureau, and some were southern white unionists who had already helped establish leagues in the hill country. But increasingly important were African Americans who had served in the U.S. Army, attended early freedmen's conventions, or preached the gospel to the emerging black congregations of the post-emancipation South, especially ministers of the African Methodist Episcopal Church. Theirs was, to say the least, arduous and extremely dangerous work; intent on mobilizing freedpeople, organizers often fell vulnerable to swift and deadly retaliation at the hands of white landowners and vigilantes. Secrecy and armed self-defense were therefore essential ingredients of successful campaigns.

The success that Union League organizers enjoyed could scarcely have been predicted. Even Radical Republicans in Congress who pressed the issues of black civil and political equality with greatest energy worried as to whose benefit the black vote would redound. After all, former slaves had never participated in what was ordinarily a rough world of electoral politics, and in the absence of significant land reform almost all of them still depended on former slaveholders for their livelihoods. Would they not then be subject to a host of coercive tactics designed to control their political activities or render them inert? Would they not succumb to the direct power of former owners and local Democratic bosses who might have even more political muscle now that the federal ratio had been vitiated and blacks counted the same as whites for the purposes of apportionment? These were unsettling questions for Republicans to contemplate. Yet in remarkable ways, freedpeople confounded these fears. Building on sensibilities, communications networks, subterranean relations and institutions, and spiritual communities they had cobbled together under slavery, they registered to vote in overwhelming numbers and resisted both the overtures and the threats of white Democrats. They marched to the polls in legions and participated in the writing of new state constitutions that reconstructed the body politic of what had been a slave society. With few exceptions, they lent their electoral support to the Republican Party. At a very critical moment, they enabled the Republicans to expand and strengthen their regime.

The developing political alliance between the Republican state and the former slaves, mediated at the grass roots by the Union League and party activists, was at once logical, necessary, and deeply problematic. Beyond question, there was a shared interest—forged in the crucible of war—in many of the projects essential to Republican nation-state building: emancipation, the military defeat of the slaveholders, the creation of birthright citizenship, universal manhood suffrage, the empowerment of the federal government, the establishment of the Republican Party in the rebellious South, and the use of federal institutions— notably the army and the Freedmen's Bureau—to protect the lives and rights of those loyal to the party and the national state. Although some Democrats hoped to "secure the good will and confidence of the negro" and tried to court their votes, few African Americans took the bait. It was the Republicans, not the Democrats, they clearly recognized, who had advanced the cause of emancipation, armed the slaves, celebrated the end of the slaveholders' rebellion, embraced civil and political equality, and made an effort to empower the freedpeople. Only those who were almost wholly cut off from black communities or wholly dependent on the patronage of whites—and who, in the Deep South, had often been free before the war—did the Democrats' bidding.

Republicans at the national and state levels saw African Americans, especially the former slaves, as crucial allies in their own efforts to build the party in the South and secure their power and authority over the nation. The alliance was a product of expediency as well as principle; outside the small districts of unionism to be found in eastern Kentucky and Tennessee, western North Carolina, northern Georgia, Alabama, and Arkansas, and sections of Missouri, Republican hopes of securing a base among white southerners proved chimerical. While most southern whites, including those who had owned slaves, accepted the abolition of slavery as a fait accompli, and some, especially former slave owners, found assurance in the Republican commitment to protecting the plantation sector, few could abide black enfranchisement. They saw the black vote and the political mobilizations it enabled as an illegitimate outrage inflicted on the South by a tyrannical—Black Republican—central state and as an immense threat to the reconstitution of social relations on the only basis—black subordination and submission—they believed tolerable. They had little use for the notion of federal sovereignty or the cultural and political demands it entailed, and once it was apparent that the "old allegiances" of the ex-slaves could not be reactivated, that they could not acquire "a strong personal influence over the negroes," they either withdrew from the political arena or battled to overturn Republican rule by any means at their disposal.

Former slaves were therefore the most numerous and reliable allies the Republicans had for the task of incorporating the rebellious states into their new nation-state. But the alliance was as tense as it was extraordinary. However much they might have shared a commitment to free labor, civic equality, and political democratization, Republican leaders and freedpeople occupied very different, and inherently antagonistic, social positions. Republicans had put together a complex coalition but their policy-making heart increasingly

beat for the interests of manufacturers, financiers, and other propertied producers; they were concerned with advancing the industrialization of the country,
stabilizing money and credit, revitalizing the cotton economy, and drawing
more and more of the United States into the capitalist marketplace. For their
part, freedpeople had their own forms of social differentiation based on place of
birth and residency, crop cultures, skills, ancestry, and kinship networks, but
they were overwhelmingly working people who owned very little in the way of
land or other productive resources and had to labor for white employers chiefly
in the fields, as well as on the docks, in mines, on railroads and other types of
transportation, in forests, and in towns and cities. Their aspiration was to
escape economic dependency and provide for themselves; short of that, they
struggled to limit their exploitation, boost their wages and crop shares, crawl
out from under the thumbs of whites, rebuild their communities, and use the
political process to increase their leverage. Never before or since has a section of
the American working class been as closely aligned with a political party as
former slaves were with the Republicans. But it was not "their" party.

For a time, especially in the early phases of Military Reconstruction, the
alliance not only held but offered the varied participants political rewards well
beyond what any of them could have anticipated. African American activism
was the key. Despite dangers and direct threats—"All the blacks who vote
against my ticket shall walk the plank," the Georgia Democrat Howell Cobb
vented—they organized their communities, rallied to the Republican banner,
and turned out to vote in stunning numbers (often 80 to 90 percent of those
eligible). This process of mobilization, so crucial to what was achieved, reflected
both the deep legacies of slavery and the new possibilities of freedom. Freedpeople tapped the "grapevine telegraph" to communicate with one another, utilized traditions of secrecy and self-defense to secure their meeting places,
followed leaders who had won influence and respect as slaves as well as those
who stepped out front with the advent of emancipation (especially those who
served in the U.S. Army), and constructed new institutions of community life.
Religious congregations, which had their roots in slavery, became particularly
important. Their ministers—who earned livelihoods principally as farmers,
croppers, and laborers—often had special talents for speaking, teaching,
resolving conflicts, and linking secular and spiritual concerns, not to mention
the ability to read and write, all of which were necessary in the arenas of formal
politics. Congregation members, linked by kinship, labor, and residential proximity, had long used this cultural space for deliberating on matters of vital
interest to one another as well as for worshipping God. Where the congregations could claim church buildings, they were also the sites of schools, Union

League meetings, and early benevolent societies: very much the centers of community life.

Politics, as this suggests, was for African Americans very much a collective undertaking, one that blurred the lines of gender and age. Granted, the franchise was extended only to black men, and without doubt it tipped the balances of community power and authority further in their direction at a time when social relations were generally being renegotiated with the end of slavery. But participation, and important forms of decision making, were more widely dispersed, connecting the electoral with other arenas of local social and political life. Black women attended rallies and meetings along with black men and took the occasion to make their sentiments known. So deeply did they become involved with the expression of partisan loyalties that the vote itself could be regarded as something of a household and family property. Some of them gathered and transmitted necessary intelligence (as did children), some taught in rural schools, and some helped defend public assemblies from attack. Where possible, they accompanied voting-age men to the ballot box, providing added cover, showing the extent of community support, and steeling the nerves of the men.

Yet freedwomen might well have made their most powerful and distinctive contribution to the developing political culture of their communities as enforcers. Manipulating gender conventions and the expectations of courtship and sexual favor, they both shamed reluctant men into performing their political duties and wreaked the most intimate and humiliating vengeance on those who strayed from the fold. It was a central way in which the discipline required for survival and success was imposed and solidarity maintained. "The negroes are as intolerant of opposition as the whites," a conservative white South Carolinian observed at the time, ostracizing, expelling, and even killing "all of their own" who "would turn democrats." And by his lights, the "women are worse than the men, refusing to talk to or marry a renegade, and aiding in mobbing him."

Black electoral support enabled the Republican Party to strengthen its hold on the national government as the rebellious states began to secure readmission, and to extend its reach into the South. In 1868, black voters gave the Republican presidential candidate, Ulysses S. Grant, the majority of popular votes cast (he only won a minority of the white vote) and, owing to their turnout in the rebellious states, a comfortable margin in the Electoral College as well (he won six of them). As these states began to hold elections under new constitutions that enfranchised African American men and disfranchised some of the rebels, the Republicans then won control of the governorships and legislatures almost everywhere (Virginia was the exception) and took charge of

county and municipal governments in many places, but especially in the plantation districts where larger slaveholding planters—most of them rebels—had
previously ruled. It was a political revolution of the sort that few modern societies have ever witnessed, displacing a wealthy and formidable elite that claimed
local sovereignty with one directly tied to the newly proclaimed sovereignty of
the nation-state.

In no way was the political revolution more arresting or consequential than
in the election to office of African Americans, most of whom had recently been
slaves. Two black men—Hiram R. Revels and Blanche K. Bruce, both from
Mississippi—were elevated to the U.S. Senate (Revels took the seat previously
occupied by the rebel chief, Jefferson Davis); sixteen black men, many from the
secessionist stronghold of South Carolina, would sit in the House of Representatives. But as dramatic as this was, black office holding in the states and localities
counted for even more. Nearly three hundred blacks served in constitutional
conventions called under the auspices of Military Reconstruction, where they
helped move state governments in far more inclusive and democratic directions.
More than a hundred won election or appointment to posts having jurisdiction
over entire states, including lieutenant governor (one of whom, P. B. S. Pinchback, would briefly serve as governor of Louisiana when Henry Clay Warmoth
was impeached), and nearly eight hundred took seats in state legislatures, in
some cases forming majorities (South Carolina and Mississippi) or near majorities (Louisiana), where they battled to create new post-emancipation societies.
"The body is almost wholly a Black Parliament," a northern journalist found in
the South Carolina statehouse. "The Speaker is black, the Clerk is black, the
door-keepers are black, the little pages are black, the chairman of the Ways and
Means is black, and the chaplain is coal black." Reflecting on the "orators and
statesmen" who had once walked the aisles, all he could now see was "the spectacle of a society turned bottomside up."

Yet such a "spectacle" was nowhere more compellingly in evidence than in
the rural counties in which former slaves composed the majority of the population. There, in the bailiwick of slaveholding clans and their clients, black men—
perhaps as many as fourteen or fifteen hundred of them—would now hold
the levers of power: as jurors, magistrates, county commissioners, tax assessors, school superintendents, coroners, election officials, constables, and even
sheriffs. It was a political transition and inversion unprecedented in the region,
nation, or (with the exception of Haiti) the hemisphere, and one that most directly threatened the social order as white southerners knew it. "There is not
half so much interest on the part of democrats in this State about Congress as
there is about the Legislature, or ordinaries or sheriffs," Georgia's black Republican leader Henry McNeal Turner explained. "They do not care so much about

Congress admitting negroes to their halls . . . but they don't want the negroes over them at home."

Aghast, white Democrats screamed about the advent of "Negro rule," and the term has long stuck as a way of capturing what many regarded—then and later—as the illegitimacies of Reconstruction politics. In fact, it was whites, not blacks, who predominated among Republican leaders and officeholders during this period, especially in the most visible and formidable seats of power. National offices like senators and congressmen as well as statewide posts were filled overwhelmingly by white men. Governorships (except for Pinchback's brief reign) were filled exclusively by white men, and outside South Carolina, Mississippi, and Louisiana, Republican legislative delegations were majority white. Even on the local level, including the plantation districts, most of the offices—and especially those with police, juridical, and taxing power (sheriffs, magistrates, assessors, and treasurers)—were held by whites.

But what the idea of "Negro rule" did capture was the significant shift in political power that Military Reconstruction made possible: from the former slaveholding elite toward a collection of groups who had been outsiders to the official arenas of southern politics. In addition to the freedmen, they included white northerners (known derisively as carpetbaggers) who had served in the U.S. Army and the Freedmen's Bureau, had taken up planting or merchandising, or had engaged in teaching and missionary work; white southerners (known even more derisively as scalawags) who had been unionists or unenthusiastic rebels, had been non-slaveholders and small slaveholders, or had lived beyond the immediate orbit of the planter class; black northerners, some having earlier escaped enslavement, who had acquired education and skills, had joined the Union military effort, or had served as ministers and missionaries for the AME Church; and some black southerners who had been free before the war. Together, they were substantially less wealthy, less experienced politically, and less committed to perpetuating the old plantation order while, for the most part, owing their positions to black votes.

Although their programs and achievements varied from place to place, the Republican regimes that took charge of the rebellious states beginning in 1868 began to carry out reforms and innovations that simultaneously rebuilt the region's infrastructure, reconfigured its public life, adjusted the balances of local power, and tied the fortunes of its new governments closely to the national state. Republicans were responsible for creating the first systems of public education (serving whites as well as blacks, though in a segregated fashion, except in New Orleans, where some of the schools were integrated between 1870 and 1875) while establishing or significantly augmenting the resources of an assortment of public institutions: hospitals, asylums, orphanages, and penitentiaries. They increased taxes and shifted the burdens from individuals (slaves, head taxes, and licensing fees) to real and personal property, in some cases forcing plantation land onto the market. In alliance with railroad developers, they attended to the repair of lines destroyed during the war and the construction of new ones that reached into districts previously on the edge of the market economy, thereby linking the South more directly with the Northeast and the Midwest. They generally centralized the power of political appointments, putting it in the hands of the governors, blocked the attempts of planters to enforce the dependency of black laborers, outlawed corporal punishment, and reduced both the number of capital offenses and the penalties for minor crimes. They liberalized access to divorce, granted property rights to married women, and enabled African Americans to sit on juries as well as sue and testify in court. It was a far cry from the old order, when slaveholders ruled over their sovereign domains—serving as patriarch, judge, and juror—when rail and river transportation mainly connected the plantation belt with southern ports, and when the public sector was scarcely more than a shell.

But the Republican political revolution provoked turmoil. Former slaveholders, most of whom were now aligned with the Democratic Party, recognized that the circuits of power and authority were being rerouted and their ability to enforce the submission of black workers seriously compromised. Thus, when their efforts to make emancipated slaves into political clients came to little, they turned very quickly to the methods of political battle that were so central to the maintenance of order under slavery: paramilitarism. It was, in an important sense, a continuation of the militarization of southern society that produced the militias and slave patrols of the antebellum era, the companies that composed the rebel armies during the war, and then the vigilante outfits that attempted to disarm and repress newly emancipated slaves, leaving them at the mercy of former owners. Including a wide assortment of local units often grouped under the rubric of the "Ku Klux Klan," these paramilitaries were generally composed of rebel officers, cavalrymen, and privates—young war veterans—who had been paroled or allowed to desert without surrendering their arms, ammunition, and horses. They began to patrol the countryside, harassing and punishing freedpeople who took advantage of their freedom, showed signs of economic independence, or behaved in ways that were regarded as insubordinate. But more than anything else, they moved against local black leaders and their white allies: Union League organizers, grassroots black activists, candidates for office, sympathetic teachers and ministers, and African Americans determined to vote for the Republican Party. Many black leaders were assassinated or driven from their homes, families and communities were terrorized, and schools and churches were burned to the ground; victims would also include

Republican congressmen, state legislators, and county officeholders. So fierce and successful could the paramilitaries be that in 1868 they enabled the Democrats to carry the presidential electoral votes of Georgia and Louisiana.

The looming question was whether the federal government and the loyal state governments in the South would use the political and military means at their disposal to protect Republican voters and officeholders and secure the power of their regimes. For a time, the answer was yes. Although the Grant administration did not increase troop strength, federal soldiers were dispatched to quell serious disturbances and suppress the most egregious examples of vigilantism; Congress, in turn, launched an investigation of the Klan that eventuated in legislation (known as the Enforcement Acts of 1870 and 1871) outlawing "conspiracies" that deprived blacks of their civil and political rights. Hundreds of perpetrators were arrested and indicted in the Carolinas, Mississippi, and Alabama, and while few convictions were obtained, many Klan leaders fled these states. The back of the Klan was effectively broken. Closer to the ground, some of the Republican governors—especially those who were hardened veterans of the hostilities that had been raging—reorganized state militias (sometimes with black troops heavily represented) and put them to good use, notably in Klan-infested areas.

Yet the political temper of the times was shifting away from the Radical faction of the Republican Party and toward the more numerous moderates. The result was a retraction of the imperial arms that the federal state had been extending from its full embrace of emancipation in 1863 through the passage of the Reconstruction Acts of 1867. It was in part the empowerment of former slaves and in part the growing influence of financial and industrial interests in policy-making circles. What would a radical agenda in the South mean for the governance and political economy of the rest of the country? Grant's renomination for president in 1872 and his campaign revealed both the strength of moderation and the public exhaustion with federal interventionism. The election itself, which Grant won by overwhelming margins in the popular (56 percent) and electoral votes, seemed to suggest that Republican rule over the nation-state no longer depended on a loyal and reliably Republican South.

But perhaps even more significant was the panic of 1873, its painful economic effect, and the widespread retrenchments it ushered in. Not only were the financial and manufacturing sectors of the Republican coalition hard hit and the corrupt practices that had sealed their marriage to the national state exposed, but the labor unrest that suddenly erupted began to shake their confidence. Hundreds of textile, railroad, and mine workers struck against wage cuts, and massive demonstrations in industrializing cities of the Northeast and the Midwest called upon the municipal and state governments to commence public works projects. The thousands who gathered in New York City's Tompkins Square in January 1874 demanding "work or bread" provoked a police crackdown and a new era of "extreme repression" against working-class activists. Small wonder that northern employers and financiers felt a growing sympathy and kinship with southern planters who complained about the laziness, insolence, and political insubordination of their black laborers. And small wonder that the Grant administration had less and less enthusiasm for coming to the aid of embattled Republican officials at the state and local levels in the South, for responding to the "annual autumnal outbreaks" with the dispatch of U.S. troops. When, in such an atmosphere, the Democratic Party reclaimed control of the House of Representatives in 1874, the imperial arms of the Republican state were weakened, and their ability to guide a variety of ambitious projects conceived during the War of the Rebellion were placed in jeopardy.

If the panic and its aftermath exacerbated the class tensions between Republican leaders at the national level and black constituents in the South, it also strained tensions of class and race among southern Republicans themselves. Well before the panic, black Republicans were coming to feel ill at ease with the leadership that white Republicans were willing to provide. Although they recognized that whites had educations and political experience worthy of deference, they resented their own status as junior partners in the coalition and felt that their aspirations and concerns were poorly understood or ignored, their claims to a fair share of offices rejected, their vulnerabilities to violence and coercion insufficiently addressed. One black South Carolinian bitterly complained about the white Republicans who made "loud and big promises to the freedmen till they got elected to office, then did not do one single thing," who refused to support the nomination of "a colored man" for major office, who "removed a number of black trial justices," and who "disarmed a number of black militia companies." "The first duty of any race of people," he thundered, "is to see to their own interests specially."

Black discontent soon forced white Republican officeholders, especially the governors, to make a critical choice: they could attend more fully to the "interests" of their black supporters and risk alienating their white ones, not to mention the national leadership; or they could try to curry the favor of moderate Democrats by cutting taxes and spending, decrying "corruption," championing "reform," and offering Democrats a share of the patronage and offices. Most chose the latter—reflecting in part the disposition toward financial retrenchment. But it was to little avail. Democrats had no inclination or need to join hands with white Republicans; they preferred to rally southern whites against the threat of "Negro rule" and rely on paramilitaries to achieve what ballots might fail to do: drive the Republicans and their black supporters from political power.

The Klan might have been the target of federal harassment, but at all events it was too diffuse and uncoordinated to dislodge Republican regimes in more than limited areas. Far more effective in this work were rifle clubs—known variously as the White Leagues or the Red Shirts—the true arms of the Democratic Party and very much fixed upon dismantling and destroying the opposition. Using networks of kinship, patronage, and military service that crossed county lines, they brought a reign of political terror into the plantation districts and eventually to the doors of the state legislatures. Democratic rifle clubs attacked Republican meetings and provoked what were called "riots" that claimed the lives of many blacks in attendance. They targeted local black leaders (white Republican leaders, too) for brutal beatings and murder. They threatened prospective voters and then, heavily armed, menaced them at the polls. Even if the Republicans managed to win elections, the rifle clubs either tried to prevent successful candidates from taking office or drove them off once they did. More and more counties were "redeemed" in this way, effectively undermining Republican state and local regimes or isolating them in a rising sea of paramilitarism. In Louisiana, while several thousand White Leaguers brazenly attempted to oust the Republican governor and legislature in 1874 (failing only because after-the-fact intervention by federal troops reversed their coup), their rural counterparts did them better: they crippled or overthrew Republican officials in at least eight parishes in a wave of bloody violence. Red River Parish was particularly gruesome. There, in August, the duly elected sheriff, tax collector, and justice of the peace together with a registrar, a Republican attorney, and several black supporters were summarily slaughtered near the county seat of Coushatta.

Quite remarkably, African Americans maintained their loyalty to the Republican Party, and in fact, as white Republicanism shrank in the face of paramilitarism and black assertiveness, they became the mainstays of the party, providing the support in states like South Carolina, Mississippi, and Louisiana that enabled Republican regimes to hold on. Black office holding in the South grew over the course of the early 1870s and might have peaked around 1874. In some localities, black arms-bearing militancy effectively stared down the rifle clubs. For all of their saber rattling, night riding, and terrorism, the Democrats, without massive electoral fraud, would have remained on the losing end, out of power, especially in the Deep South, where black political strength was greatest. Democrats found it, and would continue to find it, extremely difficult to suppress the political energies of African Americans that had been released by the War of the Rebellion and the struggle over the meaning of emancipation.

Yet it was also clear that the imperial arms of the Republican state would only extend so far. They had crushed the slaveholders' rebellion, abolished slavery, fortified the power of the federal government, established national citizenship, and organized the party in the rebellious states with a social base that had previously been enslaved. They had also imposed martial law and prescribed a raft of political and social conditions that had to be met before those states could regain their status in what was now a nation-state. This was the political and social revolution that had been made, and for that revolution to continue or to be fully preserved, the force of federal arms would need to be flexed for some time to come. But the long-term interests of the Republican Party were increasingly on the side of property and capital, not of the black laborers who had made the revolution possible and whose lives and rights were most in jeopardy.

Thermidor came in 1876. That year brought disputed elections for the presidency of the United States and for control over the governments of South Carolina, Louisiana, and Florida, and their outcomes were closely linked. The Democratic nominee, Samuel J. Tilden of New York, had won the popular national vote and was one vote shy of a majority in the Electoral College; the Republican nominee, Rutherford B. Hayes of Ohio, trailed in the popular vote and needed all the electoral votes of South Carolina, Louisiana, and Florida to prevail. An electoral commission was impaneled to try to sort it out before the term of Ulysses S. Grant came to an end and a serious crisis unfolded. Meanwhile, dual governments took shape in South Carolina and Louisiana: Republican legislators and governors who claimed legitimate power sat in their chambers surrounded by rifle clubs in service to rival Democrats demanding their surrender. Only Grant's stationing of U.S. Army troops near the capitol buildings kept the guns silent. Some expressed fear that a new civil war threatened on the horizon.

But it was a deal among the rulers rather than a war between them that came to fruition. The electoral commission, with a Republican majority on it, decided for Hayes, thereby extending the party's hold on the executive branch of the federal government. Hayes then offered more than an olive branch to the Democrats who had been defeated. A war veteran himself, he called for the "permanent pacification" of the country, putting an "end to bayonet rule." Shortly thereafter, he ordered the federal troops in New Orleans and Columbia, South Carolina, to withdraw from their posts and return to their barracks. The results were not hard to fathom. The last Republican Reconstruction governments crumpled, and Democratic "home rule" took full hold across the Deep South. Less visible, though equally consequential, one of the foundations of the modern American political economy was also set in place.

Colonialism in the Trans-Mississippi West

The imperial arms of the national state remained far more robust in the trans-Mississippi West, and General Philip Sheridan would play a significant role in directing them. Having run afoul of President Andrew Johnson for carrying out the very requirements of Military Reconstruction that congressional Republicans had prescribed—Johnson depicted his administration of the Fifth Military District as "one of absolute tyranny"—Sheridan was reassigned to the Department of the Missouri in August 1867 after only a few short months on the job. There he would carry a different portfolio, though one no less crucial to the state-building projects that Republicans had imagined. Rather than completing the suppression of the slaveholders' rebellion, protecting the new rights of former slaves, and helping to lay the foundation for a new structure of governance in the rebellious states, he would be enforcing the sovereign authority of the federal government and the principles of property and economy to which it was now devoted by completing the suppression of what were regarded as rebellious Native Americans.

Much had been or was being decided as Sheridan took up his post at Fort Leavenworth, Kansas. The tribes in Indian Territory who had aligned with the Confederacy had been punished, their black slaves emancipated, and their land claims thrown into jeopardy. The treaty system that had long framed relations between the federal government and Indian peoples was about to be jettisoned, the political sovereignty of Indians—limited as it was—no longer recognized. The building of a transportation infrastructure (chiefly railroads), the exploitation of newly discovered mineral resources, and the security of settler colonialists in the interior West would be privileged, while the lands that Native populations used for subsistence, trade, and habitation would be appropriated. And the reservation, on which the Native peoples were to be confined and "civilized," would be embraced by policy makers and reformers alike as the solution to the "Indian problem." Although the U.S. Department of the Interior rather than the War Department remained in control of Indian "affairs," it was the army, under the command of officers like Philip Sheridan, that was charged with carrying out the policies, and like Sheridan many of the other army officers—Oliver Otis Howard, Nelson A. Miles, E. O. C. Ord, Edward Canby, John Pope—not only were veterans of the War of the Rebellion but had done tours of service in the occupied South as well.

Still, whatever had been determined as to the direction of federal policy, the process of implementing it would not be easy. The Indian peoples of the Great Plains and the interior West were among the most formidable on the North American continent. The Sioux, Yankton, Crow, and Cheyenne to the north, the Comanche, Arapaho, (southern) Cheyenne, and Kiowa to the south, and the Apache, Navajo, and Ute to the southwest had, over the course of the late eighteenth and the nineteenth centuries, generally become fierce, equestrian-based hunters and warriors. They had constructed intricate trading networks involving American, Mexican, and Canadian merchants, engaged in extensive captive economies, and terrorized populations across expansive borderlands. Some had fended off a variety of adversaries, aggressively enlarging their territories, striking fear into the hearts of those they threatened to raid. Although warfare and disease had diminished their numbers over the years and strategies for survival created political divisions among them, few were ready to abandon their ways of life for the "civilization" that the federal government appeared ready to offer. The Sioux uprising of 1862 gave clear notice of the battle lines that could quickly be drawn.

Even when tribal bands, or portions of them, appeared ready to capitulate by moving onto reservations, it was often with an understanding that they would not be wholly dependent on government subsistence or forced to give up the hunt for the plow or submit to the spiritual directions of Christian missionaries. The Kiowa chief Satanta (White Bear) who signed the Treaty of Medicine Lodge in October 1867—which officially moved Kiowas and Comanches out of western Texas and onto reservation lands in Indian Territory—nonetheless pushed back against some of its demands. "All of the land south of the Arkansas [River] belongs to the Kiowas and Comanches, and I don't want to give away any of it," he told the peace commissioners appointed by President Johnson. "I have heard that you want to settle us on a reservation near the mountains. I don't want to settle there. . . . I love the land and the buffalo. . . . I love to roam over the wide prairie, and when I do I feel free and happy, but when we settle down we grow pale and die." Miles to the north, the proposed Treaty of Fort Laramie (1868), which involved a retreat to reservations and raised the ire of militant Sioux bands (those under Sitting Bull and Crazy Horse would not sign), still permitted hunting rights on lands outside the reservations "so long as the buffalo may range there" and required the abandonment of U.S. Army forts along the contested—and game-rich—Bozeman Trail leading to Montana. "We want to live as we have been raised, hunting the animals of the prairie," one of the allied Crow leaders insisted. "Do not speak of shutting us up on reservations and making us cultivate the land."

The divisions among many of the western tribes and the very different understandings that Indian signatories brought to the agreements they entered into all but ensured that the subsequent "peace policy" of the Grant administration (1869–77)—"conquest through kindness"—would quickly collapse. After all, the policy combined "concentration" (on reservations) and "civilization" (education, missionizing, and sedentary agriculture) with the summary repression of Native bands who refused to submit. Many did refuse. Across the Southwest from Texas to Arizona, Comanches, Kiowas, Navajos, and Apaches continued raiding across the U.S.-Mexican border and hunting outside the boundaries of reservations. In the Northwest, Modocs and non-treaty Nez Perces, the latter most famously represented by Young Joseph's band, struggled to avoid confinement on reservations and, in the case of the Nez Perce, trekked nearly seventeen hundred miles in the process. Not far off to the east, between the Yellowstone River of Montana and the Black Hills of South Dakota, renegade Sioux, Cheyennes, and Arapahos, rejecting the settlement at Fort Laramie, established a center of armed resistance. Mineral strikes—silver in the Colorado Rockies and gold in the Black Hills in the early 1870s—only intensified the determination of both the Native peoples to defend their social and cultural lifeways and the American nation-state to impose order along the paths of western development.

The U.S. military stood ready for engagement, and by the early 1870s President Grant himself was losing patience. General Sheridan, eager to move against cross-border raiding in southern Texas, called for a "campaign of annihilation, obliteration, and complete destruction," and together with General in Chief Sherman would redeploy the methods of "total war" they had honed during the War of the Rebellion. In what is known as the Red River War (1874–75) in Texas, Sheridan moved to invade the Indians' winter camps, drive them from their habitations, destroy their access to subsistence, and pursue them relentlessly until they surrendered. Before long, suffering from attack and the elements, the Comanche, Cheyenne, Arapaho, and Kiowa gave up the fight. As seventy-four of their leaders were shipped off for imprisonment in St. Augustine, Florida, they swallowed the bitter pill and settled for good on assigned reservations. Never again would they take up arms against the United States.

But tactics such as these proved more difficult to implement in the northern plains, where the Sioux refused to sell or lease the gold-laden Black Hills and the army set out to bring them and their allies to submission. Sheridan's plan of striking the Indians in their winter camps was nearly impossible to accomplish owing to the intense cold and heavy snow. Later assaults on Native villages provoked successful counterattacks and forced hasty withdrawals. Troops trying to converge on the militant bands were met with sniper fire and ambush. Although twenty-five hundred strong, the army could claim few clear military victories to show for its efforts. "They are brave and ready to fight for their country," the Oglala Sioux chief Red Cloud said of the militants in the spring of 1876. "They are not afraid of the soldiers nor of their chief. . . . Every lodge will send its young men, and they will all say of the Great Father's dogs, 'Let them come.'" Heedless of the message, the soldiers came—and to disastrous effect. Brigadier

Native peoples' reservations in the United States in 1883.
Map by Hiram Price and Paul T. Brodie.

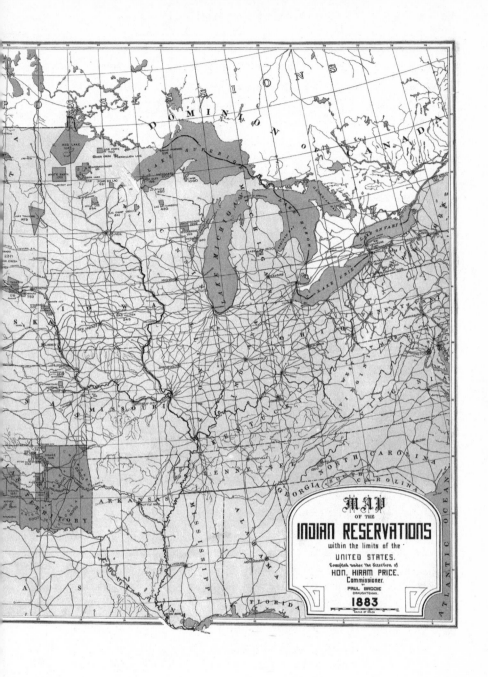

MAP
OF THE
INDIAN RESERVATIONS
within the limits of the
UNITED STATES.
Compiled under the direction of
HON. HIRAM PRICE,
Commissioner.
BY
PAUL BRODIE,
DRAUGHTSMAN.
1883

General George Crook met Crazy Horse in battle that June and failed to defeat him; the self-regarding and overconfident lieutenant colonel George Armstrong Custer fared much worse. Commanding the Seventh Cavalry, Custer headed toward the Little Bighorn (what the Sioux called the Greasy Grass) and, ignoring the warnings of his Crow and Arikara scouts, divided his men and launched an attack on what was an unusually large village. Hours later, they all lay dead. A "massacre" and "last stand" it would be called; the episode came to public light days later, on July 4, 1876, the centennial of American independence.

Militarily, the Sioux and their allies fought the U.S. Army to a standstill, and if casualties are to be counted, they clearly won. Roughly twice as many soldiers as Indian warriors were killed over the course of the "Great Sioux War." But the larger strategic vision of Sheridan—keeping the militants on the run, compromising their subsistence, subjecting them to the elements, wearing them down—eventually succeeded. Although army officers called for more troops and heavier armaments in the wake of Custer's defeat, Congress probably acted more effectively in the summer of 1876 by refusing appropriations to subsist the Sioux until they relinquished all their territorial claims, including to the Black Hills. Agency Indians (those who had remained on reservations and were already dependent on government support) quickly agreed, and even as Sitting Bull fled to Canada and Crazy Horse to the Powder River country, many of the militants began to surrender. Before very long, Crazy Horse (1877) and Sitting Bull (1881) gave up, too. Only the Apache in the Southwest, under the leadership of Geronimo, still held out.

Yet it was as much the long arm of a new political economy as the clenched fists of the U.S. Army that resulted in the subjugation and colonial containment of the western Indians. To be sure, once many of the Plains peoples turned to equestrianism in the eighteenth century, the bison population—on which they depended for food, clothing, and habitation—was subject to larger slaughters. By the mid-nineteenth century, the bison were in steady decline. For a time, some of the most powerful of the tribes might have benefited from the increased trade in skins that the equestrian hunt afforded, but as the railroads penetrated the plains and the mechanization of tanning made possible the mass production of leather goods, the consequences were catastrophic. White buffalo hunters with long-bore rifles soon made their way out to the grasslands and felled the buffalo in numbers that had previously been unimaginable. Divested of their subsistence base, Indians almost everywhere had little choice but to accept the reservation and the government dependency that went along with it. In an important sense, it was a process of enclosure that destroyed alternative modes of life and cleared the way for the capitalist development of the trans-Mississippi West. As General William Sherman observed in his annual report of 1880,

"Prosperous farms and cattle ranches exist where ten years ago no man could venture. This is largely due to the soldier, but in equal, if not greater measure, to the adventurous pioneers themselves, and to the new and greatest of civilizers, the railroad."

The surrender of Native populations to their fate on reservations scattered across the interior West enabled federal officials and social reformers to engage in the type of colonial administration they had long seen as the ultimate goal: cultural uplift and assimilation. Having little but contempt for Indian practices, values, or spirituality—regarding them as vestiges of savagery, depravity, and heathenism—they hoped to offer a path to "civilization" by tutoring their charges in the virtues of individualism, private property, hard work, patriarchal families, and the Christian faith. The ultimate goal was "detribalization" and the end of the reservations themselves. Not surprisingly, many of the reformers, like Oliver Otis Howard, Clinton B. Fisk, and Samuel Chapman Armstrong, had previously offered similar lessons to the former slaves in the rebellious states, with a view to detaching them from perceived superstitions, sloth, and barbarism and turning them into self-motivated and materially oriented workers. The new white guardians built schools and churches on reservation lands, with different denominations assigned to different reservations; they encouraged farming and livestock raising; and they established police and law courts staffed by Native American residents. The Indian, an attendee at the Lake Mohonk Conference of Friends of the Indian insisted, must be made "intelligently selfish," gotten "out of the blanket and into trousers,—and trousers with a pocket in them, and a pocket that aches to be filled with dollars!"

Especially controversial was the advent of off-reservation boarding schools. These were a response to the dilemmas of reservation-based education, where Indian children might be socialized in the new dispositions by teachers and missionaries while remaining embedded in families and communities in which the old ways still prevailed. Richard Henry Pratt, who as an army captain had accompanied Indian prisoners to St. Augustine after the Red River War and fancied himself an authority on the Native American character, believed he saw the light. "In Indian civilization," he told a religious convention, "I am a Baptist because I believe in immersing the Indians in our civilization and when we get them under holding them there until they are thoroughly soaked." With government support, Pratt founded the Carlisle Indian School in rural Pennsylvania in 1879—a model for the two dozen or so that followed and a close facsimile of the Hampton Normal and Agricultural Institute (which began admitting Indians around the same time) and the Tuskegee Normal and Industrial Institute, both committed to African American acculturation. Pratt had not spoken in jest. The Carlisle School practiced total immersion. Indian children were immediately given anglicized names. The boys had their hair cut, and all the students were required to wear school uniforms instead of Native clothing. They were taught reading and writing, expected to speak English only, introduced to "American" ways and values, and subjected to a highly regimented discipline replete with punishments for noncooperation. They also were generally prohibited from returning home, where they could still be exposed to "contaminating" influences, until their multiyear educations were completed.

Although Pratt and other reformers cultivated the support of tribal chiefs, and often got it, the general reception for the boarding schools among tribal people was sufficiently cool or outright hostile to require more coercive tactics. Reservation adults not only worried about the reformers' goal of "kill[ing] the Indian [to] save the man," of transforming their children "forever," but also objected to the prolonged absences and exposures to disease (which did claim the lives of a good many young students) that the schooling entailed. Indian children could therefore be forcibly removed from their reservations and transported hundreds of miles away. It was a wrenching example of the heavy-handedness that always accompanied the "civilizing" process and was to be found in an increasingly centralized Bureau of Indian Affairs, which grew in size and authority thanks to the handiwork of President Hayes's interior secretary, Carl Schurz.

A refugee from the German Revolution of 1848, an early Republican, a U.S. Army general, and a onetime advocate for the freedpeople, Schurz became a staunch civil service reformer looking to weed out the corruption and cronyism rampant in the bureau and among Indian agents in the field. He insisted on appointing bureau inspectors and having them report directly to him, another feature of nation-state formation that the War of the Rebellion made possible. The bureau not only oversaw educational work on the reservations and the distribution of annuities but, by the mid-1880s, moved against a variety of Native practices deemed unacceptable or retrograde in what amounted to a frontal assault on Indian culture and institutions. Using its control over subsistence and the threat of imprisonment, the bureau banned polygamy, "medicine making," bride payments, funerary rituals, and religious ceremonies such as the Sun Dance, which had a central place in the spiritual and social lives of the Lakota.

Yet, as reformers and federal officials alike recognized, the key to "assimilation" was "detribalization," and the key to "detribalization" was eradication of the land base and communal practices that sustained tribal culture. As the commissioner of Indian affairs put it, "Tribal relations should be broken up, socialism destroyed and the family and autonomy of the individual substituted." However much educating the younger generation of Native peoples and repressing the particularly objectionable customs of the older might conduce to such an end—and there was not much evidence for a rapid transition on either account—the structure of landholding and land use remained the greatest obstacle. To that end, Congress took the measure of long-standing reform sensibilities and struck at the last foundation of the Indian way of life. Led by the Massachusetts senator Henry L. Dawes, a Republican veteran of the antislavery movement and Reconstruction struggles who occupied the seat vacated by Charles Sumner, Congress enacted the General Allotment Act (also known as the Dawes Severalty Act) in 1887. Embracing ideas of family, individualism, and private property, the act authorized the president to survey reservation lands, have them divided into allotments of up to 160 acres, and make them available to Indian family heads, something in the manner of the Homestead Act. In an effort to protect the allotments against predatory speculators, the federal government would hold them in trust for twenty-five years—they could not be sold during that time—and then extend fee-simple possession to the Indian occupants. Those who agreed to take the allotments would also become citizens of the United States, a status from which Native Americans had previously been excluded, while reservation land that was not subject to allotment—"surplus" lands—would be made available for purchase and white settlement.

In many respects, the Dawes Act completed the process and embodied the contradictions of earlier federal policy in the rebellious South. Native Americans, like African Americans before them, would be rescued from the bonds of communalism (as blacks had been rescued from the bonds of slavery) and, through their embrace of private ownership, made full members of the American nation. Indeed, the Dawes Act was greeted by reformers, much like the passage of the Fourteenth Amendment two decades earlier, as an immensely "important measure" ushering in a "new epoch in Indian affairs." It was, as the secretary of the interior waxed, "practically a general naturalization law for American Indians." But in more immediate and practical terms—as was also true two decades earlier—the act served to dispossess them of the few hedges they had against the imperial arms of the national state while privileging the objectives of the nation-state's entrepreneurial allies. Unlike former slaves, they were not "freed to" be wage laborers and croppers on plantations in a new political economy; they were rather "freed from" control over lands coveted by settlers, mine owners, railroad builders, and merchandisers.

Not surprisingly, just as the freedpeople's rights and protections under the Fourteenth Amendment were steadily whittled away, so were the provisions of the Dawes Act revised to enable alienation and hasten the great white land rushes of the late nineteenth century. By the 1890s, the allotment process had been further extended to Indian Territory (previously exempted), marginalizing the semi-sovereign claims of the Five Civilized Tribes and preparing the way for the new state of Oklahoma. The 155,632,312 acres of land that Native peoples held in 1881 had declined to 77,865,373 acres by the turn of the twentieth century (or by more than half), of which only 5,409,530 had been allotted.

Citizenship was another matter. Although most reformers imagined that Indians would become "intelligent citizen[s] of the United States," questions abounded among federal officials and the wider public as to their "readiness" and "approximate fitness," all the more so once Republicans soured on their own alliance with African Americans in the South and left them prey to white Democrats. "After swallowing four million black slaves," the former secessionist and now Interior Department secretary, L. Q. C. Lamar, opined to a New York reform audience, "we need not strain at this." The Dawes Act thus offered the sort of compromise that suggested the limits of belonging that a nation-state might prescribe: while effectively placing all Native Americans under the jurisdiction of the federal government (as opposed to their own tribal laws and institutions), it granted citizenship only to those who "voluntarily" took up allotments "separate and apart from any tribe of Indians." Those who remained on the shrinking reservations and maintained their tribal connections—a considerable number—continued to be excluded from the "equal protection of the laws."

But they were also fashioning new identities and ways of living. Try as the federal government might to penalize reservation Indians through isolation and dependency, the reservation could in fact become a site of cultural and economic creativity—and of resistance to the projects of the state. Indians regularly traversed reservation boundaries, often in defiance of government regulations and pass requirements, to visit one another and to exchange labor and goods, extending lines of communication and interethnic relations (especially through intermarriage) that had been in the making for decades. In so doing, they deepened their own tribal attachments while developing a sense of pan-tribal Indianness that would find dramatic expression in the anticolonial Ghost Dance movement of 1890 in Lakota country—which occasioned a massive U.S. Army mobilization—and then resurface in a variety of forms for decades to come.

The colonial subjugation of Native peoples may seem like a discrete aspect of the history of the trans-Mississippi West during the late nineteenth century, but it was symptomatic of a far more general dynamic of power. The Republican Party had, from the first, been intent on organizing the region around "free" rather than "slave" labor—even in the face of the Supreme Court's *Dred Scott* decision—and on ensuring the reach and authority of the federal government there. When, as a result of the election of 1860, the party took command of what was left of the federal state, that intention became even more compelling, not simply because of the Native Americans who held sway on the plains and in the Southwest, but also because of the secessionist sentiment that percolated in many quarters, especially on the Pacific coast. President Lincoln's determination to hold Fort Sumter in April 1861 was just as surely a signal to separatist elements in the West as it was to rebels in the South that he meant to defend the Union and enforce the sovereignty of its governmental center. Very quickly, he and congressional Republicans moved to give that sovereign authority a firm economic, political, and cultural basis in the West. They enacted homestead legislation to promote white agricultural settlement, provided extremely generous incentives for the construction of a transcontinental railroad, abolished slavery in those areas under federal jurisdiction, reorganized military districts with a view to raising more volunteers and keeping disloyalty in check, suppressed the Sioux rebellion, and passed a bill outlawing polygamy, one of the "twin relics of barbarism" defined by the party (slavery being the other), with an eye on the Mormons of Utah who had been resisting federal suzerainty since the 1850s.

But perhaps nothing more clearly exemplified the developing colonial structure of the West than the creation and maintenance of large territories. Dakota, Colorado, and Nevada were established in 1861, Arizona and Idaho in 1863, and Montana in 1864, joining New Mexico and Utah, which had been carved out during congressional battles over the spoils of the U.S.-Mexican War. These territories covered immense stretches of the central plains, the desert Southwest, and the Rocky Mountains and were already known to be rich in gold, silver, and other precious metals. They also fell subject to the direct power of the federal government and especially the president, who appointed the leading officials: the territorial governor, secretary, and the court justices. Lincoln was able to remove at least fifteen Democrats from offices in territories that had been organized before his tenure and appoint at least thirty officers in the new ones. Plum patronage positions they were, and, almost always, they went to politically loyal people who were outsiders to the territories in which they were to serve. "There are candidates here," wrote one Colorado judge, "but it will be unsafe . . . to appoint them." "Ignore all applications from New Mexico," another official advised, "and appoint well known and reliable Republicans who have never been here."

What usually emerged in the territories were political "rings," composed mainly of lawyers, businessmen, and political appointees, who formed close alliances with the major party in national power (mostly the Republicans) and with the dominant developmental interests (railroads, ranchers, land speculators, and mine operators) in their domain while ruling, for the most part, with heavy hands over culturally complex populations. They had small patience for the concerns or well-being of either Native American or Hispanic denizens while often taking the first opportunity to cash in on networks of trade and supply or on federal funds destined for reservations. They could use their access to federal patronage and dollars to strengthen their hold on popularly elected territorial legislatures. And neither they nor their patrons in the national government had very much incentive to transform the new territories into states.

Indeed, the western territories were distinguished not only by their physical size but also by the extended period of time that elapsed between their initial organization by Congress and their eventual admission to the Union as states. Whereas new territories east of the Mississippi River moved toward statehood very rapidly (an average of thirteen years), those west of the Mississippi commonly remained under federal jurisdiction for decades: New Mexico for sixty-two years, Arizona for forty-nine, Utah for forty-six, Dakota for twenty-eight, Idaho for twenty-seven, Montana for twenty-five, and Wyoming for twenty-two. The only exceptions were Colorado, which had a fifteen-year territorial period, and Nevada, admitted after only three years as a territory, though chiefly to help ensure Lincoln's reelection in 1864. (The average for all was more than thirty years.)

Yet the dynamic of colonial rule differed from territory to territory. Utah presented many of the same challenges that the states of the rebellious South did and, as a consequence, underwent a similar process of "reconstruction." Mormon settlers of the late 1840s, fleeing persecution east of the Mississippi River, had expressed loyalty to the federal Constitution while claiming semi-sovereignty over their own affairs, which included a highly insular and communitarian economy, a veritable theocracy, and the practice of polygamy. Not surprisingly, they sought admission to the Union—as the State of Deseret—on more than one occasion during the 1850s and did what they could to limit federal interference; in 1857, their rebellion against federal political appointees provoked President James Buchanan to send troops there. But the Mormons' staunchest opponents were members of the new Republican Party who saw a strong connection between slavery and plural marriage. Both, in the Republicans' view, promoted the evils of despotism, licentiousness, and violence; both threatened the foundations of a stable republic.

Although the Morrill Anti-Bigamy Act of 1862 proved impossible to enforce, the Republican state moved in a number of directions to undermine Mormon power. Congress began by creating new territories on either side—Colorado to the east and Nevada to the west—to hedge in Utah's possible expansion and even considered a bill to "blot out the Territory" entirely by dividing it fully between Colorado and Nevada, thus disposing of "the Mormon question." Federal troops were then sent in from California, ostensibly to curb Ute raiding but also to keep Utah's rebellious denizens under close watch. Before long, Congress was entertaining an assortment of bills designed to dismantle polygamy and the

Mormon Church hierarchy through land confiscation, taxation, disfranchisement, loyalty oaths, and criminal prosecutions, much as Radical Republicans
looked to punish rebel leaders and reconstruct the rebellious South.

The late 1870s and the 1880s witnessed a full-scale assault against Mormon social and political organization. Linking the imperial arms of Congress
and the federal courts, including the Supreme Court of the United States, the
offensive occurred at the very time that retreat was under way in the South. In
a striking departure from the jurisprudence of the Slaughterhouse Cases (1873)
and the Civil Rights Cases (1883), the Court ruled in *Reynolds v. United States*
(1879) that polygamists had no right to practice a form of marriage prohibited
by Congress. Federal law enforcement officials then began indicting offenders,
including pregnant women in plural marriages (for fornication), restricting
their political privileges, supervising the dissolution of the Church corporation,
and taking hold of Church assets.

By 1890, the Mormon leadership had had enough. That year, the presiding
Church elder, citing divine revelation, issued a "manifesto" that proclaimed the
end of polygamy and the secularization of territorial politics, preparing the way
for the return of confiscated property, the pardoning of convicted polygamists,
and the admission of Utah to the Union. The Democratic congressman John
Randolph Tucker of Virginia, who co-sponsored a bill in 1887 that struck decisively at polygamy and the foundations of Church power (the Edmunds-Tucker
Act), captured the imperial meaning of the moment. Just as we "dissolve tribal
relations of the Indians in order to make the Indian a good citizen," he declared,
"so we shatter the fabric of this church organization in order to make each
member a free citizen of the Territory of Utah."

The territories of New Mexico and Arizona raised similar issues of incorporation, though with a very different cast of characters. In both cases, their territorial origins were associated with the struggle over the future of slavery and
the slaveholders' rebellion: New Mexico, organized on the basis of popular sovereignty after the armistice of 1850, enacted a slave code and housed more
than a few secessionist sympathizers; Arizona was first established by the rebel
government and then, in quick response, was made a federal territory by Congress. In both cases, the Anglo settlers were outnumbered by peoples with distinctive ethnic identities and liminal civil and political standing in the United
States: Spanish-descended inhabitants who had been in place before the U.S.-
Mexican War but whose citizenship had not yet been granted, and Indians
(Pueblos, Navajos, Apaches) who were battling ferociously against confinement
to reservations. In both cases, political rings held sway—the famed Santa Fe
ring in New Mexico most notably—and managed to enrich themselves in landholdings owing to Republican patronage and connections. And in both cases,

the arrival of the railroad marked a developmental turning point, enabling the exploitation of silver and copper mines and the influx of American settlers either from the east or from the west.

But the move from territory to statehood was complicated by a number of fears. Those of Hispanic descent worried that admission to the Union would likely secure the power and cultural dispositions of Anglo elites who would impose their taxes, public schools, land claims, ideas about suffrage, and anti-Catholic policies. White Democrats, many of whom had been born and raised in the rebellious states of the South, worried that statehood would entrench the rule of Republicans in alliance with Hispanic supporters. But most important was a sense widely shared among Republicans and Democrats alike, in the territories and in the national capital, that neither New Mexico nor Arizona was yet "ready" for statehood, that their Hispanic majorities—who could succeed in ruling the states in democratic elections—were really a "foreign people" speaking an "alien language" and were insufficiently "Americanized." Not for the first time or last would the federal government have to decide whether "the Constitution followed the flag" and, if so, how? Albert Beveridge, the chair of the U.S. Senate's Committee on Territories in the early twentieth century, embraced this view after a tour of the central plains and the Southwest. Reflecting on what he found, Beveridge contrasted "American" Oklahoma with "frontier" Arizona and "Mexican" New Mexico and described the Hispanic residents as passive, uneducated, and indolent—perhaps even "treasonous in their apparent refusal to learn English." Small wonder that he recommended statehood for Oklahoma alone. Only a growing number of Anglos, which portended a shift in the overall demographic balances, made the admission of New Mexico and Arizona possible, and not until 1912, as the last of the continental territories to become states.

Other territories of the trans-Mississippi West—the Dakotas, Idaho, Washington, Wyoming, and Montana—gained admission to the Union earlier but not by very much. Sometimes bitter factional struggles made it difficult to write and ratify new state constitutions; more often, Congress refused to pass enabling legislation owing to the "conditions" its members found there: "problems" they associated with Native Americans, Hispanics, and Mormons, with political party building, or with securing the authority of the nation-state. Political leaders and intellectuals, both inside and outside the federal government, quite simply came to see the western territories as "colonies" and policies designed to deal with Native Americans or "foreign" ethnic groups as important precedents for the future. "There may be no difference between the form of government of a territory and that of a colony," one of them intoned. Senator Henry Dawes, who sponsored the General Allotment Act of 1887, seemed comfortable with this view, suggesting how the trans-Mississippi West could serve as a proving ground for the challenges that awaited an imperial power. Efforts to manage the Indians, he argued, should guide dealings with "other alien races whose future has been put in our keeping."

Traversing the Border

When General Philip Sheridan turned his eyes south of Texas to the turbulence rocking Mexico in 1866, he was impressed by the extent of American support for the struggle against the French-imposed ruler Maximilian. "During the winter and spring of 1866 we continued covertly supplying arms and ammunition to the Liberals—sending as many as 30,000 muskets from the Baton Rouge Arsenal alone," Sheridan recorded, "and by mid-summer Juarez, having organized a pretty good sized army, was in possession of the whole line of the Rio Grande." But more than weaponry was involved in this apparent alliance. Mexican Liberals had been courting potential American investors for some time, and since 1865 millions of dollars in Mexican bonds had been purchased by American financiers and manufacturers who themselves had been enriched and empowered during the War of the Rebellion and now saw opportunities beckoning in the borderlands and well into the interior of Mexico. They included James Beekman, William E. Dodge, Anson Phelps Stokes, John Jacob Astor, J. Pierpont Morgan, Henry du Pont, August Belmont, Cyrus Field, Russell Sage, and Jay Gould. Their vision was robust. As one banker who had aided the Lincoln administration put it, "With the Rebellion vanquished, the Union reestablished, never again to be assailed, and Mexico once more a free and vigorous republic, what power or combination of powers would dare to stop the western course of Empire?"

Some members of the American financial elite imagined the annexation of both northern Mexico and western Canada as part of the "course," but for most of them "empire" was chiefly commercial and closely connected with their developmental projects in the trans-Mississippi West. They looked, that is, to suppress Native populations—principally the Apache but also the Sonoran Yaqui—still intent on raiding and resisting the advance of capitalist civilization; to construct rail lines and other infrastructures linking central Mexico to the northeastern United States; to exploit the mineral and agricultural resources of the Mexican landscape; and to strengthen their positions in both the Caribbean and the Pacific basins. For this, as in the West, they needed the cooperation if not the outright encouragement of the national state as well as of provincial officials who often had minds of their own.

For a while, these goals were easier to conceive than pursue. Mexican Liberals generally shared the modernizing perspectives of Republicans in the United States. They hoped to undermine the communal holdings of Indian villages, liberalize private property, promote the fortunes of a middle class, build transportation and communication networks, commercialize agriculture, widen the base of popular political participation, and fully integrate their country into the international market economy and culture. Yet they smarted from the defeats and humiliations of the war with the United States during the 1840s and rightly worried that a flood of American investments could compromise the sovereignty of their already troubled country. They also faced growing pressure from American bondholders for repayment, part of a foreign debt that proved increasingly difficult for Mexico to manage. The Juárez and then the Sebastián Lerdo de Tejada regimes began to offer concessions, especially to railroad men like Thomas Scott of the Pennsylvania and bankers like J. Pierpont Morgan, but did so haphazardly despite strong pressure from the U.S. minister William Starke Rosecrans (a Civil War general and himself an investor). Lerdo went so far as to repudiate some of the Mexican debt, cancel American railroad contracts, and reject a bilateral trade agreement with the United States.

The turning point came with the ascendancy of Porfirio Díaz. An army officer and elite landowner from the southern state of Oaxaca who had distinguished himself during the recent war with the French, Díaz had had his eyes on the Mexican presidency since the early 1870s. In 1877, after organizing a coup against Lerdo, he achieved his goal and set out to consolidate his power and modernize Mexico. Díaz immediately moved to break the grip of the provincial bosses (caciques) on the peripheries, especially in the north, by installing officials (*jefes políticos*) loyal to him—not unlike what the Republicans did in the territories of the trans-Mississippi West—and simultaneously sought to attract foreign capital for the construction of railroads, mines, plantations, and vital communication networks. Through a mixture of incentives and coercion, Díaz strengthened the governmental center, and through the offer of generous concessions he found eager investors. It was the beginning of a three-decade-long project of state building and dictatorial rule—something of a "revolution from above" characterized, as his regime put it, by *"mucha administración y poca política"*—that has come to be known as the Porfiriato.

The timing could not have been more propitious. The very year that Díaz claimed power, the Republican Rutherford B. Hayes, who had railroad interests in Mexico, was inaugurated president after the highly contested election of 1876, and while he still had ideas about annexing some of Mexico's northern states as well as concerns about Díaz, Hayes soon sought cooperation, through the U.S. Army, with the Díaz regime: in the near term to quell cross-border raiding. For their part, American financiers based in the Northeast who were close to Hayes and supported Díaz's ascendancy in a variety of ways quickly reaped the rewards. With the assistance of compliant provincial governors, Díaz provided subsidies and rights-of-way to railroad consortia while using a heavy hand to suppress Apache raids, peasant unrest, and labor union radicals. Before long, new railroad lines were heading south toward Mexico City from Laredo, Matamoros, Eagle Pass, El Paso, and Nogales, linking up with a number of American roads traversing the Southwest or converging on El Paso, Albuquerque, Tucson, and Phoenix. They included the Southern Pacific, the Texas and Pacific, and the Atchison, Topeka, and Santa Fe. By the time the century ended, Americans not only had financed the building of roughly seventy-five hundred miles of track but also owned 80 percent of the stocks and bonds sold by Mexican railroads. Fittingly, the Mexican Central Railway, the system's main artery, was incorporated in Massachusetts in 1880.

As in the trans-Mississippi West, the railroads were an entering wedge for other American investments in the Mexican economy, none more consequential than in the mineral sector. The intervention of the Mexican state again proved crucial, marking as it did the completion of the Mexican Central with the passage of a new mining code that, for the first time, allowed landowners rights to the resources lying beneath the soil. Drawing upon their previous experience in the Rocky Mountains and especially the desert Southwest, American investors—the Guggenheims, Rockefellers, Stillmans, Harrimans, Goulds, Phelpses, and Dodges—brought in new technologies and their own engineers and foremen to extract the ores, hired Mexican workers to perform the dangerous tasks underground, and constructed trunk rail lines (*minerales*) into remote zones to transport the ore to smelters in the United States. Eventually, they built smelting facilities as well.

Silver mining was at the heart of the imperial undertaking, and Americans, led by the Guggenheims, came to dominate centers in Chihuahua, Sonora, and Durango to the west, San Luis Potosí and Coahuila to the east, and Guanajuato farther to the south. Little by little, they gained controlling interest in silver production and then, as they had already been doing on the U.S. side of the border, turned their attention to copper and petroleum. In the process, they created an interconnected industrial borderland that linked mining towns like Tombstone, Bisbee, Gleeson, and Douglas on the U.S. side with Cananea, Nacozari, Magdalena, and Moctezuma on the Mexican. "Twenty years ago . . . as remote and inaccessible as Africa is today," an American geologist would write at the turn of the century of the changing transnational landscape, "now by the magic of the desert conquering railway, American enterprise and mining exploration, there is not a mountain but what has been scanned; not an acre that has not been surveyed; hardly a stone that has not been scrutinized."

What was, in effect, the extension of developmental patterns already in evidence in the trans-Mississippi West came to define other investments in land use, agricultural production, and corporate organization. Availing themselves of Díaz-inspired privatization of peasant landholdings and of his willingness to grant them exemptions from prohibitions on foreign land purchases, American investors commenced a massive landgrab while finding their way into other sectors of the Mexican economy. Mine owners snatched up adjacent properties in part to furnish rail connections, water, power, and food for their operations, turning them into the sorts of company towns that had already sprung up from Montana and Idaho to Colorado and Arizona. Some of the moneyed Americans established large ranches, many thousands of acres in scale, both for the meat and hides they provided and to diversify their expanding portfolios. Bankers, import-export merchants, and manufacturers like Cyrus McCormick of International Harvester put their funds into the production of coffee and sugar in Veracruz, henequen in the Yucatán, and rubber (drawn from the guayule bush) in Chiapas to the south and the Sonoran deserts to the northwest. To these may be added timber companies and ironworks. Before the end of the century, more than one-third of the Mexican landmass was owned by foreigners, most of which—130 million acres—was in American hands: this at the very time that Díaz's assault on the communalism of indigenous villages was rendering over 90 percent of the Mexican peasantry landless.

But there were wider implications as well. Just as the trans-Mississippi West served as a staging ground for the extension of America's imperial economic arms into Mexico, so too did the various projects of American investors in Mexico, from mining to agriculture to lumber to shipping to credit, prepare the way for a new type of U.S. hegemony in the Western Hemisphere and beyond. For a time, the process was gradual but from the late 1870s notable nonetheless. American banking interests began extending loans to landowners and nascent developers in Central America and the Caribbean and investing in infrastructure projects with a view to building a canal across the isthmus. American manufacturers sold advanced machinery and other technologies to creole producers. American merchants, shipping companies, and refiners helped organize the export trade, especially in sugar and other tropical commodities (sugar refining became the leading industry in New York City), turning the United States into the principal market even for societies that remained under European colonial rule. And the American nation-state, driven by Republican expansionists like James G. Blaine, negotiated a series of reciprocity treaties that simultaneously strengthened the position of the United States in hemispheric trade and challenged the position of the British, the chief European rival.

The Spanish colony of Cuba was an important case in point. American involvement with Cuba reached back into the eighteenth century and intensified in the early nineteenth as the sugar and slave economy took off. Northeastern-based mercantile companies established houses in Havana and other ports on the island, provided credit, became involved in slave trading, bought up some of the sugar crop, and acquired a few sugar and coffee estates. American political interests, to be found chiefly, though not exclusively, in the Democratic Party, pressed for annexation in what seemed an inevitable outcome—even John Quincy Adams saw "laws of political gravitation" at work—until the War of the Rebellion intervened. Little American contact, other than the arrival of disgruntled Confederates, occurred immediately thereafter.

But with the end of Cuba's first independence movement in 1878, known as the Ten Years' War (it failed), new possibilities opened without the need for annexation. American investors, generally from the financial sector, found creole planters desperate for capital to rebuild their sugar plantations and mills and through a combination of foreclosures and opportunistic purchases began to buy up properties, including the sixty-thousand-acre Constancia plantation in Cienfuegos, recognized as the largest sugar estate in the world. American dollars flowed to other areas of the Cuban economy as well—utilities, tobacco, mining, transportation—while the growing volume of trade made the United States Cuba's most important partner by far. Indeed, as the U.S. consul Ramon O. Williams put it in the 1880s, "De facto, Cuba is already inside the commercial union of the United States. . . . The Island is now entirely dependent upon the market of the United States . . . [and the] existence of the sugar plantations, the railroads, the export and import trades . . . each including hundreds of minor industries . . . are now directly related to the market of the United States to the extent of 94 percent of their employment."

Similar, though less substantial, projects were to be found elsewhere in the Caribbean basin, setting the groundwork for much more formidable corporate undertakings before the end of the century. In Nicaragua, the regime that came to power after William Walker's failed coup combined conservative politics with economic modernization and, like the Porfiriato, looked to reward export producers (mainly coffee in this case) and infrastructure developers with subsidies and a variety of legal reforms that made the acquisition of property and the accumulation of laborers more feasible. American investors trained their eyes on the country, initially believing it the most favorable place for an isthmian canal, and American cultural as well as economic influence grew accordingly. In neighboring Costa Rica, the American entrepreneur Henry Meiggs was awarded a contract in 1871 to build a railroad from the capital of San José to the Caribbean port of Limón. But when the government defaulted on its payments, Meiggs's successor (and relative) managed to extract 800,000 acres of land, which was soon producing and exporting bananas and would later be organized as the United Fruit Company.

The question of annexation turned up more significantly not in Central America or the Caribbean (though Grant failed in an effort to annex Santo Domingo)—increasingly regarded as the American "Mediterranean"—but rather in the distant Pacific archipelago of Hawai'i. It would be a lengthy and tumultuous process that resembled the approach of federal officials and social reformers to Native Americans on the North American continent—and produced a similar outcome. Just as the western hemispheric landmass had been populated by migrants who crossed over from northeastern Asia, so Hawai'i had been settled as early as the fourth century c.e. by Polynesians who had been navigating slowly across the South Pacific. Their descendants eventually organized four socially complex island kingdoms, which then struggled against one another for supremacy. By the turn of the nineteenth century, that struggle had been won, and the islands were unified under the rule of Kamehameha, a strong leader who established a hereditary dynasty. But he, and especially his immediate successors during the first half of the nineteenth century, cast worried eyes on threats to their sovereign authority. For good reason. Since the mid-eighteenth century, Hawai'i had emerged as something of an economic and cultural crossroads, serving as a refueling and provisioning station for European and American merchants and whaling vessels, some involved in the Pacific and Indian Ocean trade, who established centers of maritime commerce in Honolulu and Lahaina. By the 1820s, American missionaries, chiefly from New England, had arrived with their version of spiritual practice and "civilization" for the benefit of the Hawai'ian natives. Among them were the parents of Samuel Chapman Armstrong, himself born in Maui, and who would serve in the U.S. Army, command black troops, and go on to establish the Hampton Normal and Agricultural Institute to educate both African Americans (including Booker T. Washington) and Native Americans.

Rather than attempting to resist the foreign challenge directly, Hawai'i's rulers chose instead—somewhat in the manner of the Cherokees in North America—to protect their sovereignty by accommodating the westerners: by converting to Christianity and embracing Euro-American concepts of law, private property, and political representation. Their hope was that by showing themselves to be "civilized" and "advancing" by Western standards, they would win international respectability as an independent nation. To these ends, they organized an elective legislature, began publishing newspapers, and enacted a land reform program (known as the Great Māhele) that privatized property previously owned by the kingdom and permitted foreigners to purchase it in fee simple. It proved to be an enormous transformation of the political and cultural cartography of the islands, and for a time the strategy appeared to work. Great Britain and France issued a joint declaration recognizing Hawai'ian sovereignty, and although some annexationist sentiment was already bubbling among Americans there, the U.S. government signed the Treaty of Friendship, Commerce, and Navigation with Kamehameha III in 1849, which clearly acknowledged the independence of the Hawai'ian kingdom and made provision for commercial reciprocity between the two countries. In what became known as the Tyler Doctrine (for President John Tyler in a message to Congress), the United States had earlier insisted that it sought "no exclusive control over the Hawaiian Government" and accepted Hawai'i's independence so long as European powers did not themselves attempt to take possession of the islands.

Yet as was true for Native Americans, the cultural and political accommodationism of the Hawai'ians proved to be a weak barrier against the American developmental juggernaut. The legal and political reforms enacted by Hawai'ian rulers allowed economically ambitious Americans—many of whom were the children of missionaries if not missionaries themselves—to build a foundation of capitalist agriculture, especially for the cultivation of sugarcane. Slowly in the 1850s and far more rapidly after a reciprocity treaty gave Hawai'ian sugar duty-free access to the U.S. market (1875), a plantation economy took off and reshaped the relations of power and the demographic composition of the islands. American planters and merchants found common economic interests, further securing their alliance through intermarriage. And with African slavery unraveling across the globe, they looked—as did their counterparts elsewhere—for sources of contract labor. They turned first to the Chinese who were already working in mines and on railroad construction crews in the trans-Mississippi West (as well as in various parts of southeastern Asia) but found them unreliable once their initial contracts expired. Next they recruited Portuguese laborers, many from the Azores, and then Japanese, Koreans, and Filipinos. By 1890, less than half the population of the islands was native Hawai'ian.

Yet even as they thrived economically, planting interests together with Americans in the mercantile and missionary communities increasingly complained about the character of the Hawai'ian rulers and the powers the Hawai'ians could allegedly wield. They talked of corrupt practices, venality, wastefulness, and backwardness much as elite reformers in the United States spoke of urban bosses and political machines, not to mention the Reconstruction South. And as the language and logic of white supremacy came to suffuse the perspectives of Euro-American imperialists generally, they questioned whether Hawai'ians were capable of governing themselves, let alone anybody else. In this, missionaries and their descendants did a great deal of the cultural work. By the late 1880s, Americans had begun to hatch a political insurrection. Led by Lorrin Thurston and Sanford Dole, they formed the Hawaiian League with its own paramilitary arm (much in the fashion of southern and western politics). They wrote a new constitution that stripped the king (Kalakaua at this point) of many powers and shifted them to the legislature, which was now to be chosen by a highly circumscribed electorate. In the summer of 1887, they dumped it in Kalakaua's lap with the demand (backed by the threat of force) that he submit. With few options at his disposal, Kalakaua reluctantly signed what was known, appropriately, as the Bayonet Constitution. Although they had not yet taken full control of the government, Americans, whose goal was annexation, had clearly staged a successful coup and were now in a position to envelop the political body of Hawai'i ever more tightly within their imperial grasp.

William Seward's Imperial Eyes

Well before the 1887 coup that installed annexation-minded Americans in the seats of power in Hawai'i, William H. Seward had imagined its "quiet absorption" into the United States. Best known as a New York governor, U.S. senator, Radical Republican, candidate for the presidency in 1860, and secretary of state in Lincoln's cabinet, Seward also had a wide-angled imperial vision. He was not interested in establishing sugar plantations or any other American-based industries there or anywhere else, including Mexico, nor was he interested in promoting American settlement overseas. He had also cooled on an early goal of having Canada and Mexico join the Union. What did interest him was American commercial supremacy in the Pacific and control over the waterborne highways that led to Asia. "The empire of the seas alone is the real empire," he insisted, and Asia would be "the prize . . . the chief theater of events in the world's great hereafter." So fixed was Seward on the importance of the Pacific to America's future that this icon of antislavery rhetoric ("the irrepressible conflict" he called the battle between slavery and freedom) wanted newly conquered California admitted to the Union as quickly as possible "even if she had come as a slave state" to prevent its "severance." This, more than the secession of the rebellious states of the South, to him would have meant the "dismemberment of the empire."

While continuing to serve as secretary of state under President Johnson, Seward looked hungrily at a number of sites stretching from the Caribbean basin west, not for the purpose of conquest and colonization, but rather to establish coaling stations and commercial entrepôts for the trade with Asia. Imagining an isthmian canal in the near future, he saw Santo Domingo and some of the islands of the French West Indies as strategically important, but made no diplomatic headway. A visit to the Danish Virgin Islands, however, led to Seward's signing a treaty for their annexation, although the Senate refused to approve it. Better luck came to him in the central Pacific, where what are now known as the Midway Islands were annexed. But Seward's greatest achievement, at least by his own lights (although not in the view of many contemporaries: Seward's "ice box" some called it), was the purchase of Alaska from the Russians for just over $7 million in 1867. Well aware of long-term commercial activity in this Russian-controlled (though Native American–occupied) territory and of the Russian desire to pull back after the disastrous Crimean War, Seward saw Alaska's acquisition both as a means to extend U.S. dominion over North America and as a vital coaling station to Japan and China. He sought, that is, "possession of the American continent and control over the world." Seward clearly recognized the relation between commercial and political power and knew that the threat of military force would be necessary to secure American imperial objectives. Yet he also frowned on the use of force as a method of territorial aggrandizement—he would not permit Sheridan to cross the border during a developing Mexican civil war involving Maximilian and the French—insisting on what he regarded as voluntary action. Indeed, when Seward gazed toward Asia, and especially toward China, whose potential market left American merchants and manufacturers agape, he was intent on respecting the sovereignty of the societies there while cooperating with other western nations to maintain equal commercial opportunities. The Burlingame Treaty, signed and ratified in 1868, not only acknowledged China's territorial integrity but also abolished the coolie trade, encouraged Chinese immigration, and guaranteed reciprocal privileges for each of the nation's citizens abroad. Although it would be another three decades before the term came into common usage, Seward plainly envisioned the framework for the "Open Door."

Seward had by no means abandoned interest in the American domestic sphere. Far from it. His very idea of empire intricately linked domestic and foreign affairs and, in fact, knew no clear borders or boundaries. Commercial supremacy across the globe, he believed, required a strong and stable social order at home, built upon flourishing agricultural and industrial economies and encouraged by a national government ready to support the aspirations of merchants, manufacturers, and farmers. Seward called for a transcontinental railroad as early as the 1840s, advocated a protective tariff, and opposed the expansion of slavery in part because he thought it would render the United States unfit to pursue the kind of empire he imagined. He looked for ways to repair the damage of secession before it was irreversible (he suggested waging war against Britain and France). After Lincoln's assassination (and his own narrow escape), he backed Johnson's conciliatory approach to the rebellious states in the service of national unity.

In an important sense, Seward recognized the complex imperial tendencies of emerging nation-states, operating as they did both inside and outside their presumed territorial borders, and thus struggled to extend the reach of the imperial arms that unfolded in so many directions across and beyond the United States in the years after the War of the Rebellion. Almost invariably, that is, nation-states define themselves in relation to constellations of values—either specifically national or "universal"—that they expect to have embraced. They exalt ideas of citizenship and belonging that undermine previously existing forms of personal and group sovereignties. They champion a "rule of law" that stands as an alternative to the long-prevailing rough justice of local communities. Nation-states use the means of transportation, communication, police power, and knowledge to expand their authority over all of the territory they claim. They enumerate and classify the people who live within their borders (usually by means of a census), and explore and map their physical terrain. They establish frameworks for various social relations (labor, gender, family) and privilege certain types of cultural and spiritual behaviors that they regard as "civilized." And they commonly offer incentives (negative as well as positive) to citizens and noncitizens alike to discard their parochialism and "backwardness" and instead accept what is seen as the modern and proper way of doing things.

Not surprisingly, nation-states generally have great interest in education and other sorts of "missionizing" activities, and they nearly always come into being in close connection to movements of social and political reform—oftentimes modified or defeated—that aim at promoting new forms of character, participation, representation, market orientation, and faith. Nation-states, as William Seward presciently glimpsed, are perpetually and necessarily colonizing their own domains even as they prepare to find new ones.

CHAPTER ELEVEN

Alternative Paths

Scenes of struggle during the Great Railroad Strike of July 1877.
Frank Leslie's Illustrated Newspaper, August 11, 1877.

Antimonopoly

The epiphany came "like a flash" as he rode on horseback through the Oakland hills. Henry George had been in California since the late 1850s, an ambitious and peripatetic soul who left his birthplace of Philadelphia at the age of sixteen, joined the crew of a merchantman out of New York, made port in Melbourne and Calcutta, apprenticed as a printer on his return, and then, in the midst of the severe economic downturn in 1857, headed west with an eye on Oregon and the new gold rush to British Columbia. Like many others who followed the course of American empire in hopes of fortune, George was quickly disappointed and ended up in San Francisco searching for opportunity. His typesetting skills opened some doors and got him involved in a few journalistic ventures, though for more than a decade it was a very bumpy road. Finally, in the early 1870s, George found some stability. Pooling his small savings, he became a partner in and then editor of San Francisco's *Daily Evening Post*.

Having grown up in a household of Jacksonian Democrats, George was simultaneously attracted by the frontier character of California and shocked by the speculative mania that seemed to produce mansions and shanties. "One millionaire involves the existence of just so many proletarians," he wrote. Of a pastoral bent and very much beholden to the virtues of a small-scale society of farmers, artisans, and tradesmen, he was particularly riled by the land grants that shifted large sections of the public domain into private hands. As early as 1868, he published a piece called "What the Railroad Will Bring Us" and then followed with the pamphlets *The Subsidy Question and the Democratic Party* and *Our Land and Land Policy* (both in 1871), together lamenting that the "landgrabbers have had it pretty much their own way in California." How was it, George wondered, that "advancing poverty" came with "advancing wealth"?

The answer jolted him in the Oakland hills when one of the locals told of a man who could sell land for $1,000 an acre. "With the growth of population," George now recognized, "land grows in value, and the men who work it must pay for the privilege." Shortly thereafter, he began to write a book he would call *Progress and Poverty*. It was neither a pamphlet nor a polemic; it was rather a lengthy (more than five hundred pages) and closely reasoned treatise in political economy that challenged the assumptions and arguments of the classical political economists, especially David Ricardo and Thomas Malthus. And it was devoted to exploring what he saw as the central contradiction of modern society: how, "where the conditions to which material progress everywhere tends are most fully realized . . . we find the deepest poverty, the sharpest struggle for existence, and the most enforced idleness."

George had little patience for the view that "progress and poverty" could be explained either by population growth pressing on subsistence or by the "fixed" nature of the wage fund. There was, he insisted, "no warrant" to assume that population increased faster than subsistence; he could find no case of poverty being attributable to increasing population. As for wages, the mistake was in assuming that they were paid out of existing capital rather than out of the products of labor. Indeed, *Progress and Poverty* imagined a dynamic and diversified economy in which land (all "natural opportunities," as he saw it) served as the foundation, labor ("all human exertion") transformed the resources of land into wealth, and the wealth used to produce more wealth could be regarded as capital. The more the population grew, the more the number of laborers multiplied, the higher the wages—the very products of labor—should be. George saw no inherent conflict between labor and capital and instead argued that "the merchant or storekeeper is . . . as truly a producer as is the manufacturer, or farmer, and his stock or capital is as much devoted to production as theirs."

What, then, was the problem? How could such economic dynamism give rise to such poverty and inequality? Here, George's western perspective seemed crucial. Land, which was the basic means of production and wealth for all, had not only been taken out of the public domain for private use but through government largesse and speculation had come to be "monopolized" by a few wealthy men. In California, where railroad construction encouraged engrossment in anticipation of rising land values, and as mining companies bought up extensive tracts in anticipation of mineral exploitation, this was especially in evidence. The results could be seen in the effective "rent" that was charged for access to land's resources, rent that increased with labor's productive power and shut labor out from gainful employment while forcing wages down. "The great cause of inequality in the distribution of wealth," George proclaimed, "is inequality in the ownership of land."

Although George believed that the ideals of socialism were "grand and noble," and the only way to truly remedy the evil he saw was to "make land common property," he did not favor "restricting landownership." "An equal distribution of land" he thought "impossible." Rather, George favored a policy of taxation—it would later be called the single tax—that would be equivalent to the value of rent and thereby discourage speculative investment and monopolization. "If we concede to priority of possession the undisturbed use of the land," he reasoned, "we reconcile the fixity of tenure which is necessary for improvement with a full and complete recognition of the equal rights of all to the use of the land."

Progress and Poverty does not make for light or easy reading. It does not tell riveting or heartrending stories or deploy extravagant or millennial language. George builds his case slowly. He invokes the classical political economists. He draws wide-ranging historical analogies. And he offers up densely constructed arguments. But when the book was published in 1879, it struck a remarkable popular chord and catapulted George to national and international fame. Over the course of the nineteenth century, only the Bible and *Uncle Tom's Cabin* sold more copies in the United States. Within a decade, he would run for mayor of New York City on an independent labor ticket and, while losing, would outpoll the young Theodore Roosevelt. There is no real mystery. With great moral power, Henry George and *Progress and Poverty* tapped into what could be called the "antimonopoly" sensibilities that were widespread in the country, energized by the very inequalities that George identified and by the intensifying struggles that the advance of capitalism was producing.

Antimonopoly had deep roots in American political culture, as it did in the wider Atlantic world. It germinated in the intellectual soil of republicanism, which had long sought alternatives to forms of concentrated power that made for tyranny, and was tilled by economically independent citizens devoted to the public good. During the 1820s and 1830s, antimonopoly found expression among early labor reformers and Workingmen's parties—and favor among European radicals with artisan sensibilities—who pushed back against the market intensifications of the era. It informed Andrew Jackson's "war" against the "monster" national bank, portrayed as the personal machine of the wealthy Nicholas Biddle, as well as popular suspicions of paper money, considered the vehicle of greedy "speculators" and the bane of sturdy "producers." By the 1840s and 1850s, it had become an important component of the antislavery critique of the slave South, warning voters in the Northeast and the Midwest that a small slaveholding minority had accumulated massive wealth and reduced the non-slaveholding white majority, along with the slaves, to abject dependency. But as a developing set of political beliefs that attracted mass support, antimonopoly really took shape as the War of the Rebellion drew to a close and the character of the postwar social order—and the new American nation-state—began to be contested. And the question of money was at the very center.

In a sense, "paper money" and "hard money" (specie) remained the poles of struggle, but the advocates of each switched sides, and the issues became far more complex. Three decades earlier, as the market economy spread through the American hinterlands, wary producers saw specie as a hedge against their economic vulnerabilities. Gold and silver coins were widely recognized as mediums of exchange. They had a tangibility that other mediums lacked. In modest supply, they circulated with local promissory notes to facilitate trade in the goods that supplemented subsistence. Paper currency, however, was printed by state banks, promoted speculation, was not always convertible into specie, and often traded at a discount. The severe panic of 1837 was widely blamed on the excesses associated with paper money, and once the smoke cleared during the 1840s, many state legislatures moved to either regulate the issuing banks or abolish them outright.

The dynamic changed when the federal government, to help finance its war against the rebellious South, created a national banking system and issued over $400 million in greenbacks, paper currency that was accepted for taxes and exchange, even though it could not be redeemed in specie. Together, they established a new framework for capital accumulation and investment while being directly at odds in the constituencies they favored. On the one hand, newly chartered national banks were left in private hands and, owing to capital and loan requirements for their operations, gave the advantage to cities and larger-scale economic institutions. On the other hand, greenbacks put the federal government—and the public more generally—in control of the money supply and gave smaller producers in towns and rural districts better access to the cash they needed for their shops, farms, and debts. Thus the battle lines were redrawn. No longer did the money issue simply pit West against East or countryside against city, nor even inflationists against sound-money advocates. The battle lines cut across class and regional divides and conjured alternative political economies.

Labor reformers, emboldened by the upsurge of economic activity during the war and the prospect for shaping postwar policy, were the first to step forward. Organized in the National Labor Union (1866), an umbrella group that linked them with trade unionists, they denounced the national banking system as a promoter of money monopoly and insisted that the federal government had the responsibility to set interest rates, make loans, and print money sufficient to satisfy the needs of production. In this, they were influenced by the writings of Edward Kellogg, a late Jacksonian-era merchant and monetary theorist who saw the manipulation of interest rates by private financial interests as leading to the degradation of labor, and of Alexander Campbell, a small-town midwestern mayor and manufacturing booster who developed Kellogg's ideas and influenced the adoption of wartime greenbacks. "Our objective point," the National Labor Union president and iron molder, William Sylvis, maintained, "is a new monetary system, a system that will take from a few men the power to control the money, and give to the people a cheap, secure, and abundant currency."

The National Labor Union gave rise to the National Labor Party and then the Labor Reform Party, antimonopoly parties built on greenback platforms, both of which quickly failed. But after the panic of 1873, greenback sentiment spread among a wide range of producers who saw monetary contraction as the cause of the crisis. They knew what they were up against. Congress had already determined to pay the public debt in gold rather than in greenbacks (a boon to creditors) and then, in 1875, to allow federal banknotes to be redeemed in specie as a way of removing greenbacks from circulation (it was known as the Resumption Act). First meeting in Indiana in late 1874, a coalition of antimonopolists soon launched the Greenback Labor Party, which demanded the repeal of specie resumption, endorsed a plan to adjust the volume of currency to the needs of economic growth (the essence of greenbackism), and called "the full development of all business—agricultural, mining, manufacturing, and commercial"—the "paramount duty of government."

Greenback ideas, as central features of antimonopolism, won the allegiance of a great many agricultural producers and small manufacturers who had begun to chafe at the exploitative practices of railroads and creditors or felt themselves heirs to the Jacksonian equal rights tradition. More than a few had already found their way into local antimonopoly and reform movements, and they were especially numerous in New England, parts of the Middle Atlantic, the upper plains, the Rocky Mountains, and the Far West. Yet labor reformers and unionists, harking back to the National Labor Union and Radical Republicanism, were very much at the heart. They included Radicals like Alexander Campbell and Wendell Phillips but were particularly numerous among miners, shoemakers, iron molders, shipbuilders, and printers, whose union leaders had shown a strong affinity for currency reform. In 1876, the Greenback Labor Party first contested for office; by 1878, it claimed nearly 15 percent of the votes nationwide and between 20 and 25 percent in New England, the northern plains, the Rocky Mountain states, and the Pacific coast. More than twenty members of Congress owed their seats to Greenback votes. Yet the strongest showings came on the state and local levels, most notably in industrial and mining towns, some in alliance with other independent and labor parties, where, as in Toledo, Ohio, Greenbackers swept the city and some of the county posts and sent two of their candidates to the state legislature.

Although greenbackism did not yet threaten to vie for significant national power, its growing constituencies forced the two major parties to take notice. Indeed, in the developing battle over the character of the financial system and particularly after the panic of 1873 triggered a steep depression, Republicans and Democrats alike faced dissension within their ranks. The fissures were sharpest in the Democratic Party as a variety of western interests—agricultural producers, urban workers, small-town shopkeepers—challenged the financially conservative eastern wing in the name of monetary reform. Many were captivated by the "plan" of Ohio's George H. Pendleton—a former congressman and vice presidential candidate, and later senator—which contained an assortment of greenback remedies (such as paying bondholders in greenbacks not gold), and their strength would grow over the next two decades. For their part, the Republicans, who had defeated their inflationist wing during the late 1860s and seemed firmly attached to sound money and the gold standard, nonetheless felt pressure from constituents in states like Colorado and Nevada, where a series of rich silver strikes stoked the call for a more flexible currency. Thus, at the very time that greenbackism was gaining traction, the notion of inflating the money supply by coining silver as well as gold came on the political table.

Historians often see silver and greenbacks as two sides of an inflationist political coin, but this was hardly the case. Although Greenbackers often supported silver coinage as a means of increasing the currency in circulation and reducing interest rates, and although financial conservatives often regarded silver as a dire threat to the stability of the economic system, the limited monetization of silver increasingly won the support of mainstream Republicans and Democrats as an accommodation to economic distress and as an alternative to greenbackism. Coining silver in addition to gold did not challenge the structure of the national banking system, nor did it permit the expansion of paper currency; if anything, increasing the supply of specie would hasten the redemption and retirement of the greenbacks that remained in circulation. In 1878, a moderate silver policy won out: Congress passed, over the Republican president Rutherford B. Hayes's veto, the Bland-Allison Act, which required the Treasury Department to coin a limited number of silver dollars ($2 million to $4 million) per month at the ratio of sixteen parts silver to one part gold.

Greenbackers imagined something very different. As part of a larger antimonopoly politics, they wanted the national banking system scaled back or abolished, the currency supply placed in the hands of the federal government, and the circulation of greenbacks increased or decreased as the productive requirements of the country demanded. They hoped to limit the power of bankers and financiers to carry out monetary contractions, manipulate interest rates, and enrich themselves at the expense of ordinary citizens. And they looked to combat the growing concentrations of wealth and power that private control of the monetary system promoted. They envisioned, instead, a vibrant political economy built around an array of producers whose needs—access to the market, credit, land, transportation, and networks of communication—would be secured and advanced by the state.

By the late 1870s, the antimonopoly impulse was to be found in many corners of the United States, and it reacted to the shifting balances of power in the postwar political economy: balances that had come to favor northeastern financial and industrial elites and forced many other areas of the country to shoulder the costs of capitalist development. For a time, antimonopoly encouraged cross-class coalitions in smaller towns and rural districts as skilled workers and shopkeepers, landowners and tenant farmers alike, suffered the consequences of various forms of "monopolization." They increasingly complained of high freight rates demanded by railroad corporations, high interest rates charged by bankers and merchants, massive land engrossments carried out by speculators and ranchers, wage cuts imposed by large manufacturers, and corrupt political practices that monopolists engaged in and benefited from. Like Greenbackers, with whom they generally sympathized if not supported, they looked to devise public policies and institutions not only to readjust the balances but also to reconstruct the social order.

The political tremors were quickly felt. In the corn and wheat belts of the upper Mississippi Valley and the lower Midwest, across the hops and dairy farms of the Middle Atlantic, and in some of the cash-crop districts of the Southeast, the Patrons of Husbandry (also known as the Grange) joined hands with other aggrieved shippers and producers in calling for state and municipal railroad regulation and for the creation of marketing and purchasing cooperatives to weaken the hold of "middle men." In Texas, the fledgling Farmers' Alliance, established "for the purpose of bettering the conditions of the agricultural classes," sought to protect the crops and livestock of farm operators, talked of establishing local cooperatives, and briefly coalesced with Greenbackers in local elections. But more than any other organization, the Knights of Labor wove together the threads of antimonopolism and pointed to the directions that anti-monopoly would travel; it also exposed the limits of antimonopoly as a political movement and social vision.

Little is known about the origins of the Knights, though it appears that the organization first emerged among tailors in Philadelphia during the late 1860s. But amid a surge of trade unionism fired by agitation for the eight-hour work-day, the Knights launched what would be a fitful and then meteoric course of growth. The heyday came in the mid-1880s, when they could boast nearly three-quarters of a million members, yet the foundations were clearly set during the late 1870s. Built around local and district assemblies, the Knights of Labor was far more inclusive than any previous labor organization, open to skilled and unskilled workers, blacks and whites, "irrespective of sex," together with sympathetic shopkeepers, merchants, and manufacturers. Only bankers, stockbrokers, lawyers, gamblers, and liquor dealers—those associated in the antimonopoly outlook with idleness, vice, and corruption—were explicitly barred. Significantly, when they met in Reading, Pennsylvania, in 1879 for their first national convention, the Knights chose Terence V. Powderly, a machinist and the Green-back Labor mayor of nearby Scranton, as its president.

The goals that energized the Knights harked back, in part, to the currents of antebellum labor reform. They demanded the abolition of contract and convict labor, the implementation of more equitable taxation (a graduated income tax in this case), and land policies that favored "actual settlers" rather than "railroads and speculators," suggesting a heavy tax on "all lands now held for speculative purposes." But the Knights took account as well of the new political economy—the "alarming development and aggressiveness of great capitalists and corporations"—and the aspirations of the "producing masses" within it. They called for bureaus of labor statistics, government protection for the "health and safety" of workers, the establishment of "co-operative institutions," and a "national monetary system" built around the principles of greenbackism. Eventually, they would favor public ownership of the railroads and telegraphs. But the issue with which the Knights were to become most closely identified, and the one that brought forth their distinctive contribution to antimonopoly, was the eight-hour workday.

The hours of labor are often regarded as bread-and-butter issues that speak chiefly to the material interests of workers. But for those who began to rally around the cause of the eight-hour workday—as early as the 1830s, though in more organized fashion as the War of the Rebellion drew to a close—it represented something far more sweeping. To be sure, reducing the hours of labor (ten had become the norm, though a great many workers, women and children as well as men, had much longer daily stints) promised to lighten the physical burdens of manual labor and improve the workers' health and personal welfare. The developing arguments, however, were as much about the nature of power in the workplace as they were about the extent of free time.

Supporters of an eight-hour workday tied an expansive view of political democracy to a critique of the perils of the new capitalist order. Like the labor reformers who came before them, they believed that wage work threatened economic dependency and that long hours on the job made for a species of slavery—"wage slavery" they termed it—in which employers effectively "monopolized" all of the waking hours of their employees. After working ten, eleven, or twelve hours, there was little time for families, communities, or themselves. The eight-hour workday, as advocates imagined it, not only improved the material conditions of labor; it strengthened working-class households and social institutions and enabled workers to pursue education, culture, and, most important, the obligations of citizenship: to participate in political life and governance. "Eight hours for work, eight hours for rest, eight hours for what we will!" was the mobilizing slogan. Together with monetary and land reform and the promotion of producers' cooperatives, the eight-hour workday was heralded as striking a blow against the "wages system" and setting the basis for a new sort of commonwealth.

How encompassing would this commonwealth be? The Knights claimed to open their assemblies to the "industrial masses . . . irrespective of party, race, and sex," and in this they were bold and pioneering. Unions had customarily been built around specific trades and skilled workers who sought protection from the assaults of their employers as well as the incursions of those capable of diluting the integrity and respectability of their crafts: the unskilled, women, and blacks chief among them. Although the National Labor Union had invited African American workers to "co-operate with us," it was the Knights who recognized that "unity" was necessary to the task of "organizing and directing the power of the industrial masses" and that unity required a far more expansive outreach. Early on, recruits to the Knights came principally from the ranks of the urban skilled, especially in southeastern Pennsylvania and New Jersey. But by the late 1870s, as the organization moved into the nearby anthracite fields and then extended its arms across much of the country, semiskilled and unskilled workers began to form assemblies or joined those designated as "mixed."

In metropolitan areas, they included "lumber yard employees," "coal unloaders," "freight handlers," and "laborers," as well as tailors, shoemakers, carpenters, and iron molders. In smaller towns and rural areas, they included coal miners, farmers, farm laborers, renters, and coopers. The women who came into the organization were often shoe, textile, and garment workers, mainly from the Northeast, who had a tradition of collective action; the African Americans, overwhelmingly from the South, included sawmill workers, coal miners, farmers, and "plantation hands," especially in areas in which effective political mobilizations had followed emancipation. As of the mid-1880s, women and African Americans accounted for about 10 percent of the Knights' membership each.

Some of the Knights' assemblies, particularly those in the countryside, included women as well as men; in the towns and cities, female workers—carpet weavers, laundresses, bookbinders, domestics, and tailoresses as well as shoe and cotton operatives—for the most part established their own assemblies. But whether in rural or urban districts, almost none of the assemblies were integrated by race. Even where there was a great deal of organizational activity, as in the coal mines around Birmingham, Alabama, the cotton fields of south-central Arkansas, the tobacco factories in Durham, North Carolina, and the commercial zones of Houston, Texas, white and black Knights formed separate assemblies. Although Terence Powderly insisted that the order "recognize[d] no line of race, creed, politics, or color," the reality on the ground, where a good deal of autonomy prevailed, belied the principle. Segregated assemblies might join hands in labor actions, but white members, as one in Alabama put it, objected "to working in the same assembly with the negroes."

Whatever ambiguity there was as to the participation of women and African Americans—and national leaders like Powderly tended to take a far more inclusive view than the rank and file—the members of the Knights were of one mind when it came to the Chinese. They were to be utterly excluded from the order. Here, the Knights embraced a perspective, a movement, that had been developing in California since the 1850s and traveled very rapidly eastward as the War of the Rebellion ended and a new nation-state began to define the boundaries of its authority. Working first in the placer mines in California gold country, then on the construction crews of railroads like the Central Pacific, and eventually finding their way into an assortment of manufacturing and domestic employments, the Chinese—who would compose nearly one-quarter of California's labor force—confounded ideas of belonging that many Americans had increasingly come to embrace. They were regarded as "semi-barbarians" and "heathens," an inferior race of people, who were "incapable of assimilating." They had been brought to the United States in groups by a small cabal of merchants; they did not form families (they were overwhelmingly male) or practice any Christian faith; and the few women among them were assumed to be disease-ridden prostitutes. Some observers likened the Chinese to the Indians in their otherness and insisted that both came from the same Asian stock. Significantly, the Chinese also shared the fate of Indians when it came to civil and political standing in the United States. They were shut out. "I am not in favor of giving the rights of citizenship or the right of suffrage to either pagans or heathen," the Republican senator Frederick T. Frelinghuysen declared during the debate over the Fifteenth Amendment, expressing the white Christian nationalism that the party cultivated since its birth. "I am not in favor of taking steps backward into the slough of ignorance and of vice, even under the cry of progress."

Yet for many workers and their allies, what proved most unsettling about the Chinese was their apparent status as contract laborers, indebted and beholden to merchants and employers, utterly dependent and submissive, able to survive on the lowest of wages. In an age of emancipation, when the shackles of slavery and servitude were being cast off and labor declared free, the Chinese seemed to be reinscribing a form of bondage into the American political economy. "It is slavery in another form," a California newspaper charged, warning that the "noble" victory over "the slave-power" could be undone. The preferred term for the Chinese was "coolie," and anti-coolie clubs surfaced in the San Francisco area as early as the 1850s. They demanded an end to the "trade" that brought them, organized boycotts of Chinese-made goods, prohibited them from some of the crafts, and, at times, moved to drive them out by violent means. In the late 1870s, a powerful Workingmen's Party took control of San Francisco's city government on a vicious anti-Chinese platform and helped write a new state constitution that denied "any Chinese or Mongolian" either suffrage rights or employment on public works.

So strong did anti-Chinese sentiment become that it soon bridged the partisan threshold and demanded summary measures. Despite the Burlingame Treaty (1868) that lent China most favored nation status and encouraged immigration, Democrats and Republicans in Congress increasingly coalesced around a new policy of outright exclusion. The Chinese, they argued, were "aliens to our civilization . . . and clogs to the free movement of Christian civilization and enlightened progress," threatening to turn Americans into "a mongrel race . . . and a civilization half pagan, half Christian, semi-oriental, altogether mixed and very bad." The only dissent came from the residues of Radical Republicanism in New England, but it was to little effect. More than a few supporters of Chinese exclusion saw themselves completing the work of abolitionism, extirpating the final vestiges of slavery from the land. It would not be the last time that the hard fist of cultural imperialism was justified in the language of antislavery moralism.

In May 1882, by overwhelming margins, Congress thus passed and the Republican president, Chester A. Arthur, signed a bill banning the immigration of all "Chinese laborers . . . both skilled and unskilled" for a decade (the law was renewed until 1943). Not incidentally, this Chinese Exclusion Act came at the very time that the federal government was abandoning African American supporters to the tender mercies of their former owners in the South, completing the confinement of Native Americans to reservations (soon with the offer of citizenship if they gave up their tribal ways and embraced the values of Christian civilization), and conferring on corporations the status of citizenship under the Fourteenth Amendment.

It is not clear whether Henry George grasped these connections when he voiced his support for Chinese exclusion—and for the Workingmen's Party—from his home state of California. Like most others who shared this view, George believed that the Chinese were "utter heathens, treacherous, sensual, cowardly, and cruel . . . an infusible element." But George also feared that Chinese immigration would depress wages, promote the monopolies of the railroad companies and land engrossers who hired them, and move a tide of coolieism across the country. The consequence would be an exacerbated version of the very social fate that *Progress and Poverty* was written to expose: "to make the rich richer, and the poor poorer; to make nabobs and princes of our capitalists, and crush our working classes into the dust; to substitute a population of serfs and their masters for that population of intelligent freemen who are our glory and strength." Yet on what basis could the victims of monopolization, those who had apparently been rendered dependent and submissive, who seemed outside the civilization of "producers," be included in the struggle for an alternative America? This was the challenge and dilemma at the heart of antimonopoly movements.

Insurrections

The Knights of Labor began its period of remarkable growth in the wake of an unprecedented strike against some of the nation's largest railroad companies. Provoked by a series of wage cuts, the strike commenced in mid-July 1877, spread very rapidly from east to west, involved thousands of workers, and effectively shut down lines of vital rail traffic for days. Yet the idea of a "strike" does not adequately capture the tenor and dynamics of what proved to be an explosive social and political episode. Almost everywhere, striking railroad workers won the support of local residents—craftsmen, laborers, shopkeepers, merchandisers—who saw the railroads as the embodiments of the monopolistic practices that were pressing down on them and endangering their communities. In some places, they left their own jobs in solidarity; in some, they created new institutions of governance and hoped to expand the demands to include monetary reform and industrial regulation; in some, they armed themselves, dug trenches, and took control of the railroads and telegraphs; in some, they torched railroad yards and rolling stock; and in some, they engaged in combinations of these activities. So convulsive, extensive, and threatening did the Great Railroad Strike of 1877 become that more than a few officials, including the U.S. secretary of war, described it as an "insurrection" and moved to crush it with military force.

In the intense economic environment that the panic of 1873 and the subsequent depression produced, railroad companies, faced with large fixed costs and ruinous rate wars, shored up their resources or avoided bankruptcy by slashing wages. During the first months of 1877, some of the biggest and most powerful roads, including the New York Central, the Pennsylvania, the Erie, and the Baltimore and Ohio (B&O), announced cuts of roughly 10 percent, and company executives expressed little concern about the ramifications. As John Garrett, president of the B&O, put it, previous "strikes had been easily broken and the men easily replaced." "Labor," in Garrett's view, "lacked unity and was, thanks to the depression, amenable to company discipline." Garrett was sufficiently confident about the company's position that much like the Pennsylvania and the New York Central, the B&O continued to pay substantial dividends to stockholders while instituting the second of two wage cuts within a period of less than a year.

The workers had other ideas. Many had suffered through wage cuts for the previous few years and were nursing other job-related grievances; some had begun to organize secret, oath-bound unions. The B&O was especially notorious for its low pay, and when word of another wage cut leaked out, large sections of its labor force—brakemen, firemen, switchmen, and conductors, as well as engineers—determined to act. On Monday, July 16, in Martinsburg, West Virginia, hundreds of B&O workers struck the line and prevented freight trains from moving through. By evening, the strike had spread to Baltimore, accompanied by considerable popular unrest, then rippled out to the towns of Ohio, like Newark, where several branches of the B&O converged. With great speed, the strike jumped to the Pennsylvania Railroad, the Chicago, Burlington, and Quincy, the Atchison, Topeka, and Santa Fe, the Illinois Central, and the Texas Central, erupting with special force in cities like Pittsburgh, Chicago, St. Louis, Kansas City, and Galveston, as well as in small towns like Cumberland, Maryland. Eventually, San Francisco felt the impact. Only New England and the former rebellious South were spared.

Although the strikes appeared spontaneous, they in fact built upon actions that had taken place earlier in the decade when at least eighteen roads in the Northeast, the Midwest, and the upper South were affected. Aggrieved railroad workers, organizing locally, usually in small towns and without the aid of unions, had halted the flow of rail traffic while enlisting strong community support. Harassing strikebreakers, supplying food to the workers, sermonizing against the companies, and tending to marooned passengers, townspeople who had strong personal ties to the strikers defined limits to the power and authority of the railroads. On occasion, strikers and their local allies went further. They disabled locomotives, ripped up track, and cut telegraph wires, prompting the industry's *Railroad Gazette* to warn that they were in "flat rebellion, not simply against the companies . . . but against the law of the land," and deserved only "bayonets." Sometimes bayonets they got, as governors called in units of the state militias when popular disruptions overwhelmed the resources of town sheriffs and police.

In 1877, much of this was replayed on a larger and more turbulent stage. Whether in cities or small towns, workers could depend on substantial public support across class and ethnic lines. Indeed, in many cases the strike became just one component of what—as the *Railroad Gazette* suggested—can only be described as a popular rebellion that fed on long-standing grievances against the railroads: their scale and arrogance, their financial manipulations and political corruption, their monopolistic power, and their utter disregard for the welfare of the communities they traversed. Railroad tracks were ordinarily laid not on the edges of urban spaces but directly through main streets and neighborhoods, without gates or trestles, often where working people lived in densest numbers. The noise, smoke, and congestion, the dangers to pedestrians and children, the threats of runaway cars, had steadily worsened, and efforts on the part of residents and municipal governments to hold the roads accountable had come to little. Small wonder that the strike unleashed popular outrage. Striking workers were in fact only a minority in many of the crowds that quickly formed; it was the rail workers' allies who often played outsized roles in halting the trains and destroying railroad property.

The strike reverberated far and wide. In Chicago, with large and politicized populations of German, Scandinavian, and eastern European immigrants— and with a cadre of savvy and articulate socialists—the railroad upheavals spread into the heavily industrialized districts and briefly threatened to shut down the entire city. In St. Louis, also boasting a substantial German immigrant presence, a general strike—the first in an American industrial city—was successfully called, thanks in good part to the work and influence of the socialist Workingmen's Party of the United States (soon to be reorganized as the Socialist Labor Party, or SLP). An executive committee was quickly established, and efforts were made to form a workers' assembly to bring delegates together from the Workingmen's Party and the city's organized trades. "This strike," one of the leaders predicted, "will extend to all kinds of business, and in the end capitalists and the government must grant at least a portion of the rights demanded." There, as in Chicago, Kansas City, and many other urban centers, those rights came to include an eight-hour workday, child labor regulation, banking and currency reform, and the nationalization of the railroads.

Sympathies for the strikers not only crossed class lines but often reached the constabularies and even the state militias and thus set in motion a new sort of military escalation. The situation in Martinsburg, West Virginia, proved typical. When the strike broke out there, the mayor called on the local police to clear the tracks and coax the men back to work; they dragged their feet about doing either. A frustrated B&O official then contacted Governor Henry M. Mathews and asked him to send in the militia. Two companies, one from Martinsburg, were soon on the scene, but they seemed more interested in fraternizing with the strikers than in getting the trains rolling. A militia officer who observed the unfolding events warned the governor that the strikers would be standing arm in arm with the entire population of Martinsburg in resisting any effort to escort trains through the town.

Governor Mathews credited the report and quickly sought more substantial assistance. Although federal troops had rarely gotten involved in labor disputes, he did not hesitate to wire President Rutherford B. Hayes about the "unlawful combinations and domestic violence now existing in Martinsburg" and ask the president to send two or three hundred U.S. Army regulars. Mathews found a willing ally. Hayes, recently inaugurated after a bitter and disputed election contest, was ready to assert his authority and perhaps assure his wealthy backers. Even more to the point, as governor of Ohio just a year earlier, Hayes had sent in militia forces to "crush out" a strike of coal miners. Now he ordered his secretary of war to dispatch the troops. The U.S. Army was hardly flush with manpower. Many of the troops were engaged in wars against the Apache, Nez Perce, and Sioux and were thereby deployed over an immense territory from the Rio Grande to the Pacific coast and to the upper plains; others were in the process of being withdrawn from the former rebellious South. But General Winfield Scott Hancock, who commanded the Division of the Atlantic, believed that "the insurrection" had to be quelled "by all possible means," and he instructed his departmental subordinates in the East, the South, and the Gulf to find the men. Within days, other state governors, terrified by visions of the "Paris Commune" in their midst, followed Mathews's lead and called for federal troops to suppress popular disturbances in Baltimore, Buffalo, Pittsburgh, Terre Haute, Louisville, Chicago, and St. Louis. In the end, more than three thousand U.S. Army soldiers became involved.

Not present in overwhelming numbers, the federal troops were nevertheless intimidating and effective. They had no ties to the communities they occupied, were well armed, and carried out orders that plainly favored the railroad companies over the workers. They enabled freight traffic to resume, protected strikebreakers brought in to man the trains and tracks, and broke up meetings of strikers and union sympathizers; at times, they enforced federal court injunctions to similar effects. By the end of July, the strike had collapsed, though neither the railroad companies nor their class allies across the country could take much comfort in their apparent victory. There could be no denying that the struggle between "labor and capital" had become the central social "question" of the time or that the public temper was increasingly hostile to capital. In the view of the *New York Times*, "The days are over in which this country could rejoice in its freedom from the elements of social strife which have long abounded in the old countries." President Hayes himself would note that "the strikers have been put down by force," and there were both new calls for "citizen" militias to guard the interests of capital and new questions about the future of popular governance. "Universal suffrage is a standing menace to all stable and good government," one wealthy critic proclaimed. "Its twin sister is the commune with its labor unions, etc."

Despite its forcible suppression, the strike's energizing effects on workers and producers proved more enduring. So rapidly spreading and militant was the strike's character that more than a few railroad companies looked to settle quickly, yielding almost entirely to the strikers' demands. "I see nothing but to give in & restore pay or tie up everything," an official with the Chicago, Burlington, and Quincy Railroad groaned. "Public opinion . . . inclines to say we ought to fix it up." In unprecedented ways, skilled and unskilled workers—and on occasion black and white workers—joined hands in protest, expressing grievances that were shared by neighboring merchants, shopkeepers, and small manufacturers. The Greenback Labor Party entered a period of impressive electoral activity, and the Knights of Labor began a period of very rapid organization. As the labor leader Samuel Gompers later remembered, "The railroad strike of 1877 was the tocsin that sounded a ringing message of hope to us all."

There is an important sense in which the two decades following the panic of 1873 traced an arc of popular discontent and rebelliousness that simultaneously gave the lie to the moral and cultural sway of the financial and industrial bourgeoisie while imagining alternative sorts of societies to the one so swiftly and radically being constructed. The unrest clearly fed off the ideas and relations that antimonopoly was meant to protect and was further nourished by the intellectual and political currents brought to the United States by new waves of European immigrants, a good many of whom had been influenced by republicanism, socialism, and internationalism and, in some cases, had fled defeated struggles on the Continent. "Scratch the surface . . . in every city on the American continent," Wendell Phillips remarked, "and you will find the causes which created the Commune." That was precisely what elites in all corners of the country had come to fear. As the Haitian Revolution did for antebellum slaveholders, the image of the Paris Commune—when workers and their left-wing allies briefly took control of the French capital in 1871—hung over the rocky road of postbellum capitalist development. Accordingly, the U.S. Senate in the early 1880s saw fit to conduct what would be a multivolume investigation of "the relations between labor and capital."

Strike activity increased rather than diminished in the aftermath of 1877. Statistics compiled by the U.S. commissioner of labor show that more than 450 strikes involving well over 100,000 workers took place annually over the next seven years; then, in 1886, the numbers escalated dramatically to over 1,400 strikes involving more than 400,000 workers. Only about half of the strikes were called by unions, and most erupted over wage-related issues—very much the pattern that had been in evidence since the early 1870s—attesting to their localized and politically rebellious nature. In smaller towns and semirural areas, strikers continued to push back against what they viewed as the arbitrary power of employers who often had no ties, other than investments, to their communities, and they could usually depend on the sympathy and support of non-strikers to whom they were tied by kinship or economic interdependence. In larger cities, striking workers might look to the aid of central labor unions and trades assemblies that were being organized in Boston, New York, and Pittsburgh, in Chicago, Detroit, and St. Louis, and in Denver and San Francisco and that offered a range of material and political resources, including havens for socialists and the developing labor press.

Dynamics such as these were also to be found in the areas of the plantation South in which field hands had local and state political allies. Responding to cuts in task payments as well as to remuneration in scrip (redeemable only at the company store) rather than cash, rice workers in the South Carolina low country launched a massive strike in 1876. Mobilized in squads, sometimes numbering in the hundreds, they moved from plantation to plantation—with horns, drums, and clubs—rallying fellow workers and pressuring those still in the fields to join their ranks. Alarmed, the planters sought a "strong hand" to restore "order." But they could not find one. Many of the local officials, including trial justices, were black Republicans, the state militia was composed chiefly of low-country blacks who either sympathized with the strike or actively participated in it, and the governor—Daniel H. Chamberlain—was a Republican who refused to intervene on the planters' side. What Chamberlain did do was send Robert Smalls, the former slave, Republican organizer, and now congressman, to negotiate a settlement. Before long, the planters yielded, and strikers who had been arrested were brought before a black trial justice; the charges against them were summarily dismissed.

Four years later, a similar strike erupted in the sugar parishes of lower Louisiana, where intense struggles had roiled the plantations since the early 1870s. Price increases rather than wage cuts were the tinderbox in 1880, and the strikers—led principally by day laborers—marched from estate to estate crying that "the colored people are a nation and must stand together." Very quickly, they drew up a "constitution," which a hostile observer believed was the basis for a "visionary government," and resolved to hold out for "a dollar a day" while promising "a severe thrashing" to laborers who refused to join them. The governor at the time—after the ouster of the Reconstruction government—was a white Democrat who immediately ordered in the militia; white officials in one of the parishes had fourteen blacks regarded as "ringleaders" arrested for trespass. But another of the parish sheriffs was black, "unwilling or unable to make arrests," and a black state senator and emerging political boss, Henry Demas, in the manner of Robert Smalls, sympathized with the strikers and stepped in as a mediator. Although the "war like movements" of the white state militia effectively ended the strike, Demas had many of the arrested strikers released, and the Workingmen's Protective and Mutual Aid Association of Donaldsonville, with at least thirteen branches, was established to enforce contracts and defend laborers against the "rapacity" of storekeepers.

The construction of organizational bases such as these enabled the Knights of

Labor to move into the sugar parishes during the early 1880s and forge a network of assemblies (at least twenty but probably closer to forty) composed of "plantation hands," "farm hands," and "laborers." It was indicative of an enormous surge of labor mobilization spearheaded by the Knights. By 1886, the Knights could claim nearly ten thousand assemblies nationwide with roughly three-quarters of a million members. The densest concentrations of assemblies stretched from New England through the industrial belts of the Middle Atlantic and the Midwest and into the plains states of Iowa, Missouri, and Kansas, but there were numerous assemblies in the mining districts of the Rockies and especially around Puget Sound and San Francisco Bay on the West Coast. Many of these were in cities and towns, but the Knights also moved into the countryside to embrace "farmers," "miners," and "railroad employees," among others. Throughout, most of the new recruits were semiskilled and unskilled workers; perhaps as many as sixty thousand were women.

Organizing drives in the former rebellious South are revealing in this regard. Pushing out from beachheads in Richmond, Raleigh, Birmingham, Little Rock, New Orleans, and Galveston into the small-town and rural areas, the Knights succeeded in establishing nearly two thousand local assemblies during the 1880s, about two-thirds of which were to be found in agricultural counties. As in the sugar parishes of Louisiana, there was intense recruiting in Arkansas, Texas, Alabama, and North Carolina, particularly in the country districts, bringing in "farmers," "carpenters," "lumbermen," "mechanics," "farm renters," "washerwomen," "saw mill hands," and "laborers," many of whom were black and in separate assemblies. To these efforts of the Knights could be added those of the Cooperative Workers of America, based in South Carolina, the Agricultural Wheel, based in Arkansas, and especially the Colored Farmers' Alliance, which spread across the Deep South from its wellspring in Texas, all of which filled chiefly with black laborers (the Wheel included white insurgents as well).

The supreme irony is that for all of the Knights' work and all of the strikes that shook the country, the Knights' national leadership, especially Terence Powderly, took a dim view of strikes and related agitation. In part, it was a strategic issue: Powderly hoped to build a large organization with a committed rank and file, and while strikes brought new members in at a rapid pace, they also attracted "newcomers" who were not of the "quality the Order had sought in the past" and risked deflating the membership if and when they failed. "The remedy," Powderly told a general meeting in 1880, "lie [sic] not in the suicidal strike, but . . . in thorough, effective organization." But perhaps to an even greater extent, the trouble was ideological. The leadership of the Knights remained beholden to antimonopoly sensibilities that, despite offering thunderous critiques of postbellum capitalism, construed the world as divided between "producers" (including many employers) and "non-producers," between those who created wealth and those who accumulated and manipulated it, between those who were "virtuous" and those who were "corrupt." "I curse the word class," Powderly roared, and he set his sights on the task of abolishing "wage slavery."

Yet "thorough organization" or "arbitration," which the Knights called for in their founding document, could not fend off the assaults of employers who unilaterally cut wages or abrogated work rules. This is why more militancy and experimentation were to be found on the ground. During the early 1880s, the Knights' recruiting typically accelerated after a series of successful strikes, especially against large railroad companies, such as the Union Pacific, which instituted wage cuts of 10–25 percent in 1884. Although "not a shop on the system was organized," a walkout began in Denver. Within two days, "all branch lines" from Omaha, Nebraska, to Ogden, Utah, were shut down. The company was forced to rescind the cuts; the Knights then reaped the rewards.

A similar sequence played out on an even larger scale in the next year, 1885, when workers struck Jay Gould's massive "Southwest System." Gould was a good target. Much like other "moneyed men" of the late nineteenth century, he had made his fortune during the Civil War era in financial speculation, mostly by "watering" railroad stock, not to mention by trying to corner the gold market. By the early 1880s, he had turned his eyes to the railroads and come to control an empire stretching from Illinois through Colorado and Texas, including the Texas and Pacific, the Missouri Pacific, the International–Great Northern, the Wabash, St. Louis, and Pacific, the St. Louis and Iron Mountain, and the Missouri, Kansas, and Texas. When Gould then came into conflict with Collis P. Huntington's Southern Pacific, they agreed to form a pool and share the spoils. The Gould empire would ultimately include fifteen thousand miles of track, making it, in the estimation of one newspaper, the "largest combination of roads . . . of any one individual or corporation in the world." To top it off, and to confirm his notoriety as the great monopolist of the time, Gould took over the New York *World* and the Western Union Telegraph and thereby controlled vital means of communication as well as transportation.

The strike began among workers on the Wabash Railroad in small towns of Missouri after Gould slashed wages and hours, and it quickly spread to other Gould lines across Texas, Kansas, Missouri, Illinois, and Indiana. Once again, the strikers won the sympathy and support of the public and much of the press both because of the dire circumstances—"actual privations stared them and their families in the face"—in which many of the railroad workers found themselves and because of Gould's reputation for greed and financial peculation. To many, it appeared that Gould was the consummate "robber baron," enriching himself at the workers' expense; no one was amused by his later boast that he "could hire one half of the working class to kill the other half." Within two weeks, Gould railroad officials saw the handwriting on the wall and sat down at the table with strike leaders, agreeing to restore wages, accept work rules among engineers, and hire back striking workers even if they were affiliated with the Knights. "No such victory has ever been secured in this nation or any other," a St. Louis newspaper declared, and it was an enormous spur to the Knights' organizing not only among railroad workers but also among a wide assortment of working men and women: from iron and steel mills, to construction sites, to laundries, to stone quarries. Still, there was a good deal of skepticism as to the readiness of the companies to meet the terms of the new "contract," and workers in the local assemblies were often more emboldened than their national leaders thought wise.

What was the first phase of the Great Southwest Strike occurred in a context of nationwide agitation and expectation over the central labor issue of the postbellum era: the eight-hour workday. Although the federal government had enacted eight-hour legislation for mechanics and laborers in its employ, and although some states and municipalities (including Illinois) had done the same, the law was generally resisted by employers and rarely enforced by public authorities; for their part, the courts ruled that eight-hour laws violated the cardinal principle of the new industrial economy—freedom of contract. But optimism had been growing in labor's ranks, and the Knights of Labor, flooded with thousands of new recruits, set its sights on achieving the goal. The Knights looked to the spring of 1886, and the city of Chicago emerged as the epicenter of protest.

Chicago seemed an ideal setting. By the 1880s, it had become an industrial as well as commercial city, and its population was growing at a breathtaking rate, certainly faster than New York's. It was the western terminus for all major railroads east of the Mississippi and the eastern terminus for many of those in the trans-Mississippi West. It had attracted pioneering manufacturers and retailers like Cyrus McCormick, George Pullman, Philip Armour, and Marshall Field, along with political radicals and revolutionaries from various parts of the United States and Europe who found an increasingly sympathetic audience among the city's enormous working-class base. About 40 percent of Chicago's total population and nearly 60 percent of its workforce were immigrants—Germans, Poles, Slavs, Scandinavians, and Irish most prominently—who filled the large factories, machine shops, rolling mills, and packinghouses, formed ethnic organizations, engaged in urban politics, organized at their workplaces and in their neighborhoods, and subscribed to foreign-language and socialist newspapers. The daily *Arbeiter-Zeitung*, given over to socialism, had a circulation of twenty thousand. For nearly twenty years, workers in Chicago had been demanding an eight-hour workday.

Few if any other cities in the United States seethed as intensely with popular discontent or benefited from the number of articulate and committed radicals as Chicago. Over time, political organizers in the many working-class wards, with their own roots in Germany, Ireland, and even Alabama, wove together threads of antimonopolism, greenbackism, Irish nationalism, and socialism as they struggled to challenge the power of the city's capitalists. Some had come to call themselves anarchists, though their dream of self-governing communities of producers might have had more in common with antimonopolists than it did with Proudhon and Bakunin, the French and Russian theorists of anarchism. At all events, there was in the air a mix of Karl Marx, revolutionary French republicanism, and Tom Paine, and a growing feeling among working people that the eight-hour workday was within their grasp. Even the anarchists temporarily abandoned their critique of conventional popular protests and labor goals—they had once dismissed the eight-hour workday as "soothing syrup for babies"—to ride the political wave. May 1, 1886, was set as the day for concerted action in Chicago and around the country, though agitation commenced weeks before. Pressing their employers as early as March, nearly fifty thousand Chicago workers had won an eight-hour day by the end of April, the Chicago City Council had approved an eight-hour workday for public employees, and eight-hour rallies had begun to break out in major industrial centers from the East to the West. When May 1 arrived, hundreds of thousands of workers participated in demonstrations, and at least 350,000 nationwide joined what was a coordinated general strike; between 40,000 and 60,000 of them, unskilled and skilled alike, were in Chicago, where, in the words of one observer, "no smoke curled up from the tall chimneys of factories and mills." Then, with disastrous speed, the movement unraveled.

The first setback had nothing directly to do with the eight-hour agitation. In March, after a railroad worker was fired for attending a union meeting in Marshall, Texas, the Knights of Labor again struck the Gould system of the Southwest, this time with even greater fury. It was a reflection of worker suspicions over the previous year's agreement, which in many cases was slow to be implemented if it was implemented at all. The strike spread north to Illinois, Missouri, Arkansas, and Kansas (including East St. Louis, Kansas City, and Little Rock) and west toward Dallas and Fort Worth. Perhaps 200,000, a good many in sympathy strikes, became involved, but compared with 1885, the strike took ominous turns. As striking railroad workers at many points seized control of shops and roundhouses and disabled locomotives, pitched battles broke out, first between them and deputized private guards—including the Pinkertons, a detective agency that had once provided security for President Lincoln—and then with state militias and Texas Rangers who had been called in by the governors of Missouri and Texas. Amid the escalating violence, public support for the strike wilted, and the more conservative railroad brotherhoods refused to join. Equally devastating, state and federal courts issued unprecedented injunctions "against the interference with the traffic of the railways," a devastating blow. Under growing pressure, Terence Powderly and the Knights' General Executive Board threw in the towel and ordered members back to work, having gained nothing and with the momentum clearly in the companies' favor. Word of labor's setback reached Chicago on May 3.

That very day, closer to home, workers and police clashed outside the McCormick Reaper Works on Chicago's Southwest Side, where striking iron molders had been locked out and strikebreakers hired in. It was a hair-trigger environment. In the years after the city's Great Fire of 1871 and the Great Railroad Strike of 1877, the police department had expanded significantly to become the nation's first effective antistrike force. It had already seen action on numerous occasions and, in turn, inspired workers to create their own military units as means of defense. At McCormick's, armed with clubs and pistols, the police were ready when strikers and strikebreakers began to fight. Roughly two hundred of them at the scene quickly attacked the strikers, beating and firing at them, in a show of lethal brutality. When the smoke finally cleared, at least two of the striking workers lay dead, and many more had been injured.

Among those who regrouped were several anarchists who issued a "Revenge" circular and met to plan a response. After much discussion and disagreement, they decided to hold a protest rally the next evening, May 4, at the Haymarket, not far from the city center. Although the attendance did not exceed three thousand and the speeches of well-known organizers like August Spies and Albert Parsons were regarded as "tame"—the mayor was there for a time and reported this—the police eventually moved in to disperse what was left of the crowd. Suddenly a bomb was thrown and exploded in the square. Gunfire broke out, largely if not exclusively on the part of the police, and as a *Chicago Tribune* reporter put it, "wild carnage" ensued. "The police were in a condition of mind that permitted no resistance," he observed, "for they were blinded by passion and unable to distinguish between the peaceful citizen and Nihilist assassin." Seven police officers and four workers were killed; about sixty officers sustained wounds together with a much higher number of civilian attendees, many of whom fled the scene as quickly as possible.

Accounts of the "Haymarket bombing" remain in dispute to this day. Was there a conspiracy on the part of the anarchists? Was this a massacre carried out by the police? Who threw the bomb? What is not in dispute is the aftermath. In a frenzy of political fear, eight anarchists were rounded up, put on trial, and hastily convicted of conspiracy in the bombing. Despite denying the charges against them, four would be hanged, one would commit suicide in prison, one would be sentenced to fifteen years in prison, and two would have their death sentences commuted to life imprisonment (they were later pardoned, in 1893, by Illinois's reform governor, John Peter Altgeld, who criticized the trial proceedings).

Working people and radical intellectuals in the United States and around the world were shocked and outraged by the trial's outcome. They had come to admire the Haymarket martyrs for their courage in maintaining their innocence and in going to their deaths or jail cells without renouncing their beliefs, and they denounced Chicago elites for their cowardice and vindictiveness. Some might have known that Albert Parsons had previously stared down political harassment when he organized for the Republican Party and championed black rights in eastern Texas before heading north with his mixed-race wife, Lucy, who had likely been enslaved. The threads of Reconstruction-era radicalism were well twined and could not easily be severed by "redemption" or geography.

In any event, the Haymarket anarchists would truly live on, becoming international symbols of the struggle for justice against the lethal arm of the capitalist state. But the popular movement that had been growing for over a decade would never fully recover from these blows. The Knights of Labor began a precipitous decline, and what appeared to be a vibrant and increasingly confident labor movement would have to lick its wounds and reassess its goals.

Redefining the Republic

But in the shorter term, the consequences were not nearly so apparent, and even in the immediate aftermath of Haymarket and the Great Southwest defeat popular energies remained high. "New political forces" were still emerging, the labor journalist John Swinton could write. And so it seemed in New York City, where the fall of 1886 saw an important mayoral election. Incensed by court injunctions against strikers, the city's large Central Labor Union determined to enter the electoral arena, organizing the United Labor Party and then choosing Henry George as its candidate. George had no real ties to New York, but ever since the publication of *Progress and Poverty* he had been gaining an enthusiastic following among laboring people and producers, many of whom read and discussed the book at their places of work. During the early 1880s, George had traveled on two occasions to Ireland, where his theories on land monopoly resonated powerfully with the Irish Land League (on both sides of the Atlantic); he had also lectured to local assemblies of the Knights of Labor across the United States. By 1886, according to the Central Labor Union, George's "name had become a household word to millions who recognized him as a leader whose teachings would yet lead them out of the house of bondage," and George had already argued that a land tax would offer a solution to New York's overcrowded tenement housing.

The United Labor Party included a land tax in its platform together with demands for shorter hours, higher wages, municipal ownership of public transportation, and an end to police interference in strikes and workers' meetings. The George campaign made a special effort to target the city's landlords as the wealthy parasites who fed off laborers and the poor. "We are wage-workers and tenants," its campaign paper proclaimed. "We should vote for a man who proposes . . . to bring about legislation by which wage-slavery and land monopoly shall be abolished." It was more than enough to conjure fears of the French Revolution and the "Commune" among bourgeois New Yorkers and propel them to mobilize in defense of "property and order." Joining hands were the Union League, the Dry Goods Merchants, the Committee of One Hundred, and the Business Men's Association, and there were calls for Democrats and Republicans to close ranks behind a suitable candidate. They didn't, and the November polling results were sobering. The Democrat Abram Hewitt managed to win but with only 41 percent of the vote in an election marked by high turnout. George, who did very well in the working-class wards and attracted a good many Irish Catholic votes that would ordinarily have gone Democratic, finished second with 31 percent. A distant third was the Republican candidate, Theodore Roosevelt.

Among Henry George's supporters for mayor of New York City was the Knights of Labor president, Terence Powderly. It was a bit of a surprise. Since the early 1880s, Powderly had spoken as strongly against the Knights' involvement in electoral politics as he did against their embrace of strikes. Like some other labor leaders of the time, he was reflecting on the brief but largely unsuccessful history of the Greenback Labor Party that seemed to hold such promise before faltering amid electoral defeats, and therefore saw mainstream politics as a distraction from the important task of "thorough organization." Yet as was true for strikes, so too for politics: on the ground, Knights' assemblies marched to their own drummers, and although the organization did not formally establish political parties of its own, it backed an assortment of independent labor tickets for municipal, county, and state offices. Between 1885 and 1888, the Knights of Labor effectively ran tickets—called Union Labor, United Labor, Workingmen, Independents, even Knights of Labor—in almost two hundred cities and towns in thirty-four states and four territories and reported electoral victories in roughly one-third of them. Some were in the major metropolitan centers of Chicago, New York, San Francisco, Pittsburgh, Baltimore, Detroit, and Denver. Others were in small towns like Eureka, California; Marion, Indiana;

Boone, Iowa; Alliance, Ohio; Red Wing, Minnesota; Water Valley, Mississippi; and Gardiner, Maine.

No set platform or list of demands unified these labor tickets. Almost everywhere, they called for an eight-hour workday and related hours legislation and looked to improve municipal and social services to benefit working-class communities. At times, they called for minimum daily wages, the end of subcontracting, the extension of streetcar lines, producer cooperatives, or public works projects. Sometimes they simply wished to run municipalities themselves and demonstrate that they could do so with greater reach and efficiency. But given the racial and ethnic complexities of working-class America, most remarkable was the range of cities and towns in which the Knights put together winning coalitions. They won elections in Rochester, New Hampshire, a textile- and boot-making town that had customarily gone Republican and had a labor force composed of Yankees, French Canadians, Irish, and British. They won in Kansas City, Kansas, a railroad hub and meatpacking city that had customarily gone Democratic and included a diverse labor force of native-born whites, African Americans, Irish, Germans, and British. They won in Richmond, Virginia, a tobacco and small manufacturing center with a mixed political tradition and a labor force that was about 50 percent black. And they won in Milwaukee, Wisconsin, a growing city with a diverse industrial base (though with especially prominent breweries) that had large contingents of Germans and Poles. Throughout, in pursuit of a more democratic republic established on a base of producers of many sorts, the sensibilities of antimonopoly and the mechanisms of the electoral arena seemed to go, vividly and powerfully, into the making of a politically constituted class of working people.

The Knights' efforts, both at the workplace and in electoral politics, benefited, particularly in the former rebellious South, from the political mobilization of African Americans that Civil War emancipations had unleashed. Indeed, if any part of the country approximated the image of the Paris Commune, it was the urban and rural South, most notably in an arc stretching from Virginia out to Texas. There—as we have seen—owing to the Reconstruction Acts of 1867, the apex of Radical Republicanism, former slaves and free people of color not only won the franchise on terms enjoyed by other Americans but, mostly in alliance with the Republican Party, came to hold the levers of power, serving in offices their previous owners had once occupied. And there, in the very heart of the old regime—to an extent we have not appreciated—African Americans not only managed to invert the composition of political office holding but also struggled to construct an alternative political path, to place their own imprints on the shape of the Republic. In so doing, they established some genuine bases of black power that proved difficult to dislodge.

One of those bases was Georgia's McIntosh County, at the southern end of the antebellum rice kingdom and home to some of the Old South's wealthiest planter aristocrats. The county's staple crop economy had unraveled during and immediately after the Civil War, and by the spring of 1868 the county had experienced a revolutionary recomposition of its political power structure. In place of the grandees, their kinsmen, and white clients, black men now served as county clerk, county ordinary, justice of the peace, constable, city marshal, and election registrar and represented the county in the general assembly and the state senate. Before long, they would also serve as sheriff, deputy sheriff, coroner, election manager, and city alderman, not to mention as jurors and bailiffs. A dense and generationally rooted black population that outnumbered whites by a factor of nearly three, the departure of planter families in the face of wartime federal incursions, and the effects of Sherman's Field Orders No. 15 made possible this stunning transition, but a remarkable and energetic leader from afar proved to be the lightning rod: Tunis G. Campbell.

Campbell was one of many northern black men who brought considerable talents and resources to the task of reconstructing the slave South, but few built such a formidable local following or invited such intense controversy. Born and raised in New Jersey and New York, and too old to enlist in active military service during the War of the Rebellion, Campbell set out for Union-occupied Port Royal, South Carolina, in the summer of 1863 in hopes of assisting in the education of the freedpeople and the promotion of democracy. Commissioned in the spring of 1865 as superintendent of the Georgia Sea Islands and already convinced of the need for "separatism for strength," Campbell first established freed colonies on St. Catherines and Sapelo islands and then, owing to federal harassment, shifted his base to the mainland of McIntosh County, where he and many of his followers could be found when Congress initiated Military Reconstruction.

Campbell had developed a keen understanding of the essentials of political power and the aspirations of freed communities. Advancing $1,000 from prior savings, he leased a large plantation from Union sympathizers and divided it among black families who would control the plots and pay an annual rent in kind. He wrote a constitution and organized the BelleVille Farmers Association to function much like a local government with elected officials. And he gained appointment as an election registrar, thereby enrolling and educating prospective black voters in McIntosh and two adjoining counties. By the summer of 1867, a Freedmen's Bureau agent found the colony in "a most promising condition economically" and the hundred-odd residents preparing to erect a schoolhouse. In November, Campbell was selected as a delegate to the state constitutional convention, and the following April Campbell's son was elected to the statehouse, while Campbell himself became state senator and local justice of the peace.

Although Campbell's political control was nowhere nearly so "absolute" as white detractors claimed, he did wield great influence. An elder in the AME Zion Church as well as the leader of the BelleVille colony and holder of several political offices, he could play the roles most closely attuned to the needs of rural freedpeople and speak a language that resonated with their political sensibilities. Frequently calling county blacks together, he seemed to mix practical advice and "good republican doctrine" with a spiritual cadence and fervor. Equally impervious to bribery and intimidation, Campbell won deep and abiding personal support and used it to build a political machine and grassroots organization, replete with a citizens' militia company. While Republican prospects in the state of Georgia and most black initiatives on the local level there began to either flounder or meet strong conservative resistance, black power in McIntosh County continued to grow and become more entrenched.

Nowhere were the implications more evident or irritating to white planters than in Campbell's justice court. With two black constables to assist him, and eventually a black sheriff and deputy sheriff to lend muscle, Campbell provided black laborers with new leverage in their relations with white employers. Showing no patience for the mistreatment, insults, swindles, and personal abuse to which the freedpeople were customarily subjected, he had the accused arrested, brought before his bench, and, if found guilty, fined. Not surprisingly, local planters became indignant. "He is tyrannical overbearing and determines questions not upon principles of law but by his individual prejudice and caprice," one complained, and his "teachings [are] calculated to destroy the efficiency of labor in this section and inaugurate a reign of terror." For their part, freedpeople often left the plantations "en masse" to attend Campbell's court and associated political meetings and, by one account, commonly returned with "a disposition to refuse to enter into contracts, or if already made to violate them." It would not be long before McIntosh County whites launched a series of vindictive, and ultimately successful, attacks against Campbell. But it would be years before black power in the county was fully broken, and never would there be a return to the old order. During the twentieth century, there was an atmosphere of moderation between blacks and whites and an economic landscape in which three of four black families owned their homes.

McIntosh County, Georgia, was a rarity in the reach and duration of black political power, yet it was not unexampled. Especially where African Americans composed population majorities and availed themselves of political opportunities made possible by the Union League and the Republican Party, important enclaves could take shape. In Edgefield County, South Carolina, well-organized and armed black Republicans gained control of the county courthouse despite the concerted opposition of Democratic clubs and agricultural societies. Led by the charismatic former slave and U.S. Army sergeant Prince Rivers—who was said to have made "Toussaint perfectly intelligible"—they challenged the power of local landowners and advanced the cause of African American community development. By 1872, white planters felt the squeeze of higher taxes and complained that they could not get a fair hearing in the trial justices' courts; two years later, black schoolchildren outnumbered white by a ratio of two to one, while black and white teachers received identical pay.

In the counties of the Mississippi delta, aided by white Republican activists, blacks began to claim seats on local governing boards, win election as magistrates, constables, and state legislators, and sit on juries. In Claiborne County, amid a Republican sweep, three of five supervisors, several justices of the peace, and the sheriff were black. In Madison County, grand and petit juries were "mostly composed" of blacks, and local whites complained that "they had a board of supervisors there . . . none of whom could write his name." In Issaquena County, blacks eventually held all five seats on the board of supervisors, and in Warren County, with Vicksburg as the county seat, blacks would hold the office of sheriff, circuit clerk, treasurer, and justice of the peace while briefly controlling the board of supervisors. When a correspondent for the AME's *Christian Recorder* arrived in Greenville, Mississippi, in the spring of 1871, he marveled that "there were two juries empanelled with about two-thirds colored men" and noted that "the courthouse yard was crowded with the descendants of Africa." Four years later, a visitor to Leflore County found that nine of eleven justices of the peace were "negroes" and "white property-holders are compelled to appear and submit to their judgment on questions of law, upon which sometimes great interest depends." A total of thirteen counties, composing about one-third of Mississippi's black population, elected black sheriffs, and even after Republicans fell from power in the state, blacks would often retain a share of local offices in "fusion" agreements with Democrats.

At the other end of the Deep South, in Washington County, Texas, black power was hitched to a biracial and multiethnic Republican Party that took the reins of county government in 1870 and held them for over a decade. Although blacks routinely yielded the offices of sheriff, district judge, and county judge to their white allies, they did claim most of the nominations for state legislature and eventually served as clerks of courts, treasurers, deputies, and justices of the peace. Perhaps more consequentially, they were heavily represented on grand and petit juries. Together they helped promote black access to local offices and gave black defendants meaningful protection. Much of eastern Texas thus resisted the full consequences of Democratic "redemption," and the effective mobilization of black voters together with the experience of black officeholders would draw the attention of white insurgents, first Greenbackers and then Populists.

The analogy of the "Paris Commune," of course, suggests not only the enormous transition in power from the propertied to the propertyless, from capital to labor—the utter reconfiguration of the Republic—but also the ferocity of the counterattack that was, in so many places, launched. Republican claimants, white and black, in the plantation districts had a great many obstacles to scale, though winning elective office was not necessarily enough to allow them to wield power. They had to post bond, take their oaths, and often fight off white paramilitaries who rejected the results and wanted their heads. The showdown was particularly bloody in Grant Parish, Louisiana, where black radicals led by William Ward, a former slave and a U.S. Army veteran, had mobilized their laboring base, activated a militia company, and arrested whites suspected of violating the federal Enforcement Acts. Ward was a skilled carpenter and an experienced soldier and was not to be intimidated. He drilled Republican loyalists and in 1872 headed up the parish ticket that sent him to the state legislature. When it seemed that conservative rivals might be given the green light by the Louisiana governor to assume office instead of them in the parish seat of Colfax, Ward and his supporters seized possession of the courthouse.

Rumors quickly spread that the conservatives intended to retake the courthouse and hang the black radicals, and Ward had no reason to doubt what was coming. Thus, when an armed party led by a local planter and reputed Klan leader approached Colfax on April 1, they found it well defended and had to retreat. Skirmishing over the next few days further polarized the situation and led black men, women, and children from the surrounding countryside to flee to Colfax for protection. Recognizing that they lacked the numbers and firepower to dislodge Ward and his supporters on their own, the conservatives called for "reinforcements," and a "veritable army" of vigilantes from neighboring parishes assembled rapidly "to suppress negro domination."

Like their radical counterparts in the streets of Paris in 1871, the blacks began to dig in, building an earthwork around the courthouse, fashioning crude artillery out of pipe, and, led by the women, scouring the countryside at night for provisions. But truth was that only eighty of their number had arms, and looking out at well-equipped white paramilitaries numbering roughly three hundred, they too needed reinforcements. On April 9, with a few other black leaders, Ward slipped out of Colfax and headed to New Orleans hoping to summon state and federal troops. Before he could return, on Easter Sunday morning, April 13, the whites delivered an ultimatum, demanding control of the courthouse and offering the blacks safe passage if they would surrender their arms. When Levin Allen, another U.S. Army veteran who was left in charge, refused, the whites opened fire. The battle raged for nearly two hours. By the time it was over, more than one hundred African Americans lay dead, felled in hails of bullets or shot execution style after they were taken prisoner.

When government officials finally arrived on the scene, all they found was the aftermath of what had been the bloodiest episode of a very bloody Reconstruction era. Federal authorities did arrest ninety-eight of the conservative vigilantes for violating the Enforcement Acts—which made various kinds of political harassment and terrorism federal offenses—and managed to bring some to trial. Three were convicted. Yet, as a dramatic sign of the times, their convictions were appealed to the U.S. Supreme Court, which, in the *Cruikshank* case of 1876, overturned them. The Enforcement Acts were unconstitutional, the justices determined, because the equal protection clause of the Fourteenth Amendment only outlawed violations of black civil rights by the states; violations on the part of individuals were beyond the reach of the federal government and instead were left to the jurisdiction of states and localities, which, by then, had mostly been restored to Democratic rule. The Republican president, Rutherford B. Hayes, effectively bowed to the Court's decision in early 1877, when he ordered the U.S. Army of Occupation to return to their barracks rather than support the claims of Republican governments in South Carolina and Louisiana to remain in power. There the soldiers awaited further assignments. Fittingly, by mid-July some were being sent north on a new mission: to suppress the escalating strikes on the nation's railroads.

The reestablishment of "home"—meaning white Democratic—rule in the former rebellious states of the South was a process of signal importance in the political history of the United States. It ended prospects for a Republican alliance that accorded freedmen an important position in party affairs and policy and showed that the Radical faction had been pushed to the margins. The willingness of the national Republican Party to permit its southern regimes to fall—first in Virginia, Georgia, Alabama, Texas, and Arkansas, then in Mississippi, South Carolina, Louisiana, and Florida—indicated that the new ruling coalition in American politics could well link big financial and industrial interests in the Northeast with big landed, commercial, and mining interests in the South and the West.

But even amid the defeats of 1877, that was not yet clear, and the materials to construct very different political coalitions, including those organized chiefly around small producers and working people and around alternatives to the type of market economy then emerging, were very much intact. The freedmen themselves had not been vanquished politically. Despite losing vital allies in control of the southern state governments and militant leaders on the ground, they continued to vote in substantial numbers; in densely populated districts of the Carolinas and Georgia, the Mississippi Valley, and eastern Texas, they also continued to elect representatives to state and local office and to wield meaningful power. So well organized did African Americans remain in some of the plantation counties that both conservative Democrats and especially white insurgents influenced by antimonopolism sought an alliance with them.

Nowhere did such an interracial alliance prove more consequential than in Virginia. It would not have been expected. Alone among the former rebellious states, Virginia did not give rise to a Republican Reconstruction regime. Instead, a "Conservative" coalition, based on urban mercantile, banking, and railroad interests, came to power. But in the black-majority counties of the Tidewater and the Southside, freedmen mobilized successfully and elected to the state legislature almost seventy of their number, many of whom had skills, land, extensive kinship ties, and strong connections to local aid societies and churches. And when Conservatives determined to pay off the large state debt in full by increasing taxes and cutting back on social services, including public education, their own coalition fractured. A broad front of opposition developed in the rural areas, most notably in the western part of the state, where there had been few slaves, and in early 1879 they formed a party called the Readjusters, committed to scaling down the debt and reclaiming power from the urban and financial elites known as the Funders.

From the first, white Readjusters reached out to black Republicans—they hoped to bring together "the people of Virginia without distinction of color"—knowing very well that African Americans had strong bases in more than twenty-five of the state's counties and also that by the late 1870s they had more than their share of dissatisfactions with the white Republican Party leadership. But the moment might have passed were it not for a shrewd and tireless politician who headed up the Readjuster movement: William Mahone. A Confederate general, lifelong Democrat, and railroad president, Mahone hardly fit the bill of an insurgent. He was, however, politically ambitious (he had been blocked by the Democrats) and, trained as an engineer, had a keen sense of how he might build political bridges. Quickly, he met with black members of the state assembly and learned that only attentiveness to their concerns would allay suspicions about what the Readjusters intended. The price for black support would be a share of the state's patronage, offices at various levels of government, the abolition of the whipping post (a relic of slavery), repeal of the state's poll tax as a prerequisite for voting, and provision for public schools across the state.

Mahone made certain that these demands were included in the Readjuster platform, and Virginia blacks soon flocked to the party's standard. So impressive was the mobilization—Mahone collected detailed information on the grassroots leadership in every Virginia county and arranged to pay poll taxes where necessary—that within two election cycles—between 1879 and 1883—Mahone was elevated to the U.S. Senate, the Readjusters won control of both the governorship and the state legislature, and most of the party's platform was enacted. It was the sort of outcome that Radical Republicans had initially hoped for throughout the former rebellious South: a ruling coalition that joined freedmen with yeoman whites in the interest of small-scale producers. And it was a stunning example of insurgencies that began to erupt from Georgia to Texas, showing the fault lines in Democratic home rule. Either aligned with the Greenback Labor Party or designating themselves as Independents, the insurgents had their base of support in non-plantation districts (including new coal-mining areas) while they looked to curry the votes of disgruntled black Republicans. To that end, they called, variously, for an end to election fraud, the repeal of new poll taxes, the abolition of convict leasing, and increased funding for public schools. "A free ballot and a fair count" was their cry and bid for a political biracialism.

Among these Deep South insurgencies, none emerged to stronger effect than in east-central Texas. There Republicans first "fused" with Greenbackers in the late 1870s and then, in a number of counties, helped build interracial coalitions that gained and held on to power, sometimes for years. Hard times in the rural districts, for humble whites and blacks alike, proved to be the starting point for a course that seemed to defy Democratic white supremacy, but strong local leadership and the experience of working together served as the motor keeping these extraordinary democratic experiments in motion. It seemed indicative of a developing political culture in the state of Texas, where the South met and meshed with the West, where German and Mexican immigrants resided in significant numbers, and where oppositional politics found fertile soil. No state gave a greater proportion of its votes in national elections to the Greenbackers than Texas. Nor did many other states see such intensely overlapping economic booms and busts in the 1870s and 1880s: in cotton farming, cattle ranching, mining, and railroads. Here the prospects for building a popular movement linking town and country appeared particularly auspicious.

Constructing a Cooperative Commonwealth

Only weeks after the defeat of the Great Railroad Strike of 1877, an organization that would come to be known as the Farmers' Alliance sprang up in east-central Texas, not far from Dallas and Fort Worth. It did so in the context of a bitter fence-cutting war that set small farmers and stock raisers against large land syndicates and ranchers—a version of the fencing and enclosure struggles that were erupting across the South and the plains as capitalist property rights took hold and common use rights that had long prevailed were dismantled—and, in the process, catalyzed antimonopoly sentiments. The area became a Greenback stronghold. Before long, the Knights of Labor was also organizing farmers as well as miners and railroad workers; nearby Erath County was a coal-mining center, and two railroad lines, including the Texas and Pacific, were moving through. Thanks to a growing cadre of lecturers, the Alliance soon expanded across Texas. As the cotton economy continued to deteriorate, it spread through much of the Deep South and, where possible, cultivated close relations with the Knights and "anti-monopoly leagues." Thus, when the Alliance met in Cleburne, Texas, in 1886, shortly after the collapse of the Great Southwest Strike, its demands included recognition of trade unions and cooperative stores, taxation of railroads and corporations, a mechanics' and laborers' lien law, the abolition of convict leasing, an end to alien landownership, the taxation of land held for speculative purposes, the removal of fences from public and school lands, the passage of an interstate commerce law, the establishment of a national bureau of labor statistics, and a greenback-based monetary system.

Much the same took place as Alliance organizations began to appear in the Dakotas, Nebraska, Minnesota, Iowa, and Kansas and then in the Rocky Mountains and the Far West. Indeed, miners and railroad workers played a particularly prominent part in Colorado, Montana, and Wyoming, mostly in association with the Knights of Labor, and they might be joined, especially in California, by followers of Henry George and Edward Bellamy, the latter in growing numbers of Nationalist Clubs that commemorated the utopian collectivist society elaborated in Bellamy's best-selling *Looking Backward* (1888). What linked all these efforts, in the South and the West, was the tumultuous experience of capitalist development, the powerful spirit of antimonopoly, and an interest in cooperative alternatives to the hegemony of market relations.

Cooperatives could come in many forms and surely drew upon practices of mutuality that had deep histories in rural, village, and urban communities alike. They included cooperatives to sell crops like cotton, purchase supplies needed on farms and in working-class neighborhoods, mine coal, make shoes, bake bread, mold iron, construct machines, and fashion clothing. From the outset, the Knights of Labor encouraged the formation of "producer cooperatives," which had in fact been part of the manufacturing landscape since the 1830s. As many as five hundred might have been established nationwide during the postbellum period and perhaps as many as three hundred in the years from 1884 to 1888 alone. For their part, the Grange and other agricultural societies often attempted to organize cooperatives for the buying and selling of goods, and the Farmers' Alliance established "cooperative exchanges" on the local and state levels, most of which were hampered by inadequate capital. But the crowning idea, and one that potentially challenged the fundamental relations of the market economy, was the "subtreasury system."

The brainchild of the Texas Alliance man Charles Macune, the subtreasury system was to be a federally financed and operated network of warehouses to which agricultural operators (farmers, planters, and tenants) could bring and store their crops and, on that basis, have access to necessary credit at very low rates of interest. The crops, in turn, could be held back until market conditions improved and thus fetch higher prices than would otherwise be the case. Subtreasuries were, that is, cooperatives on a massive scale that would, simultaneously, sidestep unfavorable capital markets responsible for driving up local interest rates and skirt the cotton sellers and brokers who, flooding the international market after harvest, drove prices down. They would not only use government power to strengthen agricultural producers but weaken the position of finance capital in the political economy. When, therefore, the Farmers' Alliance met in St. Louis in 1889 to draft a national platform, the delegates included the subtreasury along with six other planks that reflected greenback and antimonopoly roots: the abolition of national banks, a greenback currency, government ownership of the means of transportation and communication, the prohibition of alien landownership, equitable taxation, and the free and unlimited coinage of silver. By that time, the Alliance had well over half a million members and was growing at a rapid pace.

Like the Knights of Labor, the Farmers' Alliance, especially in the South, was cautious about entering the political arena as an independent party. Partisan loyalties remained strong across the country, and Republicans and Democrats alike occupied formidable structural positions from which to combat insurgencies: organized nationally, they had devoted clients in the press; they dominated most branches of government (including the judiciaries); they benefited enormously from winner-take-all systems of voting; and, of course, they had very substantial resources at their disposals. What's more, the route to insurgency differed from region to region. In the plains and the Far West, the Republicans were the dominant party. In the South, the Democrats held sway. And in much of the Rocky Mountain West and the upper plains, the federal government controlled the territories. In one section of the country, insurgents would have to break with Republicans; in another, they would have to break with Democrats; and throughout they would have to join hands across a chasm that the War of the Rebellion had opened.

Equally, if not more important, the Farmers' Alliance, like the antimonopoly movement more generally, was strained by its own social tensions. The leadership was generally composed of substantial farmers and planters who were deeply involved in the commercial economy. The rank and file included farmers, tenants, and even sharecroppers who either had been staple growers for some time or, more likely, had been caught up in the rapid expansion of market relations that the outcome of the War of the Rebellion enabled in both the South and the West. What they all shared was an experience of exploitation in the sphere of exchange owing to the concentrations of control in finance, marketing, and transportation. They suffered as well from limited access to policy making in the federal government because the balances of power in the postbellum political economy did not favor them. Broad antimonopoly sensibilities and interest in monetary inflation unified their outlooks. But they remained divided by various forms of social differentiation that marked the countryside.

These were crucially important in the former rebellious South, where the slave plantation had given way, in the absence of land reform, to the tenant and sharecropper plantation presided over by a planter turned landlord. As a landowner and agricultural operator, the planter was not all that different from the yeoman. Both owned real property, headed households, and exploited the labor of economic dependents, and both suffered from declining crop prices and high interest and freight rates. Yet as landlords, planters came to occupy a distinctive social position. Not only did they employ (mostly) black workers on their land, sometimes in substantial numbers, but they often moved into small-scale merchandising to exert greater control over their laborers. Debt, after all, proved to be an effective means of tying a labor force down. Themselves links in the new chains of credit and marketing, moreover, they looked askance at proposals that might disrupt the way they did business and offer black sharecroppers and tenants a more independent footing.

The southern wing of the Farmers' Alliance, therefore, excluded African Americans from membership (overwhelmingly laborers, blacks formed their own Colored Farmers' Alliance). It was more divided over both the subtreasury plan and the prospect of independent politics than was true in the West. Although the white and black Alliances made some gestures of mutual support and shared an interest in cooperatives, there was no talk of a merger and a great deal of suspicion on either side. The distrust then exploded into fury in 1891 when the Colored Farmers' Alliance supported a cotton pickers' strike and the white Farmers' Alliance helped to crush it. Not the best of prospects for breaking the hold of the white supremacist Democrats. Indeed, while the southern Alliance planned to work through the Democratic Party, by demanding that candidates for office publicly endorse the organization's platform (the "Alliance yardstick"), insurgent westerners were ready to take bolder steps. From the Dakotas to Colorado to Kansas, they fielded their own tickets—called Alliance, Independent, and People's parties—and scored notable successes. In the congressional elections of 1890, local People's Party candidates in Kansas, where mobilization was particularly strong, won five of the seven seats. One disgruntled Republican described the campaign as "a composite of [Victor] Hugo's pictures of the French Revolution and a western religious revival."

What permitted an independent political movement to emerge nationally was the failure of the southern Alliance strategy to join forces with the Democrats. On the one hand, they succeeded in electing Alliance-endorsed candidates across the South, taking hold of governorships, legislatures, and nearly twenty seats in Congress. On the other hand, they soon discovered that their newly elected Democratic "friends" would do little to enact the Alliance program or even speak in its support. By 1892, there seemed little alternative to following an independent path, and in Omaha that July a substantial portion of the southern Alliance—predominantly small farm owners—broke off and joined with insurgents from the plains and the Mountain West to form the national People's, or Populist, Party.

The Populist platform ratified in Omaha expressed, perhaps better than any other document of the period, the vision and limits of antimonopoly politics, together with the cooperative impulse that gave those politics their social distinctiveness. Like the Alliance, Knights, and Greenbackers before them, Populists called for a "permanent and perpetual . . . union of the labor forces of the United States" and demanded the abolition of national banks; a greenback currency "as much as possible in the hands of the people"; a graduated income tax; an end to alien landownership and the ownership of land by railroads and corporations "in excess of their actual needs" (the lands to be "reclaimed by the government and held for actual settlers"); and government ownership of the railroads and telegraphs. Like the Alliance, they included the "free and unlimited coinage of silver and gold at the present legal ratio of 16 to 1" and the radically cooperativist "subtreasury plan."

The platform's preamble, drafted by the fiery Minnesota farmer, lawyer, congressman, and writer Ignatius Donnelly, defined the moral and political stakes. He denounced the "corruption" that dominated the political system, the muzzling of the press, the "hireling standing army unrecognized by our laws" (like the Pinkertons), the pauperization of labor, the appropriation of the power to create money, and the many other dangers that threatened the Republic. "From the same prolific womb of government injustice," he thundered, "we breed the two great classes—tramps and millionaires." Instead, Donnelly argued, the Populists believed "that the power of government—in other words, of the people—should be expanded . . . to the end that oppression, injustice, and poverty shall eventually cease in the land." Yet in a series of attached resolutions that supported "a free ballot and a fair count" and the struggle for an eight-hour workday, the Populists also condemned the opening of "our ports to the pauper and criminal classes of the world" and called for "the further restriction of undesirable emigration," a reminder of the hostility that still fell upon those who were regarded as most dependent, whatever their racial or ethnic origins.

Newly minted as the party was, the Populists did remarkably well in the national elections of 1892. They won the electoral votes of five states (North Dakota, Kansas, Colorado, Idaho, and Nevada) thanks to coalitions of farmers and workers and attracted more than one-third of the popular vote in five others (South Dakota, Nebraska, Wyoming, Oregon, and Alabama). Overall, the Populists received more than a million votes in the presidential election (about 9 percent of all ballots cast) and won congressional races in Minnesota, Colorado, Kansas, Nebraska, California, and North Carolina, governorships in Kansas and Colorado, and legislative seats in many other states of the South and the West. Two years later, as the consequences of the panic of 1893 deepened, they did better still, especially in the southern states of Texas, Georgia, Alabama, and North Carolina, where white farmers in the non-plantation districts lent growing support. This was no small achievement because Democrats accused Populists in the South of undermining white supremacy and often sought to prevent them from casting their ballots.

The moment was ripe internationally. The decline of commodity prices, especially of major agricultural staples, was a worldwide phenomenon as the countryside across much of the globe came to pay the costs of capitalist industrialization. Major migrations, especially of landless or land-poor peasants, either to urban centers relatively nearby or to major sites of economic activity across the oceans represented one of the ramifications. So too did the formation of agricultural electoral blocs—where landowners retained influence in state policy—in the interests of tariffs on imported grains or the establishment of rural cooperatives. But as in the United States, there were explosions as well: the land war in Ireland, peasant risings and the emergence of anarchism in Spain, rural unrest in Sicily and the Balkans, a millennial movement in the Brazilian northeast, anticolonial battles in Cuba and the Philippines, and the Boxer Rebellion in China. It was a time of massive, if imbalanced, struggle in the developing capitalist world between town and country, industry and agriculture, metropole and colony.

The fate of the southern Populist explosion would depend on the party's ability to forge some sort of alliance with black voters who ordinarily backed the Republicans. Only that way could they win solid majorities. They had a model in the Readjusters of Virginia who attempted to accommodate the interests of African Americans in tangible ways. But the Populists had no William Mahone to lead the way, and they suffered accordingly. Some of their leaders, like Tom Watson in Georgia and H. S. P. "Stump" Ashby in Texas, appropriated a language of protest in which blacks and whites could be imagined as participants in the same civil and political arenas, suffering similar problems and having common stakes in a political battle. And at the grass roots, some organizers could tell blacks that "your race today, like ours, is groaning under the oppression of taxation and the low estimate placed on labor" and that "to better our condition means to better yours."

It seemed enough to gain the endorsement of the Colored Farmers' Alliance and perhaps the votes of African Americans who had some experience working with white insurgents in previous years. It also helped cement a successful alliance between Populists and Republicans in North Carolina—they won control of both houses of the state legislature in 1894 and remained a force for several years—chiefly because the deal also involved "divid[ing] the county offices with the negroes," which, one Democrat said with a sigh, "takes like fire with" them. For the most part, however, Populists ignored or were inattentive to black concerns and were rarely willing to nominate them for office or provide them with important leadership positions. They were happy to get black votes but reluctant to give blacks power, and so the black support that Populists received tended to be lukewarm and decline over time.

Given its character as a movement—one of petty, property-owning producers—the Populists probably reached the boundaries of their political prospects in 1894; misgivings about the role of the state, the working of the subtreasury system, and the place of African Americans hampered their ability to enlarge their coalition and compete for genuine national power. Ironically, the best prospects for an alternative path inspired by Populism were soon to be found in a changing Democratic Party. In some of the southern states, Democrats responded to the Populist challenge by moving in reform directions that the party had previously resisted. Many Democrats were, of course, Farmers' Alliance members to begin with and shared antimonopoly sensibilities, even if they did not fully embrace the Alliance program. A few also addressed issues of concern to black constituents and, like Georgia's governor, William J. Northen, pushed to increase funding for black schools while publicly denouncing lynch mobs. But the most important developments occurred on the national level as the inflationist wing of the party, based principally in the South and the West, looked to challenge the gold wing based in the Northeast. It had, in truth, been a long-standing struggle, but the panic of 1893 and the subsequent depression—the deepest the nation had yet experienced—strengthened their hand, all the more so as President Grover Cleveland of New York, himself a Democrat, responded to the crisis by tightening rather than loosening the money supply.

By 1896, pressured by Populism as well as by widespread labor unrest, the inflationist Democrats won out and, although they rejected both the subtreasury and government ownership of the railroads and telegraphs, nonetheless showed the deep imprint of antimonopolism. Their platform lashed out at the national banking system ("Congress alone has the power to coin and issue money"), denounced "the absorption of wealth by the few, the consolidation of our leading railroad systems, and the formation of trusts and pools," and demanded the free and unlimited coinage of silver. To exemplify the changing of the party's guard, the convention, meeting in Chicago, chose as its presidential candidate a young congressman and silverite from the state of Nebraska who, in a ringing keynote speech, warned that "mankind" risked being crucified "upon a cross of gold." His name was William Jennings Bryan. Recognizing their affinities, or bitterly swallowing their pride, most of the Populists reluctantly signed on and battled for the future of the country.

Building Blocks of Social Democracy

The national election of 1896 proved to be a defining moment in American political history, and it went badly for those who had antimonopoly dispositions and hoped to readjust the balances of the nation's political economy to the benefit of workers, petty producers, small towns, agricultural districts, the South, and the West. After three decades of closely contested elections, multiplying insurgencies, greenback-inspired platforms, antimonopoly mobilizations, and the organization of the largest third party in the country's history, the Republican Party consolidated its ascendancy. Although the Republican presidential candidate, William McKinley of Ohio, received only 51 percent of the popular vote, he won a landslide in the Electoral College (271 of 447 votes) by sweeping the states of the Northeast, the Middle Atlantic, the Midwest, and the Far West, leaving the South, the Great Plains, and the Rocky Mountain West united in defeat. McKinley was aided by the remarkable and inventive campaign tactics of Mark Hanna, who helped raise $3.5 million (five times what the Democrats raised and equivalent to about $100 million in today's dollars) from frightened members of the elite and set an example of the advertised politics so familiar to the twentieth century. In uneasy control of the national government since the time of the War of the Rebellion, the Republicans would now dominate for more than the next three decades. The industrial and financial sections of the United States thereby became the ruling "core"; the agricultural and extractive sections of the country were left as the "peripheries," as "regions" in relation to the "center." The national banking system would be preserved, the railroads and telegraphs would remain in private hands, and talk of greenbacks and free silver would be banished to the margins. In 1900, the McKinley administration put the United States officially on the gold standard.

It seemed emblematic of a series of moments over the previous decade when capital flexed its powerful muscles and many working people and petty producers took it on their collective chin. After the failures of 1886, which sent the Knights of Labor reeling and buried the movement for the eight-hour workday, laborers saw that large corporations had little patience for their organizational weapons and were ready to enlist the military arm of the state on the slightest provocation. One of the first showdowns came at Andrew Carnegie's Homestead steelworks, just outside Pittsburgh, where the Amalgamated Association of Iron and Steel Workers had won a collective bargaining agreement after a successful strike in 1889. Homestead management quickly complained about the constant "interference" of some "busybody representing the Amalgamated," and by 1892 Carnegie had decided to lower the boom. Through his hard-nosed superintendent Henry Clay Frick, he instituted a 20 percent wage cut and locked the workers out in an attempt to break the hold of the union. Pitched gun battles soon erupted between strikers and Pinkerton guards brought in to protect strikebreakers, and both sides took heavy casualties. But as in the Great Southwest Strike, the tide fully turned when the Pennsylvania governor ordered in eight thousand state troops who, refusing to fraternize with the strikers, enabled strikebreakers to fire up the machinery and renew steel production.

Farther to the west, an even bigger, and more consequential, struggle was brewing in the town of Pullman, just south of Chicago. The sleeping-car magnate George Pullman had built what he and many other observers regarded as a veritable paradise for his company's employees: a town replete with housing, retail stores, parks, banks, churches, and libraries meant to stand in stark contrast to the congestion, tenements, and dangerous political influences to be found in the city. But there was no democracy on the ground, just the paternalism of Pullman and his managers. Thus, when the company cut wages (though not dividends) by 30–50 percent in the spring of 1894 while leaving rents and company store prices intact, the workers pushed back. They had the support of the newly organized American Railway Union (ARU), fresh from a victory over James J. Hill's Northern Pacific Railway. Led by Eugene V. Debs, the ARU recruited unskilled as well as skilled workers, and when Pullman fired the local leaders and locked the workers out, the union (despite Debs's misgivings) called a nationwide boycott of Pullman cars. For a time, it appeared as if the ARU might again have the upper hand. As many as 250,000 workers in twenty-seven states honored the boycott, and rail transport between Chicago and the Pacific coast had, in the words of one industry spokesman, been "fought to a standstill." But the Pullman company still had strong cards to play. Instead of looking to the intervention of Illinois's governor, John Peter Altgeld, a reformer who was sympathetic to the strikers, company officials went directly to the federal government. It made sense. President Cleveland's attorney general, Richard Olney, was as powerful an ally as the Pullman company could have wished for. A longtime railroad lawyer, Olney continued to serve on several railroad boards—including one involved in the strike—even after becoming attorney general, and he took the opportunity to crush what he saw as a radical threat to federal authority and business interests. Obtaining a blanket injunction against the ARU for interfering with the mails and interstate commerce (under the provisions of the recently enacted Sherman Antitrust Act), Olney ordered the strikers to desist and, when they refused, sent in federal troops under the command of General Nelson A. Miles, best known for battling Native Americans in the trans-Mississippi West. In relatively short order, the trains were rolling, the strike was broken, and Debs was hauled off to prison, where he served a six-month sentence for contempt of court.

The outlook for working people and agricultural producers appeared grim indeed. Yet as the smoke of defeat began to settle, it also became clear that the political mobilizations of the previous three decades—around the eight-hour workday, collective bargaining, greenbackism, public ownership of the rails and telegraphs, producer and consumer cooperatives, and antimonopoly more generally—were not without notable effect. Challenging the power of financial and industrial capital and the hegemony of market relations, insurgents in town and country alike helped to shift the center of political gravity and intellectual discourse away from the pieties of individualism, competition, and laissez-faire and toward a new conception of the state and civil society, a new compact involving an activist government and broader notions of social responsibility. As counterpoints to classical liberalism, the dissident movements of Populism, socialism, and social democracy came to nourish one another in important new mixes.

The political journey of the ARU's leader, Eugene Debs, offers a revealing example. Born in the small town of Terre Haute, Indiana, in 1855, Debs became a locomotive fireman and loyal Democrat who, while concerned for the downtrodden, also imagined a world in which capital and labor could cooperate and settle their differences amicably. Although rising to a leadership position in the Brotherhood of Locomotive Firemen, Debs was cool (as many of the railroad brotherhoods were) to the tactic of the strike, given the enormous power of corporations. But the events at Homestead in 1892 helped move him to embrace the industrial unionism of the ARU (so long as members were "white"), and then the panic of 1893 together with the struggle at Pullman convinced him that the Democrats were as closely allied with large corporations as the Republicans. Workers, he came to believe, had to chart an independent course. Even before the Pullman boycott was over, Debs, who had campaigned for the Democrat Grover Cleveland in the past, thus announced, "I am a Populist, and I favor wiping out both old parties so they will never come to power again. I have been a Democrat all my life and I am ashamed to admit it." So noteworthy was his political conversion that over the next couple of years Debs was approached about running for Illinois governor and then president on the People's Party ticket.

Yet during the months he sat in a McHenry County, Illinois, jail cell, Debs began to have another road to Damascus experience. He read the works of Edward Bellamy, Laurence Gronlund, and the Marxist Karl Kautsky, and, visited by the German American socialist Victor Berger (who left him a copy of Marx's *Capital*), the British trade union radical Keir Hardie, and the Chicago labor activist Thomas J. Morgan, he talked socialism and the need for international cooperation among working people. He already subscribed to the *Coming Nation* published by the American socialist J. A. Wayland and, while continuing to edit the *Railway Times*, thought deeply about the social questions of the day. Once released, Debs campaigned for William Jennings Bryan in 1896, but in the aftermath of Bryan's defeat he set out on a new political path, though one that showed the influence of antimonopolism and Populism. "The issue is Socialism versus Capitalism," Debs wrote. "I am for Socialism because I am for humanity. We have been cursed with the reign of gold long enough. Money constitutes no proper basis of civilization. The time has come to regenerate society—we are on the eve of a universal change."

The socialism that Debs advocated had contested meanings and complex roots in transatlantic thought and movements of the early nineteenth century. The first glimmerings were in evidence among land reformers, communitarians, radical republicans, and utopians of the 1820s and 1830s who used the Enlightenment's intellectual heritage of reason and science as means of combating the contagions of industrialism and of tying material progress to social cooperation. Many of the original disciples—Claude Henri de Saint-Simon, Charles Fourier, Robert Owen—were themselves children of the Enlightenment who had faith in the productive power of new technologies but bridled at the competitive struggles that developing market economies inevitably spawned. Their ideas initially gained traction among artisans and some middle-class reformers, and they surely informed demands for a "social" republic that could be heard on the European continent in 1830 and 1848 and for the working-class franchise pursued by the British Chartists. But it was not until the 1850s and 1860s that socialism fully entered the political vocabulary of the Atlantic world and became linked chiefly to mobilizations of working people. Karl Marx's *Communist Manifesto* (1848) and subsequent organization of the International Workingmen's Association (the First International in 1864) were signal moments in this process.

Even so, socialism remained less a specific program or vision than a set of political predispositions—counterpoints to liberal individualism, market competition, economic hierarchies, and elite rule. What socialists generally shared were commitments to "society," mutual cooperation, political democratization, social justice, and worker empowerment. They pressed for the establishment of parliamentary regimes (sometimes in alliance with radical liberals and republicans), for the expansion of the elective franchise, for the organization of trades and workplaces, for the construction of international networks of solidarity, and for major readjustments in the balance of social power. They also fought among themselves over the appropriate strategies and tactics of struggle. Some scoffed at parliamentary means, insisting instead on the necessity of devising alternative institutions or engaging in insurrection; most others, especially after the defeat of the Paris Commune, saw the wisdom in a range of activities (not to mention the perils of insurrectionism) and pushed toward a working-class political movement of national and transnational dimensions. By the last quarter of the nineteenth century, socialists were in the process of helping to build the first mass political parties in Europe, the largest and most consequential of which was the German Social Democratic Party (SPD) founded in 1875, in the immediate wake of the panic.

Small wonder that German immigrants figured significantly in the development of socialism in the United States. Waves of German refugees from the 1848 revolutions, the activities of the First International, and Bismarck's antisocialist laws had enormous influence on the liberal and radical currents of American politics. They boosted the antislavery movement of the 1850s, the wartime course of emancipation in the 1860s, the unfolding of federal Reconstruction policy, and then the emergence of grassroots socialism in the 1870s and 1880s, chiefly in the urban centers of the Middle Atlantic and the Midwest: from New York out to Chicago and Milwaukee, and down to St. Louis. German socialists built institutional networks that traversed international borders. They established daily newspapers, created women's auxiliaries, and became active in trade union organizing (including the American Federation of Labor, or AFL). They supported striking workers, formed alliances with antimonopoly radicals, and, at times, lent their votes to the campaigns of independent labor tickets and the Socialist Labor Party. They would be joined by native-born radicals who had moved through greenbackism, the Knights of Labor, and Populism, especially out in Kansas, Texas, Arkansas, and Oklahoma; by women's rights activists, including those involved in the temperance movement, who were deeply concerned about the exploitation of women and children at the workplace; by settlement house workers who became deeply involved with struggling immigrant communities in teeming industrial metropoles; by growing numbers of intellectuals in the rapidly professionalizing social sciences who mounted critiques of industrialism (many of whom had studied in German universities); and by evangelical Christians who redefined the notions of personal responsibility consecrated by the Great Awakening into what became known as the social gospel.

The most committed socialists not only threw themselves into the fight against capitalism but also battled among themselves over the best political path to be charted: whether to focus on industrial organizing, build dual unions, mobilize for revolution, or participate in the formal electoral sphere. These were the very issues that roiled socialists across Europe and gave rise to a number of sectarian tendencies, including anarchism and syndicalism. In the United States, several of these tendencies found an uneasy home when, in 1901, Eugene Debs, Victor Berger, and the Russian-born socialist and labor activist Morris Hillquit helped found the Socialist Party. Over the next two decades, with Debs as its standard-bearer, the party would win hundreds of thousands of votes (nearly one million in 1912) and elect mayors, city councilmen, and state legislators from California and Idaho, Wisconsin and Minnesota, Louisiana and Oklahoma, Ohio and Pennsylvania, and New York and New Jersey. Organized socialism had clearly established a beachhead on the American political landscape.

Perhaps more important, during the last two decades of the nineteenth century and the first decade of the twentieth, socialist ideas and ideals took hold among a broad range of producers—workers, farmers, and the petit bourgeoisie— as well as intellectuals and reformers who might never have aligned with, or voted for, a socialist party but who nonetheless sought alternatives to or modifications in the prevailing "wages" system. Some became aware of the social democratic thought that was emerging in Germany, France, and Britain and that was rejecting orthodox Marxism with its emphasis on revolution and the proletariat in favor of a more "evolutionary" road to socialism. Some, like Henry George, Edward Bellamy, and Henry Demarest Lloyd, built upon the logic of antimonopoly to envision collectivist possibilities. A great many felt the energies of moral revitalization that Christianity, once a bedfellow of industrialism, could provide, criticizing capitalism as "the defender of privilege."

Indeed, a political culture of social democracy might well have been the most significant legacy that the great struggles of the late nineteenth century bequeathed to the country's future. And nowhere did social democracy assume more distinctively American form than in the trans-Mississippi West. There among miners, lumberjacks, migrant farm laborers, and railroad workers, as well as Bellamyites and Georgists, radicalized members of the middle class, and a new breed of reformer and social scientist, new ideas and practices—a new social and political consciousness—had been taking special shape. As in much of the country, they reflected the inheritances of antimonopoly, trade unionism, greenbackism, and Populism. But they also showed the discrete circumstances of economic development, labor, and politics: the enormous power of corporate railroad, mining, and land companies; the extremely dangerous conditions of work and the mutualism that such dangers bred; the high demand for skilled and unskilled laborers that scattered populations created; strong ties between middling and working people; and the relative weakness of partisan structures and identities that made the electoral arena a promising site for political struggle. Levels of unionization were high, and militancy was pronounced, especially among coal, silver, and copper miners. The Knights of Labor had engaged in some of its epic battles along broad reaches of the Southwest. Populists recruited workers as well as small farmers in the plains and mountain states and registered signal gains. And socialism found some of its most powerful expressions in the press and on the hustings. Labor and independent political tickets flourished, sympathetic local and state officials were often elected, and in some places an eight-hour workday was established and defended.

More than in any other part of the country, the power and greed of corporate capital was most nakedly in evidence in the trans-Mississippi West, and here was where social democratic solutions seemed to gain most traction. There was support for government ownership of railroads, telegraphs, and telephones, for various forms of direct democracy and woman suffrage, for new types of taxation including the Henry George–inspired single tax, and for municipal control of social services. There was also support for the industrial unionism that the Knights of Labor commenced and both the Western Federation of Miners and the Industrial Workers of the World (IWW) would carry into the twentieth century. It was in the "peripheries," in other words, that the cultural and political alternatives to capitalism gained some of their firmest footing and richest nourishments.

And in the "peripheries" too—southern as well as western—there were glimmerings of new dispositions that seemed capable of breaking the boundaries long imposed by race and dependency on dissenting currents of thought and politics. They were not the result of idealism or ideological transformations; they grew out of pragmatic concerns and institutional developments, of the expansion of proletarianized work and the mobilizations that could go along with it. They were to be seen not in the industrial or agricultural heartlands but on the docks along the Gulf and Atlantic coasts, in the coal mines of the Alabama, Oklahoma, and Kansas hills, and in the lumber camps of the Louisiana and Texas piney woods. They were the products of a biracial unionism made possible by the organizational efforts of black workers and white socialists and by the recognition on the part of white workers that in industries with traditions of black employment this was the only way forward. The biracialism of these moments involved limited social fraternizing and continuing lines of separation; often, as was the case with the Knights of Labor, black and white workers would be in racially distinct locals, and tensions among them could easily flare up. But they also found ways to struggle together, even in the face of their employers' efforts to divide them, to appreciate each other's strengths and experience, and to imagine outcomes where all might benefit. To be sure, it wasn't all that much. Yet it was much more than might have been expected, and it set the vital groundwork for far greater social democratic possibilities in the future.

CHAPTER TWELVE

Reconstructions

Banker and financier J. Pierpont Morgan leading investors and politicians along the path of corporate consolidation. Art by Udo J. Keppler, *Puck*, September 17, 1902.

Social Reconstruction

Among the first to join the Socialist Party of America in 1901 was Florence Kelley. Daughter of William D. "Pig-Iron" Kelley, one of the founders of the Republican Party, a powerful congressman, and a mainstay of its Radical wing, she was early exposed to the currents of abolitionism and women's rights and set out in a direction that the enormous transformations of the postwar period both made possible and seemed to demand. Availing herself of new educational opportunities for middle-class women, she attended Cornell University, where she gravitated to the new social sciences, became interested in issues of child welfare, and ultimately finished a thesis on the subject that earned publication. Equally consequential was a four-year stay in Europe, much of it in Germany, where she embraced Marxian socialism, entered the orbit of the fledgling Social Democratic Party, married a Russian socialist, and returned to the United States as a wife and mother. Along the way, she began a correspondence with Karl Marx's collaborator, Friedrich Engels, and translated his influential work *The Condition of the Working-Class in England* into English for a wider readership.

For a time, Florence Kelley mixed interests in the struggles of working women and children—writing essays in their support and helping to establish the Philadelphia Working Women's Society—with the politics of the Socialist Labor Party, an American extension of the German SPD. But differences with the SLP's German-language orientation and its Lassallean views (emphasizing direct political action as opposed to trade unionism) led her to break with the party and turn more fully to the travails of working people in general and women and children in particular. She soon met up with Jane Addams, who had returned from her own unsettling trip to Europe to help launch the settlement house movement on the West Side of Chicago. With a base in Addams's Hull House, Kelley looked to train young women in domestic work, won appointment as special agent of the Illinois Bureau of Labor Statistics, and, during the governorship of John Peter Altgeld, became state factory inspector.

Although Kelley's lifelong attachment to socialism set her apart, her political journey in many ways marked the road from antebellum reform to what became known as Progressivism and exemplified the central part that women activists played in laying it out. Building on the bedrocks of evangelicalism, abolitionism, and women's rights, they pioneered new tactics of political mobilization, missionizing, and voluntarism that were tested in the conflagrations of warfare and then in the social traumas of industrial capitalism. Generally from middle-class families of the Northeast, the Midwest, and the Pacific coast, often born in the 1850s and 1860s, many chafed at the limited expectations that Victorian culture prescribed. They enrolled in institutions of higher learning that either sought out or agreed to admit women (owing to Civil War–era land-grant legislation), and then had arresting encounters with the poverty and deprivation that had come to plague the world of industrial workers. In the process, they rejected the pieties of social Darwinism and liberal individualism and instead advanced new ideas of social responsibility and the role of the state as a vehicle of reform.

It might have appeared that settlement house reformers, social workers, teachers, and nurses were merely carrying on the work of antebellum predecessors who had "visited" poor women in their neighborhood tenements, sought to provide relief to needy widows, or tried to "rescue" prostitutes while solidifying their own bourgeois identities. And to some extent, this is the case. The social dynamics bore close resemblance, the class prerogatives were clearly in evidence, and the moral imperatives were often in full display. There is a powerful sense in which "uplift" to a set of cultural ideals remained the principal objective. But how problems were understood and the solutions imagined had changed in important ways.

Nothing was more important to this change than the massive struggles and conflicts that engulfed the United States and much of the Atlantic world during the second half of the nineteenth century. The revolutionary political eruptions that marked the path of nation building in Germany, Italy, and France, the abolition of slavery across the Americas, and the epic slaughter and social challenges that accompanied the War of the Rebellion fostered new interconnections while highlighting the transformative possibilities of an activist state. Equally significant, the rapid advance of capitalist relations, in countryside and town, agriculture and industry, not only produced dislocations on a global scale but led, from Berlin to San Francisco, Chicago to Mexico City, to new battles between labor and capital. And nowhere were those battles bloodier and more convulsive than in the United States. Late nineteenth-century reformers like Florence Kelley, Jane Addams, and the health and settlement house worker Lillian Wald were heirs not simply to antebellum pioneers but also to those women who, in the many hundreds, reshaped the cultural and political landscape of the nation: to women who gravitated during the war to organizations like the U.S. Sanitary Commission and the Western Sanitary Commission, which tended to the health of U.S. soldiers and ex-slaves in hospitals, kitchens, and encampments; to women who signed, in the many thousands, petitions in support of the Thirteenth Amendment to the Constitution abolishing slavery; to women who headed south with the American Missionary Association and other church-related groups to minister to the freedpeople, and west to minister to Native Americans on newly established reservations; and to women who mobilized unsuccessfully to have women, as well as African American men, politically enfranchised. They were heirs, that is, to a generation of women who, in their own experience, came to see the reach of social problems that a modernizing world was creating, to recognize how different groups of people could be the products of specific circumstances, and to view the political arena as a vital sphere of struggle.

They were, as well, witnesses to the ways in which industrial capitalism was reshaping the landscape of American cities as unprecedented numbers of immigrants—chiefly from southern and eastern Europe—fled the commodifications of land and labor in their homelands and flooded into the urban United States between 1870 and 1914. They saw the crowded tenements and residential enclaves that Poles, Italians, Slavs, Germans, Jews, and Bohemians came to occupy, the rampant un- and underemployment that beset them during especially severe cycles of economic distress, the lack of adequate lighting and sanitation, and the exploitation of women and children who had to contribute to family and community economies. All of this shocked them out of middle-class complacency and inspired them to do "useful" work. They also saw the bitter conflicts that were continuously erupting between employers and laborers, some turning into pitched street battles, as the "old relationships" of the workplace steadily disintegrated. For Jane Addams and Florence Kelley, the Pullman strike of 1894 was an especially shocking and revealing episode. "We do not like to acknowledge," Addams observed, "that Americans are divided into two nations."

Settlement houses, which spread across the face of industrializing America between the late 1880s and the second decade of the twentieth century, provided a range of social services for the working-class neighborhoods in which they were ordinarily located. Especially in the largest cities, they offered child care and kindergartens, lectures and adult education classes, job training and theatrical productions, shelters and public baths. Before long, Protestant and Catholic churches devised their own settlements and programs, as did the nondenominational Young Men's Christian Association and the Salvation Army, both of which had origins in mid-century London and eventually spread to the United States.

As this might suggest, the settlement house movement and other vectors of urban social reform in the late nineteenth and early twentieth centuries developed in close association with a new sense of social awareness, particularly among Protestants. Proponents of what was known as the social gospel, clergy from a number of denominations—most of whom grew up and continued to preach in industrializing cities—sought to apply what they regarded as Christian ethics to social problems, turning evangelicalism into a motor of social justice. At the radical edge, men like Walter Rauschenbusch, who was born in

Rochester and preached in New York City's Hell's Kitchen, attacked both the poverty and inequality that industrial capitalism was creating and the individualism that evangelicalism had once so forcefully advanced. "Capitalism set out as the opponent of privilege and the champion of freedom," Rauschenbusch wrote, "it has ended by being the defender of privilege and the intrenchment of autocracy." Together with the ministers Lyman Abbott, Josiah Strong, and Washington Gladden, he exhorted his listeners to embrace the "next great principle . . . association." "New forms of association must be created. Our disorganized, competitive life must pass into an organic cooperative life," he urged. Rauschenbusch was something of a Christian socialist, but what he shared with many other advocates of the social gospel was an interest in applying "the teaching of Jesus and the total message of Christian salvation to society," a vision of the city "as a nerve center" and "storm center of our civilization," and a desire to join hands with intellectuals, reformers, and political leaders at the local and national level to advance a project of what Gladden called "reconstruction." Rauschenbusch had supported the New York mayoral campaign of Henry George in 1886, started a Christian socialist newspaper, *For the Right*, three years later, and exercised a growing influence on social scientists, philosophers, and educators like Richard T. Ely (both Rauschenbusch and Ely studied in Germany in the late 1870s) who were laying the groundwork of social democratic and progressive thought. Indeed, the social gospel not only lent progressive reform much of its moral fervor—from its sense of crisis to its notions of transformation—but also provided a language that spoke to the personal struggles and visions of many of the reformers themselves. Not surprisingly, the social gospel would come to connect the roughest urban neighborhoods with the highest reaches of the national state.

Few movements saw the intersection of these cultural impulses with the project of "reconstruction" more directly than that for temperance and prohibition. The movement already had a lengthy history, surpassing any other social reform of the antebellum era in popular appeal and making a significant dent in the consumption of alcoholic beverages, especially in the evangelical belts of the Northeast and the Midwest. But antebellum temperance supporters tended to see what they called "enslavement to demon rum" as a product of personal failings that the embrace of Christ and self-improvement were meant to break. When the movement took off again in the 1870s, however, alcoholism was increasingly seen in a broad social context—as cause and consequence—and its eradication understood as requiring a number of cultural and political interventions. This was especially true for the Woman's Christian Temperance Union (WCTU), headed up for the last twenty years of the nineteenth century by Frances Willard and easily the most prominent and powerful organization of its kind.

Born near Rochester, New York, and growing up in small-town Wisconsin, Willard was educated at North Western Female College in Evanston, Illinois, and came to temperance in part as a result of personal and family crises (including the alcoholism of her brother). But Willard's ambitions were broadly based in relation both to prohibition and to prohibition's place in the universe of reform. Under Willard's leadership, the WCTU adopted a "do everything" model, pressing for liquor laws, temperance education in the schools, and grassroots mobilizations while at the same time embracing labor reform, child welfare legislation, municipal sanitation, anti-polygamy laws, and woman suffrage, which she saw as essential to the necessary political progress. Willard's feminism did not reject domesticity but instead used it as a moral center for social change. Soon she was rubbing shoulders with Jane Addams, Richard T. Ely, and Washington Gladden, most notably at annual summer retreats in Chautauqua, New York, where hundreds of middle-class women and men came for a week or two to enjoy leisure activities and listen to the ideas of progressive thinkers.

These reformers were part of a transatlantic network of activists and intellectuals who, in coming to grips with the repercussions of industrial capitalism, were redefining the terms and institutional bases of political engagement. Like Rauschenbusch, Kelley, Ely, and Addams, they had studied and traveled abroad, especially in Germany and Britain, become familiar with new social democratic discourses circulating around the German Social Democratic Party and the British Fabian socialists, and witnessed a variety of experiments in welfare policy and city planning (social insurance in Germany, missions to the poor in London, Baron Haussmann's architectural makeovers in Paris); they had also influenced—and were in turn influenced by—the emergence of professional fields of social science and economics in the United States devoted in good part to the study of contemporary social problems. Many of the pioneering social scientists and economists of the period were themselves trained in German universities where graduate research programs had been initiated and soon became the models for American counterparts such as the one at Johns Hopkins University.

Almost invariably, "socialism" formed part of their language and vision. They rejected models of atomized societies organized around the individual in favor of new ones based on social groups and other collectivities; they cast critical eyes on "competition" and emphasized the need for "cooperation"; and they saw the state—at various levels—as the engine of transformation and reconstruction, whether in its regulatory function for workplaces and dwellings or its ownership of public utilities and management of urban affairs. As Lyman Abbott intoned, "Individualism is the characteristic of simple barbarism, not of republican civilization." Many such critics and reformers embraced the long-standing movement for an eight-hour workday, but to this they added advocacy for child labor legislation, tenement house reform, the regulation of sweatshops, and taxes on large incomes and inherited wealth. Some supported the recognition of unions. When Florence Kelley helped found the National Consumers League with Jane Addams and Josephine Lowell in 1899, they hoped to promote safer and less exploitative working conditions through the power that consumers—in their minds mostly women—could wield in the marketplace: a tactic their abolitionist forebears had deployed in boycotting slave-produced goods.

Yet what separated new "progressive" reformers—female and male alike—from the socialists whose perspectives and ideas they often borrowed was a resistance to empowering the very people whose lives they seemed devoted to improving. For all the information they gathered about how the "other half" lived and worked, for all their attempts to mitigate exploitation, improve health, and increase educational opportunities, for all their efforts to protect women and children, they spoke principally to other members of the middle and upper classes and upheld standards of comportment, aspiration, and respectability that were familiar to themselves. Some exoticized their subjects, trying to identify the "primitive needs" of the communities they tended, aiming to carry out a social reconstruction that would be conducive to civic progress and peace—a reconstruction that educated experts like themselves, not workers and immigrants whom they meant to benefit, would direct.

Indeed, they seemed ready to bring out heavier ammunition. Whereas reformers of an earlier day looked to persuade, exhort, and convert those who had fallen or succumbed to their darker selves, progressives were more willing to compel change, to use the levers of the state to attack alcoholism, illiteracy, corruption, infectious disease, prostitution, greed, and labor exploitation. In so doing, they began to lay the foundation of what would—decades later—become the welfare state while at the same time lending moral authority to projects of defining the destinies of peoples both in the United States and elsewhere in the world.

Corporate Reconstruction

Few Americans were more concerned about the social unrest and class conflict of the late nineteenth century than the members of the emerging industrial and financial elite, and their dominant reaction was fear. Quick to put strikes, political insurgencies, and popular critiques of capitalism in an international context of revolutionary agitation and socialism, they increasingly worried that the tide of radicalism, if not abated, might soon sweep over them. Everywhere they looked, discontent seemed to be bubbling to the surface and then erupting into squalls and violent tempests. Movements for the eight-hour workday, greenbacks, the regulation of railroads and other big businesses, and calls for the nationalization of the means of transportation and communication had been disturbing the landscape, challenging the hegemony of the marketplace, and perhaps even threatening the sanctity of private property. The railroad president James J. Hill was not alone in fretting about a "reign of terror [that] exists in the large centres." For some, Populism and the silver crusade of William Jennings Bryan were the last straws, "the representative[s] of anarchy, socialism, and a debased currency."

To be sure, large employers and their political allies in legislatures and the courts had inflicted major defeats on working people along a variety of fronts: at the workplace, in municipal politics, and in the staple-producing countryside. But these might be seen as only temporary setbacks; strike activity continued to mount and socialist ideas were gaining traction not only among workers but among the educated middle class. Widespread popular revulsion at the excesses of railroad and mining companies, and at the corrupt practices of manufacturers and financiers, was forcing the major political" parties to take notice. Congress, under pressure from a variety of "populist" and "provincial" constituencies, passed the Interstate Commerce Act (1887), which established a commission to monitor railroad rates, followed by the Sherman Antitrust Act (1890), which outlawed "contracts" or "combinations" in "restraint of trade among the several States, or with foreign nations," all signs of ongoing struggles over the shape and direction of the political economy.

There was no single response to what was perceived as a crisis, and some saw little alternative to digging in their heels and fending off the challenges by any means. But there also arose, among some of the largest and most influential industrial and financial capitalists, what amounted to a developing social movement of their own, devoted to reconstructing both the institutions of economic life and the relations between the economy and the state. The movement had no clear center or official leadership, no constitution, preamble, or set of demands. It rather assumed the form of private associations, lobbying groups, informal networks, and alliances in the intellectual and political worlds, which together fashioned arguments, perspectives, and policies. In effect, they created a new sense of reality that took the measure of opponents among small manufacturers and merchants on the one side and the organized working class on the other while attempting to construct the property relations and judicial rules of a new political economy. Those who composed this movement disagreed and fought among themselves over the terms and balances and, in so doing, established political battle lines that would endure well into the twentieth century. But if they rallied under any one banner, it might have read, "corporate capitalism and the administered marketplace."

It is commonplace to equate American industrialization with the corporation, and given the importance of the railroads there is some reason for this. But until the very end of the nineteenth century, the corporate form was not widespread among manufacturers, even those who were building large and increasingly integrated establishments. Ownership of firms usually resided in individuals, families, and partnerships, and capital was raised by tapping personal resources, reinvesting profits, or borrowing from commercial lenders. The surge in incorporations did not commence until the late 1880s and early 1890s and arose from a number of developments: the limited usefulness, legal and otherwise, of pools and trusts as means of expanding power in the market; the growing ties between industrial and financial capital; and the green light that the courts and some state legislatures gave to corporate ambitions. The increasing centrality of the corporation to the economy of the United States—well established by the end of the first decade of the twentieth century—was not simply a matter of wealth and scale, or a quantitative growth; it was a qualitative leap and represented a new form of capitalism.

What, then, was new? The corporation embodied novel forms of property and new sets of social relations. No longer would ownership rest in only a few hands, or management face unlimited liability in case of debt or suit, or assets be tied to particular places and take mainly tangible form, or companies be prohibited from controlling other companies. Formal ownership would be "socialized" among shareholders, liability limited, and boards of directors vested with legal powers. And, at least in some states, corporations could cast their nets very widely. At the same time, capital would increasingly be raised through the institutions that were either born or dramatically strengthened by the government requirements of suppressing the slaveholders' rebellion—the stock and bond markets, brokerage houses, and investment banks—and assume the form of assets that could far exceed the value of a corporation's plant and equipment.

This did not happen through the "invisible hand" of the competitive market; it happened because of precedents in the area of incorporation, especially involving railroads, and because of political and legal interventions that lent corporations new rights as "individuals" in the eyes of the law. Beginning in 1886, in *Santa Clara County v. Southern Pacific Railroad,* a case involving taxation, the Supreme Court suggested that corporations had the same rights of due process as "natural persons" under the Fifth and Fourteenth Amendments to the Constitution. Four years later, when it crafted the Sherman Antitrust Act, Congress followed suit. It not only outlawed "every contract, combination . . . or conspiracy in restraint of trade" but also explicitly stipulated that "the word 'person' or 'persons,' whenever used in this act, shall be deemed to include corporations and associations." With these rulings, the corporate form would simultaneously enjoy protection from aggressive regulations and taxation imposed by the state at all levels to which individuals were not subject, as well as the status of a discrete type of property that individuals could not hold.

"Restraint of trade" raised a great many questions about the practices in which large firms, whether incorporated or not, could engage. To this day, the issue hovers over the corporate world and its quest for control over markets. But as "pools" and "trusts" came under public fire in the late nineteenth century, some states stepped in to increase the leverage corporations could have (incorporation took place in states because there was no federal incorporation law). New Jersey, in 1889, was especially generous. It permitted corporations to hold stock in other corporations even if they were located in different states and thereby gave legal standing to what was known as the holding company: corporations that existed solely for the purpose of gaining ownership rights in other corporations. Small wonder that by the turn of the twentieth century two-thirds of all firms valued at $10 million or more were incorporated in New Jersey, wherever they did their main business.

The question of what constituted an illegal "restraint of trade" was contested ground for the next two decades, and for a time a slim majority on the Supreme Court, led by Associate Justice John Marshall Harlan of Kentucky, ruled in favor of strict enforcement. Only in 1911, in the *Standard Oil* and *American Tobacco Company* cases (with Harlan the lone dissenter), did the Court establish what was known as the "rule of reason," distinguishing between reasonable and unreasonable restraints, as the common law had long prescribed. At all events, pressure for such a ruling had been building among both business and political leaders ever since the Sherman Antitrust Act had passed, and at no point did the Court suggest that the size of a corporation was, in itself, grounds for deeming it an illegal combination. In 1895, in *United States v. E. C. Knight Company*, the Court ruled that the American Sugar Refining Company (derisively known as the Sugar Trust) did not violate the Sherman Act even though it controlled 95 percent of the refining market. Presidents Theodore Roosevelt and William Howard Taft soon accepted the premise, as did a number of prominent economists, all of whom had come to embrace large-scale institutions as foundational to a modern society.

But in a sense, they were riding a wave of corporate consolidation that had, by the late 1890s, become something of a tsunami, when massive amounts of capital rushed in from the tottering railroad industry to far more attractive industrial securities. Next came the corporate reorganization spurred by the panic of 1893 and the subsequent depression. Between 1894 and 1897 alone, railroads with over forty thousand miles of track and over $2.5 billion in assets were aggregated in foreclosure sales. Much of this was financed by J. Pierpont Morgan and a handful of other investment bankers. By 1906, two-thirds of the nation's track mileage was controlled by only seven groups of investors: chief among them the Vanderbilt, Gould, Harriman, and, of course, Morgan railroads. In the meantime, between 1897 and 1902, as economic growth resumed, Morgan and John D. Rockefeller presided over a massive "merger movement" that restructured the metals, food products, petroleum, chemical, coal, machinery, and transportation industries. Almost three thousand mergers occurred, by far the greatest number in 1899. By the time the consolidation tide had receded, the three hundred largest combinations controlled nearly half of the nation's manufacturing capital. Among them were such giants as U.S. Steel, Du Pont, General Electric, Standard Oil, and American Tobacco.

Reconstruction went beyond securing the corporate form and greatly enlarging its reach; it also involved reconfiguring the internal structure of the corporate enterprise, especially at the workplace. The economic crises spanning the early 1870s through the mid-1890s disrupted capital flows, promoted deflation, and augmented the pressures of an intensely competitive marketplace, all of which, in the eyes of many manufacturers, reduced or undercut profit margins. When the crunch came, as it did at various points—especially after the panics of 1873 and 1893—they struggled to survive by cutting costs, wages in particular, and trying to ward off the resulting resistance of their workers. Those who did pull through often looked to increase their leverage in the market by scooping up the losers and experimenting with new ways to manage the volatilities of pricing, production, and distribution. Pools, trusts, holding companies, and corporate consolidations represented some of what they came up with.

But they also became interested in sweeping aside a significant roadblock on the shop floor, where skilled workers with the technical knowledge required to make the goods retained important power. Drawing upon deeply rooted craft traditions, workers were often able to exert influence or control over the organization, pace, and remunerative practices of labor, even in factory settings: sometimes through formal work rules, particularly if they had established trade unions; sometimes in alliance with foremen who determined the nature and rates of pay; and sometimes through less formal means of group-enforced ethical codes. Mechanization was one way for employers to attack this problem, enabling semiskilled machine tenders with little experience of the craft to replace their skilled counterparts. Specialization and homogenization were still others. Yet what became increasingly attractive to the larger enterprises was a more sweeping reconstruction that came to be known as scientific management.

"Scientific" or "systematic" management reflected both the growing inter-connections between science and industry and the growing sense among corporate managers that the capitalist crises of the late nineteenth century could only be overcome by bringing order to the ways in which business was done. A new cohort of engineers, absorbed in redesigning the material flows of the steel, electrical, and chemical industries, was aghast at the chaos, wastefulness, and inefficiency they saw in manufacturing plants, whether at the point of production or among those involved with bookkeeping and cost accounting. In their view, too much power and authority rested with workers and foremen, too little with supervisors and managers. The locus of power, they believed, had to shift. The productive process had to be organized from the top down rather than the bottom up.

No one was more important in devising and advancing this sort of reconstruction than Frederick Winslow Taylor. Born to a wealthy Quaker family in Philadelphia in 1856, Taylor could easily have been destined for a career in law or finance; his father had hands in both worlds. Fittingly, he was educated at the elite Phillips Exeter Academy and went on to pass the entrance exams for Harvard. But Taylor ended up choosing a very different path. He apprenticed as a machinist and then went to work, initially as a machine-shop laborer, at the nearby Midvale Steel Company in 1878. Quickly rising in the ranks (in part because of family connections), he became a foreman and ultimately research director and chief engineer. By the time he moved on to the Manufacturing Investment Company of Philadelphia (1890) and Bethlehem Steel (1898), establishing his own consulting firm along the way, he had well-formed ideas about how to "systematize shop management and manufacturing costs." Eventually, they were encapsulated in his book *The Principles of Scientific Management* (1911).

Taylor was driven to distraction by the very craft practices that skilled workers deployed to protect themselves from undue exploitation on the job. He and other critics called it "soldiering." Owing to work rules, collective pressure, or lack of incentives, Taylor believed, workers simply did not labor as hard or as steadily as they could, to the detriment of efficiency and productivity. Scientific study would prescribe the solution: centralize planning and routing; standardize work, pay, and accounting; place the workforce under close supervision and provide better training; and use wage incentives. The first step, as Taylor saw it, was for management to gather "all of the great mass of traditional knowledge, which in the past has been in the heads of the workmen . . . and has been acquired through years of experience." Further examination of each stage of production, including what were called "time and motion studies," would expand the technical authority of managers and diminish that of workers while routinizing the tasks. "It is only through enforced standardization of methods, enforced adoption of the best implements and working conditions, and enforced cooperation that this faster work can be assured," Taylor wrote. "And the duty of enforcing the adoption of standards and enforcing this cooperation rests with management alone."

For all his own bravado, Taylor's direct influence was slow to take hold, in good measure because workers themselves found new ways to struggle against his methods. "We object to being reduced to a scientific formula," one Davenport, Iowa, machinist thundered. Before 1917, just thirty factories nationwide had been organized along the lines that Taylor prescribed. But Taylor's was only the most comprehensive version of a new approach to management/labor relations that shared his goals of embedding control in the hands of employers and using that control to reorder and streamline manufacturing operations. And in this arena, significant progress occurred. Before the turn of the twentieth century, a great many metal, textile, and machine-making companies had constructed new plants that were designed to rationalize the flow of materials and fabrication, while "efficiency," "organization," and "standardization" became the mantras for corporate capitalists, engineers, and social scientists alike.

These mantras were the key words of a developing ideology that began to take hold among business, political, and academic leaders who imagined a new social compact as an alternative to the ferocious social struggles they saw all around them. They frowned at the intense competition that seemed to drag the market economy through cycles of volatility, as well as the attachment to small-scale production that was to be found among populist constituencies in many parts of the United States. They frowned, too, at the tenets of a mid-nineteenth-century liberalism that postulated a world of atomized and self-owning individuals who pursued their interests and independence, not to mention a republicanism that fortified antimonopoly in its various forms. Instead, they viewed the emergence of large corporations and financial institutions as the sign of modern times and the guarantor of economic stability, and they increasingly embraced a new ethic of partnerships and cooperation—involving capital, labor, and the state—as the best means of promoting social peace. In the process, they fashioned a new liberalism (some have called it corporate liberalism) that attempted to square corporate capitalism with the mechanisms of democratic governance.

Emblematic of this orientation—and of the private associations that helped advance the social movement of corporate capitalists—was the National Civic Federation (NCF). Founded in Chicago in 1900 by the educator and journalist Ralph M. Easley, it drew membership from business, labor, and the "public." Bankers and industrialists clearly dominated, many from a significant number of the largest corporations in the United States. The NCF's first president was Mark

Hanna, the Ohio senator, political operative, and major industrialist. Corporate participants composed a who's who of wealth and power in the country: August Belmont, Charles Francis Adams, Franklin MacVeagh, Andrew Carnegie, Cyrus McCormick, George B. Cortelyou, and several partners from J. Pierpont Morgan's investment bank. But labor's members were the leaders of some of the largest trade unions in the country, notably the machinists, mine workers, iron molders, railway brotherhoods, boot and shoe makers, and carpenters. And the "public" was made up of a cross section of journalists, ministers, academics, and prominent political leaders, Grover Cleveland, William Howard Taft, Columbia University's Nicholas Murray Butler, Harvard's Charles W. Eliot, and the archbishop of Minneapolis, John Ireland, chief among them.

What NCF members shared was an interest in meeting the challenges of industrialization and a willingness both to experiment with new approaches and to marshal the state as a mechanism of reform and reconstruction. They were concerned not only with popular resistance to the size and practices of business enterprises but also with the uncertainties of regulation, especially in the area of antitrust. They aimed to engage with issues of social and banking reform and to help craft legislation that would put the Sherman Antitrust Act on a surer and less threatening footing. They organized conferences (including one on combinations and trusts), sought to mobilize public opinion behind their cause, worked with the executive and legislative branches of the state and federal governments, and, at times, drew up model bills. It could be tough sledding. Their opponents were to be found not only among socialists on the left but among smaller and more traditional industrialists organized in the National Association of Manufacturers—known to some in the NCF as the "anarchists." There were false starts and defeats. Yet over time, NCF perspectives and lobbying contributed to the shape of the Clayton Antitrust Act (1914) and the Federal Trade Commission Act (1914) and to the establishment of the Federal Reserve System (1913), which together consecrated the legal and institutional form of the corporation, implemented a regulatory apparatus acceptable to corporate capital, and created a more centralized and asset-based banking structure.

Most of all, NCF members focused on the labor question and the radicalizing consequences of bitter struggles between employers and employees. Some had come to accept the need for conservative unionism, others for less formal methods to mediate disputes. Mark Hanna's "plan [was] to have organized union labor Americanized in the best sense and thoroughly educated to an understanding of its responsibilities and in this way make it an ally of the capitalist, rather than a foe with which to grapple." To this end, he headed up the NCF's "Industrial Department" with a view toward establishing a basis for collective bargaining (it did not get very far). More generally, the NCF, through its

"Welfare" and "Trade Agreements" departments, engaged with the issues of workmen's compensation (pressing either for state laws or for private business initiatives), child labor, industry-wide contracts, and broader company responsibilities to its labor force, all in the interests of acknowledging the new organizational realities of the workplace and modulating their political dynamics. Over the course of a dozen years, the NCF built institutions and networks to educate corporate leaders, address special types of abuse and exploitation, promote cooperation between capital and labor, and establish alliances with political officials in Congress and the state legislatures with an eye toward imposing regulative uniformity.

Among the members of the NCF, and its long-serving first vice president, was Samuel Gompers, head of the American Federation of Labor. His involvement anchored labor's leg of the NCF tripod and was neither unexpected nor out of character; in many ways, it reflected the reconstruction of unionism that Gompers and the AFL were trying to carry out. Still, it appeared to be a long way from his intellectual and political roots. A London-born immigrant of Dutch ancestry, Gompers arrived in New York City in 1863, learned the cigar-making trade from his father, and was quickly swept into the political world of the Lower East Side, with its vibrant currents of Marxism and socialism. Before long, he was a leader in the Cigar Makers' International Union, and although he once belonged to the Knights of Labor and sympathized with the New York mayoral candidacy of Henry George, he generally viewed the electoral activities of organized workingmen with discomfort and suspicion. Together with his fellow cigar maker Adolph Strasser, a Hungarian immigrant, Gompers came to reject a raft of labor and antimonopoly reform movements—greenbacks, cooperatives, regulatory legislation—and instead focused on organization at the workplace, on building trade unions and strengthening their leverage with employers. It was, in effect, a brand of syndicalism (the control and management of industrial enterprises by organized workers) that would be called "pure and simple unionism."

If anything, the many defeats of the 1880s and early 1890s—in the electoral arena and in strikes that relied on community support—as well as the destructive effect of court rulings and injunctions confirmed Gompers's sensibilities. Nothing struck him more tellingly than a New York Court of Appeals decision in 1885 to overturn legislation regulating tenement house labor that he had fought to have enacted: a decision that "nullified . . . our work." "Labor," Gompers would proclaim, "does not depend on legislation. It asks . . . no favors from the State. It wants to be let alone and to be allowed to exercise its rights." When he helped organize the American Federation of Labor in 1886, the very year that the Knights of Labor reached the apogee of its influence and then began to crumble, Gompers imagined a course that would revitalize and reconstruct working-class power.

The AFL was a federation of trade unions in which the idea of craft autonomy figured powerfully. And whatever Gompers's views about the appropriate course of unionism, it was difficult for him to steer the politics of the affiliated unions. In an 1894 plebiscite, more than half of the AFL's unions endorsed a socialist platform that called for "independent labor politics," an eight-hour day for all workers, and public ownership of industry. Yet over the course of the 1890s and into the early twentieth century, judicial interventions to break strikes and boycotts (in some cases by invoking the Sherman Antitrust Act) and overturn favorable labor legislation, together with the thumping defeats of Populism and the free-silver crusade, convinced even radicals and socialists in the AFL of the futility of electoral politics and pushed many of them toward Gompers's position. Unlike their counterparts in the 1870s and 1880s who talked of dismantling the "wages system" and formed alliances with antimonopolists, the leadership of the AFL increasingly accepted the reality and likely permanence of a large-scale, corporate-dominated political economy and struggled to find a stable and secure berth for unions within it.

This recognition, together with an upsurge in AFL membership around the turn of the century when the economy was on an uptick, helped bring Gompers and some other union leaders—including John Mitchell of the United Mine Workers, Daniel Keefe of the Longshoremen, and J. W. Sullivan of the Typographers—into an association with the NCF and its corporate liberal vision. What Gompers did not embrace was a new reliance on the state; "voluntarism," with its emphasis on unions and the workplace as the locus of struggle, remained central to his philosophy—that is to say, except for immigration restriction, especially concerning the Chinese, for which he welcomed federal government support. "One need but read the history of the toilers," he later wrote, "to learn how potent has been the power vested in the constituted authorities of the time to twist laws intended to be of interest to the workers to their very undoing, even to the verge of tyranny and enslavement."

Yet the syndicalist tendency that Gompers and others in the AFL leadership embodied had ripple effects well beyond the AFL, especially when unemployment was low and workers had their best chances to organize. It fueled the rise of the Industrial Workers of the World in 1905, which, in the spirit of the Knights of Labor, took special interest in the unskilled, together with the growth and militancy of trade unions that came to pursue industry-wide organization (mobilizing unskilled and semiskilled workers) and collective control over the conditions of work as a response to scientific management. The International Ladies' Garment Workers' Union staged general strikes in New York

City that brought thousands of women workers into the fray. A massive textile strike in Lawrence, Massachusetts, in 1912, aided by the IWW, involved well over twenty thousand laborers from as many as fifty different nationalities. Mine fields from northeastern Pennsylvania, to southern Colorado, to northern Idaho were ablaze with class warfare led by the United Mine Workers and the even more militant Western Federation of Miners. Socialists had come to exert important influence in a number of industrial unions, including some within the net of the AFL. By the end of the second decade of the twentieth century, more and more workers had won an eight-hour day, not as a result of legislation, but as the fruit of strikes and worker mobilizations. While the American economy had plainly been reconstructed in a corporate image, new fields of struggle had accordingly been established and the balances of power had yet to be determined.

Political Reconstruction

Samuel Gompers and other AFL leaders who sought to steer labor away from involvement with the state were outliers not only in associations like the NCF but also in the political arena more generally. By the end of the nineteenth century, a growing proportion of Americans from the wheat fields of Kansas to the corporate headquarters of lower New York had come to see the state—at all levels—as central to resolving the challenges of industrial capitalism. In good measure, they had embraced the thinking of popular antimonopoly movements—the Greenbackers, Knights of Labor, and Populists—that blamed the woes of producers on political corruption and believed that only an empowered state could tame the excesses of big business, even as they rejected either the critique or the proposed remedies. Which is to say it was the intellectual, as well as political, mobilization of workers and yeoman farmers that paved the way for a new construct of the state in corporate capitalist society.

And their ideas lived on even after they suffered political defeats of their own. It is easy to catalog the failed initiatives, whether greenbacks or free silver or the subtreasury or the eight-hour workday or the single tax, in reckoning the results of popular radicalism during the last three decades of the nineteenth century. But we must not forget that a great deal of political energy remained at the state and local levels, imbuing Progressivism with its democratic content while revealing its enduring links with antimonopolism and Populism. Much of that democratic energy was to be seen in an arc stretching from the Midwest across the northern plains and then down the Pacific coast. State legislatures that were more responsive to popular pressures led the way in attempts to rein in the abusive practices of railroads, mining companies, and other large industrial enterprises, even if those achievements were then overturned by the courts. The battles were especially intense in California as a broad spectrum of farmers, workers, and small-business people mobilized against the power of the Southern Pacific Railroad, derisively known as the Octopus, because its "tentacles" controlled large parts of the state's economy and politics. Coalitions of labor unions, progressive reformers, and socialists pressed for municipal regulation or outright ownership of utilities and public transportation—"gas and water socialism," as some called it—in cities large and small: Cleveland, Toledo, Milwaukee, Jersey City, Los Angeles, and San Francisco, to name but a few. In North Dakota, the threads of Populism and socialism would go into the making of the Nonpartisan League, which demanded public ownership of grain elevators, flour mills, and packinghouses, state grain inspection and insurance programs, and a state-operated bank. Many of these states led the way in establishing railroad commissions, workmen's compensation, more popular access to decision making, and woman suffrage. Indeed, well before the ratification of the Nineteenth Amendment (1920), women had gained the right to vote in Wyoming, Utah, Colorado, Idaho, Washington, California, Arizona, Kansas, Oregon, Montana, and Nevada.

Perhaps the most arresting example of a reenvisioning of the state and civil society came in Oregon and particularly in the city of Portland during the first two decades of the twentieth century. There a formidable coalition of workers and middle-class radicals, many of whom were influenced by Henry George, formed the People's Power League and made their presence felt. Regarding themselves as advocates for "the interests of the producing and industrial classes," they sought to "defend a citizen's rights against injustice by powerful corporations." Led by the remarkable William U'Ren, who worked as a miner, lawyer, and newspaper editor before encountering *Progress and Poverty*, they not only pioneered many progressive political measures—initiative and referendum, direct primaries, the popular election of U.S. senators—but also championed woman suffrage and utterly reimagined the structure of popular government. Reaching back to Pennsylvania's Revolutionary-era constitution, they agitated for a unicameral legislature, and availing themselves of international currents of political thought, they called for proportional representation based on occupation, including female wage workers and housewives.

These elements of the "Oregon System" remain ahead of our time; other elements of left-wing Progressivism would play important roles in building America's version of social democracy during the 1930s. But the political reconstruction that would be most consequential involved both the federal government's role in administering the national economy and the redefinition, at all levels, of what democratic governance was to mean. In some respects, the reconstruction was breathtaking in its speed, especially as to political discourse. Before the turn of the twentieth century, demands for federal regulatory action came chiefly from insurgent parties fired by antimonopoly politics. Thereafter, and for the next two decades, the debate infusing each of the major parties was not over whether the federal government should establish a regulatory apparatus but rather over how it should be done and where the regulatory power should reside. Radicalism and antitrust opened the doors and conjured the threat. The social movement of corporate capitalists struggled to diminish that threat and channel popular anger into policies that could discipline their excesses in the name of the public interest while providing an environment for corporate activity marked by stability, security, and legal uniformity.

The transition was visible by the late 1880s, especially with the passage of the Interstate Commerce Act and the Sherman Antitrust Act, but the implications were hazy until the first half decade of the twentieth century when leaders of the executive branch—presidents in particular—helped define a new framework in the face of Supreme Court rulings that still looked back to principles of "unrestricted competition." The young Theodore Roosevelt, a Republican, who ascended to the presidency after the assassination of William McKinley in 1901, stood out in this regard. "When I became president," he later recalled, the power that the "National Government" had "was either not exercised at all or exercised with utter inefficiency." That he meant to rectify. On the one hand, Roosevelt had little patience either for the excesses and arrogance of corporate capital or for the rigidity and traditionalism of the governing class. He had a notion of the "public interest" to which, he believed, all organizations of capital and labor must submit and of activist leadership designed to reinvigorate the federal state. On the other hand, he fully accepted the corporation and other large-scale enterprises as the bases of a modern and prosperous economy and worried about the consequences of both judicial restraint and socialist mobilizations.

For most of his two terms, Roosevelt aimed to rein in the heavy-handed tactics of big business, rally public opinion in favor of "reasonable" restraints of trade, and find an administrative formula for asserting authority over the corporate sector without inviting interference from the courts. He even intervened directly in a bitter anthracite miners' strike in 1902, forcing the company to the bargaining table with the help of the United Mine Workers and the NCF. Throughout this period, Roosevelt was in close contact with the National Civic Federation, and together they worked to fashion legislation that would establish a federal structure of licensing and incorporation using an executive agency as the means of policy and enforcement. Indeed, from the end of his second term until his run for the presidency in 1912 as the candidate of the Progressive

"Bull Moose" Party, Roosevelt increasingly moved in a statist direction: while conceding private ownership, Roosevelt came to think of corporations more as public utilities whose operations would require strict accountability and subordination to federal oversight, and thus whose very property relations could be reconfigured. This Roosevelt saw—invoking the figure of Abraham Lincoln against Wendell Phillips and John Brown—as the alternative to the "country [being] divided into two parties, one containing the bulk of property owners and conservative people, the other the bulk of wage earners and the less prosperous people," to class war and "an extreme and radical democracy." He would call it the New Nationalism, and given his imperial ambitions across the hemisphere and the Pacific it potentially edged toward fascism.

Roosevelt's successor, the Republican William Howard Taft, initially seemed ready to follow in the path that Roosevelt had been laying out. Along with a growing cross section of groups associated with the National Civic Federation, they seemed to share an interest in accepting the dominance of corporate institutions in the economy, legalizing "reasonable" restraints of trade, authorizing federal regulation of interstate commerce, and establishing an administrative agency at the federal level that could do the regulating. Taft was also open to federal incorporation and licensing toward the ends of regulation. But he was far more hesitant about the statism that Roosevelt came to advocate, about a federal role that appeared nearer to direction than to regulation. And following the Supreme Court's "rule of reason" decisions in 1911, Taft made public a policy move that had clearly been under way beforehand: toward judicial supremacy in determining the legality of corporate practices and toward corporate (as opposed to federal) administration of the interstate marketplace. With this, Taft and Roosevelt had a formal political break, and Roosevelt decided to seek election to the presidency as an independent.

The main beneficiary of the warfare in the Republican Party was Woodrow Wilson. Born in Virginia, educated at Princeton, the University of Virginia, and the graduate school at Johns Hopkins, where he formed a strong intellectual bond with Frederick Jackson Turner, Wilson served as president of Princeton University and then as a reform governor of New Jersey. He came to represent what could be called the corporate and cosmopolitan wing of the Democratic Party, which had been controlled since 1896 by William Jennings Bryan and the agrarians of the South and the West. Wilson saw "business [as] the foundation of every other relationship" and, like both Roosevelt and Taft, believed that the corporation was a fundamental component of a modern society. Like them, too, he sought a "middle ground" in the expansion of the state's regulatory reach between socialism and "the old laissez faire." "No one questions the necessity for a firm and comprehensive regulation of business operations," he maintained. In a four-way contest in 1912, in which Republicans divided between Roosevelt and Taft and the Socialist Party's standard-bearer Eugene V. Debs won nearly one million votes, Wilson was elected president. He was only the second Democrat to win the presidency since the Civil War and the first southerner to sit in the White House since Andrew Johnson.

During the campaign, Wilson attempted to distinguish himself from his Republican opponents by insisting, "Ours is a program of liberty, and theirs is a program of regulation." This he called—appropriating the phrase from the jurist, and his economic adviser, Louis D. Brandeis—the New Freedom. Yet the "middle ground" Wilson quickly defined was in fact between Roosevelt and Taft, between a statist and a statutory/judicial model of federal regulation. Although he regarded the steady shift in power and authority from the states to the national government as something of a natural evolution, and as necessary to order and stability, Wilson rejected a regulatory apparatus that subordinated the corporation and other business interests to the state, as Roosevelt had come to advocate. Rather, he sought to walk a line between the concerns of his agrarian and labor constituents as to big capital and the fears of corporate and financial interests as to the expansion of state supervision.

The results emerged from Congress in 1914. The Clayton Antitrust Act encompassed an array of statutory prohibitions as to monopolistic practices—in pricing, mergers, stockholding, directorships, and liability—while exempting labor unions from antitrust prosecution (which employers had used the Sherman Act to accomplish and labor leaders had been desperate to stop). "The labor of a human being is not a commodity or an article of commerce," the legislation now stipulated, and "labor organizations [should be] permitted to carry out their legitimate objective."

But labor's exemption was on the hollow side—no specific actions were delineated—and corporate unease about the issue of enforcement was mitigated by the almost simultaneous passage of the act establishing the Federal Trade Commission (FTC), whose members would be appointed by the president and confirmed by Congress. The FTC was authorized to look into "unfair methods of competition" and issue "cease and desist" orders. Yet corporations would not be required to register with the commission or submit their contracts, books, and investment portfolios for commission approval; the FTC could only use its discretion to request reports and investigate allegations of antitrust violations, ultimately making recommendations to Congress and the Justice Department. And the commission's membership was expected to come from the private sector, from those tied to or conversant with the business world or those with special expertise in corporate practice. Here, it seemed, was a new model for the relationship between the state and the corporate economy, one that required nearly three decades of initiation and experimentation to bring to fruition and that would establish an institutional basis for the next century.

Ideas about order, expertise, and proper management not only helped frame the role of the regulatory state; they also came to raise serious doubts about the workings of political democracy. Those doubts were half a century in the making. Ever since the 1840s and 1850s, sections of the American elite had begun to pull back from their earlier embrace of democratic reforms. For the first time, growing numbers of people who were either poor or in some condition of dependency sought the political rights that most white men had come to enjoy. Some were people of color who were free or freed and pressed for civil and political equality in states where slavery had been officially outlawed; some were women who, energized by religious beliefs and their experience in social reform movements, demanded the vote as a natural right. A great many were recent immigrants, including hundreds of thousands from Ireland, who were propertyless, unskilled by urban standards, and Catholic, and who gravitated to the Democratic Party. Defenders of white male privilege, most in the Whig and then Republican Party, sent these efforts down to defeat, defining clearer boundaries of formal political participation, in part by organizing a nativist movement. In the process, they gave notice of the political dilemmas that the development of industrial capitalism might pose.

This political backlash was reversed by the revolutionary eruption of the War of the Rebellion and the abolition of slavery, which together made possible an unprecedented and almost unimagined expansion of civil and political rights. Never before in modern history was so large a population of former slaves invested with citizenship and the right to vote, and never before was such a remarkable enfranchisement then tied to demands for woman suffrage and labor mobilizations. But it did not take very long for elite political concerns of the last antebellum decades to reassert themselves. As the urban population and the ranks of wage earners continued to swell, as immigration increasingly brought to the country men and women who were not Protestants and did not speak English, as the working class began to organize in new ways and win the support of a broader ethnic community, and as free laborers came to include those who had previously been in legal subjection, alarms began to sound.

Not surprisingly, the alarmists tended to be of Protestant and Anglo-Saxon background, often residents of industrializing cities, and mostly from the world of commerce and the professions. Many of them read or wrote for liberal reform publications like the *Nation, Harper's Weekly,* the *North American Review,* and the *Atlantic Monthly.* They fretted incessantly about a world they felt they had lost and a dangerous new one they seemed to have inherited. "A New England village of olden time," the historian Francis Parkman bemoaned in 1878, "would have been safely and well governed by the votes of every man in it; but now that the village has grown into a populous city, with its factories and workshops, its acres of tenement-houses, and thousands and tens of thousands of restless workmen, foreigners for the most part, to whom liberty means license and politics means plunder . . . whose ears are open to the promptings of every rascally agitator, the case is completely changed, and universal suffrage becomes a questionable blessing."

Parkman blamed the changed situation on "an invasion of peasants . . . an ignorant proletariat," and in this sense he was more and more of a mind with the former slaveholders in the South, who determined to fight black suffrage and political power by any means necessary, and with land barons, developers, and even white workingmen in the West, who cast hostile eyes on the ethnically complex populations around them, especially the Mexicans and Chinese. Together they spoke a language of "corruption," "dishonesty," "vice," "demagoguery," "illiteracy," and "illegitimacy" that had come to contaminate the ballot box and political arena, of "diseases" that had spread through the "body politic." As Charles Francis Adams Jr. saw it, "Universal suffrage can only mean in plain English the government of ignorance and vice: it means a European, and especially Celtic, proletariat on the Atlantic coast; an African proletariat on the shores of the Gulf, and a Chinese proletariat on the Pacific." The enemies were Reconstruction, popular democracy, and birthright citizenship; by the late 1870s, the disgruntled elites seemed ready to join hands in a postwar "reunion" and reclaim the nation's politics from its usurpers, to "cleanse" the electorate and "purify" the ballot box, securing "educated men" in their proper place as the governing class.

For all their wealth, knowledge, and power, they did not have an easy time. Industrial cities and towns had already felt the effects of working-class political power, and many of them were constructing machines—usually through the auspices of the Democratic Party—that attended to the needs of new immigrants in return for their votes. In some, workers composed the majority of the electorate and had gained experience in local governance. The Fourteenth and Fifteenth Amendments to the Constitution, moreover, guaranteed the equal protection of the laws and prohibited disfranchisement on the basis of "race, color, or previous condition of servitude," complicating efforts in the southern states to roll back the effects of Radical Reconstruction.

A period of experimentation thus ensued. In the Far West, a movement to deny citizenship to the Chinese and then exclude them entirely from the country won enormous support from a cross section of the public. In the Southwest, New Mexico and Arizona remained in a prolonged territorial status while refusing to move forward on the citizenship claims that those of Mexican descent had been assured under the Treaty of Guadalupe Hidalgo. In the states of the former rebellious South, the Democrats who had toppled Republican regimes began to impose poll taxes together with new registration and ballot box laws designed to discourage the participation of poor black voters. And in the urban Northeast, reformers looked to literacy and residency requirements, to less frequent and at-large elections, and to the creation of special municipal boards with powers over taxation and expenditures, to be selected only by property owners (and therefore taxpayers). "The right of voting cannot be taken away," the *Atlantic Monthly* concluded in 1879, "but the subjects of voting can be much reduced." But, more than anything else, it was the social and political upheavals of the 1880s and 1890s—advanced by Greenbackers, Knights of Labor, members of the Colored Farmers' Alliance, black Republicans, striking workers, and Populists—that gave the momentum for political "reform" a decisive push. The achievements were most sweeping and hardfisted in the Deep South, where planters and other Democrats from black-majority districts had begun to look for a "scheme" to "remove from the sphere of politics in the state the ignorant and unpatriotic negro." Mississippi led the way in 1890 with a constitutional convention that sidestepped the Fifteenth Amendment by legislating "against [the black man's] habits and weaknesses." The new constitution required prospective voters to live in the state for two years and the election district for one, to register at least four months before an election, to pay a cumulative poll tax of $2, and "to read" or "to understand" or to "give a reasonable interpretation" of "any section of the [state] constitution" to the satisfaction of the appointed registrar.

Known as the Mississippi Plan, the new constitution exploited black poverty, mobility, and illiteracy while giving enormous discretionary authority to registrars put in place by Democratic officeholders. And in one way or another, it was used as a model by many of the other southern states later in the decade or very early in the next one: first by South Carolina in 1895 and then by Louisiana, Alabama, and Virginia (which called constitutional conventions) and by North Carolina, Texas, and Georgia (which passed constitutional amendments), following fast upon the Supreme Court's decision in *Williams v. Mississippi* (1898), which gave disfranchisement the federal green light. The "scheme" worked; everywhere blacks evaporated from the voting rolls—only a handful continued to vote—and what came to be called the "solid" Democratic South took shape. For the guardians of white supremacy, the new constitutions and amendments, replete with disfranchising devices, marked the true end of Reconstruction.

Or, perhaps, it was part of a new political reconstruction of the country. The Mississippi Plan might have been a centerpiece of Jim Crow in the South, but it in fact cobbled together electoral remedies that were being deployed elsewhere, including in the North and the West. By the turn of the twentieth century, liberal fears of what Theodore Roosevelt would describe as "radical democracy" had won greater intellectual legitimacy from the technocratic currents of Progressivism. Universal suffrage and democratic politics, in the view of many progressives, were not only dangerous but also cumbersome and inefficient. They played to the emotions and narrow self-interest of voters and allowed the uneducated and the inexperienced to get their hands on the levers of power. Venality and mismanagement thereby reigned supreme, the public interest was ignored, and conflict rather than cooperation prevailed. Partisanship itself, one of the main features of nineteenth-century political culture, became an object of suspicion, an example of what turned politics into a mass spectacle driven by greed and blind loyalties. Like liberal reformers before them, many progressives wondered if popular democracy was compatible with the successful management of large polities, but rather than looking to an older governing elite as an alternative, they preferred the rule of expertise, of men trained to tackle social and political affairs, of those who were not tied to particular constituencies and could stand above the fray of party and patronage.

None of the states or municipalities outside the Deep South enacted the full package of measures that ended the participation of black voters there along with a large portion of poor white ones whose political dispositions were thought objectionable. But many, especially in the industrial belt stretching from the Northeast out through the Midwest, considered or enacted pieces of the package: literacy and residency requirements; the exclusion of paupers, aliens, and felons; and taxpaying provisions for the exercise of the franchise. There were other initiatives, however, that had the virtue of appearing more modern and rational, more likely to promote political independence and combat fraud, more consonant with good governance. Almost everywhere in the decades after the War of the Rebellion, systems of voter registration were devised—they varied from state to state in their particulars—ostensibly to prevent ineligible voters from casting ballots and to reduce the chaos that often engulfed polling places on Election Day. In large urban areas, especially where immigrants were able to elect their candidates to the municipal council or the mayor's office, reformers pressed for redistricting and at-large elections in order to weaken political machines and empower officials who could represent the "entire" city instead of smaller wards within it. Some reformers went further in the direction of "city managers" who would be appointed rather than elected (replacing mayors) and presumably would not be dependent on any one political party. Once the Australian (secret) ballot was first used in 1888 (in Louisville), it was widely adopted as a means of ensuring the voter's ability to register choices and preventing interference from partisan operatives or nosy employers, but it also prevented illiterate voters from receiving assistance at the ballot box.

By the time of the First World War, and certainly by the 1920s, this political reconstruction established many of the features of American politics that would prevail across the twentieth century. These included the diminishing significance of partisanship, the bureaucratization of political parties and institutions of government, the increasing importance of nonelected officials in policy-making positions, and the use of cumbersome registration procedures. In large part as a consequence, these also included the dramatic decline in popular participation in elections at all levels of the state. The decline was steepest in the Deep South states, where the Mississippi Plan framed the dynamics of political life. Black turnout quickly dropped to about 5 percent of those eligible to vote, but white turnout also dropped precipitously; indeed, from 1896 to 1916, average southern turnout in presidential elections plunged from 64 percent to 32 percent and then fell further to only 20 percent by 1924. In the North and the West, the drop in voter turnout was not nearly so steep, but it was substantial nonetheless: in 1896, voter turnout averaged around 83 percent; by 1916, around 65 percent; and by 1924, around 58 percent. Everywhere voter turnout was lower still in off-year and local elections.

The one area in which political reconstruction witnessed a clear expansion in the universe of participation was woman suffrage. But it was a lengthy, complex, and contradictory process. Part of a century-long struggle waged by women's rights activists who had come up through a variety of reform movements, especially abolitionism, the campaign for the franchise was a rocky one. Surfacing in the late 1840s and the 1850s, most famously at Seneca Falls, New York, suffrage advocates threaded the Age of Revolution's ideas of natural rights into demands for political as well as civil equality. Their "Declaration of Sentiments" seemed in many ways a capstone to the Declaration of Independence, and its resounding rejection by white men—often with ridicule—was a bruising one.

Yet it was not long before the door of possibility opened anew. The War of the Rebellion and its increasingly radical trajectory toward emancipation, birthright citizenship, and a black male franchise pushed forcefully at the boundaries of change. Elizabeth Cady Stanton, in a moment of optimism, hoped to advance woman and black suffrage but soon discovered that her erstwhile male allies in the battle to save the Union and free the slaves were ready to break ranks in order to empower the freedmen and save the Republican Party. Even Charles Sumner, who introduced a petition for woman suffrage in the U.S. Senate in 1866, nonetheless let his colleagues off the hook: "I do not think this is a proper time for the consideration of that question." For Stanton, Susan B. Anthony, Lucy Stone, and a great many other suffrage organizers and followers, it was a galling betrayal, not only because the Fifteenth Amendment did not include "sex" in its protected categories for "the right to vote," but also because the Fourteenth Amendment, in its section encouraging an African American franchise, explicitly equated voters with "males." Groaning about the "colored man" being "enfranchised before the woman," Stanton then revealed her own class and racial outlook. "I would not trust him with all my rights," she maintained, "degraded, oppressed himself, he would be more despotic with the governing power than even our Saxon rulers are."

The suffrage movement quickly fractured amid bitterness and recrimination, a testament both to the depth of its opposition and to its own social and cultural limitations. Composed chiefly of white, Protestant women of the educated middle class, the movement had little to say to working women or men, let alone to black women, even of the urban "better classes," who were beginning to establish reform organizations of their own. Given the economic crises of the 1870s and 1880s and the growing mobilizations against the reach of political democracy as it was, the woman suffrage question was put further on the defensive if not entirely pushed to the margins. When a reunification was attempted in 1890, with the founding of the National American Woman Suffrage Association (NAWSA), the arguments of the suffragists seemed a far cry from the "Declaration of Sentiments." Instead of claiming the franchise as a natural right, they spoke of the positive effect that women could have on a corrupt political system awash in class and ethnic antagonisms.

Indeed, some suffrage advocates spoke of the female franchise as an essential counterweight to the voting power of ignorant and alien men. Carrie Chapman Catt, who became involved with the NAWSA and eventually ascended to its leadership, insisted that "there has arisen in America a class of men not intelligent, not patriotic, not moral, nor yet not pedigreed . . . who nominate officials, at the polls through corrupt means . . . [then] elect them and by bribery, it is they who secure the passage of many a legislative measure." By Catt's lights, enfranchising native-born women was the surest means to save the "American Republic." "The census of 1890 proves," she observed, "that women hold the solution in their hands." In the South, where opposition to woman suffrage was especially strong, female supporters like Rebecca Latimer Felton, Kate Gordon, and Belle Kearney took Catt's perspective even further, associating their enfranchisement with the forces of white supremacy. Like Catt, they portrayed white women as the embodiments of moral virtue and civilization while making what was called the "statistical argument," that adding them to the voter rolls would more than neutralize the numbers of eligible black men. "Anglo-Saxon women," Kearney told a NAWSA convention in 1903, were "the medium through which to retain the supremacy of the white race over the African." For three days, in fact, the Mississippi disfranchisement convention of 1890 debated the wisdom of a female franchise before enacting the elements of its better-known "plan."

If emphasizing the cultural attributes that women might bring to a vicious male world of politics seemed more likely to soften the opposition to woman suffrage, it did not really work. Despite efforts to press ahead on referenda in some of the states or on bills in state legislatures, there was precious little to show for it—except as to partial suffrage, which would enable women to vote in only selective elections, usually involving school boards. But early in the twentieth century, there was a new and militant spark. While notions of moral guardianship did not disappear from suffragists' vocabularies, a younger generation of activists began to push the NAWSA toward alliances that dramatically broadened its base. Embodying the best energies of Progressivism, they built local organizations, reached out across class lines to women and men, sought the support of trade unions, and took their demands to the streets in suffrage spectacles. Speaking before a NAWSA convention in 1906, Florence Kelley, who had taken up the cause of women and child labor, admonished, "I have rarely heard a ringing suffrage speech which did not refer to the 'ignorant and degraded' men, or the 'ignorant immigrants' as our masters . . . [and] this is what the workingmen are used to hear applied to themselves by their enemies in times of strike."

By the second decade of the twentieth century, woman suffrage was fast becoming a mass movement—something it had never been before—bringing together a coalition of social reformers (including socialists) who saw the franchise as a means of empowering working people and of progressives who understood women's rights as an important component of modernity. Support came from the AFL and the Socialist Party as well as from the Progressive Party of Theodore Roosevelt, not to mention from newer and more militant organizations like the Equality League of Self-Supporting Women, the Congressional Union, and the National Woman's Party, led by the internationalist Alice Paul. The National Association for the Advancement of Colored People (NAACP) came on board too, arguing in its journal, the *Crisis*, that "votes for women mean votes for black women." When, in the midst of national mobilization during World War I, President Woodrow Wilson publicly described woman suffrage "as a war measure," the path to the enactment of the Nineteenth Amendment to the Constitution was finally cleared: the "right to vote" could no longer be "denied or abridged . . . on account of sex."

What of its reach and impact? Ever since the 1890s, educated black women who set out to fight the ferocious racism of the time saw in woman suffrage a way to turn back the massive assault on black civil and political rights. Through organizations like the National Association of Colored Women, whose motto was "lifting as we climb," they aligned themselves with both the NAWSA and the WCTU in efforts to promote women's full enfranchisement. Yet cooperation was limited. For all the outreach that white suffrage activists attempted, they did little to cross a color line that was being more deeply drawn than ever before. Political reconstruction would greatly enlarge the sphere of prospective participants, but its capitulation—indeed contribution—to white supremacy was indicative of a politics meant to shift power further away from the grassroots. When celebrations over the Nineteenth Amendment died down, the fears of its opponents were never realized. Although the size of the electorate almost doubled, the overall turnout rates continued to slide. For the time being, that is to say, woman suffrage seemed to reinforce rather than reorient a political culture that had been taking shape for more than three decades. And because of disfranchisement in the South, black women would have no better opportunities than black men to make their presence felt in the arenas of formal politics.

Racial Reconstruction

No one better reflected the temper and trajectory of "race" in the United States around the turn of the twentieth century than Booker T. Washington. A former slave who was educated at the Hampton Institute in Virginia and then, beginning in 1881, headed up the new Tuskegee Normal and Industrial Institute in the heart of the Alabama Black Belt, Washington made a name for himself by instructing black students in pedagogy and the manual arts and by cultivating the support of conservative and philanthropic whites from near and far. By the mid-1890s, his renown had earned him an invitation to speak before a large, and racially mixed, audience at Atlanta's Cotton States and International Exposition in September 1895, and he delivered an address that would give him even greater notoriety. Arguing that it had been a mistake for the federal government to enfranchise African American men, that Reconstruction had been a misguided experiment, that agitation for social equality was "extremest folly," and that African Americans would mostly live by the sweat of their brows, he called on his black listeners to "cast down your buckets where you are": in effect, to accept the world of the Jim Crow South that they inhabited—as opposed to emigrating—improve themselves as best they could, and contribute to the prosperity of the region. "In all things purely social we can be as separate as the fingers," Washington famously said, with his white audience undoubtedly in mind, "yet one as the hand in all things essential to mutual progress."

Although praise flooded in from many quarters, critics would call the speech "the Atlanta Compromise."

It was a troubling and propitious moment. Earlier that year, Frederick Douglass, the fugitive slave, abolitionist, and great champion of civil and political equality, had died, and as Washington spoke in Atlanta, South Carolina was following Mississippi in disfranchising African American men. Hundreds of blacks were being lynched across the Deep South for refusing the submission that whites demanded of them, and southern states were passing laws to separate blacks and whites in public life. Allies among Republicans and Populists, who had some interest in maintaining black political rights, were fewer and fewer, and the Democratic Party in the South was increasingly dominated by radical white supremacists. Recognizing the dangers that black men and women faced, and the apparent futility of fighting back, Washington counseled something of a truce and looked for a solution to what was called the "Negro problem."

The "Negro problem" was not new to the late nineteenth century. It had been central to the white encounter with African Americans since at least the late eighteenth century and was not about squaring the principles of the Republic with slavery and its exploitative aftermath but about controlling a population that had been released from traditional restraints and was regarded as a potential menace. For Thomas Jefferson, the "problem" was imagining how white and black people could live together in peace under conditions of freedom, and the "solution" he ventured—and that remained a centerpiece of emancipationist thought well into the War of the Rebellion—was colonization. The "problem" then deepened after slavery was fully abolished, and especially by the 1880s and 1890s, as African Americans continued to press for a freedom they found meaningful and as the first generation of whites and blacks born in the post-emancipation era began meeting each other as young adults in the southern states. The results were unsettling and often explosive. The etiquettes and expectations of slavery were gone, but save for the enforced submission of African Americans new ones had yet to take their place. Black people were a "problem," in the view of white observers, because they were in the United States, and white people had to figure out how to move on with their business without becoming mired in conflicts with blacks or utilizing too many valuable resources to control them. The "Negro problem," that is, was really a "white problem," and first and foremost it seemed to be one of "management."

There can be little doubt that the Deep South, and especially the rural and small-town districts, pulsed with racial violence during the 1880s and 1890s, a reflection, in part, of black political fortitude after the fall of the Republican Reconstruction regimes. Insurgent politics in Virginia and Texas and mobilizations by the

Knights of Labor and the Colored Farmers' Alliance in Louisiana, Mississippi, Arkansas, and South Carolina led to brutal confrontations that often took the lives of militant black leaders. But it was the gruesome upsurge in lynchings—mob executions, often before hundreds of onlookers—that seemed most indicative of the unstable social order. Lynchings were most likely to occur in cotton-growing counties with large and demographically volatile black populations, and their victims tended to be young black men relatively new to the areas in which they lived. The tensions and conflicts of the rural economy, especially strains between landlords and tenants or debtors and creditors, often figured in the provocation: most of the lynching victims stood accused of murder, arson, assault, and theft rather than rape or other sexual transgressions, as Ida B. Wells demonstrated over a century ago. Between the early 1880s and the mid-1890s, the number of lynchings increased rapidly; in the year Booker T. Washington spoke in Atlanta, and for most of the decade, an African American was lynched, on average, approximately every three days.

The racial violence was by no means an exclusively southern affair. Although the overwhelming majority of African Americans still lived in the South, the black population of many northern cities was steadily increasing in the decades after the War of the Rebellion. Race riots together with politically motivated attacks exploded sporadically in large cities like New York, Philadelphia, and Chicago as well as in small ones like Akron, Ohio, and Springfield, Illinois. In the Pacific Northwest, the violence turned against the Chinese, who had already been prohibited from immigrating to the United States as of 1882. White mobs, composed mostly of workers who feared for their economic prospects, attempted to drive the Chinese out of Eureka, California, Seattle and Tacoma, Washington, and Rock Springs, Wyoming, during the 1880s. In Rock Springs, twenty-five of the Chinese died when their section of town was torched and left smoldering. Small wonder that the Chinese population of the United States, concentrated in the Far West, dropped by one-third between 1890 and 1910 and by as much as half in California, where most of the Chinese had come to reside.

That accusations of rape and miscegenation became central to the discourse of lynching, not only in the South, but elsewhere in the country, suggests what participants in lynch mobs saw at stake. On the one hand, they depended on having control over the apparatus of the state (or at least on the cooperation of the state to avoid prosecution). On the other hand, they rejected state institutions as the appropriate channels for enacting popular justice; rejected, that is, the notion that all individuals should be subject to the authority of the laws and judicial system instead of the direct domination of the "community." In many cases, lynching victims had already been arrested and charged; in some cases, they had been convicted and sentenced to summary punishments. But the accused were none-theless hauled out of jail, often with the sheriff looking on, and, in the crude par-lance of lynching, "dispatched" or "launched into eternity," at times accompanied by bloodthirsty and sexualized rituals of dismemberment.

Feeding on deep cultures of social and political violence, lynch mobs thus sought to reestablish the boundaries that they believed were being traversed (by the state or by alien "racial" groups), to crush the attacks and violations they associated with the weakening of their own authority in the face of the destabilizing and centralizing trends of the age. And no boundaries or viola-tions were more intimate and fundamental than those of patriarchy, house-hold, gender, and sexuality. For just as slavery was constructed around the reproductive capacity of females—the law determined in the late seventeenth century that the status of enslavement would follow that of the mother—so did the reconstruction of race toward the end of the nineteenth century entail the heightened patrolling of sexual contact. Lynching served as the lethal hand, the regulation of marriage the civil.

Laws against interracial sex and marriage have a history as long as the colonial settlement of North America, and certainly as long as that of African-descended slavery, but they became more comprehensive and widespread after the fall of Reconstruction regimes in the South. Legitimated by new "scientific" theories of race that placed Caucasians atop a hierarchy of innate difference, miscegenation laws were reenacted in a growing number of states, especially of the South and the West, both as a means of protecting the biological integrity (and alleged superiority) of white people and as a way of marking new racial categories. In the states of the South, the laws barred marriage between whites and blacks and, in the process, helped define the "one drop" rule of racializa-tion, a contrived method of bringing clarity to an inherently opaque concept. Mississippi, South Carolina, and Alabama wrote these prohibitions into the very constitutions that disfranchised African American men. In the West, and especially the Far West, miscegenation laws would be far more capacious and come to encompass Chinese, Japanese, Kanakas (Hawai'ians), Malays, Mongo-lians, and Native Americans as well as blacks. Despite the questions they raised about the equal protection clause of the Fourteenth Amendment, to say noth-ing of freedom of contract, the statutes were generally upheld by judges who instead invoked the "laws of nature" and, accordingly, the "police power of the State."

Miscegenation laws were only some of the products of new racial and socio-logical thinking that emphasized separation, or segregation, as crucial to the management of modern civil and political society. And as was true for inter-marriage, gender and sexuality often emerged as flash points for action. To be sure, practices of racial separation were deeply embedded in the United States, constraining forms of interaction under slavery and its immediate aftermath. Racial separation, or more precisely exclusion, prevailed in much of the Northeast and the Midwest during the first half of the nineteenth century, whether at polling places or in public spaces. Even abolitionists could follow its imperatives in their own organizations and activities. Indeed, what we call segregation, especially of the residential variety, has been a feature of urban life for centuries and in its racial aspects has certainly been in evidence since the eighteenth century.

Yet the impulses toward comprehensive segregation became overpowering toward the end of the nineteenth century, not as a throwback to an earlier day of personal domination, but as an accompaniment to the forces of modernization: to the rapid development of cities, industries, and transportation networks that would bring large numbers of people together in new and impersonal ways. Segregation was understood by its advocates as a thoroughly modern way to organize—to choreograph—the social worlds of different racial groups and as a liberal alternative to violent encounters on the one side and the empowerment of those regarded as "inferior" or "backward" on the other. It also proved central to the formation of states. The almost simultaneous emergence of state-mandated segregation in the American South and in South Africa is revealing. Although the policy components often differed, segregation in both places developed most thoroughly in newer cities tied to newer industries where newer states sought to extend their reach. In South Africa, segregation came quickly after the establishment of the Union of South Africa (1910) and was concentrated in the gold- and diamond-mining districts of the Transvaal to satisfy the escalating demand for labor and to mediate potential conflicts between African and Afrikaner workers. In the American South, segregation followed the establishment of Democratic "home rule" in the states and was to be seen in its most aggressive forms not in the older cities of the Atlantic Seaboard and the Gulf Coast but in the industrializing and commercializing towns of the interior—Charlotte, Durham, Spartanburg, Atlanta, Birmingham, and Nashville—and on the lines of transportation between and within them.

Not surprisingly, the initial forays into de jure segregation came in two of the institutions that typified the South's lurch toward modernity and were places where males and females came together in physical proximity: the new public schools established by Reconstruction governments and, by the late 1880s and early 1890s, the railroads and streetcars that traversed the region. Segregation ordinances then spread to virtually all areas of public life—parks, theaters, waiting rooms, drinking fountains, restrooms. They snowballed during the late 1890s and the first decade of the twentieth century, once black men were disfranchised and the Supreme Court of the United States in *Plessy v. Ferguson* (1896), with John Marshall Harlan the lone dissenter, ruled that separate accommodations neither stamped "the colored race with a badge of inferiority" nor violated the rights of African Americans under the Thirteenth and Fourteenth Amendments. (Harlan utterly rejected these claims, finding the "arbitrary separation of citizens, on the basis of race . . . a badge of servitude wholly inconsistent with the civil freedom and equality before the law established by the Constitution.") Arch-segregationists indulged fantasies of legislating racially divided city blocks as well as separating white and black landholding districts in the countryside, neither of which succeeded.

Retrograde as these laws may seem, they reflected the sort of liberal thinking that resonated with social reformers in many parts of the country. Edgar Gardner Murphy, an Episcopal minister in Alabama who was deeply disturbed by the racial violence that engulfed the rural and small-town South, became a prominent intellectual conduit. While viewing blacks as a childlike race in need of guidance, Murphy insisted that they did not have to be terrorized into submission because they showed "a preference for amnesty" and an instinct for "self-conservation" when confronted with the power of whites. Separation, he and others of similar mind believed, was both a recognition of different capacities and an encouragement to racial pride and integrity, especially if accompanied by the treatment and education that promoted friendship and cooperation. Booker T. Washington was thereby regarded as the model of black leadership and foresight, "the greatest man save General Lee, born in the South in a hundred years," one of them exclaimed. "The industrial education of the negro," Murphy wrote, "is intended to supply under the conditions of freedom, those elements of skill, those conditions of industrial peace, that our fathers supplied under the conditions of slavery." And, he added, "it was not without significance that no graduate of Hampton or Tuskegee has ever been charged with assault upon a woman."

Murphy's ideas won an appreciative reception in northern progressive circles where reformers had been searching for a new perspective on "race relations." Murphy was viewed by some as "a prophet, a reformer, and a historian," an alternative to the "sectional fanaticism" of the South; his writings won high praise in many progressive journals and newspapers. Walter Rauschenbusch, one of the leaders of the social gospel movement who conceded that the "Negro problem" seemed both "tragic" and "insoluble," could nonetheless term it the duty of whites to take "our black brother by the hand [and] urge him along the road of steady and intelligent labor, of property rights, of family fidelity . . . and of pride and joy in his race achievements." President Theodore Roosevelt, beset by controversy over inviting Booker T. Washington to the White House and appointing blacks to office, called upon Murphy for advice in 1904 and soon considered him "one of the men to follow in reference to the Negro question."

Racial segregation did not rush forward with the same legal torrent in the Northeast and the Midwest that it did in the South, but it was increasingly encompassing and hardfisted. In part, its effects were to be seen during the last decades of the nineteenth century in ethnic and racial enclaves that dotted industrializing cities, where "Nigger Hill," "New Guinea," and "Little Africa" joined "Little Italy," "Polonia," "Greektown," and "Pilsen." But the lines of separation were hardened less by state or municipal statutes than by neighborhood protective associations and real estate interests, which played upon concerns about declining property values and the transmission of diseases like tuberculosis. Restrictive covenants backed by threats of personal violence (the Ku Klux Klan would be energized by these fears across the urban North) worked as effectively as legislation. They also left their imprint on schools, which appeared as segregated as those in the South. Private establishments, like restaurants, theaters, and hotels, which remained beyond the reach of the Fourteenth Amendment, simply refused to serve black people. By the second decade of the twentieth century, under the administration of President Woodrow Wilson, southern progressive, the federal bureaucracy segregated any African Americans who managed to escape dismissal.

Yet, however much they might have regarded segregation as a scientifically supported and rational method for organizing "race relations" in urban areas, offering it as an alternative to the horrific violence of the southern countryside, progressives of various sorts often turned a blind eye to what was going on all around them. In Wilmington, North Carolina (1898), and Atlanta, Georgia (1906)—and in some smaller cities and towns—Jim Crow was ushered in not by the cool heads of "modernists" but by the brutal violence of white mobs who responded to tense local elections and allegations of sexual violations by hunting down blacks and destroying their communities. W. E. B. Du Bois, who was teaching at Atlanta University but off doing research in Alabama when the riot occurred there, hurried back in a state of near hysteria to protect his wife and daughter. He knew what he was up against; he sat out in front of the dormitory where they lived with a shotgun. "The Atlanta riot was if anything worse than reports," he later wrote. Sanitized as it might have become in a search for racial order, Jim Crow flowed through the streets as it did through the fields, on currents of blood.

Still, as a measure of the consensus that racial reconstruction was establishing in ruling and progressive circles, there was remarkably little resistance let alone protest. The Republican Party had long since abandoned its black constituents in favor of the party's "lily-white" faction in the South, which no longer threatened to achieve power. Theodore Roosevelt, who had briefly consulted with Booker T. Washington, went so far as to congratulate "those brave and earnest men of the South who in the face of fearful difficulties are doing all that men can do for the betterment alike of white and black." Neither Populists, socialists, nor trade unionists, scorning "social equality" even as they pursued black votes, were prepared to raise alarms; most seemed content to accept the separations and exclusions that they practiced in their own organizations.

The only voices to register dissent came from the intended victims: African Americans who struggled to articulate a critique, find an ally, or influence the discussion and debate. The most that those in the South could do was slow the wheels of disfranchisement or ready themselves to meet the challenges of poll taxes and literacy requirements. Washington himself worked behind the scenes, unsuccessfully, so that "the Negro [could] have some humble share in choosing those who shall rule over him." But when it came to segregation, even these voices were muffled.

They were muffled in part because of the power and influence of Booker T. Washington over many African Americans and their leaders. But opposition to him and what was termed the Tuskegee machine had also been growing among black journalists, educators, ministers, and professionals, chiefly in the urban North, who had come to political maturity with Reconstruction-era expectations and were in no mood to cast their buckets down anywhere. Spearheaded by William Monroe Trotter and W. E. B. Du Bois, they rejected Washington's accommodationism as well as his high-handed treatment of black critics and determined to organize "aggressive action on the part of men who believe in Negro freedom and growth." First meeting on the unsegregated Canadian side of Niagara Falls in 1905, they drew participants from much of the country, even a few from the South, and agreed to a "Declaration of Principles" that was as far removed from the Atlanta Compromise in tone and substance as could be imagined. Insisting on full political rights and calling discrimination on account of race or color "barbarous," the declaration refused "to allow the impression to remain that the Negro American assents to his inferiority, [that] he is submissive under oppression and apologetic before insults. . . . [T]he voice of protest of ten million Americans must never cease to assail the ears of their fellows, so long as America is unjust." It was known as the Niagara Movement, and four years later the ringing demands for civil and political equality in the "Declaration of Principles" went into the making of the interracial National Association for the Advancement of Colored People, which would help shape black politics for decades to come.

Well before he helped establish the Niagara Movement, Du Bois reflected on the development of race in the United States, asking African Americans, "How does it feel to be a problem?" and writing of the "two-ness—an American, a Negro"—that he believed they inevitably experienced. But in much of the southern countryside, former slaves and the descendants of slaves were charting their own way forward and thereby contributing in distinctive ways to the late nineteenth-century making of race. They had long struggled to put their freedom on a safe and independent foundation, seeking land or tenancies that might allow them strong measures of self-governance. Many had joined with or supported the Union League and the Republican Party, had voted and perhaps held office, had defended their families and communities from the wrath of paramilitaries, and might well have aligned with political insurgencies of the 1880s and 1890s toward that end. Yet over time, owing to aspirations as well as defeats, growing numbers of them, especially in the plantation districts, came to believe that their security and future prospects lay in separating themselves as much as possible from southern whites.

Such an impulse toward separatism, which had deep roots in their enslavement, did not signal a tacit acceptance of the destruction of the civil and political rights they had fought so hard to retain or of the official segregation then being imposed. African Americans regarded all of these as despicable indignities and humiliations. Nonetheless, they had come to see their survival and growth as best served by turning further inward, by pursuing self-reliance even more fully than before. Some of Booker T. Washington's perspectives thus resonated with their own sensibilities and goals, though their response was not necessarily Washingtonian. Popular interest in African emigrationism (which Washington vehemently opposed) revived dramatically in the mid- to late 1880s, especially in Arkansas, Mississippi, and Florida. "The Negro in the South . . . is moneyless homeless and he is Friendless," one prospective emigrant wrote, "we are . . . lynch and kill. . . . We see no Betterse in the future fo the Negro here." Between 1886 and 1892, more than 450 African Americans left small towns and counties in search of homes in Liberia, while hundreds of others tried desperately to follow them. Many more were attracted to "black towns," which first appeared in the immediate post-emancipation period and then multiplied from the late 1870s on as the hopes of Reconstruction faded and the opportunities for black people faded with them. Some of the towns grew up on the prairies of Kansas as black migrants moved west from Tennessee and Kentucky or north through the Mississippi Valley from Louisiana and Mississippi; still others emerged across the Deep South from South Carolina out to Texas and then north to Oklahoma, where more than twenty were established. As was true at Mound Bayou, Mississippi, perhaps the best known of them, they were usually built around large family groups and, with names like Freetown, New Rising Star, Klondike, Peace, New Africa, and Bookman (to commemorate the name of its founder), were determined to organize their lives and politics as they saw fit.

Elsewhere in the South, petty accumulations of land and personal property that some African Americans had struggled mightily to attain could become hubs around which kinship groups could circulate and find relative stability. In the early twentieth century, several families of Archers in the hills just outside the Mississippi delta established a "family rent group" and leased a hilltop of more than four hundred acres known to them as the Place. Led by their "patriarch," John Perry Archer, who also happened to be a Baptist minister, they not only produced cotton and corn but also planted potato, vegetable, and orchard crops, raised livestock, and built smokehouses and a blacksmith shop. As best as possible, they avoided borrowing and paid their bills on time to keep white creditors—and much of the "outside world"—at bay. When, therefore, one of their group traveled to Mound Bayou to hear Booker T. Washington speak, he found much with which to agree, though he adamantly rejected Washington's "philosophy of casting down one's bucket wherever one was." "This smacked of the white man's idea that black people should be satisfied with what they had rather than make any attempt to better themselves," he charged.

There and in hundreds of other settlements—some clustered on tenant plantations, some at the edges of market towns, some composed mainly of sharecroppers and others of squatters, virtually all held together by kinship, faith, schools, and benevolent societies—the webs of community and peoplehood were spun, toughened further by the fierce and quotidian repression that whites could bring upon them. To these may be added the outposts of black teachers, ministers, storekeepers, physicians, and tradesmen who simultaneously serviced and aimed to "uplift" the poor working folk around them, pressed together by the tighter racial boundaries that whites were setting yet mindful of the independence and respectability that they hoped to display. Gradually, they too embraced "race," not as a mark of exclusion or inferiority, but as a symbol of dignity and pride, of achievement in the face of enormous obstacles, and of solidarity in the face of personal forms of domination. Before long, Marcus Garvey would excite their imaginations with a new language of blackness and of race as power. Race, that is, was being reconstructed on both sides of a color line now drawn more deeply than ever.

Imperial Reconstruction

When Nelson A. Miles, commanding general of the U.S. Army, arrived in the Philippines in October 1902 to survey what remained of the Filipino "insurgency," he seemed to embody the arc of American imperial projects growing out of the War of the Rebellion. As a young man in the U.S. Army, without a West Point pedigree, he had earned distinction on the battlefields of the Virginia peninsula, Antietam, Spotsylvania, Cold Harbor, and Petersburg, eventually being brevetted major general and put in charge of an army corps. Soon after the cessation of major hostilities, Miles was sent to Fortress Monroe and then to the new District of North Carolina, along the way meeting and marrying the niece of William T. Sherman. But rather than being left to engage for long in the reconstruction of the rebellious South, he was dispatched to the reconstruction of the rebellious West, spending most of the next quarter century out in the trans-Mississippi territories fighting the Kiowa, Comanche, Sioux, Nez Perce, and Apache, bringing both Chief Joseph and Geronimo to heel, before leading the brutal suppression of the Ghost Dance movement. So well regarded was he (not least by himself) that when the Pullman strike erupted in 1894 and threatened to disrupt rail traffic across the United States, Miles was put in command of the federal troops ordered to suppress it.

Nelson Miles saw political and cultural continuities linking all of these episodes. Writing in the *North American Review* in August 1894, he likened the Pullman strike to the Confederate and Indian rebellions, as yet another battle in the "war of civilization" waged against enemies who would bring "famine, pestilence, and death" to prosperous communities and "blow down the beautiful arch of our sovereignty—the hope of humanity, the citadel of liberty, independence, the temple of happiness for all mankind." In its defiance of court injunctions and "allegiance to their dictator Eugene V. Debs," the strike was, he believed, an insurrection against the federal government, very much deserving of the military's heavy hand. Veteran that Miles was of civil and Indian warfare, he requested permission to fire on the striking crowd.

Miles was not alone in his perspective. Observers spoke in 1894 of the "Chicago Indians" and more generally might depict striking workers as "Digger Indian white men," anarchist women as "squaws," and street protests as "war dances." Senator Henry Dawes identified a strong resemblance between the values of Native Americans and those of radical laborers, suggesting that each had an affinity with "Henry George's system," and he had little trouble comparing the army's challenges in the Philippines with those of the interior West. Theodore Roosevelt heartily agreed. "Every argument that can be made for the Filipinos could be made for the Apaches," Roosevelt railed. "Every word that can be said of Aguinaldo could be said for Sitting Bull."

There was more than a little to all of this. Ever since moving forcefully against the slaveholders' rebellion in the 1860s, the newly constructed American nation-state had been extending its imperial arms across a variety of spaces. Chiefly through the military, it abolished slavery, subdued rebel slaveholders, established a framework for national citizenship, enfranchised freedmen, reorganized governments in the rebellious states, encouraged the formation of male-headed households, promoted the spread of Christianity, and upheld the rule of contract in the world of the marketplace. Looking west, it financed railroad development, created large territories under federal jurisdiction, extended its sovereignty over Indian peoples while punishing those who resisted being confined to reservations, and refused to turn territories into states before they met an assortment of political and cultural criteria. In the process, the American nation-state enabled a new class of finance capitalists to turn their eyes toward Mexico, Central America, and the Pacific, searched for new markets in Asia, and expanded the size of the navy. Small wonder that in 1898, when popular insurrections against Spanish rule created political instabilities in Cuba and the Philippines, the U.S. government took the opportunity to bring "civilization" to the "backward" peoples of color there. It seemed only an extension of a mission more than three decades old, with military personnel serving as bridges: much of the officer corps in the Philippines had previously been in Indian service in the West, and most of the troops on the ground had been recruited from the western states and territories. The South and especially the West were proving grounds for new American imperial ambitions overseas.

Yet it would be a mistake to see only continuities in these regards. While imperial energies had been highly charged since the founding of the Republic, they had also been tied chiefly to specific commercial and political goals: to trade across the hemisphere and in the great Pacific, to the struggle between slaveholders and non-slaveholders for breathing space and leverage in the federal government, to security against the encroachments of rival European powers, and to the expansion of national authority over all points within its territorial borders. Together they represented the energies and objectives of an agro-commercial union becoming a nation-state. To be sure, men like William Seward and James G. Blaine had, in the 1860s, 1870s, and 1880s, begun to envision a new type of American empire organized around access to international markets, reciprocity agreements with foreign states, and sea-lanes to Asia, but these were preludes to a larger imperial reconstruction that would transform American society and the place of the United States in the world. Unlike the European scramble of the last decades of the nineteenth century, this imperial reconstruction would involve not so much the establishment and administration of formal colonies as the formation of American zones of authority and influence, in thrall to private investors but backed by the military arm of the nation-state. And it would be the product of a crisis of political economy, cultural authority, colonial power, and class.

Imperial reconstruction occurred in a context not only of serious domestic unrest but also of anticolonial and nationalist rebellions that, although brewing for several decades, erupted forcefully during the 1890s and very early years of the twentieth century. With complex dynamics and social bases, they either struggled for political independence, as in Cuba and the Philippines, or pushed back against the reach and arrogance of imperial powers, as among the Boxers in China or the Boers in southern Africa. They also availed themselves of newly globalized networks of communication—newspapers, travel, academic institutions, political organizations—to stay informed and to feed off each other. Filipino nationalists embraced the constitutional framework of their Cuban counterparts; Chinese nationalists followed the unfolding of events in Cuba and the Philippines; the Chinese and the Filipinos studied the Boers' battles against British imperialism. Some would touch bases personally through the mediation of liberals, anarchists, and socialists in Paris, London, New York, Singapore, and Hong Kong. Together they disrupted the march of empire and set potential limits to the sway of capital.

Almost everywhere, these movements showed the marks of western political and intellectual currents in their familiarity with liberal institutions and their concern for the trappings of modernity. But almost everywhere, too, they were tied to more indigenous and often prophetic traditions that looked to sever the cultural arms of the colonizers entirely or to the aspirations of former slaves and peasants who imagined a different sort of justice from what liberalism might prescribe. At times, especially where Anglo-European colonialism had a lengthy history, the movements might evince a syncretic cultural and spiritual caste, combining elements of Christianity with non-Christian folk beliefs. In the Philippines, the Tagalog-speaking Katipunans, founded in 1892 in the face of growing Spanish repression and the commodification of landholdings, spread their message from the outskirts of Manila into the countryside of Luzon, turning the narrative of Christ's suffering—the *pasyon*—to revolutionary ends. They would provide the spark for the 1896 uprising against the Spanish colonizers.

Well before American troops and officials encountered the effects of this uprising on the other side of the Pacific, they saw a smaller version emerge among colonized people within their own borders. As reservation Indians across the northern plains struggled with the impact of their military defeats and of federal pressure for detribalization, they learned of a prophet, a "New Messiah," beyond the He Ska (Rocky Mountains) known as Wovoka. Living among the Paiutes in a remote corner of Nevada, Wovoka spoke of being "taken up to the other world" at a time of solar eclipse where he "saw God, with all the people who had died long ago engaged in their oldtime sports and occupations." Although he counseled living "in peace with the whites," Wovoka also predicted "a great change . . . ushered in by a trembling of the earth" when Native peoples would alone be left to occupy their lands. And to hasten that day, Wovoka instructed the various delegations who visited him—Lakotas, Cheyennes, Arapahos—to perform a ghost dance "every six weeks" and to "make a feast" along with it. "When the earth shakes do not be afraid," he assured them. "It will not hurt you."

Word of Wovoka and his prophecy quickly spread by means of intertribal visits in 1889 and 1890, especially among those bands who had rejected cooperation with the United States and had long resisted submission to reservations. Leaders like Sitting Bull, Kicking Bear, Red Cloud, Hump, and Big Foot now thought that the political and cultural assaults of the whites might be turned back and that their white tormentors might be destroyed or removed from among them. Some of the Sioux donned ghost dresses and shirts that they believed were invulnerable to bullets, while the dancers conjured visions of a world regenerated by Native peoples.

But word—and alarm—spread as well through the reservation agencies and to federal officials of dangerous portents, of a rising in the making, and by September 1890 the newly promoted general Miles had learned of them. Long a critic of the Interior Department's management of Indian affairs, Miles had been looking to increase the size of the army and demonstrate its ability to move swiftly against Native American unrest. Now an opportunity seemed to fall into his lap. Accepting the talk of violent Indian intentions, Miles concluded that "there never has been a time when the Indians were as well armed and equipped for war as the present." In short order, thousands of federal troops were summoned and deployed in what became the largest single military operation since the War of the Rebellion. Although alternative tactics were available and the Indians for the most part were chastened, the momentum headed toward a show of overwhelming force. Before it was over in late December, Sitting Bull had been arrested and murdered, and perhaps three hundred Lakotas, many women and children, had been massacred at a spot on the Pine Ridge reservation known as Wounded Knee Creek. Miles gave the orders, but the carnage was carried out by the Seventh Cavalry, once the command of George Armstrong Custer, in what might well have been an act of vengeance for the Little Bighorn.

The Ghost Dance movement may be regarded as the end of mass Native American resistance to the authority of the American state as well as the passing of a pan-tribalism that decades of struggle and the reservation itself had nurtured. Its suppression would serve as a clear indication of the lines of belonging that the nation-state would tolerate: drawn between those who accepted the offer of inclusion and citizenship under the auspices of the Dawes Act and those who rejected it and were left to the isolation, wardship, and virtual apartheid of the reservation. Cultural and political activities—large ceremonies—meant to cross those lines, to construct alternative forms of attachment and belonging, would be dealt with summarily. There and elsewhere in the interior West, the reach of constitutionalism was constantly being tested, as histories of conquest and colonialism, of lengthy territorializations and new ethnic exclusions, challenged notions of birthright citizenship and statehood incorporation. How were the borders of the United States to be construed, and what did those borders mean for the populations residing within them? Could territories remain indefinitely under federal jurisdiction? What sort of political space did Indian reservations compose? And what might the relation be between territories within the borders of the United States and newly acquired territories outside them?

These questions had become particularly pressing by the end of the nineteenth century as the American nation-state extended its reach well beyond its formal borders, though much of the impulse derived from issues of political economy. The deep depressions of the 1870s and 1890s and the social turmoil that they produced left policy makers and industrialists searching for explanations and remedies. Many blamed excessive competition for sapping their profits and driving manufacturers in destructive directions. Others blamed labor strikes for disrupting operations and preventing employers from rationalizing the organization of their shops. Still others worried about the outflow of gold and the dangers of a devalued currency should greenbacks or bimetallism triumph. But by the mid-1890s, there appeared to be a developing consensus: the problem was that industrialists, embracing new technologies with high fixed costs, were producing far more than the American public could consume—it was generally called overproduction—and the solution was that industrialists not only needed to consolidate their enterprises but also desperately required new markets abroad, especially in Latin America and Asia. "When an article was produced by a small manufacturer," Andrew Carnegie reflected, "it was an easy matter for him to limit or even stop production. As manufacturing is carried on today, in enormous establishments, with five or ten million dollars of capital invested . . . the article is produced for months, and in some cases . . . for years . . . without profit . . . or interest on capital."

To be sure, since the mid-nineteenth century, following leads in Britain and France, American retailers had been experimenting with new ways of selling manufactured goods, especially to an expanding urban middle class. Some of them had started, and continued to operate, in the wholesale trade; others had roots in particular product lines like clothing. At all events, they began establishing retail consolidations known as department stores. With family names like Macy's (New York City), Wanamaker's (Philadelphia), and Marshall Field's (Chicago), these large stores centralized the sale of many different types of commodities that individual purchasers had customarily found in a scattering of specialty shops, and thereby created spatially interconnected marketplaces. Later in the century, mail-order houses—the midwestern Montgomery Ward and Sears, Roebuck and Company being the best-known examples—effectively moved new opportunities for consumption out of large cities and into smaller towns and rural districts, where they joined traveling salesmen in introducing a range of goods that local merchants and dry goods stores were in no position to stock. Perhaps most consequential, both the department stores and the mail-order houses gave rise to advertising agencies that, through various media but especially newspapers and periodicals, cultivated new awareness of and tastes for foods, clothing, furnishings, and nascent household technologies. Together they went into the making of a consumer culture that would take hold by the first decades of the twentieth century and eventually transform the dynamics of the national and international economies.

Yet these transformations were on the distant horizon in the 1890s, and the problem of overproduction sat front and center. Some investors had been putting their capital into projects—railroads, mines, plantations—in Mexico, Central America, and the broad Caribbean basin. By the 1890s, American investors had over $50 million in Cuba alone, and the United States had become the island's major trading partner. Others, notably in the manufacturing sector, looked hungrily at Asia, especially at China, to which textile exports were already growing rapidly. The combination of reciprocity treaties, which proved especially valuable in Latin America, and access to the markets of the Pacific, which Seward pursued as a policy objective years earlier, seemed the best means of solving the crisis within a framework of capitalist relations. As Alfred T. Mahan, who campaigned for a great battleship fleet as a necessary accompaniment to American commerce, saw it, the choice was between promoting consumption at home through "socialistic" measures and finding markets across what he called the new "frontier," the oceans. For Mahan, as for Seward, colonial outposts were valuable principally as coaling stations and provisioning stops along the way to the greater prize of foreign markets. In 1899, Secretary of State John Hay, responding to the scramble for the China trade, lent an enduring rubric to such a framework when he called upon European powers (the Germans, Russians, and British most notably) to respect Chinese territorial integrity and accept equitable commercial opportunity for all foreigners there. It was known as the Open Door.

The urgency with which Hay enunciated the Open Door reflected a new position the United States had come to occupy both in the western Pacific and in the Caribbean as a result of warfare against Spanish colonizers and nationalist insurgents. It was not necessarily destined to be so. Ever since the 1860s, Spain's authority had been contested in its remaining colonies of Cuba and the Philippines, with demands for political reform, greater autonomy, or outright independence. In Cuba, the struggle was initially confined to the less developed eastern end of the island, where disgruntled creole landholders and slaveholders joined hands with slaves and free blacks in an effort to overthrow the Spanish regime. By the late 1880s, they had won some concessions together with the abolition of slavery but fell short of their main goals. In the Philippines, years of peasant unrest were deepened by the discontent of educated Filipinos, often of Chinese extraction (*ilustrados,* as they were known), who hoped to cast off the retrograde chains of colonial rule and create a modern society. In the mid-1890s, both of these insurgencies reached a new intensity and threatened to overturn the established order. With the aid of exiled activists like José Martí, the Cubans reignited their independence movement in 1895 and, this time, mobilized an army fifty thousand strong that marched into the western districts where large sugar plantations held sway. They imagined a new republic based, at least rhetorically, on equality between the races. A year later, the Katipunans launched a campaign in the Philippines that would involve a tense alliance between the leaders Andrés Bonifacio and Emilio Aguinaldo, but one that also exposed the weaknesses of the Spanish.

Americans focused principally on events in Cuba, which had been of long-standing interest and where investors had already become deeply involved, but there was no uniformity of opinion as to what might be done. The cause of Cuba Libre had substantial support, both inside Congress and out, while the Cleveland and McKinley administrations took a cautious stance, encouraging the Spanish to end repression against the insurgents, embrace reforms, and perhaps grant autonomy to the island. Yet as the insurgency moved west on the shoulders of a multiracial army, fears among creole and American business concerns mounted. The U.S. minister to Spain, Stewart Woodford, insisting that the insurgency was "confined almost entirely to negroes," warned that "Cuban independence is absolutely impossible as a permanent solution of the difficulty, since independence can only result in a continuous war of the races . . . a second Santo Domingo." He was not alone in urging annexation.

President McKinley, who with Mark Hanna represented the corporate wing of the Republican Party, then stepped in to play a defining role. A strong advocate of reciprocity agreements, the gold standard, and greater executive authority in foreign affairs, he was less interested in annexation than in expanding the perimeters of U.S. economic power. Believing, by early 1898, that the Spanish had lost control in Cuba, he sent the navy's battleship *Maine* to Havana Harbor to maintain order and safeguard American property. When the *Maine* was subsequently destroyed in what was likely an accidental explosion, he was ready to implement his goals. Rather than recognizing Cuban independence and the leadership of the insurgents, he called on Congress to declare war against Spain while renouncing any intention "to exercise sovereignty, jurisdiction, or control" over the island (the provision was known as the Teller Amendment to the congressional resolution). Shortly thereafter, McKinley turned to the Pacific and asked Congress for another resolution, this one to annex the Hawai'ian Islands. It was the last phase of a prolonged battle over the future of Hawai'i, where American sugar planters wielded great power but had failed to convince the public at home of the wisdom of annexation and had rankled the Japanese who were well represented in the Hawai'ian population. With war looming and his eyes on Asian markets, McKinley now claimed that Hawai'i was necessary to the United States as a military base. "We need Hawaii just as much and a good deal more than we did California," he declared. "It is manifest destiny." Congress yielded in a close vote.

What of the Philippines? Unlike in Cuba, the United States had few direct economic involvements in the Philippines, though, like Hawai'i, the archipelago was regarded as a potential stepping-stone to the wider Asian trade. The U.S. Navy had already made the Philippines an objective in the event of hostilities with Spain, and in January 1898 Theodore Roosevelt, then assistant secretary of the navy, took the initiative in ordering Admiral George Dewey to attack Manila if war broke out. It was a presumptuous move on Roosevelt's part but also one with larger social significance. Roosevelt ached for war not as a throwback to the martial cults of the past but as a way to invigorate sections of the upper class—such as his own—that, he believed, were being overrun by the grasping and nationally oriented ambitions of a new class of industrial and finance capitalists. "I should welcome any war," he confided, "for I think this country needs one." Roosevelt had nothing but scorn for the effete scions of regional elites who looked warily at the onset of modernity and had little enthusiasm for the pursuit of American power overseas. Indeed, Roosevelt's own life, growing up sickly in a female-dominated household of the old New York gentry but then turning himself into a tough-talking, game-hunting, virile politician who relished the American West (and wrote its history), seemed a parable of the sort of class transformation he wished to bring about. Although McKinley tossed out some of Roosevelt's recommendations, he nonetheless let the orders to Dewey stand, and on May 1, 1898, Dewey's fleet sailed into Manila Bay. Once the shooting started, Manila fell in a matter of hours, Cuba in a matter of months. For his part, Roosevelt resigned his post, formed a cavalry regiment, departed for Cuba, and, on Kettle Hill in July, led his troops over "open ground" in the face of "the best modern repeating rifles." Two hundred of his men died, and possibly one thousand more were wounded, but they would claim the victory. It was, Roosevelt later recalled, "the great day of my life."

Rapid as it was, military victory over the Spanish brought choices as well as perils. Insurgents in Cuba and the Philippines entertained hope that American intervention might clear their road to independence. The Teller Amendment, after all, abjured annexation and seemed to recognize Cuban sovereignty, and in the Philippines the insurgent leader Emilio Aguinaldo, who had been forced into exile by the Spanish, returned after Dewey's triumph and imagined something of an alliance taking shape. But in neither case was the McKinley administration willing to stoke the revolutionary fires, doubting as it did the capacity of Cubans and Filipinos to rule themselves. "Self-government!" one U.S. Army officer in Cuba exclaimed. "Why those people are no more fit for self-government than gunpowder is for hell . . . no more capable of self-government than the savages of Africa." Attempting to exert requisite American control while maintaining the appearance of Cuban self-governance, McKinley's new secretary of war, Elihu Root, a prominent corporate lawyer, crafted a set of conditions that the "independent" Cuban government was required to accept: prohibiting Cuba from signing international treaties that might give other foreign nations influence, requiring the sale or lease of Cuban territory to the United States for coaling and naval stations (the origin of the U.S. base at Guantánamo Bay), and permitting the United States to intervene in Cuban affairs "for the preservation of Cuban independence [and] the maintenance of a government adequate for the protection of life, property, and individual liberty." Enacted in 1901 as the Platt Amendment to an army appropriations bill, these conditions, despite strong Cuban objections, were then shoehorned into the island's constitution and regarded as the terms for ending American occupation. "None of us thought," the well-known insurgent General Máximo Gómez angrily declared, "that [peace] would be followed by a military occupation by our allies, who treat us as a people incapable of acting for ourselves, and who have reduced us to obedience, to submission, and to a tutelage imposed by the force of circumstances." It was a bitter pill.

Yet circumstances were even more complex in the Philippines, where, unlike in Cuba, the issue of annexation was quickly on the table. While Dewey's fleet destroyed the Spanish, McKinley sent five thousand troops to occupy Manila and, having decided to reject any of Emilio Aguinaldo's "political claims," upped the deployment to nearly forty thousand by the summer. It was to be a tough and protracted fight, especially after Aguinaldo declared independence and organized his own government in Malolos, not far from Manila. From early on, U.S. troops and political officials spoke of the conflict in racialized terms, referring to the Filipinos as "niggers" and "gugus." "No cruelty is too severe for these brainless monkeys who can appreciate no sense of honor, kindness, or justice," one soldier sneered; "I am in my glory when I can sight some dark skin and pull the trigger," crowed another. But as much as anything else, it was the struggle against Native Americans in the trans-Mississippi West that framed the nature of the operation. Major General Adna Chaffee, who spent years fighting Comanches, Kiowas, Apaches, and Cheyennes on the plains after serving in the War of the Rebellion, was said to have "brought the Indian Wars with him to the Philippines and wanted to treat the recalcitrant Filipinos the way he had the Apaches in Arizona—by herding them onto reservations." When Aguinaldo's forces turned to guerrilla warfare to better combat large-scale American assaults, the Indian analogy seemed to be confirmed, and the brutality of the engagements further escalated.

Comparing the Filipinos to Native American enemies in the West clearly reinforced the view of many policy makers that they were no more suited to self-rule than the Cubans. "What alchemy," the Republican senator Albert Beveridge asked, "will change the oriental quality of their blood, and set the self-governing currents of the American pouring through their Malay veins?" Yet, rather than "herding them onto reservations," McKinley seemed more interested in turning all of the Philippines into a reservation: placing the archipelago fully under American jurisdiction by means of annexation. It was a move compelled, in the main, not by a racial choreography but by Manila's strategic value in relation to the great China market. If the Europeans succeeded in dividing up China and "we fail to establish ourselves with a large port and with territory in the East," the Massachusetts senator Henry Cabot Lodge advised, it would be nothing short of disastrous. "We must have new markets unless we would be visited by declines in wages and by great industrial disturbances. . . . The old theory of competing in foreign markets merely by the price of the product is no longer practicable [and] a navy, coaling stations and ports in the East . . . have become essential conditions in our time."

Still, the annexation of a distant and multicultural territory was a bold move, and like the annexation of Hawai'i it provoked significant opposition. Indeed, the debate over McKinley's annexation treaty revealed the fault lines of a changing political economy as well as the lineaments of an imperial reconstruction. Supporters of annexation predictably argued that ample precedent was to be found in the acquisitions of Louisiana, Alaska, and parts of Mexico; that it was the duty of the United States to "educate the Filipinos, and uplift and civilize and Christianize them"; that the country's "priceless principles [would] undergo no change under the tropical sun"; and that "enormous material benefits [would come] to our trade, our industries, and our labor." "We have had colonies in this country ever since we ceased to be colonies ourselves," one senator confidently intoned.

Not long after, when occupation forces learned of indigenous forms of slavery practiced among the Moros in the southern islands of the Philippines, annexationists could further pride themselves on putting colonialism in the service of abolitionism.

Opponents, generally known as anti-imperialists (though in truth they were simply anti-annexationists), staked out political ground high and low. At their best, they doubted that annexation had any basis in the Constitution and feared it would transform the United States into a "vulgar, commonplace empire founded upon physical force, controlling subject races and vassal states, in which one class must forever rule, and other classes must forever obey." The Republic, quite simply, could not survive under such circumstances. Jane Addams, who helped to organize anti-imperialists in Chicago, insisted "that the forcible subjugation of a . . . people [represented] open disloyalty to the distinctive principles of our government." Mark Twain was more biting: "Shall we go on conferring our Civilization upon the peoples that sit in darkness . . . or shall we sober up and sit down and think it over first?" The Democratic Party, with William Jennings Bryan again as its standard-bearer in 1900, insisted, ironically playing off Lincoln's "house divided," that "no nation can long endure half republic and half empire." As Henry Cabot Lodge, who led the floor fight for annexation, conceded, if the anti-imperialists were proved correct, "our whole past record of expansion is a crime."

But anti-annexationism had a far darker side, and even high-mindedness could be tethered to it. Annexing the Philippines, many warned, would open the United States to a "mess of Asiatic pottage," challenge white supremacy, devalue democracy, and degrade white American labor. "The racial differences between the Oriental and Western races are never to be eradicated," it was said. "The two races could never amalgamate." As Stanford's president, David Starr Jordan, had it, "Civilization is suffocated in the tropics, . . . nature's asylum for degenerates [and] . . . neither the people nor the institutions of the United States can ever occupy the Philippines." South Carolina's senator Benjamin Tillman, an arch-segregationist who was especially vocal in the anti-imperialist cause, mocked the annexationist argument that Filipinos were incapable of governing themselves. Those "who are now contending for a different policy in Hawaii and the Philippines," he declared, "gave the slaves of the South not only self-government, but they forced on the white men of the South, at the point of the bayonet, the rule and dominion of those ex-slaves."

Roosevelt disparaged the anti-annexationists as "men of a bygone age," and, condescension aside, he had a deeper point. With some exception, those who opposed the annexation of the Philippines in the U.S. Senate were either New England patricians, some with strong antislavery credentials, or Democrats from the South and the Midwest, some members of older aristocratic families, whose vision remained provincial and who embodied the remnants of an agro-commercial economy that was being dramatically superseded. They cast critical eyes on the modernizing and centralizing trends of the age and worried about the social and political consequences of the new imperial ambitions. The annexationists, by way of contrast, not only were heavily concentrated in the Republican Party but also represented the nation's growing metropolitan centers, which rested on a foundation of industry and finance, and the hinterlands that were connected to them. Many, like Roosevelt and Lodge (themselves renegades from the provincial elite), were young, energetic, and "progressive," comfortable with a new role in the world for the United States, and eager to export what they regarded as a superior culture and set of institutions. They were at or near the leading edge of the various reconstructions of the period. What both sides unfortunately held in common was a Darwinian-influenced view of human prospects and a strong belief in social hierarchies organized around race that appeared to order both the country and the globe.

If nothing else, the U.S. occupation of Cuba and the Philippines demonstrated that popular struggles for independence and self-determination might well threaten the very world that progressives were hoping to construct. The merger movement that coincided with these occupations, producing vast new sources of capital, greatly increased U.S. investments overseas, especially in Latin America, but at the same time intensified patterns of exploitation and corruption where those investments were made. The political ripple effects were being felt in Venezuela and the Dominican Republic, with European creditors as well as American investors looking to shake the financial trees.

Theodore Roosevelt, who became president after McKinley's assassination in 1901 and quickly described interventions against "barbarous and semi-barbarous peoples" as "a most regrettable but necessary international police duty," then built upon the principles of the Platt Amendment and offered a framework for the exercise of American power in the hemisphere. Rejecting any hunger for land, annexation, or "aggrandizement," Roosevelt told Congress in 1904 that all the United States desired was "to see the neighboring countries stable, orderly, and prosperous" and that "any country whose people conduct themselves well can count upon our hearty friendship . . . [and] need fear no interference from the United States." But there was an explicit threat attached. "Chronic wrongdoing, or an impotence which results in a general loosening of the ties of civilized society," he declared in the language of hyper-masculinity, "may . . . ultimately require intervention by some civilized nation, and in the Western Hemisphere the adherence of the United States to the Monroe Doctrine may force the United States . . . to the exercise of an international police power."

It became known as the Roosevelt Corollary to the Monroe Doctrine and would be invoked to justify many army occupations in the Caribbean basin over the next several decades.

In essence, the Roosevelt Corollary designated the nations of the Western Hemisphere as effective protectorates of the United States: they were permitted self-rule, and their citizens the rights their governments accorded, so long as they could protect themselves from "instabilities," which General Leonard Wood famously described as "money at six percent." Then the "big stick" of Roosevelt and his successors could be wielded. But what of the Philippines, and of Puerto Rico and Guam, which together were ceded to the United States by Spain in 1898? What were they as political entities, and what civil and political standing did their populations enjoy? In principle, they could have been regarded as federal territories, much the way Louisiana and the Mexican cession were, capable of becoming states and subject to the full reach of the Constitution. But few imagined this as a possibility on racial, cultural, or logistical grounds; after all, there were enough misgivings about making some of the territories of the trans-Mississippi West into states.

Instead, owing to the congressional Foraker Act of 1900 and to a series of Supreme Court decisions between 1901 and 1910, collectively known as the Insular Cases, a new political status was inscribed into law. The recently annexed territories would be "unincorporated," left to congressional authority, and their peoples would have certain "fundamental" rights, though not full rights of citizenship as guaranteed by the Constitution. In the convoluted language of the Court, which had previously upheld segregation in *Plessy v. Ferguson*, these territories were not "foreign countr[ies]" in "an international sense," yet at the same time were "foreign to the United States in a domestic sense," not "incorporated," but "merely appurtenant thereto as a possession." They were "insular" to themselves in governance, not beholden to territorial precedent in political terms, while remaining under the sovereign power of the United States. It was a proclamation both of segregation from the American body politic and of civil inferiority within the realm of federal jurisdiction. To the question of whether, in this new imperial order consecrated by the Insular Cases, the "Constitution would follow the flag," Elihu Root cleverly remarked, "The Constitution indeed follows the flag, but it doesn't quite catch up."

Among the territories that fell to the logic of the Supreme Court's rulings in the Insular Cases was the newly acquired Canal Zone running through the Republic of Panama, and it was here that the fruits of imperial reconstruction were fully to be realized. American interest in an isthmian crossing stretched back at least to the California gold rush of the mid-nineteenth century and intensified as the Pacific trade grew in volume. Far more than the transcontinental railroad system, it would be the gateway to Asia. The sticking point was whether Nicaragua or Panama would be a better site (Nicaragua presented fewer engineering hurdles), but the die was effectively cast when the French set out to build a canal across the Isthmus of Panama in 1880. After nearly twenty years, they gave it up, and with Roosevelt in the presidency the United States quickly moved in, though, ironically, not before helping Panamanian insurgents achieve political independence at the expense of Colombia. The reward for the United States was complete and perpetual control, as "if it were sovereign," over a strip of land roughly ten miles wide and thirty miles long in return for $10 million and a yearly payment of $250,000.

Completed over a period of ten years, the canal proved to be a colossal feat of engineering and a transforming event in the development of the global economy. This was how many observers viewed it at the time and how it has mostly been remembered since. But it was also the embodiment of many elements that would define the new American empire. The zone was a territorial possession of the United States, though, like the Philippines and Puerto Rico, "insular" in terms of governance. It was run with a stern hand by an appointed governor—the engineer and army veteran George Washington Goethals being the first of them—who had no interest in democratic forms and little tolerance for labor unrest. The workforce composed a hierarchy of skill and privilege associated with race and national origins, and various types of segregation and discrimination structured virtually every corner of zone life. The managerial and highly skilled positions were the province of white Americans and Europeans; lesser and unskilled jobs were filled by migrants of Mediterranean descent and especially by Afro-Caribbeans, most of whom came to Panama from the sugar plantation island of Barbados. The distinctions were further reinforced by a system of payment that remunerated workers from the United States with gold currency and the unskilled from elsewhere with devalued Panamanian silver. African Americans, relatively few in number, occupied a liminal status: they were acknowledged as citizens of the United States but also placed on the "silver" payrolls. It seemed very much a mix of the American South and the Union of South Africa.

As an "insular" territory, the Canal Zone had its own justice system, which was tied closely to the executive branch of its government. There were no jury trials—Roosevelt did ultimately grant them in capital cases—nor was there judicial review; the only appeal that convicted offenders had was to the embassies of their home countries. The legal culture, having little to do with the U.S. Constitution and Bill of Rights, was a mélange of Colombian, Panamanian, and American practices, and large numbers of workers were arrested for a variety of infractions and generally set to hard labor in the zone's penitentiaries. And although the zone was formally set off from the Republic of Panama, tensions inevitably spilled over the border between them—especially in the nearby capital of Panama City—and the United States exercised an influence over politics, finance, and landholding that called Panamanian sovereignty into question.

Yet for many American progressives, even those on Progressivism's left wing, the Canal Zone became a source of great interest and often admiration. Here, many of them believed, was an example of the sort of partnership that they were trying to promote within the United States: between an activist state, scientific and managerial expertise, and technological prowess and efficiency. Little troubled by the political and labor hierarchies that had been constructed—most of them, of course, had come to accept segregation as sensible and necessary—they instead relished what they saw as the potential wonders of statism. Some even glimpsed a resemblance between the order of the zone and Henry George's dream of government ownership of the land. For them, it was possible to imagine an American empire exemplified in the Canal Zone, not as a threat to the Republic or a blot on the Constitution, but as an extension of the social experimentation they were so eager to carry on. Many clearly thrilled at the canal's completion, ahead of schedule, in mid-August 1914 and might have followed with fascination the great Panama-Pacific International Exposition in San Francisco the next year meant to celebrate the canal's opening. But they undoubtedly noticed, too, that the guns of world war had already begun firing and the rumblings of revolution were already being heard.

Revolution, War, and the Borders of Power

Mexican revolutionary Pancho Villa, circa 1908.

Revolution on the Border

Several months before the Panama Canal was completed and the first shots of what would be a thirty-year world war were fired, President Woodrow Wilson faced a foreign policy crisis. It was neither on the far side of the Atlantic nor of the Pacific, not in Europe or Asia, but directly to the south in the bordering country of Mexico. And it was the product of a revolution that had already engulfed most corners of Mexican society and would ultimately cast a long and enduring shadow over the twentieth-century Americas, if not the entire globe.

Brewing for more than a decade, the revolution had begun in 1910 as a rebellion against the authoritarian regime of Porfirio Díaz. A military hero in the struggle against the French in the 1860s, Díaz had claimed the presidency in 1877. He centralized power, brought many of the regional bosses (caciques) to heel, and furthered the modernization projects of his liberal predecessors. It was a version of nation building that was embraced by both the United States and Canada, though with its own peculiarities. Díaz offered incentives to foreign investors—Americans chief among them—to construct railroads and develop mines, plantations, oil rigs, and ranches, and he enabled hacienda owners to continue encroaching upon the communal lands of peasant villages. He skillfully fashioned concentric rings of cronies and clients, including a group of technocrats known as the *científicos*, while strengthening the federal army (*los federales*) and the rural constabularies (*rurales*), which lent his regime legitimacy and ballast.

There was more than a little resemblance to the Gilded Age United States, where foreign capital continued to assume developmental importance, Indian lands were steadily appropriated, and political corruption ran rampant, save that Díaz saw no reason to bow very much to democratic forms. He entrenched himself in the presidency and did not intend to give it up; he was reelected without opposition on six consecutive occasions. Americans who appreciated the economic opportunities Díaz offered them paid no mind. After all, they were having their own reservations about the workings of democracy at home and trying, in various ways, to limit its reach. "If I were a poet I should write eulogies; if I were a musician I should compose triumphal marches; if I were a Mexican I should feel that the steadfast loyalty of a lifetime would not be too much to give in return for the blessings that he has brought to my country," Secretary of State Elihu Root exulted in 1907. Díaz was, as Root saw it, "one of the great men to be held up for the hero-worship of mankind."

Yet by 1907 the regime's edifice of power was beginning to crack. Peasant discontent intensified, especially in Mexico's south-central states such as Morelos and in north-central states such as Durango, where haciendas and plantations had accelerated moves against surrounding villages to expand their crop acreage and accumulate a larger labor force. Nearly four-fifths of all rural communities and nearly half of the rural population were enveloped by hacienda boundaries. Farther to the northwest, in the mountains and foothills (the *serrano*), more independent peasants and rancheros chafed at the political demands of the Díaz regime and threw up their own share of social bandits who harassed the representatives of the central government. Railroad workers and miners, whose numbers had grown very rapidly, launched militant strikes, some in collaboration with socialists and anarchists. And the export booms in oil, copper, and henequen that had fortified Díaz's projects were punctured by the serious financial panic of that year, adding stress to the cities and the countryside alike.

But like many rebellions turned revolutions, Mexico's commenced with a political rising of disgruntled members of the elite and their middle-class allies who sought to end the Díaz dictatorship and reform the system that sustained it. They found a leader in Francisco Madero, the scion of a wealthy landed family from the northeastern state of Coahuila, who determined to deny Díaz yet another term by running as the presidential candidate of the Anti-reelectionist Party in 1910. In a characteristic bit of chicanery, Díaz had Madero arrested on charges of sedition until the election was over and Díaz could claim victory. Then, sensing the political backlash, he had Madero released. Rather than risk further trouble, Madero hopped a northbound train, crossed the border into El Paso, Texas, and continued plotting an alternative road to power: an insurrection for November.

U.S. officials left Madero alone despite the entreaties of Díaz. They did not show the same consideration to Ricardo and Enrique Flores Magón, voices of the anarcho-syndicalist Left and allies of the Industrial Workers of the World, who had fled the Díaz regime and attempted to continue publishing their anti-capitalist paper, *Regeneración*, first in San Antonio, then in St. Louis and Los Angeles, before suffering arrest and imprisonment in 1907. Perhaps it was a growing sense in the administration of President William Howard Taft that Díaz's days were numbered; perhaps it was the dissatisfaction of American business interests over the favor that Díaz had recently shown British investors; perhaps it was simply a choice, on this occasion, for noninterference in Mexican affairs. At all events, Madero was given free rein to organize, and when he finally returned to Mexican soil, unrest had spread across much of the country, especially in the *serrano* of the northwest and in the villages and haciendas of the sprawling rural districts, in anticipation of a great change in the offing.

The Porfiriato crumbled with remarkable speed. In late May 1911, the once all-powerful Díaz quietly shipped out from Veracruz, and soon thereafter Madero marched into Mexico City. Yet the forces of revolution had already moved well beyond what Madero was prepared to pursue. For him, the revolution was chiefly political rather than social; he had no program other than displacing Díaz and, indeed, had agreed to maintain the Porfirian officer corps, headed by General Victoriano Huerta. It was a salve to many of Madero's bourgeois supporters, who wanted the preservation of order above all else, but a shocker to his more humble allies who imagined they would now recover lands that had been taken from them and local power that had been usurped. Small wonder that Madero quickly had a rebellion on his own hands.

In fact, Madero had several rebellions on his hands. As historians have long recognized, there was not one but "many" Mexicos, complicating the project of nation building from the time of independence in 1810. The rapidity of regime change preceding the Porfiriato testified to the many social bases of power across the country and the difficulties of constructing stable ruling coalitions. Although Madero took the reins of leadership, the ouster of Díaz required a groundswell of highly localized—and armed—popular movements that Madero neither controlled nor knew very much about. And they were easy to reignite. Two of the most important developed under Pascual Orozco in northern Chihuahua (one of the bases of Maderismo) and Emiliano Zapata in southern Morelos, each rather different in character. What they shared was deep anger at Madero's reluctance to attack the foundations of Porfirian political power and an abiding intent to extend the reach of the revolution. Zapata and his peasant followers crafted the Plan de Ayala in late November 1911, which not only called for the overthrow of Madero—already deemed a tyrant and traitor—but demanded an agrarian reform designed to benefit peasants at the expense of hacendados and punish those who opposed them. For his part, Orozco, who rebelled a few months later, denounced the corruption of the Madero administration and its apparent subservience to the United States while advocating the nationalization of the railroads, the improvement of wages and conditions for workers, and immediate consideration of the agrarian question.

Besieged from several directions, Madero reached into the Porfirian bag, mobilizing the federal army to save his regime. For a time, with the aid of General Huerta, he seemed to be succeeding, especially against Orozco's forces. But as onetime Díaz loyalists joined the fray, looking for a "Porfiriato *sin* Porfirio," the pressure proved too great. Conspiring in part with the U.S. ambassador in Mexico City, Huerta betrayed Madero and, in early 1913, launched a coup d'état against him. Quickly consolidating his power, Huerta received the support of most provincial governors as well as the *federales*. His only misstep turned out to be a major one: Huerta had Madero assassinated and, in so doing, created a martyr out of a failed leader.

Among those whose support Huerta did not secure were an increasingly powerful leader from Chihuahua named Francisco "Pancho" Villa and the governor of Coahuila, Venustiano Carranza. Villa was deeply loyal to Madero despite his limitations; Carranza had more doubts about Madero, especially his seeming weakness. But they both vowed to topple Huerta, joining together in Carranza's Plan de Guadalupe and fighting under a broad banner of "Constitutionalism." It was an unwieldy coalition of forces, all the more so with Zapatistas, inspired by an agrarian vision, battling on in Morelos. Villa and Carranza would become bitter rivals. For the time being, though, they set their sights on Huerta and, to that end, also hoped to win some assistance from the United States, chiefly in the form of weapons and supplies.

There was some cause for optimism in this regard. Although President Wilson had assumed a stance of "watchful waiting" in relation to political developments in Mexico, he refused to extend diplomatic recognition to the Huerta regime and made no secret of his distaste for the methods Huerta deployed to seize power. "There can be no certain prospect of peace in America until General Huerta has surrendered his usurped authority in Mexico," Wilson told Congress in December 1913, "such pretended governments will not be countenanced or dealt with by the Government of the United States." Wilson also had an assortment of Texans advising him, some in the cabinet, who worried about the fate of American interests. Thus, when a group of U.S. sailors who had come ashore in the gulf port of Tampico on a routine stop for fuel was briefly detained by local Huerta officials, Wilson was quick to move. Insisting that the "dignity" of the United States and the "rights" of its citizens had been "flouted," Wilson ordered the bombardment and marine occupation of nearby Veracruz, Mexico's most important port, with plans on the table for extending the occupation into Tampico and Mexico City.

It was all too familiar. While Wilson had portrayed the United States as "champions" of "constitutional government in America" and had spoken in a less bellicose and more idealistic language, he also took pages from the diplomatic playbooks of James K. Polk and especially Theodore Roosevelt. Comparing the "situation in Mexico" to that of "France at the time of the Revolution," Wilson argued that Mexico now needed "the strong guiding hand of the great nation on this continent that . . . must assist these warring people back into the paths of quiet and prosperity." Only in this way would the world see "that the Monroe Doctrine means unselfish friendship for our neighbors." The blow to Huerta was substantial, and when U.S. forces finally departed Veracruz, they left behind a large cache of arms that Carranza's Constitutionalists eagerly grabbed up.

Time was plainly running out on Huerta. By early summer, Villa's army, fortified in part by arms that had flowed across the Texas-Mexico border ("watchful waiting" also involved the relaxation of an American arms embargo), had marched south and captured the central Mexican city of Zacatecas; Zapata's troops had taken control of deeply contested Morelos; and Carranza continued to close the vise, though he was intent on keeping Villa on the political sidelines. In July, yielding to the inevitable, Huerta resigned and followed Díaz's path to the sea, in this case boarding a German cruiser for Jamaica and then Barcelona. The next month, as war in Europe erupted, the Sonoran Álvaro Obregón, with Carranza's blessing, led his army into Mexico City and opened yet another chapter in the revolution.

Reconfiguring Borders of Race and Politics

Woodrow Wilson's international rhetorical idealism did not extend to African Americans or to the concept of racial inclusion, but as he enabled the spirit of *Plessy v. Ferguson* to infect the institutions of the federal government, the racial and political landscape of the country was beginning to shift under his very feet. In truth, the signs of change had been in evidence since at least the 1870s when some former slaves, mainly in the cotton districts of the Deep South, talked of leaving the South and organized for migration to Kansas, Liberia, or some territory in the trans-Mississippi West. In the meantime, black workers had been on the move from the worn-out plantation lands of the Southeast to the newly developing ones of the Arkansas-Mississippi delta, from rural districts to the towns and cities of the southern states, and from the plantations and farms to the lumber and sawmill camps, turpentine camps, and coal mines stretching from the Atlantic and Gulf coasts up through the Appalachians. By the 1890s, as Jim Crow devoured the region, there were new signs, particularly among young black men and women born into a world of freedom and particularly in the states of the upper South, of a northerly reorientation of migration, across the Ohio River and the Mason-Dixon Line, which fugitives from slavery had once traversed, to New York and Philadelphia, Pittsburgh and Cleveland, Detroit and Chicago.

The streams of northward migration turned into a flood during the second decade of the twentieth century, tapping communities farther southward, from Texas through the states of the Gulf Coast to Georgia and Florida. As the drumbeats of European war initiated a massive mobilization of industrial production and manpower, meaningful employment outside the South now beckoned for African Americans, and encouraged by labor recruiters, railroad companies, and repression at home, thousands responded by taking to the rails, rivers, and roads. Joining them were thousands more of African descent, chiefly from the Caribbean, who fled economic distress, natural disasters, and changes in colonial policies—as some had done during the building of the Panama Canal—and headed principally to the Northeast. It proved to be a kaleidoscope of political and cultural intensity, not seen since the War of the Rebellion, that would turn regional inventions like jazz and the blues into national idioms, give birth to astonishing literary and artistic creativity, infuse modernism with special energy, provide a new base for social democracy, and construct the sorts of diasporic politics—with their complex blend of racial nationalism and anticolonialism—that would swirl through the next half century.

Perhaps the greatest embodiment of this transformation was an African Jamaican named Marcus Garvey. An artisan and political agitator from rural St. Ann's Bay who spent time in Kingston and London—mixing there with Afro-Caribbeans and Pan-Africanists interested in mounting opposition to British colonialism—Garvey came to New York City in 1916 along with the early waves of migrants from the South. After a whirlwind tour of the United States, he returned to Harlem, established a branch of the organization he had founded in Jamaica known as the Universal Negro Improvement Association (UNIA), began publishing a newspaper, the *Negro World*, and commenced the work of mobilization. He was remarkably successful. By the early 1920s, the membership of the UNIA numbered in the many thousands, and Garvey's following in the United States, from the rural and small-town South to the small-town and urban North, might have exceeded one million. Ultimately encompassing forty-two countries, mainly in the Caribbean, Latin America, and Africa, Garvey's became the largest and most formidable Pan-African movement the world has seen.

Although influenced by Booker T. Washington's message of self-help and material improvement as well as by nineteenth-century "civilizationism," Garvey nonetheless rejected the possibility of a meaningful accommodation with whites. Only when blacks could claim an independent and powerful African nation of their own, he argued, would they be able to prosper and achieve rights and respect either there or anywhere else. Indeed, Garvey's vision was, at once, nationalist and anticolonial. He called not so much (as is customarily thought) for African repatriation as for a movement to oust European colonizers and to establish a basis for black self-governance, a movement that would link "every member of the race in every part of the world" who, wherever their residence, were "citizens of Africa." At a time of wanton repression and very grim prospects for African Americans, Garvey's project of black empowerment electrified black audiences and amassed an enormous following even among those who never joined the UNIA. "We may make progress in America, the West Indies and other foreign countries," he told them, "but there will never be any real lasting progress until the Negro makes of Africa a strong . . . Republic to lend protection to the success we make in foreign lands." Garvey called for agitation and collective struggle toward that end and spoke of likely allies in China, India, Egypt, and Ireland and of the forceful example left by the rise of Japan.

Garvey's attention to such potential allies and his interest in what the Japanese had done were not misplaced. The first decades of the twentieth century witnessed the emergence of nationalist and anticolonial movements there as well as in Iran, Turkey, Korea, and southern Africa that began to shake imperial structures old and new, anticipating the dynamics of global conflagration that erupted in 1914. The Japanese, showing the results of modernizing impulses unleashed by the Meiji Restoration, had inflicted a humiliating defeat on the Russian Empire in 1905; for Garvey, they were not only a power to be reckoned with on the international scene but also, as a nation-state with a significant military arm, a source of protection for those of the Japanese diaspora. An enlarged cast of historical actors, now encompassing the Pacific and Indian oceans together with the Atlantic, was stepping onto the global stage. And, as the European imperial powers slaughtered each other on the western and eastern fronts, they also battled on the African continent and in the Middle East, recruiting thousands of soldiers from their colonies, while the Japanese took the opportunity to enter the fray (declaring war on Germany) and strengthen their position in parts of China, notably Manchuria. In the meantime, the Pan-African Conference, first held in London in 1900, would be poised to meet again in Paris once the shooting stopped.

The prospects for a different world order, one less beholden to imperialism, coming out of the bloodbath of warfare were heightened by President Wilson's words and aspirations. It was not necessarily to be expected despite the label of the "New Freedom" that he attached to his first election campaign. Wilson had signed both the Clayton Act and the Federal Trade Commission Act in early 1914—concessions to the "reality" of corporate power that were already common in the industrial Euro-Atlantic—and in his Mexican interventions of that time he took up a well-deployed American imperial stance. As the United States moved toward a potential war footing, Wilson also embraced statist policies he had once criticized: creating the War Industries Board, the War Labor Policies Board, the Council of National Defense, and a number of other centrally directed projects designed to oversee the nation's economy and civil society, not to mention repress the antiwar Left. Yet even before he called upon Congress to declare war on Germany, Wilson spoke of a "peace without victory" and a new global compact based on self-determination, the consent of the governed, the equality of nations, and international cooperation to resolve conflicts. Many of these ideas were then encapsulated by his "Fourteen Points," the explicit statement of war aims once the United States had become directly involved.

Wilson's idealism in these regards immediately catapulted him to great prominence internationally, perhaps as the leading voice for the shaping of a postwar world. But in ways he had scarcely anticipated, his words and principles riveted the attention of those struggling against European colonialism and in pursuit of various forms of nationalism—so much so that for a time he surpassed the prestige of V. I. Lenin, who had also called for a "self-determination" explicitly directed at the dismantling of European colonial empires. Circulating globally through print media, Wilson's rhetoric not only stirred the optimism of colonial peoples but also helped ignite movements from Egypt and India to China and Korea that then erupted as the war appeared to end. "Ideas—universal ideas, have a knack of rubbing off all geographical limitations," the Indian nationalist Lala Lajpat Rai observed in 1918. "It is impossible that the noble truths uttered by President Wilson . . . could be limited in their application. Henceforth, his words are going to be the war cry of all small and subject and oppressed nationalities in the world." It was more than a "Wilsonian moment." It was—from St. Petersburg to Berlin to Paris to Seattle, as from Delhi to Seoul to Cairo—a revolutionary moment that would resonate across much of the twentieth century. But for the United States, much of what that century would hold in store had still to play out in Mexico and the borderlands of the Southwest.

The Reach of Revolution

When Ricardo and Enrique Flores Magón fled the persecution of the Porfirio Díaz regime in 1904 and began republishing *Regeneración* on the American side of the border, they found allies in a radical network that included socialists, the Western Federation of Miners, and the IWW. Two years later, after forming what they called the Partido Liberal Mexicano (PLM), they announced a program that anticipated many of the vectors of subsequent revolutionary activism: free speech, the end to Díaz's reelections, the abolition of military conscription, protections for "Indians," agrarian reforms, minimum wages, an eight-hour workday, and child labor legislation. *Regeneración* also found a substantial readership among Mexicans in southern Texas (Tejanos)—its circulation neared twenty thousand in the United States—who were feeling the harsh effects of a social and political transformation that destabilized a world with which they had long been familiar.

It proved a combustible mix. As late as the turn of the twentieth century, the land in southernmost Texas between the Nueces and the Rio Grande rivers had resisted the developmental changes that were sweeping the trans-Mississippi West since the War of the Rebellion. Over 90 percent of the population was ethnic Mexican, and the economy was organized chiefly around small-scale ranching and farming with a wide distribution of landownership. Those of

Anglo descent tended to reside in the towns and constituted something of an elite, but they had also made a variety of cultural and political accommodations with the Tejano majority. They learned Spanish, intermarried, often converted to Catholicism, and helped construct a political system organized around Tejano voting and office holding. At a time when Jim Crow was demanding rigid racial hierarchies and exclusions throughout Texas and the rest of the South, the Nueces "strip" clearly stood apart, more like northern Mexico in its social relations and cultural dispensations. For a U.S. Army officer, the area was "an American Congo."

That changed with the coming of the St. Louis, Brownsville, and Mexico Railway in 1904, the very year the Flores Magón brothers crossed the border. With breakneck speed, real estate developers lured thousands of Anglo farmers into the region with promises of an agricultural boom, and together they began to disrupt the social and political structure. Many Tejano cultivators and ranchers faced challenges to their property holdings in good part because land titles, dating back to the Treaty of Guadalupe Hidalgo, were complicated and at times impossible to retrieve. Thousands of acres changed hands, and as land prices rose precipitously, Tejanos who had been dispossessed slipped into the ranks of field hands for the aggressive agricultural entrepreneurs.

The new Anglo farmers and ranchers had no more respect for the region's political ways than they did for its economic ways. Rejecting any dependence on Tejano voters or officeholders, on the clientelist politics they claimed to abhor, and determined to control the levers of local government—especially taxation—to advance their projects, they turned instead to the time-tested methods that had proved so effective in disempowering African Americans across the South, including in eastern Texas: disfranchisement. Poll taxes, white primaries, and then the elimination of interpreters at voting places not only dramatically reduced Tejanos' electoral participation but ended their access to political power for decades. The Anglo newcomers turned as well to the codes of Jim Crow, especially in the budding towns of the river valleys, rigidifying what had been relatively fluid interactions of ethnicity and race. It was a dreadfully meaningful moment and an indication of how widely this system had come to be embedded in the United States: many of the white farmers and entrepreneurs were from the Midwest rather than the South.

There was no one response to the crisis. Some Tejanos struggled to preserve elements of the interethnic political machine that had operated to spread the benefits of local patronage. Others, especially merchants and small-business men, sought to reach an accommodation with the new order, calling for equal economic opportunities, nondiscriminatory education, respect for Mexican culture, and ethnic pluralism. In 1911, they gathered in Laredo for the Primer

Congreso Mexicanista, the largest assembly devoted to ethnic Mexican civil rights up to that time, and formed the Gran Liga Mexicanista, a forerunner of the League of United Latin American Citizens (LULAC), which would come to resemble the NAACP.

Yet for many of the Tejanos who bore the brunt of the capitalist trans-formation—small ranchers and ranch hands, skilled laborers, artisans, and shopkeepers—the response was more radical. Some had been drawn into locals established by the Socialist Party and some into the socialist Land League. More were influenced by the Flores Magóns and their paper, *Regener-ación*, some joining the PLM with visions of uniting "with American, Italian, Polish, and Negro *compañeros.*" All took keen note of the revolution unfolding across the border and the possibilities that it might open for those of Mexican ancestry, wherever they might reside. It was in this context, and behind a veil of secrecy, that the Plan de San Diego was hatched in the small southern Texas town of that name. Little is known about the making of the plan, however, save that among the signatories were readers of *Regeneración.*

The plan was an extraordinary document, so much so that there were, and are, doubts about its authenticity. It captured many of the radical currents of the time, from racial and ethnic nationalism to socialism and anticolonialism, while imagining an entirely different geopolitical future for the North Ameri-can continent. The plan called for the rising of the Liberating Army for Races and Peoples to commence against the United States on February 20, 1915, and immediately proclaim "the liberty of the individuals of the black race." The army's sights would then be set on establishing the "independence" of the states of Texas, New Mexico, Arizona, Colorado, and California, of which "the Repub-lic of Mexico was robbed in the most perfidious manner by North American imperialism," and on helping blacks to obtain six other American states out of which they "may form . . . a republic and they may be therefore independent." Guided by the Supreme Revolutionary Congress based in San Diego, Texas, the Liberating Army would also seek to win the support of Apaches and other Native peoples in return for the restoration of lands that had been taken from them by the governments of the United States and Mexico. No mercy would be shown to prisoners taken in this rebellion or to Anglo males sixteen years of age or older, and depending on the course of revolution in Mexico, the indepen-dent states of the Southwest might eventually rejoin their former country.

Very early in 1915, the plan was inadvertently revealed to public view when a man carrying the document into Texas from northern Mexico was arrested on the suspicions of another Tejano; February 20 passed without incident, and after a flurry of concern in the Anglo population the alarm subsided. Then, during the summer months, a series of cross-border attacks began, with raiding parties numbering between twenty and eighty. Called bandits and *sediciosos*, they moved up and down the Rio Grande valley, targeting ranches—most run by Anglos, though some by Tejanos regarded as complicit in the agricultural boom—stealing horses and other property, and at times killing the owners. They torched railroad trestles and cut telegraph lines. Although none of the *sediciosos* explicitly identified themselves with the plan, some appear to have insisted that "this section of the country was taken away from Mexico, and does not really belong to the United States." Another attack, this on a corner of the sprawling King Ranch, was carried out by sixty raiders hoisting a red flag emblazoned with the inscription "*igualdad e independencia.*"

That the revolution in Mexico had entered a particularly convulsive and bloody phase was very much part of the drama. The revolutionary factions that had briefly allied toward the end of toppling the Huerta dictatorship went to the sword over the political direction of the struggle soon thereafter. The peasant armies of Zapata in the south and, especially, Villa in the north, energized by the goal of agrarian reform, battled the forces of Carranza and Obregón, more given over to gradualism and modernization. For a time, it looked as though the Zapatistas and Villistas might prevail, and Villa worked to cultivate the favor of the United States. Owing to his knowledge of the dynamic north of Mexico, he had some supporters in the Wilson administration. At all events, the civil war between the factions (La Bola) created openings and alliances for the *sediciosos*, who regularly retreated into Tamaulipas and received assistance from the Carrancistas in control of that state's borderlands.

Although the Zapatistas and Villistas were briefly poised to gain the upper hand in the revolution, they plainly lacked what the Carrancistas and Obregonistas possessed: a national vision and the political skills to bring it about. Zapata and Villa had deeply loyal followers who were nonetheless focused on redressing local grievances and bolstering their villages; their program was revolutionary, but their horizons were mostly parochial. Carranza and Obregón looked to the big picture, to a reformed and revitalized Mexico with calculated bows to the demands of peasants and workers. Over time, this cosmopolitanism helped them on the field of battle (Obregón was a keen student of European warfare) as well as in the arena of diplomacy. Recognizing the radical dangers that Zapatistas and Villistas might represent if they came to rule (American business interests almost uniformly opposed them) and aiming to suppress the troubles in southern Texas, the Wilson administration threw its support to Carranza, and Carranza quickly moved against the *sediciosos*.

The harassment brought to bear by Carranza in Mexico was nothing compared with the repression unleashed in Texas. Anglo vigilantes and Texas Rangers lynched suspected *sediciosos* and more generally terrorized Tejanos in the southern Texas countryside. Many Tejanos consequently fled toward the relative safety of Brownsville or even across the border into Mexico, while Anglos took the opportunity to secure their dominance over the region. The manager of the King Ranch, reflecting the views of other large ranchers, called for the establishment of martial law and "concentration camps along the river," together with the building of a border road "for the use of the military." An Anglo lawyer went so far as to suggest "that we ought to compel all Mexican residents on the Border to go across the river until the troubles were over, and then go out and shoot all that were left." Exterminism was not, in the end, the main vehicle of Anglo rule; political reorganization, with disfranchisement, segregation, and the creation of new counties, proved more effective and lasting. But the toll was heavy. Several thousand Tejanos may have been murdered before relative quiet returned. "The cry was often heard," one Tejano leader reported, "'we have to make this a white man's country!!'"

Pancho Villa had his own troubles. The Wilson administration's recognition of Carranza was a major blow to Villa's military and political prospects; it cut off the flow of needed supplies and limited his maneuvering room. Villa returned the favor initially by attacking American interests at various points in northern Mexico, and then, in March 1916, with several hundred men, he crossed into the United States and raided the town of Columbus, New Mexico, where a cavalry unit was stationed. Wilson responded several days later by ordering Brigadier General John Pershing, a veteran of the Indian Wars and the Philippine insurrection, into Mexico on a "punitive expedition" meant to capture Villa and defang his army. It was not Pershing's first military foray into the northern Mexico desert lands. Years earlier, he had pursued Geronimo there and was now puffed up with greater ambitions. He soon had more than ten thousand American troops on the ground and called for an occupation of the entire country. "One must be a fool indeed to think that people half savaged and wholly ignorant will ever form a republic," Pershing's deputy pronounced. "A despot is all they know and want."

Wilson had no interest in such an occupation, and that was undoubtedly a good decision. Pershing could not even manage to bring in Villa. Over the course of ten months, Pershing and his troops hunted Villa across a wide area but to no avail. All the punitive expedition accomplished before it was withdrawn in February 1917 was angering Carranza for its violation of Mexican sovereignty and enhancing the popular reputation of Villa, whose army again grew in size. Indeed, amid the disarray created by Pershing across stretches of northern Mexico, *sedicioso* raids into Texas resumed and brought tensions between the governments of the United States and Mexico near to the boiling point. Wilson considered a declaration of war, pointing to Carranza's inability to secure the border, before coming to his senses.

Ironically, it was another version of the Plan de San Diego, one proffered by the Germans, that was to be the final step toward American involvement in the European war. Desperate to turn the tide in what had become a stalemated struggle, Germany decided to launch unrestricted submarine warfare and hoped to tie up the United States in Mexico to blunt the likely response. To that end, the German foreign secretary, Arthur Zimmermann, with Villa's recent raid apparently in mind, raised the possibility of Mexico "reconquer[ing] its former territories in Texas, New Mexico, and Arizona" in return for allying with Germany in a war against the United States. Zimmermann's telegram to this effect was intercepted in March 1917, and although Carranza had brushed off the proposal, one month later Wilson asked Congress for a declaration of war against Germany. General Pershing was then appointed commander of the American Expeditionary Force in Europe, a reward perhaps for his meritorious service in Mexico.

Although Wilson's vision of a postwar world organized around the principle of self-determination lifted the hopes of anticolonial movements around the globe, his invasions of revolutionary Mexico suggested what the boundaries of such a principle might be. Wilson never really contemplated the potential reach of self-determination, and although he did not specifically exclude colonized peoples of color from its reach, he thought of it chiefly in a European context. As Wilson's secretary of state Robert Lansing later maintained, self-determination was not meant to apply to "races, peoples, or communities whose state of barbarism or ignorance deprive them of the capacity to choose intelligently their political affiliations." This is hardly surprising. Wilson was a southerner, thought black and nonwhite people inferior or backward, viewed Reconstruction as a nightmare (he hailed the film *The Birth of a Nation*), brought racial segregation and exclusion into the federal bureaucracy, and, after the annexation treaty was signed in 1898, jumped on the imperial bandwagon. Even in retrospect, he never spoke favorably of the aspirations of Cubans and Filipinos for self-determination in their struggles against Spanish colonizers. At best, self-determination for colonial dependencies could be seen as a gradual process, extended "if they be fit to receive it"; it would not in Wilson's hands, as it was in Lenin's, be the entering wedge of a critique of Euro-American imperialism.

Yet the revolution in Mexico posed challenges that neither Cuba nor the Philippines had. It was simultaneously the last great bourgeois revolution of the seventeenth, eighteenth, and nineteenth centuries and the first great peasant revolution of the twentieth. And it created a distinctive state that extended the revolutionary impulses for decades. Indeed, the simultaneity became evident in 1917 as Carranza began to consolidate his power and a convention drafted a new constitution for Mexico.

Looking back to the constitution of 1857 that the brief Huerta dictatorship had brazenly violated, Carranza hoped the new document would secure federal supremacy, define Mexican nationality and the individual rights that went along with it, strengthen the executive, and deepen liberal anticlericalism while moving lightly in the areas of social reform. He hoped, that is, to establish a framework that could bring peace between factions and some rewards to the rural and urban masses who supported the revolution without jeopardizing the property and developmental basis of the regime or the further capitalist modernization of Mexico.

What he got was something rather different. Meeting in Querétaro, northwest of Mexico City, the constitutional convention was quickly dominated by the "Jacobins," a group influenced by social experimentation in some of the states (not to mention radical currents in the Euro-Atlantic world) and far more committed to social rights, contingent notions of property, worker empowerment, and agrarian reform. They crafted a remarkable constitution, resonating with ideas of the Flores Magóns, that guaranteed universal education, an eight-hour workday, a minimum wage, profit sharing, equal pay for equal work "regardless of sex or nationality," considerations for pregnant and nursing women who worked, workmen's compensation, and the right to organize, strike, and bargain collectively. The constitution made ownership of lands, waters, and natural resources conditional on the will of the national state, gave the state the right to place limits on the use of private property as "the public interest may demand," and restricted property ownership to Mexicans or Mexican companies, a far cry from the orientation of the Porfiriato. Foreigners would be able to establish property ownership only with the permission of the state and if the property was at least a hundred kilometers from a territorial border. Equally important, the constitution made provision for the division of large estates, the protection of smallholdings, and the return of communal lands that had previously been despoiled.

It was a constitution that brimmed with economic nationalism, political liberalism, and social democracy, one that constructed a more inclusive polity than had ever existed in Mexico or, for that matter, anywhere else in the world, and yet one that mixed corporatist and localist features in the name of modernization and social justice. But it was one thing to encode the principles and quite another to carry them through. Over the next six years, while land reform moved forward incrementally, the struggle over the direction and fate of the revolution continued its turbulent and bloody course. Initially, Zapata, then Carranza and Villa, were felled by assassins; Obregón would meet a similar fate in 1928. In the meantime, the first large-scale migration of ethnic Mexicans into the United States commenced, and the rule of the caudillos gave way to the formation of a political party—the Partido Nacional Revolucionario—that would govern Mexico for decades (it morphed into the PRI) in the name of the "revolution."

The stage was then set for the emergence of Lázaro Cárdenas, who moved the revolution into its last and most radical phase. During the Depression-worn 1930s, he not only accelerated land confiscations and redistributions (totaling fifty million acres, twice the acreage of his predecessors combined) and encouraged strikes among workers who had "always suffered injustices, disregard, and privations" but also nationalized all foreign-owned companies, especially in the sectors where American investments were concentrated: oil, mining, railroads, electrical power, and communications. It was a signal historical moment in the hemisphere. While the United States had tried to turn Mexico—much as it did Cuba, Panama, and the Caribbean basin—into a protectorate, with borders that could easily be traversed in the service of economic and political power, the Mexicans pushed back and marked a new border in defense of their revolution.

None of this was clear as an armistice in 1919 suspended the fighting in what would be thirty years of global warfare. The United States, having sought "peace without victory," emerged with a great victory of its own: as the most formidable power in the world. It could not have been readily expected. Six decades earlier, the country had been unhinged by the largest of a series of rebellions, this by slaveholders who had ridden the cotton plant to enormous wealth, and both Britain and France had waited to preside over the formal dissolution. At the very least, they imagined a United States seriously weakened and unable to fend off their own encroachments in the hemisphere, as the French move into Mexico suggested. But in mobilizing to defeat the slaveholders' challenge, the Republican state empowered new classes of industrialists and financiers and sought to extend its authority over the far reaches of American territory. Forcing the rebellious states to surrender, abolishing the slave property that had undergirded their power, enlisting slaves into the military, establishing birthright citizenship, and giving their party a basis in the South, the Republicans also proclaimed the sovereignty of a new nation-state.

For a time, this social and political revolution moved further than anyone could have imagined in 1861, certainly further than any revolution of its time had moved. Former slaves were voting, holding office, and helping to create new polities and civil societies. Former slaveholders had been deprived of their most valuable property, weakened on the ground, and driven from effective national power. Petty producers were fighting to assert popular control over the greenback money supply, and skilled workers were fighting for an eight-hour day; new national organizations like the Knights of Labor called for an end to the "wages system." A battle for the future of the nation was clearly being waged, and in large part its outcome would be determined in the South and in the trans-Mississippi West, where many of the boundaries of power would be tested.

Indeed, it was there that the patterns of development that supported nineteenth-century American capitalism were most sharply in evidence, on the land, in mines, on the railroads, and in a variety of workplaces. And it was there that the nation-state revealed its imperial dispositions, imposing martial law, creating large territories under its jurisdiction, suppressing Indian counter-sovereignties, and demanding adherence to a set of legal and cultural norms as the price of inclusion. By the end of the century, the battle was being won—with the aid of the courts and the military arms of the state—by the owners of capital, factories, and large landholdings. But in the massive struggles of ideas and wills and ways, there were major reckonings and adjustments, so that the reconstructions undertaken as of the 1890s would show the marks of the losers as well as the winners and of the lessons being learned in what some were calling America's "colonies" within its own borders. The corporate capitalism that began to emerge was something new and could not help but energize the social democracy it tried mightily to absorb.

The imperial projects of the 1890s and early twentieth century plainly owed to experiences in the South, the West, and the southwestern borderlands, but they were new as well. They were no longer given over to the encouragement of settler colonialism as had been the case across the continent for most of the nineteenth century, nor did they imagine the sorts of territorial colonies that Europe's powers had been accumulating in Africa and Asia (though the annexation of the Philippines came close). They looked instead to maintaining economic and political "order" in the hemisphere while making the world safe for trade in the goods that the United States produced and the resources it needed to consume. This, after all, might be a way to keep the peace at home without yielding to the redistributionist demands offered up by a raft of popular movements. It would be a world in which the borders of American nationhood were well secured while the borders of American power remained limitless.

Yet as the United States emerged from the armistice and the Versailles accords as the nation whose power and ambitions were most in ascendancy, there were also signs of potential limits in the future. The Bolshevik Revolution toppled Eurasia's mightiest empire and established the world's first socialist regime. Popular movements of the Left and the Right erupted across the European continent and Japan and, like the Bolsheviks, defined themselves against the world order that the United States seemed to be advancing. People of color in Asia, Africa, and the African diaspora began pushing back against the racialized imperialisms to which they had been subjected and forging new alliances. And within the United States itself, the massive labor unrest and racial violence of 1919 suggested that social peace would not easily be bought.

But it might have been in neighboring Mexico, often overlooked in the moment, that the challenges to a world over which the United States now hoped to preside were most readily in evidence. It was there that the disruptive forces of capitalism, especially in the countryside, provoked their initial revolutionary backlash. There that ideals of nationalism, anticolonialism, and social democracy mixed in a most explosive way. There that party and state would eventually become almost indistinguishable. There that the nationalization of economic resources and foreign-owned property would seek to chart another road forward. And it was there, on the border of the United States, that the long nineteenth century first gave way to the twentieth.

Acknowledgments

Books such as this one, which have been quite some time in the making, benefit from so many forms of advice and encouragement that I fear overlooking or not adequately acknowledging all of them. If I do neglect to mention an individual or institution, please let me apologize at the outset. But I shall do my best, and I am happy to note as many of my large debts as possible.

I should first like to express my thanks to the School of Arts & Sciences at the University of Pennsylvania, and to Dean Rebecca Bushnell in particular, for her generosity in enabling me to take the leave time necessary to research and then write this book. Sincere thanks as well to the National Endowment for the Humanities for a year-long fellowship that helped fund some of that leave time.

Many of the ideas that found their way into this book took shape in graduate seminars I taught during the past decade at the University of Pennsylvania and in papers and lectures I have had the opportunity to present at conferences and to university history departments. I'd like to thank the outstanding Penn students who challenged me in a variety of ways, especially Jessie Regunberg, Roberto Saba, Evgenia Schnayder Shoop, Kevin Waite, and Emma Teitelman, who read the entire manuscript and gave me the benefit of their criticisms over the course of two extended meetings. Emma Teitelman was also of great help in putting together the book's bibliographic essay as well as the collection of images that appear in its pages.

I'd like to thank those in attendance for presentations at the Johns Hopkins University (especially Philip Morgan and Michael Johnson), Emory University (especially Gyanendra Pandey), the University of Wisconsin (especially Stephen Kantrowitz), the State University of New York at Geneseo (especially Justin Behrand), the conference "Beyond Freedom: New Directions in the Study of Emancipation" at Yale University, the Robert Fortenbaugh Memorial Lecture at Gettysburg College, the Frank L. Klement Lecture at Marquette University, the Program on the Study of Capitalism at Harvard University (especially Sven Beckert, Alexander Keyssar, Christine Desan, and Liat Spiro), the conference "The World the Civil War Made" at Penn State University (especially Greg Downs and Kate Masur), the conference "Race, Labor, and Citizenship in the Post-Emancipation South" at the College of Charleston, the symposium "W. E. B Du Bois's *Black Reconstruction* in America" at Duke University, the conference

"Remaking North American Sovereignty" at the University of Calgary's Banff Centre (especially Frank Towers and Tom Bender), the Shelby Cullom Davis Center at Princeton University, and the conference "Civil War Wests" sponsored by Southern Methodist University (especially Adam Arenson and Andrew Graybill).

Eric Foner did me the great honor of inviting me to write this book for the Penguin History of the United States series that he edits, an honor all the more humbling and daunting given his own powerful contributions to the fields and years this book covers. He was also very generous and supportive in allowing me to find my way through it and offering—with remarkable speed and insight—editorial comments and suggestions. I am deeply grateful to him. I am extremely grateful, as well, to a number of good friends and colleagues who have read portions, or all, of the manuscript, have saved me from errors, and, most of all, have encouraged me to take the risks I was interested in: Sven Beckert, Justin Behrend, Ira Berlin, Junot Diaz, Gregory Downs, Karl Jacoby, Benjamin Johnson, Larry Powell, Jonathan Prude, Amy Stanley, and Tom Summerhill. At Penguin (now Penguin Random House), Wendy Wolf showed me more patience than I deserved and then more enthusiasm than I expected; I thank her sincerely for both.

Susan Wishingrad came into my life as I was completing this book and did a great deal to help me finish it. Artist, lawyer, intellectual, she read the manuscript with great understanding and insight, pushed me in some directions I had neglected to follow, and gave me confidence in the book's potential appeal to a wider interested readership. Equally if not more important, she taught me more than she knows about what is meaningful and joyous in life.

My son Declan and daughter Saoirse have watched this book unfold and, on more than one occasion, have helped me through rough going of various sorts. They have also read portions of the book and let me know if it did or didn't make sense—and their instincts were invariably on the mark. But most of all they have amazed and rewarded me with their intellectual and athletic gifts, their humor, their worldliness, their fantastic company, their warmth, their heart, and their incredible love. I don't know what I've done to deserve them, and surely don't know what I'd do—or would have done—without them.

This book has a special dedication: to the many students, especially graduate students, I've taught over the years at the University of Delaware, the University of California, San Diego, Northwestern University, New York University, and the University of Pennsylvania, and to the students I've worked with in a number of community-based programs in Chicago and Philadelphia. There's often a sense that teaching and learning are something of a vertical experience: the one dispenses knowledge and the other imbibes it. No one who participates in education knows this to be true, but I've had the great fortune to discover first-hand that teaching is always most about learning, and that those of us who teach are often the greatest of the beneficiaries. My research and writing, as well as my teaching, have been influenced immeasurably by students who have pushed back, questioned my assumptions, challenged my interpretive logic, and taken off in directions I never thought to pursue myself. For them, and especially for the ones who have gone on to become wonderful scholars and teachers in their own right, who continue to teach me and inspire me with their commitment and insight, I dedicate this book.

Bibliography

Writing a book such as this—one that is simultaneously "synthetic" and interpretive—was only possible because of many years of thinking, researching, writing, and teaching about the history of the nineteenth century, the development of capitalism, the abolition of slavery, popular struggles to reshape the organization of society, the rise of nation-states, and the lineaments of empire. But the book is also very much indebted to the work and imagination of a great many scholars—historians, political scientists, social theorists, and anthropologists among them—who have opened my eyes to problems large and small and have challenged me to think harder and more deeply about this important historical period.

Needless to say, a full and fair accounting of this scholarship, not to mention the original source material on which it is based, would require many more pages than I have here. Thus, I will try to identify the work that I have found most important and useful for each of the chapters and the topics embraced by them, privileging books rather than articles, and secondary sources rather than either published primary or archival records. Especially significant articles will be noted, as will original source material that is readily accessible for scholars and general readers alike.

Prologue

My understanding of the nineteenth and early twentieth centuries, not only in the United States but in the larger world of which it was an integral part, owes to some remarkable scholars who have helped me conceptualize the geographical dimensions, the social and political dynamics, the fields of force, and the chronological markers. They include Eric J. Hobsbawm, especially his multivolume *The Age of Revolution: Europe, 1789–1848* (New York: World, 1962), *The Age of Capital, 1848–1875* (New York: Scribner, 1975), *The Age of Empire, 1875–1914* (New York: Pantheon, 1987), and *The Age of Extremes: A History of the World, 1914–1991* (New York: Pantheon, 1994), as well as his *Primitive Rebels: Studies in Archaic Forms of Social Movement in the 19th and 20th Centuries* (New York: W. W. Norton, 1965), *Labouring Men: Studies in the History of Labour* (New York: Basic Books, 1964), and *Nations and Nationalism Since 1780: Programme, Myth, Reality* (New York: Cambridge University Press, 1990); Barrington Moore Jr., *Social Origins of Dictatorship and Democracy: Lord and Peasant in the Making of the Modern World* (Boston: Beacon Press, 1966); E. P. Thompson, *Making of the English Working Class* (New York: Vintage, 1963), *Whigs and Hunters: The Origins of the Black Act* (New York: Pantheon, 1976), and *Customs in Common* (London: Merlin Press, 1991); James C. Scott, *Domination and the Arts of Resistance: Hidden Transcripts* (New Haven, Conn.: Yale University Press, 1990), *Seeing Like a State: How Certain Schemes to Improve the Human Condition Have Failed* (New Haven, Conn.: Yale University Press, 1998), and *The Art of Not Being Governed: An Upland History of Southeast Asia* (New Haven, Conn.: Yale University Press, 2009);

Benedict Anderson, *Imagined Communities: Reflections on the Origins and Spread of Nationalism* (London: Verso, 1983); Ranajit Guha, *Elementary Aspects of Peasant Insurgency in Colonial India* (Durham, N.C.: Duke University Press, 1999); Dipesh Chakrabarty, *Provincializing Europe: Postcolonial Thought and Historical Difference* (Princeton, N.J.: Princeton University Press, 2000); David Brion Davis, *The Problem of Slavery in the Age of Revolution, 1770–1823* (Ithaca, N.Y.: Cornell University Press, 1975); Partha Chatterjee, *The Politics of the Governed: Reflections on Popular Politics in Most of the World* (New York: Columbia University Press, 2004); D. W. Meinig, *The Shaping of America: A Geographical Perspective on 500 Years of History*, 4 vols. (New Haven, Conn.: Yale University Press, 1986–2006); Thomas Bender, *A Nation Among Nations: America's Place in World History* (New York: Hill and Wang, 2006); C. A. Bayly, *The Birth of the Modern World, 1780–1914* (London: Wiley-Blackwell, 2003); Florencia Mallon, *The Defense of Community in Peru's Central Highlands: Peasant Struggle and Capitalist Transition, 1860–1940* (Princeton, N.J.: Princeton University Press, 1983); Barbara Weinstein, *The Amazon Rubber Boom, 1850–1920* (Stanford, Calif.: Stanford University Press, 1983).

My understanding of empires as political, cultural, and historical state formations has been advanced by Frederick Cooper and Jane Burbank, *Empires in World History: Power and the Politics of Difference* (Princeton, N.J.: Princeton University Press, 2010); Charles S. Maier, *Among Empires: American Ascendancy and Its Predecessors* (Cambridge, Mass.: Harvard University Press, 2007); Ann Laura Stoler, *Carnal Knowledge and Imperial Power: Race and the Intimate in Colonial Rule* (Berkeley: University of California Press, 2002); Frederick Cooper and Ann Laura Stoler, eds., *Tensions of Empire: Colonial Cultures in a Bourgeois World* (Berkeley: University of California Press, 1997); Frederick Cooper, *Colonialism in Question: Theory, Knowledge, History* (Berkeley: University of California Press, 2005); Edward Said, *Orientalism* (New York: Vintage, 1979) and *Culture and Imperialism* (New York: Alfred A. Knopf, 1993); J. H. Elliott, *Empires of the Atlantic World: Britain and Spain in America, 1492–1830* (New Haven, Conn.: Yale University Press, 2006); Richard Price, *Making Empire: Colonial Encounters and the Creation of Imperial Rule in Nineteenth-Century Africa* (New York: Cambridge University Press, 2008); William Appleman Williams, *The Roots of Modern American Empire* (New York: Vintage, 1970).

My understanding of the relations and development of capitalism has been shaped by Maurice Dobb, *Studies in the Development of Capitalism* (New York: International, 1947); Rodney Hilton, ed., *The Transition from Feudalism to Capitalism* (London: New Left Books, 1976); T. H. Ashton and C. H. E. Philpin, eds., *The Brenner Debate: Agrarian Class Structure and Economic Development in Preindustrial Europe* (Cambridge, U.K.: Cambridge University Press, 1987); Immanuel Wallerstein, *The Modern World System*, 4 vols. (Berkeley: University of California Press, 2011); Fernand Braudel, *Civilization and Capitalism*, 3 vols. (New York: Harper and Row, 1982–84); Ellen Meiksins Wood, *The Origin of Capitalism: A Longer View* (London: Verso, 2002); C. B. Macpherson, *The Political Theory of Possessive Individualism: Hobbes to Locke* (Oxford: Oxford University Press, 1975); Karl Polanyi, *The Great Transformation: The Political and Economic Origins of Our Time* (Boston: Beacon Press, 1957); Eugene D. Genovese, *The Political Economy of Slavery: Studies in the Society and Economy of the Slave South* (New York: Pantheon, 1965); Sven Beckert, *Empire of Cotton: A Global History* (New York: Alfred A. Knopf, 2014); John Tutino, *Making a New World: Founding Capitalism in the Bajío and Spanish North*

America (Durham, N.C.: Duke University Press, 2011); Kenneth Pomeranz, *The Great Divergence: China, Europe, and the Making of the Modern World Economy* (Princeton, N.J.: Princeton University Press, 2001); Sidney Mintz, *Sweetness and Power: The Place of Sugar in Modern History* (New York: Penguin, 1986); David Harvey, *The Condition of Postmodernity: An Inquiry into the Origins of Cultural Change* (Oxford: Blackwell, 1990); Antonio Gramsci, *Selections from the Prison Notebooks*, ed. and trans. Quintin Hoare and Geoffrey N. Smith (New York: International, 1971); Jürgen Habermas, *The Structural Transformation of the Public Sphere*, trans. Thomas Burger (Cambridge, Mass.: MIT Press, 1989).

Ambitious and influential treatments of the nineteenth-century United States include Sean Wilentz, *The Rise of American Democracy: Jefferson to Lincoln* (New York: W. W. Norton, 2005); T. J. Jackson Lears, *Rebirth of a Nation: The Making of Modern America, 1877–1920* (New York: Harper Perennial, 2010); Rogers Smith, *Civic Ideals: Conflicting Visions of Citizenship in U.S. History* (New Haven, Conn.: Yale University Press, 1999); Eric Foner, *The Story of American Freedom* (New York: W. W. Norton, 1998); Richard White, *It's Your Misfortune and None of My Own: A New History of the American West* (Norman: University of Oklahoma Press, 1993); William Appleman Williams, *The Contours of American History* (Chicago: Quadrangle Books, 1961); Alexander Keyssar, *The Right to Vote: The Contested History of Democracy in the United States* (New York: Basic Books, 2000). Also see the impressive world survey by Jürgen Osterhammel, *The Transformation of the World: A Global History of the Nineteenth Century* (Princeton, N.J.: Princeton University Press, 2014).

Chapter One: Borderlands

My thinking about the concept of borderlands has been influenced by a growing body of literature interested in exploring the liminal spaces in which social relations, cultures, and claims to sovereign authority make contact, struggle, and reshape one another. For an important statement that speaks to many of the larger themes of this book, see Jeremy Adelman and Stephen Aron, "From Borderlands to Borders: Empires, Nation-States, and the People in Between in North America," *American Historical Review* 104 (June 1999): 814–41. Also see Herbert E. Bolton, *The Spanish Borderlands: A Chronicle of Old Florida and the Southwest* (New Haven, Conn.: Yale University Press, 1921); Richard White, *The Middle Ground: Indians, Empires, and Republics in the Great Lakes Region* (New York: Cambridge University Press, 1991); Pekka Hämäläinen and Samuel Truett, "On Borderlands," *Journal of American History* 98, no. 2 (Sept. 2011): 338–61; Stephen Aron, *American Confluence: The Missouri Frontier from Borderland to Border States* (Bloomington: Indiana University Press, 2006); Samuel Truett and Elliott Young, eds., *Continental Crossroads: Remapping U.S.-Mexico Borderlands History* (Durham, N.C.: Duke University Press, 2004); David J. Weber, "Turner, the Boltonians, and the Borderlands," *American Historical Review* 91 (Feb. 1986): 66–81; Karl Jacoby, *Shadows at Dawn: A Borderlands Massacre and the Violence of History* (New York: Penguin Press, 2008); Albert L. Hurtado, "Parkmanizing the Spanish Borderlands: Bolton, Turner, and the Historians' World," *Western Historical Quarterly* 26 (Summer 1995): 149–67. For a searching treatment of the broader Atlantic context that interrogates the legal complexities of sovereignty in the early modern period, see Lauren Benton, *A Search for Sovereignty: Law and Geography in European Empires, 1400–1900* (New York: Cambridge University Press, 2010).

For the early history of independent Mexico and the struggle between center and periphery, see Timothy Anna, *Forging Mexico, 1821–1835* (Lincoln: University of Nebraska Press, 1998); Christon I. Archer, ed., *The Birth of Modern Mexico, 1780–1824* (Wilmington, Del.: Rowman and Littlefield, 2003); Timothy J. Henderson, *The Mexican Wars for Independence* (New York: Hill and Wang, 2009); Enrique Krauze, *Siglo de caudillos: Biografía política de México, 1810–1910* (Barcelona: Tusquets, 1994); Jan Bazant, "From Independence to the Liberal Republic, 1821–1867," in *Mexico Since Independence*, ed. Leslie Bethell (Cambridge, U.K.: Cambridge University Press, 1991), 1–48; Stuart F. Voss, *On the Periphery of Nineteenth-Century Mexico: Sonora and Sinaloa, 1810–1877* (Tucson: University of Arizona Press, 1982); Cynthia Radding, *Wandering Peoples: Ethnic Spaces and Ecological Frontiers in Northwestern Mexico* (Durham, N.C.: Duke University Press, 1997); Will Fowler, *Santa Anna of Mexico* (Lincoln: University of Nebraska Press, 2009); Jaime Rodriguez, ed., *The Independence of Mexico and the Creation of the New Nation* (Los Angeles: UCLA Latin American Center Publications, University of California, 1989); David Weber, *The Mexican Frontier, 1821–1846* (Albuquerque: University of New Mexico Press, 1982); Andrés Reséndez, *Changing National Identities at the Frontier: Texas and New Mexico, 1800–1850* (New York: Cambridge University Press, 2005).

The literature on Native societies on the North American continent has become vast, sophisticated, and challenging in its implications for how we approach the history of the United States. Among the works that I have found most important, especially for the late eighteenth and early nineteenth centuries, are Daniel Richter, *Facing East from Indian Country: A Native History of Early America* (Cambridge, Mass.: Harvard University Press, 2003); James Merrell, *The Indians' New World: Catawbas and Their Neighbors from European Contact Through the Era of Removal* (Chapel Hill: University of North Carolina Press, 1989); Pekka Hämäläinen, *The Comanche Empire* (New Haven, Conn.: Yale University Press, 2008); Richard White, *The Roots of Dependency: Subsistence, Environment, and Social Change Among the Choctaws, Pawnees, and Navajos* (Lincoln: University of Nebraska Press, 1983); James F. Brooks, *Captives and Cousins: Slavery, Kinship, and Community in the Southwest Borderlands* (Chapel Hill: University of North Carolina Press, 2002); Juliana Barr, *Peace Came in the Form of a Woman: Indians and Spaniards in the Texas Borderlands* (Chapel Hill: University of North Carolina Press, 2007); Ned Blackhawk, *Violence over the Land: Indians and Empires in the Early American West* (Cambridge, Mass.: Harvard University Press, 2004); Kathleen DuVal, *The Native Ground: Indians and Colonists in the Heart of the Continent* (Philadelphia: University of Pennsylvania Press, 2006); Lance R. Blyth, *Chiricahua and Janos: Communities of Violence in the Southwestern Borderlands, 1680–1880* (Lincoln: University of Nebraska Press, 2012); Tiya Miles, *Ties That Bind: The Story of an Afro-Cherokee Family in Slavery and Freedom* (Berkeley: University of California Press, 2005); Gregory Evans Dowd, *A Spirited Resistance: The North American Indians' Struggle for Unity, 1745–1815* (Baltimore: Johns Hopkins University Press, 1993); Claudio Saunt, *A New Order of Things: Property, Power, and the Transformation of the Creek Indians, 1733–1816* (New York: Cambridge University Press, 1999); William G. McLoughlin, *Cherokee Renaissance in the New Republic* (Princeton, N.J.: Princeton University Press, 1986); Stephen Warren, *The Shawnees and Their Neighbors, 1795–1870* (Urbana: University of Illinois Press, 2008).

The settlement and conflicts eventuating in the Texas Revolution have long been surrounded in myth and misinformation; they have become the stuff of folklore. But for serious scholarly treatments that suggest the many contingencies, see Gregg Cantrell, *Stephen F. Austin: Empresario of Texas* (New Haven, Conn.: Yale University Press, 1999); Randolph B. Campbell, *An Empire for Slavery: The Peculiar Institution in Texas, 1821–1865* (Baton Rouge: Louisiana State University Press, 1989); Gary Clayton Anderson, *The Conquest of Texas: Ethnic Cleansing in the Promised Land, 1820–1875* (Norman: University of Oklahoma Press, 2005); Carlos Castañeda, ed., *The Mexican Side of the Texas Revolution* (Dallas: P. L. Turner, 1928); José Enrique de la Peña, *With Santa Anna in Texas: A Personal Narrative of the Revolution*, trans. and ed. Carmen Perry (1936; College Station: Texas A&M University Press, 1975); Paul Lack, *The Texas Revolutionary Experience: A Political and Social History, 1835–1836* (College Station: Texas A&M University Press, 1992); William C. Binkley, *The Texas Revolution* (Baton Rouge: Louisiana State University Press, 1952); David Montejano, *Anglos and Mexicans in the Making of Texas, 1836–1986* (Austin: University of Texas Press, 1987); Andrés Tijerina, *Tejanos and Texas Under the Mexican Flag, 1821–1836* (College Station: Texas A&M University Press, 1994); Alwyn Barr, *Texans in Revolt: The Battle for San Antonio, 1835* (Austin: University of Texas Press, 1990); Stephen L. Hardin, *Texas Iliad: A Military History of the Texas Revolution, 1835–1836* (Austin: University of Texas Press, 1994); James W. Pohl and Stephen L. Hardin, "The Military History of the Texas Revolution," *Southwestern Historical Quarterly* 89 (Jan. 1986): 269–308.

On the imperial visions of early political leaders and policy makers in the United States, see Peter S. Onuf, *Jefferson's Empire: The Language of American Nationhood* (Charlottesville: University Press of Virginia, 2000); Eliga H. Gould, *Among the Powers of the Earth: The American Revolution and the Making of a New World Empire* (Cambridge, Mass.: Harvard University Press, 2014); J. C. A. Stagg, *Borderlines in the Borderlands: James Madison and the Spanish American Frontier, 1776–1821* (New Haven, Conn.: Yale University Press, 2009); Jay Sexton, *The Monroe Doctrine: Empire and Nation in Nineteenth-Century America* (New York: Hill and Wang, 2011); Bradford Perkins, *The Creation of a Republican Empire, 1776–1865* (New York: Cambridge University Press, 1993); Robert W. Tucker and David C. Hendrickson, *Empire of Liberty: The Statecraft of Thomas Jefferson* (New York: Oxford University Press, 1992); David C. Hendrickson, *Union, Nation, or Empire: The American Debate over International Relations, 1789–1941* (Lawrence: University Press of Kansas, 2009); Marc Egnal, *A Mighty Empire: The Origins of the American Revolution* (Ithaca, N.Y.: Cornell University Press, 1988); Jack Greene, *Peripheries and Center: Constitutional Development in the Extended Polities of the British Empire and the United States, 1607–1788* (Athens: University of Georgia Press, 1986).

On the Haitian Revolution and its relation to imperial ambitions in the United States and the purchase of Louisiana, see C. L. R. James, *Black Jacobins: Toussaint L'Ouverture and the San Domingo Revolution* (1939; New York: Vintage, 1963); Laurent Dubois, *Avengers of the New World: The Story of the Haitian Revolution* (Cambridge, Mass.: Harvard University Press, 2004); David P. Geggus, ed., *The Impact of the Haitian Revolution in the Atlantic World* (Columbia: University of South Carolina Press, 2001); Gordon S. Brown, *Toussaint's Clause: The Founding Fathers and the Haitian Revolution* (Jackson: University Press of Mississippi, 2005); Jon Kukla, *A Wilderness So Immense: The Louisiana Purchase and the Destiny of America* (New York: Anchor Books, 2004); Thomas Fleming, *The Louisiana Purchase* (New York: Wiley, 2003); Robert D. Bush, *The Louisiana Purchase in Global Context* (New York: Routledge, 2013); Lawrence N. Powell, *The*

Accidental City: Improvising New Orleans (Cambridge, Mass.: Harvard University Press, 2012); Peter J. Kastor, *The Nation's Crucible: The Louisiana Purchase and the Creation of America* (New Haven, Conn.: Yale University Press, 2004); Laurent Dubois, "The Haitian Revolution and the Sale of Louisiana," in *Empires of the Imagination: Transatlantic Histories of the Louisiana Purchase*, ed. Peter J. Kastor and Francois Weil (Charlottesville: University of Virginia Press, 2009), 93–113; Robert Paquette, "Revolutionary St. Domingue in the Making of Territorial Louisiana," in *A Turbulent Time: The French Revolution and the Greater Caribbean*, ed. David Barry Gaspar and David P. Geggus (Bloomington: Indiana University Press, 1997), 204–25; Tim Matthewson, *A Proslavery Foreign Policy: Haitian-American Relations during the Early Republic* (Westport, Conn.: Praeger, 2003).

On imperial expansion and the efforts to dislodge Native peoples through military, political, and diplomatic means as well as Native American resistance, see Reginald Horsman, *Expansion and American Indian Policy, 1783–1812* (East Lansing: Michigan State University Press, 1967); Theda Perdue, *Slavery and the Evolution of Cherokee Society, 1540–1866* (Knoxville: University of Tennessee Press, 1979); Theda Perdue and Michael D. Green, *The Cherokee Nation and the Trail of Tears* (New York: Penguin Press, 2007); Kevin Mulroy, *Freedom on the Border: The Seminole Maroons in Florida, the Indian Territory, Coahuila, and Texas* (Lubbock: Texas Tech University Press, 1993); Kenneth Porter, *Black Seminoles: History of a Freedom-Seeking People* (Gainesville: University Press of Florida, 1996) and *The Negro on the American Frontier* (New York: Arno Press, 1971); Jane Landers, *Black Society in Spanish Florida* (Urbana: University of Illinois Press, 1999); Ronald N. Satz, *American Indian Policy in the Jacksonian Era* (Lincoln: University of Nebraska Press, 1975); Michael P. Rogin, *Fathers and Children: Andrew Jackson and the Subjugation of the American Indian* (New York: Vintage, 1975); John K. Mahon, *History of the Second Seminole War, 1835–1842* (Gainesville: University Presses of Florida, 1985); Michael D. Green, *The Politics of Indian Removal: Creek Government and Society in Crisis* (Lincoln: University of Nebraska Press, 1982); Daniel Littlefield, *Africans and Seminoles: From Removal to Emancipation* (Westport, Conn.: Greenwood Press, 1977); Anthony F. C. Wallace, *The Long Bitter Trail: Andrew Jackson and the Indians* (New York: Hill and Wang, 1993); Tim A. Garrison, *The Legal Ideology of Indian Removal: The Southern Judiciary and the Sovereignty of Native American Nations* (Athens: University of Georgia Press, 2002); Francis P. Prucha, *The Great Father: The United States Government and the American Indians*, vol. 1 (Lincoln: University of Nebraska Press, 1984); Francis P. Prucha, ed., *Documents of United States Indian Policy* (Lincoln: University of Nebraska Press, 2000). For an important contextual argument, see James H. Merrell, "American Nations Old and New: Reflections on Indians in the Early Republic," *Native Americans and the Early Republic*, ed. Frederick E. Hoxie, Ronald Hoffman, and Peter J. Albert (Charlottesville: University Press of Virginia, 1999), 333–53.

Chapter Two: Slavery and Political Culture

The literature on the early development of antislavery in the broad Atlantic world is enormous, but any interested reader must begin with David Brion Davis's multivolume masterwork on the problem of slavery: *The Problem of Slavery in Western Culture* (Ithaca, N.Y.: Cornell University Press, 1966); *The Problem of Slavery in the Age of Revolution, 1770–1823* (Ithaca, N.Y.: Cornell University Press, 1975); and most recently *The Problem of Slavery in the Age of Emancipation* (New York: Alfred A. Knopf, 2014). Also important are Eric Williams, *Capitalism and Slavery* (Chapel Hill: University of North Carolina Press, 1944); Christopher L. Brown, *Moral Capital: Foundations of British Abolitionism* (Chapel Hill: University of North Carolina Press, 2006); Robin Blackburn, *The American Crucible: Slavery, Emancipation, and Human Rights* (London: Verso, 2011) and *The Overthrow of Colonial Slavery, 1776–1848* (London: Verso, 1988); Manisha Sinha, *The Slave's Cause: A History of Abolition* (New Haven, Conn.: Yale University Press, 2016); David Eltis, *Economic Growth and the Ending of the Atlantic Slave Trade* (Oxford: Oxford University Press, 1987); Catherine Hall, *Civilizing Subjects: Colony and Metropole in the English Imagination, 1830–1867* (Chicago: University of Chicago Press, 2002); Sibylle Fischer, *Modernity Disavowed: Haiti and the Cultures of Slavery in the Age of Revolution* (Durham, N.C.: Duke University Press, 2004); Thomas Holt, *The Problem of Freedom: Race, Labor, and Politics in Jamaica and Britain, 1832–1938* (Baltimore: Johns Hopkins University Press, 1992); Diana Paton, *No Bond but the Law: Punishment, Race, and Gender in Jamaican State Formation, 1780–1870* (Durham, N.C.: Duke University Press, 2004); Jean R. Soderlund, *Quakers and Slavery: A Divided Spirit* (Princeton, N.J.: Princeton University Press, 1985); P. J. Staudenraus, *The African Colonization Movement, 1816–1868* (New York: Columbia University Press, 1961); Eric Burin, *Slavery and the Peculiar Solution: A History of the American Colonization Society* (Gainesville: University Press of Florida, 2008). On Benjamin Lundy, see Merton L. Dillon, *Benjamin Lundy and the Struggle for Negro Freedom* (Urbana: University of Illinois Press, 1966).

The role of slaves and free people of color in advancing the goals of antislavery and in helping to build an early movement have, until fairly recently, been overlooked or outright ignored despite the revolutionary and rebellious convulsions of the age. But a growing body of literature has been rectifying this oversight and painting a picture of the cultural and political complexities of the African Atlantic. Among the best works with a hemispheric perspective are John K. Thornton, *Africa and Africans in the Making of the Atlantic World, 1400–1800* (New York: Cambridge University Press, 1993); Emilia Viotti da Costa, *Crowns of Glory, Tears of Blood: The Demerara Slave Rebellion of 1823* (New York: Oxford University Press, 1994); Michael Craton, *Testing the Chains: Resistance to Slavery in the British West Indies* (Ithaca, N.Y.: Cornell University Press, 1982); Vincent Brown, *The Reaper's Garden: Death and Power in the World of Atlantic Slavery* (Cambridge, Mass.: Harvard University Press, 2008); Ada Ferrer, *Freedom's Mirror: Cuba and Haiti in the Age of Revolution* (New York: Cambridge University Press, 2014); Matt D. Childs, *The Aponte Rebellion in Cuba and the Struggle Against Atlantic Slavery* (Chapel Hill: University of North Carolina Press, 2006); Robert Paquette, *Sugar Is Made with Blood: The Conspiracy of La Escalera and the Conflict Between Empires over Slavery in Cuba* (Middletown, Conn.: Wesleyan University Press, 1988); Greg Grandin, *The Empire of Necessity: Slavery, Freedom, and Deception in the New World* (New York: Picador, 2014); Gelien Matthews, *Caribbean Slave Revolts and the British Abolitionist Movement* (Baton Rouge: Louisiana State University Press, 2006); Alvin O. Thompson, *Flight to Freedom: African Runaways and Maroons in the Americas* (Kingston: University of the West Indies Press, 2006).

For the early American republic, see Gary Nash, *Forging Freedom: The Formation of Philadelphia's Free Black Community, 1720–1840* (Cambridge, Mass.: Harvard University Press, 1988); Richard S. Newman, *The Transformation of American Abolitionism: Fighting*

Slavery in the Early Republic (Chapel Hill: University of North Carolina Press, 2002) and *Freedom's Prophet: Bishop Richard Allen, the AME Church, and the Black Founding Fathers* (New York: New York University Press, 2008); Peter Hinks, *To Awaken My Afflicted Brethren: David Walker and the Problem of Antebellum Slave Resistance* (University Park: Pennsylvania State University Press, 1997); James Sidbury, *Ploughshares into Swords: Race, Rebellion, and Identity in Gabriel's Virginia, 1730–1810* (New York: Cambridge University Press, 1997); Douglas R. Egerton, *He Shall Go Out Free: The Lives of Denmark Vesey* (Oxford: Rowman and Littlefield, 2004) and *Gabriel's Rebellion: The Virginia Slave Conspiracies of 1800 and 1802* (Chapel Hill: University of North Carolina Press, 1993); Herbert Aptheker, *American Negro Slave Revolts* (New York: Columbia University Press, 1943); Sylvia Frey, *Water from a Rock: Black Resistance in a Revolutionary Age* (Princeton, N.J.: Princeton University Press, 1991); Jane Landers, *Atlantic Creoles in the Age of Revolutions* (Cambridge, Mass.: Harvard University Press, 2010); Eric Foner, *Gateway to Freedom: The Hidden History of the Underground Railroad* (New York: W. W. Norton, 2015); Graham Russell Gao Hodges, *David Ruggles: A Radical Black Abolitionist and the Underground Railroad in New York City* (Chapel Hill: University of North Carolina Press, 2010); James O. Horton and Lois E. Horton, *In Hope of Liberty: Culture, Community, and Protest Among Northern Free Blacks, 1700–1860* (New York: Oxford University Press, 1997); Leslie Harris, *In the Shadow of Slavery: African Americans in New York City, 1626–1863* (Chicago: University of Chicago Press, 2004); Julie Winch, *Philadelphia's Black Elite: Activism, Accommodation, and the Struggle for Autonomy, 1787–1848* (Philadelphia: Temple University Press, 1988); Eddie S. Glaude Jr., *Exodus! Religion, Race, and Nation in Early Nineteenth-Century Black America* (Chicago: University of Chicago Press, 2000); Ira Berlin and Ronald Hoffman, eds., *Slavery and Freedom in the Age of the American Revolution* (Charlottesville: University Press of Virginia, 1983); Patrick Rael, *Black Identity and Black Protest in the Antebellum North* (Chapel Hill: University of North Carolina Press, 2002); Floyd J. Miller, *The Search for a Black Nationality: Black Colonization and Emigration, 1787–1863* (Urbana: University of Illinois Press, 1975); Michael Gomez, *Exchanging Our Country Marks: The Transformation of African Identities in the Colonial and Antebellum South* (Chapel Hill: University of North Carolina Press, 1998). Especially valuable are the selections in Dorothy Porter, ed., *Early Negro Writing, 1760–1837* (Boston: Beacon Press, 1971).

On the emancipation process in the states of the Northeast, the Middle Atlantic, and the upper South, see Arthur Zilversmit, *The First Emancipation: The Abolition of Slavery in the North* (Chicago: University of Chicago Press, 1967); Ira Berlin, *The Long Emancipation: The Demise of Slavery in the United States* (Cambridge, Mass.: Harvard University Press, 2015); Gary B. Nash and Jean R. Soderlund, *Freedom by Degrees: Emancipation in Pennsylvania and Its Aftermath* (New York: Oxford University Press, 1991); Shane White, *Somewhat More Independent: The End of Slavery in New York City, 1770–1810* (Athens: University of Georgia Press, 1991); Steven Hahn, *The Political Worlds of Slavery and Freedom* (Cambridge, Mass.: Harvard University Press, 2009); Joanne Pope Melish, *Disowning Slavery: Gradual Emancipation and "Race" in New England, 1790–1860* (Ithaca, N.Y.: Cornell University Press, 1998); David N. Gellman, *Emancipating New York: The Politics of Slavery and Freedom, 1777–1827* (Baton Rouge: Louisiana State University Press, 2006); Ira Berlin, *Slaves Without Masters: The Free Negro in the Antebellum South* (New York: Pantheon, 1974); Eva S. Wolf, *Race and Liberty in the*

New Nation: Emancipation in Virginia from the Revolution to Nat Turner's Rebellion (Baton Rouge: Louisiana State University Press, 2006).

On the emergence of radical abolitionism and its social and organizational dimensions, see Aileen Kraditor, *Means and Ends in American Abolitionism: Garrison and His Critics on Strategy and Tactics, 1834–1850* (New York: Pantheon, 1967); Ronald G. Walters, *The Antislavery Appeal: American Abolitionism After 1830* (Baltimore: Johns Hopkins University Press, 1976); Paul Goodman, *Of One Blood: Abolitionism and the Origins of Racial Equality* (Berkeley: University of California Press, 1998); Martin Duberman, ed., *The Antislavery Vanguard: New Essays on Abolitonists* (Princeton, N.J.: Princeton University Press, 1965); Thomas Bender, ed., *The Antislavery Debate: Capitalism and Abolitionism as a Problem in Historical Materialism* (Berkeley: University of California Press, 1992); Lewis Perry, *Radical Abolitionism: Anarchy and the Government of God in Antislavery Thought* (Ithaca, N.Y.: Cornell University Press, 1983); Henry Mayer, *All on Fire: William Lloyd Garrison and the Abolition of Slavery* (New York: W. W. Norton, 1998); Edward Magdol, *The Antislavery Rank and File: A Social Profile of the Abolitionists' Constituency* (Westport, Conn.: Greenwood Press, 1986); James Brewer Stewart, *Holy Warriors: The Abolitionists and American Slavery* (New York: Hill and Wang, 1996); Bertram Wyatt-Brown, *Lewis Tappan and the Evangelical War Against Slavery* (Cleveland: Press of Case Western Reserve University, 1969); Timothy McCarthy and John Stauffer, eds., *Prophets of Protest: Reconsidering the History of American Abolitionism* (New York: New Press, 2006); John R. McKivigan, *The War Against Proslavery Religion: Abolitionism and the Northern Churches, 1830–1865* (Ithaca, N.Y.: Cornell University Press, 1984).

On women abolitionists and their pioneering politics, see Jean Fagan Yellin and John C. Van Horne, eds., *The Abolitionist Sisterhood: Women's Political Culture in Antebellum America* (Ithaca, N.Y.: Cornell University Press, 1994); Gerda Lerner, *The Grimké Sisters from South Carolina: Pioneers for Women's Rights and Abolition* (1967; Chapel Hill: University of North Carolina Press, 2004); Julie Roy Jeffrey, *The Great Silent Army of Abolitionism: Ordinary Women in the Antislavery Movement* (Chapel Hill: University of North Carolina Press, 1998); Debra Gold Hansen, *Strained Sisterhood: Gender and Class in the Boston Female Anti-slavery Society* (Amherst: University of Massachusetts Press, 1993); Blanche G. Hersch, *The Slavery of Sex: Female Abolitionists in America* (Urbana: University of Illinois Press, 1978); Susan Zaeske, *Signatures of Citizenship: Petitioning, Antislavery, and Women's Political Identity* (Chapel Hill: University of North Carolina Press, 2003).

On anti-abolitionism and the turbulent political culture of the period, see Leonard Richards, *"Gentlemen of Property and Standing": Anti-abolitionist Mobs in Jacksonian America* (New York: Oxford University Press, 1970); Michael Feldberg, *The Turbulent Era: Riot and Disorder in Jacksonian America* (New York: Oxford University Press, 1970); David Grimsted, *American Mobbing, 1828–1861: Toward Civil War* (New York: Oxford University Press, 1998); Paul Gilje, *The Road to Mobocracy: Popular Disorder in New York City, 1763–1834* (Chapel Hill: University of North Carolina Press, 1987); Amy Greenberg, *Cause for Alarm: The Volunteer Fire Department in the Nineteenth-Century City* (Princeton, N.J.: Princeton University Press, 1998); Bertram Wyatt-Brown, *Southern Honor: Ethics and Behavior in the Old South* (New York: Oxford University Press, 1982).

On the changing politics and sensibilities of slaveholders in the southern states, see William W. Freehling, *The Road to Disunion, 1776–1854: The Secessionists at Bay* (New

York: Oxford University Press, 1990); Lacy Ford, *Deliver Us from Evil: The Slavery Question in the Old South* (New York: Oxford University Press, 2009); William W. Freehling, *Prelude to Civil War: The Nullification Crisis in South Carolina, 1816–1836* (New York: Harper and Row, 1964); Richard Ellis, *The Union at Risk: Jacksonian Democracy, States' Rights, and the Nullification Crisis* (New York: Oxford University Press, 1987); Drew Gilpin Faust, *James Henry Hammond and the Old South: A Design for Mastery* (Baton Rouge: Louisiana State University Press, 1985); Matthew Mason, *Slavery and Politics in the Early American Republic* (Chapel Hill: University of North Carolina Press, 2006); Robert P. Forbes, *The Missouri Compromise and Its Aftermath: Slavery and the Meaning of America* (Chapel Hill: University of North Carolina Press, 2007); Adam Rothman, *Slave Country: American Expansion and the Origins of the Deep South* (Cambridge, Mass.: Harvard University Press, 2005); Eugene D. Genovese and Elizabeth Fox-Genovese, *The Mind of the Master Class: History and Faith in the Southern Slaveholders' Worldview* (New York: Cambridge University Press, 2005) and *Slavery in Black and White: Class and Race in the Southern Slaveholders' New World Order* (New York: Cambridge University Press, 2008); Larry E. Tise, *Proslavery: A History of the Defense of Slavery in America, 1701–1840* (Athens: University of Georgia Press, 1987); Michael O'Brien, *Conjectures of Order: Intellectual Life and the American South, 1810–1860*, 2 vols. (Chapel Hill: University of North Carolina Press, 2004).

For the more general context of cultural change and social reform, see Richard Carwardine, *Transatlantic Revivalism: Popular Evangelicalism in Britain and America, 1790–1865* (Westport, Conn.: Greenwood Press, 1978); Robert Abzug, *Cosmos Crumbling: American Reform and the Religious Imagination* (New York: Oxford University Press, 1994); Whitney Cross, *The Burned-Over District: The Social and Intellectual History of Enthusiastic Religion in Western New York, 1800–1850* (Ithaca, N.Y.: Cornell University Press, 1950); Mary P. Ryan, *Cradle of the Middle Class: The Family in Oneida County, New York, 1790–1865* (New York: Cambridge University Press, 1981); Kathryn Kish Sklar, *Catherine Beecher: A Study in American Domesticity* (New York: W. W. Norton, 1976); Nancy F. Cott, *The Bonds of Womanhood: "Woman's Sphere" in New England, 1780–1835* (New Haven, Conn.: Yale University Press, 1978); Michael Meranze, *Laboratories of Virtue: Punishment, Revolution, and Authority in Philadelphia, 1760–1835* (Chapel Hill: University of North Carolina Press, 1996); Lori Ginzberg, *Women and the Work of Benevolence: Morality, Politics, and Class in the Nineteenth-Century United States* (New Haven, Conn.: Yale University Press, 1990); Anne M. Boylan, *The Origins of Women's Activism: New York and Boston, 1797–1840* (Chapel Hill: University of North Carolina Press, 2002); Michael Katz, *The Irony of Early School Reform: Educational Innovation in Mid-nineteenth Century Massachusetts* (Boston: Beacon Press, 1972); David J. Rothman, *The Discovery of the Asylum: Social Order and Disorder in the New Republic* (Boston: Little, Brown, 1971); W. J. Rorabaugh, *The Alcoholic Republic: An American Tradition* (New York: Oxford University Press, 1979); Nancy Hewitt, *Women's Activism and Social Change: Rochester, New York, 1822–1872* (Ithaca, N.Y.: Cornell University Press, 1984); Alice Felt Tyler, *Freedom's Ferment: Phases of American Social History from the Colonial Period to the Outbreak of the Civil War* (1944; New York: Harper and Row, 1961).

On some of the more radical cultural and political trends of the period that sought to challenge fundamental relations—in certain cases including slavery—of the early republic, see Christopher Clark, *The Communitarian Moment: The Radical Challenge of the*

Northampton Association (Amherst: University of Massachusetts Press, 1995); Carl J. Guarneri, *The Utopian Alternative: Fourierism in Nineteenth-Century America* (Ithaca, N.Y.: Cornell University Press, 1991); J. F. C. Harrison, *Quest for the New Moral World: Robert Owen and the Owenites in Britain and America* (New York: Scribner, 1969); Arthur Bestor, *Backwoods Utopias: The Sectarian Origins and the Owenite Phase of Communitarian Socialism in America, 1663–1829,* 2nd ed. (Philadelphia: University of Pennsylvania Press, 1970); Paul Johnson and Sean Wilentz, *The Kingdom of Matthias: A Story of Sex and Salvation in Nineteenth-Century America* (New York: Oxford University Press, 1994); Jonathan H. Earle, *Jacksonian Antislavery and the Politics of Free Soil, 1824–1854* (Chapel Hill: University of North Carolina Press, 2004); Gail Bederman, "Revisiting Nashoba: Slavery, Utopia, and Frances Wright in America, 1818–1826," *American Literary History* 17 (Autumn 2005): 438–59; and especially the early chapters of Sean Wilentz, *Chants Democratic: New York City and the Rise of the American Working Class, 1788–1850* (New York: Oxford University Press, 1984).

Chapter Three: Markets, Money, and Class

The early decades of the nineteenth century are generally associated with what is known as the market revolution, by which is meant an enormous expansion and extension of commercial activity, early industrialization, and a transformation in social and cultural life related to economic modernization. I have chosen a different conceptual approach—I have termed it "market intensification"—but have also benefited from the large literature that explores the market revolution in its many aspects. For an excellent overview, see Stanley Engerman and Robert E. Gallman, eds., *The Cambridge Economic History of the United States: The Long Nineteenth Century* (Cambridge, U.K.: Cambridge University Press, 2000). Also see Charles Sellers, *The Market Revolution: Jacksonian America, 1815–1846* (New York: Oxford University Press, 1991); Melvyn Stokes and Stephen Conway, eds., *The Market Revolution in America: Social, Political, and Religious Expressions, 1800–1880* (Charlottesville: University Press of Virginia, 1996); Paul E. Johnson, *A Shopkeeper's Millennium: Society and Revivals in Rochester, New York, 1815–1837* (New York: Hill and Wang, 1978); Daniel Walker Howe, *What Hath God Wrought? The Transformation of America, 1815–1848* (New York: Oxford University Press, 2007).

On the panic of 1837, a signal moment in this process, and the circuits of international trade connected with it, see Jessica M. Lepler, *The Many Panics of 1837: People, Politics, and the Creation of a Transnational Financial Crisis* (New York: Cambridge University Press, 2013); Scott R. Nelson, *A Nation of Deadbeats: An Uncommon History of America's Financial Disasters* (New York: Alfred A. Knopf, 2012); Peter Temin, *The Jacksonian Economy* (New York: W. W. Norton, 1969); John M. McFaul, *The Politics of Jacksonian Finance* (Ithaca, N.Y.: Cornell University Press, 1972). For the Pacific trade in silver and other goods, involving Mexico, China, and the United States, see James R. Fichter, *So Great a Proffit: How the East Indies Trade Transformed Anglo-American Capitalism* (Cambridge, Mass.: Harvard University Press, 2010); Kenneth Pomeranz, *The Great Divergence: China, Europe, and the Making of the Modern World Economy* (Princeton, N.J.: Princeton University Press, 2000); John Tutino, *Making a New World: Founding Capitalism in the Bajío and Spanish North America* (Durham, N.C.: Duke University Press, 2011).

On money, banking, and the "bank war," see Bray Hammond, *Banks and Politics in America from the Revolution to the Civil War* (Princeton, N.J.: Princeton University Press, 1957); Naomi Lamoreaux, *Insider Lending: Banks, Personal Connections, and Economic Development in Industrial New England* (New York: Cambridge University Press, 1994); Stephen Mihm, *A Nation of Counterfeiters: Capitalists, Con Men, and the Making of the United States* (Cambridge, Mass.: Harvard University Press, 2007); James Willard Hurst, *A Legal History of Money in the United States, 1774–1970* (Lincoln: University of Nebraska Press, 1973); Edward Balleisen, *Navigating Failure: Bankruptcy and Commercial Society in Antebellum America* (Chapel Hill: University of North Carolina Press, 2001); Howard Bodenhorn, *A History of Banking in Antebellum America: Financial Markets and Economic Development in an Era of Nation-Building* (New York: Cambridge University Press, 2000); Bruce H. Mann, *A Republic of Debtors: Bankruptcy in the Age of American Independence* (Cambridge, Mass.: Harvard University Press, 2002); Robert Wright, *The Wealth of Nations Rediscovered: Integration and Expansion in American Financial Markets, 1780–1850* (Cambridge, Mass.: Harvard University Press, 2002); Christine Desan, *Making Money: Coin, Currency, and the Coming of Capitalism* (New York: Oxford University Press, 2015); Robert Remini, *Andrew Jackson and the Bank War* (New York: W. W. Norton, 1967).

On the expansion of the economic infrastructure of the United States and developing regional linkages, see George Rogers Taylor, *The Transportation Revolution, 1815–1860* (New York: Harper and Row, 1958); Carter Goodrich, *Government Promotion of American Canals and Railroads, 1800–1890* (New York: Columbia University Press, 1965); Leland H. Jenks, *The Migration of British Capital to 1875* (New York: Alfred A. Knopf, 1927); Alfred D. Chandler Jr., *The Visible Hand: The Managerial Revolution in American Business* (Cambridge, Mass.: Harvard University Press, 1977); John L. Larson, *Internal Improvement: National Public Works and the Promise of Popular Government in the Early United States* (Chapel Hill: University of North Carolina Press, 2001); Paul F. Paskoff, *Troubled Waters: Steamboats, Disasters, River Improvements, and American Public Policy, 1821–1860* (Baton Rouge: Louisiana State University Press, 2007); Robert G. Albion, *The Rise of New York Port, 1815–1860* (New York: Scribner, 1939); Douglass C. North, *The Economic Growth of the United States, 1790–1860* (New York: W. W. Norton, 1961); Stuart W. Bruchey, *The Roots of American Economic Growth, 1607–1861* (New York: Harper and Row, 1965; William Cronon, *Nature's Metropolis: Chicago and the Great West* (New York: W. W. Norton, 1991).

On the cotton boom and the expansion of the cotton plantation economy, see Lewis C. Gray, *History of Agriculture in the Southern United States to 1860*, 2 vols. (Washington, D.C.: Smithsonian Institution, 1933); Angela Lakwete, *Inventing the Cotton Gin: Machine and Myth in Antebellum America* (Baltimore: Johns Hopkins University Press, 2003); Sven Beckert, *Empire of Cotton: A Global History* (New York: Alfred A. Knopf, 2014); John H. Moore, *The Emergence of the Cotton Kingdom in the Old Southwest: Mississippi, 1770–1860* (Baton Rouge: Louisiana State University Press, 1988).

On the dynamics of the slave plantation system, see Eugene D. Genovese, *The Political Economy of Slavery: Studies in the Society and Economy of the Slave South* (New York: Pantheon, 1965); Robert Fogel and Stanley Engerman, *Time on the Cross: The Economics of American Negro Slavery* (Boston: Little, Brown, 1974); Gavin Wright, *The Political Economy of the Cotton South: Households, Markets, and Wealth in the Nineteenth Century* (New York: W. W. Norton, 1978); Ira Berlin, *Generations of Captivity: A History of*

African-American Slaves (Cambridge, Mass.: Harvard University Press, 2003); Eugene D. Genovese, *Roll, Jordan, Roll: The World the Slaves Made* (New York: Pantheon, 1974); Richard Follett, *The Sugar Masters: Planters and Slaves in Louisiana's Cane World, 1820–1860* (Baton Rouge: Louisiana State University Press, 2006); Peter Kolchin, *Unfree Labor: American Slavery and Russian Serfdom* (Cambridge, Mass.: Harvard University Press, 1987); Walter Johnson, *Soul by Soul: Life Inside the Antebellum Slave Market* (Cambridge, Mass.: Harvard University Press, 1999); Walter Johnson, ed., *The Chattel Principle: Internal Slave Trades in the Americas* (New Haven, Conn.: Yale University Press, 2004); Michael Tadman, *Speculators and Slaves: Masters, Traders, and Slaves in the Old South* (Madison: University of Wisconsin Press, 1989); Steven Deyle, *Carry Me Back: The Domestic Slave Trade in American Life* (New York: Oxford University Press, 2006); Mark M. Smith, *Mastered by the Clock: Time, Slavery, and Freedom in the American South* (Chapel Hill: University of North Carolina Press, 1997); Edward E. Baptist, *The Half Has Never Been Told: Slavery and the Making of American Capitalism* (New York: Basic Books, 2014); Harold Woodman, *King Cotton and His Retainers: Financing and Marketing the Cotton Crop of the South* (Lexington: University of Kentucky Press, 1967); Ira Berlin and Philip Morgan, eds., *Culture and Cultivation: Labor and the Shaping of Slave Life in the Americas* (Charlottesville: University Press of Virginia, 1993); Barbara J. Fields, *Slavery and Freedom on the Middle Ground: Maryland During the Nineteenth Century* (New Haven, Conn.: Yale University Press, 1985); Erskine Clarke, *Dwelling Place: A Plantation Epic* (New Haven, Conn.: Yale University Press, 2005).

On agriculture and the countryside outside the southern plantation sector, see Paul W. Gates, *The Farmer's Age: Agriculture, 1815–1860* (New York: Harper and Row, 1960); Steven Hahn and Jonathan Prude, eds., *The Countryside in the Age of Capitalist Transformation: Essays in the Social History of Rural America* (Chapel Hill: University of North Carolina Press, 1985); James Henretta, "Families and Farms: *Mentalité* in Pre-industrial America," *William and Mary Quarterly*, 3rd ser., 35 (Jan. 1978): 3–32; Michael Merrill, "Cash Is Good to Eat: Self-Sufficiency and Exchange in the Rural Economy of the United States," *Radical History Review* 4 (1977): 42–71; Allan Kulikoff, *The Agrarian Origins of American Capitalism* (Charlottesville: University Press of Virginia, 1992); Christopher Clark, *The Roots of Rural Capitalism: Western Massachusetts, 1780–1860* (Ithaca, N.Y.: Cornell University Press, 1990); John Mack Faragher, *Sugar Creek: Life on the Illinois Prairie* (New Haven, Conn.: Yale University Press, 1986); Thomas Summerhill, *Harvest of Dissent: Agrarianism in Nineteenth-Century New York* (Urbana: University of Illinois Press, 2005); Reeve Huston, *Land and Freedom: Rural Society, Popular Protest, and Party Politics in Antebellum New York* (New York: Oxford University Press, 2000); David M. Ellis, *Landlords and Farmers in the Hudson-Mohawk Region, 1790–1850* (Ithaca, N.Y.: Cornell University Press, 1946); Winifred Rothenberg, *From Market-Places to a Market Economy: The Transformation of Rural Massachusetts, 1750–1850* (Chicago: University of Chicago Press, 1992); Nancy Grey Osterud, *Bonds of Community: The Lives of Farm Women in Nineteenth-Century New York* (Ithaca, N.Y.: Cornell University Press, 1991); Steven Stoll, *Larding the Lean Earth: Soil and Society in Nineteenth-Century America* (New York: Hill and Wang, 2002).

On the transformations of urban workplaces and labor relations and on the emergence of textile factories, see Bruce Laurie, *Artisans into Workers: Labor in Nineteenth-Century America* (New York: Hill and Wang, 1989); Alan Dawley, *Class and Community: The*

Industrial Revolution in Lynn, Massachusetts (Cambridge, Mass.: Harvard University Press, 1976); Bruce Laurie, *The Working People of Philadelphia, 1800–1850* (Philadelphia: Temple University Press, 1983); Sean Wilentz, *Chants Democratic: New York City and the Rise of the American Working Class, 1788–1850* (New York: Oxford University Press, 1984); Ronald Schultz, *The Republic of Labor: Philadelphia Artisans and the Politics of Class, 1720–1830* (New York: Oxford University Press, 1993); Steven J. Ross, *Workers on the Edge: Work, Leisure, and Politics in Industrializing Cincinnati, 1788–1890* (New York: Columbia University Press, 1985); Thomas Dublin, *Women at Work: The Transformation of Work and Community in Lowell, Massachusetts, 1826–1860* (New York: Columbia University Press, 1981); Jonathan Prude, *The Coming of Industrial Order: Town and Factory Life in Rural Massachusetts, 1810–1860* (New York: Cambridge University Press, 1983); Anthony F. C. Wallace, *Rockdale: The Growth of an American Village in the Early Industrial Revolution* (New York: W. W. Norton, 1972); David Meyer, *The Roots of American Industrialization* (Baltimore: Johns Hopkins University Press, 2003); Thomas C. Cochran, *Frontiers of Change: Early Industrialism in America* (New York: Oxford University Press, 1981); Philip Scranton, *Proprietary Capitalism: The Textile Manufacturer at Philadelphia, 1800–1885* (New York: Cambridge University Press, 1983); Jeanne Boydston, *Home and Work: Housework, Wages, and the Ideology of Labor in the Early Republic* (New York: Oxford University Press, 1990).

On the many coercive dimensions that shaped workers and labor relations, see Robert Steinfeld, *The Invention of Free Labor: The Employment Relation in English and American Law and Culture, 1350–1870* (Chapel Hill: University of North Carolina Press, 1991); Christopher L. Tomlins, *Law, Labor, and Ideology in the Early American Republic* (New York: Cambridge University Press, 1993); Seth Rockman, *Scraping By: Wage Labor, Slavery, and Survival in Early Baltimore* (Baltimore: Johns Hopkins University Press, 2009); Christopher M. Osborne, "Invisible Hands: Slaves, Bound Laborers, and the Development of Western Pennsylvania," *Pennsylvania History* 72 (Jan. 2005): 77–99; Paul Finkelman, "Evading the Ordinance: The Persistence of Bondage in Indiana and Illinois," *Journal of the Early Republic* 6 (Winter 1986): 343–70; Peter Way, *Common Labor: Workers and the Digging of North American Canals, 1780–1860* (Baltimore: Johns Hopkins University Press, 1993); David Montgomery, *Citizen Worker: The Experience of Workers in the United States with Democracy and the Free Market During the Nineteenth Century* (New York: Cambridge University Press, 1993); Jonathan A. Glickstein, *Concepts of Free Labor in Antebellum America* (New Haven, Conn.: Yale University Press, 1991); Amy Dru Stanley, *From Bondage to Contract: Wage Labor, Marriage, and the Market in the Age of Emancipation* (New York: Cambridge University Press, 1998).

On the character, culture, and constituencies of the new mass political parties of the "Jacksonian" era, see James Roger Sharp, *The Jacksonians Versus the Banks: Politics in the States After the Panic of 1837* (New York: Columbia University Press, 1970); Amy Bridges, *A City in the Republic: Antebellum New York and the Origins of Machine Politics* (New York: Cambridge University Press, 1984); Daniel Walker Howe, *The Political Culture of the American Whigs* (Chicago: University of Chicago Press, 1984); John Ashworth, *Agrarians and Aristocrats: Party Ideologies in the United States, 1837–1846* (Cambridge, U.K.: Cambridge University Press, 1983); Lee Benson, *The Concept of Jacksonian Democracy: New York as a Test Case* (Princeton, N.J.: Princeton University Press, 1961); Jean H. Baker, *Affairs of Party: The Political Culture of Northern Democrats in the Mid-nineteenth Century* (Ithaca, N.Y.: Cornell University Press, 1983); Ronald Formisano, *The Transformation of Political Culture: Massachusetts Parties, 1790s–1840s* (New York: Oxford University Press, 1983); Richard P. McCormick, *The Second American Party System: Party Formation in the Jacksonian Era* (Chapel Hill: University of North Carolina Press, 1968); Marvin Meyers, *The Jacksonian Persuasion: Politics and Belief* (Stanford, Calif.: Stanford University Press, 1957); John Ashworth, *Slavery, Capitalism, and Politics in the Antebellum Republic: Commerce and Compromise, 1820–1850* (New York: Cambridge University Press, 1995); Harry L. Watson, *Liberty and Power: The Politics of Jacksonian America* (New York: Hill and Wang, 1990); Jonathan H. Earle, *Jacksonian Antislavery and the Politics of Free Soil, 1824–1854* (Chapel Hill: University of North Carolina Press, 2004).

On the social struggles and cultural developments that went into "class making" during this period, see Christine Stansell, *City of Women: Sex and Class in New York, 1789–1860* (New York: Alfred A. Knopf, 1986); David R. Roediger, *The Wages of Whiteness: Race and the Making of the American Working Class* (London: Verso, 1991); Eric Lott, *Love and Theft: Blackface Minstrelsy and the American Working Class* (New York: Oxford University Press, 1993); Walter Hugins, *Jacksonian Democracy and the Working Class* (Stanford, Calif.: Stanford University Press, 1960); Sven Beckert, "Merchants and Manufacturers in the Antebellum North," in *Ruling America: A History of Wealth and Power in a Democracy*, ed. Steve Fraser and Gary Gerstle (Cambridge, Mass.: Harvard University Press, 2005), 92–122; Stuart Blumin, *The Emergence of the Middle Class: Social Experience in the American City, 1760–1900* (New York: Cambridge University Press, 1989); Brian Luskey, *On the Make: Clerks and the Quest for Capital in Nineteenth-Century America* (New York: New York University Press, 2010); Jeffrey Sklansky, *The Soul's Economy: Market Society and Selfhood in American Thought, 1820–1920* (Chapel Hill: University of North Carolina Press, 2002); Karen Halttunen, *Confidence Men and Painted Women: A Study of Middle-Class Culture in America, 1830–1870* (New Haven, Conn.: Yale University Press, 1982); Mary P. Ryan, *Cradle of the Middle Class: The Family in Oneida County, New York, 1790–1865* (New York: Cambridge University Press, 1981); Drew Gilpin Faust, *James Henry Hammond and the Old South: A Design for Mastery* (Baton Rouge: Louisiana State University Press, 1982); Tom Downey, *Planting a Capitalist South: Masters, Merchants, and Manufacturers in the Southern Interior, 1790–1860* (Baton Rouge: Louisiana State University Press, 2006); Walter Johnson, *River of Dark Dreams: Slavery and Empire in the Cotton Kingdom* (Cambridge, Mass.: Harvard University Press, 2013); Jonathan Daniel Wells, *Origins of the Southern Middle Class, 1800–1861* (Chapel Hill: University of North Carolina Press, 2003); James David Miller, *South by Southwest: Planter Emigration and Identity in the Slave South* (Charlottesville: University of Virginia Press, 2002); Eugene D. Genovese and Elizabeth Fox-Genovese, *The Mind of the Master Class: History and Faith in the Southern Slaveholders' Worldview* (New York: Cambridge University Press, 2005); Eugene D. Genovese, *The World the Slaveholders Made: Two Essays in Interpretation* (New York: Pantheon, 1969); James Oakes, *The Ruling Race: A History of American Slaveholders* (New York: Alfred A. Knopf, 1982).

Chapter Four: Continentalism

Historians are beginning to recognize that the march of American settlement across the North American continent was not simply a process of "expansion" but also one of conquest, colonialism, and imperial design in which the Pacific loomed as the great attraction. For important scholarship on these matters, not all of which share this perspective, see Norman Graebner, *Empire on the Pacific: A Study in American Continental Expansion* (New York: Ronald Press, 1955); Walter Nugent, *Habits of Empire: A History of American Expansion* (New York: Alfred A. Knopf, 2008); Michael Golay, *The Tide of Empire: America's March to the Pacific* (Hoboken, N.J.: John Wiley and Sons, 2003); Tom Chaffin, *Pathfinder: John Charles Frémont and the Course of American Empire* (New York: Hill and Wang, 2003); Frederick Merk, *The Monroe Doctrine and American Expansionism, 1843–1849* (New York: Alfred A. Knopf, 1966); Bradford Perkins, *The Creation of a Republican Empire, 1776–1865* (Cambridge, Mass.: Harvard University Press, 1995); William H. Goetzman, *When the Eagle Screamed: The Romantic Horizons in American Diplomacy, 1800–1860* (New York: Alfred A. Knopf, 1966) and *Exploration and Empire: The Explorer and the Scientist in the Winning of the American West* (New York: Alfred A. Knopf, 1966); John Schroeder, *Shaping a Maritime Empire: The Commercial and Diplomatic Role of the American Navy, 1829–1861* (Westport, Conn.: Greenwood Press, 1965); Howard Jones, *To the Webster-Ashburton Treaty: A Study in Anglo-American Relations, 1783–1843* (Chapel Hill: University of North Carolina Press, 1977); Sam W. Haynes and Christopher Morris, eds., *Manifest Destiny and Empire: American Antebellum Expansionism* (College Station: Texas A&M Press, 1997); David A. Johnson, *Founding the Far West: California, Oregon, and Nevada, 1840–1890* (Berkeley: University of California Press, 1992); Anders Stephanson, *Manifest Destiny: American Expansionism and the Empire of Right* (New York: Hill and Wang, 1995); William E. Weeks, *Building the Continental Empire: American Expansion from the Revolution to the Civil War* (Chicago: Ivan R. Dee, 1996); Shelley Streeby, *American Sensations: Class, Empire, and the Production of Popular Culture* (Berkeley: University of California Press, 2002); Amy Kaplan, *The Anarchy of Empire in the Making of U.S. Culture* (Cambridge, Mass.: Harvard University Press, 2005); Patricia N. Limerick, *The Legacy of Conquest: The Unbroken Past of the American West* (New York: W. W. Norton, 1987); Richard Slotkin, *Regeneration Through Violence: The Mythology of the American Frontier, 1660–1860* (Middleton, Conn.: Wesleyan University Press, 1973); Henry Nash Smith, *Virgin Land: The American West as Symbol and Myth* (Cambridge, Mass.: Harvard University Press, 1950). For an international perspective, see John C. Weaver, *The Great Land Rush and the Making of the Modern World, 1600–1900* (Montreal: McGill-Queens University Press, 2003).

On Texas annexation and the political conflicts it created, see Joel Silbey, *The Storm over Texas: The Annexation Controversy and the Road to Civil War* (New York: W. W. Norton, 2005); Gary Clayton Anderson, *The Conquest of Texas: Ethnic Cleansing in the Promised Land, 1820–1875* (Norman: University of Oklahoma Press, 2005); Michael A. Morrison, *Slavery and the American West: The Eclipse of Manifest Destiny and the Coming of the Civil War* (Chapel Hill: University of North Carolina Press, 1997); Yonatan Eyal, *The Young America Movement and the Transformation of the Democratic Party, 1828–1861* (New York: Cambridge University Press, 2007); Amy Greenberg, *Manifest Manhood and the Antebellum American Empire* (New York: Cambridge University Press, 2005); Thomas R. Hietala, *Manifest Design: Anxious Aggrandizement in Late Jacksonian America* (Ithaca, N.Y.: Cornell University Press, 1985); Mark Lause, *Young America: Land, Labor, and the Republican Community* (Urbana: University of Illinois Press, 2005); David Pletcher, *The Diplomacy of Annexation: Texas, Oregon, and the Mexican War* (Columbia: University of Missouri Press, 1973); William W. Freehling, *The Road to Disunion: The Secessionists at*

Bay, 1776–1854 (New York: Oxford University Press, 1990); John Ashworth, *Slavery, Capitalism, and Politics in the Antebellum Republic: Commerce and Compromise, 1820–1850* (New York: Cambridge University Press, 1995); Frederick Merk, *Slavery and the Annexation of Texas* (New York: Alfred A. Knopf, 1972); Norman E. Tutorow, *Texas Annexation and the Mexican War: A Political Study of the Old Northwest* (Palo Alto, Calif.: Chadwick House, 1978).

The U.S.-Mexican War and its broad political and imperial context are now getting the attention they deserve. For some of the most important works, see Brian DeLay, *War of a Thousand Deserts: Indian Raids and the U.S.-Mexican War* (New Haven, Conn.: Yale University Press, 2008); Amy S. Greenberg, *A Wicked War: Polk, Clay, Lincoln, and the 1846 U.S. Invasion of Mexico* (New York: Vintage, 2012); David Weber, *The Mexican Frontier, 1821–1846* (Albuquerque: University of New Mexico Press, 1982); Paul Foos, *A Short, Offhand, Killing Affair: Soldiers and Social Conflict During the Mexican-American War* (Chapel Hill: University of North Carolina Press, 2002); Richard Griswold del Castillo, *The Treaty of Guadalupe Hidalgo: A Legacy of Conflict* (Norman: University of Oklahoma Press, 1990); Rachel St. John, *A Line in the Sand: A History of the Western U.S.-Mexico Border* (Princeton, N.J.: Princeton University Press, 2011); Reginald Horsman, *Race and Manifest Destiny: The Origins of American Racial Anglo-Saxonism* (Cambridge, Mass.: Harvard University Press, 1981); Robert W. Merry, *A Country of Vast Designs: James K. Polk, the Mexican War, and the Conquest of the American Continent* (New York: Simon and Schuster, 2010). For the Mexican as well as the American perspective, also see Timothy J. Henderson, *A Glorious Defeat: Mexico and Its War with the United States* (New York: Hill and Wang, 2007); Neal Harlow, *California Conquered: War and Peace on the Pacific, 1846–1850* (Berkeley: University of California Press, 1982); Sergio Ortega Noriega, *Un ensayo de historia regional: El noroeste de México, 1530–1880* (Mexico City: Universidad Nacional Autónoma de México, 1993); Pedro Santoni, *Mexicans at Arms: Puro Federalists and the Politics of War, 1845–1848* (Fort Worth: Texas Christian University Press, 1996); Otis Singletary, *The Mexican War* (Chicago: University of Chicago Press, 1960); Joseph Wheelan, *Invading Mexico: America's Continental Dream and the Mexican War, 1846–1848* (New York: Carroll and Graf, 2007); Irving Levinson, *Wars Within War: Mexican Guerrillas, Domestic Elites, and the United States of America, 1846–1848* (Fort Worth: Texas Christian University Press, 2005); Arnoldo De León, *The Tejano Community, 1836–1900* (Albuquerque: University of New Mexico Press, 1982); María E. Montoya, *Translating Property: The Maxwell Land Grant and the Conflict over Land in the American West, 1840–1900* (Berkeley: University of California Press, 2002); Leonard Pitt, *The Decline of the Californios: A Social History of the Spanish-Speaking Californians, 1846–1890* (Berkeley: University of California Press, 1970); Paula Rebert, *La Gran Línea: Mapping the United States–Mexican Boundary, 1849–1857* (Austin: University of Texas Press, 2005); James M. McCaffrey, *Army of Manifest Destiny: The American Soldier in the Mexican War, 1846–1848* (New York: New York University Press, 1992); Samuel W. Haynes, *James K. Polk and the Expansionist Impulse* (New York: Longman, 1997); Robert W. Johannsen, *To the Halls of Montezuma: The Mexican War in American Imagination* (New York: Oxford University Press, 1985).

Especially good on the California gold rush and its ramifications are Susan Lee Johnson, *Roaring Camp: The Social World of the California Gold Rush* (New York: W. W. Norton, 2000); Brian Roberts, *American Alchemy: The California Gold Rush and Middle-Class*

Culture (Chapel Hill: University of North Carolina Press, 2000); Leonard L. Richards, *The California Gold Rush and the Coming of the Civil War* (New York: Vintage, 2007). But also see H. W. Brands, *The Age of Gold: The California Gold Rush and the New American Dream* (New York: Anchor, 2001); J. S. Holiday, *The World Rushed In: The California Gold Rush Experience* (Norman: University of Oklahoma Press, 2002); James J. Rawls and Robert J. Orsi, *The Golden State: Mining and Economic Development in Gold Rush California* (Berkeley: University of California Press, 1999); Paula M. Marks, *Precious Dust: The American Gold Rush Era, 1848–1900* (New York: W. Morrow, 1994); Aims McGuinness, *Path of Empire: Panama and the California Gold Rush* (Ithaca, N.Y.: Cornell University Press, 2008); Richard J. Orsi and Kevin Starr, eds., *Rooted in Barbarous Soil: People, Culture, and Community in Gold Rush California* (Berkeley: University of California Press, 2000); Kenneth N. Owens, ed., *Riches for All: The California Gold Rush and the World* (Lincoln: University of Nebraska Press, 2002); Rodman W. Paul and Elliott West, *Mining Frontiers of the Far West, 1848–1880* (Albuquerque: University of New Mexico Press, 2001); Malcolm J. Rohrbough, *Days of Gold: The California Gold Rush and the American Nation* (Berkeley: University of California Press, 1997); Robert M. Senkewicz, *Vigilantes in Gold Rush San Francisco* (Stanford, Calif.: Stanford University Press, 1985); David Vaught, *After the Gold Rush: Tarnished Dreams in the Sacramento Valley* (Baltimore: Johns Hopkins University Press, 2007).

On the making of what has come to be known as the "compromise" or "armistice" of 1850, see David Potter, *The Impending Crisis, 1848–1861* (New York: Harper and Row, 1976); Holman Hamilton, *Prologue to Conflict: The Crisis and Compromise of 1850* (Lexington: University of Kentucky Press, 1964); Fergus M. Bordewich, *The Great Debate: Henry Clay, Stephen Douglas, and the Compromise That Preserved the Union* (New York: Simon and Schuster, 2013); Chaplain W. Morrison, *Democratic Politics and Sectionalism: The Wilmot Proviso Controversy* (Chapel Hill: University of North Carolina Press, 1967); Mark J. Stegmaier, *Texas, New Mexico, and the Compromise of 1850* (Kent, Ohio: Kent State University Press, 1996); Robert W. Johannsen, *Stephen A. Douglas* (New York: Oxford University Press, 1973); Robert V. Remini, *At the Edge of the Precipice: Henry Clay and the Compromise That Saved the Union* (New York: Basic Books, 2011). On the Mormon migrations and the development of Mormon Utah, see Richard Bushman, *Joseph Smith: Rough Stone Rolling* (New York: Vintage, 2007); Leonard J. Arrington, *Great Basin Kingdom: An Economic History of the Latter-Day Saints, 1830–1900* (1958; Urbana: University of Illinois Press, 2005); Sarah Barringer Gordon, *The Mormon Question: Polygamy and Constitutional Conflict in Nineteenth-Century America* (Chapel Hill: University of North Carolina Press, 2002).

Chapter Five: Border Wars

During the mid-1850s, many of the borders of social and political life in the United States were being challenged and traversed in new ways, provoking conflicts that would explode soon thereafter. On the increasingly convulsive politics that went into the making of the Kansas-Nebraska Act and then the violent battle over slavery in Kansas, see Robert W. Johannsen, *Stephen A. Douglas* (New York: Oxford University Press, 1973); David M. Potter, *The Impending Crisis, 1848–1861* (New York: Harper and Row, 1976); William W. Freehling, *The Road to Disunion, 1776–1854: The Secessionists at Bay* (New York: Oxford University Press, 1990); Michael Holt, *The Political Crisis of the 1850s* (New York: Wiley, 1978); Joel Silbey, *The Partisan Imperative: The Dynamics of*

American Politics Before the Civil War (New York: Oxford University Press, 1985); James Rawley, *Race and Politics: "Bleeding Kansas" and the Coming of the Civil War* (Lincoln: University of Nebraska Press, 1969); Nicole Etcheson, *Bleeding Kansas: Contested Liberty in the Civil War Era* (Lawrence: University Press of Kansas, 2004); Gunja SenGupta, *For God and Mammon: Evangelicals and Entrepreneurs, Masters and Slaves in Territorial Kansas, 1854–1860* (Athens: University of Georgia Press, 1996); David S. Reynolds, *John Brown, Abolitionist: The Man Who Killed Slavery, Sparked the Civil War, and Seeded Civil Rights* (New York: Alfred A. Knopf, 2005); W. E. B. Du Bois, *John Brown* (1919; New York: Oxford University Press, 2007); Robert McGlone, *John Brown's War Against Slavery* (New York: Cambridge University Press, 2009); Gerald W. Wolff, *The Kansas-Nebraska Bill: Party, Section, and the Coming of the Civil War* (New York: Revisionist Press, 1977).

On the imperial visions of Deep South slaveholders and the filibustering operations that some of them supported, see Walter Johnson, *River of Dark Dreams: Slavery and Empire in the Cotton Kingdom* (Cambridge, Mass.: Harvard University Press, 2013); Matthew Karp, *This Vast Southern Empire: Slaveholders at the Helm of American Foreign Policy* (Cambridge, Mass.: Harvard University Press, 2016); Robert E. May, *The Southern Dream of a Caribbean Empire, 1854–1861* (Baton Rouge: Louisiana State University Press, 1973), *Manifest Destiny's Underworld: Filibustering in Antebellum America* (Chapel Hill: University of North Carolina Press, 2002), and *John A. Quitman: Old South Crusader* (Baton Rouge: Louisiana State University Press, 1995); James Byrne, *Albert Gallatin Brown: Radical Southern Nationalist* (New York: D. Appleton, 1937); Matthew Guterl, *American Mediterranean: Southern Slaveholders in the Age of Emancipation* (Cambridge, Mass.: Harvard University Press, 2008); William Barney, *The Road to Secession: A New Perspective on the Old South* (New York: Praeger, 1972); Enrico Dal Lago, *Agrarian Elites: American Slaveholders and Southern Italian Landowners, 1815–1869* (Baton Rouge: Louisiana State University Press, 2005); Eugene D. Genovese, *The World the Slaveholders Made: Two Essays in Interpretation* (New York: Pantheon, 1969); Robert Bonner, *Mastering America: Southern Slaveholders and the Crisis of American Nationhood* (New York: Cambridge University Press, 2009); Charles H. Brown, *Agents of Manifest Destiny: The Lives and Times of the Filibusters* (Chapel Hill: University of North Carolina Press, 1980); Michel Gobat, *Confronting the American Dream: Nicaragua Under U.S. Imperial Rule* (Durham, N.C.: Duke University Press, 2005); Tom Chaffin, *Fatal Glory: Narciso López and the First Clandestine U.S. War Against Cuba* (Charlottesville: University Press of Virginia, 1996).

On the development of political antislavery, see Eric Foner, *Politics and Ideology in the Age of the Civil War* (New York: Oxford University Press, 1980); Richard H. Sewell, *Ballots for Freedom: Antislavery Politics in the United States, 1837–1860* (New York: W. W. Norton, 1976); R. J. M. Blackett, *Building an Antislavery Wall: Black Americans and the Atlantic Abolitionist Movement, 1830–1860* (Baton Rouge: Louisiana State University Press, 1983); Bruce Levine, *Half Slave and Half Free: The Roots of the Civil War* (New York: Hill and Wang, 1992) and *The Spirit of 1848: German Immigrants, Labor Conflict, and the Coming of the Civil War* (Urbana: University of Illinois Press, 1992); Frederick J. Blue, *The Free Soilers: Third Party Politics, 1848–1854* (Urbana: University of Illinois Press, 1973); Michael Holt, *Forging a Majority: The Formation of the Republican Party in Pittsburgh, 1848–1860* (New Haven, Conn.: Yale University Press, 1969); William E. Gienapp, *The Origins of the Republican Party, 1852–1856* (New York: Oxford University Press, 1987);

Eugene H. Berwanger, *The Frontier Against Slavery: Western Anti-Negro Prejudice and the Slavery Extension Controversy* (Urbana: University of Illinois Press, 1967); Thomas D. Morris, *Free Men All: The Personal Liberty Laws of the North, 1780–1860* (Baltimore: Johns Hopkins University Press, 1974); James Oakes, *The Scorpion's Sting: Antislavery and the Coming of the Civil War* (New York: W. W. Norton, 2014).

On new patterns of immigration and the rise of nativism, see Dirk Hoerder, *Cultures in Contact: World Migrations in the Second Millennium* (Durham, N.C.: Duke University Press, 2010); Samuel Clark, *Social Origins of the Irish Land War* (Princeton, N.J.: Princeton University Press, 1979); Dale T. Knobel, *Paddy and the Republic: Ethnicity and Nationalism in Antebellum America* (Middletown, Conn.: Wesleyan University Press, 1986); Cormac Grada, *The Great Irish Famine* (Cambridge, U.K.: Cambridge University Press, 1989); Kevin Kenny, *Making Sense of the Molly Maguires* (New York: Cambridge University Press, 1998); Tyler Anbinder, *Nativism and Slavery: The Northern Know Nothings and the Politics of the 1850s* (New York: Oxford University Press, 1992); Michael Holt, *The Rise and Fall of the American Whig Party: Jacksonian Politics and the Onset of the Civil War* (New York: Oxford University Press, 1999); Ray Allen Billington, *The Protestant Crusade, 1800–1860: A Study of the Origins of American Nativism* (New York: Macmillan, 1938); Noel Ignatiev, *How the Irish Became White* (New York: Routledge, 1995); Alexander Saxton, *The Rise and Fall of the White Republic: Class Politics and Mass Culture in Nineteenth-Century America* (London: Verso, 1991); Michael Feldberg, *The Philadelphia Riots of 1844: A Study of Ethnic Conflict* (Westport, Conn.: Greenwood Press, 1975); Michael Katz, *The Irony of Early School Reform* (Boston: Beacon Press, 1972); David Montgomery, "The Shuttle and the Cross: Weavers and Artisans in the Kensington Riots of 1844," *Journal of Social History* 5 (Summer 1972): 411–46.

On the developing struggle for women's rights, see Judith Wellman, *The Road to Seneca Falls: Elizabeth Cady Stanton and the First Women's Rights Convention* (Urbana: University of Illinois Press, 2004); Lori Ginzberg, *Elizabeth Cady Stanton: An American Life* (New York: Hill and Wang, 2009) and *Untidy Origins: A Story of Woman's Rights in Antebellum New York* (Chapel Hill: University of North Carolina Press, 2005); Ellen Carol DuBois, *Feminism and Suffrage: The Emergence of an Independent Women's Movement in America, 1848–1869* (Ithaca, N.Y.: Cornell University Press, 1978); Nancy Isenberg, *Sex and Citizenship in Antebellum America* (Chapel Hill: University of North Carolina Press, 1998); Linda Kerber, *No Constitutional Right to Be Ladies: Women and the Obligations of Citizenship* (New York: Hill and Wang, 1999); Margaret H. McFadden, *Golden Cables of Sympathy: The Transatlantic Sources of Nineteenth-Century Feminism* (Lexington: University Press of Kentucky, 1999); Nancy Hewitt, *Women's Activism and Social Change: Rochester, New York, 1822–1870* (Ithaca, N.Y.: Cornell University Press, 1984); Bonnie S. Anderson, *Joyous Greetings: The First International Women's Movement, 1830–1860* (New York: Oxford University Press, 2000); Ann Braude, *Radical Spirits: Spiritualism and Women's Rights in Nineteenth-Century America* (Boston: Beacon Press, 1989); Kathryn Kish Sklar and James Brewer Stewart, eds., *Women's Rights and Transatlantic Antislavery in the Age of Emancipation* (New Haven, Conn.: Yale University Press, 2007); Kathryn Kish Sklar, *Women's Rights Emerges Within the Antislavery Movement, 1830–1870: A Brief History with Documents* (Boston: Bedford/St. Martin's, 2000).

On the multifaceted and international African American struggle against slavery and for civil and political equality during this period, see Stanley W. Campbell, *Slave*

Catchers: Enforcement of the Fugitive Slave Law, 1850–1860 (Chapel Hill: University of North Carolina Press, 1968); Eric Foner, *Gateway to Freedom: The Hidden History of the Underground Railroad* (New York: W. W. Norton, 2015); R. J. M. Blackett, *Making Freedom: The Underground Railroad and the Politics of Slavery* (Chapel Hill: University of North Carolina Press, 2013); William Still, *The Underground Rail Road* (Philadelphia: Porter and Coates, 1872); Larry Gara, *The Liberty Line: The Legend of the Underground Railroad* (Lexington: University of Kentucky Press, 1961); Fergus M. Bordewich, *Bound for Canaan: The Underground Railroad and the War for the Soul of America* (New York: Harper-Collins, 2005); Stanley Harrold, *Border War: Fighting over Slavery Before the Civil War* (Chapel Hill: University of North Carolina Press, 2010); Herbert Aptheker, *American Negro Slave Revolts* (New York: Columbia University Press, 1943); Stephanie H. M. Camp, *Closer to Freedom: Enslaved Women and Everyday Resistance in the Plantation South* (Chapel Hill: University of North Carolina Press, 2004); Howard H. Bell, *A Survey of the Negro Convention Movement, 1830–1861* (New York: Arno Press, 1969); Thomas P. Slaughter, *Bloody Dawn: The Christiana Riot and Racial Violence in the Antebellum North* (New York: Oxford University Press, 1991); John Stauffer, *Black Hearts of Men: Radical Abolitionism and the Transformation of Race* (Cambridge, Mass.: Harvard University Press, 2002); John Hope Franklin and Loren Schweninger, *Runaway Slaves: Rebels on the Plantation* (New York: Oxford University Press, 1999); George Hendrick and Willene Hendrick, *The Creole Mutiny: A Tale of Revolt Aboard a Slave Ship* (Chicago: Ivan R. Dee, 2003); Albert J. Von Frank, *The Trial of Anthony Burns: Freedom and Slavery in Emerson's Boston* (Cambridge, Mass.: Harvard University Press, 1998); Jane Pease and William H. Pease, *They Who Would Be Free: Blacks Search for Freedom* (New York: Atheneum, 1974); Marcus Rediker, *The* Amistad *Rebellion: An Atlantic Odyssey of Slavery and Freedom* (New York: Penguin Press, 2013); Stephen Kantrowitz, *More Than Freedom: Fighting for Black Citizenship in a White Republic, 1829–1889* (New York: Penguin Press, 2012).

On the making of the *Dred Scott* decision, see Don Fehrenbacher, *The Dred Scott Case: Its Significance for American Law and Politics* (New York: Oxford University Press, 1978); Mark A. Graber, *Dred Scott and the Problem of Constitutional Evil* (New York: Cambridge University Press, 2006); Adam Arenson, *The Great Heart of the Republic: St. Louis and the Cultural Civil War* (Cambridge, Mass.: Harvard University Press, 2011); Lea Vander Velde, *Redemption Songs: Suing for Freedom Before Dred Scott* (New York: Oxford University Press, 2011) and *Mrs. Dred Scott: A Life on Slavery's Frontier* (New York: Oxford University Press, 2009); Austin Allen, *Origins of the Dred Scott Case: Jacksonian Jurisprudence and the Supreme Court, 1837–1857* (Athens: University of Georgia Press, 2006).

Chapter Six: Death of a Union

The historical literature of the Civil War era, from the struggle over the fate of the Union to the end of Reconstruction, is enormous and of high quality. Here I will note the works that I found most useful and influential in writing the relevant chapters. On the emergence of the Republican Party, Abraham Lincoln, and Lincoln's debates with Stephen Douglas, see Eric Foner, *Free Soil, Free Labor, Free Men: The Ideology of the Republican Party Before the Civil War* (New York: Oxford University Press, 1970) and *The Fiery Trial: Abraham Lincoln and American Slavery* (New York: W. W. Norton, 2010); Eric Foner, ed., *Our Lincoln: New Perspectives on Lincoln and His World* (New York: W. W. Norton,

2008); David Donald, *Lincoln* (New York: Touchstone, 1995); Don E. Fehrenbacher, *Prelude to Greatness: Lincoln in the 1850s* (Stanford, Calif.: Stanford University Press, 1962); Harry V. Jaffa, *Crisis of the House Divided: An Interpretation of the Issues in the Lincoln-Douglas Debates* (Garden City, N.Y.: Doubleday, 1959); Robert E. May, *Slavery, Race, and Conquest in the Tropics: Lincoln, Douglas, and the Future of Latin America* (New York: Cambridge University Press, 2013); Vernon Burton, *The Age of Lincoln* (New York: Hill and Wang, 2008); James Oakes, *The Radical and the Republican: Frederick Douglass, Abraham Lincoln, and the Triumph of Antislavery Politics* (New York: W. W. Norton, 2008); Allan Nevins, *The Ordeal of the Union*, 4 vols. (New York: Scribner, 1947–50); David Donald, *Charles Sumner and the Coming of the Civil War* (New York: Alfred A. Knopf, 1960); William E. Gienapp, *The Origins of the Republican Party, 1852–1856* (New York: Oxford University Press, 1987); Michael F. Holt, *The Political Crisis of the 1850s* (New York: W. W. Norton, 1983); Kenneth Stampp, *America in 1857: A Nation on the Brink* (New York: Oxford University Press, 1990); Elizabeth R. Varon, *Disunion! The Coming of the American Civil War, 1789–1859* (Chapel Hill: University of North Carolina Press, 2010); Robert W. Johannsen, *Stephen A. Douglas* (New York: Oxford University Press, 1973); John Majewski, *A House Dividing: Economic Development in Pennsylvania and Virginia Before the Civil War* (New York: Cambridge University Press, 2000); James L. Huston, *The Panic of 1857 and the Coming of the Civil War* (Baton Rouge: Louisiana State University Press, 1987); Roy F. Nichols, *The Disruption of American Democracy* (New York: Macmillan, 1948); Richard Sewell, *A House Divided: Sectionalism and Civil War, 1848–1865* (Baltimore: Johns Hopkins University Press, 1988); David Zarefsky, *Lincoln, Douglas, and Slavery: In the Crucible of Public Debate* (Chicago: University of Chicago Press, 1990).

On developing secessionist politics in the slave states, see John Ashworth, *Slavery, Capitalism, and Politics in the Antebellum Republic: The Coming of the Civil War, 1850–1861* (New York: Cambridge University Press, 2007); William W. Freehling, *The Road to Disunion: Secessionists Triumphant, 1854–1861* (New York: Oxford University Press, 2007); Avery O. Craven, *The Growth of Southern Nationalism, 1848–1861* (Baton Rouge: Louisiana State University Press, 1953); Lacy K. Ford, *Origins of Southern Radicalism: The South Carolina Upcountry, 1800–1860* (New York: Oxford University Press, 1988); J. Mills Thornton III, *Politics and Power in a Slave Society: Alabama, 1800–1860* (Baton Rouge: Louisiana State University Press, 1978); Eric H. Walther, *The Fire-Eaters* (Baton Rouge: Louisiana State University Press, 1992); William L. Barney, *The Road to Secession: A New Perspective on the Old South* (New York: Praeger, 1972); Manisha Sinha, *The Counterrevolution of Slavery: Politics and Ideology in Antebellum South Carolina* (Chapel Hill: University of North Carolina Press, 2000); Stephanie McCurry, *Masters of Small Worlds: Yeoman Households, Gender Relations, and the Political Culture of the Antebellum South Carolina Low Country* (New York: Oxford University Press, 1995); Frank Towers, *The Urban South and the Coming of the Civil War* (Charlottesville: University of Virginia Press, 2004); Christopher J. Olsen, *Political Culture and Secession in Mississippi: Masculinity, Honor, and the Antiparty Tradition, 1830–1860* (New York: Oxford University Press, 2000); John C. Inscoe, *Mountain Masters, Slavery, and the Sectional Crisis in Western North Carolina* (Knoxville: University of Tennessee Press, 1989); Mitchell Snay, *Gospel of Disunion: Religion and Separatism in the Antebellum South* (New York: Cambridge University Press, 1993); Joseph P. Reidy, *From Slavery to Agrarian Capitalism in the Cotton Plantation South: Central Georgia, 1800–1880* (Chapel Hill: University of North Carolina Press, 1992); Drew Gilpin

Faust, *James Henry Hammond and the Old South: A Design for Mastery* (Baton Rouge: Louisiana State University Press, 1982); John McCardell, *The Idea of a Southern Nation: Southern Nationalists and Southern Nationalism* (New York: W. W. Norton, 1979); David M. Potter, *The South and the Sectional Conflict* (Baton Rouge: Louisiana State University Press, 1968).

On slave politics and expectations during the 1850s, see Steven Hahn, *A Nation Under Our Feet: Black Politics in the Rural South from Slavery to the Great Migration* (Cambridge, Mass.: Harvard University Press, 2003); Anthony E. Kaye, *Joining Places: Slave Neighborhoods in the Old South* (Chapel Hill: University of North Carolina Press, 2007); William Link, *Roots of Secession: Slavery and Politics in Antebellum Virginia* (Chapel Hill: University of North Carolina Press, 2003); Merton Dillon, *Slavery Attacked: Southern Slaves and Their Allies, 1619–1865* (Baton Rouge: Louisiana State University Press, 1990); Herbert Aptheker, *American Negro Slave Revolts* (New York: Columbia University Press, 1943); William Webb, *The History of William Webb, Composed by Himself* (Detroit: E. Hoekstra, 1873); Stephanie Camp, *Closer to Freedom: Enslaved Women and Everyday Resistance in the Plantation South* (Chapel Hill: University of North Carolina Press, 2004).

On the election of 1860, the dynamics of secession, and the outbreak of warfare, see Douglas R. Egerton, *Year of Meteors: Stephen Douglas, Abraham Lincoln, and the Election That Brought on the Civil War* (New York: Bloomsbury Press, 2013); A. James Fuller, ed., *The Election of 1860 Reconsidered* (Kent, Ohio: Kent State University Press, 2013); David M. Potter, *The Impending Crisis, 1848–1861* (New York: Harper and Row, 1976) and *Lincoln and His Party in the Secession Crisis* (New Haven, Conn.: Yale University Press, 1942); Daniel W. Crofts, *Reluctant Confederates: Upper South Unionists in the Secession Crisis* (Chapel Hill: University of North Carolina Press, 1989); Kenneth Stampp, *And the War Came: The North and the Secession Crisis, 1860–1861* (Baton Rouge: Louisiana State University Press, 1950); Michael P. Johnson, *Toward a Patriarchal Republic: The Secession of Georgia* (Baton Rouge: Louisiana State University Press, 1977); Steven Channing, *Crisis of Fear: Secession in South Carolina* (New York: W. W. Norton, 1970); William L. Barney, *The Secessionist Impulse: Alabama and Mississippi in 1860* (Princeton, N.J.: Princeton University Press, 1974); J. Carlyle Sitterson, *The Secession Movement in North Carolina* (Chapel Hill: University of North Carolina Press, 1939); James M. Woods, *Rebellion and Realignment: Arkansas's Road to Secession* (Fayetteville: University of Arkansas Press, 1987); William W. Freehling and Craig Simpson, eds., *Showdown in Virginia: The 1861 Convention and the Fate of the Union* (Charlottesville: University of Virginia Press, 2010) and *Secession Debated: Georgia's Showdown in 1860* (New York: Oxford University Press, 1992); Ralph A. Wooster, *The Secession Conventions of the South* (Princeton, N.J.: Princeton University Press, 1962); Tony Horwitz, *Midnight Rising: John Brown and the Raid That Sparked the Civil War* (New York: Henry Holt, 2012); Jonathan Earle, *John Brown's Raid on Harpers Ferry: A Brief History with Documents* (Boston: Bedford/St. Martin's, 2008); Charles B. Dew, *Apostles of Disunion: Southern Secession Commissioners and the Causes of the Civil War* (Charlottesville: University Press of Virginia, 2001); Robert G. Gunderson, *Old Gentlemen's Convention: The Washington Peace Conference of 1861* (Madison: University of Wisconsin Press, 1961); Robert Cook, William Barney, and Elizabeth Varon, *Secession Winter: When the Union Fell Apart* (Baltimore: Johns Hopkins University Press, 2013); Emory M. Thomas, *The Confederacy as a Revolutionary Experience* (Englewood Cliffs, N.J.: Prentice-Hall, 1971).

For an international context of the struggle over slavery, slaveholder rebellion, and secessionism, see Eugene D. Genovese, *The World the Slaveholders Made: Two Essays in Interpretation* (New York: Pantheon, 1969); Don H. Doyle, ed., *Secession as an International Phenomenon: From America's Civil War to Contemporary Separatist Movements* (Athens: University of Georgia Press, 2010); Don H. Doyle, *Nations Divided: America, Italy, and the Southern Question* (Athens: University of Georgia Press, 2002); Brian Schoen, *The Fragile Fabric of Union: Cotton, Federal Politics, and the Global Origins of the Civil War* (Baltimore: Johns Hopkins University Press, 2009); Edward Rugemer, *The Problem of Emancipation: The Caribbean Roots of the American Civil War* (Baton Rouge: Louisiana State University Press, 2009); Sven Beckert, *Empire of Cotton: A Global History* (New York: Alfred A. Knopf, 2014); Shearer Davis Bowman, *Masters and Lords: Mid-19th Century U.S. Planters and Prussian Junkers* (New York: Oxford University Press, 1993); Enrico Dal Lago, *Agrarian Elites: American Slaveholders and Southern Italian Landowners, 1815–1861* (Baton Rouge: Louisiana State University Press, 2005) and *American Slavery, Atlantic Slavery, and Beyond: The U.S. "Peculiar Institution" in International Perspective* (Boulder, Colo.: Paradigm, 2013); Peter Kolchin, *Unfree Labor: American Slavery and Russian Serfdom* (Cambridge, Mass.: Harvard University Press, 1987) and *A Sphinx on the American Land: The Nineteenth-Century South in Comparative Perspective* (Baton Rouge: Louisiana State University Press, 2003); Rajmohan Gandhi, *A Tale of Two Revolts: India's Mutiny and the American Civil War* (London: Haus, 2011).

Chapter Seven: Birth of a Nation

The military, and related political and diplomatic, history of the War of the Rebellion could easily fill several libraries with the volumes that have been published, but relatively few have focused on the trans-Mississippi West. Important starting points for a wide-angled picture would be James M. McPherson, *Battle Cry of Freedom: The Civil War Era* (New York: Oxford University Press, 1988); Allan Nevins, *The War for the Union*, 4 vols. (New York: Scribner, 1959–71); Herman Hattaway and Archer Jones, *How the North Won: A Military History of the Civil War* (Urbana: University of Illinois Press, 1983); Richard E. Beringer et al., *Why the South Lost the Civil War* (Athens: University of Georgia Press, 1986). On the West, see Alvin Josephy Jr., *The Civil War in the American West* (New York: Alfred A. Knopf, 1991); Donald S. Frazier, *Blood and Treasure: Confederate Empire in the Southwest* (College Station: Texas A&M University Press, 1995); Adam Arenson and Andrew Graybill, eds., *Civil War Wests: Testing the Limits of the United States* (Berkeley: University of California Press, 2015); Virginia Scharff, ed., *Empire and Liberty: The Civil War and the West* (Berkeley: University of California Press, 2015); Ray C. Colton, *The Civil War in the Western Territories: Arizona, Colorado, New Mexico, and Utah* (Norman: University of Oklahoma Press, 1959); Clarissa W. Confer, *The Cherokee Nation in the Civil War* (Norman: University of Oklahoma Press, 2007); Mary Jane Warde, *When the Wolf Came: The Civil War and the Indian Territory* (Fayetteville: University of Arkansas Press, 2013); Howard Lamar, *The Far Southwest: A Territorial History* (New Haven, Conn.: Yale University Press, 1966).

On the early phases of foreign relations involving both the Union and the Confederacy, as well as the international context of the war, see Don H. Doyle, *The Cause of All Nations: An International History of the American Civil War* (New York: Basic Books, 2014); Howard Jones, *Blue and Gray Diplomacy: A History of Union and Confederate*

Foreign Relations (Chapel Hill: University of North Carolina Press, 2010) and *Union in Peril: The Crisis over British Intervention in the Civil War* (Chapel Hill: University of North Carolina Press, 1992); Robert E. May, ed., *The Union, the Confederacy, and the Atlantic Rim* (Gainesville: University Press of Florida, 2013); Frank L. Owsley, *King Cotton Diplomacy: Foreign Relations of the Confederate States of America* (Chicago: University of Chicago Press, 1959); Jay Monaghan, *Abraham Lincoln Deals with Foreign Affairs* (Indianapolis: Bobbs-Merrill, 1945); Jay Sexton, *Debtor Diplomacy: Finance and American Foreign Relations in the Civil War Era, 1837–1873* (New York: Oxford University Press, 2005); Christopher Dickey, *Our Man in Charleston: Britain's Secret Agent in the Civil War South* (New York: Crown, 2015); R. J. M. Blackett, *Divided Hearts: Britain and the American Civil War* (Baton Rouge: Louisiana State University Press, 2000); Amanda Foreman, *A World on Fire: Britain's Crucial Role in the American Civil War* (New York: Random House, 2012); Mary Ellison, *Support for Secession: Lancashire and the American Civil War* (Chicago: University of Chicago Press, 1972); Lynn M. Case and Warren F. Spencer, *The United States and France: Civil War Diplomacy* (Philadelphia: University of Pennsylvania Press, 1970); Charles M. Hubbard, *The Burden of Confederate Diplomacy* (Knoxville: University of Tennessee Press, 2000).

On the state-building initiatives of the Lincoln administration involving money, credit, tariffs, land, the creation of territories, and railroads, see Richard F. Bensel, *Yankee Leviathan: The Origins of Central State Authority in America, 1859–1877* (New York: Cambridge University Press, 1990); Leonard P. Curry, *Blueprint for Modern America: Nonmilitary Legislation of the First Civil War Congress* (Nashville: Vanderbilt University Press, 1968); Heather Cox Richardson, *The Greatest Nation of the Earth: Republican Economic Policies During the Civil War* (Cambridge, Mass.: Harvard University Press, 1997); Gabor S. Boritt, *Lincoln and the Economics of the American Dream* (Memphis: Memphis State University Press, 1978); Paul W. Gates, *Agriculture and the American Civil War* (New York: Alfred A. Knopf, 1965); Bray Hammond, *Sovereignty and an Empty Purse: Banks and Politics in the Civil War* (Princeton, N.J.: Princeton University Press, 1970); Robert P. Sharkey, *Money, Class, and Party: An Economic Study of Civil War and Reconstruction* (Baltimore: Johns Hopkins University Press, 1959); Phillip Shaw Paludan, *The Presidency of Abraham Lincoln* (Lawrence: University Press of Kansas, 1994) and *A People's Contest: The Union and Civil War, 1861–1865* (Lawrence: University Press of Kansas, 1988); Ralph Andreano, ed., *The Economic Impact of the American Civil War* (New York: Schenkman, 1967); David Montgomery, *Beyond Equality: Labor and the Radical Republicans, 1862–1872* (New York: Alfred A. Knopf, 1967); Earl S. Pomeroy, *The Territories and the United States: Studies in Colonial Administration* (Philadelphia: University of Pennsylvania Press, 1947); Richard White, *Railroaded: The Transcontinentals and the Making of Modern America* (New York: W. W. Norton, 2011); Thomas Weber, *The Northern Railroads in the Civil War, 1861–1865* (Bloomington: Indiana University Press, 1952); Mark R. Wilson, *The Business of Civil War: Military Mobilization and the State, 1861–1865* (Baltimore: Johns Hopkins University Press, 2006); John Fabian Witt, *Lincoln's Code: The Laws of War in American History* (New York: Free Press, 2012); Laura Edwards, *A Legal History of the Civil War and Reconstruction* (New York: Cambridge University Press, 2015); Michael S. Green, *Freedom, Union, and Power: Lincoln and His Party During the Civil War* (New York: Fordham University Press, 2004); Edward Hagerman, *The American Civil War and the Origins of Modern Warfare* (Bloomington: Indiana University Press, 1988).

On the Sioux rebellion on the plains and the beginnings of the Indian Wars, see David A. Nichols, *Lincoln and the Indians: Civil War Policy and Politics* (Urbana: University of Illinois Press, 1978); Jeffrey Ostler, *The Plains Sioux and U.S. Colonialism: From Lewis and Clark to Wounded Knee* (New York: Cambridge University Press, 2004); Hank H. Cox, *Lincoln and the Sioux Uprising of 1862* (Nashville: Cumberland House, 2005); Gary C. Anderson, ed., *Through Dakota Eyes: Narrative Accounts of the Minnesota Indian War of 1862* (St. Paul: Minnesota Historical Society, 1988); Gary C. Anderson, *Kinsmen of Another Kind: Dakota-White Relations in the Upper Mississippi Valley, 1650–1862* (Lincoln: University of Nebraska Press, 1984); C. M. Oehler, *The Great Sioux Uprising* (1959; New York: Da Capo Press, 1997); Robert Utley, *The Indian Frontier of the American West, 1846–1890* (Albuquerque: University of New Mexico Press, 1984); Laurence M. Hauptman, *Between Two Fires: American Indians in the Civil War* (New York: Free Press, 1995); Roy W. Meyer, *History of the Santee Sioux: United States Policy on Trial* (Lincoln: University of Nebraska Press, 1967); Annie Heloise Abel, *The American Indian in the Civil War, 1862–1865* (1919; Lincoln: University of Nebraska Press, 1992); Elliott West, *The Contested Plains: Indians, Goldseekers, and the Rush to Colorado* (Lawrence: University Press of Kansas, 1998); Richard W. Etulain, ed., *Lincoln Looks West: From the Mississippi to the Pacific* (Carbondale: Southern Illinois University Press, 2010).

On the slaves' rebellion and the development of the emancipation process, see Steven Hahn, *The Political Worlds of Slavery and Freedom* (Cambridge, Mass.: Harvard University Press, 2009); Ira Berlin et al., *Slaves No More: Three Essays on Emancipation and the Civil War* (New York: Cambridge University Press, 1992); Ira Berlin et al., eds., *Freedom: A Documentary History of Emancipation, 1861–1867*, 4 vols. (New York: Cambridge University Press, 1983–93); James Oakes, *Freedom National: The Destruction of Slavery in the United States, 1861–1865* (New York: W. W. Norton, 2012); Leon Litwack, *Been in the Storm So Long: The Aftermath of Slavery* (New York: Alfred A. Knopf, 1979); John Hope Franklin, *The Emancipation Proclamation* (Garden City, N.Y.: Doubleday, 1963); Michael Vorenberg, *The Emancipation Proclamation: A Brief History with Documents* (Boston: Bedford/St. Martin's, 2010); W. E. B. Du Bois, *Black Reconstruction in America, 1860–1880* (1935; New York: Free Press, 1998); Silvana R. Siddali, *From Property to Person: Slavery and the Confiscation Acts, 1861–1862* (Baton Rouge: Louisiana State University Press, 2005); Barbara J. Fields, *Slavery and Freedom on the Middle Ground: Maryland During the Nineteenth Century* (New Haven, Conn.: Yale University Press, 1985); Willie Lee Rose, *Rehearsal for Reconstruction: The Port Royal Experiment* (Indianapolis: Bobbs-Merrill, 1964); Armstead L. Robinson, *Bitter Fruits of Bondage: The Demise of Slavery and the Collapse of the Confederacy, 1861–1865* (Charlottesville: University of Virginia Press, 2005); Thavolia Glymph, *Out of the House of Bondage: The Transformation of the Plantation Household* (New York: Cambridge University Press, 2008); James M. McPherson, *The Negro's Civil War: How American Negroes Felt and Acted During the War for the Union* (New York: Vintage, 1965); David W. Blight, *Frederick Douglass' Civil War: Keeping Faith in Jubilee* (Baton Rouge: Louisiana State University Press, 1991); Benjamin Quarles, *The Negro in the Civil War* (Boston: Beacon Press, 1953); Matthew J. Clavin, *Toussaint Louverture and the American Civil War: The Promise and Perils of a Second Haitian Revolution* (Philadelphia: University of Pennsylvania Press, 2011).

On Lincoln's views on slavery and his embrace of emancipation, see Eric Foner, *The Fiery Trial: Abraham Lincoln and American Slavery* (New York: W. W. Norton, 2010);

Louis P. Masur, *Lincoln's Hundred Days: The Emancipation Proclamation and the War for the Union* (Cambridge, Mass.: Harvard University Press, 2012); William K. Klingaman, *Lincoln and the Road to Emancipation, 1861–1865* (New York: Viking, 2001); LaWanda Cox, *Lincoln and Black Freedom: A Study in Presidential Leadership* (Columbia: University of South Carolina Press, 1981); David Herbert Donald, *Lincoln* (New York: Touchstone, 1995); Kate Masur, *An Example for All the Land: Emancipation and the Struggle over Equality in Washington, D.C.* (Chapel Hill: University of North Carolina Press, 2010); James M. McPherson, *Abraham Lincoln and the Second American Revolution* (New York: Oxford University Press, 1990); Michael P. Johnson, ed., *Abraham Lincoln, Slavery, and the Civil War: Selected Writings and Speeches* (Boston: Bedford/St. Martin's, 2001); John Hope Franklin, *The Emancipation Proclamation* (Garden City, N.Y.: Doubleday, 1965); William Blair and Karen Younger, eds., *Lincoln's Proclamation: Emancipation Reconsidered* (Chapel Hill: University of North Carolina Press, 2009).

On resistance to the policies of the Lincoln administration within the Union, see Frank L. Klement, *The Copperheads in the Middle West* (Chicago: University of Chicago Press, 1960) and *The Limits of Dissent: Clement L. Vallandigham and the Civil War* (New York: Fordham University Press, 1999); Jennifer L. Weber, *The Copperheads: The Rise and Fall of Lincoln's Opponents in the North* (New York: Oxford University Press, 2006); Iver Bernstein, *The New York City Draft Riots: Their Significance for American Society and Politics in the Age of the Civil War* (New York: Oxford University Press, 1990); Grace Palladino, *Another Civil War: Labor, Capital, and the State in the Anthracite Regions of Pennsylvania, 1840–1868* (Urbana: University of Illinois Press, 1990); Joel H. Silbey, *A Respectable Minority: The Democratic Party in the Civil War Era, 1860–1868* (New York: W. W. Norton, 1977); Kevin Kenny, *Making Sense of the Molly Maguires* (New York: Oxford University Press, 1998).

On the context for the Gettysburg Address, see Garry Wills, *Lincoln at Gettysburg: The Words That Remade America* (New York: Touchstone, 1992); Martin P. Johnson, *Writing the Gettysburg Address* (Lawrence: University Press of Kansas, 2013); George M. Fredrickson, *The Inner Civil War: Northern Intellectuals and the Crisis of the Union* (New York: Harper and Row, 1965); Edmund Wilson, *Patriotic Gore: Studies in the Literature of the American Civil War* (New York: Oxford University Press, 1962); James M. McPherson, *Crossroads of Freedom: Antietam* (New York: Oxford University Press, 2002); Allen Guelzo, *Gettysburg: The Last Invasion* (New York: Vintage, 2014); T. Harry Williams, *Lincoln and His Generals* (New York: Alfred A. Knopf, 1952); Archer Jones, *Confederate Strategy from Shiloh to Vicksburg* (Baton Rouge: Louisiana State University Press, 1961); Andre M. Fleche, *The Revolution of 1861: The American Civil War in the Age of Nationalist Conflict* (Chapel Hill: University of North Carolina Press, 2014); Mark Neely, *Abraham Lincoln and Civil Liberties* (New York: Oxford University Press, 1991); Drew Gilpin Faust, *This Republic of Suffering: Death and the American Civil War* (New York: Alfred A. Knopf, 2008); Vernon Burton, *The Age of Lincoln* (New York: Hill and Wang, 2007).

Chapter Eight: Defining a Nation-State

On the development of federal policy toward the rebellious South, see Eric Foner, *Reconstruction: America's Unfinished Revolution, 1863–1877* (New York: Harper and Row, 1988); Herman Belz, *Reconstructing the Union: Theory and Policy During the Civil War* (Westport, Conn.: Greenwood Press, 1969); Richard H. Abbott, *The Republican Party and the South, 1855–1877: The First Southern Strategy* (Chapel Hill: University of North Carolina Press, 1986); W. R. Brock, *An American Crisis: Congress and Reconstruction, 1865–1867* (New York: Harper and Row, 1963); Allan Bogue, *The Earnest Men: Republicans of the Civil War Senate* (Ithaca, N.Y.: Cornell University Press, 1981); Louis Masur, *Lincoln's Last Speech: Wartime Reconstruction and the Crisis of Reunion* (New York: Oxford University Press, 2015); Michael Les Benedict, *A Compromise of Principle: Congressional Republicans and Reconstruction, 1863–1869* (New York: W. W. Norton, 1974); William C. Harris, *With Charity for All: Lincoln and the Restoration of the Union* (Lexington: University Press of Kentucky, 1997); Earl M. Maltz, *Civil Rights, the Constitution, and Congress, 1863–1869* (Lawrence: University Press of Kansas, 1990); William A. Blair, *With Malice Toward Some: Treason and Loyalty in the Civil War Era* (Chapel Hill: University of North Carolina Press, 2014); Mark Summers, *The Ordeal of Reunion: A New History of Reconstruction* (Chapel Hill: University of North Carolina Press, 2014).

On early policies regarding the freedpeople and experiments in free labor, see Ira Berlin et al., eds., *Freedom: A Documentary History of Emancipation, 1861–1867*, ser. 1, vol. 3, *The Wartime Genesis of Free Labor: The Lower South* (New York: Cambridge University Press, 1990); Ira Berlin et al., eds., *Freedom: A Documentary History of Emancipation, 1861–1867*, ser. 1, vol. 2, *The Wartime Genesis of Free Labor: The Upper South* (New York: Cambridge University Press, 1993); Robert Dale Owen et al., *Final Report of the American Freedmen's Inquiry Commission* (Washington, D.C., 1864); Lawrence N. Powell, *New Masters: Northern Planters in the Civil War and Reconstruction* (New Haven, Conn.: Yale University Press, 1980); Willie Lee Rose, *Rehearsal for Reconstruction: The Port Royal Experiment* (Indianapolis: Bobbs-Merrill, 1964); James Oakes, *Freedom National: The Destruction of Slavery in the United States, 1861–1865* (New York: W. W. Norton, 2014); Louis Gerteis, *From Contraband to Freedman: Federal Policy Toward Southern Blacks, 1861–1865* (Westport, Conn.: Greenwood Press, 1973); Joseph G. Dawson III, *Army Generals and Reconstruction: Louisiana, 1862–1877* (Baton Rouge: Louisiana State University Press, 1982); Peyton McCrary, *Abraham Lincoln and Reconstruction: The Louisiana Experiment* (Princeton, N.J.: Princeton University Press, 1978); LaWanda Cox, *Lincoln and Black Freedom: A Study in Presidential Leadership* (Columbia: University of Missouri Press, 1981); Janet Sharp Hermann, *The Pursuit of a Dream* (New York: Oxford University Press, 1981); Paul Cimbala and Randall Miller, eds., *The Freedmen's Bureau and Reconstruction: Reconsiderations* (New York: Fordham University Press, 1999); Judith Ann Giesberg, *Civil War Sisterhood: The U.S. Sanitary Commission and Women's Politics in Transition* (Boston: Northeastern University Press, 2000); Joe M. Richardson, *Christian Reconstruction: The American Missionary Association and Southern Blacks, 1861–1890* (Athens: University of Georgia Press, 1986).

On federal policy toward Native Americans and the warfare in the West, see David A. Nichols, *Lincoln and the Indians: Civil War Policy and Politics* (Urbana: University of Illinois Press, 1978); Ari Kelman, *A Misplaced Massacre: Struggling over the Memory of Sand Creek* (Cambridge, Mass.: Harvard University Press, 2013); Jerome A. Greene and Douglas D. Scott, *Finding Sand Creek: History, Archeology, and the 1864 Massacre Site* (Norman: University of Oklahoma Press, 2004); Robert Utley, *The Indian Frontier of the American West, 1846–1890* (Albuquerque: University of New Mexico Press, 1984); Alvin M. Josephy Jr., *The Civil War in the American West* (New York: Alfred A. Knopf, 1991); Karl Jacoby, *Shadows at Dawn: A Borderlands Massacre and the Violence of History*

(New York: Penguin, 2008); Francis P. Prucha, *The Great Father: The U.S. and the American Indians*, 2 vols. (Lincoln: University of Nebraska Press, 1984); C. Joseph Genetin-Palawa, *Crooked Paths to Allotment: The Fight over Indian Policy After the Civil War* (Chapel Hill: University of North Carolina Press, 2012); M. Thomas Bailey, *Reconstruction in Indian Territory: A Story of Avarice, Discrimination, and Opportunism* (Port Washington, N.Y.: Kennikat Press, 1972); Annie Heloise Abel, *The American Indian and the End of the Confederacy, 1863–1866* (1925; repr., Lincoln: University of Nebraska Press, 1993); Clarissa W. Confer, *The Cherokee Nation in the Civil War* (Norman: University of Oklahoma Press, 2012).

On the military participation of African Americans during the War of the Rebellion and the wartime mobilizations of African Americans, slave and free, see Ira Berlin et al., eds., *Freedom: A Documentary History of Emancipation, 1861–1867*, ser. 2, *The Black Military Experience* (New York: Cambridge University Press, 1982); Benjamin Quarles, *The Negro in the Civil War* (Boston: Little, Brown, 1953); Joseph T. Wilson, *The Black Phalanx: A History of Negro Soldiers of the United States in the Wars of 1775–1812, 1861–1865* (Hartford, Conn.: American, 1890); James M. McPherson, *The Negro's Civil War: How American Negroes Felt and Acted During the War for the Union* (New York: Vintage, 1965); Dudley T. Cornish, *The Sable Arm: Negro Troops in the Union Army, 1861–1865* (1956; New York: W. W. Norton, 1966); Joseph T. Glatthaar, *Forged in Battle: The Civil War Alliance of Black Soldiers and White Officers* (New York: Free Press, 1989); Edwin S. Redkey, ed., *A Grand Army of Black Men: Letters from African-American Soldiers in the Union Army* (New York: Cambridge University Press, 1992); Thomas Wentworth Higginson, *Army Life in a Black Regiment* (1869; Boston: Beacon Press, 1962); Steven Hahn, *A Nation Under Our Feet: Black Political Struggles in the Rural South from Slavery to the Great Migration* (Cambridge, Mass.: Harvard University Press, 2003); Ted Tunnell, *Crucible of Reconstruction: War, Radicalism, and Race in Louisiana, 1862–1877* (Baton Rouge: Louisiana State University Press, 1984); Leon Litwack, *Been in the Storm So Long: The Aftermath of Slavery* (New York: Alfred A. Knopf, 1979); Stephen D. Kantrowitz, *More Than Freedom: Fighting for Black Citizenship in a White Republic, 1829–1889* (New York: Penguin, 2012); Hugh Davis, *"We Will Be Satisfied with Nothing Less": The African-American Struggle for Equal Rights in the North During Reconstruction* (Ithaca, N.Y.: Cornell University Press, 2011); James M. McPherson, *The Struggle for Equality: Abolitionists and the Negro in the Civil War and Reconstruction* (Princeton, N.J.: Princeton University Press, 1964); David Roediger, *Seizing Freedom: Slave Emancipation and Liberty for All* (London: Verso, 2014).

On the military and political unraveling of the Confederate rebellion, see Bruce Levine, *The Fall of the House of Dixie: How the Civil War Remade the American South* (New York: Random House, 2013) and *Confederate Emancipation: Southern Plans to Free and Arm Slaves During the Civil War* (New York: Oxford University Press, 2006); Armstead L. Robinson, *Bitter Fruits of Bondage: The Demise of Slavery and the Collapse of the Confederacy, 1861–1865* (Charlottesville: University of Virginia Press, 2005); Emory M. Thomas, *The Confederate Nation, 1861–1865* (New York: Harper and Row, 1979); Victoria E. Bynum, *The Free State of Jones: Mississippi's Longest Civil War* (Chapel Hill: University of North Carolina Press, 2001); David Williams et al., *Plain Folk in a Rich Man's War: Class and Dissent in Confederate Georgia* (Gainesville: University Press of Florida, 2002); Stephanie McCurry, *Confederate Reckoning* (Cambridge, Mass.: Harvard University

Press, 2010); William W. Freehling, *The South Versus the South: How Anti-Confederate Southerners Shaped the Course of the Civil War* (New York: Oxford University Press, 2001); Charles W. Ramsdell, *Behind the Lines in the Southern Confederacy* (Baton Rouge: Louisiana State University Press, 1944); Ella Lonn, *Desertion During the Civil War* (Gloucester, Mass.: Peter Smith, 1966); Bell Wiley, *The Plain People of the Confederacy* (Baton Rouge: Louisiana State University Press, 1944); George C. Rable, *The Confederate Republic: A Revolution Against Politics* (Chapel Hill: University of North Carolina Press, 2007); James M. McPherson, *Embattled Rebel: Jefferson Davis as Commander in Chief* (New York: Penguin, 2014); Gary W. Gallagher, *The Confederate War* (Cambridge, Mass.: Harvard University Press, 1999); Drew Gilpin Faust, *The Creation of Confederate Nationalism* (Baton Rouge: Louisiana State University Press, 1988) and *Mothers of Invention: Women of the Slaveholding South in the American Civil War* (Chapel Hill: University of North Carolina Press, 2004).

On the tumultuous transition from the Lincoln to the Johnson administration and the dynamics of presidential Reconstruction, see Gregory P. Downs, *After Appomattox: Military Occupation and the Ends of War* (Cambridge, Mass.: Harvard University Press, 2015); Martha Hodes, *Mourning Lincoln* (New Haven, Conn.: Yale University Press, 2015); Eric McKitrick, *Andrew Johnson and Reconstruction* (Chicago: University of Chicago Press, 1960); Eric Foner, *The Fiery Trial: Abraham Lincoln and American Slavery* (New York: W. W. Norton, 2010); Michael Perman, *Reunion Without Compromise: The South and Reconstruction, 1865–1868* (Cambridge, U.K.: Cambridge University Press, 1973); Dan T. Carter, *When the War Was Over: The Failure of Self-Reconstruction in the South, 1865–1867* (Baton Rouge: Louisiana State University Press, 1985); LaWanda Cox and John H. Cox, *Politics, Principle, and Prejudice, 1865–1866: Dilemma of Reconstruction America* (New York: Macmillan, 1963); Brooks D. Simpson, *Let Us Have Peace: Ulysses S. Grant and the Politics of War and Reconstruction, 1861–1868* (Chapel Hill: University of North Carolina Press, 1991); William C. Harris, *Presidential Reconstruction in Mississippi* (Baton Rouge: Louisiana State University Press, 1967).

On African Americans and the land question, see Steven Hahn et al., eds., *Freedom: A Documentary History of Emancipation, 1861–1867*, ser. 3, vol. 1, *Land and Labor in 1865* (Chapel Hill: University of North Carolina Press, 2008); Steven Hahn, "'Extravagant Expectations of Freedom': Rumor, Political Struggle, and the Christmas Insurrection Scare of 1865 in the American South," *Past and Present* 157 (Nov. 1997): 122–58; Steven Hahn et al., eds., "The Terrain of Freedom: The Struggle over the Meaning of Free Labour in the U.S. South," *History Workshop Journal* 22 (1986): 108–30; Edward Magdol, *A Right to the Land: Essays on the Freedmen's Community* (Westport, Conn.: Greenwood Press, 1977); Claude F. Oubre, *Forty Acres and a Mule: The Freedmen's Bureau and Black Land Ownership* (Baton Rouge: Louisiana State University Press, 1978); William McFeely, *Yankee Stepfather: O. O. Howard and the Freedmen* (New York: W. W. Norton, 1968); Michael Lanza, *Agrarianism and Reconstruction Politics: The Southern Homestead Act* (Baton Rouge: Louisiana State University Press, 1990); Joel Williamson, *After Slavery: The Negro in South Carolina During Reconstruction, 1861–1877* (Chapel Hill: University of North Carolina Press, 1965).

On the making and limits of Military (Radical) Reconstruction, see W. E. B. Du Bois, *Black Reconstruction in America, 1860–1880* (New York: Russell and Russell, 1935); Michael Vorenberg, *Final Freedom: The Civil War, the Abolition of Slavery, and the*

Thirteenth Amendment (New York: Cambridge University Press, 2004); Leonard L. Richards, *Who Freed the Slaves? The Fight over the Thirteenth Amendment* (Chicago: University of Chicago Press, 2015); Hans L. Trefousse, *The Radical Republicans: Lincoln's Vanguard for Racial Justice* (New York: Alfred A. Knopf, 1969); David Donald, *Charles Sumner and the Rights of Man* (New York: Alfred A. Knopf, 1970); Eric Foner, *Politics and Ideology in the Age of the Civil War* (New York: Oxford University Press, 1980); Robert J. Kaczorowski, *The Politics of Judicial Interpretation: The Federal Courts, the Department of Justice, and Civil Rights, 1866–1876* (New York: Fordham University Press, 1985); Herman Belz, *Emancipation and Equal Rights: Politics and Constitutionalism in the Civil War Era* (New York: W. W. Norton, 1978); Harold M. Hyman, *A More Perfect Union: The Impact of the Civil War and Reconstruction on the Constitution* (Boston: Houghton Mifflin, 1975); Gerard Magliocca, *American Founding Son: John Bingham and the Invention of the Fourteenth Amendment* (New York: New York University Press, 2013); Laura Edwards, *A Legal History of the Civil War and Reconstruction: A Nation of Rights* (New York: Cambridge University Press, 2015); Ellen Carol DuBois, *Feminism and Suffrage: The Emergence of an Independent Women's Movement in America* (Ithaca, N.Y.: Cornell University Press, 1978); Faye E. Dudden, *A Fighting Chance: The Struggle over Woman Suffrage and Black Suffrage in Reconstruction America* (New York: Oxford University Press, 2011); Jean H. Baker, ed., *Votes for Women: The Struggle for Suffrage Revisited* (New York: Oxford University Press, 2002); Jean H. Baker, *Sisters: The Lives of American Suffragists* (New York: Hill and Wang, 2006).

Chapter Nine: Capitalism

The advance of capitalism in the United States depended on a host of important interconnections: national and international markets, new forms of finance, transportation and communication networks, and the support of the state at several levels. As this chapter suggests, it was a rocky and uneven course punctuated by crisis. On the emergence of finance capital and the panic of 1873, see Richard Franklin Bensel, *Yankee Leviathan: The Origins of Central State Authority in America* (New York: Cambridge University Press, 1990); Robert Sharkey, *Money, Class, and Party: An Economic Study of the Civil War and Reconstruction* (Baltimore: Johns Hopkins University Press, 1960); Irwin Unger, *The Greenback Era: A Social and Political History of American Finance, 1865–1879* (Princeton, N.J.: Princeton University Press, 1964); Jonathan Levy, *Freaks of Fortune: The Emerging World of Capitalism and Risk in America* (Cambridge, Mass.: Harvard University Press, 2012); M. John Lubetkin, *Jay Cooke's Gamble: The Northern Pacific, the Sioux, and the Panic of 1873* (Norman: University of Oklahoma Press, 2006); Henrietta Larson, *Jay Cooke* (Cambridge, Mass.: Harvard University Press, 1936); Jean Strouse, *Morgan: American Financier* (New York: Random House, 1999); Ron Chernow, *The House of Morgan: An American Banking Dynasty and the Rise of Modern Finance* (New York: Grove Press, 2010); Richard White, *Railroaded: The Transcontinentals and the Making of Modern America* (New York: W. W. Norton, 2011); Scott R. Nelson, *A Nation of Deadbeats: An Uncommon History of America's Financial Disasters* (New York: Alfred A. Knopf, 2012); Jack Beatty, *The Age of Betrayal: The Triumph of Money in America, 1865–1900* (New York: Alfred A. Knopf, 2007); Leland H. Jenks, *The Migration of British Capital to 1875* (New York: Alfred A. Knopf, 1927); Dolores Greenberg, *Financiers and Railroads, 1869–1889* (East Brunswick, N.J.: Associated University Presses, 1980);

David T. Gilchrist and W. David Lewis, eds., *Economic Change in the Civil War Era* (Green-ville, Del.: Hagley Foundation, 1965); Steve Fraser, *Every Man a Speculator: A History of Wall Street in American Life* (New York: Harper Perennial, 2006); Margaret G. Myers, *The New York Money Market: Origins and Development* (New York: Columbia University Press, 1931).

On the transformation of the post-emancipation southern economy, see Thavolia Glymph and John J. Kushma, eds., *Essays on the Postbellum Southern Economy* (College Station: Texas A&M University Press, 1985); C. Vann Woodward, *Origins of the New South, 1877–1913* (Baton Rouge: Louisiana State University Press, 1951); Barbara J. Fields, *Slavery and Freedom on the Middle Ground: Maryland During the Nineteenth Century* (New Haven, Conn.: Yale University Press, 1985); Harold D. Woodman, *King Cotton and His Retainers: Financing and Marketing the Cotton Crop of the South* (Lexington: University of Kentucky Press, 1967) and *New South, New Law: The Legal Foundations of Labor and Credit Relations in the Postbellum South* (Baton Rouge: Louisiana State University Press, 1995); Gavin Wright, *Old South, New South: Revolutions in the Southern Economy Since the Civil War* (New York: Basic Books, 1985); Gerald Jaynes, *Branches Without Roots: The Genesis of the Black Working Class in the American South, 1862–1882* (New York: Oxford University Press, 1986); Roger Ransom and Richard Sutch, *One Kind of Freedom: The Economic Consequences of Emancipation* (New York: Cambridge University Press, 1977); Sharon Ann Holt, *Making Freedom Pay: North Carolina Freed People Working for Themselves, 1865–1900* (Athens: University of Georgia Press, 2000); Jay R. Mandle, *The Roots of Black Poverty: The Southern Plantation Economy After the Civil War* (Durham, N.C.: Duke University Press, 1978); Julie Saville, *The Work of Reconstruction: From Slave to Wage Laborer in South Carolina, 1860–1870* (New York: Cambridge University Press, 1994); Leslie Schwalm, *A Hard Fight for We: Women's Transition from Slavery to Freedom in South Carolina* (Urbana: University of Illinois Press, 1997); Joseph P. Reidy, *From Slavery to Agrarian Capitalism in the Cotton Plantation South: Central Georgia, 1800–1880* (Chapel Hill: University of North Carolina Press, 1992); Jeffrey Kerr-Ritchie, *Freedpeople in the Tobacco South: Virginia, 1860–1900* (Chapel Hill: University of North Carolina Press, 1997); John Rodrigue, *Reconstruction in the Cane Fields: From Slavery to Free Labor in Louisiana's Sugar Parishes, 1862–1880* (Baton Rouge: Louisiana State University Press, 2001); Steven Hahn, *The Roots of Southern Populism: Yeoman Farmers and the Transformation of the Georgia Upcountry, 1850–1890* (New York: Oxford University Press, 1983); Michael Wayne, *The Reshaping of Plantation Society: The Natchez District, 1860–1880* (Baton Rouge: Louisiana State University Press, 1983); Jonathan M. Wiener, *Social Origins of the New South: Alabama, 1860–1885* (Baton Rouge: Louisiana State University Press, 1978); Alex Lichtenstein, *Twice the Work of Free Labor: The Political Economy of Convict Labor in the New South* (London: Verso, 1996); Tera Hunter, *To 'Joy My Freedom: Southern Black Women's Lives and Labor After the Civil War* (Cambridge, Mass.: Harvard University Press, 1997); Jacqueline Jones, *Labor of Love, Labor of Sorrow: Black Women, Work, and the Family from Slavery to the Present* (New York: Basic Books, 1985); Dylan Penningroth, *The Claims of Kinfolk: African-American Property and Community in the Nineteenth-Century South* (Chapel Hill: University of North Carolina Press, 2003); Dwight B. Billings, *Planters and the Making of a "New South": Class, Politics, and Development in North Carolina, 1865–1900* (Chapel Hill: University of North Carolina Press, 1979); Crandall Shifflett, *Coal Towns: Life, Work, and Culture in the Company*

Towns of Southern Appalachia, 1880–1960 (Knoxville: University of Tennessee Press, 1991); David L. Carlton, *Mill and Town in South Carolina, 1880–1920* (Baton Rouge: Louisiana State University Press, 1982); Pete Daniel, *Breaking the Land: The Enclosure of Cotton, Tobacco, and Rice Cultures* (Urbana: University of Illinois Press, 1984); Don H. Doyle, *New Men, New Cities, New South: Atlanta, Nashville, Charleston, Mobile, 1860–1910* (Chapel Hill: University of North Carolina Press, 1990); Neil Foley, *The White Scourge: Mexicans, Blacks, and Poor Whites in Texas Cotton Culture* (Berkeley: University of California Press, 1997).

For an international perspective on the development of post-emancipation societies, see Eric Foner, *Nothing but Freedom: Emancipation and Its Legacy* (Baton Rouge: Louisiana State University Press, 1982); Thomas Holt, *The Problem of Freedom: Race, Labor, and Politics in Jamaica and Britain, 1832–1938* (Baltimore: Johns Hopkins University Press, 1992); Rebecca J. Scott, *Degrees of Freedom: Louisiana and Cuba After Slavery* (Cambridge, Mass.: Harvard University Press, 2005); Pamela Scully and Diana Paton, eds., *Gender and Slave Emancipation in the Atlantic World* (Durham, N.C.: Duke University Press, 2005); Peter Kolchin, *A Sphinx on the Land: The Nineteenth-Century South in Comparative Perspective* (Baton Rouge: Louisiana State University Press, 2003); Frederick Cooper et al., *Beyond Slavery: Explorations of Race, Labor, and Citizenship in Postemancipation Societies* (Chapel Hill: University of North Carolina Press, 2000); Sven Beckert, *Empire of Cotton: A Global History* (New York: Alfred A. Knopf, 2014).

On the transformation of the countryside in the trans-Mississippi West, see Fred A. Shannon, *The Farmer's Last Frontier: Agriculture, 1860–1897* (New York: Harper and Row, 1945); Gilbert Fite, *The Farmers' Frontier, 1865–1900* (New York: Holt, Rinehart and Winston, 1966); Rodman Paul, *The Far West and the Great Plains in Transition, 1859–1900* (New York: Harper and Row, 1988) and *The Mining Frontier of the Far West, 1848–1880* (Albuquerque: University of New Mexico Press, 1963); Donald J. Pisani, *From the Family Farm to Agribusiness: The Irrigation Crusade in California and the West, 1850–1930* (New York: Cambridge University Press, 2000); Richard Lingenfelter, *The Hardrock Miners: A History of the Mining Labor Movement in the American West, 1863–1893* (Berkeley: University of California Press, 1974); Thomas Andrews, *Killing for Coal: America's Deadliest Labor War* (Cambridge, Mass.: Harvard University Press, 2008); Linda Gordon, *The Great Arizona Orphan Abduction* (Cambridge, Mass.: Harvard University Press, 2001); Samuel Truett, *Fugitive Landscapes: The Forgotten History of the U.S.-Mexico Borderlands* (New Haven, Conn.: Yale University Press, 2006); Sarah Deutsch, *No Separate Refuge: Class, Culture, and Gender on the Anglo-Hispanic Frontier in the American Southwest, 1880–1940* (New York: Oxford University Press, 1987); Frank Tobias Higbie, *Indispensable Outcasts: Hobo Workers and Community in the American Midwest, 1880–1930* (Urbana: University of Illinois Press, 2003); Cecilia Danysk, *Hired Hands: Labour and the Development of Prairie Agriculture, 1880–1930* (Toronto: McClellan and Stewart, 1995); Cletus Daniel, *Bitter Harvest: A History of California Farmworkers, 1870–1941* (Ithaca, N.Y.: Cornell University Press, 1981); Deborah Fink, *Agrarian Women: Wives and Mothers in Rural Nebraska, 1880–1940* (Chapel Hill: University of North Carolina Press, 1992); María E. Montoya, *Translating Property: The Maxwell Land Grant and the Conflict over Land in the American West, 1840–1900* (Berkeley: University of California Press, 2002); Sucheng Chan, *This Bittersweet Soil: The Chinese in California Agriculture, 1860–1910* (Berkeley: University of California Press, 1986).

On the transformations in agriculture of the Northeast, see Thomas Summerhill, *Harvest of Dissent: Agrarianism in Nineteenth-Century New York* (Urbana: University of Illinois Press, 2005); Hal Barron, *Those Who Stayed Behind: Rural Society in Nineteenth-Century New England* (New York: Cambridge University Press, 1988) and *Mixed Harvest: The Second Great Transformation in the Rural North, 1870–1930* (Chapel Hill: University of North Carolina Press, 1997); Cindy Hahamovitch, *The Fruits of Their Labor: Atlantic Coast Farmworkers and the Making of Migrant Poverty, 1870–1945* (Chapel Hill: University of North Carolina Press, 1997).

On the patterns of postbellum industrialization, see Edward Kirkland, *Industry Comes of Age: Business, Labor, and Public Policy, 1860–1897* (Chicago: Quadrangle Books, 1961); Walter Licht, *Industrializing America: The Nineteenth Century* (Baltimore: Johns Hopkins University Press, 1995); David M. Gordon et al., *Segmented Work, Divided Workers: The Historical Transformation of Labor in the United States* (New York: Cambridge University Press, 1982); Richard Franklin Bensel, *The Political Economy of American Industrialization, 1877–1900* (New York: Cambridge University Press, 2000); Alexander M. Keyssar, *Out of Work: The First Century of Unemployment in Massachusetts* (New York: Cambridge University Press, 1986); Walter Licht, *Working for the Railroad: The Organization of Work in the Nineteenth Century* (Princeton, N.J.: Princeton University Press, 1983); David Montgomery, *The Fall of the House of Labor: The Workplace, the State, and American Labor Activism, 1865–1925* (New York: Cambridge University Press, 1987) and *Workers' Control in America: Studies in the History of Work, Technology, and Labor Struggles* (New York: Cambridge University Press, 1979); Daniel Nelson, *Managers and Workers: Origins of the New Factory System in the United States, 1880–1920* (Madison: University of Wisconsin Press, 1975); William G. Roy, *Socializing Capital: The Rise of the Large Industrial Corporation in America* (Princeton, N.J.: Princeton University Press, 1997); Alfred Chandler, *The Visible Hand: The Managerial Revolution in American Business* (Cambridge, Mass.: Harvard University Press, 1977); David Nasaw, *Andrew Carnegie* (New York: Penguin, 2007); T. J. Stiles, *The First Tycoon: The Epic Life of Cornelius Vanderbilt* (New York: Vintage, 2010); Ron Chernow, *Titan: The Life of John D. Rockefeller Sr.* (New York: Vintage, 2004); Olivier Zunz, *Making America Corporate* (Chicago: University of Chicago Press, 1992); Alice Kessler-Harris, *Out to Work: A History of Wage-Earning Women in the United States* (New York: Oxford University Press, 1982); Jacqueline Jones, *The Dispossessed: America's Underclasses from the Civil War to the Present* (New York: Basic Books, 1992); Katherine Benton-Cohen, *Borderline Americans: Racial Division and Labor War in the Arizona Borderlands* (Cambridge, Mass.: Harvard University Press, 2009); David Brody, *Steelworkers in America: The Non-union Era* (Cambridge, Mass.: Harvard University Press, 1960); David Katzman, *Seven Days a Week: Women and Domestic Service in Industrializing America* (New York: Oxford University Press, 1978); Judith A. McGaw, *Most Wonderful Machine: Mechanization and Social Change in Berkshire Paper Making, 1801–1885* (Princeton, N.J.: Princeton University Press, 1987); Joanne Meyerowitz, *Women Adrift: Independent Wage Earners in Chicago, 1880–1930* (Chicago: University of Chicago Press, 1988); Joshua Rosenbloom, *Looking for Work, Searching for Workers: American Labor Markets During Industrialization* (New York: Cambridge University Press, 2002); Philip Scranton, *Endless Novelty: Specialty Production and American Industrialization, 1865–1925* (Princeton, N.J.: Princeton University Press, 1997); Daniel Walkowitz, *Worker City, Company Town: Iron and Cotton-Worker Protests in Troy and Cohoes, New York,*

1855–84 (Urbana: University of Illinois Press, 1978); Francis G. Couvares, *The Remaking of Pittsburgh: Class and Culture in an Industrializing City, 1877–1919* (Albany: State University of New York Press, 1984).

On immigration and industrialization, see Herbert Gutman, *Work, Culture, and Society in Industrializing America* (New York: Alfred A. Knopf, 1976); Gunther Peck, *Reinventing Free Labor: Padrones and Immigrant Workers in the North American West, 1880–1930* (New York: Cambridge University Press, 2000); Roger Daniels, *Asian America: Chinese and Japanese in the United States Since 1850* (Seattle: University of Washington Press, 1988) and *Coming to America: A History of Immigration and Ethnicity in American Life* (New York: HarperCollins, 1990); John Bodnar, *Immigration and Industrialization: Ethnicity in an American Mill Town, 1870–1940* (Pittsburgh: University of Pittsburgh Press, 1977); Jon Gjerde, *From Peasants to Farmers: The Migration from Balestrand, Norway, to the Upper Midwest* (New York: Cambridge University Press, 1985); Madeline Yuan-yin Hsu, *Dreaming of Gold, Dreaming of Home: Transnationalism and Migration Between the United States and South China, 1882–1943* (Stanford, Calif.: Stanford University Press, 2000); Erika Lee, *At America's Gates: Chinese Immigration During the Exclusion Era, 1882–1943* (Chapel Hill: University of North Carolina Press, 2003); Kerby Miller, *Emigrants and Exiles: Ireland and the Irish Exodus to North America* (New York: Oxford University Press, 1985); Mae Ngai, *Impossible Subjects: Illegal Aliens and the Making of Modern America* (Princeton, N.J.: Princeton University Press, 2004).

On the cultural, intellectual, and class currents that flowed in relation to the development of capitalism, see T. J. Jackson Lears, *Rebirth of a Nation: The Making of Modern America, 1877–1920* (New York: HarperCollins, 2009); Richard Hofstadter, *Social Darwinism in American Thought* (Philadelphia: University of Pennsylvania Press, 1944); Alan Trachtenberg, *The Incorporation of America: Culture and Society in the Gilded Age* (New York: W. W. Norton, 1982); Nancy L. Cohen, *The Reconstruction of American Liberalism, 1865–1914* (Chapel Hill: University of North Carolina Press, 2002); Sven Beckert, *The Monied Metropolis: New York City and the Consolidation of the American Bourgeoisie, 1850–1896* (New York: Cambridge University Press, 2001); Jeffrey Sklansky, *The Soul's Economy: Market Society and Selfhood in American Thought, 1820–1920* (Chapel Hill: University of North Carolina Press, 2002); John G. Sproat, *"The Best Men": Liberal Reformers in the Gilded Age* (New York: Oxford University Press, 1968); Stuart Blumin, *The Emergence of the Middle Class: Social Experience in the American City, 1769–1900* (New York: Cambridge University Press, 1989); Daniel Rodgers, *The Work Ethic in Industrial America, 1850–1920* (Chicago: University of Chicago Press, 1979).

On the role of the courts and the military arm of the state in the development of capitalist social relations, see Amy Dru Stanley, *From Bondage to Contract: Wage Labor, Marriage, and the Market in the Age of Emancipation* (New York: Cambridge University Press, 1998); David Montgomery, *Citizen Worker: The Experience of Workers in the United States with Democracy and the Free Market During the Nineteenth Century* (New York: Cambridge University Press, 1993); Stephen Skowronek, *Building a New American State: The Expansion of National Administrative Capacities, 1877–1920* (New York: Cambridge University Press, 1982); Karen Orren, *Belated Feudalism: Labor, the Law, and Liberal Development in the United States* (New York: Cambridge University Press, 1991); Clayton D. Laurie and Ronald H. Cole, *The Role of Federal Military Forces in Domestic Disorders, 1877–1945* (Washington, D.C.: Department of the Army, 1997); William E. Forbath,

Law and the Shaping of the American Labor Movement (Cambridge, Mass.: Harvard University Press, 1991); Morton Horwitz, *The Transformation of American Law, 1870–1960: The Crisis of Legal Orthodoxy* (New York: Oxford University Press, 1992); James Willard Hurst, *Law and Markets in the United States: Different Modes of Bargaining Among Interests* (Madison: University of Wisconsin Press, 1982); Christopher L. Tomlins, *The State and the Unions: Labor Relations, Law, and the Organized Labor Movement, 1880–1960* (New York: Cambridge University Press, 1985); Michael Grossberg and Christopher Tomlins, eds., *The Cambridge History of Law in America*, vol. 2, *The Long Nineteenth Century (1789–1920)* (New York: Cambridge University Press, 2011); Barbara Young Welke, *Recasting American Liberty: Gender, Race, Law, and the Railroad Revolution, 1865–1920* (New York: Cambridge University Press, 2001) and *Law and the Borders of Belonging in the Long Nineteenth Century United States* (New York: Cambridge University Press, 2010); Eric H. Monkkonen, *The Police in Urban America, 1860–1920* (New York: Cambridge University Press, 2004); Jerry Cooper, *The Rise of the National Guard: The Evolution of the American Militia, 1865–1920* (Lincoln, Neb.: Bison Books, 2002).

Chapter Ten: Imperial Arms

I have tried to conceptualize Reconstruction as part of the imperial projects of the new American nation-state, especially in its radical phase that effectively ended the rebellion and brought about a brief but consequential political revolution in the former rebellious states. On the advent and dimensions of Military (Radical) Reconstruction, see Eric Foner, *Reconstruction: America's Unfinished Revolution, 1863–1877* (New York: Harper and Row, 1988); W. E. B. Du Bois, *Black Reconstruction in America, 1860–1880* (New York: Russell and Russell, 1935); Steven Hahn, *A Nation Under Our Feet: Black Political Struggles in the Rural South from Slavery to the Great Migration* (Cambridge, Mass.: Harvard University Press, 2003); Thomas Holt, *White over Black: Negro Political Leadership in South Carolina During Reconstruction* (Urbana: University of Illinois Press, 1977); Bruce Baker et al., eds., *After Slavery: Race, Labor, and Citizenship in the Reconstruction South* (Gainesville: University Press of Florida, 2013); Justin Behrend, *Reconstructing Democracy: Grassroots Black Politics in the Deep South After the Civil War* (Athens: University of Georgia Press, 2015); Aaron Astor, *Rebels on the Border: Civil War, Emancipation, and Reconstruction in Kentucky and Missouri* (Baton Rouge: Louisiana State University Press, 2012); Ronald E. Butchart, *Schooling the Freed People: Teaching, Learning, and the Struggles for Black Freedom* (Chapel Hill: University of North Carolina Press, 2010); David Cecelski, *The Fire of Freedom: Abraham Galloway and the Slaves' Civil War* (Chapel Hill: University of North Carolina Press, 2012); Laura Edwards, *Gendered Strife and Confusion: The Political Culture of Reconstruction* (Urbana: University of Illinois Press, 1997); William McKee Evans, *Ballots and Fence Rails: Reconstruction on the Lower Cape Fear* (Chapel Hill: University of North Carolina Press, 1966); Michael Fitzgerald, *The Union League Movement in the Deep South: Politics and Agricultural Change During Reconstruction* (Baton Rouge: Louisiana State University Press, 1989) and *Urban Emancipation: Popular Politics in Reconstruction Mobile* (Baton Rouge: Louisiana State University Press, 2002); Robert F. Engs, *Freedom's First Generation: Black Hampton, Virginia, 1861–1890* (New York: Fordham University Press, 2004); Richard L. Hume and Jerry B. Gough, *Blacks, Carpetbaggers, and Scalawags: The Constitutional Conventions of Radical Reconstruction* (Baton Rouge: Louisiana State University Press, 2008); Richard

Follett et al., *Slavery's Ghost: The Problem of Freedom in the Age of Emancipation* (Baltimore: Johns Hopkins University Press, 2012); Eric Foner, *Freedom's Lawmakers: A Directory of Black Officeholders During Reconstruction* (Baton Rouge: Louisiana State University Press, 1996); Richard N. Current, *Those Terrible Carpetbaggers: A Reinterpretation* (New York: Oxford University Press, 1988); Clarence Walker, *A Rock in a Weary Land: The African Methodist Episcopal Church During the Civil War and Reconstruction* (Baton Rouge: Louisiana State University Press, 1982); Carol Faulkner, *Women's Radical Reconstruction: The Freedmen's Aid Movement* (Philadelphia: University of Pennsylvania Press, 2004); Charles Vincent, *Black Legislators in Louisiana During Reconstruction* (Baton Rouge: Louisiana State University Press, 1977); William C. Harris, *The Day of the Carpetbagger: Republican Reconstruction in Mississippi* (Baton Rouge: Louisiana State University Press, 1979); William E. Montgomery, *Under Their Own Vine and Fig Tree: The African-American Church in the South, 1865–1900* (Baton Rouge: Louisiana State University Press, 1993); Robert C. Morris, *Reading, 'Riting, and Reconstruction: The Education of Freedmen in the South, 1861–1870* (Chicago: University of Chicago Press, 1981); Carl Moneyhon, *The Impact of the Civil War and Reconstruction on Arkansas: Persistence in the Midst of Ruin* (Baton Rouge: Louisiana State University Press, 1994); Ted Tunnell, *Crucible of Reconstruction: War, Radicalism, and Race in Louisiana, 1862–1877* (Baton Rouge: Louisiana State University Press, 1992); Xi Wang, *The Trial of Democracy: Black Suffrage and Northern Republicans, 1860–1910* (Athens: University of Georgia Press, 1997); Edmund Lee Drago, *Black Politicians and Reconstruction in Georgia: A Splendid Failure* (Baton Rouge: Louisiana State University Press, 1982); James A. Baggett, *The Scalawags: Southern Dissenters in the Civil War and Reconstruction* (Baton Rouge: Louisiana State University Press, 2003); Victoria Bynum, *The Free State of Jones: Mississippi's Longest Civil War* (Chapel Hill: University of North Carolina Press, 2001); Richard O. Curry, ed., *Radicalism, Racism, and Party Realignment: The Border States During Reconstruction* (Baltimore: Johns Hopkins University Press, 1969); Peter Bardaglio, *Reconstructing the Household: Families, Sex, and the Law in the Nineteenth Century* (Chapel Hill: University of North Carolina Press, 1995); Mary Farmer-Kaiser, *Freedwomen and the Freedmen's Bureau: Race, Gender, and Public Policy in the Age of Emancipation* (New York: Fordham University Press, 2010).

On paramilitary violence and the process of overthrowing Reconstruction regimes in the rebellious states, see Allen Trelease, *White Terror: The Ku Klux Klan Conspiracy and Southern Reconstruction* (New York: Harper and Row, 1971); Gladys Marie Fry, *Night Riders in Black Folk History* (Athens: University of Georgia Press, 1975); George C. Rable, *But There Was No Peace: The Role of Violence in the Politics of Reconstruction* (Athens: University of Georgia Press, 1984); Carole Emberton, *Beyond Redemption: Race, Violence, and the American South After the Civil War* (Chicago: University of Chicago Press, 2013); Nicholas Lemann, *Redemption: The Last Battle of the Civil War* (New York: Farrar, Straus and Giroux, 2006); LeeAnna Keith, *The Colfax Massacre: The Untold Story of Black Power, White Terror, and the Death of Reconstruction* (New York: Oxford University Press, 2008); Hannah Rosen, *Terror at the Heart of Freedom: Citizenship, Sexual Violence, and the Meaning of Race in the Postemancipation South* (Chapel Hill: University of North Carolina Press, 2009); Lou Faulkner Williams, *The Great South Carolina Ku Klux Klan Trials, 1871–1872* (Athens: University of Georgia Press, 1996); Scott R. Nelson, *Iron Confederacies: Southern Railways, Klan Violence, and Reconstruction* (Chapel Hill: University of North Carolina Press, 1999);

Richard Zuczek, *State of Rebellion: Reconstruction in South Carolina* (Columbia: University of South Carolina Press, 1996); Michael Perman, *The Road to Redemption: Southern Politics, 1869–1879* (Chapel Hill: University of North Carolina Press, 1984); William Gillette, *Retreat from Reconstruction, 1869–1879* (Baton Rouge: Louisiana State University Press, 1979); William McFeely, *Grant: A Biography* (New York: W. W. Norton, 1981); Jean Edward Smith, *Grant* (New York: Simon and Schuster, 2002); Heather Cox Richardson, *The Death of Reconstruction: Race, Labor, and Politics in the Post–Civil War North, 1865–1901* (Cambridge, Mass.: Harvard University Press, 2001); Ronald M. Labbé and Jonathan Lurie, *The Slaughterhouse Cases: Regulation, Reconstruction, and the Fourteenth Amendment* (Lawrence: University Press of Kansas, 2005); Vincent P. DeSantis, *Republicans Face the Southern Question* (Baltimore: Johns Hopkins University Press, 1959); C. Vann Woodward, *Reunion and Reaction: The Compromise of 1877 and the End of Reconstruction* (Boston: Little, Brown, 1951); Michael F. Holt, *By One Vote: The Disputed Presidential Election of 1876* (Lawrence: University Press of Kansas, 2008); Andrew L. Slap, *Doom of Reconstruction: The Liberal Republicans in the Civil War Era* (New York: Fordham University Press, 2006); Keith A. Polakoff, *The Politics of Inertia: The Election of 1876 and the End of Reconstruction* (Baton Rouge: Louisiana State University Press, 1973); Ari Hoogenboom, *Rutherford B. Hayes: Warrior and President* (Lawrence: University Press of Kansas, 1995).

The Reconstruction imperial projects in the trans-Mississippi West were rather different from in the South, concerning as they did Native peoples and the federal territories rather than the rebellious states and the freedpeople. See Jeffrey Ostler, *The Plains Sioux and U.S. Colonialism: From Lewis and Clark to Wounded Knee* (New York: Cambridge University Press, 2004); Francis P. Prucha, *American Indian Policy in Crisis: Christian Reformers and the Indian, 1865–1900* (Norman: University of Oklahoma Press, 1976); Frederick Hoxie, *A Final Promise: The Campaign to Assimilate Indians, 1880–1920* (Lincoln: University of Nebraska Press, 2001); Stephen J. Rockwell, *Indian Affairs and the Administrative State in the Nineteenth Century* (New York: Cambridge University Press, 2010); Frank Rzeczkowski, *Uniting the Tribes: The Rise and Fall of Pan-Indian Community on the Crow Reservation* (Lawrence: University Press of Kansas, 2012); Robert W. Mardock, *Reformers and the American Indian* (Columbia: University of Missouri Press, 1971); Robert Wooster, *The Military and United States Indian Policy, 1865–1903* (New Haven, Conn.: Yale University Press, 1988); Andrew R. Graybill, *Policing the Great Plains: Rangers, Mounties, and the North American Frontier, 1875–1910* (Lincoln: University of Nebraska Press, 2007); David W. Adams, *Education for Extinction: American Indians and the Boarding School Experience, 1875–1928* (Lawrence: University Press of Kansas, 1995); Cathleen D. Cahill, *Federal Fathers and Mothers: A Social History of United States Indian Service, 1869–1933* (Chapel Hill: University of North Carolina Press, 2011); M. C. Coleman, *American Indian Children at School, 1850–1930* (Jackson: University Press of Mississippi, 1993); C. Joseph Genetin-Pilawa, *Crooked Paths to Allotment: The Fight over Federal Indian Policy After the Civil War* (Chapel Hill: University of North Carolina Press, 2012); Emily Greenwald, *Reconfiguring the Reservation: The Nez Perces, Jicarilla Apaches, and the Dawes Act* (Albuquerque: University of New Mexico Press, 2002); Sidney Harring, *Crow Dog's Case: American Indian Sovereignty, Tribal Law, and United States Law in the Nineteenth Century* (New York: Cambridge University Press, 1994); Curtis Hinsley, *The Smithsonian and the American Indian: Making a Moral Anthropology in Victorian America* (Washington, D.C.: Smithsonian Institution Press, 1994); Margaret D. Jacobs, *White Mother to a Dark*

Race: Settler Colonialism, Maternalism, and the Removal of Indigenous Children in the American West and Australia, 1880–1940 (Lincoln: University of Nebraska Press, 2009); Robert H. Keller Jr., *American Protestantism and United States Indian Policy, 1869–1882* (Lincoln: University of Nebraska Press, 1983); D. S. Otis, *The Dawes Act and the Allotment of Lands* (Norman: University of Oklahoma Press, 1973); Robert Utley, *Frontier Regulars: The U.S. Army and the Indian, 1866–1891* (Lincoln: Bison Books, 1984) and *The Indian Frontier of the American West, 1846–1890* (Albuquerque: University of New Mexico Press, 2003); Wilcomb Washburn, *The Assault on Indian Tribalism: The General Allotment Law (Dawes Act) of 1887* (New York: Lippincott, 1975); Heather Cox Richardson, *West from Appomattox: The Reconstruction of America After the Civil War* (New Haven, Conn.: Yale University Press, 2007); Sarah Barringer Gordon, *The Mormon Question: Polygamy and Constitutional Conflict in Nineteenth-Century America* (Chapel Hill: University of North Carolina Press, 2002); Howard R. Lamar, *The Far Southwest, 1846–1912: A Territorial History* (New Haven, Conn.: Yale University Press, 1965); Earl S. Pomeroy, *The Territories and the United States, 1861–1890: Studies in Colonial Administration* (Philadelphia: University of Pennsylvania Press, 1947); Elliot West, *The Last Indian War: The Nez Perce Story* (New York: Oxford University Press, 2009).

On the international and overseas reach of the federal state in the postwar era, see Walter LaFeber, *The New Empire: An Interpretation of American Expansion, 1860–1898* (Ithaca, N.Y.: Cornell University Press, 1963) and *Cambridge History of American Foreign Relations: The American Search for Opportunity, 1865–1913* (New York: Cambridge University Press, 1993); Walter Nugent, *Habits of Empire: A History of American Expansion* (New York: Alfred A. Knopf, 2008); Eric Love, *Race over Empire: Racism and U.S. Imperialism, 1865–1900* (Chapel Hill: University of North Carolina Press, 2004); Tom E. Terrill, *The Tariff, Politics, and American Foreign Policy* (Westport, Conn.: Greenwood Press, 1973); John Mason Hart, *Empire and Revolution: The Americans in Mexico Since the Civil War* (Berkeley: University of California Press, 2002); Juan Mora-Torres, *The Making of the Mexican Border: The State, Capitalism, and Society in Nuevo León, 1848–1910* (Austin: University of Texas Press, 2001); Friedrich Katz and Claudio Lomnitz, *El Porfiriato y la Revolución en la historia de México: Una conversación* (Mexico City: Era, 2011); Paul Vanderwood, *Disorder and Progress: Bandits, Police, and Mexican Development* (Lincoln: University of Nebraska Press, 1981); Miguel Tinker Salas, *A la sombra de las águilas: Sonora y la transformación de la frontera durante el Porfiriato* (Mexico City: Fondo de Cultura Económica, 2010); Gilbert M. Joseph, *Revolution from Without: Yucatán, Mexico, and the United States, 1880–1924* (New York: Cambridge University Press, 1982); Thomas David Schoonover, *Dollars over Dominion: The Triumph of Liberalism in Mexican-American Relations, 1861–1867* (Baton Rouge: Louisiana State University Press, 1978); Ada Ferrer, *Insurgent Cuba: Race, Nation, and Revolution, 1868–1898* (Chapel Hill: University of North Carolina Press, 1999); Rebecca J. Scott, *Degrees of Freedom: Louisiana and Cuba After Slavery* (Cambridge, Mass.: Harvard University Press, 2005); Louis A. Pérez Jr., *Cuba and the United States in History and Historiography* (Athens: University of Georgia Press, 1990); Jules Benjamin, *The United States and Cuba: Hegemony and Dependent Development, 1880–1934* (Pittsburgh: University of Pittsburgh Press, 1977); José M. Hernández, *Cuba and the United States: Intervention and Militarism, 1868–1933* (Austin: University of Texas Press, 1993); Michel Gobat, *Confronting the American Dream: Nicaragua Under U.S. Imperial Rule* (Durham, N.C.: Duke University Press, 2005); Akira Iriye, *Pacific*

Estrangement: Japanese and American Expansion, 1897–1911 (Cambridge, Mass.: Harvard University Press, 1972); Sally E. Merry, *Colonizing Hawai'i: The Cultural Power of Law* (Princeton, N.J.: Princeton University Press, 2000); Noenoe Silva, *Aloha Betrayed: Native Hawaiian Resistance to American Colonialism* (Durham, N.C.: Duke University Press, 2004); Jonathan Kay Kamakawiwo'ole Osorio, *Dismembering Lāhui: A History of the Hawaiian Nation to 1887* (Honolulu: University of Hawaii Press, 2002); David L. Anderson, *Imperialism and Idealism: American Diplomats in China, 1861–1898* (Bloomington: Indiana University Press, 1985); Ernest N. Paolino, *The Foundations of American Empire: William Henry Seward and American Foreign Policy* (Ithaca, N.Y.: Cornell University Press, 1973). And for a broad view, see Gregory P. Downs and Kate Masur, eds., *The World the Civil War Made* (Chapel Hill: University of North Carolina Press, 2015).

Chapter Eleven: Alternative Paths

On antimonopoly politics and the issues and institutions that nourished it, see Gretchen Ritter, *Goldbugs and Greenbacks: The Antimonopoly Tradition and the Politics of Finance in America, 1865–1896* (New York: Cambridge University Press, 1999); Richard F. Bensel, *The Political Economy of American Industrialization, 1877–1900* (New York: Cambridge University Press, 2000); Irwin Unger, *The Greenback Era: A Social and Political History of American Finance, 1865–1879* (Princeton, N.J.: Princeton University Press, 1964); David Montgomery, *Beyond Equality: Labor and the Radical Republicans, 1862–1872* (New York: Alfred A. Knopf, 1967); Philip S. Foner, *History of the Labor Movement in the United States: From Colonial Times to the Founding of the American Federation of Labor* (New York: International, 1947); Bruce Laurie, *Artisans into Workers: Labor in Nineteenth-Century America* (New York: Hill and Wang,1989); Alex Gourevitch, *From Slavery to the Cooperative Commonwealth: Labor and Republican Liberty in the Nineteenth Century* (New York: Cambridge University Press, 2015); Kim Voss, *The Making of American Exceptionalism: The Knights of Labor and Class Formation in the Nineteenth Century* (Ithaca, N.Y.: Cornell University Press, 1993); Robert E. Weir, *Beyond Labor's Veil: The Culture of the Knights of Labor* (University Park: Pennsylvania State University Press, 1996); Craig Phelan, *Grand Master Workman: Terence Powderly and the Knights of Labor* (Westport, Conn.: Greenwood Press, 2000); Gerald N. Grob, *Workers and Utopia: A Study of Ideological Conflict in the American Labor Movement, 1865–1900* (Evanston, Ill.: Northwestern University Press, 1961); Roy Rosenzweig, *Eight Hours for What We Will: Workers and Leisure in an Industrial City, 1870–1920* (New York: Cambridge University Press, 1985); Allen Weinstein, *Prelude to Populism: The Origins of the Silver Issue, 1867–1878* (New Haven, Conn.: Yale University Press, 1970); Tamara Venit Shelton, *A Squatter's Republic: Land and the Politics of Monopoly in California, 1850–1900* (Berkeley: University of California Press, 2013); Anna George de Mille, *Henry George: Citizen of the World* (Westport, Conn.: Greenwood Press, 1972); Edward T. O'Donnell, *Henry George and the Crisis of Inequality: Progress and Poverty in the Gilded Age* (New York: Columbia University Press, 2015); John L. Thomas, *Alternative America: Henry George, Edward Bellamy, Henry Demarest Lloyd, and the Adversary Tradition* (Cambridge, Mass.: Harvard University Press, 1983); Elwood P. Lawrence, *Henry George and the British Isles* (East Lansing: Michigan State University Press, 1957); Mae Ngai, *Impossible Subjects: Illegal Aliens and the Making of Modern America* (Princeton, N.J.: Princeton University Press, 2004); Alexander Saxton, *The Indispens-*

able Enemy: Labor and the Anti-Chinese Movement in California (Berkeley: University of California Press, 1975); John Soennichsen, *The Chinese Exclusion Act of 1882* (Santa Barbara, Calif.: ABC-CLIO, 2011); Najia Aarim-Heriot, *Chinese Immigrants, African Americans, and Racial Anxiety in the United States, 1848–82* (Urbana: University of Illinois Press, 2003); and an essential starting point, Henry George, *Progress and Poverty: An Enquiry into the Cause of Industrial Depressions, and of Increase of Want with Increase of Wealth; the Remedy* (1881; Garden City, N.Y.: Doubleday, 1926).

On the arc of labor strikes and mobilizations between 1877 and 1886, see David O. Stowell, *Streets, Railroads, and the Great Strike of 1877* (Chicago: University of Chicago Press, 1999); David O. Stowell, ed., *The Great Strikes of 1877* (Urbana: University of Illinois Press, 2008); Shelton Stromquist, *A Generation of Boomers: The Patterns of Railroad Labor Conflict in the Nineteenth Century* (Urbana: University of Illinois Press, 1983); Walter Licht, *Working for the Railroad: The Organization of Work in the Nineteenth Century* (Princeton, N.J.: Princeton University Press, 1983) and *Industrializing America: The Nineteenth Century* (Baltimore: Johns Hopkins University Press, 1995); Robert V. Bruce, *1877: Year of Violence* (Indianapolis: Bobbs-Merrill, 1959); David Montgomery, "Strikes in Nineteenth-Century America," *Social Science History* 4 (Winter 1980): 81–104; Norman Ware, *The Labor Movement in the United States, 1865–1895: A Study in Democracy* (New York: Alfred A. Knopf, 1967); Theresa Case, *The Great Southwest Railroad Strike and Free Labor* (College Station: Texas A&M University Press, 2010); Ruth Allen, *The Great Southwest Strike* (Austin: University of Texas Press, 1942); Mary H. Blewett, *Men, Women, and Work: Class, Gender, and Protest in the New England Shoe Industry, 1780–1910* (Urbana: University of Illinois Press, 1990); Gerald D. Eggert, *Railroad Labor Disputes: The Beginnings of Federal Strike Policy* (Ann Arbor: University of Michigan Press, 1967); Clayton D. Laurie and Ronald H. Cole, *The Role of Federal Military Forces in Domestic Disorders, 1877–1945* (Washington, D.C.: U.S. Army, 1997); Ira Katznelson and Aristide R. Zolberg, eds., *Working-Class Formation: Nineteenth-Century Patterns in Western Europe and the United States* (Princeton, N.J.: Princeton University Press, 1986); Richard Oestreicher, *Solidarity and Fragmentation: Working People and Class Consciousness in Detroit, 1875–1900* (Urbana: University of Illinois Press, 1986); Richard Schneirov, *Labor and Urban Politics: Class Conflict and the Origins of Modern Liberalism in Chicago, 1864–1897* (Urbana: University of Illinois Press, 1998); Carl Smith, *Urban Disorder and the Shape of Belief: The Great Chicago Fire, the Haymarket Bomb, and the Model Town of Pullman* (Chicago: University of Chicago Press, 1995); David M. Emmons, *The Butte Irish: Class and Ethnicity in an American Mining Town, 1875–1925* (Urbana: University of Illinois Press, 1989); Jonathan Garlock, ed., *Guide to Local Assemblies of the Knights of Labor* (Westport, Conn.: Greenwood Press, 1982); John Rodrigue, *Reconstruction in the Cane Fields: From Slavery to Free Labor in Louisiana's Sugar Parishes, 1862–1880* (Baton Rouge: Louisiana State University Press, 2001); Eric Foner, *Nothing but Freedom: Emancipation and Its Legacy* (Baton Rouge: Louisiana State University Press, 1982); James R. Green, *Death in the Haymarket: The Story of Chicago, the First Labor Movement, and the Bombing That Divided Gilded Age America* (New York: Pantheon, 2006); Paul Avrich, *The Haymarket Tragedy* (Princeton, N.J.: Princeton University Press, 1984); Timothy Messer-Kruse, *The Haymarket Conspiracy: Transatlantic Anarchist Networks* (Urbana: University of Illinois Press, 2012).

On labor, popular politics, and grassroots efforts to redefine the Republic, see Leon Fink, *Workingmen's Democracy: The Knights of Labor and American Politics* (Urbana: University of Illinois Press, 1985); David Montgomery, *Citizen Worker: The Experience of Workers in the United States with Democracy and the Free Market During the Nineteenth Century* (New York: Cambridge University Press, 1993); John B. Jentz and Richard Schneirov, *Chicago in the Age of Capital: Class, Politics, and Democracy During the Civil War and Reconstruction* (Urbana: University of Illinois Press, 2012); Clare Dahlberg, *Producers' Cooperatives in the United States, 1865–1890* (Pittsburgh: University of Pittsburgh Press, 1977); Steven Leikin, *The Practical Utopians: American Workers and the Cooperative Movement in the Gilded Age* (Detroit: Wayne State University Press, 2004); Russell Duncan, *Freedom's Shore: Tunis Campbell and the Georgia Freedmen* (Athens: University of Georgia Press, 1986); Steven Hahn, *A Nation Under Our Feet: Black Political Struggles in the Rural South from Slavery to the Great Migration* (Cambridge, Mass.: Harvard University Press, 2003); Jane Dailey, *Before Jim Crow: The Politics of Race in Postemancipation Virginia* (Chapel Hill: University of North Carolina Press, 2000); Matthew Hild, *Greenbackers, Knights of Labor, and Populists: Farmer-Labor Insurgency in the Late-Nineteenth-Century South* (Athens: University of Georgia Press, 2007); Peter Rachleff, *Black Labor in Richmond, 1865–1890* (Urbana: University of Illinois Press, 1989); LeeAnna Keith, *The Colfax Massacre: The Untold Story of Black Power, White Terror, and the Death of Reconstruction* (New York: Oxford University Press, 2009); Charles Lane, *The Day Freedom Died: The Colfax Massacre, the Supreme Court, and the Betrayal of Reconstruction* (New York: Henry Holt, 2009); Susan Levine, *Labor's True Woman: Carpet Weavers, Industrialization, and Labor Reform in the Gilded Age* (Philadelphia: Temple University Press, 1984); Gwendolyn Mink, *Old Labor and New Immigrants in American Political Development: Union, Party, and State, 1875–1920* (Ithaca, N.Y.: Cornell University Press, 1986); Michael Pierce, *Striking with the Ballot: Ohio Labor and the Populist Party* (DeKalb: Northern Illinois University Press, 2010); Victoria Hattam, *Labor Visions and State Power: The Origins of Business Unionism in the United States* (Princeton, N.J.: Princeton University Press, 1993); Sven Beckert, *The Monied Metropolis: New York City and the Consolidation of the American Bourgeoisie, 1850–1896* (New York: Cambridge University Press, 2001); Margaret Garb, *Freedom's Ballot: African-American Political Struggles in Chicago from Abolition to the Great Migration* (Chicago: University of Chicago Press, 2014).

On efforts to build a cooperative commonwealth and mobilizations of rural and urban producers during the 1880s and 1890s, see Lawrence C. Goodwyn, *Democratic Promise: The Populist Moment in America* (New York: Oxford University Press, 1976); John D. Hicks, *The Populist Revolt: A History of the Farmers' Alliance and the People's Party* (Minneapolis: University of Minnesota Press, 1931); C. Vann Woodward, *Origins of the New South, 1877–1913* (Baton Rouge: Louisiana State University Press, 1951) and *Tom Watson: Agrarian Rebel* (New York: Macmillan, 1938); Robert C. McMath Jr., *American Populism: A Social History, 1877–1898* (New York: Hill and Wang, 1993) and *Populist Vanguard: A History of the Southern Farmers' Alliance* (Chapel Hill: University of North Carolina Press, 1975); Charles Postel, *The Populist Vision* (New York: Oxford University Press, 2007); Michael Schwartz, *Radical Protest and Social Structure: The Southern Farmers' Alliance and Cotton Tenancy, 1880–1890* (New York: Academic Press, 1976); Barton C. Shaw, *The Wool-Hat Boys: Georgia's Populist Party* (Baton Rouge: Louisiana State University Press, 1984); Roscoe Martin, *The People's Party in Texas: A Study in Third Party*

Politics (Austin: University of Texas Press, 1933); Omar H. Ali, *Black Populism in the New South, 1886–1900* (Jackson: University Press of Mississippi, 2010); Peter Argersinger, *The Limits of Agrarian Radicalism: Western Populism and American Politics* (Lawrence: University Press of Kansas, 1995); Donna Barnes, *Farmers in Rebellion: The Rise and Fall of the Southern Farmers' Alliance and People's Party in Texas* (Austin: University of Texas Press, 1984); James M. Beeby, *Revolt of the Tar Heels: The North Carolina Populist Movement, 1890–1901* (Jackson: University Press of Mississippi, 2008); James M. Beeby, ed., *Populism in the South Revisited: New Interpretations and New Departures* (Jackson: University Press of Mississippi, 2012); Jeffrey Ostler, *Prairie Populism: The Fate of Agrarian Radicalism in Kansas, Nebraska, and Iowa, 1880–1892* (Lawrence: University Press of Kansas, 1993); Bruce Palmer, *"Man over Money": The Southern Populist Critique of American Capitalism* (Chapel Hill: University of North Carolina Press, 1980); Steven Hahn, *The Roots of Southern Populism: Yeoman Farmers and the Transformation of the Georgia Upcountry, 1850–1890* (New York: Oxford University Press, 1983); Norman Pollack, *The Populist Response to Industrial America* (Cambridge, Mass.: Harvard University Press, 1962); William Ivy Hair, *Bourbonism and Agrarian Protest: Louisiana Politics, 1877–1900* (Baton Rouge: Louisiana State University Press, 1969); James L. Hunt, *Marion Butler and American Populism* (Chapel Hill: University of North Carolina Press, 2003); Gerald H. Gaither, *Blacks and the Populist Movement: Ballots and Bigotry in the New South* (Tuscaloosa: University of Alabama Press, 1977); Joseph Gerteis, *Class and the Color Line: Interracial Class Coalition in the Knights of Labor and the Populist Movement* (Durham, N.C.: Duke University Press, 2007); James E. Wright, *The Politics of Populism: Dissent in Colorado* (New Haven, Conn.: Yale University Press, 1974); Michael Kazin, *The Populist Persuasion: An American History* (New York: Basic Books, 1995) and *A Godly Hero: The Life of William Jennings Bryan* (New York: Alfred A. Knopf, 2006); Robert Cherny, *A Righteous Cause: The Life of William Jennings Bryan* (Norman: University of Oklahoma Press, 1994); Joseph Creech, *Righteous Indignation: Religion and the Populist Revolution* (Urbana: University of Illinois Press, 2006); Gregory P. Downs, *Declarations of Dependence: The Long Reconstruction of Popular Politics in the South, 1861–1908* (Chapel Hill: University of North Carolina Press, 2011).

On the election of 1896 and its aftermath, see Robert F. Durden, *The Climax of Populism: The Election of 1896* (Lexington: University of Kentucky Press, 1965); R. Hal Williams, *Realigning America: McKinley, Bryan, and the Remarkable Election of 1896* (Lawrence: University Press of Kansas, 2010); Paul Krause, *The Battle for Homestead, 1880–1892: Politics, Culture, and Steel* (Pittsburgh: University of Pittsburgh Press, 1992); David Papke, *The Pullman Case: The Clash of Labor and Capital in Industrial America* (Lawrence: University Press of Kansas, 1999); Richard Schneirov et al., eds., *The Pullman Strike and the Crisis of the 1890s: Essays on Labor and Politics* (Urbana: University of Illinois Press, 1999); Carlos Schwantes, *Coxey's Army: An American Odyssey* (1985; Moscow: University of Idaho Press, 1994); Nick Salvatore, *Eugene V. Debs: Citizen and Socialist* (Urbana: University of Illinois Press, 1984); Ray Ginger, *Eugene V. Debs: The Making of an American Radical* (New Brunswick, N.J.: Rutgers University Press, 1947); James Weinstein, *The Decline of Socialism in America, 1912–1925* (New York: Vintage, 1967); Mari Jo Buhle, *Women and American Socialism, 1870–1920* (Urbana: University of Illinois Press, 1983); James R. Green, *Grassroots Socialism: Radical Movements in the Southwest, 1895–1943* (Baton Rouge: Louisiana State University Press, 1978); Eric Arnesen, *Waterfront*

Workers of New Orleans: Race, Class, and Politics, 1863–1923 (New York: Oxford University Press, 1991); Daniel Letwin, *The Challenge of Interracial Unionism: Alabama Coal Miners, 1878–1921* (Chapel Hill: University of North Carolina Press, 1998); Karin A. Shapiro, *A New South Rebellion: The Battle Against Convict Labor in the Tennessee Coalfields, 1871–1896* (Chapel Hill: University of North Carolina Press, 1998); Robert D. Johnston, *The Radical Middle Class: Populist Democracy and the Question of Capitalism in Progressive Era Portland, Oregon* (Princeton, N.J.: Princeton University Press, 2003); Ardis Cameron, *Radicals of the Worst Sort: Laboring Women in Lawrence, Massachusetts, 1860–1912* (Urbana: University of Illinois Press, 1993).

For a broader context of popular movements, see Geoff Eley, *Forging Democracy: The History of the Left in Europe, 1850–2000* (New York: Oxford University Press, 2002); E. P. Thompson, *William Morris: Romantic to Revolutionary* (1955; New York: Pantheon, 1976); Benedict Anderson, *The Age of Globalization: Anarchists and the Anticolonial Imagination* (London: Verso, 2005); Kristin Ross, *Communal Luxury: The Political Imaginary of the Paris Commune* (London: Verso, 2015); Temma Kaplan, *The Anarchists of Andalusia, 1868–1903* (Princeton, N.J.: Princeton University Press, 1977); Eric J. Hobsbawm, *Workers: Worlds of Labor* (New York: Pantheon, 1984).

Chapter Twelve: Reconstructions

The literature on what is conventionally known as the Progressive Era, or, what I have called Reconstructions, is wide and very deep. I have benefited enormously from it. On the developing cultural and intellectual currents—and experimentation—and on the larger impulses that gave rise to "social" reconstruction, see Daniel Rodgers, *Atlantic Crossings: Social Politics in a Progressive Age* (Cambridge, Mass.: Harvard University Press, 1998); Michael McGerr, *A Fierce Discontent: The Rise and Fall of the Progressive Movement in America, 1870–1920* (New York: Oxford University Press, 2003); James T. Kloppenberg, *Uncertain Victory: Social Democracy and Progressivism in European and American Thought, 1870–1920* (New York: Oxford University Press, 1986); Robert H. Wiebe, *The Search for Order, 1877–1920* (New York: Hill and Wang, 1967); Daniel Aron, *Men of Good Hope: A Story of American Progressives* (New York: Oxford University Press, 1951); Richard Hofstadter, *The Age of Reform: From Bryan to FDR* (New York: Alfred A. Knopf, 1955); Kathryn Kish Sklar, *Florence Kelley and the Nation's Work: The Rise of Women's Political Culture, 1830–1900* (New Haven, Conn.: Yale University Press, 1997); Paul Boyer, *Urban Masses and Moral Order in America, 1820–1920* (Cambridge, Mass.: Harvard University Press, 1992); Nancy L. Cohen, *The Reconstruction of American Liberalism, 1865–1914* (Chapel Hill: University of North Carolina Press, 2002); Philip Ethington, *The Public City: The Political Construction of Urban Life in San Francisco, 1850–1900* (New York: Cambridge University Press, 1994); Louise W. Knight, *Citizen: Jane Addams and the Struggle for Democracy* (Chicago: University of Chicago Press, 2006); Victoria B. Brown, *The Education of Jane Addams* (Philadelphia: University of Pennsylvania Press, 2007); Christopher Lasch, *The New Radicalism in America, 1889–1963* (New York: Vintage, 1965); T. J. Jackson Lears, *No Place of Grace: Antimodernism and the Transformation of American Culture, 1880–1920* (New York: Pantheon, 1981); Alan Dawley, *Struggles for Justice: Social Responsibility and the Liberal State* (Cambridge, Mass.: Harvard University Press, 1993); Molly Ladd-Taylor, *Mother-Work: Women, Child Welfare, and the State, 1890–1930* (Urbana: University of Illinois Press, 1994); Ruth H. Crocker, *Social*

Work and Social Order: The Settlement Movement in Two Industrial Cities, 1889–1930 (Urbana: University of Illinois Press, 1992); Allen F. Davis, *Spearheads for Reform: The Social Settlements and the Progressive Movement, 1880–1914* (New Brunswick, N.J.: Rutgers University Press, 1984); Ruth Bordin, *Frances Willard: A Biography* (Chapel Hill: University of North Carolina Press, 2014); Lisa McGirr, *The War on Alcohol: Prohibition and the Rise of the American State* (New York: W. W. Norton, 2015); Leslie Butler, *Critical Americans: Victorian Intellectuals and Transatlantic Liberal Reform* (Chapel Hill: University of North Carolina Press, 2007); Mina Carson, *Settlement Folk: Social Thought and the American Settlement Movement, 1885–1930* (Chicago: University of Chicago Press, 1990); Sarah Deutsch, *Women and the City: Gender, Space, and Power in Boston, 1870–1940* (New York: Oxford University Press, 2000); Donald K. Gorrell, *The Age of Social Responsibility: The Social Gospel in the Progressive Era, 1900–1920* (Macon, Ga.: Mercer University Press, 1988); Christopher Evans, *The Kingdom Is Always But Coming: A Life of Walter Rauschenbusch* (Waco, Tex.: Baylor University Press, 2010); Ronald C. White and C. Howard Hopkins, *The Social Gospel: Religion and Reform in Changing America* (Philadelphia: Temple University Press, 1976); Ellen Fitzpatrick, *Endless Crusade: Women Social Scientists and Progressive Reform* (New York: Oxford University Press, 1990); Maureen Flanagan, *America Reformed: Progressives and Progressivism, 1890s–1920s* (New York: Oxford University Press, 2007); Linda Gordon, *Pitied but Not Entitled: Single Mothers and the History of Welfare, 1890–1935* (New York: Free Press, 1994); Thomas L. Haskell, *The Emergence of Professional Social Science: The American Social Science Association and the Nineteenth-Century Crisis of Authority* (Urbana: University of Illinois Press, 1977); Shelton Stromquist, *Re-inventing "the People": The Progressive Movement, the Class Problem, and the Origins of Modern Liberalism* (Urbana: University of Illinois Press, 2006); David A. Moss, *Socializing Security: Progressive-Era Economists and the Origins of American Social Policy* (Cambridge, Mass.: Harvard University Press, 1995); Robin Muncy, *Creating a Female Dominion in American Reform, 1890–1935* (New York: Oxford University Press, 1991); Dorothy Ross, *The Origins of American Social Science* (New York: Cambridge University Press, 1991).

On the dimensions and dynamics of "corporate" reconstruction, see Martin J. Sklar, *The Corporate Reconstruction of American Capitalism, 1890–1916* (New York: Cambridge University Press, 1988); Alfred D. Chandler, *The Visible Hand: The Managerial Revolution in American Business* (Cambridge, Mass.: Harvard University Press, 1977); David Gordon et al., *Segmented Work, Divided Workers: The Historical Transformation of Labor in the United States* (New York: Cambridge University Press, 1982); David Montgomery, *The Fall of the House of Labor: The Workplace, the State, and American Labor Activism, 1865–1925* (New York: Cambridge University Press, 1987) and *Workers' Control in America: Studies in the History of Work, Technology, and Labor Struggles* (New York: Cambridge University Press, 1979); William G. Robbins, *Socializing Capital: The Rise of the Large Industrial Corporation in America* (Princeton, N.J.: Princeton University Press, 1997); David F. Noble, *America by Design: Science, Technology, and the Rise of Corporate Capitalism* (New York: Vintage, 1977); Harry Braverman, *Labor and Monopoly Capital: The Degradation of Work in the Twentieth Century* (New York: Monthly Review Press, 1974); Julie Greene, *Pure and Simple Politics: The American Federation of Labor and Political Activism, 1881–1917* (New York: Cambridge University Press, 2006); James Weinstein, *The Corporate Ideal in the Liberal State, 1900–1918* (Boston: Beacon Press, 1968); R. Jeffrey Lustig, *Corporate Liberalism:*

The Origins of Modern American Political Theory, 1880–1920 (Berkeley: University of California Press, 1982); William Leach, *Land of Desire: Merchants, Power, and the Rise of a New American Culture* (New York: Vintage, 1994); Olivier Zunz, *Making America Corporate, 1870–1920* (Chicago: University of Chicago Press, 1990); Gerald Berk, *The Constitution of American Industrial Order, 1865–1917* (Baltimore: Johns Hopkins University Press, 1994); Stuart Ewen, *Captains of Consciousness: Advertising and the Social Roots of the Consumer Culture* (New York: McGraw-Hill, 1977); T. J. Jackson Lears, *Fables of Abundance: A Cultural History of Advertising in America* (New York: Basic Books, 1995); Naomi R. Lamoreaux, *The Great Merger Movement in American Business, 1895–1904* (Cambridge, Mass.: Harvard University Press, 1985); Daniel Nelson, *Frederick W. Taylor and the Rise of Scientific Management* (Madison: University of Wisconsin Press, 1980); Hugh G. J. Aiken, *Scientific Management in Action: Taylorism at Watertown Arsenal, 1908–1915* (Princeton, N.J.: Princeton University Press, 1985); Marguerite Green, *The National Civic Federation and the American Labor Movement, 1900–1925* (Westport, Conn.: Greenwood Press, 1973); Craig Phelan, *Divided Loyalties: The Public and Private Life of Labor Leader John Lewis* (Albany: State University of New York Press, 1994); Scott R. Bowman, *The Modern Corporation and American Political Thought: Law, Power, and Ideology* (University Park: Pennsylvania State University Press, 1996); William E. Forbath, *Law and the Shaping of the American Labor Movement* (Cambridge, Mass.: Harvard University Press, 1995); Frank Dobbin, *Forging Industrial Policy: The United States, Britain, and France in the Railway Age* (Cambridge, U.K.: Cambridge University Press, 1994); Neil Fligstein, *The Transformation of Corporate Control* (Cambridge, Mass.: Harvard University Press, 1990); Walter A. Friedman, *Birth of a Salesman: The Transformation of Selling in America* (Cambridge, Mass.: Harvard University Press, 2004); Louis Galambos and Joseph Pratt, *The Rise of the Corporate Commonwealth* (New York: Basic Books, 1988); Kristin Hoganson, *Consumers' Imperium: The Global Production of American Domesticity, 1865–1920* (Chapel Hill: University of North Carolina Press, 2007); Nikki Mandell, *The Corporation as Family: The Gendering of Corporate Welfare, 1890–1930* (Chapel Hill: University of North Carolina Press, 2002); Herbert Hovenkamp, *Enterprise and American Law, 1836–1937* (Cambridge, Mass.: Harvard University Press, 1991); Richard John, *Network Nation: Inventing American Telecommunications* (Cambridge, Mass.: Harvard University Press, 2010); Kenneth Lipartito, ed., *Constructing Corporate America: History, Politics, Culture* (New York: Oxford University Press, 2004).

On the expanding regulatory apparatus of the state at various levels, as well as efforts to redefine the boundaries of the political arena, see Stephen Skowronek, *Building a New American State: The Expansion of National Administrative Capacity, 1877–1920* (New York: Cambridge University Press, 1982); Thomas McCaw, *Prophets of Regulation: Charles Francis Adams, Louis D. Brandeis, James M. Landis, Alfred E. Kahn* (Cambridge, Mass.: Harvard University Press, 1984); Gabriel Kolko, *The Triumph of Conservatism: A Reinterpretation of American History, 1900–1916* (New York: Free Press, 1963) and *Railroads and Reform, 1877–1916* (Princeton, N.J.: Princeton University Press, 1965); Robert H. Wiebe, *Businessmen and Reform: A Study of the Progressive Movement* (Cambridge, Mass.: Harvard University Press, 1962); Steven Usselman, *Regulating Railroad Innovation: Business, Technology, and Politics in America, 1840–1920* (New York: Cambridge University Press, 2002); Barbara Young Welke, *Recasting American Liberty: Gender, Race, Law, and the Railroad Revolution, 1865–1920* (New York: Cambridge University Press, 2001); John Milton

Cooper, *The Warrior and the Priest: Woodrow Wilson and Theodore Roosevelt* (Cambridge, Mass.: Harvard University Press, 1983); John Morton Blum, *The Republican Roosevelt* (Cambridge, Mass.: Harvard University Press, 1954); Sidney M. Milkis, *Theodore Roosevelt, the Progressive Party, and the Transformation of American Democracy* (Lawrence: University Press of Kansas, 2009); Bruce Bringhurst, *Antitrust and the Oil Monopoly: The Standard Oil Cases, 1890–1911* (Westport, Conn.: Greenwood Press, 1979); E. Thomas Sullivan, ed., *The Political Economy of the Sherman Act: The First Hundred Years* (New York: Oxford University Press, 1991); Elizabeth Sanders, *Roots of Reform: Farmers, Workers, and the American State, 1877–1917* (Chicago: University of Chicago Press, 1999); Robert Johnston, *The Radical Middle Class: Populist Democracy and the Question of Capitalism in Progressive-Era Portland, Oregon* (Princeton, N.J.: Princeton University Press, 2003); Gwendolyn Mink, *Old Labor and New Immigrants in American Political Development: Union, Party, and State, 1875–1920* (Ithaca, N.Y.: Cornell University Press, 1986); Robert Angevine, *The Railroad and the State: War, Politics, and Technology in Nineteenth-Century America* (Stanford, Calif.: Stanford University Press, 2004); Gerald Berk, *Louis D. Brandeis and the Making of Regulated Competition, 1900–1932* (New York: Cambridge University Press, 2009); Tony A. Freyer, *Regulating Big Business: Antitrust in Great Britain and America, 1880–1990* (New York: Cambridge University Press, 1992); Robert Harrison, *Congress, Progressive Reform, and the New American State* (New York: Cambridge University Press, 2004); Hendrik Hartog, *Public Property and Private Power: The Corporation of the City of New York in American Law, 1730–1870* (Chapel Hill: University of North Carolina Press, 1983); Morton Keller, *Regulating a New Society: Public Policy and Social Change in America* (Cambridge, Mass.: Harvard University Press, 1994); Michael McGerr, *The Decline of Popular Politics: The American North, 1865–1928* (New York: Oxford University Press, 1986); Kevin Mattson, *Creating a Democratic Public: The Struggle for Urban Participatory Democracy During the Progressive Era* (University Park: Pennsylvania State University Press, 1998); J. Morgan Kousser, *The Shaping of Southern Politics: Suffrage Restriction and the Establishment of the One-Party South, 1880–1910* (New Haven, Conn.: Yale University Press, 1974); Michael Perman, *Struggle for Mastery: Disfranchisement in the South, 1888–1908* (Chapel Hill: University of North Carolina Press, 2001); Suzanne M. Marilley, *Woman Suffrage and the Origins of Liberal Feminism in the United States, 1820–1920* (Cambridge, Mass.: Harvard University Press, 1996); Rebecca Mead, *How the Vote Was Won: Woman Suffrage in the Western United States, 1868–1914* (New York: New York University Press, 2004); Louise M. Newman, *White Women's Rights: The Racial Origins of Feminism in the United States* (New York: Oxford University Press, 1999); Rosalyn Terborg-Penn, *African-American Women in the Struggle for the Vote, 1850–1920* (Bloomington: Indiana University Press, 1998); Allison L. Sneider, *Suffragists in an Imperial Age: U.S. Expansion and the Woman Question, 1870–1929* (New York: Oxford University Press, 2008); Sarah Hunter Graham, *Woman Suffrage and the New Democracy* (New Haven, Conn.: Yale University Press, 1996); Marjorie Spruill Wheeler, *New Women of the New South: The Leaders of the Woman Suffrage Movement in the Southern States* (New York: Oxford University Press, 1993); Gayle Gullett, *Becoming Citizens: The Emergence and Development of California's Women's Movement, 1880–1911* (Urbana: University of Illinois Press, 2000); Alexander Keyssar, *The Right to Vote: The Contested History of Democracy in the United States* (New York: Basic Books, 2000; William J. Novak, *The People's Welfare: Law and Regulation in Nineteenth-Century America* (Chapel Hill: University of North Carolina Press, 1996).

On the construction of "race" in a national and international context, see C. Vann Woodward, *Origins of the New South, 1877–1913* (Baton Rouge: Louisiana State University Press, 1951) and *The Strange Career of Jim Crow* (New York: Oxford University Press, 1955); George M. Fredrickson, *The Black Image in the White Mind: The Debate on African-American Character and Destiny, 1817–1914* (New York: Harper and Row, 1971) and *White Supremacy: A Comparative Study in American and South African History* (New York: Oxford University Press, 1981); John Cell, *The Highest Stage of White Supremacy: The Origins of Segregation in South Africa and the United States* (New York: Cambridge University Press, 1982); Carl H. Nightingale, *Segregation: A Global History* (Chicago: University of Chicago Press, 2012); Howard Rabinowitz, *Race Relations in the Urban South, 1865–1890* (Urbana: University of Illinois Press, 1980); Edward L. Ayers, *The Promise of the New South: Life After Reconstruction* (New York: Oxford University Press, 1993); Joel Williamson, *Crucible of Race: Black-White Relations in America Since Emancipation* (New York: Oxford University Press, 1984); Leon F. Litwack, *Trouble in Mind: Black Southerners in the Age of Jim Crow* (New York: Alfred A. Knopf, 1998); Natalie J. Ring, *The Problem South: Region, Empire, and the New Liberal State, 1880–1930* (Athens: University of Georgia Press, 2012); Glenda E. Gilmore, *Gender and Jim Crow: Women and the Politics of White Supremacy in North Carolina, 1896–1920* (Chapel Hill: University of North Carolina Press, 1996); Louis R. Harlan, *Booker T. Washington*, 2 vols. (New York: Oxford University Press, 1972, 1983); Robert J. Norrell, *Up from History: The Life of Booker T. Washington* (Cambridge, Mass.: Harvard University Press, 2009); David Levering Lewis, *W. E. B. Du Bois: Biography of a Race, 1868–1919* (New York: Henry Holt, 1993); W. Fitzhugh Brundage, *Lynching in the New South: Georgia and Virginia, 1880–1930* (Urbana: University of Illinois Press, 1993); W. Fitzhugh Brundage, ed., *Under Sentence of Death: Lynching in the South* (Chapel Hill: University of North Carolina Press, 1997); Stewart E. Tolnay and E. M. Beck, *A Festival of Violence: An Analysis of Southern Lynchings, 1882–1930* (Urbana: University of Illinois Press, 1995); Amy L. Wood, *Lynching and Spectacle: Witnessing Racial Violence in America, 1890–1940* (Chapel Hill: University of North Carolina Press, 2009); Paula J. Giddings, *Ida, a Sword Among the Lions: Ida B. Wells and the Campaign Against Lynching* (New York: Amistad Press, 2008); Mia Bay, *To Tell the Truth Freely: The Life of Ida B. Wells* (New York: Hill and Wang, 2009); Crystal M. Feimster, *Southern Horrors: Women and the Politics of Rape and Lynching* (Cambridge, Mass.: Harvard University Press, 2011); Diane M. Sommerville, *Rape and Race in the Nineteenth-Century South* (Chapel Hill: University of North Carolina Press, 2004); Peggy Pascoe, *What Comes Naturally: Miscegenation Law and the Making of Race in America* (New York: Oxford University Press, 2009); Laura L. Lovett, *Conceiving the Future: Pronatalism, Reproduction, and the Family in the United States, 1890–1930* (Chapel Hill: University of North Carolina Press, 2007); Evelyn Brooks Higginbotham, *Righteous Discontent: The Women's Movement in the Black Baptist Church, 1880–1920* (Cambridge, Mass.: Harvard University Press, 1993); Michelle Mitchell, *Righteous Propagation: African Americans and the Politics of Racial Destiny After Reconstruction* (Chapel Hill: University of North Carolina Press, 2004); Stephanie Shaw, *What a Woman Ought to Be and Do: Black Professional Women Workers During the Jim Crow Era* (Chicago: University of Chicago Press, 2006); Martha Hodes, *Black Women, White Men: Illicit Sex in the Nineteenth-Century South* (New Haven, Conn.: Yale University Press, 1997); Martha S. Jones, *All Bound Up Together: The Woman Question in African-American Public Culture,*

1830–1900 (Chapel Hill: University of North Carolina Press, 2007); J. Douglas Smith, *Managing White Supremacy: Race, Politics, and Citizenship in Jim Crow Virginia* (Chapel Hill: University of North Carolina Press, 2002); Grace E. Hale, *Making Whiteness: The Culture of Segregation in the South, 1890–1940* (New York: Pantheon, 1998); Neil McMillen, *Dark Journey: Black Mississippians in the Age of Jim Crow* (Urbana: University of Illinois Press, 1989); Edward J. Blum, *Reforging the White Republic: Race, Religion, and American Nationalism, 1865–1898* (Baton Rouge: Louisiana State University Press, 2005); Edward J. Larson, *Race, Sex, and Science: Eugenics in the Deep South* (Baltimore: Johns Hopkins University Press, 1995); John Haller, *Outcasts from Evolution: Scientific Attitudes of Racial Inferiority, 1859–1900* (Carbondale: Southern Illinois University Press, 1995); Gregory M. Dorr, *Segregation's Science: Eugenics and Society in Virginia* (Charlottesville: University of Virginia Press, 2008); John Ettling, *The Germ of Laziness: Rockefeller Philanthropy and Public Health in the New South* (Cambridge, Mass.: Harvard University Press, 1981); Pete Daniel, *The Shadow of Slavery: Peonage of the South, 1901–1969* (Urbana: University of Illinois Press, 1972); William Cohen, *At Freedom's Edge: Black Mobility and the Southern White Quest for Racial Control, 1861–1915* (Baton Rouge: Louisiana State University Press, 1991); David S. Cecelski and Timothy B. Tyson, eds., *Democracy Betrayed: The Wilmington Race Riot of 1898 and Its Legacy* (Chapel Hill: University of North Carolina Press, 1998); Jane Turner Censer, *The Reconstruction of White Southern Womanhood, 1865–1895* (Baton Rouge: Louisiana State University Press, 2003); Gaines M. Foster, *Ghosts of the Confederacy: Defeat, the Lost Cause, and the Emergence of the New South, 1865–1913* (New York: Oxford University Press, 1987); Stephen Kantrowitz, *Ben Tillman and the Reconstruction of White Supremacy* (Chapel Hill: University of North Carolina Press, 2000); Blair L. M. Kelley, *Right to Ride: Streetcar Boycotts and African-American Citizenship in the Era of Plessy v. Ferguson* (Chapel Hill: University of North Carolina Press, 2010); William A. Link, *The Paradox of Southern Progressivism* (Chapel Hill: University of North Carolina Press, 1992); Charles A. Lofgren, *The Plessy Case: A Legal-Historical Interpretation* (New York: Oxford University Press, 1987); Mark Schultz, *The Rural Face of White Supremacy: Beyond Jim Crow* (Urbana: University of Illinois Press, 2005); J. William Harris, *Deep Souths: Delta, Piedmont, and Sea Island Society in the Age of Segregation* (Baltimore: Johns Hopkins University Press, 2001); Gregory P. Downs, *Declarations of Dependence: The Long Reconstruction of Popular Politics in the South, 1861–1908* (Chapel Hill: University of North Carolina Press, 2011); David W. Blight, *Race and Reunion: The Civil War in American Memory* (Cambridge, Mass.: Harvard University Press, 2001).

On the reconfiguration of American empire, see William Appleman Williams, *The Tragedy of American Diplomacy* (New York: World, 1959); Walter LaFeber, *The New Empire: An Interpretation of American Expansion, 1860–1898* (Ithaca, N.Y.: Cornell University Press, 1963) and *Inevitable Revolutions: The United States in Central America* (New York: W. W. Norton, 1983); Greg Grandin, *Empire's Workshop: Latin America, the United States, and the Rise of the New Imperialism* (New York: Henry Holt, 2007); Amy S. Kaplan, *The Anarchy of Empire in the Making of U.S. Culture* (Cambridge, Mass.: Harvard University Press, 2002); Emily S. Rosenberg, *Spreading the Dream: American Economic and Cultural Expansion, 1890–1945* (New York: Hill and Wang, 1982); Michael Adas, *Dominance by Design: Technological Imperatives and America's Civilizing Mission* (Cambridge, Mass.: Harvard University Press, 2006); César Ayala, *American Sugar Kingdom: The Plantation Economy of the Spanish Caribbean, 1898–1934* (Chapel Hill: University of North Carolina Press, 1999); Willard B. Gatewood Jr., *Black Americans and the White*

Man's Burden, 1898–1903 (Urbana: University of Illinois Press, 1975); Gail Bederman, *Manliness and Civilization: A Cultural History of Gender and Race in the United States, 1880–1917* (Chicago: University of Chicago Press, 1995); Kristin Hoganson, *Fighting for American Manhood: How Gender Politics Provoked the Spanish-American and Philippine-American Wars* (New Haven, Conn.: Yale University Press, 1998); Matthew Frye Jacobson, *Barbarian Virtues: The United States Encounters Foreign Peoples at Home and Abroad, 1876–1917* (New York: Hill and Wang, 2000); Akira Iriye, *Pacific Estrangement: Japanese and American Expansion, 1897–1911* (Cambridge, Mass.: Harvard University Press, 1972); Michael Salman, *The Embarrassment of Slavery: Controversies over Bondage and Nationalism in the American Colonial Philippines* (Berkeley: University of California Press, 2001); Ian Tyrell and Jay Sexton, eds., *Empire's Twin: U.S. Anti-imperialism from the Founding Era to the Age of Terror* (Ithaca, N.Y.: Cornell University Press, 2015); Robert Beisner, *Twelve Against Empire: The Anti-imperialists, 1898–1900* (New York: McGraw-Hill, 1968); Christopher Lasch, *The World of Nations: Reflections on American History, Politics, and Culture* (New York: Vintage, 1973); Sondra Herman, *Eleven Against War: Studies in American Internationalist Thought* (Stanford, Calif.: Stanford University Press, 1969); Paul Kramer, *The Blood of Government: Race, Empire, the United States, and the Philippines* (Chapel Hill: University of North Carolina Press, 2006); Julie Greene, *The Canal Builders: Making America's Empire at the Panama Canal* (New York: Penguin Press, 2009); Stanley Karnow, *In Our Image: America's Empire in the Philippines* (New York: Random House, 1989); Reynaldo Clemeña Ileto, *Pasyon and Revolution: Popular Movements in the Philippines, 1840–1910* (Manila: Ateneo de Manila University Press, 1979); Glenn A. May, *Social Engineering in the Philippines: The Aims, Execution, and Impact of American Colonial Policy, 1900–1913* (Westport, Conn.: Greenwood Press, 1980); Alfred W. McCoy, *Policing America's Empire: The United States, the Philippines, and the Rise of the Surveillance State* (Madison: University of Wisconsin Press, 2009); Alfred A. McCoy and Francisco Scarano, eds., *Colonial Crucible: Empire in the Making of the Modern American State* (Madison: University of Wisconsin Press, 2009); Warwick Anderson, *Colonial Pathologies: American Tropical Medicine, Race, and Hygiene in the Philippines* (Durham, N.C.: Duke University Press, 2006); Vicente Rafael, *White Love and Other Events in Filipino History* (Durham, N.C.: Duke University Press, 2000); Jules Benjamin, *The United States and Cuba: Hegemony and Dependent Development, 1880–1934* (Pittsburgh: University of Pittsburgh Press, 1977); J. F. Offner, *An Unwanted War: The Diplomacy of the United States and Spain over Cuba, 1895–1898* (Chapel Hill: University of North Carolina Press, 1992); Louis Pérez, *The War of 1898: The United States and Cuba in History and Historiography* (Chapel Hill: University of North Carolina, 1998); H. W. Brands, *Bound to Empire: The United States and the Philippines* (New York: Oxford University Press, 1992); Pedro A. Cabán, *Constructing a Colonial People: Puerto Rico and the United States, 1898–1932* (Boulder, Colo.: Westview Press, 1999); Jason M. Colby, *The Business of Empire: United Fruit, Race, and U.S. Expansion in Central America* (Ithaca, N.Y.: Cornell University Press, 2011); Phillip Darby, *The Three Faces of Imperialism: British and American Approaches to Asia and Africa, 1870–1970* (New Haven, Conn.: Yale University Press, 1987); John H. Coatsworth, *Central America and the United States: The Clients and the Colossus* (New York: Twayne, 1994); Richard H. Collin, *Theodore Roosevelt's Caribbean: The Panama Canal, the Monroe Doctrine, and the Latin American Context* (Baton Rouge: Louisiana State University Press, 1990); Eileen Suárez Findlay, *Imposing Decency: The Politics of*

Sexuality and Rape in Puerto Rico, 1870–1920 (Durham, N.C.: Duke University Press, 1999); Julian Go, *American Empire and the Politics of Meaning: Elite Political Cultures in the Philippines and Puerto Rico During U.S. Colonialism* (Durham, N.C.: Duke University Press, 2008); Julian Go and Anne L. Foster, eds., *The American Colonial State in the Philippines: A Global Perspective* (Durham, N.C.: Duke University Press, 2003); David Healy, *Drive to Hegemony: The United States and the Caribbean, 1898–1917* (Madison: University of Wisconsin Press, 1988); Jerry Israel, *Progressivism and the Open Door: America and China, 1905–1921* (Pittsburgh: University of Pittsburgh Press, 1971); Jane Hunter, *The Gospel of Gentility: American Women Missionaries in Turn-of-the-Century China* (New Haven, Conn.: Yale University Press, 1984); J. Kehaulani Kauanui, *Hawaiian Blood: Colonialism and the Politics of Sovereignty and Indigeneity* (Durham, N.C.: Duke University Press, 2008); Gary Y. Okihiro, *Island World: A History of Hawai'i and the United States* (Berkeley: University of California Press, 2008); Thomas J. Osborne, *"Empire Can Wait": American Opposition to Hawaiian Annexation, 1893–1898* (Kent, Ohio: Kent State University Press, 1981); Noenoe K. Silva, *Aloha Betrayed: Native Hawaiian Resistance to American Colonialism* (Durham, N.C.: Duke University Press, 2004); Lester D. Langley and Thomas Schoonover, *The Banana Men: American Mercenaries and Entrepreneurs in Central America, 1880–1930* (Lexington: University Press of Kentucky, 1995); Thomas McCormick, *The China Market: America's Quest for Informal Empire, 1893–1901* (Chicago: Quadrangle Books, 1967); Daniel S. Margolies, *Spaces of Law in American Foreign Relations: Extradition and Extraterritoriality in the Borderlands and Beyond, 1877–1898* (Athens: University of Georgia Press, 2011); Kal Raustiala, *Does the Constitution Follow the Flag? The Evolution of Territoriality in American Law* (New York: Oxford University Press, 2009); Mary A. Renda, *Taking Haiti: Military Occupation and the Culture of U.S. Imperialism, 1915–1940* (Chapel Hill: University of North Carolina Press, 2001); Bartholomew H. Sparrow, *The Insular Cases and the Emergence of American Empire* (Lawrence: University Press of Kansas, 2006); Ian Tyrrell, *Reforming the World: The Creation of America's Moral Empire* (Princeton, N.J.: Princeton University Press, 2010); Cyrus Veeser, *A World Safe for Capitalism: Dollar Diplomacy and America's Rise to Global Power* (New York: Columbia University Press, 2002); Laura Wexler, *Tender Violence: Domestic Visions in an Age of U.S. Imperialism* (Chapel Hill: University of North Carolina Press, 2000).

Epilogue: Revolution, War, and the Borders of Power

On the Mexican Revolution and its complex relation to the United States and the world, see Alan Knight, *The Mexican Revolution*, 2 vols. (New York: Cambridge University Press, 1986); John Womack Jr., *Zapata and the Mexican Revolution* (New York: Vintage, 1968); Friedrich Katz, *The Life and Times of Pancho Villa* (Stanford, Calif.: Stanford University Press, 1998) and *The Secret War in Mexico: Europe, the United States, and the Mexican Revolution* (Chicago: University of Chicago Press, 1981); Friedrich Katz and Claudio Lomnitz, *El Porfiriato y la Revolución en la historia de México* (Mexico City: Era, 2011); Gilbert M. Joseph, *Revolution from Without: Yucatán, Mexico, and the United States, 1880–1924* (New York: Cambridge University Press, 1982); Gilbert M. Joseph and Jürgen Buchenau, *Mexico's Once and Future Revolution: Social Upheaval and the Challenge of Rule Since the Late Nineteenth Century* (Durham, N.C.: Duke University Press, 2013); Adolfo Gilly, *The Mexican Revolution* (London: Verso, 1983); John Mason Hart, *Empire and Revolution: The Americans in Mexico Since the Civil War* (Berkeley: University of California Press, 2002) and *Revolutionary Mexico: The Coming and Process of the Mexican Revolution* (Berkeley: University of California Press, 1987); Claudio Lomnitz, *The Return of Comrade Ricardo Flores Magón* (New York: Zone Books, 2014); Benjamin H. Johnson, *Revolution in Texas: How a Forgotten Rebellion and Its Bloody Suppression Turned Mexicans into Americans* (New Haven, Conn.: Yale University Press, 2003); Allen Wells and Gilbert M. Joseph, *Summer of Discontent, Seasons of Upheaval: Elite Politics and Rural Insurgency in Yucatán, 1876–1915* (Stanford, Calif.: Stanford University Press, 1996); Paul Hart, *Bitter Harvest: The Social Transformation of Morelos, Mexico, and the Origins of the Zapatista Revolution, 1840–1910* (Albuquerque: University of New Mexico Press, 2005); John Tutino, *From Insurrection to Revolution in Mexico: Social Bases of Agrarian Violence, 1750–1940* (Princeton, N.J.: Princeton University Press, 1986); Elena Poniatowska, *Las Soldaderas: Women of the Mexican Revolution* (Mexico City: Era, 2006); John S. D. Eisenhower, *Intervention! The United States and the Mexican Revolution, 1913–1917* (New York: W. W. Norton, 1993).

On Woodrow Wilson, colonialism, and the vision for a postwar world, see Erez Manela, *The Wilsonian Moment: Self-Determination and the International Origins of Anticolonial Nationalism* (New York: Oxford University Press, 2007); Robert Gerwarth and Erez Manela, eds., *Empires at War, 1911–1923* (New York: Oxford University Press, 2014); Adam Tooze, *The Deluge: The Great War, America, and the Remaking of the Global Order, 1916–1931* (New York: Viking Press, 2014); John Milton Cooper Jr., *Reconsidering Woodrow Wilson: Progressivism, Internationalism, War, and Peace* (Princeton, N.J.: Woodrow Wilson Center Press, 2008); N. Gordon Levin Jr., *Woodrow Wilson and World Politics: America's Response to War and Revolution* (New York: Oxford University Press, 1970).

On the Great Migration, Marcus Garvey, and a new Pan-Africanism, see James R. Grossman, *Land of Hope: Chicago, Black Southerners, and the Great Migration* (Chicago: University of Chicago Press, 1986); Peter Gottlieb, *Making Their Own Way: Southern Blacks' Migration to Pittsburgh, 1916–1930* (Urbana: University of Illinois Press, 1987); Kimberley L. Phillips, *AlabamaNorth: African-American Migrants, Community, and Working-Class Activism in Cleveland, 1915–45* (Urbana: University of Illinois Press, 1999); Earl Lewis, *In Their Own Interests: Race, Class, and Power in Twentieth-Century Norfolk, Virginia* (Berkeley: University of California Press, 1991); Joe William Trotter, ed., *The Great Migration in Historical Perspective: New Dimensions of Race, Class, and Gender* (Bloomington: Indiana University Press, 1991); Winston James, *Holding Aloft the Banner of Ethiopia: Caribbean Radicalism in Early Twentieth-Century America* (London: Verso, 1998); Adam Ewing, *The Age of Garvey: How a Jamaican Activist Created a Mass Movement and Changed Global Black Politics* (Princeton, N.J.: Princeton University Press, 2014); Tony Martin, *Race First: The Ideological and Organizational Struggles of Marcus Garvey and the Universal Negro Improvement Association* (Westport, Conn.: Greenwood Press, 1976); Mary G. Rolinson, *Grassroots Garveyism: The Universal Negro Improvement Association in the Rural South, 1920–1927* (Chapel Hill: University of North Carolina Press, 2007); Judith Stein, *The World of Marcus Garvey: Race and Class in Modern Society* (Baton Rouge: Louisiana State University Press, 1986); Steven Hahn, *The Political Worlds of Slavery and Freedom* (Cambridge, Mass.: Harvard University Press, 2009); C. L. R. James and Robin D. G. Kelley, *A History of the Pan-African Revolt* (1938; Chicago: C. H. Kerr, 2012); Brent H. Edwards, *The Practice of Diaspora: Literature, Translation, and the Rise of Black Internationalism* (Cambridge, Mass.: Harvard University Press, 2003); Robin D. G. Kelley, *Freedom Dreams: The Black Radical Imagination* (Boston: Beacon Press, 2002); James T. Campbell, *Songs of Zion: The African Methodist Episcopal Church in the United States and South Africa* (Chapel Hill: University of North Carolina Press, 1998); Barbara Foley, *Spectres of 1919: Class and Nation in the Making of the New Negro* (Urbana: University of Illinois Press, 2003); Andrew Zimmerman, *Alabama in Africa: Booker T. Washington, the German Empire, and the Globalization of the New South* (Princeton, N.J.: Princeton University Press, 2010); Nikhil Pal Singh, *Black Is a Country: Race and the Unfinished Struggle for Democracy* (Cambridge, Mass.: Harvard University Press, 2004).

Index